Visual Processes in Reading and Reading Disabilities

Visual Processes in Reading and Reading Disabilities

Edited by

Dale M. Willows
Ontario Institute for Studies in Education

Richard S. Kruk
University of Wollongong, Australia

Evelyne Corcos
Glendon College—York University, Ontario

1993

LAWRENCE ERLBAUM ASSOCIATES, PUBLISHERS
Hillsdale, New Jersey   Hove and London

Lawrence Erlbaum Associates, Inc., Publishers
365 Broadway
Hillsdale, New Jersey 07642

Library of Congress Cataloging-in-Publication Data

Visual processes in reading and reading disabilities / edited by Dale
   M. Willows, Richard S. Kruk, Evelyne Corcos.
      p.   c.m.
   Includes bibliographical references and index.
   ISBN 0-8058-0900-7. — ISBN 0-8058-1332-2 (pbk.)
   1. Reading, Psychology of.   2. Reading disability.   3. Visual
perception.   I.   Willows, Dale M.   II. Kruk, Richard S.
III. Corcos, Evelyne.
BF456.R2V57   1993
150.14—dc20   93-26065
                                                         CIP

Books published by Lawrence Erlbaum Associates are printed on acid-free
paper, and their bindings are chosen for strength and durability.

Printed in the United States of America
10   9   8   7   6   5   4   3   2   1

Contents

Preface

Over the last 25 years, reading processes have been the focus of an enormous amount of research in experimental psychology as well as in other disciplines. Although the theories and models that have emerged from this research have greatly advanced our understanding, the contribution of visual processing factors to normal reading acquisition and to reading disabilities has been relatively neglected in the literature.

Reading and writing are distinct from the language processes of speaking and listening largely by virtue of the fact that a visual modality is involved. Hence, one would expect that the visual processes in reading would be the subject of a great deal of theory and research. Surprisingly, however, although there has been a considerable amount of relevant research, it is widely scattered both geographically and in terms of disciplines, and until very recently there have been no substantial reviews or books concerned with visual aspects of normal reading or of reading disabilities.

The purpose of this volume is to bring together a broad range of evidence that concerns the role of visual information in normal reading processes and in reading disabilities. Because reading processes are of concern to a diverse multidisciplinary group that includes cognitive scientists, speech and language pathologists, optometrists, neuropsychologists, psycholinguists, clinicians, and educators, this book should be of interest to a broad readership.

The volume begins with an introduction by Keith Stanovich, who places the book within the larger context of the general literature on reading processes and reading disabilities. This introduction is followed by five major sections, each including a number of chapters. Part I provides some background on the ways that visual processes have been viewed in the field of reading in the past; Part II considers the neuropsychological foundation of visual processes in reading; Part III examines the role of basic visual processes in normal reading acquisition and in skilled reading; Part IV explores the contribution of visual processing deficits to reading disabilities; and Part V discusses some of the parameters that affect visual processing in various situations. In the concluding chapter, Keith Rayner points to future directions for research in the field of visual processes in reading and reading disabilities.

In chapter 1, Richard Venezky charts the origins and history of knowledge relating to the visual component in reading. He accomplishes this task in three ways. First, he describes the visual changes in writing which resulted from pressures to make text more readable as more people gained access to printed material. Next, he examines the contribution of early experimental psychology in providing the means to evaluate psychophysical phenomena and the early preoccupation with reaction time for reading letters and words, with eye movements, and with perceptual span and field of vision while overlooking contributions of the different types of memory. Finally, he chronicles the early investigations of reading disabilities and "word blindness" as described by Hinshelwood, Kerr, and Morgan, Orton's neurological model, and optometric explanations focusing on visual fatigue. Venezky also highlights the visual perspective contained in the educational views of Gates, Monroe, and Robinson to complete his historical account.

In chapter 2, Dale Willows and Megan Terepocki explore the phenomenon of letter-orientation reversals that, since Orton's early work in the field of reading disabilities, has been identified as a characteristic symptom of dyslexia and has been thought to provoke evidence that some type of visual processing deficit underlies reading disabilities. Their chapter begins by describing earlier historical and clinical contexts in which reversal errors became of special interest to the field of reading disabilities, and it goes on to describe the more modern context in which reversal errors may warrant a fresh look. Beginning with a discussion of some key methodological issues, they review the research evidence on *static reversals,* distinguishing them from *kinetic reversals* (transpositions). The literature is considered under the rubrics of reversals of nonalphabetic stimuli, reversals of isolated letters, letter orientation errors in the context of nonwords, letter orientation errors in the context of words, and letter reversal incidence in writing. The authors conclude that although some theorists have argued that letter-orientation reversals are of little theoretical interest in understanding reading disabilities, reversals may represent an intriguing piece in the puzzle of dyslexia, and further, more conceptually coherent research is much needed.

In chapter 3, Michael Corballis and Ivan Beale examine the work of Orton in order to clarify aspects of Orton's theory which they believe are commonly misrepresented and, at the same time, to argue for a modified version of Orton's position. They note that according to Orton the problem experienced by disabled readers is not with seeing or recognizing objects but with associating printed words with meaning. They consider the weakness in Orton's theory to be his explanation of how the brain works. Corballis and Beale describe how present conceptualizations of brain processes argue against Orton's notion that the left hemisphere records information in its correct orientation whereas the right hemisphere records the image left-reversed, the idea that dyslexics see a reversed image. Instead, they suggest that the left–right orientation pattern of a trace is reversed not when the information is encoded, but rather when it is transferred from one hemisphere to the other and consequently when it is remembered. Corballis and Beale discuss reversal errors and the relationship between laterality and reading disability. Finally, they describe how contemporary neuropsychological theories (Geschwind, Annette, and Galaburda) are compatible with a modified version of Orton's theory that highlights the importance of directional sense and the ability to discriminate mirror-image letters in reading. Their discussion leads directly into Part II, Neuropsychological Bases of Visual Processes.

In chapter 4, Stephen Lehmkuhle explains the neurological basis of visual processes in reading. He describes visual perception as a unitary experience that gives little indication to the individual of the separate processes that make up the visual experience. He outlines the anatomical, physiological, and psychophysical organization of the magnocellular (M) and the parvocellular (P) visual pathways. He continues with a discussion of disease and M and P pathways, reporting on pathological states in which the M pathway might be selectively compromised. The chapter ends with a description of how a deficit in the M pathway may manifest itself in dyslexia, and how such a deficit may result in unstable visual processing and impeded reading.

In chapter 5, Bruno Breitmeyer outlines the literature on parallel visual processing channels. His review begins by tracing the development of the theory of sustained and transient visual channels, linking psychophysical and neurophysiological perspectives. He discusses current controversies in the area, describing how the two channels operate in both normal and disabled readers. He raises the issue that deficits in transient-like pathways across sensory modalities may have a common underlying mechanism, which could relate the diversity of symptoms that point to subtypes of reading disability.

In chapter 6, a special form of reading disability, *neglect dyslexia,* is discussed by Jane Riddoch and Glyn Humphreys. They define this unusual form of dyslexia, relate it to the wider neglect syndrome, and describe symptomology of visual neglect under different reading conditions, including text and single word reading. They evaluate several theoretical explanations, and conclude that an impairment in attentional abilities offers a suitable account of current data on visual neglect.

Part III focuses on basic visual processes in normal reading acquisition and in skilled reading. In chapter 7, Dominic Massaro and Thomas Sanocki present a theoretical framework to explain the processing of visual information in word recognition. They consider visual processes to be fundamental to reading letters, but they emphasize that the processing of text also involves nonvisual information (orthographic, syntactic, lexical). Because letters are processed before words are identified, they present a Fuzzy Logical Model of Perception (FLMP) to explain letter recognition and this model is contrasted with an Interactive Activation Model (IAM). Massaro and Sanocki argue on the side of the FLMP as they account for a wider range of experimental findings. They conclude that letters are recognized on the basis of both global features and local or font-tuning features. This conclusion is used to explain the downfall of the i.t.a. alphabet which was restricted to modifying global features, and Massaro and Sanocki are hopeful about the outcome of studies evaluating a Graphophonic alphabet based on a FLMP.

In chapter 8, Evelyne Corcos and Dale Willows examine orthographic information from a print perspective adopting a frequency definition that highlights the probability of letters and letter sequences in various spatial positions within words. They limit their literature review to studies that do not intentionally integrate the processing of orthographic information with that of phonological and morphological information. Studies of adults and children of varying ages and reading-skill levels are presented to demonstrate a strong relationship between the acquisition of orthographic knowledge and visual familiarity. They conclude that further studies should assess the importance of exposure to print at the lexical level.

Alexander Pollatsek's chapter provides a general introduction to the topic of eye movements in reading. He highlights the finding that reading typically involves a word-by-word pattern of eye-movements, and outlines the functionality of this pattern. He reviews the literature on relevant aspects of text processing, proposes a model of eye-movement programming in reading, and, finally, compares two approaches to the use of eye-movement data for the study of text processing. He argues for the use of fixation time as an ordinal measure of cognitive processing during reading.

Continuing the theme of eye movements in reading, Alan Kennedy shows how new technological advances may have unanticipated effects on reading. Kennedy examines the effects of video display of text on eye-movement control of readers who process text presented in this manner. He begins with a review of the literature examining processing differences for text presented on screen and hard copy. He then reports data on differences in processing strategies of typists, as people who frequently encounter text on computer screens. He outlines possible mechanisms to explain the differences, introduces the notion of *optimal viewing positions,* and reports recent data on eye-movement control of typists and nontypists as a function of screen refresh rate. He shows that typists adopt a specific reading strategy when reading text, even in nontyping situations, which involves an increased frequency of small within-word saccades produced in response to pulsation-induced mislocations of eye-movements. He reports that the effects of screen pulsation are observed at refresh frequencies well above estimates of normal fusion, and suggests that increasing the refresh rate of displays may reduce the perceptible flicker of screen-presented text.

In chapter 11, Laurie Beth Feldman examines skilled reading in Serbo-Croatian, a language that can be written with the Roman or Cyrillic alphabet. This provides a unique opportunity to study visual effects relying on the features of the alphabet of the text. Feldman reviews studies of words and pseudowords presented in the same alphabet or in the two different alphabets at pre-lexical and post-lexical stages of processing. She concludes that the alphabetic context primarily helps to augment the processing of phonologically ambiguous words, and that this effect, therefore, originates in the mapping of phonemes and graphemes.

In chapter 12, Dale Willows, Richard Kruk and Evelyne Corcos explore the role of visual processing deficits in reading disabilities. Their review scrutinizes a broad range of literature addressing the fundamental question of whether or not there are disabled/normal reader differences in basic visual processes. The literature is organized around the stage of visual processing examined, early or late. Studies that involve assessment of the processing of visual information within the first few hundred milliseconds after it reaches the eye (i.e., reflecting sensation and perception) are included in the section on early visual processing whereas studies that involve retention, recognition and/or reproduction of visual information after it has disappeared from view (i.e., reflecting memory in addition to perceptual processes) are included in the section on later visual processing. On the basis of a critical examination of this literature directly investigating disabled/normal reader differences in early and later visual processes, the authors conclude that there is a need to reexamine the widely held belief that visual processing deficits are not related to reading disabilities.

In chapter 13, Catherine Watson and Dale Willows take a different tack. By reviewing the large literature on subtypes of learning/reading disabilities, they address the question of whether there may be a visual-processing-deficit subtype among the reading disabled. Many clinicians and researchers have long argued that the reading disabled represent a heterogeneous group, and some have suggested that there may be relatively homogeneous subgroups or subtypes among the reading disabled. Both clinical and multivariate statistical approaches have been used in attempts to reveal subtypes among the reading disabled. As the authors point out, this literature involves diverse approaches to subject selection and widely varied test batteries. Nevertheless, they argue that, taken together, the subtyping literature has produced considerable evidence that disabled readers differ among themselves with respect to their visual processing abilities. Watson and Willows conclude by raising several possibilities to explain the fairly consistent finding of a visual-processing-deficit subtype among the reading disabled and by suggesting a focus for future research.

In an extended review of the current literature of early visual processes and reading disability, William Lovegrove and Mary Williams describe the converging evidence from psychophysical and physiological investigations showing that a large proportion of disabled readers are deficient in transient visual processing. Referring to studies of visual masking, they report that the nature of the deficit involves the time course of visual processing; the transient system of disabled readers responds less efficiently than that of normal readers, resulting in a less effective pattern of inhibition of the sustained visual channel response. They also outline recent studies indicating that temporal aspects of transient system functioning can be affected by the physical properties of the text—namely wavelength. The authors end by suggesting that a normal pattern of visual processing in disabled readers can be reestablished depending on the wavelength properties of text.

In chapter 15, John Stein summarizes research examining "visual dyslexics"—children who exhibit deficits in ocular-motor control—from a variety of perspectives. He provides evidence showing that many disabled readers exhibit unstable binocular fixation. This results in visual confusion and leads to the perception of unstable visual images. Moreover, these children have poor visual location sense, which makes words appear jumbled, and this may explain the difficulties that disabled readers experience in reading nonwords. He provides data showing that monocular occlusion may lead to improved binocular stability and, ultimately, better reading performance. Finally, he relates the findings of studies of phonological and visuospatial deficiencies, suggesting that both types of deficiency may arise from a common developmental disorder, possibly involving the magnocellular neural system.

Philip Seymour and Henryka Evans also examine the connection between visual processes and dyslexia. They propose that reading difficulties in dyslexia may occur at several different stages in their model: in early visual processing, in either a visual (object) processor or a visual (orthographic) processor exclusive to processing print, or in the central reading processes that incorporate higher cognitive and language aspects. Seymour and Evans present evidence reinforcing the notion that dyslexics represent a heterogeneous population and demonstrate that some dyslexics have a prominent difficulty at the visual orthographic level. They conclude that visual deficits in dyslexia reside in a visual orthographic processor.

In chapter 17, Richard Olson and Helen Forsberg outline studies of eye-movement behavior of normal and disabled readers in reading and nonreading tasks. The evidence they report indicates that there are no differences in eye-movement behavior between disabled and reading-age-matched control groups. Minor differences between disabled and chronological-age-matched control groups are not attributed to visual processes. Their findings are contrasted with earlier research showing significant differences in eye movements between normal and disabled readers. The authors argue against the use of eye-movement measures as screening tests for reading disability, or the use of remediation practices that focus on eye-movement patterns. Research investigating individual differences in eye-movement behavior is also reviewed. The authors report significant correlations between reading and nonreading eye-movements. They also discuss individual differences in eye-movements in relation to performance on visual and language tasks, as well as genetic influences. Evidence of genetic involvement in comparisons of identical and fraternal twins is reported. The chapter ends with the authors drawing a link between the eye-movement data reported and findings of transient channel deficits in disabled readers, and suggesting the possibility of a common underlying neurological deficiency for both visual and phonological processing deficits.

In chapter 18, P. G. Aaron and Jean-Claude Guillemard examine the relationship between developmental dyslexia and visual processes, particularly with reference to artistic skill. They maintain that the contribution of visual memory as an independent component of reading is not clearly established. The status of visual memory in reading is examined by raising the questions of whether word recognition and spelling skills can come about by superior visual memory alone, and whether visual memory skills are also related to superior orthographic memory. These questions are addressed in a novel way by presenting case studies of well-known artists who have shown evidence of developmental dyslexia. It is assumed that artists have superior visual skills, and that their symptoms of dyslexia cannot be attributed to visual skills (of the type involved in the creation of works of art). On the basis of their analysis, the authors conclude that superior visual processing skills can be observed with disabled readers. They point to other, nonvisual processing skills that may have contributed to the reading difficulties of the artists studied.

Part V, the last section of the book, focuses on optometric and ergonomic parameters influencing visual processes. In chapter 19, Ralph Garzia discusses the association between visual functioning and reading from a clinical, optometric perspective. He begins by outlining the visual functions required for efficient reading, including accurate acuity, oculomotor control, accommodation and vergence responses, and the impact of letter size, illumination, contrast, and glare. He then discusses common visual abnormalities observed during reading, as well as reading-behavior and perceptual abnormalities. He outlines the relationship between visual skills and reading, touching on studies of the relation between visual anomalies and reading disability, showing that a considerable degree of confusion and misunderstanding remains in this area. He further discusses correlations between visual functions and reading performance, as well as developmental, reading level, and subtyping issues. The chapter ends with a discussion of visual assessment and screening practices for optometric visual deficits in disabled readers.

Arnold Wilkins argues, in chapter 20, that visual discomfort associated with reading is a consequence of successive lines of text resembling a stripe pattern. Some individuals are much more sensitive to the effect of stripes and therefore are more likely to experience eye-strain, headaches and visual distortions when reading. Wilkins describes modifications to minimize these adverse effects: covering the lines not being read; wearing tinted glasses with the tint specifically selected for an individual; and altering the spatial and temporal characteristics of text to improve its perceptibility. Wilkins proposes a theory of visual discomfort to explain the phenomena and presents supporting evidence from children with visual dyslexia.

In another report of unanticipated consequences of a new technology, Richard Kruk's chapter outlines research concerned with the effects of computer monitor presentation of text on reading performance. This chapter focuses on legibility and ergonomics issues, discussing characteristics unique to computer-presented text that may affect reading performance. He outlines both hardware- and software-dependent factors found to significantly affect visual processing and reading. He ends by suggesting that a feasible model for explaining monitor legibility and effects on reading should be based on the spatial frequency characteristics of monitor-presented text.

In the concluding chapter, Keith Rayner discusses the direction of research and theory in visual processing as it relates to normal and disabled reading. He does not foresee a paradigm shift as a result of new information in the field. Instead, he expects new information, particularly about neurophysiological mechanisms associated with reading, to simply refine existing models. In the field of dyslexia, Rayner submits that both visual perceptual and language deficits probably contribute to reading disabilities. He suggests, however, a move away from a disease and/or single-cause model of dyslexia in order to acknowledge the diversity existing among dyslexics, evident in their reactions to remedial interventions. Finally, Rayner argues that an understanding of dyslexia is contingent on gaining a greater understanding of skilled reading.

—Dale M. Willows
—Richard S. Kruk
—Evelyne Corcos

Acknowledgments

Thirteen years ago, after having spent more than a decade as a basic researcher in the field of reading, I (the senior editor) took a sabbatical leave from my position in the Department of Psychology at the University of Waterloo and undertook a clinical internship at a highly respected learning center (The McGill-Montreal Children's Hospital Learning Center). There I had the privilege of working with an outstanding team of clinicians—with credentials in such fields as psychology, education, linguistics, and communication disorders—who, for many years, had been assessing students' learning disabilities and developing and implementing programs for them. By working with these experts, I hoped to determine whether the theories and models emanating from basic reading research seemed to have validity and utility in the real world of practice. As a result of my experiences there, I became convinced that what seemed relatively clear cut in theory was far from it in practice. In particular, as someone whose primary research program was focused on the role of linguistic (semantic, syntactic, and phonological) processes in reading, it came as a genuine shock to me to discover a range of phenomena in the reading and writing of the learning disabled that seemed to suggest an involvement of visual processing deficits, in addition to linguistic deficiencies. At the time, the psycholinguistic view was dominant in the field of reading, and reading disabilities were ascribed to linguistic deficits in phonological, morphological, semantic, and syntactic processes, to the exclusion of visual factors.

In an attempt to explore what role, if any, visual processes might have in reading disabilities, I (with Evelyne Corcos) undertook an extensive literature review. One puzzling finding from the review was that, although few North American researchers seemed interested in the role of visual factors in reading disabilities, researchers farther afield, in Australia, New Zealand, the United Kingdom, and some other European countries were involved in programmatic study of the visual processing of disabled readers. In an attempt to better understand the motivation for the work that was going on overseas, I travelled on another sabbatical in 1987 to meet William Lovegrove at the University of Wollongong in Australia and Michael Corballis at the University of Auckland in New Zealand. Both of these visits encouraged me in my growing conviction that "the case"—concerning the potential relation between visual processing deficits and reading disabilities—was not yet closed, and that it had been closed prematurely in North America, probably because of the Zeitgeist in experimental psychology, as much as any weight of evidence.

Taken together, then, both clinical observations and careful review of research evidence led me to conclude that it was time for a fresh look at what role visual processes have in normal reading and at how inefficiencies in visual processing might impact on reading performance and skill. Thus, I set out to bring together the latest evidence concerning the nature of the involvement of visual processes in normal reading and in reading disabilities. This book is the product of that effort.

Because the topic of "visual processes in reading and reading disabilities" was fundamentally unpopular among most North American reading researchers, the plan for this book would never have been actualized without the help and inspiration of a number of people. For the role they had in "opening my eyes" to the complexity of learning disabilities in reading and writing, I am greatly indebted to the staff who were at The McGill-Montreal Children's Hospital Learning Center during my sabbatical there in 1980. Very special thanks are owed to Margie Golick and Sybil Schwartz who shared so generously of their knowledge and skills, and who have remained as special friends and unpaid consultants over the years since. For their encouragement and very helpful suggestions in the early planning stage of the book, I am also greatly indebted to Bill Lovegrove and Mike Corballis. I found in them an openness to ideas that were virtual heresy in North American theoretical circles at the time. Bill Lovegrove offered a wealth of suggestions that had considerable impact on the form and content of the book. Mike Corballis, Dick Venezky, Uta Frith, John Kershner, and Max Coltheart also made suggestions that were most helpful in establishing the final list of contributors. My current and former students, particularly Evelyne Corcos, Richard Kruk, Megan Terepocki,   Karen Sumbler, and Catherine Watson, have served as a source of intellectual challenge and enormous support throughout this endeavor.

At a personal level, I want to express my deepest appreciation and affection to my partner Jack Quarter who has been an unfailing source of confidence and encouragement for me. Without his patience and love I would certainly never have been able to see the project through.

—Dale M. Willows

Contributors

P. G. Aaron, *Department of Educational and School Psychology, Indiana State University, Terre Haute, IN 47809, U.S.A.*

Ivan L. Beale, *Department of Psychology, University of Auckland, Private Bag 92019, Auckland, New Zealand*

Bruno G. Breitmeyer, *Department of Psychology, University of Houston, Houston, TX 77204-5341, U.S.A.*

Michael C. Corballis, *Department of Psychology, University of Auckland, Private Bag 92019, Auckland, New Zealand*

Evelyne Corcos, *Department of Psychology, Glendon College-York University, 2275 Bayview Avenue, Toronto, Ontario M4N 3M6, Canada*

Henryka M. Evans, *Department of Psychology, University of Dundee, Dundee DD1 4HN, Scotland*

Laurie Beth Feldman, *Department of Psychology, SS 112, SUNY - Albany (and Haskins Laboratories, New Haven, CT), Albany, NY 12222, U.S.A.*

Helen Forsberg, *Department of Psychology, University of Colorado, Box 345, Boulder, CO 80309, U.S.A.*

Ralph P. Garzia, *School of Optometry, University of Missouri - St. Louis, St. Louis, MO 63121-4499, U.S.A.*

Jean-Claude Guillemard, *Past president, International School Psychology Association, 9 Allee Brahms, La Croix Saint Jacques, 91410 Dourdan, France*

Glyn W. Humphreys, *Cognitive Science Research Centre, School of Psychology, University of Birmingham, Birmingham B15 2TT, England*

Alan Kennedy, *Department of Psychology, University of Dundee, Dundee DD1 4HN, Scotland*

Richard S. Kruk, *Department of Psychology, University of Wollongong, P.O. Box 1144, Northfields Ave., Wollongong, N.S.W. 2500, Australia*

Stephen Lehmkuhle, *School of Optometry, University of Missouri - St. Louis, St. Louis, MO 63121-4499, U.S.A.*

William J. Lovegrove, *Dean, School of Graduate Studies, University of Wollongong, P.O. Box 1144, Northfields Ave., Wollongong, N.S.W. 2500, Australia*

Dominic W. Massaro, *Program in Experimental Psychology, University of California-Santa Cruz, Clark Kerr Hall, Santa Cruz, CA 95064, U.S.A.*

Richard K. Olson, *Department of Psychology, University of Colorado, Box 345, Boulder, CO 80309, U.S.A.*

Alexander Pollatsek, *Department of Psychology, University of Massachusetts, Amherst, MA 01003, U.S.A.*

Keith Rayner, *Department of Psychology, University of Massachusetts, Amherst, MA 01003, U.S.A.*

M. Jane Riddoch, *Cognitive Science Research Centre, School of Psychology, University of Birmingham, Birmingham B15 2TT, England*

Thomas Sanocki, *Department of Psychology, University of South Florida, Tampa, FL 33620, U.S.A.*

Philip H. K. Seymour, *Department of Psychology, University of Dundee, Dundee DD1 4HN, Scotland*

Keith E. Stanovich, *Department of Instruction and Special Education, Ontario Institute for Studies in Education, 252 Bloor Street West, Toronto, Ontario M5S 1V6, Canada*

John F. Stein, *Laboratory of Physiology, Oxford University, Parks Road, Oxford OX1 3PT, England*

Megan Terepocki, *Department of Applied Psychology, Ontario Institute for Studies in Education, 252 Bloor Street West, Toronto, Ontario M5S 1V6, Canada*

Richard L. Venezky, *Unidel Professor of Educational Studies, Department of Educational Studies, University of Delaware, Newark, DE 19716, U.S.A.*

Catherine Watson, *Department of Curriculum, Ontario Institute for Studies in Education, 252 Bloor Street West, Toronto, Ontario M5S 1V6, Canada*

Arnold J. Wilkins, *Medical Research Council, Applied Psychology Unit, 15 Chaucer Road, Cambridge CB2 2EF, England*

Mary C. Williams, *Department of Psychology, University of New Orleans, New Orleans, LA 70148, U.S.A.*

Dale M. Willows, *Department of Instruction and Special Education, Ontario Institute for Studies in Education, 252 Bloor Street West, Toronto, Ontario M5S 1V6, Canada*

Introduction

Keith E. Stanovich
Ontario Institute for Studies in Education

A book such as this is long overdue. Because the reading process begins with print arrayed visually on the page, one would think that visual processes would have been one of the first topics to be studied by reading researchers and one of the most intensely investigated. However, the history of reading research is often curious (Venezky, 1977). Although the visual perception of words has at times been the subject of intense scrutiny by experimental psychologists (e.g., Carr & Pollatsek, 1985; Estes, 1977; Paap, Newsome, McDonald, & Schvaneveldt, 1982) processes of visual perception have often been neglected by reading researchers. General theories of reading often give short shrift to visual processes. The knowledge of visual word processing gained from the investigations of experimental psychologists has not been integrated into general reading theories.

At times, this work seems to have been willfully ignored by the reading education community. A case in point concerns the research on the functional visual stimulus in reading using eye movement technologies (see Balota, Pollatsek, & Rayner, 1985; Kennedy, chap. 10, this volume; Pollatsek, chap. 9, this volume). Proponents of top-down theories of reading that emphasize hypothesis testing as a processing mechanism (see Stanovich, 1986, for a discussion) have chosen to ignore findings indicating that, during reading, the sampling of visual information is relatively dense and that visual features are not minimally sampled but instead are rather exhaustively processed, even when the word is highly predictable (Ehrlich & Rayner, 1981; Pollatsek, Rayner, & Balota, 1986).

Work on visual processes in reading has had most of its impact on theory through discussions of the causes of reading disability. The idea of visual deficits as a cause of reading disability has, of course, been much discussed. However, this discussion—for all its popularity in the general media—has not been matched by a commensurately intense research effort. This volume collects some of the best work on the possibility of visual processing deficits in dyslexia from ongoing programmatic research efforts. One thing that has hampered efforts to understand the role of visual processing in reading disability is that the small body of research that does exist is scattered throughout numerous books and journals—some of the latter being sources (e.g., *Vision Research*) that are not regularly read or cited by readers of the more mainstream reading research literature (e.g., *Reading Research Quarterly*). We have, for a long time, needed an edited volume that brings some of the best of this work under one cover.

Another factor that has hampered our understanding of the role of visual processing in reading disability is that the issue has been couched in the form of a debate. There is, of course, nothing wrong with a debate per se. But unfortunately—as often happens in the education field—this debate was set in an overly simplified, either/or fashion where a gain for one hypothesis (e.g., phonological processing deficits) was automatically seen as a loss for another (e.g., visual processing deficits). Possible complexities such as the co-occurence of processing deficits were likely to be ignored. This volume is most definitely not in the tradition of these shopworn debates.

The general approach taken by the editors of this volume is akin to that adopted by Marilyn Adams in her monumental synthesis of research on beginning reading: *Beginning to Read: Thinking and Learning About Print*. When commissioned by Congress to produce a summary of what is known about beginning reading and the teaching of reading, Adams chose not to couch her work in the language of the phonics versus whole word or phonics versus whole language debates. Instead, what Adams did was to place her entire discussion of beginning reading within the context of general models of reading-related processes in cognitive psychology. Thus, when Adams did begin to discuss more specific aspects of teaching, classroom practice, and the debate over phonics, those issues were grounded in the complexity of general models of complex information processing (including connectionist modeling).

The approach taken by the editors of the current volume is similar in that, via a judicious choice of topics and authors, they attempt to ground the debate about the role of visual deficits in reading disability in what is known more generally about visual processes in reading and the neuropsychology of visual processing. If this book had no purpose other than to foster a more complex debate about visual deficits and to set the debate in the context of information processing and neuropsychological theories of reading, it would have achieved something of scientific importance. But in addition to this, the book should help to more fully integrate knowledge about visual processing into general theories of normal reading.

In short, this volume is an ideal place for students to begin their study of visual processes in reading. Additionally, it should command the attention of even those investigators whose research has focused on language difficulties as the cause of reading disability (myself among them). This volume should help to ensure that investigations of differing processing loci for reading disability do not take place in totally different literatures with no cross-fertilization. There are several edited volumes that collect data and theory on phonological processes in reading (e.g., Brady & Shankweiler, 1992; Shankweiler & Liberman, 1989; Stanovich, 1988). This volume is unique in providing a companion work on visual processes, but one set within a broad framework. I predict it will become a benchmark publication.

REFERENCES

Adams, M. J. (1990). *Beginning to read: Thinking and learning about print.* Cambridge, MA: MIT Press.

Balota, D., Pollatsek, A., & Rayner, K. (1985). The interaction of contextual constraints and parafoveal visual information in reading. *Cognitive Psychology, 17,* 364–390.

Brady, S., & Shankweiler, D. (Eds.). (1992). *Phonological processes in literacy.* Hillsdale, NJ: Lawrence Erlbaum Associates.

Carr, T. H., & Pollatsek, A. (1985). Recognizing printed words: A look at current models. In D. Besner, T. G. Waller, & G. E. MacKinnon (Eds.), *Reading research: Advances in theory and practice* (Vol. 5, pp. 1–82). Orlando, FL: Academic Press.

Ehrlich, S., & Rayner, K. (1981). Contextual effects on word perception and eye movements during reading. *Journal of Verbal Learning and Verbal Behavior, 20,* 641–655.

Estes, W. (1977). On the interaction of perception and memory in reading. In D. LaBerge & S. J. Samuels (Eds.), *Basic processes in reading: Perception and comprehension* (pp. 1–25). Hillsdale, NJ: Lawrence Erlbaum Associates.

Paap, K. R., Newsome, S. L., McDonald, J. E., & Schvaneveldt, R. W. (1982). An activation-verification model for letter and word recognition: The word superiority effect. *Psychological Review, 89,* 573–594.

Pollatsek, A., Rayner, K., & Balota, D. A. (1986). Inferences about eye movement control from the perceptual span in reading. *Perception & Psychophysics, 40,* 123–130D.

Shankweiler, D., & Liberman, I. Y. (Eds.). (1989). *Phonology and reading disability: Solving the reading puzzle.* Ann Arbor: University of Michigan Press.

Stanovich, K. E. (1986). Matthew effects in reading: Some consequences of individual differences in the acquisition of literacy. *Reading Research Quarterly, 21,* 360–407.

Stanovich, K. E. (Ed.). (1988). *Children's reading and the development of phonological awareness.* Detroit: Wayne State University Press.

Venezky, R. L. (1977). Research on reading processes: A historical perspective. *American Psychologist, 32,* 339–345.

BACKGROUND

1 History of Interest in the Visual Component of Reading

Richard L. Venezky
University of Delaware

Reading is a psychological process that is, under normal conditions, driven by visual input that initiates recognition and comprehension activities. That the reader interacts with the text, integrates previously acquired knowledge with local text information, and generates hypotheses about what might occur next in the text does not negate the critical initiation role played by the letters, words, punctuation, and other graphic characteristics of the page. Just how the optical and neurological systems transform these light–dark contrasts into meaningful information has occupied several generations of experimental psychologists, neurologists, and ophthalmologists. What we now know about visual processing in reading is amply summarized by the chapters that follow. The mission of this chapter is to explore the origins of this knowledge, that is, the history of interest in the visual component of reading.

The core of this chapter is a review of early work in experimental psychology that involved reading. This is the period of Cattell and Dodge, Quantz and Dearborn, Javal and Gates, and of the chronoscope, the Cattell fall screen, the plaster of Paris cornea cup, and the spark record. A parallel interest is the history of investigations of reading disabilities—the realm of Hinshelwood and Orton, of Gates, Monroe, and Robinson, and of many others. But a third area is also of interest to this chapter because it provides clues to the extent to which visual considerations influenced the evolution of writing systems and of the English alphabet in particular. The development of Egyptian and Sumerian writing, of the Phoenician syllabaries, of the Greek and Roman alphabets, and of the letter styles of these alphabets provide a testing ground for hypotheses about visual considerations in the evolution of writing.

Although the scribes in the Nile valley who were responsible for the transition from hieroglyphic to demotic writing left no committee meeting records or design statements, we can nevertheless inspect the various forms of writing through this transition and make judgments about their impacts on the reader and the writer. Similarly, we can analyze the differences between Carolingian minuscules and Gothic book hand and make parallel judgments, and so on across the vast set of changes in scripts and manuscript styles that collectively constitute the history of writing and printing. The search in these cases is both for evidence that visual considerations potentially motivated a change and for evidence to the contrary. That is, changes that make manuscripts and printed pages more difficult to read are equally important because they indicate that the requirements of the reader were either not understood or were secondary to more pressing issues, such as the need to conserve parchment.

This chapter attends to three major areas where the interests just described are manifest: first, the premodern history of reading and writing; then the first 50 years or so of experimental psychology's investigations of reading and spelling; and finally the earlier studies of visual properties in reading disabilities.

THE VISUAL ELEMENT
IN PREMODERN WRITING

In the 6,000 to 8,000 years that have intervened since the earliest records of writing, dramatic changes have occurred in the symbols employed to represent sound and meaning, in the marks deployed to indicate grammatical and semantic boundaries, and in the format of the manuscript and printed page. Egyptian and Sumerian logograms yielded to syllabic symbols, and in Phoenician and Greek cultures, to an alphabet. Phoenician letter forms were redrawn in a variety of forms to yield lapidary Roman capitals, uncials, half-uncials, Carolingian minuscules, gothic, italic, Bodoni, and many other styles. Space became a standard word boundary marker; periods, commas, colons, and the like were assigned respectable roles; titles and subtitles were incorporated; and pages were numbered.

From the boustrophedon writing of the oldest Greek inscriptions, with no word divisions and with the direction of reading changing from left to right and from right to left at alternate lines, to the manuscript book that coexisted with the first printed specimens of the mid-15th century, the appearance of texts was radically transformed. To what degree do these changes indicate an awareness of the visual processing needs of the reader? Can we locate within the transformations that occurred in writing systems, alphabet styles, and page characteristics, any tendencies toward more scannable and more readable documents? Can what we know now about the visual processing habits of the reader help explain any changes that occurred prior to the modern, research-based period?

This section explores this question, bringing in evidence from the period that extends from the earliest records of writing until the adoption of "modern" type styles and page formats in the 16th century. The basic conclusion presented here purports that the reader's ability to extract sound and sense rarely can be invoked to explain changes during this period. The premodern period, for reasons presented shortly, was not a time when visual processing was consciously or unconsciously considered. Exceptions do exist, for example in the introduction in the 7th century of chapter divisions in biblical texts (Saenger, 1972), but the majority of changes that might be attributed to visual considerations could also have been motivated by nonvisual factors.

The Premodern Reader

In considering text and alphabet design prior to the modern period, it is important to clarify the potential audiences involved in each period. Prior to the Renaissance, the reading public was limited to a relatively small percentage of the population in most countries. For ancient scripts, the audience was even more circumscribed, consisting primarily of scribes, and a limited number of bureaucrats and learned noblemen. Ancient Greek texts could be written without word divisions because only a small number of individuals were expected to read them, and most of these people were scribes themselves. When Judaism centered on the temple in Jerusalem, the holy texts were read mostly by the priestly group that administered the temple rituals. A Semitic script that recorded only consonants was adequate for these situations. But with the destruction of the Second Temple and the diaspora, sacred texts were read by a multitude of rabbis and teachers, dispersed throughout the known world. Vowel marking systems were required to ensure uniformity of pronunciation.

Similarly, the elaborate abbreviation systems of Greek and Latin were easily adapted for English at a time when most of the those literate in the vernacular were clerics. But with the widespread literacy that evolved through the Renaissance and post-Renaissance periods, esoteric abbreviations were a barrier to understanding and were complicated to teach; consequently they were reduced to a handful by the middle of the 16th century.

A second factor to consider is the nature of reading itself. Although some learned individuals even from classical times probably read at more than 250 words per minute silently, the vast majority of readers prior to the time of Chaucer probably read slowly and orally. Although opinions differ on the nature and extent of silent reading prior to modern times (cf. Chaytor, 1945; Hendrickson, 1929; Saenger, 1982), most who write on this topic tend to agree that silent reading was not the norm until at least the 15th century, if not later. Without the need to scan quickly and to read silently (and therefore rapidly), many imperfections in script and format could be tolerated.

Influences on Script and Format

What influenced change in script and page format prior to the modern period? Three factors appear to be especially influential: technology, cost, and impression on the reader/viewer.

Technology. A common theme that extends from the earliest recorded times until almost 100 years after the introduction of movable type printing is the priority of scribal needs over reading ease. In each case cited here, however, the technology of writing introduced the primary constraints. For example, cuneiform evolved in Lower Mesopotamia where clay was readily available and where a technology developed very early for its acquisition and use. The predecessors of cuneiform were pictographs and then so-called line characters, developed through simplification of the pictographs. In time a syllabary of about 350 symbols developed, each symbol composed of a different combination of wedge-shaped signs. Changes over time in the forms of the symbols appear to have been dictated by the constraints of the writing system, which consisted of soft clay tablets into which the symbols were recorded through the pressure of a reed stylus, rather than through concessions to the reader. In reviewing the transitions from outline characters (c. 4500 B.C.), to archaic cuneiform (c. 2500 B.C.), to Assyrian (c. 700 B.C.), to late Babylonian (c. 500 B.C.), Sarton (1952, p. 64) speculated, "As the speed of writing increased, the characters were necessarily simplified; various forms of cursive or shorthand changed the appearance of the script profoundly."

A similar argument can be made for Egyptian hieroglyphics, which were inscribed on papyrus with a reed pen. But given the greater freedom for scribal innovation that such a technology offers over that of the Sumerians, a wider range of symbol forms could be incorporated. Hieroglyphics are assumed to have descended also from an earlier pictographic system that was simplified over time to facilitate writing. In time, the hieroglyphic system was simplified even further to produce a cursive or running hand (the hieratic script) and then reduced further to a shorthand, called the demotic. Both of these latter two scripts were visually divorced from the original hieroglyphic symbols, thus once again favoring the needs of the writer over the reader.

Once alphabets were fully developed, letter styles often developed in response to technological considerations. For example, Roman stone carving led to the design of what are called lapidary Roman capitals or Trajan capitals, after the inscriptions incised on a column erected by the emperor Trajan around 114 A.D. These letter forms are highly geometric and are especially adapted for chiseling into stone. For writing on parchment or papyrus, rustic capitals, a more condensed alphabet with thinned verticals, was more common. According to Boyd (1973, p. 61), "Practical writing habits are . . . seen to be partly responsible for the changing styles of book hands through the centuries."

Cost. A second factor that took precedence over visual processing was production cost, as measured by the amount of writing material consumed and the amount of time required by the scribe. The former consideration led to techniques for crowding as much writing as possible on the page; the latter led to scripts that were easy to produce. Until modern times, writing materials were relatively expensive. Even paper production, until the introduction of wood pulp, was an expensive component of book making. Under Tiberius, papyrus became so scarce that its distribution was regulated (*Pliny,* cited in Sarton, 1952, p. 24, fn. 14). In later times the high cost of vellum led to a search for alphabets that would allow a greater number of words per sheet than existing hands. This was one of the motivations for the development of the Carolingian minuscules under Charlemagne (Boorstin, 1983, p. 496). By the 13th century, as the demand for parchment rapidly increased, new scripts were introduced with more condensed letters. One of these, Gothic, is estimated by Jackson (1981) to have required only one-third of the page area consumed by the same height Carolingian letters.

Besides developing scripts that were more condensed, medieval scribes originated an elaborate system of abbreviations for Greek and Latin that were, by the Norman Conquest, established in English documents. This system was fully developed by the year 1200, after which no new abbreviation marks were developed for Latin. A major expansion in the use of abbreviations occurred in the 13th century with the introduction of the Gothic book hand. This use of abbreviations was "an attribute which makes Gothic writing rather cryptic and much more difficult to read than the best handwriting of the twelfth century" (Boyd, 1973, p. 64). During the late Middle Ages a number of the abbreviation signs fell into disuse but the system of abbreviations was carried into printing and survived for another several centuries before being reduced to the two basic forms we have today. Speeding this decline was an English act of 1731 that required the use of English in domestic records, "replacing Latin, French, and any other language," and specified that all writing in such documents be "in words at length and not abbreviated" (cited in Hector, 1966, p. 23).

The consequences of expensive writing materials were more crowded and highly abbreviated texts, as attempts were made to pack as many words as possible into a given area. Classical Latin scribes did not ordinarily separate words; where ambiguity would result, however, either spaces or a point (*punctum*) was used. The avoidance of word spaces should not be taken as evidence for a lack of understanding of the concept of word, however, as suggested by Saenger (1982). Glossaries, interlinear word glosses, and various mechanisms for separating words in sentences are ample proof of a word sense from this and from earlier periods. (In Hebrew and Arabic, for example, special forms of letters developed for word-final position. In Arabic this was extended to other word positions and to a larger number of letters than Hebrew.)

Impression.   Writing, particularly through the medieval period, often served to impress or to awe the semiliterate and the illiterate. Many early English charters served this purpose, as did many ecclesiastical documents. The *Book of Kells,* a beautifully illuminated Irish text from about 700 A.D., is a stunning example of this function of writing. Although it contains the earliest example of Irish half-uncial script, from which lowercase letters evolved, and elaborate, multicolor artwork, the text itself is riddled with errors. "Parts of sentences are omitted, a whole page is repeated by accident, letters had to be rewritten to replace incorrect ones, and there are other defects in the organization" (Jackson, 1981, p. 60). Few attempts were made by the scribes who worked on the book to correct the textual errors. "What seemed to matter most to the scribes who made this book was the magical pictorial imagery they were weaving for the eye of the mind" (p. 61).

Readership.   As already mentioned, a number of orthographic and graphic devices have evolved under the pressure of an expanded readership for a script. Hebrew, for example, was for centuries written only with consonants. Speakers of the language could, with context, supply the missing vowels because Hebrew, like the other Semitic languages, distinguishes meanings primarily with consonants, using vowels to mark grammatical forms. In time, several "weak" consonants *(aleph, he, waw, yod)* began to appear occasionally as indicators of vowel quality. These *matres lectionis* or "mothers of reading," eventually became regular vowel indicators, thus producing a form of writing called *scriptio plene.* But *scriptio plene* could only indicate 4 of the 10 vowels reconstructed for ancient Hebrew and therefore did not result in a full alphabetic system (Gelb, 1963). In the 8th century of the common era, however, at least three different systems for indicating complete vocalizations evolved: Babylonian, Palestinian, and Tiberian. The latter two were primarily superlinear, the last, mostly sublinear. Of these three, only the Tiberian has survived (Chomsky, 1957). As stated earlier, the primary motivation for the vowel indicators was the expanded and dispersed readership that evolved after the destruction of the Second Temple. Because correct pronunciation of the holy scriptures was desired, and a small group of priests no longer were the main readers, a complete system for generating pronunciation became a necessity.

English spelling represents another case where expanded usage of an orthography led to concessions to the reader. Although English orthography evolved toward a standard of sorts through the Renaissance, it was not until English was restored as the language of Parliament that standardization of spelling became an issue (Fisher, 1977). Yet even after the introduction of printing, spelling regularity was often sacrificed to printing convenience. For example, many English words retained a final *e* in the 15th and 16th centuries, even though the *e* was no longer pronounced. The early English printers would sometimes include or delete the *e* to achieve proper justification of a line.

The Minim Problem

The clearest evidence for visual considerations in orthographic or graphic changes prior to the 16th century occurs in relation to what is called the *minim problem.* By the late 12th century, a condensed, upright form of Carolingian minuscules had developed, with most of the curves excluded. Downstrokes tended to be heavy, with horizonal and diagonal connectors quite thin. A succession of three downstrokes might represent *in, ni, m, iii, ui, iu,* or *w.*

> The risk of misreading is perhaps at its greatest when the manuscript presents a succession of "minims," the short perpendicular strokes which in varying numbers compose the manuscript letters *i* (often equivalent to *j*), *m, n,* and *u* (often equivalent to *v*). Words whose written forms consist wholly or predominantly of successive minims are particularly frequent in Latin: common examples are *nimium, minimum, annuum, immunis, innumeri.* Medieval scribes are seldom at pains to indicate the position, or even the presence, of *i,* and after 1200 very few of them make any visible distinction between *n* and *u, m* and *ni* (in, ui, iu), and so forth. (Hector, 1966, p. 27)

Beginning in the 13th century a number of changes occurred in English orthographic practices that could be interpreted as steps toward solving the minim problem, that is, steps toward making manuscripts more legible. These changes were (a) substituting *o* for short *u* in contiguity with *m, n, u,* and so forth; (b) reversing *hw* to *wh;* and (c) substituting *y* for *i* in contiguity with *m, n, u,* and so forth. Some of these changes, such as the use of *y* as a variant of *i,* resulted from similar Norman practices; others, like the reversal of *hw* occurred only in English. In the latter change, a phonologically accurate spelling (*hw*) was sacrificed for a more legible one (*wh*).

On the replacement of *u* by *o* when *u* represented a short vowel (e.g., *wolf, woman, worm; above, dove, love; monk, money; come, some*), Scragg (1974, p. 44) agreed that visual factors were important when *u* was adjacent to *v* (which was then identical to *u*) and *w* (which was written *uu*), but doubts that this same argument can be applied to words in which *u* was adjacent to *m* or *n.* Several purely graphic changes also occurred at this time, apparently motivated by the minim problem. One was the addition of a mark over *i,* which according to Pyles (1964), developed from a faint sloping line that Middle English scribes introduced to distinguish *i* from adjacent *m, n,* and *u,* and to distinguish *ii* from *u.*

A second change was the development of a tailed form of *i,* which eventually became modern *j.* "The same cause that led to the dotting of *i* contributed largely to the formation of *j,* originally merely a lengthened or tailed *i* used finally as a more distinctive form, especially when two *i*'s came together, as in *ingenij,* or in the numerals *ij, iij, viij,* etc" (Oxford English Dictionary, Vol. 5, p. 517). *I* and *j,* like *u* and *v,* were not differentiated in early modern English writing. However, by the 16th century some writers used *i* exclusively for vowels and *j* only for consonants. But complete separation did not occur until nearly the middle of the 19th century.

A third graphic change involved the distribution of the curved and angular forms of *u* (*u* and *v*), which were used in Old and Middle English indiscriminantly for both consonant and vowel values. Middle English scribes began to use *v* initially and *u* elsewhere, regardless of whether they represented consonant or vowel. However, when a *u* would be adjacent to *m* or *n,* an exception was made for legibility through the substitution of *v* (Pyles, 1964).

Summary

Until the masses could read and print became competitive in the marketplace, changes in writing styles, fonts, and page formats favored the interests of the writer/printer over those of the reader. Transitions from pictograms to syllabaries may have been driven as much by economy of memory as by scribal convenience, but the adoption of more condensed scripts and of elaborate systems of abbreviations were most probably driven by a desire to economize on parchment and scribal time. A few exceptions to this pattern occurred, as in the development of Carolingian minuscules under Charlemagne and in some spelling and graphic alterations to reduce confusability of script, but until at least the end of the 18th century the eyes of the reader were not a systematic consideration in writing or printing.

VISUAL PROCESSING IN EARLY STUDIES OF READING

The earliest empirical studies on the visual aspects of reading were concerned with legibility of print. In Paris in the 1790s, two typefaces were compared for legibility by measuring the closest distances at which experts could no longer read them (Updike, 1928). In 1827, Charles Babbage (of mechanical calculator fame) evaluated the effects of different shades of paper on legibility through majority vote (Pyke, 1926). But the true beginnings of the psychological investigation of reading are marked not by these early explorations of legibility but by the inauguration of Wundt's laboratory at the University of Leipzig in the late 1870s.

One of Wundt's experimental interests was the speed of mental events and the dominant paradigm for studying this factor was the reaction time experiment, with Donder's subtractive procedure used to isolate the time factors for different stages of processing (Cattell, 1888). Reading was a convenient and familiar process for measuring reaction times of mental activity, so for a brief period printed letters, words, and sentences occupied stage center in the psychological laboratory.

For our purposes the central figure in Leipzig was not Wilhelm Wundt, but James McKeen Cattell, an American who spent 3 years with Wundt as a graduate student, receiving his doctorate from Leipzig in 1886. Cattell was one of a steady stream of U.S. graduate students, including Joseph Mayer Rice, Lincoln Steffens, and Gertrude Stein, who made pilgrimages to the psychological laboratories of Germany. While at Leipzig, Cattell concentrated on individual differences, yet he is most remembered among reading researchers for his work on letter and word recognition, legibility, and the span of attention.

In two articles published in the mid-1880s (Cattell, 1885, 1886), Cattell described three seminal experiments in the visual processing of print. The first (1885) demonstrated that at brief exposure intervals, accomplished readers could read three or four randomly selected letters or two randomly selected words. This result, which contrasted with Valentius' claim (cited in Schmidt, 1917) that letters were perceived separately in word perception, was for many years cited as evidence in support of teaching reading via whole word methods.

Another experiment demonstrated that naming times for single words decreased as more words to be named were in view simultaneously. The parallel processing implied by this result is responsible for the eye-voice span first reported by Quantz (1897–1898), but not investigated thoroughly until Buswell (1920). The third study was similar to the first two, except the task was to read aloud connected and unconnected words and letters. In general, Cattell found that competent readers required about twice as much time to read the unconnected as the connected material. (On Cattell's studies, see also Dearborn, 1914.)

At the same time that Wundt was initially stocking his laboratory in Leipzig, Emile Javal, a French ophthalmologist, was studying eye movements in reading, as well as the legibility of print. Javal's discovery that the eyes in reading moved *par saccades* or jumps contradicted the prevailing views on eye control and motivated similar studies throughout Europe and later, North America (Javal, 1879).

From the middle 1880s until the beginnings of the educational testing movement (c. 1911), perceptual studies of reading were common in experimental psychology. Although the first studies were done in Europe (Paris, Leipzig, Halle, etc.), by the early 1900s active experimental psychology laboratories existed in North America, including Yale (Judd, McAllister, Stelle), Brown (Delabarre), Columbia (Cattell), Wesleyan (Dodge), Clark (Huey), and Wisconsin (Quantz, Dearborn). By 1908 three major experimental studies of reading had been published (Dearborn, 1906; Huey, 1908; Quantz, 1897–1898), a stage-by-stage processing model proposed, subvocal speech analyzed, and pronunciations of pseudowords collected. The primary issues explored during this golden era—word recognition, eye movements, field of vision, and perceptual span—are summarized here. A fuller account is given in Venezky (1984), which is the basis for this discussion.

Word Recognition

Word perception was, as it is today, one of the central mysteries of the reading process. Erdmann and Dodge (1898) demonstrated that words could be read at a distance at which their constituent letters could not be identified. This result, which was later misinterpreted as support for a wholeword instructional strategy, was consistent with Cattell's (1886) finding that the perceptual span for letters in meaningful words was considerably greater than the span for letters in random strings. Adding further support to the holistic explanation was a study reported by Pillsbury (1897) in which subjects were asked to identify words in which a letter was either omitted, blurred with an overtyped *x,* or replaced by another letter. These words were exposed for brief durations and the subjects were asked not only to identify each word but to comment on any letters that were not clearly seen. Subjects tended not to report many of the letters that were altered and in some cases even insisted that a replaced letter was clearly seen. (Omissions were detected in 40% of the cases, replacements in 22%, and blurs in only 14%.)

Opposition to the whole-word recognition school focused mainly on letters and letter features. Goldscheider and Muller (1893) found that misreadings of briefly exposed words were more frequent if certain "determining letters" were absent than if other "indifferent letters" were missing. Zeitler (1900), whose work is summarized at length in Huey (1908), derived a theory of "dominant letters" from studying which letters were reported most accurately in misreadings of tachistoscopically presented words. Messmer (1904) also found evidence for perception mediated by "dominating" letters or complexes. Long letters that projected above the line tended to dominate more than those that projected below the line, but attention during recognition pauses can also wander, allowing other parts of the word to affect the response.

In general, the German psychologists supported word recognition mediated by letters and letter groups, whereas North American psychologists argued for total form. An exception on this side of the Atlantic was Hamilton (1907), who supported neither a pure word shape nor a dominant letter theory. Hamilton, who taught at the New York Training School for Teachers, had worked as a student with many of the leading U.S. psychologists at the beginning of the 20th century: W. L. Bryan and J. A. Bergstrom at Indiana University, J. R. Angell and J. B. Watson at the University of Chicago, and E. L. Thorndike and R. S. Woodworth at Columbia, where Hamilton received his doctorate. As part of his dissertation study, Hamilton examined the reading under brief exposure times of short sentences, phrases, and words. The subjects related orally after each trial what they read, including their degree of certainty for each word or word part, and their subjective description of their impressions.

As would be expected, the subjects read more in connected sentences than they did in miscellaneous phrases, and more in miscellaneous phrases than for miscellaneous words (for the same exposure times). In a second experiment, paragraphs were exposed line by line, with repeated exposures until full recognition was achieved. Subjects reported not only the words that they recognized but also partial impressions. Hamilton (1907) concluded that for adults, word recognition for familiar words occurred through general features—word shape, length, certain determining letters. "But when some unfavorable condition arises or when the words are strange or difficult, additional distinctions within the word are required, in which case the parts of the word must be brought more or less clearly to consciousness according to the degree of the complexity or unfamiliarity" (p. 52). Hamilton (1907, p. 53) spoke of a "conscious resort to such analysis," implying that the reader controlled the recognition strategy, deploying different procedures for different processing tasks. Included in this same report was a reference to stages of word processing, with a comment that introspection, which was a common experimental procedure at that time, was not too useful for demonstrating the various stages.

As was common at the time, Hamilton inferred that his results with adults were sufficient evidence for deciding how children should be taught. "In the first place it has been found that in every form of experiment in reading which has been undertaken, the influence of context as a condition of word recognition is strongly in evidence. . . . The value of these facts as a warrant for the pedagogical practise of presenting reading lessons in the form of whole compositions is obvious" (p. 52).

Dearborn (1906) attempted to resolve the word recognition controversy through eye movement recordings, but mistakenly assumed that changes in attention, as would occur during word perception mediated by letters, would necessarily be accompanied by fixation changes. Not finding any, he declared firmly for word shape. Huey (1908), although concluding that word form was the primary cue for recognition, hedged somewhat on the role that letters might play in this process. The general condition of word perception theories in the early 20th century, however, was aptly described by Huey (1908), who wrote, perhaps for the entire century: "It is very difficult to draw final conclusions concerning visual perception in reading" (p. 102).

Eye Movements

One of the most controversial issues in the golden era of reading research concerned the nature of perception during reading, and especially the question of whether or not perception occurred while the eyes were moving. Cattell suggested that it did, but experiments by Erdmann and Dodge (1898) and Dodge (1900, 1907) produced evidence to the contrary. For those who held that visual perception did not occur during eye movements, a further controversy developed over the inhibitory mechanism. Dodge (1900) held that optical blurring was the cause, and Holt (1903) attributed it to a central inhibitory process. (More recently, demonstrations of the correctness of Dodge's position have been published by Volkmann, 1962, and Uttal and Smith, 1968.) Related to this issue was a conflict over the regularity of eye movements. Javal claimed that the eyes paused on every tenth letter in reading. Huey (1908), although not supporting the specific span of 10 letters, nevertheless held that eye movements were rhythmic. Erdmann and Dodge (1898), on the other hand, stressed the irregularities in eye movements due to individual differences and to differences in reading materials. In contrast to this view, Dearborn (1906) concluded that length of line, and not sentence form or subject matter, conditioned the fixation pattern. He, nevertheless, did find large individual differences in motor habits, and noted especially the differences evidenced by the same subject in successive readings of the same passage.

Much less controversial were conclusions drawn about the nature of fixations during reading. Huey (1898) observed that fixations often involved small movements of the eye around a limited area. Both McAllister (1905) and Dearborn (1906) investigated this phenomenon, the latter finding that readjustments tended to occur primarily during the fixations at the beginning and end of a line. Data were also accumulated on the number of fixations made on lines of different lengths, on the negative relationship between this variable and reading speed, and on the places within a line where the eyes are most likely to fixate. Investigation of this latter variable is perhaps the most important contribution of Dearborn's (1906) dissertation study. By comparing eye movements during successive rereadings of the same passages, Dearborn concluded that sequences of small function words required relatively more fixations than longer content words because they could not readily be fused into larger units. "Since they [prepositions, conjunctions, etc.] occur now with one word and now with another, they cannot without danger of error be fused into larger wholes, and, for that reason, they must, except where the content gives the connection, be separately perceived" (p. 85).

Dearborn (1906) was also the first to investigate the role of orthographic structure and pronounceability in reading. Using rows of unrelated nonsense words (five words per row) as stimuli, Dearborn obtained eye movement records from adult readers. From an analysis of these records and of the structure of the nonsense words, he concluded the following:

> The length of the [fixation] pause is due in part to the sequence of letters. If that is the normal or more common sequence of words, such as "werq," "wopi," "gero," "apli," "enfa," the association process is less interfered with; such combinations as "ciuo," "weao," "dpin" disappoint the association expectancy and the time taken for perception is longer. A second and perhaps more important element is that of the ease of pronunciation . . . articulation or some form of motor expression is undoubtably one of the factors which determine the length of the fixation pauses in general. (p. 65)

Although Dearborn's concept of common (i.e., English-like) letter sequences is slightly askew (the final *q* in *werq*, for example, does not occur in English spelling), his suggestions about the role of orthographic structure and pronounce-ability were unusual for his time. Not until the work of E. J. Gibson and her colleagues in the early 1960s (e.g., Gibson, Pick, Osser, & Hammond, 1962) was this issue revived, and it remains unresolved today.

Eye movements returned to a position of prominence beginning in the 1920s as part of the debate over the relative values of oral and silent reading. Judd and Buswell (1922), for example, used eye movement comparisons to emphasize the differences between oral and silent reading. In the 1930s a variety of studies (e.g., Anderson & Swanson, 1937; Fairbanks, 1937; Swanson, 1937), using methodologies similar to those of Judd and Buswell (1922), concluded the op-posite, that is, that the two processes were highly similar. Most of these studies made simple, correlational comparisons between oral and silent reading factors. For example, Anderson and Swanson (1937), using college students, found high correlations between oral and silent reading for pause duration, fixation frequen-cy, and reading rate.

The first comparison of eye movements across languages and writing systems was made by Gray (1956). Eye movements and reading rates were recorded in the reading laboratory at the University of Chicago for 78 adults, almost all of whom were graduate students in universities in and around Chicago. Included were competent speakers of Arabic, Burmese, Chinese, English, French, Hebrew, Hindi, Japanese, Korean, Navaho, Spanish, Thai, Urdu, and Yoruba. No significant differences in eye movement patterns were found across the lan-guages involved. In all cases, fixation durations for oral reading were longer than those for silent reading. The average number of words recognized per fixation also did not vary between oral and silent reading, except for English and French, where small differences were found. How "word" was defined for languages like Arabic, Hebrew, and Chinese was not described, however. (The definition, if consistent within a language, would affect only the comparisons across lan-guages.)

Field of Vision and Perceptual Span

Cattell's studies established that the field of distinct vision and the perceptual span were different entities, the latter depending on the subject's ability to group stimuli into larger units. Erdmann and Dodge (1898) found similar results, using isolated letters, words, and sentences. Quantz (1897–98) approached this prob-lem by interrupting the reading stimulus during reading and counting the number of words that could be produced beyond this point. The resulting eye–voice span was found to vary not only by individual, but also by place in the line where the interruption occurred. The span was longest at the beginning of the line and shortest at the end. Hamilton (1907), like Cattell (1886) and Erdmann and Dodge (1898), used a tachistoscopic exposure of sentences, but asked his subjects to report everything they could resolve of the stimulus, including image shape and first letters. He found that even when whole words were not resolved, various word features were nevertheless correctly retained.

More typical, however, of work on span of attention during this period is a study by Griffing (1896) in which subjects from grade one through college attempted to identify briefly exposed capital letters. Each exposure contained six randomly drawn letters, arranged in two rows of three letters each. Exposure durations were 0.1s and 1s; each subject received 10 trials at each exposure duration. Subjects showed continual improvement with increasing grade level, with the advantage of increased exposure time decreasing steadily over the same age span. Although Griffing's main concern was attention, he was not willing to attribute the entire experimental effect to this factor. He was clearly aware of immediate memory problems, mentioning the "ability to receive and retain a number of simultaneous retinal impressions."

Huey (1908) also clearly distinguished between the field of vision, as measured with nonredundant materials and perceptual span, which depended on predictive ability. Earlier studies had shown that more material was generally recognized to the right than to the left of the fixation point in reading and that unusually long strings of words might be recognized in a single fixation if the words were meaningfully connected. However, with randomly selected letters, only four or five could be recognized at once. Huey (1908) also summarized work showing that with longer strings of unrelated letters (e.g., 6–7), the first and last letters were most easily recognized.

Using the letters *n* and *u,* Ruediger found that the size of the visual field varied with the size and legibility of the test letter and its distance from the eye. By measuring the reading rates and numbers of fixations per line for his subjects, Ruediger also found that the size of the visual field did not relate to either reading speed or fixation pattern. He concluded that reading rate was primarily a function of the speed of comprehension processes that occurred after word perception.

Other issues, such as the integration of information across fixations were also investigated (Dearborn, 1906; Dockeray, 1910), but by the time adequate instrumentation was available for such work, educational psychology had separated from experimental psychology and shifted its attention to schooling and testing, whereas experimental psychology was beginning its transition away from an interest in mental events, moving toward the long winter of behaviorism.

Summary

By the end of 1911 the first volume of the *Journal of Educational Psychology* had been issued and Thorndike's handwriting scale was published. Behaviorism was ready to emerge on the psychological scene, to share the foreground with educational testing and school efficiency. Research on visual factors would continue, particularly on eye movements (Fairbanks, 1937; C. T. Gray, 1917; Judd

& Buswell, 1922; Tinker, 1946), but the pace would be slower and more to the periphery of reading research. The intensity of work on visual factors and the excitement of discovery that characterized the golden era would not reappear until after the passage of the Cooperative Research Act of 1954.

DISABILITIES, ABNORMALITIES, AND ANOMALIES

Interest in the visual aspects of reading disability, abnormality, or anomaly began in the 19th century and continues to the present time. Depending on the investigator, observations on such reading defects served to further theories about brain organization, ocular-muscular functioning, or reading instruction. Three basic schools have developed on reading disability, each focusing on a different set of causes for reading malfunction and failure. They are to some degree in competition with each other, but each also has its own exclusive territory within which the other schools have no basis for trespassing. For convenience of discussion, these schools are called *neurological, ocular-motor,* and *psychoeducational,* although the names should be taken as approximate characterizations only, and not as definitions.

Neurological Functioning

Hinshelwood.   The neurological school originated from an interest in acquired and congenital word-blindness and has been dominated by two camps, each centered on a different view of cortical malfunctions in relation to reading. In 1895, a Glasgow eye surgeon, James Hinshelwood, published an account of acquired word-blindness, that is, of sudden loss of reading ability after damage to the brain (Hinshelwood, 1895). In the following year, two accounts of congenital word-blindness appeared in England. One, from James Kerr, medical officer of health in the city of Bradford, mentioned briefly in an essay on school hygiene a boy of normal or above-normal intelligence who could "spell the separate letters" but was word-blind (cited in Critchley, 1964, p. 7). The second account came from Dr. W. Pringle Morgan, a general practitioner in the English town of Seaford, and was published in the *British Medical Journal* (Morgan, 1896). Morgan described some of the characteristics of a 14-year-old boy, also of normal or above-normal intelligence, who had good ability in arithmetic and algebra but could not learn to read. Morgan assumed a neurological disorder as the cause of the boy's reading failure. In forwarding a copy of his article to Hinshelwood, Morgan wrote in a covering letter that word-blindness might possibly be congenital.

Although Hinshelwood, Kerr, and Morgan are generally credited with the first published accounts of word-blindness, earlier accounts from the 19th century have been found by Critchley (1964). For example, a professor from Montpelier named Lordat recounted his own recovery from a speech disorder, which included the loss for a period of time of the ability to read. Kussmaul in 1877 supposedly was the first to propose the term *word-blindness* for aphasic loss of reading ability where other intellectual abilities remained intact. In the early 1870s, Broadbent reported on a word-blindness case in which an autopsy revealed lesions in the left angular and supramarginal gyri regions—the first record of a connection between acquired word-blindness and cortical damage.

The term *dyslexia,* which is generally applied to cases of word-blindness where other intellectual functions are intact, has an uncertain history. According to Critchley (1964, p. 2), it was first proposed by Professor Berlin of Stuttgart in 1887 in a monograph entitled "Eine besondere Art der Wortblindheit (Dyslexia)." However, the *Oxford English Dictionary Supplement* (Vol. 1, 1972) cites an 1883 usage by Berlin (German dyslexie). *Dyslexia,* according to the first edition of the *Oxford English Dictionary* (vol. 3, p. 738) is "a difficulty in reading due to affection of the brain." This definition, published in 1897, differs from the definition of *word-blindness* that occurs in volume 12, but was not published until 1927: "inability to understand written or printed words when seen, owing to disease of the visual *word-centre*" (p. 283). Hinshelwood (1917) proposed a three-way distinction between *congenital dyslexia* (mildly backward readers), *congenital alexia* (inability to read by the mentally retarded), and *congenital word-blindness* (cases of pure reading defect where other functions are intact). These distinctions have not been widely subscribed, however.

Modern dictionaries do not fully agree on definitions for dyslexia, varying from simple statements of *reading disability* to more elaborate causal mechanisms, including *inability to integrate auditory and visual information.* The *International Reading Association Dictionary of Reading and Related Terms* (Harris & Hodges, 1981, p. 95) has what is probably the most accepted definition among reading educators: "A rare but definable and diagnosable form of primary reading retardation with some form of central nervous system dysfunction."

Hinshelwood, in spite of his failure to establish preferred nomenclature for the field, nevertheless was the most influential voice for almost a quarter of a century in the neurophysiology of word-blindness. Through case reports and two monographs (Hinshelwood, 1900, 1917), he elaborated a theory based on separate cortical areas for visual memory of letters, words, and general perceptual input. Word-blindness resulted from damage to the visual memory center for words and might not be accompanied by damage to any of the other visual memory centers. For example, in an 1898 report he described a 53-year-old man who lost his ability to read after a stroke, but continued to recognize letters and numbers normally, and could write to dictation and copy words.

His most intriguing case concerned a 34-year-old man who before he suffered a stroke could read fluently English, French, Latin, and Greek (Hinshelwood, 1902). The stroke left him aphasic, but still capable of naming letters and some shorter English words. Some longer words could be recognized if he spelled them aloud letter by letter, but sentences in English were beyond his immediate poststroke ability. Nevertheless, he could still read Greek fluently and with some difficulty handle Latin and French. (The Greek was tested on Homer, Xenophon, and the *New Testament.*) The man became aphasic in early July 1901 and by end of September of that year had made nearly a full recovery of his reading abilities. Hinshelwood (1902, p. 361) concluded that "in the case of a person who is able to read several languages the letter- and word-visual images of each language will be grouped together forming thus a series of separate groups within the centre."

Although the term *word-blindness* has been adopted for the anomaly discussed here, it is important to note that the problem reported is not in the primary perceptual stages of processing, but in the association of an image with a name or meaning in long-term memory. Some writers have pointed out that dyslexia could result from impairment of a specific memory center or from defects in the connecting fibers between specific centers or processing areas (e.g., Lord, Carmichael, & Dearborn, 1925; Wallin, 1920). As logical as the explanations are of impairment to specific cortical areas or to interconnections, almost all of them originated without conclusive postmortem examinations. Robinson (1946), whose review of the pre-World War II neurological evidence for reading failure is among the best available, claims that Hinshelwood did only a single postmortem examination among all of the word-blindness patients he examined. Orton (1928) concluded that no postmortem had ever been done on a patient with congenital word-blindness.

Although some educational psychologists have been highly critical of neurological theories of reading failure (e.g., Gates, 1927), the evidence for a neurological connection to acquired word-blindness is difficult to refute. In almost all cases reported, word-blindness occurred after a stroke or other form of brain trauma and disappeared generally within 6 months. Hinshelwood, although not a reading specialist, adopted early in his work a sequence of tests for picture, letter, and word naming. The patient was first shown an illustrated picture book and asked to identify and name one of the pictures (e.g., "cat"). Then the patient was asked to spell the name out loud and to name letters of the alphabet from their printed forms (both upper- and lowercase). Finally, the patient was asked to locate exemplars of the selected word in a printed text without moving his lips or hands and without spelling the word aloud.

Other reports of both acquired and congenital dyslexia from early in this century showed a similar sensitivity to different components of reading behavior. Rutherfurd (1909), for example, reported a case of a 10-year-old girl who could read short, simple words (e.g., *an, of, the, if*), but not longer or less familiar monosyllables (e.g., *first, think*). She also could not pronounce words from hearing their spellings nor could she remember words pointed out to her in the text. She could, however, identify pictures easily. Rutherfurd (1909) traced the family of his patient and found that her parents and grandparents were illiterate. Thomas (1905) also reported a family association with congenital word-blindness, as did Hinshelwood (1907), who examined four brothers with the disability. What cannot be determined from these cases, however, is whether dyslexia resulted from similar cortical defects within each family, transmitted through heredity, or if it resulted from shared combinations of environmental and educational factors, such as poor nutrition, ingestion of excessive amounts of lead or mercury, or limited schooling.

Orton.   Samuel T. Orton, director of a county medical clinic in Iowa, became interested in word-blindness in the early 1920s, but unlike Hinshelwood, focused his medical attention on lateral dominance. In a series of influential publications, Orton (1925, 1928, 1937) advanced an explanation for reading failure based on developmental changes in cortical localization. According to Orton's analysis, in the early stages of learning to read, both hemispheres participate in the recognition of letters and words. That is, the images of letters and words are projected onto both the left and right associative cortices, one being a mirror image of the other. In normal reading development, the confusing images of the nondominant hemisphere, which are reversed from those in the dominant hemisphere, are repressed. Reading disability, therefore, results from a failure of the dominant hemisphere to suppress the interfering images from the nondominant hemisphere. This defect he called *strephosymbolia,* for "twisted signs," a term that has failed to gain a place in the reading disability literature outside of the Orton school.

Orton's claims of "ambiguous occipital dominance" derived in part from high correlations he claimed to have found between reading disability and left-handedness or ambidexterity, and from a high incidence of reversals in both the reading and the writing of the reading disabled. In particular, he found mirror writing to be a direct substantiation of the reversed images he hypothesized to be stored in the nondominant hemisphere. Most reading educators, in contrast, have not found merit in Orton's claims. Gates (1936, p. 352) was one of the first to reject Orton, claiming "the idea that confused brain dominance or lack of dominance should be the cause of such reading difficulties was considered too speculative to be serviceable." The idea of mirror images or engrams he dismissed as "unacceptable to most psychologists" (p. 351). More reasoned criticisms were made by Critchley (1964), who questioned why verbal symbols would show a dysfunctionality not shared by other visual stimuli—objects, scenes, pictures, and so forth. He also questioned how such an explanation could account for confusions in the lateral direction only.

Attempts to relate eye and hand dominance with reading disability have yielded mixed results and questions remain on the proper evaluation of dominance and of the relationship of eye dominance evaluated in static situations with eye dominance during the dynamics of reading. Dearborn (1932–33) and Eames

(1934), among others, report data in support of Orton's hypothesis, derived from comparing eye-hand dominance in reading-disabled groups with the same factors in controls. Witty and Kopel (1936) and Traxler (1937), in contrast, are representative of studies in the United States that failed to support Orton. Hermann (1959), who worked in Copenhagen, also arrived at a negative conclusion on eye-hand dominance and dyslexia. More recent work, particularly that of Benton (1975), has tended to reject Orton's dominance claims. Nevertheless, the Orton Society maintains a respectable following and some educators still find favor in the dominance hypothesis (e.g., Downing & Leong, 1982). Crider's summary of this work from 1934 appears to be valid today: "The opinions advanced by Orton and Dearborn are commendable as hypotheses but they are not theories and even less are they facts" (cited in Robinson, 1946, p. 42).

Ocular-muscular Functioning.   With Javal's observations in the 1870s of the saccadic nature of the reading process came a parallel observation of visual fatigue from reading (cited in Huey, 1908, p. 387). With sustained reading, the eyes are not only traveling at a variety of different rates (e.g., about 8 feet per minute average for saccadic jumps and fixations combined and about 140 feet per minute average during return sweeps), but also starting and stopping about 146 times per minute. (Luckiesh and Moss, 1942, estimated that during 8 hours of reading, the ocular muscular mechanism will start and stop about 70,000 times.) Visual fatigue might involve fatigue of the retina as well as ocular muscular fatigue and fatigue of the optical pathways that transmit visual information to the brain. Although this is not a topic that is developed fully here, it was during the first half of this century an issue in the study of reading.

Besides Javal (1879), Griffing and Franz (1896) wrote on visual fatigue before the 20th century, as did a number of German psychologists. Huey (1908), in his *Psychology and Pedagogy of Reading,* devoted two chapters to the topic, one on the nature of visual fatigue and one on the characteristics of printed texts that contribute to decreased fatigue. Major texts on the topic did not appear, however, until the 1940s (e.g., Lukiesh and Moss, 1942, and Carmichael and Dearborn, 1947). The latter has the most extensive bibliography to be found on the topic up to that date, incorporating over 400 items, including a considerable number from the 19th century. The term *reading hygiene,* which included visual fatigue as one of its components, was not used much past the first quarter of this century. What was incorporated under this title became, in time, studies of visibility and legibility.

Educational Views

Other neurological explanations of reading failure exist, such as a functional maturational lag (Chall & Mirsky, 1978; Wixson & Lipson, 1991), but for the most part educators have been unwilling to accept single cause explanations for the range of reading disabilities that are observed in the schools. For many years the work of Hinshelwood and of Orton was ignored by educators and educational psychologists. For example, neither Huey (1908), nor Wheat (1923), nor Anderson and Dearborn (1952) devoted a single line to dyslexia or word-blindness in their texts on the psychology of reading. Brooks (1926) provided a neutral, brief description, listing it as one of 13 causes of slow silent reading, along with defective vision, lack of interest, and so forth. Gates (1927) was outright hostile toward neurological explanations, whereas Monroe (1932) and Robinson (1946) viewed faulty neurological development as one of a number of potential explanations for reading failure. Their specific views are the subject of the next section.

Gates.   The educational testing movement that began in the second decade of this century with the publication of Thorndike's (1910) handwriting scale led rapidly to a national industry in reading diagnosis and assessment. So overwhelming was the educational fascination with reading tests that by the 1920s reading research articles on testing dominated over all other topics. But the times were ripe for assessment and accountability. The massive immigration movement that extended from the 1880s until the beginning of World War I when the doors were shut had brought a dramatic increase in school enrollments. Methods were needed to determine objectively where students should be placed when they entered the school system. Then, silent reading, which began to replace oral reading at the end of the 19th century as the dominant mode of school-based reading, created a further need for objective assessment. With oral reading, the teacher need only listen, but with silent reading some probe was needed to determine if mind and eye were synchronized and efficient. Which was cause and which was effect may not be clear in this environment; silent reading may have been an outcome of overcrowded schools where teachers could not cope with either individual student needs or the din from unsynchronized oral reading. Objective, group-administered tests provided a level of assessment that was no longer possible with individual oral presentation. But whichever came first, tests were adopted wholeheartedly and have remained in the schools ever since.

In parallel with objective, standardized tests came a concern for reading failure, for the students who in the past were simply considered slow or backward. Just as Binet and Henri developed intelligence tests to identify students who had potential for learning but were not progressing as expected in the French schools, diagnostic tests for reading were developed to determine what, if anything, might be done with disabled readers. Among the work done in the first four decades of this century on diagnosis of reading disabilities, the most influential was that of Gates and his colleagues at Teachers College, Columbia University. Gates, who had been a student of Thorndike at Columbia, published *The Improvement of Reading: A Program of Diagnostic and Remedial Methods* in 1927 and a revised edition in 1936. The first edition was based on studies done prior to the end of 1926 and showed the eclectic clinical model of reading diagnosis that remains in place today.

Gates' view on reading difficulty was that "most difficulties, ranging from the least to the most serious, are . . . due primarily to failures to acquire techniques that might have been acquired had the right guidance been given at the right time" (1936, p. 17). On the Hinshelwood/Orton notions about neurological causes for reading difficulties, Gates answered,

> It is recognized that various weaknesses and defects of the bodily organs and mechanisms involved in reading may prove to be handicaps, often very serious ones. Similarly, certain individual physical or mental characteristics, such as left-handedness or volatile personality, may predispose a pupil to develop difficulty. Thus, despite the fact that physical, mental and emotional obstacles are numerous and serious, it is believed that most children of Intelligence Quotients above 70 may be taught to read if optimal methods are employed. (p. 18)

The test battery that Gates assembled covered almost every aspect of reading considered important today: vocabulary and comprehension, phonics and auditory perception, eye movements, educational background and motivation, and so forth. For visual processing, Gates placed especially strong emphasis on left-to-right visual scanning and on properly sequenced instruction. He was probably the first to recognize that word recognition habits often resulted almost directly from the classroom methods used to teach word recognition. In an earlier study (Gates & Boeker, 1923), he had found that when beginning readers were introduced to new words with differing lengths, the children selected word length as a distinguishing feature, and when trained on words of the same length, they selected small details of each word idiosyncratically. (This subject was not revived in reading research until the work of Marchbanks & Levin, 1965, and Williams, Blumberg, & Williams, 1970.)

Drawing on work by Hildreth (1934), Gates also argued that letter and word reversals were totally normal and expected for beginning readers. Shape, but not direction, was a salient cue for object recognition in the child's world up to the time that letters and numbers are encountered. Remediation that stressed overtly the correct direction for word and line scanning was suggested to overcome this problem if it persisted. Gates was especially strong in insisting on left-to-right processing of words, railing against overemphasis on word endings. He failed to recognize, however, that overemphasis on word beginnings could lead to guessing at words based on first letters, a phenomenon observed in a number of countries.

Monroe and Robinson.   Among other important studies on reading disability, the work of Monroe (1932) and Robinson (1946) was nearly as influential as that of Gates. Monroe worked on reading disability at the University of Iowa in the

1920s where she came in contact with Orton and his ideas about mirror-reading and mirror-writing. Although tests for these phenomena were included in the test batteries she developed there and later at the Illinois Institute for Juvenile Research, the hemispheric dominance component of Orton's theory was not a major factor in her work (Monroe, 1928). Monroe (1932) reported on measures of reading disability among 415 children, ranging from the mentally retarded to the intellectually gifted, and a control group of 101 average school children. The experimental subjects varied in age from about 6 to 17, and the controls varied from about 6 to 11. The range of quantitative and qualitative tests given to each student included reading and mathematics achievement, oral reading errors, intelligence, hand- and eye-preference, mirror-reading and mirror-writing, handwriting, speech and auditory discrimination, and sound blending.

Results from the visual processing measurements showed a significantly greater percentage of left-eye preference and left-eye preference with right-hand preference within the reading disability groups than among the controls. Left-eye preference was associated with fluent mirror reading, which in turn was associated with reading disability. In contrast, reversal errors in reading did not differ significantly according to eye preference. The first general conclusion drawn across the full battery of tests was that no single factor was represented in all of the remedial cases and each factor that helped differentiate the remedials from the controls could be found in a contradictory case. "It is probable that the reading defect is caused by a constellation of factors rather than by one isolating factor. Two children may therefore possess much the same impeding constitutional factor and yet one, through good environmental, methodological, and emotional factors, may overcome the disability, while the other, through poor environmental, methodological, and emotional factors, may become seriously retarded" (p. 110).

Robinson (1946) both reviewed the literature on reading disability and reported on analyses of 30 seriously retarded readers who ranged in age from 6 years 9 months to 15 years 3 months. All had IQs of at least 85 (New Stanford-Binet Intelligence Test, Form L) and each was examined by a battery of specialists, including a social worker, psychiatrist, pediatrician, neurologist, ophthalmologist, speech-correctionist, a reading specialist, and a few others. Besides achievement tests for reading, each child was tested for eye, hand, foot, and ear preference. (The other tests, covering vision, skull X-ray, hearing, etc. are not of direct interest here.) After testing, a remedial plan for each child was developed, but not all of the cases were treated by the investigator. Six of the 30 cases were judged by the neurologist to have indications of problems that could interfere with learning to read. One of these cases responded very quickly to remedial-reading training, two responded very slowly, and two were not treated.

Results from the preference tests showed a 93% agreement between hand and foot preference but only 73% agreement between hand and eye. No relationship was established, however, between eye and hand preference agreement and degree of reading disability.

The general results were similar to those found by Monroe (1932), that is, that multiple factors were usually involved in reading disability. Readers who were severely retarded in reading tended to have more anomalies than those who were less retarded, but the pattern of anomalies varied from reader to reader. Visual anomalies were the most prevalent, occurring in 73% of the cases. Social and emotional maladjustments were next in frequency of occurrence.

CONCLUSIONS

A search across the history of writing failed to find, prior to the introduction of printing, any significant attention to visual processing needs in the evolution of writing systems. Accelerating the output of the scribe/writer and minimizing the number of sheets of papyrus, parchment, or paper required for a document appeared to have been far more important than the travails of the reader. Exceptions did occur, as in the insertion of chapter titles, the slow evolution of punctuation, and perhaps even in the various changes that occurred beginning in the 13th century to break up sequences of minims.

To some degree this neglect of the reader can be explained by the limited number of literate people during the eras of interest, and by the role of reading at these times. Until the Renaissance, literacy was generally limited to clerics, administrators, and some members of the aristocracy. Although the percentage of literates varied considerably across and within countries throughout the history of writing, the idea of mass literacy, promulgated nationally, emerges only in the 19th century. Reading was primarily an oral activity and it served mainly bureaucratic and religious ends. When the appearance of the manuscript page was attended to, the goal was primarily to impress and to awe, not to enhance verbal communication. Without a mass market for print and without a common need to consume large amounts of print daily, there was little pressure on scribes or printers to produce more readable documents. Until a market occurred, competition in the production of print products was limited, and therefore the reader could not exercise a preference for more readable materials over less readable ones.

Almost no research is done on the nature of reading in earlier periods, yet this field could be explored through imitative experiments. It would, for example, be possible to do training and testing on the reading of medieval scripts, using letter search as well as other paradigms. Similarly, evidence may be available for estimating the total amount of reading that an administrator, shop owner, or trader might do during a week of work. Using data that could be obtained from studies of adult literacy, we might be able to estimate expected reading speed and possibly even degree of subvocalization in reading from earlier periods. At a minimum, legibility studies could be done of manuscript forms and of the fonts from the early period of movable type printing.

The end of the 18th century marks the beginning of the experimental study of visual factors in reading. These earliest studies, however, were totally atheoretical, as most legibility studies have tended to be since that time. With the emergence of experimental psychology in the last quarter of the 19th century, a knowledge base for studying the visual aspects of reading rapidly emerged. Equally importantly, reading was studied within a more general theoretical framework that was constructed around the speed of mental events and around perceptual processing in general. Within a period of about three decades, almost all of the visual processing problems that capture our attention today were observed and explored. Although we have far better equipment today for studying visual processing and we know far more about experimental procedures, we still return with unbridled nostalgia to Huey (1908) and the psychological milieu that he wrote about.

In doing so, we risk inflating the degree of insight and discovery that occurred then. Most experimenters prior to World War I had limited knowledge of perceptual development or of learning in general. Results from adult studies were assumed to be relevant to the instruction of the young. Except for a few experimenters like Hamilton, no one acknowledged the ability of the reader to control recognition strategies. Subjects for many studies were recruited from one's own faculty colleagues or advisors, and often from those who knew the purpose of the study and who may even have assisted in its design.

Oral report was often employed in the early studies of perception in reading, so confounding of perception and memory was frequent. Until the partial report paradigm was introduced, these factors were seldom separated. Other paradigms unknown before World War II, such as priming and the lexical decision task, have also contributed to an understanding of word recognition processing that extends far beyond what was known to Cattell or to Dodge or to Dearborn. Then, factors such as letter and word frequency and orthographic structure were poorly understood and seldom either explored or controlled in experiments. Models for visual processing were crude, at best, with limited or no appreciation of the different types of memory involved and the possibility of recoding for retention in short-term memory.

Yet even with these reservations, it is difficult to ignore the enormous progress that was made prior to World War I in understanding visual processes in reading. That we still are trying to understand how printed words are recognized, and why particular letters are often confused, and whether certain reading disabilities have a neurological basis do not mean that little was accomplished prior to the present time. Many of the old problems are still with us, as the remaining chapters of this book demonstrate, but we stand on higher ground in attacking them, thanks to what has been learned in the past.

More could be said on this topic and much of what has been said could be more tightly organized and more closely related to trends in psychology and education. Paradigms change, as Kuhn (1970) made us so aware, and many problems once thought to be pivotal to our continued existence are abandoned while formerly unnoticed issues become national concerns. With the current emphasis in reading research on assessment and on comprehension and higher level thinking, few major new research programs on word recognition will be started and no research and development center will be dedicated to this issue. Perhaps a knowledge of the rich history of interest in the visual component of reading and of the problems that remain will lead a few researchers to explore this arena.

REFERENCES

Anderson, I. H., & Dearborn, W. F. (1952). *The psychology of teaching reading.* New York: Ronald Press.

Anderson, I. H., & Swanson, D. E. (1937). Common factors in eye-movements in silent and oral reading. *Psychological Monographs, 48*(3), 61–69.

Benton, A. L. (1975). Developmental dyslexia: Neurological aspects. In W. J. Friedlander (Ed.), *Advances in neurology* (Vol. 7, pp. 1–47). New York: Raven Press.

Boorstin, D. J. (1983). *The discoverers.* New York: Random House.

Boyd, B. (1973). *Chaucer and the medieval book.* San Marino, CA: Huntington Library.

Brooks, F. D. (1926). *The applied psychology of reading.* New York: Appleton & Co.

Buswell, G. T. (1920). An experimental study of the eye-voice span in reading. *Supplementary Educational Monographs* (No. 17). Chicago: University of Chicago Press.

Carmichael, L., & Dearborn, W. F. (1947). *Reading and visual fatigue.* Boston: Houghton Mifflin.

Cattell, J. M. (1885). Ueber die Zeit der Erkennung und Benennung von Schriftzeichen, Bildern und Farben. *Philosophische Studien, 2,* 635–650.

Cattell, J. M. (1886). The time it takes to see and name objects. *Mind, 11,* 63–65.

Cattell, J. M. (1888). The psychological laboratory at Leipsic. *Mind, 13,* 37–51.

Chall, J. S., & Mirsky, A. F. (Eds.). (1978). *Education and the brain* (Yearbook of the National Society for the Study of Education, 77th. pt. 2). Chicago: National Society for the Study of Education.

Chaytor, H. J. (1945). *From script to print: An introduction to medieval vernacular literature.* Cambridge, England: Cambridge University Press.

Chomsky, W. (1957). *Hebrew: The eternal language.* Philadelphia: Jewish Publication Society.

Critchley, M. (1964). *Developmental dyslexia.* London: Heinemann.

Dearborn, W. F. (1906). The psychology of reading: An experimental study of the reading pulses and movements of the eye. *Archives of Philosophy, Psychology and Scientific Methods, 4*(4).

Dearborn, W. F. (1914). Professor Cattell's studies of perception and reading. *Archives of Psychology, 4*(30), 34–45.

Dearborn, W. F. (1932–1933). Structural factors which condition special disability in reading. *Proceedings and addresses of the fifty-seventh annual session of the American Association on Mental Deficiency, 38,* 268–283.

Dockeray, F. C. (1910). The span of vision in reading and the legibility of letters. *Journal of Educational Psychology, 1,* 123–131.

Dodge, R. (1900). Visual perception during eye movement. *Psychological Review, 7,* 454–465.

Dodge, R. (1906). Recent studies in the correlation of eye movement and visual perception. *Psychological Bulletin, 3,* 85–92.

Dodge, R. (1907). An experimental study of visual fixation. *Psychological Review Monograph Supplements, 3*(4) 1–96.

Downing, J., & Leong, C. K. (1982). *Psychology of reading.* New York: Macmillan.

Eames, T. H. (1934). Low fusion convergence as a factor in reading disability. *American Journal of Ophthalmology, 17,* 709–710.

Erdmann, R., & Dodge, R. (1898). *Psychologische Untersuchungen uber das Lesen auf Experimenteller Grundlage.* Halle: Neimeyer.

Fairbanks, G. (1937). The relation between eye-movements and voice in the oral reading of good and poor silent readers. *Psychological Monographs, 48*(3), 78–107.

Fisher, J. H. (1977). Chancery and the emergence of standard written English in the fifteenth century. *Speculum, 52,* 870–899.

Gates, A. I. (1926). A study of the role of visual perception, intelligence, and certain associative processes in reading and spelling. *Journal of Educational Psychology, 17,* 433–445.

Gates, A. I. (1927). *The improvement of reading: A program of diagnostic and remedial methods.* New York: Macmillan.

Gates, A. I. (1936). *The improvement of reading: A program of diagnostic and remedial methods* (rev. ed.). New York: Macmillan.

Gates, A. I., & Boeker, E. (1923). A study of initial stages in reading by pre-school children. *Teachers College Record, 24,* 469–488.

Gelb, I. J. (1963). *A study of writing* (rev. ed.). Chicago: University of Chicago Press.

Gibson, E. J., Pick, A., Osser, H., & Hammond, M. (1962). The role of grapheme-phoneme correspondence in the perception of words. *American Journal of Psychology, 75,* 554–570.

Goldscheider, A., & Muller, R. F. (1893). Zur Physiologie und Pathologie des Lesens. *Zeitschrift fur linische Medicin, 23,* 131–167.

Gray, C. T. (1917). Types of reading ability as exhibited through tests and laboratory experiments. *Supplementary Educational Monographs* (No. 5). Chicago: University of Chicago Press.

Gray, W. S. (1956). *The teaching of reading and writing.* Chicago: Scott, Foresman.

Griffing, H. (1896). On the development of visual perception and attention. *American Journal of Psychology, 7,* 227–236.

Griffing, H., & Franz, S. I. (1896). Conditions of fatigue in reading. *Psychological Review, 3,* 513–530.

Hamilton, F. M. (1907). The perceptual factors in reading. *Archives of Psychology, 9,* 1–56.

Harris, T. L., & Hodges, R. W. (Eds.). (1981). *A dictionary of reading and related terms.* Newark, DE: International Reading Association.

Hector, L. C. (1966). *The handwriting of English documents* (2nd ed.). London: Edward Arnold.

Hendrickson, G. L. (1929). Ancient reading. *Classical Journal, 25,* 182–196.

Hermann, K. (1959). *Reading disability: A medical study of word-blindness and related handicaps.* Springfield, IL: Charles C Thomas.

Hildreth, G. (1934). Reversals in reading and writing. *Journal of Educational Psychology, 25,* 1–20.

Hinshelwood, J. (1895). Word-blindness and visual memory. *Lancet, 2,* 1564–1570.

Hinshelwood, J. (1900). *Letter-, word- and mind-blindness.* London: Lewis.

Hinshelwood, J. (1902). Four cases of word-blindness. *Lancet, 1,* 358–363.

Hinshelwood, J. (1907). Four cases of congenital word-blindness occurring in the same family. *British Medical Journal, 2,* 1229.

Hinshelwood, J. (1917). *Congenital word-blindness.* London: Lewis.

Holt, E. B. (1903). Eye-movement and central anaesthesia. *Harvard Psychological Studies, 1* (issued as Vol. 4, *Psychological Monographs*), 3–48.

Huey, E. B. (1898). Preliminary experiments in the physiology and psychology of reading. *American Journal of Psychology, 9,* 575.

Huey, E. B. (1908). *The psychology and pedagogy of reading.* New York: Macmillan.

Jackson, D. (1981). *The story of writing.* New York: Taplinger.

Javal, L. (1879). Essai sur la physiologie de la lecture. *Annales d'Oculistique, 82,* 242–253.

Judd, C. H., & Buswell, G. T. (1922). Silent reading: A study of the various types. *Supplementary Educational Monographs* (No. 23). Chicago: University of Chicago Press.

Kuhn, T. S. (1970). *The structure of scientific revolutions* (2nd ed.). Chicago: University of Chicago Press.

Lord, E., Carmichael, L., & Dearborn, W. F. (1925). Special disabilities in learning to read and write. *Harvard Monographs in Education* (Ser. 1, Vol. 2, No. 1). Cambridge: Harvard University Press.

Luckiesh, M., & Moss, F. K. (1942). *Reading as a visual task.* New York: Van Nostrand.

Marchbanks, G., & Levin, H. (1965). Cues by which children recognize words. *Journal of Educational Psychology, 56,* 57–61.

McAllister, C. N. (1905). The fixation of points in the visual field. *Psychological Review Monograph Supplements, 7,* (1, Whole No. 29).

Messmer, O. (1904). Zur Psychologie des Lesens bei Kindern and Erwachsenen. *Archiv fur die gesamte Psychologie, 2,* 190–298.

Monroe, M. (1928). Methods for diagnosis and treatment of cases of reading disability. *Genetic Psychology Monographs* (Vol. 4, Nos. 4–5).

Monroe, M. (1932). *Children who cannot read.* Chicago: University of Chicago Press.

Morgan, W. P. (1896). A case of congenital word-blindness. *British Medical Journal, 2,* 1612–1614.

Orton, S. T. (1925). Word-blindness in school-children. *Archives of Neurology and Psychiatry, 14,* 581–615.

Orton, S. T. (1928, Sept.). An impediment in learning to read—A neurological explanation of the reading disability. *School & Society,* 286–290.

Orton, S. T. (1937). *Reading, writing and speech problems in children.* London: Chapman & Hall.

Oxford English Dictionary. (1933). Oxford: Oxford University Press.

Pillsbury, W. B. (1897). A study in apperception. *American Journal of Psychology, 8,* 315–398.

Pyke, R. L. (1926). Report on the legibility of print. *Medical Research Council Special Report Series* (No. 110). London.

Pyles, T. (1964). *The origins and development of the English language.* New York: Harcourt, Brace & World.

Quantz, J. O. (1897–98). Problems in the psychology of reading. *Psychological Monographs, 2,* (1, Whole No. 5). (Summary: *Psychological Review, 5,* 434–436.)

Robinson, H. M. (1946). *Why pupils fail in reading.* Chicago: University of Chicago Press.

Ruediger, W. C. (1907). The field of distinct vision: With reference to individual differences and their correlations. *Archives of Psychology, 1*(5), 1–68.

Rutherfurd, W. J. (1909). The aetiology of congenital word-blindness, with an example. *British Journal of Children's Diseases, 6,* 484–488.

Saenger, P. (1982). Silent reading: Its impact on late medieval script and society. *Viator, 13,* 367–414.

Sarton, G. (1952). *A history of science: Ancient science through the golden age of Greece.* Cambridge, MA: Harvard University Press.

Schmidt, W. A. (1917). An experimental study of the psychology of reading. *Supplementary Educational Monographs* (No. 2). Chicago: University of Chicago Press.

Scragg, D. G. (1974). *A history of English spelling.* Manchester, England: Manchester University Press.

Swanson, D. E. (1937). Common elements in silent and oral reading. *Psychological Monographs, 48,* 36–60.

Thomas, C. J. (1905). Congenital word-blindness and its treatment. *Ophthalmoscope, 3,* 380–385.

Thorndike, E. L. (1910). Handwriting. *Teachers College Record, 11,* 83–175.

Tinker, M. A. (1946). The study of eye movements in reading. *Psychological Bulletin, 43*, 93–120.

Traxler, A. E. (1937). *Summary and selected bibliography of research relating to the diagnosis and teaching of reading, 1930–1937*. New York: Educational Records Bureau.

Uttal, W. R., & Smith, P. (1968). Recognition of alphabetic characters during voluntary eye movement. *Perception & Psychophysics, 3*, 257–264.

Updike, D. B. (1928). A translation of the reports of Berlier and Sobry on types of Gille. *The Fleuron, 6*, 181.

Venezky, R. L. (1984). The history of reading research. In P. D. Pearson (Ed.), *Handbook of reading research* (Vol. 1, pp. 3–38). New York: Longman.

Volkmann, F. C. (1962). Vision during voluntary saccadic eye movements. *Journal of the Optical Society of America, 52*, 571–578.

Wallin, J. E. W. (1920). Congenital word-blindness: Some analyses cases. *Training School Bulletin, 17*, 76–84, 93–99.

Wheat, H. G. (1923). *The teaching of reading*. New York: Ginn.

Williams, J. P., Blumberg, E. L., & Williams, D. V. (1970). Cues used in visual word recognition. *Journal of Educational Psychology, 61*, 310–315.

Witty, P., & Kopel, D. (1936). Factors associated with the etiology of reading disability. *Journal of Educational Research, 29*, 449–59.

Wixson, K. K., & Lipson, M. Y. (1991). Perspectives on reading disability research. In R. Barr, M. L. Kamil, P. B. Mosenthal, & P. D. Pearson (Eds.), *Handbook of reading research* (Vol. 2, pp. 539–570). New York: Longman.

Zeitler, J. (1900). Tachistoskopische Untersuchungen uber das Lesen. *Philosophische Studien, 16*, 380–463.

2 The Relation of Reversal Errors to Reading Disabilities

Dale M. Willows
Megan Terepocki
Ontario Institute for Studies in Education

There are certain phenomena that appear sufficiently often in the reading and writing of individuals who have serious difficulties learning to read that clinicians have often considered them diagnostic of developmental dyslexia or specific reading disability. "Reversals" are probably the best known of these phenomena, including both *static reversals*—the confusion of mirror image letters such as *b-d,* and *f-t* in reading and writing—and *kinetic reversals*—the transposition of some or all of the letters within words so that *was* is read as *saw* and *girl* is written as *gril.* According to the clinical literature, although "these very same errors occur as the normal child learns to read; what distinguishes the dyslexic is the frequency and persistence of these errors well beyond the time at which they have become uncommon in the normal child" (Eisenberg, 1966, p. 15). In earlier years, these errors were accorded considerable attention in the literature because they were thought to provide evidence that reading disabilities are caused by some type of visual perceptual deficit. More recently however, compelling arguments have been made that reversal errors have a linguistic rather than a visual origin, and that there is little or no evidence of visual processing deficits among the reading disabled. The following quotations present a sampling of these current views:

> Recent research strongly suggests that disabled readers can perceive letter and word symbols accurately, but mislabel them in oral reading because of a basic difficulty in associating symbols with their verbal counterparts. . . . The findings indicate that a child who calls *b* for *d* or *was* for *saw* in oral reading, can perceive these symbols but mislabels them in spite of accurate perception. This suggests that the child lacks verbal rather than visual information when he makes such errors, and

thereby limits the utility of visual discrimination exercises to correct the problem. A more useful approach would supply such a child with semantic and acoustic mnemonics to help him remember the verbal counterparts of printed words, particularly those with many overlapping visual features (e.g., *b/d, was/saw*).

Additional support for the suggestion that poor readers sustain no basic disorder in visual perception and visual memory is provided by several other recent studies (Vellutino, Pruzek, Steger, & Meshoulam 1973; Vellutino, Steger, DeSetto, & Phillips 1975; Vellutino, Steger, Kaman, & DeSetto 1975). In all these investigations, poor readers performed as well as normals in short- and long-term memory of Hebrew letters and words—symbols unfamiliar to both groups. (Vellutino, Steger, Moyer, Harding, & Niles, 1977, p. 57)

Far from being a visual problem, dyslexia appears to be the consequence of limited facility in using language to code other types of information. (Vellutino, 1987, p. 34)

The hypothesis that a deficit in basic visual process is a critical cause of reading failure has garnered enormous attention in the learning disabilities and dyslexia literatures. This attention has not, however, been accompanied by a commensurate amount of solid empirical evidence. The sequencing and "reversal" errors (*b/d, was/saw*) that once loomed so large in importance have proven to be a dead end (and indeed, a useful lesson in how case study evidence can be misleading). (Stanovich, 1985, p. 70)

Although the arguments that these and other authors have made are persuasive, it may be that their conclusions are premature. To begin with, as discussed by Willows, Kruk, and Corcos (chap. 12) and by several others the evidence that there are no visual processing differences between disabled and normal readers has now been brought into question. Moreover, clinical reports of apparent difficulties among disabled readers in processing visual and/or orientation information in letters and words are not so easily dismissed. If the only characteristic phenomena in the reading and writing of developmental dyslexics were the *b/d* and *was/saw* confusions so often mentioned, then the views quoted here might be fully justified. There are, however, a number of other less-studied clinical phenomena—potentially related to reversal errors—not discussed by these authors that would seem to suggest the need to consider visual as well as linguistic factors in theories attempting to account for dyslexia.

The purpose of this chapter is to reconsider reversal errors within a "modern context." There are two main parts to the chapter. The first describes observations from the clinical literature suggesting that there is probably more to reversal errors than the linguistic confusions proposed by some authors. Because evidence obtained by the clinical approach has often been discounted by basic researchers (sometimes with good reason; see Nisbett and Ross, 1980; Stanovich, 1992), the clinical phenomena associated with reversal errors have rarely been seriously discussed in the experimental literature since the time when Hinshelwood (1917) and Orton (1925, 1931, 1937) brought them to the attention of the scientific community. Thus the first section provides a brief discussion of reversal errors, from a clinical perspective, in the context of the development of reading and writing by children with reading disabilities or *dyslexia*. The second part presents a critical review of the empirical literature on reversal errors that may have implications for understanding the potential role of visual processing factors in reading/writing disabilities. Studies involving disabled and normal readers' processing of orientation information in perception/recognition and recall/reproduction tasks are reviewed under the rubrics of reversals of non-alphabetic stimuli, reversals of isolated letters, letter orientation errors in the context of nonwords, and letter orientation errors in the context of words. Finally, in a concluding section, limitations of the reversals literature are discussed and future research directions are proposed.

REOPENING A "CLOSED CASE": THE CLINICAL PHENOMENA OF DYSLEXIA

The research data that have usually been used to dismiss the possible importance of reversal errors and/or an underlying visual/symbolic deficit in dyslexia (e.g., the Hebrew studies cited in the quotation by Vellutino and colleagues earlier) have generally come from short-term laboratory studies (for a review see Willows et al., chap. 12). None of the studies has seriously investigated the performance of subjects over time. Clinicians and educators who often work with the same children over weeks, months, and even years have an opportunity to observe patterns in the abilities and learning of reading-disabled individuals that such short-term laboratory studies cannot begin to assess.

Based on a synthesis of published clinical reports, on interviews with clinicians, as well as on our own clinical experience, we have come to recognize a characteristic developmental pattern commonly observed in the reading and writing of dyslexic individuals. This pattern has long been acknowledged by educators and clinicians, and aspects of it have been described repeatedly in clinical case studies (e.g., Boder, 1973; Doehring, 1968; Farnham-Diggory, 1978; Golick, 1978; Hinshelwood, 1917; Money, 1962, 1966; Orton, 1925, 1931, 1937; Rawson, 1982; Simpson, 1979; Spache, McIlroy, & Berg, 1981). A synopsis of the characteristic pattern of the reading and writing development of individuals who make static reversal errors and who seem to manifest some type of visual processing deficit is presented here. We have referred to these individuals as "visual dyslexics." This pattern would not be expected to appear in the development of all reading-disabled individuals because there may well be multiple factors contributing to reading disabilities (Feagans & McKinney, 1991; Hooper & Willis, 1989; Watson & Willows, chap. 13). The pattern is, however, a very common one.

A Characteristic Developmental Pattern of Visual Dyslexics

Number and Letter Recognition.   In the earliest stages of exposure to print visual dyslexics have great difficulty in recognizing numbers and letters. By the end of grade 1 they may still be unable to recognize many of the letters of the alphabet, and their misidentifications are frequently based on visual similarities between letters (e.g., *a/o, b/d, p/q, u/n, n/h, k/h, f/t, m/n, m/w*). Continuing difficulties in letter recognition are evident when uppercase letters (e.g., *M/W, C/G, O/Q, S/Z, E/F, R/K, Y/V*) and cursive writing are introduced (e.g., even as adults some visual dyslexics who are able to read print are unable to read cursive writing).

Recall of Numbers and Letters.   Even after they have mastered number and letter recognition with confidence visual dyslexics seem to have great difficulty in recalling or, "revisualizing," the form of letters to write them and may have to copy from a model for many months. It is common for the young visual dyslexic to ask "What does a (letter) *look like?*" Their printing errors reflect the same characteristic visual confusions apparent in their letter recognition. Reversals of letters and numbers and generally poor letter formation are common. In addition, in printing they confuse upper- and lowercase letters that differ by minor visual features (e.g., *K/k, P/p, J/j, T/t*), often using them interchangeably. Such difficulties are common among young children just learning to read and write, but the visual dyslexic's problems may extend over many months or years.

Spontaneous strategies employed to overcome the most persistent visual confusions (e.g., the *b/d* "reversal") often involve substituting uppercase letters or cursive letters for the lowercase printed form. Some visual dyslexics have so much difficulty learning to write cursive letters after they have learned to print that they abandon their attempts and persist in printing into adulthood, suggesting that learning a new *visual form* (because they have already mastered all of the phonemes) creates a problem for them. The handwriting of visual dyslexics is notoriously poor.

Word Recognition.   After the visual dyslexic can recognize most alphabet letters accurately, the recognition of even the highest frequency sight words (e.g., *the, is, and*) still poses a serious problem. The visual dyslexic may encounter the same word (either a content or a function word) over and over in a brief period of time and each time may guess at it or may attempt to sound it out, showing no sign of recognition. In many cases, lack of response availability does not seem a plausible interpretation. Rather, the visual dyslexic seems not to realize that the same word has appeared before. Frequently, their word recognition errors are global, in that they maintain some of the letters and the overall shape of the word but seem to reflect a failure to analyze the internal structure of the words. So, the word *either* may be substituted for *enter*.

In text, word recognition errors appear to reflect an overreliance on context. When reading aloud, visual dyslexics, who may appear to have reading comprehension problems, shows that they have substituted so many words (based both on global and contextual word substitutions) that, in essence, they have read a different story than that presented in the text. The visual dyslexic is also insensitive to another source of visual information in text, the punctuation, often apparently unaware of periods and commas.

Recall of Words.   Even after a visual dyslexic can read quite well and appears to have automatized the recognition of many words, recall of "how words look" continues as a serious problem. In spelling and written work the visual dyslexic may have great difficulty spelling ("revisualizing") even very high frequency words and often resorts to a phonic strategy (the word *of* may be spelled *ov*). Their spelling also reflects an insensitivity to orthographic patterns. (So *the* may be spelled *hte*). The visual dyslexic often seems unable to look at a word after spelling it to determine whether it is right or wrong. When asked if a word they have just printed "looks right," visual dyslexics may respond, "Words never *look right* to me."

Taken together this developmental pattern is consistent with an underlying difficulty in processing and/or remembering discrete or segmental features of visual symbolic information. There are a few specific phenomena within this pattern that would seem to argue strongly that a nonvisual interpretation *alone* is inadequate to account for the "data." The following three phenomena are examples:

1. Static reversals are daily occurrences in the writing of many visual dyslexics long after an age when other children have stopped making them. Visual dyslexics show by the form of the symbol that they know what letter or number they want to make, they simply reverse it. It is not uncommon for visual dyslexics as old as 10 or 11 years of age to print a nonreversible letter such as *j, k* or *r* in reversed orientation in their own name. There are numerous examples of these errors of orientation in the clinical literature. Orton (1937) pointed them out and they can easily be confirmed with writing samples from visual dyslexics (see Fig.

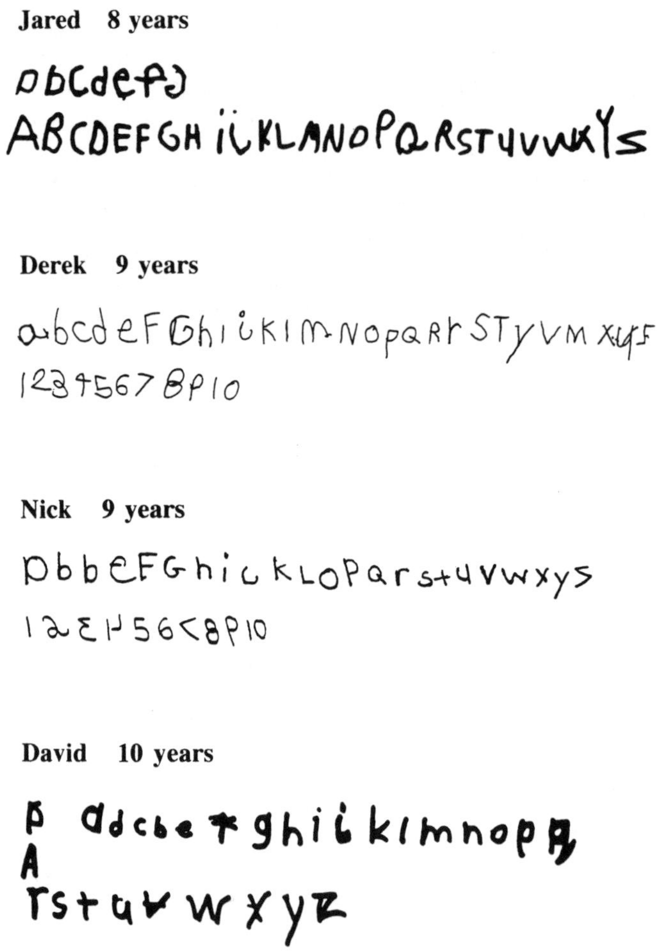

Jared   8 years

ρbϹdℯϜɔ
ABϹDEFGH iϲʁʟ∧ИOPȹRsтuvʍⱥʏs

Derek   9 years

ɑᵁbϲdℯϜGhi ϲʁiɱ-ɴopɑʀʰSTyvм xႷϜ
i2ȝ+567ϐρio

Nick   9 years

ρbbℯϜGhiϲ kʟoρɑrs+uvwxyş
i2Єiᴶ56⟨8ρio

David   10 years

ρ ddϲᵇℯ✦ghiϲ kiɱnopᵦ
A
ʀst u⩗ w x yℒ

FIG. 2.1.   Examples of "static reversals" in the writing of visual dyslexics.

2.1). These confusions about the visual form of the letter do not always involve
confusing one symbol with another, as in the case of reversible letters such as *b-
d, u-n, f-t, m-w*. Thus, a labeling or linguistic intrusion interpretation could not
account for the phenomenon.

2. A common spontaneous strategy of using uppercase *B* and/or *D* to avoid
confusing the lowercase forms of *b* and *d* suggests that the problem is not simply
with remembering labels. The use of the uppercase letters avoids a visual confusion. A less frequent, but parallel strategy, is shown when uppercase *F* and/or *T*

are used to avoid confusing the lowercase forms *f/t*. Both the *B/D* and the *F/T* strategies were documented by Orton (1931), and examples are easily found in the writing of visual dyslexics (see Fig. 2.2). The substitution of cursive letters— another visual strategy—is used to avoid confusing *s/z* and *S/Z*. These strategies were explicitly described by Louise Baker, a literate adult dyslexic, "Granted I still can't print "s," "z," "b," or "d." But I either capitalize or write the hard ones cursively. (I capitalize my "B" and "D" and cursively write my "s" and "z.") I mostly get my threes and fives backwards but that's OK—people know what I mean" (Rawson, 1982, pp. 294–295).

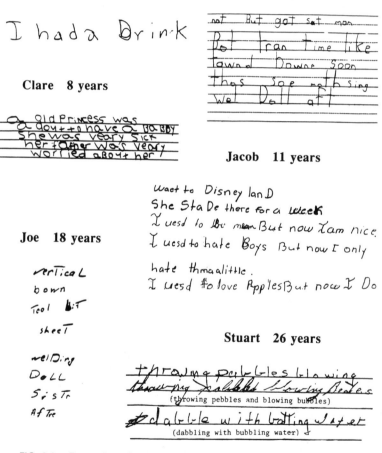

FIG. 2.2. Examples of substitutions of uppercase and cursive letters to resolve lowercase confusions by visual dyslexics.

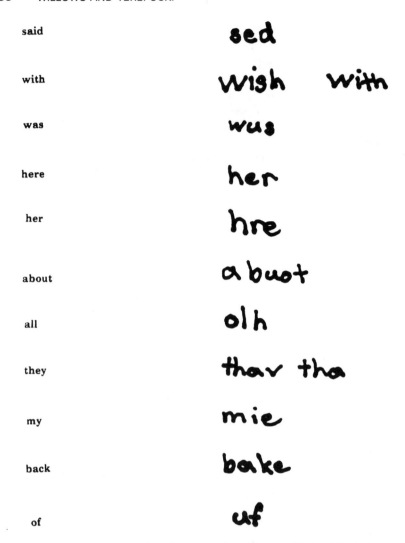

said — sed

with — wish   with

was — wus

here — her

her — hre

about — a buot

all — ol h

they — thav tha

my — mie

back — bake

of — uf

FIG. 2.3.   Examples of spelling errors by a 12-year-old visual dyslexic.

3.   In describing the spelling of visual dyslexics it is common for clinicians to observe that "it doesn't look like English." This observation reflects the fact that visual dyslexics have great difficulty learning the orthographic patterns of the language. Long after other children have learned that *t* always precedes *h* in the *th* digraph, visual dyslexics show an insensitivity to the pattern. Thus, even in a copying task visual dyslexics will transpose *th* to *ht* and not notice that a very high frequency word (e.g., *the*/*hte* or *with*/*wiht*) does not look right. (See Fig. 2.3 for examples of a visual dyslexic's spelling.) If the difficulty were based only

on labeling, then after misspelling a common orthographic pattern visual dyslexics should recognize "by sight" that it does not look right. But, the inability of visual dyslexics to check their own spelling by sight is very well known to clinicians.

These phenomena, and others in the characteristic developmental pattern of visual dyslexics suggest that the type of linguistic-intrusion interpretation of "dyslexic errors" presented in the quotations earlier is inadequate. Although there may be a wide variety of grounds on which to dismiss the older theories (such as Orton's, 1925, 1937) that have attempted to account for these phenomena and the older perceptual-training practices (such as Frostig's, 1968) that have attempted to remediate them, the phenomena themselves cannot be dismissed. They must be more thoroughly documented, and if their existence is corroborated by careful longitudinal research, then theories of reading disabilities must be modified to account for them.

Samuel Orton's View on Reversal Errors: "The Older Context"

Based on his observation of reversal errors in the reading and writing of "word blind" individuals, Orton (1925) believed that dyslexics' brains functioned differently from those of other children. Dyslexic children's apparent confusion about the orientation of letters, numbers, and words led Orton to label their problem "strephosymbolia" (i.e., twisted signs). In his view, written productions reflected information exactly as it was stored in the brain, and mirror writing was taken as evidence that information was stored in more than one orientation. At that time it was understood that the left hemisphere was involved in language storage and production, however, less was known about right hemisphere function. Orton believed that information in the right hemisphere was a mirror reflection of information in the left hemisphere. Learning to read and write involved learning to attend to the correct hemispheric image. Children normally learned to pay attention to the left hemisphere version and suppress the image from the right hemisphere. Orton's theory of dyslexia was essentially one of hemispheric imbalance: He thought that in the dyslexic individual the images from the right and left hemispheres were in competition because those from the right hemisphere were inadequately suppressed. Orton thought that visual perception and recognition functions could be performed adequately by both hemispheres but visual association that connected visual information to meaning could only be performed by the left hemisphere, and "when the left hemisphere was unable to perform that critical suppressive function, confusions and delays would result. There would be distortions of the motor output in both speech and writing, interference in the linking of visual symbols and sounds, and subsequent failure to associate sounds and meaning" (Farnham-Diggory, 1978, p. 30). Few, if any theorists, embrace Orton's view of dyslexia today, although there are present-day interpretations that are not totally inconsistent with his theory (see Corballis & Beale, chap. 3).

There is a fairly large research literature concerned with reversal errors (see review in Kaufman, 1980). Much of this literature was generated in an attempt to test Orton's hypothesis (or, as Corballis and Beale point out in chapter 3, a misinterpretation of Orton's hypothesis) during a period when views about the nature and origin of reading disabilities were considerably different than they are today. Most of the earlier research was designed (a) to compare the incidence of reversal errors among dyslexics, poor readers, and average readers in order to determine whether dyslexics' perceptions of letters and words differ from those of "normal" poor and average readers; (b) to examine factors that may be related to reversal errors in an attempt to explore other possible underlying causal mechanisms; or (c) to test the effectiveness of various interventions to reduce the incidence of reversal errors. Fundamental to much of this earlier research was the notion that problems in processing letter and word orientation are somehow causal in reading disability.

Although there is still no general agreement among theoreticians and researchers about the cause or causes of reading disability, few if any present-day theorists would consider reversal errors as potential causes of reading disability. Some might, however, consider static reversals as reflecting more general deficits in basic visual processes. Because the older literature on reversal errors comes out of a largely obsolete view of the cause of reading disabilities, much of it is essentially irrelevant to current conceptualizations of reading disability. Certain aspects of the literature, however, remain significant to current debates about reading disability in that they have relevance to the potential role of visual processing deficits in causing reading disabilities. In particular there are three questions that remain very important. First, a key question is whether or not disabled and normal readers do, in fact, differ in their ability to process orientation information in nonlinguistic stimuli. If they do, important theoretical questions are raised about the cause of the difference. Second, if there are disabled/normal reader differences in the processing of orientation information in nonlinguistic stimuli, then the next crucial question is whether or not disabled readers make significantly more reversal errors than normally achieving readers when processing linguistic stimuli in their reading and writing. Although clinicians often report a higher incidence of such errors in the work of disabled readers/writers, it is important to determine whether controlled research confirms these clinical observations. Third, the most fundamental questions are: What type of mechanism accounts for reversal errors in reading and writing, and what role does such a mechanism have in children's written language acquisition? In sum then, the purpose of this chapter is to reexamine the literature on static reversals in the light of current conceptualizations of reading disability in order to determine whether there is convincing evidence of a higher incidence of these errors among the reading disabled and to explore the possible role visual processing deficits might play in producing such errors.

REVIEW OF STATIC REVERSALS LITERATURE

This section begins with a brief discussion of a range of methodological issues that must be addressed in any research comparison of the incidence of reversal errors among disabled and normal readers. These include the distinction between orientation and sequence errors, recognition versus recall measures, types of orientation errors, definitions of unsuccessful and successful reader groups, language/labeling confounds.

Methodological Considerations

Orientation versus Sequence Reversals.   If "static reversals" (i.e., *b-d, f-t*) are a result of some sort of difficulty in processing orientation information then there is little reason to expect that they would be related to "kinetic reversals" (i.e., transpositions like *clot-colt, left-felt*), which would seem to reflect a problem with sequence rather than with orientation.[1] Many of the investigations conducted on reversal errors have reported results based on reversal tests that confounded both orientation and sequence reversals (e.g., N. L. Kaufman & A. Kaufman, 1980; Stevenson, Parker, Wilkerson, Hegion, & Fish, 1976). The current review attempts to clarify the incidence of orientation reversals and their relationship to reading disability by reporting only the results from research that considered letter orientation errors (i.e., static reversals) and sequencing errors (i.e., kinetic reversals) separately.

Recognition versus Recall Measures.   Although they are often intermixed in the literature, findings from recognition (i.e., perception and memory of symbols, as in reading) and recall (i.e., written production of symbols, as in writing) reversal measures are reviewed separately here in order to examine the potential role of increased cognitive demands on the incidence of reversals: The cognitive demands in recognition tasks are presumably not as great as those involved in recall.

---

[1]It is conceivable, however, that both types of error could be a result of a visual processing deficit that interferes with a fine-grained visual analysis of letters and words. Such a possibility would have to be examined directly in research and is not addressed here.

Types of Orientation Errors.   The literature has employed various definitions of letter orientation errors that are sometimes distinguished to reflect the axis of rotation. For instance, a "letter reversal" (or static reversal) usually refers to a "right-left," or "mirror image" reversal where the letter rotates on the vertical axis (e.g., *b-d*). Letter "inversions" pertain to letters that rotate on the horizontal axis (e.g., *b-p*). As well, a letter that rotates on its depth axis (e.g., *b-q*), may be specifically called a "rotation." For the purpose of this review, a letter orientation reversal is defined as the rotation of a letter on any of these axes (and, usually describes confusions of the letters *b, d, p, q,* or *g*). Another distinction made here pertains to letters that are "reversible" (e.g., *b-p, m-w*), which rotate to form a different letter, as opposed to "nonreversible" letters such as *x,* or *e,* which do not form another letter when rotated.

Defining Reading Groups.   A prime goal of this review is to find out if orientation errors are characteristic of subjects with reading difficulty, and if so, under what conditions. In the studies reported here, reading-disabled subjects were selected according to the common discrepancy definition that describes the disabled as having generally poor reading (i.e., written language) skills compared with average-or-above cognitive abilities. Unless otherwise noted, in the studies reviewed "dyslexic," "disabled," or "poor" readers (i.e., unsuccessful readers) were compared with "normal" or "average" readers (i.e., successful readers), matched according to chronological age and cognitive ability.

Not all comparisons in this literature are between unsuccessful and successful readers, however, and another important methodological consideration is the types of reading groups compared in the reversals literature. Based on the "medical-model" view of reading disabilities, several of the studies compared "dyslexics" (or "disabled readers") with "poor readers," sometimes without a comparison with normally achieving readers. If such studies failed to find dyslexic/poor reader differences, the results may simply indicate that reading ability is normally distributed and that both so-called dyslexics and poor readers are at the low unsuccessful-reader-end of the normal distribution. Because dyslexics (or disabled readers) and poor readers are operationally distinguished only in terms of the *degree* of their reading difficulty, and because the medical model view that considers reading disability as a distinct neuropsychological syndrome is not supported by a growing body of evidence (e.g., Perfetti, 1986; S. E. Shaywitz, Escobar, B. A. Shaywitz, Fletcher, & Makuch, 1992), the dyslexic/poor-reader comparisons in the reversals literature may be largely irrelevant in current contexts, and may fail to test for differences between unsuccessful and successful readers.

Language/Labeling Confounds.   Studies that have tried to measure visual processing in disabled and average readers are subject to language/labeling confounds when "clean" measures are not employed (Calfee, 1977; Willows,

1991). The same problem applies to reversal measures where the goal has been to understand the basic processes contributing to reversal errors. The difficulty lies in attempting to identify the incidence of reversals in reading or writing tasks—where the stimuli are necessarily alphabetic in nature—while trying to minimize the role of verbal labeling. Letter naming or decoding tasks explicitly confound verbal and visual processes because they require the subject to retrieve the grapheme label or corresponding phoneme. For this reason, the concept of reversals in this review includes the processing of orientation information in non-alphabetic stimuli, such as simple geometric shapes or line drawings, in which the identity is not confounded with orientation as it is with some alphabet letters (e.g., *b-d, n-u,* etc.).

Reversal studies that employ linguistic material are subject to confounds such as differential rates of letter and word exposure. This is an important factor when attempting to understand the outcomes of word recognition tasks because null results (especially in older subjects) might reflect the fact that subjects of all levels of reading ability are relying on a global strategy for recognizing simple words, masking potential reversal error tendencies. Conversely, group differences in younger subjects might be related to an inflated error rate in subjects less familiar with the stimulus items (most likely, the disabled-reader group). Lyle (1969) for example, found that several children could not spell the test items in a task used to elicit reversal errors. This problem likely confounds most of the studies discussed in the section on word recognition where researchers do not control for personal familiarity of sight words for all subjects. In order to exert some control over this possibility, and to examine the idea that basic processing differences may be related to reversal error rates, tasks that employed isolated letters, nonword decoding studies, and word recognition tasks are reviewed separately.

Reversals of Nonalphabetic Stimuli

There is evidence that by 4 years of age children can differentiate the spatial orientation of nonverbal shapes (Wohlwill & Wiener, 1964) and letterlike figures (Stein & Mandler, 1974). Oyama and Sato (1975) showed that by 5 years of age, children respond to various orientations of geometric shapes, and this skill is differentiated over time. Cairns and Steward (1970) extended the orientation processing research to include uppercase letters and found that young children (age 4–6) can orient letters in space with relative accuracy, and this skill improves with age. Cairns and Steward suggested that orientation difficulties beyond 6 years of age would predict reading difficulties. This section reports the relative ability of children (beyond age 6), who differ in reading skill, to accurately judge the orientation of simple forms and pictures.

In an early study of visual perceptual abilities in beginning reading, Goins (1958) required first-grade children to complete a same-different task involving reversals of pictures. In this task, half of the items (pairs of pictures) were identical, whereas in the other half of the items, one of the pictures in the pair was mirror reversed. Goins found that performance on the reversals test correlated moderately with reading achievement on an initial test ($r = .48$), with similar results obtained 5 months later ($r = .49$). It was suggested that reversals in reading may therefore be related to problems in visual space perception.

Stronger evidence that orientation processing difficulties exist to some extent in the reading-disabled population was obtained in a large-scale investigation of the correlates of reading disability. Doehring (1968) tested 10- to 14-year-olds on several measures of cognitive functioning, including the reversals test employed in Goin's study. An analysis of covariance showed that the reversals test discriminated between the two groups at the $p < .001$ level of significance. Furthermore, a multiple regression analysis indicated that, in addition to reading and spelling tests, the reversals test emerged as the third best measure to differentiate the disabled and normal readers. (The reversals test added 11.6% to the total variance accounted for.)

Other researchers have investigated the tendency for poor or disabled readers to reverse nonalphabetic stimuli in match-to-sample tasks. Wechsler and Hagin (1964), for instance, required good and poor readers in grades 1 and 3 to match an asymmetric figure to a test item located in an array of six alternative orientations of the same figure. The test was presented in both simultaneous and delayed conditions. Poor readers from both age groups were found to make significantly more errors than average readers on these tasks. Using a delayed match-to-sample paradigm Terepocki, Willows, and Kruk (1993) compared the performance of 10-year-old disabled and normal readers on a task where they were asked to match letter-like figures (Japanese characters) to samples. Each test display consisted of a figure identical to the sample as well as a mirror-reversal of it. The results showed that the groups were not distinguished on accuracy on this task, but the disabled readers responded significantly more slowly than the normal readers.

Using another type of match-to-sample task, Lyle and Goyen (1968) tested grade 2 and 3 retarded and average readers. Simple line figures and word shapes were presented tachistoscopically, in simultaneous and delayed conditions. Subjects were required to match the sample item to one of five alternative items, which consisted of two foils that were different orientations of the sample and two foils that differed from the sample on some visual feature, but not orientation. In contrast to the other research involving match-to-sample, the retarded and average readers in this study were reported not to differ in their orientation errors. While Lyle and Goyen's study did not indicate poorer disabled reader performance, the results do not necessarily contradict the outcomes obtained in other research in this section. By analyzing the proportion of reversal errors to total errors in their study, these investigators essentially asked whether reversible figures were as confusing to identify as other visually similar items, and found that they were. Had they combined errors of both types, they might well have found that the disabled readers made more errors than the normal readers overall (possibly due to a deficit in early visual processes). These concerns also apply to the single letter version of this task which is discussed in the next section. The sample item was presented for a very brief duration (100 ms), compared with the 3-s duration employed by Wechsler and Hagin, thus it is possible that early visual processes may have been tapped in Lyle and Goyen's, and Terepocki et al.'s studies while later visual processes may have been assessed in the Wechsler and Hagin research (for a discussion of early and later visual processes, see Willows et al., chap. 12).

Overall, the results of the research presented in this section are consistent with the conclusion that disabled readers from the early stages of reading through age 14 are less sensitive than average readers to the correct orientation of non-alphabetic forms. Because it is unlikely that the tests in these studies required sound-symbol coding or verbal mediation to complete them, it appears that orientation coding difficulties in general may be related to reading difficulties. Nonetheless, more than one interpretation of these findings is possible. Although the nonalphabetic tasks utilized in these studies appeared to have been relatively "clean" tests of the processing of orientation, it may be, for example, that differences on the recognition tasks involved (same/different and match-to-sample) reflect impulsivity rather than some type of orientation-processing-deficit per se. Scores from a much-used test developed by Kagan (1966), the Matching Familiar Figures (MFF) test—which was explicitly designed to test reflection/impulsivity using a match-to-sample methodology with visually similar nonalphabetic target and test items—have been found to correlate with reading achievement.

Even if the observed disabled/normal reader differences on nonalphabetic tasks do reflect some real underlying deficit in the processing of orientation information, the results of the studies do not speak directly to reading and writing tasks. Where the relationship between the orientation coding of nonalphabetic figures and letter reversal errors in reading has been examined, however, there is some evidence that nonverbal perceptual abilities and letter reversals in reading and writing are related. Lyle (1969) for example, found that scores on the Memory For Designs test (scored largely for reversals) and letter orientation and sequence reversals in reading, and letter orientation reversals in writing loaded on the same factor in a factor analysis. The remaining sections describe research that is more closely related to reversals in reading and writing, because alphabetic material is employed.

Reversals of Isolated Letters

There has been some interest in finding out if disabled readers confuse the orientation of letters outside a meaningful context. If isolated letters are reversed more frequently by disabled readers than by average readers, poor visual processing rather than linguistic factors may be implicated. Effects attributed to differences in word familiarity are also minimized in this type of task. However, the naming tasks described here are clearly confounded by verbal labeling, which means that "visual" interpretations of the results from these studies should be considered tentative.

Letter orientation difficulties in disabled readers have been investigated in match-to-sample tasks where the target item is presented briefly (ta-chistoscopically) and subjects are required to choose the matching test item from an array of confusable letters (e.g., *b, d, p, q,* and *g*). Two such studies reported that single letter reversals do not characterize grade 2 or 3 disabled readers (e.g., Lyle & Goyen, 1968) or grade 2 poor readers (Liberman, Shankweiler, Orlando, Harris, & Bell Berti, 1971). In contrast, however, Fischer, Liberman, and Shankweiler (1978) found that when compared with poor readers of the same age (the children employed in Liberman et al.'s study) disabled readers made more reversals (a mean of 14 vs. 7) on this type of task.

There are problems associated with these studies that raise questions about the outcomes. For example, Lyle and Goyen (1968) mentioned that the matching target letter was to be chosen from among alternative letters, many of which were "imperfect" reversals of the target. This may have significantly diminished the distinction between "reversed," and "visually similar" alternatives, possibly, as discussed earlier, diminishing the reversal error rate. Furthermore, Liberman et al.'s (1971) investigation, which is often cited as evidence that reversals are not characteristic of disabled readers, is not necessarily representative of that popula-tion because the "disabled" subjects were grade 2 children who scored in the lower third of the class on a test of reading ability.

Terepocki et al. (1993) also examined orientation confusions of letters and numbers by employing the same match-to-sample paradigm used for non-alphabetic stimuli. Ten-year-old disabled and normal readers matched either an identical or a mirror reversed test item (letter or number) to a normally-oriented or backward sample item. Disabled readers responded significantly more slowly than normal readers, but did not make significantly more errors, possibly reflect-ing the ease of the task for this age group. Another paradigm employed by Terepocki et al. (1993) was a continuous-performance task where upper- and lowercase nonreversible letters (e.g., *j, k, r*) were presented consecutively. Par-ticipants were required to press a key whenever a letter in reversed orientation appeared on the screen. The disabled readers made significantly more errors ($p < .005$) than normal readers on this task, but performed identically to them in an attention control condition when the target was an *x*. Together, the results from the Terepocki et al. study, (involving both the match-to-sample and continu-ous-performance paradigms) provide some fairly consistent evidence that, out-side of a meaningful (i.e., word) context, disabled readers have more difficulty identifying disoriented letters than normal readers.

Using a different approach to examine the processing of letter-orientation information, Bigsby (1985) investigated both the extent and the locus of reversible letter confusions by comparing the performance of 10-year-old dyslexics with that of reading age and chronological age controls. There were 10 children in each group with the "dyslexics" being at least 1½ years behind their reading age. The study involved a same–different task (tachistoscopic presentation) requiring letter pairs to be matched on the basis of their names or visual features; however, only the visual tasks are detailed here. Letters were presented in four conditions: physically similar (*ss, tt, nn, kk*), physically similar but reversible (*bb, dd, pp, qq*), physically different (*sr, rz, ns, mv*), and physically different but reversible (*bd, db, pq, qp*). A measure of "reversibility confusion" was obtained by evaluating the difference scores between the reversible letter pairs and nonreversible letter pairs in both the "physically similar" and "physically different" conditions. Results of this study indicated that all of the aforementioned conditions were easy for all groups (less than 10% errors) and none of the groups showed evidence of "reversibility confusion" on accuracy measures in the visual task. Response time measures revealed that both dyslexics and chronological-age controls evidenced "reversibility confusion" in the "physically different" condition only, but did not differ on any of the conditions in the visual task. Bigsby concluded therefore, that the disabled readers "function well in the visual code." It is notable, however, that despite the low error rates in the condition where letters were reversible but different (e.g., *b-d*), the dyslexics made three times as many errors as their chronological-age controls. Taking together the facts that there were only four items presented in each condition and that the sample size was relatively small (*n* = 10 per group), these null findings in the visual condition may reflect a lack of statistical power.

Letter-naming accuracy and naming speed have also been among the measures used to investigate isolated letter reversal errors. Cohn and Stricker (1979), for example, found that letter reversals (confusions of the letters *b, d, p,* or *q*) were frequently produced by grade 1 children of various letter-naming abilities. Whereas letter-naming errors decreased with competency in letter naming, the greatest proportion of reversal responses was made by children most competent at naming letters. This unexpected result was explained in terms of normal perceptual development: Because the awareness of letter parts precedes that of orientation, children can easily recognize letter names, but may still have difficulty with letter orientation. Cohn and Stricker suggested that persistent difficulty with letter orientation may indicate perceptual problems.

Letter-naming speed was investigated in a study where dyslexics and average readers across a broad age range (6–14 years old) were tested on their ability to name briefly presented letters (Grosser & Trzeciak, 1981). A tachistoscopic letter-naming task was employed where reversible letters (*b, d, p, q*) and nonreversible letters (*u, w, x, o*) were presented in separate conditions. Each letter was shown at increasing exposures until it was named accurately (threshold condition). The same letters were presented in another condition, briefly preceded by a dot mask (mask condition). The threshold reaction times for reversible letters (*b, d, p, q*) were analyzed separately in order to determine whether or not they presented unique difficulties for disabled readers. Results indicated that normal readers recognized both letter groups significantly faster than dyslexics in the threshold condition (this finding may reflect differences in early visual processes, see Willows et al., chap. 12). The dyslexics and average readers did not respond differently to the letter groups in the threshold task. Furthermore, in the masked condition, all subjects found reversible letters more difficult to recognize than nonreversible letters. The authors concluded that because the reversible letters were difficult for all subjects in the masked condition, developmental factors, and not a specific processing weakness may be contributing to the processing of these letters. These results should be interpreted with caution, however, because the distinction between reversible and nonreversible letters is questionable: The inclusion of *u* and *w* in the stimulus set of "nonreversible" letters ignores the fact that these letters can be reversed to the letters *n* and *m* respectively, through changes in orientation. Nor does the study state whether the experimental and control groups were matched on age.

One of the goals of Corballis, Macadie, Crotty, and Beale (1985) was to investigate the ability of disabled readers to identify disoriented letters. It was hypothesized that disabled readers might not show the typical response time advantage when identifying normal over backward letters, because disabled readers have been found to have a greater degree of left–right confusion than average readers. Thus, disabled and normal readers (11–13 years of age) were required to name capital letters, which were briefly presented at various orientations. The performance of the disabled readers was not significantly more impaired than normal readers on this task. Disabled readers did, however, have particular difficulty identifying the letter *G,* whereas average readers had the least difficulty with this letter. Corballis et al. suggested that this outcome might indicate visuospatial difficulties in some of the disabled readers.

No definitive conclusions about letter-reversal error rates can be reached on the basis of the findings reported in this section. Some of the results may be interpreted as indicating that disabled readers might have slightly more difficulty processing orientation information than normal readers (Bigsby, 1985; Corballis, et al., 1985), while others appear to show that disabled readers have substantially more difficulty than normal readers processing orientation in single letter recognition tasks (Terepocki et al., 1993). Moreover, although Fischer et al. (1978) did not report a statistical comparison, their results seemed to show a substantial difference between disabled and poor readers (mean reversal error rates of 14 vs. 7, respectively). This outcome is particularly noteworthy because the groups involved—disabled vs. poor rather than disabled vs. normal readers—minimized the chances of finding differences. The outcomes of still other studies seem to argue that disabled readers do not have more difficulty than average readers identifying reversible, or disoriented letters, although a range of methodological factors have been suggested to account for these null findings.

The following two sections examine reversal error incidence in the context of other letters (nonwords and words, respectively). Undertaken in the "older context" of Orton's hypothesis, a focus in most of these studies is that disabled readers may produce reversals disproportionately with respect to other types of errors. For instance, Liberman et al. (1971) found that grade 2 poor readers produced relatively few letter orientation errors in word recognition (12.7% of the errors were made by the poor readers when opportunity to make the errors was accounted for). However, because the other error categories (e.g., "vowel," "other consonant," or "reversed sequence") could all, in part, reflect general visual discrimination problems (which may also be the basis for reversal errors) the focus on relative error proportion may not be the most useful approach to the analysis of reversal errors in these tasks.

Letter Orientation Errors in the Context of Nonwords

The studies in this section required subjects to process letter-orientation information in the context of nonwords. In order to investigate the incidence of letter orientation reversals (among other errors) in disabled readers, the first two studies required subjects to read aloud monosyllabic nonwords. The use of nonwords as stimulus items in reversal tasks makes sense because this is one way of approximating the reading experience while at the same time controlling possible linguistic effects produced by familiarity with words.

Seidenberg, Bruck, Fornarolo, and Backman (1985) found that reversal errors did not distinguish 9- to 10-year-old disabled readers from poor readers on a nonword reading task. However, the comparison of interest to this review (e.g., disabled vs. good readers) was not carried out because the error rates for good readers were very low. Further, the outcomes of this study were limited because the low error rates for all groups may reflect the fact that nonwords were formed by changing only the first letter of each real word. As discussed by Werker, Bryson, and Wassenberg (1989), the disabled readers may have read the nonwords globally as if they were the real word they were derived from, thus masking potential difficulties.

Accounting for this methodological weakness, Werker and colleagues analyzed the consonant error patterns of 10- to 17-year-old "severely" disabled readers and their age- and reading-level controls. The disabled readers were divided into three groups based on discrepancies between verbal and performance Wechsler Intelligence Scale for Children-Revised (WISC-R) scores (P > V; V > P; V = P). Results indicated that none of the experimental subgroups was significantly more likely to make orientation reversals than either control group. The researchers suggested that these results were not consistent with a visual deficit hypothesis of reading difficulty. This interpretation is open to question, however, because there were only four subjects in one of the disabled reader subgroups. This group consisted of subjects who were more proficient in verbal than visual-spatial skills, so it may be that subjects in this group were those most likely to make reversal errors. Furthermore, had the reading-disabled subjects been compared with controls, as a group, different results might have been obtained. Thus, unfortunately, neither the Seidenberg et al. nor the Werker et al. study made adequate comparisons to provide answers about visual difficulties in reading disability, as manifested by reversal errors in the context of nonwords.

Also questioning whether reading disabilities reflect visual-spatial deficits, Vellutino, Smith, Steger, and Kaman (1975) included a letter-reversal measure in a test battery. Twenty-one normal and 21 disabled readers (at each of grades 2 and 6) were compared on their ability to copy, as well as to "spell out" briefly exposed (1 s) letter strings. Both age groups of disabled readers made significantly more letter orientation errors in the spelling-aloud condition, but not in the copying task. The authors interpreted the differences in terms of linguistic factors because the problems seemed to arise for disabled readers when identifying letters but not when copying them. The authors did not present mean scores for the nonword task, however, so other possible explanations, such as ceiling effects on the copying task (which appear elsewhere in the study on copying tasks), cannot be ruled out.

Other evidence of disabled readers' difficulties with reversals in nonwords was found in the previously mentioned study by Terepocki et al. Disabled and normal readers (10 years of age) were found to differ in their performance on a continuous performance task which used reversed letters in unpronounceable letter strings as target items. Subjects were asked to press a key whenever a letter string containing a mirror reversed letter appeared on the screen. The disabled readers made significantly more errors than normal readers on this task. Because the targets were embedded in letter strings rather than in words, the outcome could not reflect differences in familiarity with the test items.

Overall the outcomes of studies investigating the processing of letter-orientation information in nonwords show that disabled readers may well be distinguished from normal readers in the number of errors they produce when adequately controlled comparisons are made.

Letter Orientation Errors in the Context of Words

The research on reversals in word recognition required subjects to simply read a list of monosyllabic words aloud to the experimenter. This method of examining reversal errors controls for some of the problems associated with letter recognition tasks. It is difficult to know, for example, whether reversal errors made in single letter naming tasks, are based on the confusion of visual features or misnaming, however when letters are presented in words, the likelihood of confusing letters based on their names is minimized. Even so, there are important limitations associated with the word recognition studies described earlier.

In addition to the single letter recognition task discussed previously, Lyle and Goyen (1968) were interested in whether or not grade 2 and 3 retarded readers differed from average readers on their production of letter reversals in word recognition. Whereas there were no differences in error rate for the older subjects (grade 3), the younger retarded readers (grade 2) made significantly more letter orientation reversals as a proportion of total errors than did younger normal readers. Consistent with these results, Lyle (1969) found that when 6- to 12-year-old retarded and adequate readers were required to read aloud a list of words, letter orientation reversals were related to reading achievement (loading on the same factor in a factor analysis, loading − .83). Chronological age was positively associated with this factor indicating that younger disabled readers were more likely to reverse letters than older disabled readers.

The incidence of orientation errors in word recognition has also been examined by researchers who were primarily interested in finding out if dyslexics were distinguished from poor readers, rather than normal readers, on these measures (e.g. Fischer et al., 1978; Liberman et al., 1971; Taylor, Satz, & Friel, 1976; Seidenberg et al., 1985). The null results obtained in all of these studies do not mean that there was not a relationship between reading disability and reversal errors. By comparing with poor readers, these researchers may have compared with a group who is also at the low end of the distribution on a normal curve, thus biasing the comparison against finding differences. Different results might have been obtained had more discriminating comparisons been made. For example, Taylor et al. found that grade 2 dyslexics and poor readers combined, made significantly more letter orientation errors than a group of age-matched normal readers. It is clear from their study that children who had difficulty reading were more likely to reverse letters.

Letter Reversal Incidence in Writing

Relatively few studies have focused on the production of reversal errors in writing tasks. This omission is unfortunate because the reversal errors documented in the clinical literature are usually taken from writing samples rather than from reading where they are rarely observed, possibly because contextual constraints and word frequency factors[2] may conspire against finding them in reading. The research reviewed in this section focuses on orientation reversals produced by disabled and average readers when writing single letters and words to dictation.

---

[2]It is unlikely that young children will misread *dad* as *dab* or *rat* as *raf* because the word *dab* and the nonword *raf* are not in their lexicon.

Taking a different approach to the study of reversals, Chapman and Wedell (1972) first identified a group of children (8 years old) who reversed letters in writing and then compared them with children who did not reverse letters. The subjects were distinguished by their performance on three dictation tasks: They were asked to write 10 reversible words, 10 numbers, and 10 lowercase letters as they were named and sounded. Their findings showed that compared to the nonreversers, who were performing at their age level in reading and spelling, the reversers were approximately 2 years behind age level on reading and spelling measures. Consistent with these results, Collette (1979) found that older dyslexics (12- to 14-year-olds) and retarded readers were distinguished from adequate readers of the same age, on a letter dictation task requiring subjects to write several uppercase letters to dictation. Dyslexics were selected only if they scored at least a year below age level on various tests of visual perception, thus conclusions from this study are restricted to disabled readers predisposed to visual perceptual difficulties.

Reversals have also been observed in the spelling of dictated words. In addition to the recognition tasks described earlier, Lyle (1969) required the 6- to 12-year-old disabled and normal readers to spell a list of words to dictation, in script. As with reversals in reading, written orientation reversals and reading achievement were associated with the same factor (factor loading −.85), and decreased with age. Black (1973), on the other hand, found that less severely retarded readers, 6 to 9 years of age, did not produce a significantly different rate of orientation errors on this task. Differences between group performance in the incidence of letter reversal errors was found to be minimal and nonsignificant (20% for normal readers and 22% for retarded readers). These results are limited to mildly retarded readers, however, which may explain why Black did not find a greater discrepancy between the normal and retarded readers on this task (retarded readers were an average of .7 years reading delayed). Moreover, the results from both of these studies may well be underestimates of reversal tendencies because, in Lyle's study, subjects were required to write in script, and it is not clear if the older children in Black's study responded to the task in cursive writing (which would have reduced the reversal error rate substantially).

In contrast with the tests usually employed in the research on written reversals (e.g., copying test items or writing to dictation) Terepocki et al. (1993) devised a task where subjects printed the names of simple line drawings (selected to elicit a range of target letters). They found that 10-year-old disabled readers reversed substantially more letters than normal readers on this task.

In sum then, results from the research on written reversal errors provide some support for clinical observations that younger disabled readers (up to age 10) reverse letters in writing. There is also evidence that older disabled readers (with perceptual difficulties) tend to reverse dictated letters.

CONCLUSIONS
AND FUTURE RESEARCH DIRECTIONS

This examination of the research literature emphasizes the fact that, viewed within a modern context, the phenomena associated with reversal errors warrant further investigation. The findings from studies involving nonalphabetic stimuli indicate that the reading disabled, up to 14 years of age, have more difficulty with tasks involving orientation than normal readers. The pattern of results from studies involving letter recognition either out of, or in, the context of nonwords or words is not as consistent, and points clearly to the need for greater methodological refinement in terms of reader group comparisons, selection of test stimuli, and experimental paradigms. In addition, the few studies involving recall/production of orientation in writing show disabled/normal reader differences, but there is too little research and what there is lacks adequate experimental control to draw confident conclusions.

One overriding impression from the literature is that future researchers need to approach questions concerning "reversal errors" with greater conceptual clarity. In designing future studies it is important to keep in mind the possibility that differences in static reversal error rates in recognition tasks may reflect a genuine difficulty in some aspect of visual processing, or, on the other hand, may be a result of attention, verbal labeling, cognitive style (e.g., reflection/impulsivity), or some other factors differentiating heterogeneous groups of disabled and normal readers. If the problem of reversals has to do with some type of visual processing deficit, it is essential to be able to distinguish between potential contributing factors such as the processing of orientation information, speed of visual processing, and visual attention. A distinction should also be made between the stages of visual processing involved in each task, with "early" visual processes being examined separately from "later" (Willows et al., chap. 12).

Some of the clinical observations presented in the profile of the visual dyslexic in the beginning section of the chapter deserve more careful study. Probably because of Orton's theory, reversible-letter confusions (such as *b-d*, *p-q*, *f-t*) have, perhaps, been given a disproportionate amount of attention relative to other related clinical phenomena. The spontaneous use of uppercase letters in writing to avoid confusing the lowercase forms of reversible letters, for example, has never been formally studied in the experimental literature as far as we could determine.

In addition, the *b-d* confusion that has garnered the most attention in the literature, probably because of its greater prevalence, is not necessarily a result of the same factors that contribute to other static reversal errors. If children learn the unfamiliar visual forms of the alphabet letters by a process of "acquired distinctiveness of cues" (such that attaching names to letters helps make similar stimuli more easily distinguishable), then *b-d* may be a special case. Because the letters have both visual and some degree of phonological similarity, it may be more difficult to associate the visual forms with the appropriate sounds. The early confusability of the letters may produce a "learned confusion" such that the child knows that the pair of letters is the one that produces problems but cannot remember for sure what goes with what. Other static reversals, such as the reversal of the nonreversible letter *j* which occurs in the writing of disabled readers is, in a sense, more interesting because acquired-distinctiveness-of-cues and learned-confusion interpretations are not as compelling.

Kinetic reversals—more appropriately designated as letter transpositions—which we have not discussed in any detail in this chapter, also represent interesting clinical phenomena deserving of research attention. It seems unlikely that they have the same origin as static reversals and it is probably because of Orton's unfortunate choice of terms in referring to them as reversals that they have been conceptually confused with static reversals in the literature. Transposition errors may well share common variance with the spelling difficulties that plague disabled readers.

In any case, the phenomena of the two types of reversal errors should be documented and clarified, and the processing factors underlying each should be carefully examined. At this point, it seems about equally probable that reversal errors are a fascinating key to understanding the problems that some individuals have processing symbolic information as that they are a "red herring" leading clinicians and researchers astray.

REFERENCES

Bigsby, P. (1985). The nature of reversible letter confusion in dyslexic and normal readers: Misperception or mislabelling? *British Journal of Educational Psychology, 55,* 264–272.

Black, F. (1973). Reversal and rotation errors by normal and retarded readers. *Perceptual & Motor Skills, 36,* 895–898.

Boder, E. (1973). Developmental dyslexia: A diagnostic approach based on three atypical reading-spelling patterns. *Developmental Medicine and Child Neurology, 15,* 663–687.

Cairns, N. U., & Steward, M. S. (1970). Young children's orientation of letters as a function of axis of symmetry and stimulus alignment. *Child Development, 41,* 993–1002.

Calfee, R. C. (1977). Assessment of independent reading skills: Basic research and practical applications. In A. S. Reber & D. L. Scarborough (Eds.), *Towards a psychology of reading* (pp. 289–324). Hillsdale, NJ: Lawrence Erlbaum Associates.

Chapman, L., & Wedell, K. (1972). Perceptual-motor abilities and reversal errors in children's handwriting. *Journal of Learning Disabilities, 5,* 321–325.

Cohn, M., & Stricker, G. (1976). Inadequate perception vs. reversals. *Reading Teacher, 30,* 162–167.

Collette, M. (1979). Dyslexia and classic pathognomic signs. *Perceptual and Motor Skills, 48,* 1055–1062.

Corballis, M., Macadie, L., Crotty, A., & Beale, I. (1985). The naming of disoriented letters by normal and reading-disabled children. *Journal of Child Psychology and Psychiatry, 26,* 929–938.

Doehring, D. (1968). *Patterns of impairment in specific reading disability.* Bloomington, IN: Indiana University Press.

Eisenberg, L. (1966). The epidemiology of reading retardation and a program for preventive intervention. In J. Money & G. Schiffman (Eds.), *The disabled reader: Education of the dyslexic child* (pp. 3–7). Baltimore: Johns Hopkins University Press.

Farnham-Diggory, S. (1978). *Learning disabilities: A psychological perspective.* Cambridge, MA: Harvard University Press.

Feagans, L. V., & McKinney, J. D. (1991). Subtypes of learning disabilities: A review. In L. V. Feagans, E. J. Short, & L. J. Meltzer (Eds.), *Subtypes of learning disabilities: Theoretical perspectives and research* (pp. 3–31). Hillsdale, NJ: Lawrence Erlbaum Associates.

Fischer, W., Liberman, I., & Shankweiler, D. (1978). Reading reversals and developmental dyslexia: A further study. *Cortex, 14,* 496–510.

Frostig, M. (1968). Education of children with learning disabilities. In H. R. Myklebust (Ed.), *Progress in learning disabilities* (pp. 234–266). New York: Grune & Stratton.

Goins, J. T. (1958). Visual perceptual abilities and early reading progress. *Supplementary Educational Monographs* (No. 87). Chicago: University of Chicago Press.

Golick, M. (1978). Learning disabilities and the school age child. *Learning Disabilities: Information Please,* 1–8.

Grosser, G., & Trzeciak, G. (1981). Durations of recognition for single letters with and without visual masking by dyslexic and normal readers. *Perceptual and Motor Skills, 53,* 991–995.

Hinshelwood, J. (1917). *Congenital word-blindness.* London: Lewis.

Hooper, S. R., & Willis, W. G. (1989). *Learning disability subtyping.* New York: Springer-Verlag.

Kagan, J. (1966). Reflection-impulsivity: The generality and dynamics of conceptual tempo. *Journal of Abnormal Psychology, 71,* 17–24.

Kaufman, N. L. (1980). Review of research on reversal errors. *Perceptual and Motor Skills, 51,* 55–79.

Kaufman, N. L., & Kaufman, A. (1980). Does item content (semantic vs. figural) affect reversal errors made by black and white first graders? *Perceptual and Motor Skills, 50,* 993–994.

Liberman, I., Shankweiler, D., Orlando, C., Harris, K., & Bell Berti, F. (1971). Letter confusions and reversals of sequence in the beginning reader: Implications for Orton's theory of developmental dyslexia. *Cortex, 7,* 127–142.

Lyle, J. (1969). Reading retardation and reversal tendency: A factorial study. *Child Development, 40,* 833–843.

Lyle, J., & Goyen, J. (1968). Visual recognition, developmental lag and strephosymbolia in reading retardation. *Journal of Abnormal Psychology, 73,* 25–29.

Money, J. (1962). Dyslexia: A postconference review. In J. Money (Ed.), *Reading disability: Progress and research in dyslexia* (pp. 9–33). Baltimore: Johns Hopkins University Press.

Money, J. (1966). Case 1: Space-form deficit. In J. Money (Ed.), *The disabled reader: Education of the dyslexic child* (pp. 263–276). Baltimore: Johns Hopkins University Press.

Nisbett, R., & Ross, L. (1980). *Human inference: Strategies and shortcomings of social judgement.* Englewood Cliffs, NJ: Prentice-Hall.

Orton, S. T. (1925). "Word-blindness" in school children. *Archives of Neurology and Psychiatry, 14,* 581–615.

Orton, S. T. (1931). Special disability in spelling. *Bulletin of the Neurological Institute of New York, 1,* 166–200.

Orton, S. T. (1937). *Reading, writing and speech problems in children.* New York: Norton.

Oyama, T., & Sato, K. (1975). Relative similarity of rotated and reversed figures to the original figures as a function of children's age. *Journal of Comparative and Physiological Psychology, 88,* 110–117.

Perfetti, C. A. (1986). Continuities in reading acquisition, reading skill, and reading disability. *Remedial and Special Education, 7,* 11–21.

Rawson, M. B. (1982). Louise Baker and the Leonardo Syndrome. *Annals of Dyslexia, 32,* 289–304.

Seidenberg, M., Bruck, M., Fornarolo, G., & Backman, J. (1985). Word recognition processes of poor and disabled readers: Do they necessarily differ? *Applied Psycholinguistics, 6,* 161–180.

Shaywitz, S. E., Escobar, M. D., Shaywitz, B. A., Fletcher, J. M., & Makuch, R. (1992). Evidence that dyslexia may represent the lower tail of a normal distribution of reading ability. *New England Journal of Medicine, 326,* 145–150.

Simpson, E. (1979). *Reversals: A personal account of a victory over dyslexia.* Boston: Houghton Mifflin.

Spache, G. D., McIlroy, K., & Berg, P. C. (1981). *Case studies in reading disability.* Boston: Allyn & Bacon.

Stanovich, K. E. (1985). Explaining the variance in terms of psychological processes: What have we learned? *Annals of Dyslexia, 35,* 67–96.

Stanovich, K. E. (1992). *How to think straight about psychology* (3rd ed.). New York: Harper Collins.

Stein, N. L., & Mandler, J. M. (1974). Children's recognition of reversals of geometric figures. *Child Development, 45,* 604–615.

Stevenson, H. W., Parker, T., Wilkerson, A., Hegion, A., & Fish, E. (1976). Longitudinal study of individual differences in cognitive development and scholastic achievement. *Journal of Educational Psychology, 68,* 377–400.

Taylor, H., Satz, P. & Friel, J. (1976). Developmental dyslexia in relation to other childhood reading disorders. Significance and clinical utility. *Reading Research Quarterly, 15,* 84–81.

Terepocki, M., Willows, D. M., & Kruk, R. (1993, November). *The incidence and causes of static reversal errors in reading disability.* Paper presented at the Orton Dyslexia Society 44th Annual Conference, New Orleans, LA.

Vellutino, F. R. (1987). Dyslexia. *Scientific American, 256*(3), 34–41.

Vellutino, F. R., Pruzek, R., Steger, J. A., & Meshoulam, U. (1973). Immediate visual recall in poor and normal readers as a function of orthographic-linguistic familiarity. *Cortex, 9,* 368–384.

Vellutino, F. R., Smith, H., Steger, J. A., & Kaman, M. (1975). Reading disability: Age differences and the perceptual deficit hypothesis. *Child Development, 46,* 487–493.

Vellutino, F. R., Steger, J. A., DeSetto, L., & Phillips, F. (1975). Immediate and delayed recognition of visual stimuli in poor and normal readers. *Journal of Experimental Child Psychology, 19,* 223–232.

Vellutino, F. R., Steger, J. A., Kaman, M., & DeSetto, L. (1975). Visual form perception in deficient and normal readers as function of age and orthographic linguistic familiarity. *Cortex, 11,* 22–30.

Vellutino, F. R., Steger, J. A., Moyer, B. M., Harding, S. C., & Niles, C. J. (1977). Has the perceptual deficit hypothesis led us astray? *Journal of Learning Disabilities, 10,* 54–64.

Wechsler, D., & Hagin, R. (1964). The problem of axial rotation in reading disability. *Perceptual and Motor Skills, 19,* 319–326.

Werker, J., Bryson, S., & Wassenberg, K. (1989). Toward understanding the problem in severely disabled readers. Part II: Consonant errors. *Applied Psycholinguistics, 10,* 13–30.

Willows, D. M. (1991). Visual Processes in Learning Disabilities. In B. Y. L. Wong (Ed.), *Learning about learning disabilities* (pp. 163–193). New York: Academic Press.

Wohlwill, J. F., & Wiener, M. (1964). Discrimination of form orientation in young children. *Child Development, 35,* 1113–1125.

3 Orton Revisited: Dyslexia, Laterality, and Left–Right Confusion

Michael C. Corballis
Ivan L. Beale
University of Auckland

By far the most influential theory of developmental dyslexia, at least historically, has been that of Samuel Torrey Orton (e.g., 1937). His extensive observations in the 1920s and 1930s persuaded him that dyslexic children were especially prone to left–right confusions and reversals, such as mistaking *b* for *d* or *was* for *saw,* or writing in mirrored script. Many were also left-handed, or showed evidence of mixed laterality. Orton concluded that developmental dyslexia was due to a failure to establish a left–right sense, which was in turn caused by incomplete cerebral dominance. There are still many people who, even if they have not heard of Orton, regard dyslexia as virtually synonymous with "seeing things backward," or who regard left- or mixed-handedness as ominous signs of potential reading difficulty.

Orton's ideas fell into disrepute following World War II, at least in academic and educational circles. This was due in part to a trend away from organic theories of mental disorders, and toward theories based on depth psychology or on learning theory. The war itself may have led to the realization that psychological ills could often be traced to experience rather than constitution. Moreover, it came to be regarded as anathema to impose a label like "dyslexia," with its neurological overtones, onto a disorder that might be purely psychological in origin, and might perhaps be treated with appropriate psychological intervention. By the early 1960s dyslexia was seen as part of the more general class of "learning disabilities" and was widely viewed as an educational rather than a neurological or even a psychological problem. Yet the neurological model persisted in some quarters, fueling a continuing and often acrimonious debate on central issues such as definition, diagnosis, and classification (Kavale & Forness, 1985).

There has since been something of a counterrevolution, linked to the "cognitive revolution" of the 1960s and the subsequent rise of neuropsychology, so that once again it is respectable to seek anomalies of brain function in children labeled as dyslexic. Orton seemed to have been largely forgotten in the new wave (but see Willows and Terepocki, chap. 2), although it remains a common theme that dyslexia may be due in some way to incomplete cerebral lateralization, or a weakness in left-hemispheric function (e.g., Geschwind & Galaburda, 1987). Given the dominant role of the left hemisphere in normal language, including reading and writing, that theme has a natural insistency.

We now turn to a closer examination of Orton's theory. In fact, it is commonly misrepresented, and Orton anticipated a good deal of contemporary thinking on reading difficulties. His neurological theory does present problems, but we argue nevertheless that a modified version may still yield insights into the nature and treatment of dyslexia.

ORTON'S THEORY

According to Orton's theory, the two sides of the brain would code spatial information with opposite *parity,* or left–right orientation. This, he thought, was a simple consequence of the fact that they are themselves structural mirror images of one another. "The exact symmetrical relationship of the two hemispheres would lead us to believe that the group of cells irradiated by any visual stimulus in the right hemisphere are the exact mirrored counterpart of those in the left" (Orton, 1931, p. 166). Where one hemisphere might encode a *b,* the other would encode a *d;* or where one might register a face in left profile, the other would record it in right profile. Orton's diagram illustrating this reversal is shown in Fig. 3.1.

If this theory is correct, cerebral dominance would then be critical to mirror-image discrimination. In a person without clearly established dominance, it would be merely a matter of chance which hemisphere provided the relevant information; the person might write in either direction, or might describe a given letter as either a *b* or a *d,* depending on the hemisphere exerting control at the time. Orton named this condition *strephosymbolia* (twisted symbols). He also distinguished between *static* reversals, which are confusions of mirror-image pairs such as *b* and *d* or of near-mirror images such as *p* and *g* or *f* and *t,* and *kinetic* reversals, which represent confusions over the direction in which letters are sequenced, such as reading or writing *pradon* for *pardon, sorty* for *story,* and the like. Both kinds of reversal would be overcome, of course, if a consistent dominance and therefore a consistent left–right sense were established.

As already noted, it is often supposed that Orton's theory implies that those without established dominance would actually *see* things as though reversed. For example, Vellutino, Steger, and Kandel (1972) wrote that "it may not be true as

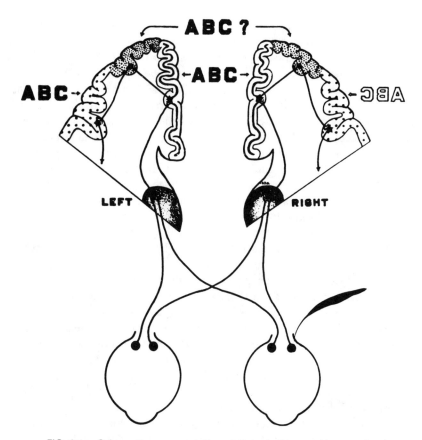

FIG. 3.1.   Schematic representation of Orton's theory of how a visual pattern (ABC) is represented in the two sides of the brain. The normally dominant representation is shown in boldface, and the normally elided one in outline. In those lacking cerebral dominance, these two representations would compete, creating left–right confusion. From " 'Word-blindness' in school children" by S. T. Orton, 1925, *Archives of Neurology & Psychiatry, 14,* pp. 581–615. Copyright 1925 by American Medical Association. Reprinted by permission.

Orton (1925, 1937) and others suggest, that the child who calls a 'b,' 'd,' or 'was,' 'saw' perceives ('sees') them as such, but rather, that he 'misreads' them, in spite of reliable perception, because he is unable to produce their precise auditory designations" (p. 107). However Orton (1931) was adamant that his theory does *not* imply that perception is reversed: "I believe that children with these problems *see as others do* but fail to elide completely one of the two antitropic engrams registered as a pattern for later comparison which forms the basis of recognition" (p. 166; our italics). Vellutino and his colleagues persistently but mistakenly referred to Orton's theory as a "perceptual deficit" theory (e.g., Vellutino, 1979).[1] They are in fact in perfect agreement with Orton when they note that disabled readers have little difficulty copying words correctly, but make many reversal errors (such as *din* for *bin, cob* for *cod, sung* for *snug,* and *lion* for *loin*) when pronouncing those words (Vellutino et al., 1972).

Nevertheless the distinction between perception and recognition is sometimes a fine one. Orton (1928b) actually distinguished three levels of visual processing, and noted that his dyslexic cases "did not have any visual defect in the ordinary sense and moreover that they did not have any defect in the second level of brain function in the visual field; i.e., they could make adequate and proper use of visual memories of objects, calling the names of objects and pictures promptly and quickly" (p. 1096). The problem arose at the third level "where association between the printed word and its meaning or concept takes place" (p. 1096).[2] In a highly automated skill like reading, it is this third level that dominates awareness, as is evident from the Stroop effect in which the meanings of words dominate the color of the ink they are printed in. Because written words are somewhat unique in that their left–right parity is critical to their understanding, left–right parity is also a dominant aspect of their visual apprehension. This is not the case with other objects or shapes, as is easily demonstrated by looking at the world through a looking glass. Most everyday objects and shapes look reasonably familiar and normal, to the point that it is not always clear whether or not they are reversed. But with text there is little doubt, because reversed text has an unfamiliar, almost eerie quality. The strange sea of reversed text may present to normal readers some sense of what the dyslexic experiences when confronted with normal text.

More recently, a distinction has been drawn between those dyslexics with a primarily visual deficit, and those with a primarily phonological deficit (e.g., Boder, 1973; Johnson & Myklebust, 1967; Pirozzolo, 1979). Boder (1973) re-fered to these subtypes as "dyseidetic" and "dysphonetic," respectively, and noted that the majority of disabled readers actually fall into the latter category. However Orton was also well aware that children often have difficulty with phonology in learning to read or write. He noted that strephosymbolic children often confuse letters representing similar sounds, such as *k* and *g, d* and *t,* or *f* and *v* (Orton, 1931). Precisely why such errors should result from strephosym-bolia is not made clear, although it is perhaps reasonable that any deficit in forming unambiguous impressions of letters would be compounded if the sounds

---

[1]For further, and related, criticism of Vellutino's work, see Willows, Kruk, and Corcos (chap. 12).

[2]The distinction between Orton's second and third levels is not entirely clear, because there seems to be little difference in principle between naming an object and naming a word. The difference seems to lie in the importance of left–right orientation in the case of words. The distinction between perceptual and associative aspects seems clear, however, and is captured in the distinction between apperceptive and associative agnosia. Dyslexia might therefore be considered a kind of associative agnosia for words.

they represent are also similar. Orton (e.g., 1929, 1931) was also highly critical of the "sight method" in teaching children to read, because this not only leaves the child at the mercy of visual reversals, but also fails to teach the phonological skills critical to the "grapheme-to-phoneme mapping" required in mastering alphabetically based scripts.

Orton anticipated a good deal of contemporary discussion of reading disability, thus one might ask why his views have been so widely ignored in the contemporary literature. Perhaps it is just an aspect of the collective amnesia that afflicts much of modern neuropsychology.[3] A more important reason, however, may be the mistaken premise on which Orton's neurological theory is based.

Contrary to Orton, there is no good reason to suppose that the two halves of the brain would simply record information with opposite left–right orientations (Corballis & Beale, 1976, 1983). Certainly, the bilateral symmetry of the brain does not force such a conclusion, any more than the symmetry of a camera lens forces symmetrical impressions on the two sides of exposed film. Orton also implied that, in the majority of people at least, the left hemisphere of the brain would record information as though correctly oriented and the right side would record it as though left–right reversed (see Fig. 3.1), but there is no reason why the left side should be so blessed and the right side cursed. And because the right side is presumed to play the greater role in spatial perception, the wonder is that those with "normal" hemispheric specialization are not forever barking up wrong trees, and getting their wires crossed.

Although this illogical aspect of Orton's theorizing may help explain why it lost favor, few have been explicit as to precisely what was wrong with it.[4] Zangwill (1960), for example, merely observed that Orton "linked his observations with a decidedly speculative theory of brain function that few have had the temerity to accept," but went on to attribute great credit to Orton "for being the first to study these problems in a systematic way and to envisage them within the framework of genetic neurology" (p. 14).

But was Orton's theory so very wrong? We next consider a modified version of it that at least removes its irrational quality.

ORTON'S THEORY MODIFIED

We suggested (Corballis & Beale, 1976, 1983) that the left–right orientation of patterns might be reversed, not in the initial laying down of traces in the hemispheres, but in the transfer of traces from one hemisphere to the other. Con-

---

[3]To cite another example, a good deal of present-day speculation on hemispheric duality is in fact a repeat of speculation that took place at the end of last century, especially in France, but few were even aware of this until Harrington (1985) pointed it out.

[4]We like to think we are among that few (Corballis & Beale, 1976, 1983).

fronted with a stimulus such as the letter *d,* both hemispheres would (naturally) record it for what it is. However each hemisphere might then transfer reversed information, so that both hemispheres now register the *b* shape as well as the *d* shape. This transfer is a property of *plasticity,* not of stimulation per se; that is, it occurs in memory formation, not in perception, so that both hemispheres "see" the letter veridically. In later recall or recognition, however, the reversal would create potential confusion as to which letter had actually been presented.

Mirror-image reversal of this sort would be a natural consequence of homotopic connections between the hemispheres; connections, that is, that join mirror-image points. If the hemispheres were symmetrical to begin with, and the homotopic connections were involved in establishing structural changes in the brain, this would ensure that the brain would tend to remain structurally symmetrical. In other words, the interhemispheric exchange would act as a process of *symmetrization.* This is sufficient in itself to guarantee mirror-image confusion, or the inability to tell left from right (Corballis, 1983, 1988; Corballis & Beale, 1970, 1976, 1983). The reason for this can be explained.

Suppose our bilaterally symmetrical organism sees the letter *b* on a screen, and correctly names it as a "bee." Now suppose the whole scene is mirror-reversed, as in a looking glass. The organism, being bilaterally symmetrical, is of course quite unaltered by mirror reversal, and its vocalization also remains unaltered; it continues to say "bee." However the *b* is now transformed by the mirror reversal into a *d.* Consequently we now see the organism inescapably calling the *d* a "bee." Quite literally, then, it cannot tell which letter is which. The same conclusion holds for any task that requires the ability to tell left from right. It should be noted that this argument applies regardless of the nature of the memory code; that is, it is not necessary to assume that events or patterns are coded in topographic fashion (Corballis & Beale, 1976).

Note also that our hypothetical symmetrical organism need have no difficulty *seeing* which way round the letter is. That is, there is no reason why it could not point to the rounded portion, or run its finger along the straight side. The problem is one of labeling, where the labels to mirror images are not themselves mirror images (Corballis & Beale, 1970). In this respect, this modified version of Orton's theory is actually more consistent with Orton's own views as to the level at which left–right problems occur than was the original version of the theory.

This discussion of interhemispheric reversal may seem little more than a Carrollian flight of fancy, but most animals, including humans, are to a high degree bilaterally symmetrical, notwithstanding the current obsession with cerebral lateralization. This is surely a consequence of the fact that, to a freely moving creature, the natural world is indifferent with respect to left and right. For example, events are equally likely to occur on either side of the body, and objects such as the bodies and faces of other animals are equally likely to appear in left or right profile. Moreover, there is an adaptive advantage in symmetrizing the remembered products of experience, because a face seen in one profile might be next encountered in the opposite profile, or a predator that pounces from one side might next pounce from the other. An active process of symmetrization would accomplish what we have termed *mirror-image generalization,* preserving a balanced response to the world around us (Corballis & Beale, 1970, 1976, 1983).

There is evidence that mirror-image generalization is indeed dependent on the interhemispheric commissures. Beale, Williams, Webster, and Corballis (1972) found that mirror-image generalization to oblique lines was abolished in the pigeon following section of the commissures, and Noonan and Axelrod (1990) reported improved left–right differentiation in the rat following section of the corpus callosum. In a reanalysis of data reported by Noble (1968), Achim and Corballis (1977) concluded that discrimination of visual mirror images by monkeys was improved following section of the anterior commissure. Many of the commissures link mirror-image points in the two hemispheres (Cummings, 1970), ensuring a left–right reversal in transfer. There is also evidence that plasticity induced in one hemisphere by peripheral denervation in the flying fox is almost immediately mirrored in the other hemisphere, presumably as a result of homotopic transfer (Calford & Tweedale, 1990). The brain seems to have been constructed in such a way as to preserve its own symmetry in the face of asymmetrical experience, or even of asymmetrical physical insult.

Unilateral brain injury sometimes brings about a systematic tendency to left–right reversal, perhaps because of a release of a reversed representation in the other hemisphere. Of 18 cases described in the literature of mirror-writing brought about by brain injury, all had left-hemispheric damage and wrote backward with the left-hand, suggesting that reversed representations had been laid down in the right hemisphere (Feinberg & Jones, 1985). Although this might seem to support Orton's original theory, we suspect that the reversal is due to interhemispheric transfer and not to the way in which the hemispheres initially record information. Representations to do with script may be initially recorded more strongly in the left hemisphere, but reversed representations due to interhemispheric transfer would then be more strongly recorded in the right. Luria (1966) also described a case of a patient with right parietal damage who drew a reversed map of Russia, suggesting that spatial information, normally more strongly represented in the right hemisphere, tends to be reversed in the left hemisphere.

Far from being a pathological condition, then, left–right confusion may actually be the consequence of an adaptive process of left–right generalization. Indeed nearly all children experience difficulty in learning mirror-image discriminations or in differentiating left from right responses (Corballis & Beale, 1970, 1976), and this is often manifest when they first learn to read and write. What, then, might left–right confusion have to do with reading disability?

LEFT–RIGHT CONFUSION
AND READING DISABILITY

First, there is a strong a priori reason for linking reading disability to left–right confusion. Reading and writing, at least in the case of horizontally arrayed scripts, are almost unique among the activities of humans (or indeed of any creatures) in that they require a consistent sense of left and right. Vocal language does not require asymmetry, nor does the use of tools or weapons—although asymmetry might be an advantage for such activities because it might allow greater specialization. But reading and writing require asymmetry, because they require the ability to tell left from right.

Second, Orton (1937) was aware that left–right confusion was a ubiquitous phenomenon, but insisted on empirical grounds that it was more pronounced among the reading disabled than among normal children:

> The errors made by a group of reading disability cases were tabulated and compared with those made by a carefully selected group of normal readers of the same grade and intelligence, and the errors of reversal were found to be significant statistically for the reading disability cases at each of the four reading grades that were studied. Not only was this so, but the frequency with which errors of reversal appeared in the work of a given case proved to correlate with the amount of retardation in reading, that is, with the severity of the disorder. (p. 151)

Although some studies, including one of our own (Corballis, Macadie, Crotty, & Beale, 1985), have failed to show any clear relation between left–right confusions and reading disability, the evidence as a whole is generally in support of such a relation (see the reviews by Kaufman, 1980, and by Willows and Terepocki, chap. 2).

Willows and her colleagues (Watson & Willows, chap. 13; Willows & Terepocki, chap. 2) suggest two factors that have weakened the evidence. First, there may be different types of reading disability, such as the dyseidetic and dysphonetic types identified by Boder (1973), and those who display the classic Orton-type pattern constitute only one type—perhaps the dyseidetic subgroup, although we saw earlier that Orton thought that strephosymbolia might lead to both visual and phonetic problems. Second, laboratory studies typically last only 15 to 20 min, and may therefore fail to reveal the sorts of problems that emerge from long-term assessment and remedial work. Indeed, there is some evidence that reversals are more characteristic of those actually diagnosed as dyslexic than of children selected from a normal classroom on the basis of poor performance on standard reading tests (Fischer, Liberman, & Shankweiler, 1978). The majority of controlled studies are based on classroom samples, which might explain why support for Orton's theory has been intermittent. Willows and Terepocki (chap. 2) note that reversal errors are very common among the cases of dyslexia they have studied.

One classic case is American writer Eileen Simpson, whose struggle with dyslexia and left–right confusion is documented in *Reversals* (1980), which reads as a virtual testimonial to Orton. Another talented dyslexic is the British mathematician Kalvis M. Jansons (1988), who describes his left–right problems as follows:

> For the first six years of my life I was essentially ambidextrous and I have always had trouble telling left from right, as do my father and brother. Often when I try to recall a scene I find it difficult to determine whether it or its mirror image is the correct representation, unless there is some cue like traffic or road signs. (p. 505)

Even Leonardo da Vinci might be taken as support for the theory (see Aaron & Guillemard, chap. 18). He was a left-hander who not only habitually wrote in mirrored script, but also exhibited the symptoms of surface dysgraphia; that is, his spelling was erratic but nearly always phonologically correct (Sartori, 1987). Another habitual mirror-writer, an adolescent girl, also displays the spelling patterns of surface dysgraphia, as in *sorce* for *source, ecenchal* for *essential, sholders* for *shoulders* (Corballis, 1983). It is possible that people with an over-developed tendency to left–right *generalization* have special difficulty in learning precisely what words look like, and therefore resort to spelling by sound rather than by sight.

LATERALITY AND READING DISABILITY

The other aspect of Orton's theory has to do with the failure of disabled readers to establish consistent cerebral dominance. Again the evidence is mixed. There has been some support for an association between left-handedness and developmental learning disorders, including reading disability, from the work of Geschwind and his colleagues (Geschwind & Behan, 1982; Geschwind & Galaburda, 1987; Schachter, Ransil, & Geschwind, 1987), but this association has been disputed on both methodological and empirical grounds by Bishop (1983, 1990).

There is some evidence however that the relation between handedness and reading ability may be nonlinear. Annett and her colleagues (Annett & Kilshaw, 1984; Annett & Manning, 1990) reported that both non-right-handers and extreme right-handers are more susceptible to reading problems than are the moderately right-handed. Moreover, Annett and Manning (1990) selected children classified as dyslexic, divided them into two groups on the basis of their intelligence scores on the Raven's Colored Progressive Matrices test (Raven, Court, & Raven, 1984), and discovered that the "dull" group were strongly right-handed, whereas the "bright" group showed little overall bias. It may be the bright group that corresponds most nearly to the profile of dyslexia as presented by Orton.

Orton thought that dyslexia might be related to opposite asymmetries on different measures, and noted in particular that of 102 cases of dyslexia in his files, 69 were of opposite handedness and eye dominance (Orton, 1937). This was corroborated by Denckla (1979), who recorded a fact that she "tried in vain to escape": Nearly two-thirds of her dyslexic patients were right-handed, right-footed, but *left*-eye dominant. Earlier, we described a mirror-writer with the symptoms of surface dyslexia; this girl is right-handed both for normal and mirror-writing, but is left-eye dominant (Corballis, 1983).

Some investigators have examined the relation between reading disability and more direct measures of cerebral lateralization. Obrzut and Boliek (1986) reviewed evidence from studies of dichotic listening, visual hemifield differences, and verbal-manual time sharing in normal and reading-disabled children, and concluded that reading-disabled children as a group show the usual left-hemispheric specialization for verbal processing, but to a lesser degree than do normal children. They also noted that it is not clear whether this reduced specialization is due to incomplete dominance, developmental delay, or neurological deficits.

Geschwind and Galaburda (1987) referred to several cases of dyslexics where autopsy has shown abnormal development of the brain, especially on the left side; these include an excess of white matter, or the presence of irregularities such as "brain warts." There is also evidence that anatomical asymmetries normally observed in the human brain are reversed or absent among those with reading or learning disabilities. In some 91% of right-handers and 73% of left-handers, the posterior part of the brain is wider on the right than on the left (LeMay, 1977), but brain scans of 24 dyslexic patients showed that this asymmetry was reversed in 10 of them, with 8 showing the usual asymmetry and 6 showing no asymmetry (Hier, LeMay, Rosenberger, & Perlo, 1981). A follow-up study revealed a similar pattern (Rosenberger & Hier, 1981), although a recent review casts some doubt on these various findings (Hynd & Semrud-Clikeman, 1989).

Just as Annett and her colleagues suggested that the relation between reading disability and handedness might be nonlinear, so it has been suggested that opposite extremes of cerebral asymmetry might be detrimental to reading. Bakker and his colleagues (e.g., Bakker, 1979, 1986; Bakker, Licht, Kok, & Bouma, 1980), classified dyslexics into *P-types*, who depend primarily on a right-hemispheric, perceptual mode, and *L-types*, who depend on a left-hemispheric, linguistic mode. They suggested that learning to read normally depends first on perceptual strategies, but linguistic strategies are more critical later on. P-type dyslexics remain fixed at the perceptual level, whereas L-types employ linguistic strategies from the start.

Bakker also developed remedial techniques based on stimulation of the supposedly weaker hemisphere. L-type dyslexics receive reading material to the left visual half-field or to the left hand to stimulate the right hemisphere, and P-types are presented with material to the right half-field or to the right hand, and in both cases there is reported improvement in reading fluency (Bakker, Bouma, &

Gardien, 1990; Bakker & Vinke, 1985). Orton (1929, 1931) also advocated the remedial use of kinesthetic stimulation, by encouraging dyslexic children to point to the words and letters while reading—a recommendation still widely followed that has gathered some empirical support (e.g., Bradley, 1981). The remedies proposed by Orton and Bakker therefore have much in common, although based on different (even opposite) rationales. Orton's aim was to increase cerebral asymmetry and instil a left–right directional sense, whereas Bakker's is to stimulate an underdeveloped or underused left hemisphere, with the aim of decreasing asymmetry rather than increasing it.

THEORETICAL PERSPECTIVES

Although Orton's theory does not feature in most current accounts, the idea that dyslexia might be related to anomalies of cerebral lateralization has persisted. How, then, might such anomalies come about? There are at least two current theoretical perspectives on this, and although they differ from Orton's they are not necessarily incompatible with it. We suggest that these two perspectives are to some extent compatible with one another, and they also leave a potential niche for Orton.

Geschwind's Theory

Geschwind and his colleagues (e.g., Geschwind & Galaburda, 1987) suggested that excessive intrauterine exposure to the male hormone testosterone, or some related substance, has an inhibitory effect on the growth of the left hemisphere, as well as on the thymus, a gland involved in the development of lymphocytes that recognize self antigens. This theory explains why men are more likely than women to be left-handed, and are more likely also to suffer from learning disabilities, including dyslexia. It also predicts that the incidence of autoimmune disorders should be associated with left-handedness and learning disabilities.

Support for this theory has been decidedly mixed (see, e.g., Bishop, 1990; Chavance et al., 1990; Hugdahl, Synnevag, & Satz, 1990; Hynd & Semrud-Clikeman, 1989). Recently, however, Galaburda switched the emphasis from autoimmune disorders and the putative role of testosterone to the nature of the variation in cerebral asymmetry and its relation to learning disorders. Instead of arguing that testosterone levels affect the development of the left hemisphere, Galaburda, Corsiglia, Rosen, and Sherman (1987) suggested that asymmetry is normally achieved by a neuronal loss on the *right* side, and testosterone (or some other influence) might interfere with this process of neuronal "pruning." The more general idea that variations in cerebral asymmetry reflect variations in *right*-hemispheric growth, whether or not testosterone is involved, is pursued by Galaburda, Rosen, and Sherman (1990).

These authors make the interesting suggestion that difficulties may arise if there is either too much or too little pruning; that is, to be too asymmetrical may be as much of an impediment as to be too symmetrical:

> Development of [cellular and connectional] structures may lead to errors in which conceivably too many neurons and interhemispheric connections might be lost on one side leading to overly reduced asymmetrical networks and callosal deficits (which we suggest characterizes the underlying substrate of the callosal agenesis syndromes). Conversely, as we believe applies to developmental dyslexia, inadequate numbers of cells may be pruned, resulting in exuberant networks that fail in ways that exaggerate the characteristics of left-handed symmetrical brains. (p. 543)

Annett's Theory

Instead of attributing variations in cerebral asymmetry to the influence of testosterone, Annett (1972, 1985) postulated control by a single gene. She called this the "right-shift" (RS) gene, because the dominant allele (RS+) shifts the distribution of handedness in favor of the right hand (Annett, 1972). More recently, Annett (1985) switched the emphasis from handedness to cerebral lateralization, so that the gene might be more properly identified as a *left*-shift gene, but to avoid left–right confusion we persist with the original terminology.

Annett's idea purported that those who inherit two recessive (RS−) alleles are essentially without any genotypic bias; that is, they are as likely to be left-handed as right-handed, and to be left as right cerebrally dominant for language. This condition increases the risk of developmental language disorders, such as dyslexia. As we saw earlier, however, Annett's work (Annett & Kilshaw, 1984; Annett & Manning, 1990) suggests that extreme right-handers might also have problems with reading and other academic skills, implying that those who inherit two dominant (RS+) alleles might also be disadvantaged. The optimal condition is therefore what she called "balanced polymorphism," with one allele of each type. It follows from the binomial theorem that the proportion of such individuals (heterozygotes) cannot exceed 50%, and Annett (1985) presented evidence that the actual proportion is indeed very close to this optimal value.

The relation between this theory and that of Galaburda et al. (1990) should now be clear. RS+ homozygotes correspond to the overly asymmetrical, overly "pruned" group, whereas RS− homozygotes are the ones with symmetrical but "exuberant" brains. That is, the RS+ gene may work through the pruning of the right hemisphere rather than the development of the left. There is no doubt considerable phenotypic variation, so these genotypes should not of course be seen as rigidly prescriptive of reading or academic disability. Rather, homozygosis may simply increase the risk of disorder.

Annett's theory implied that both left-handedness and dyslexia should tend to run in families. It was again Orton (1930) who provided the early evidence that this was so. He drew up charts of eight families over three generations, showing the incidence of ambidexterity, left-handedness, stuttering, and reading and writing problems among individuals. Of the 83 individuals concerned, 41 showed at least one of these characteristics. Similar family charts of the incidence of different kinds of reading disability have been presented by Omenn and Weber (1978).

In terms of Annett's theory, then, it is presumably the RS− homozygotes who provide the classic Orton-type of dyslexia. These are the talented dyslexics, in the mold of Leonardo or Eileen Simpson, who often attract attention through the very contrast between their otherwise superior talents and their seemingly perverse inability to read or spell. Neither Annett nor Galaburda and his colleagues made it very clear why the possession of these exuberant brains should be at all disadvantageous. It is here, we think, that Orton's theory may still contribute a degree of insight.

Because reading and writing are recent skills, and in many cultures still the preserve of the elite, it is unlikely that the ability to tell left from right was decisive in the evolution of asymmetry. Indeed, as we pointed out earlier, the advantages mostly lie with treating left and right as equivalent, especially in the natural world. The advantage of asymmetry probably had to do rather with the control of internally generated, sequential actions—or what have been termed "praxic" skills (Corballis, 1983, 1989). Orton (1928a) recognized that the lack of cerebral dominance might interfere with processes that were purely sequential, and took up the idea that it might underlie stuttering. He was unclear as to the reason, however, and it was left largely to his colleague Lee Edward Travis (1931) to pursue this theme.

Initially, then, cerebral asymmetry may have proven adaptive because it reduced the risk of interhemispheric conflict in intricate sequential skills, such as speech. But with the advent of literacy and the importance of the left–right distinction, a symmetrical brain, albeit an exuberant one, may have exacted another price—the risk of failure to develop a clear left–right sense. And if Annett's theory is correct, there will always be a proportion of the normal population in this category, because the optimal condition is a genetic compromise between symmetry and asymmetry.

Gathering the Threads

How good, then, is the evidence that the problem with those overexuberant, symmetrical brains is indeed, at root, a left–right problem? We have seen that there is at least some evidence suggesting left–right problems in those genuinely classed as dyslexic, and there are good a priori reasons for arguing that the left–right dimension is especially critical in reading and writing. Moreover, Orton's theory has no doubt suffered from the failure of others to grasp the *level* at which left–right confusion causes an impediment, and from Orton's own eccentric neurologizing. We suspect, too, that many experiments on left–right discrimination in reading-disabled children may fail to detect real left–right problems. In the typical experimental set-up, for example, there are often consistent cues, such as the experimenter sitting on one side of the child, that serve as a cue to left from right (Corballis & Beale, 1976), so that the child need not draw on an internal directional sense. An overexuberant process of *mirror-image generalization* might well create difficulties in building up reading and writing skills over the long term, and these might not be detected in simple discrimination tasks.

In any case, what better theory do we have to explain those otherwise intelligent people whose reading problems seem to be essentially those of the surface dyslexic—those who fail to apprehend the *looks* of words? One competing theory suggests that some dyslexics, at least, do indeed suffer subtle visual defects that have been characterized as an impairment of the visual transient subsystem (Lovegrove, Martin, & Slaghuis, 1986; Lovegrove & Williams, chap. 14). This results in an excess of visible persistence, such that inputs from successive fixations might tend to be superimposed. But such deficits are unlikely to be the *cause* of dyslexia because, for example, most dyslexics have severe problems in reading single words where the role of multiple fixations is minimal (Hulme, 1988). Hulme concluded that impairment of the transient system might well be an irrelevant correlate of reading problems, perhaps reflecting some minor brain damage or developmental anomaly, and where visual problems do play a direct role in dyslexia they are at a higher level. This brings us, potentially at least, back to Orton.

Another approach is to appeal to higher level perceptual "styles." As we saw earlier from the work of Bakker, it is sometimes suggested that P-type (visuospatial, dyseidetic) dyslexics are overly dependent on the right hemisphere, and may therefore adopt a holistic mode of perception that is ill-suited to reading, which requires a more analytic approach. But the question now is whether this holistic strategy is general, or whether it is specific to reading. In fact, the development of appropriate analytic procedures for processing words depends critically on a directional sense and on the discrimination of mirror-image forms.

In short, Orton's theory may provide insight as to *why* some children fail to develop such analytic procedures. The very concept of dyslexia implies a *specific* deficit, and words themselves have a specific property that sets them apart from all other patterns, at least in cultures where they are represented horizontally as strings of alphabetic characters. That property is directionality. Failure to develop the cerebral mechanisms to deal with it might therefore account for the frustrating specificity of dyslexia.

Finally, it should be said that the theories of Annett and Galaburda offer us a return to Orton for another reason; they place the emphasis, not on left- or right-hemispheric processing per se, but rather on the problems that arise from the lack of consistent cerebral asymmetry. Moreover they are not deficit theories; both stress that the exuberant unlateralized brain may have advantages that compensate for, and perhaps even outweigh, the potential disadvantages. Dyslexia should not be a cause for blame or recrimination, and in some cases it may even be a cause for celebration.

REFERENCES

Achim, A., & Corballis, M. C. (1977). Mirror-image equivalence and the anterior commissure. *Neuropsychologia, 15,* 475–478.

Annett, M. (1972). The distribution of manual asymmetry. *British Journal of Psychology, 63,* 343–358.

Annett, M. (1985). *Left, right, hand and brain.* Hillsdale, NJ: Lawrence Erlbaum Associates.

Annett, M., & Kilshaw, D. (1984). Lateral preference and skill in dyslexia: Implications of the right shift theory. *Journal of Child Psychology & Psychiatry, 25,* 357–377.

Annett, M., & Manning, D. (1990). Reading and a balanced polymorphism for laterality and ability. *Journal of Child Psychology & Psychiatry, 31,* 511–529.

Bakker, D. J. (1979). Hemispheric differences and reading strategies: Two dyslexias? *Bulletin of the Orton Society, 29,* 84–100.

Bakker, D. J. (1986). Electrophysiological validation of L- and P-type dyslexia. *Journal of Clinical & Experimental Psychology, 8,* 113.

Bakker, D. J., Bouma, A., & Gardien, C. J. (1990). Hemisphere-specific treatment of dyslexia subtypes: A field experiment. *Journal of Learning Disabilities, 23,* 433–438.

Bakker, D. J., Licht, R., Kok, A., & Bouma, A. (1980). Cortical responses to word reading by right- and left-eared normal and reading-disturbed children. *Journal of Clinical Neuropsychology, 2,* 1–12.

Bakker, D. J., & Vinke, J. (1985). Effects of hemisphere-specific stimulation on brain activity and reading in dyslexics. *Journal of Clinical & Experimental Neuropsychology, 7,* 505–525.

Beale, I. L., Williams, R. J., Webster, D. M., & Corballis, M. C. (1972). Confusion of mirror-images by pigeons and interhemispheric commissures. *Nature, 238,* 348–349.

Bishop, D. V. M. (1983). How sinister is sinistrality? *Journal of the Royal College of Physicians, London, 17,* 161–172.

Bishop, D. V. M. (1990). Handedness, clumsiness and developmental language disorders. *Neuropsychologia, 28,* 681–690.

Boder, E. (1973). Developmental dyslexia: A diagnostic approach based on three atypical reading-spelling patterns. *Developmental Medicine & Child Neurology, 15,* 663–687.

Bradley, L. (1981). The organization of motor patterns for spelling: An effective remedial strategy for backward readers. *Developmental Medicine & Child Neurology, 15,* 790–793.

Calford, M. B., & Tweedale, R. (1990). Interhemispheric transfer of plasticity in the cerebral cortex. *Science, 249,* 805–807.

Chavance, M., Dellatolas, G., Bousser, M. G., Amor, B., Grardel, B., Kahan, A., Kahn, M. F., Le Floch, J. P., & Tchobroutsky, G. (1990). Handedness, immune disorders and information bias. *Neuropsychologia, 28,* 429–442.

Corballis, M. C. (1983). *Human laterality.* New York: Academic Press.

Corballis, M. C. (1988). Recognition of disoriented shapes. *Psychological Review, 95,* 115–123.

Corballis, M. C. (1989). Laterality and human evolution. *Psychological Review, 96,* 492–505.

Corballis, M. C., & Beale, I. L. (1970). Bilateral symmetry and behavior. *Psychological Review, 77,* 451–464.

Corballis, M. C., & Beale, I. L. (1976). *The psychology of left and right.* Hillsdale, NJ: Lawrence Erlbaum Associates.

Corballis, M. C., & Beale, I. L. (1983). *The ambivalent mind.* Chicago, IL: Nelson-Hall.

Corballis, M. C., Macadie, L., Crotty, A., & Beale, I. L. (1985). The naming of disoriented letters by normal and reading-disabled children. *Journal of Child Psychology & Psychiatry, 26,* 929–938.

Cummings, W. J. K. (1970). An anatomical review of the corpus callosum. *Cortex, 6,* 1–18.

Denckla, M. (1979). Childhood learning disabilities. In K. M. Heilman & E. Valenstein (Eds.), *Clinical neuropsychology* (pp. 535–573). New York: Oxford University Press.

Feinberg, T., & Jones, G. (1985). Object reversals after parietal lobe infarction—A case report. *Cortex, 21,* 261–271.

Fischer, F. W., Liberman, I. Y., & Shankweiler, D. (1978). Reading reversals and developmental dyslexia: A further study. *Cortex, 14,* 496–510.

Galaburda, A. M., Corsiglia, J., Rosen, G. D., & Sherman, G. F. (1987). Planum temporale asymmetry, reappraisal since Geschwind and Levitsky. *Neuropsychologia, 25,* 853–868.

Galaburda, A. M., Rosen, G. D., & Sherman, G. F. (1990). Individual variability in cortical organization: Its relationship to brain laterality and implications to function. *Neuropsychologia, 28,* 529–546.

Geschwind, N., & Behan, P. (1982). Left-handedness: Association with immune disease, migraine, and developmental disorder. *Proceedings of the National Academy of Sciences, 79,* 5097–5100.

Geschwind, N., & Galaburda, A. M. (1987). *Cerebral lateralization: Biological mechanisms, associations, and pathology.* Cambridge, MA: Bradford/MIT Press.

Harrington, A. (1985). Nineteenth-century ideas on hemispheric differences and "duality of mind." *Behavioral & Brain Sciences, 8,* 617–660.

Hier, D. B., LeMay, M., Rosenberger, P. B., & Perlo, V. P. (1978). Developmental dyslexia: Evidence for a subgroup with a reversal of cerebral asymmetry. *Archives of Neurology, 35,* 90–92.

Hugdahl, K., Synnevag, B., & Satz, P. (1990). Immune and autoimmune diseases in dyslexic children. *Neuropsychologia, 28,* 673–680.

Hulme, C. (1988). The implausibility of low-level visual deficits as a cause of children's reading difficulties. *Cognitive Neuropsychology, 5,* 369–374.

Hynd, G. W., & Semrud-Clikeman, M. (1989). Dyslexia and brain morphology. *Psychological Bulletin, 106,* 447–482.

Jansons, K. M. (1988). A personal view of dyslexia and of thought without language. In L. Weiskrantz (Ed.), *Thought without language* (pp. 498–506). Oxford: Clarendon Press.

Johnson, D. J., & Myklebust, H. R. (1967). *Learning disabilities: Educational principles and practices.* New York: Grune & Stratton.

Kaufman, N. L. (1980). Review of research on reversal errors. *Perceptual & Motor Skills, 51,* 55–79.

Kavale, K. A., & Forness, S. R. (1985). Learning disability and the history of science: Paradigm or paradox? *Remedial & Special Education, 6*(4), 12–24.

LeMay, M. (1977). Asymmetries of the skull and handedness: Phrenology revisited. *Journal of Neurological Sciences, 32,* 243–253.

Lovegrove, W., Martin, F., & Slaghuis, W. (1986). A theoretical and experimental case for a visual deficit in specific reading disability. *Cognitive Neuropsychology, 2,* 225–267.

Luria, A. R. (1966). *Human brain and psychological processes.* New York: Harper & Row.

Morgan, W. P. (1896). A case of congenital word-blindness. *British Medical Journal, 2,* 1378.

Noble, J. (1968). Paradoxical transfer of mirror-image discrimination in the optic chiasm sectioned monkey. *Brain Research, 10,* 127–151.

Noonan, M., & Axelrod, S. (1990). *Improved acquisition of left–right response differentiation in rat following section of corpus callosum.* Unpublished manuscript.

Obrzut, J. E., & Boliek, C. A. (1986). Lateralization characteristics in learning disabled children. *Journal of Learning Disabilities, 19,* 308–314.

Omenn, G. S., & Weber, B. A. (1978). Dyslexia: Search for phenotypic and genetic heterogeneity. *American Journal of Medical Genetics, 1,* 333–342.

Orton, S. T. (1925). "Word-blindness" in school children. *Archives of Neurology & Psychiatry, 14,* 581–615.

Orton, S. T. (1928a). A physiological theory of reading disability and stuttering in children. *New England Journal of Medicine, 199,* 1046–1052.

Orton, S. T. (1928b). Specific reading disability—strephosymbolia. *Journal of the American Medical Association, 90,* 1095–1099.

Orton, S. T. (1929). The "sight reading" method of teaching reading as a source of reading disability. *Journal of Educational Psychology, 2,* 135–142.

Orton, S. T. (1930). Familial occurrence of disorders in the acquisition of language. *Eugenics, 3,* 140–147.

Orton, S. T. (1931). Special disability in spelling. *Bulletin of the Neurological Institute of New York, 1,* 159–192.

Orton, S. T. (1937). *Reading, writing, and speech problems in children.* New York: Norton.

Pirozzolo, F. J. (1979). *The neuropsychology of developmental reading disorders.* New York: Praeger.

Raven, J. C., Court, J. H., & Raven, J. (1984). *Manual for Raven's progressive matrices and vocabulary scales.* London: Lewis.

Rosenberger, P. B., & Hier, D. B. (1981). Cerebral asymmetry and verbal intellectual deficits. *Annals of Neurology, 38,* 300–304.

Sartori, G. (1987). Leonardo da Vinci: Omo sanza lettere. A case of surface dysgraphia? *Cognitive Neuropsychology, 4,* 1–10.

Schachter, S. C., Ransil, B. J., & Geschwind, N. (1987). Associations of handedness with hair color and learning disabilities. *Neuropsychologia, 25,* 269–276.

Simpson, E. (1980). *Reversals: A personal account of victory over dyslexia.* London: Gollancz.

Travis, L. E. (1931). *Speech pathology.* New York: Appleton.

Vellutino, F. R. (1979). *Dyslexia: Theory and research.* Cambridge, MA: MIT Press.

Vellutino, F. R., Steger, J. A., & Kandel, G. (1972). Reading disability: An investigation of the perceptual deficit hypothesis. *Cortex, 8,* 106–118.

Zangwill, O. L. (1960). *Cerebral dominance and its relation to psychological function.* Edinburgh: Oliver & Boyd.

II

NEUROPSYCHOLOGICAL BASES OF VISUAL PROCESSES

4 Neurological Basis of Visual Processes in Reading

Stephen Lehmkuhle
University of Missouri-St. Louis

Visual perception is a unitary experience that simply has no vestige of the separate processes and mechanisms that underlie the generation of the percept. An individual photoreceptor cannot uniquely convey information about spatial, temporal, and chromatic properties of the stimulus. The information is contained in the pattern of stimulation across the photoreceptors. The initial stages of retinal processing separate and collect signals in the photoreceptoral array in different ways to derive information rudimentary to the perceptions of brightness, color, shape and contour, and motion.

The initial stages of retinal processing form different channels or pathways that maintain their separability throughout the visual system. In this chapter, two such pathways are described. The magnocellular or M pathway receives and integrates input from a large number of photoreceptors across the entire extent of the retina. It receives input from both rods and all cone types. The second pathway, the parvocellular or P pathway, is much more selective about which photoreceptors provide an input and integrates the input over a fewer number of receptors primarily located in the central retina. The M pathway is expressly designed to process information quickly, whereas the P pathway processes information at a slower pace. As a consequence, the different types of visual information carried by each pathway are processed at different rates.

The M and P pathways are often referred to as parallel pathways, with the implication that the two pathways are strictly independent at all levels of visual processing. Although the M and P pathways are structurally different and receive different inputs, these pathways do interact at many levels. Nonetheless, many consider the M and P pathways as parallel because there is a division in the labor of extracting information about different stimulus attributes.

This chapter is organized in the following manner: The anatomical and physiological differences between M and P pathways are briefly outlined in the first part of the chapter. The second part presents some psychophysical experiments done in primates and humans that have attempted to elucidate the visual functions performed by each pathway. The third part describes some of the visual deficits often associated with damage to the M pathway. The chapter ends with some speculations about the contribution of the M and P pathways to reading.

ANATOMICAL CLASSIFICATIONS

Retinal ganglion cells in many species are not homogeneous in morphology. Rather, ganglion cells form several distinct heterogeneous groups that can be distinguished in terms of soma size, extent of dendritic field, diameter of axon, and projection sites. M ganglion cells have large soma, with fairly extensive dendritic fields, and large axons that project to the two ventral layers of the dorsal lateral geniculate nucleus. The P ganglion cells have smaller soma, smaller dendritic fields, medium-size axons, and project to the four dorsal layers of the geniculate nucleus. In primate, about 80% of the ganglion cells are classified as P cells, whereas 10% are classified as M cells. Density and dendritic extent are inversely related for the two cell groups, so fewer M ganglion cells with larger dendritic fields provide similar coverage of the retina as do the larger number of P cells with the smaller dendritic fields. The relative numbers of M and P ganglion cells vary with retinal eccentricity. The P ganglion cells are more dense in foveal and parafoveal regions. The M ganglion cells have a fairly even distribution across the retina (DeMonasterio, 1978; Leventhal, Rodieck, & Dreher, 1981; Perry & Cowey, 1981; Perry, Oehler, & Cowey, 1984).

The remaining ganglion cells fall into a third category referred to as W ganglion cells, which have small soma, large dendritic fields, small axons, and projections to the interlaminar zones of the dorsal lateral geniculate nucleus and to the superior colliculus (Leventhal et al., 1981).

The same morphological properties that distinguish M and P ganglion cells in the retina also characterize differences observed between M and P cells in the dorsal lateral geniculate nucleus of the thalamus. Moreover, M and P cells are clearly segregated into different laminae of the geniculate nucleus. The parvocellular layers (layers 3 to 6) contain P cells; layers 3 and 5 receive input from P ganglion cells located in the ipsilateral eye and layers 4 and 6 receive input from P ganglion cells in the contralateral eye. The magnocellular layers (layers 1 and 2) contain M cells; layer 1 receives input from M ganglion cells in the contralateral eye and layer 2 receives input from M ganglion cells in the ipsilateral eye. The projection of the P cells in the geniculate to striate cortex is via small axons with restricted terminal arbors. The projection of M cells to striate cortex is along larger axons with larger terminal arborizations (Hickey & Guillery, 1979).

It is important to note that probably less than 20% of the synaptic input onto

M and P cells in the dorsal lateral geniculate nucleus is retinal in origin. The majority of the synaptic input is from extraretinal sources, such as visual cortex and the brainstem (Sherman & Koch, 1986). It is inappropriate, therefore, to conceptualize the geniculate as a simple thalamic relay of the outputs of M and P ganglion cells onto visual cortex. The dorsal lateral geniculate nucleus contains the anatomical substrate that can substantially modify outputs of the M and P ganglion cells before reaching various cortical structures.

Much like the projections of the M and P ganglion cells, the projections of M and P geniculate cells to visual cortex are also segregated. The M geniculate cells project to layers 4b and 4c alpha in cortical area VI. The P geniculate cells project to layer 4cβ. The M and P pathways then continue through the upper layers of VI (Hubel & Wiesel, 1972; Lund & Boothe, 1975). The projections of the two pathways are distinguished in layers 1–3 of VI with use of cytochrome oxidase staining, which is a stain that marks the amount of chronic neural activity. In upper layers of VI cytochrome oxidase staining collects in small dense areas referred to as "blobs." The P and M pathways are intertwined in the blob regions and the P pathways travels through the interblob regions (Livingstone & Hubel, 1982, 1984). In cortical area VII, the cytochrome oxidase staining collects in pale, thin, and thick stripes. The pale stripes contain inputs from the P pathway; the thick stripes contain inputs from the M pathway; and the thin stripes receive mixed input (Livingstone & Hubel, 1984).

The M and P pathways continue to spread throughout a number of different extrastriate areas that involve a myriad of connections from striate and extrastriate cortical areas, the callosum, and other subcortical structures. Only the major connections are described here, and the reader is referred to several reviews on this topic for a detailed description of cortical projections (DeYoe & Van Essen, 1988; Kaas, 1986; Van Essen, 1979). The major output of the pale stripe area of VII involves the passage of the P pathway through dorsal lateral area of visual cortex and the caudal portion of the inferior temporal cortex. The M pathway makes direct connections from layer 4B in VI to the medial temporal area of cortex. The M pathway also projects indirectly to the medial temporal area via the thick stripe regions of VII. The major outputs of medial temporal area are to adjoining areas, the superior temporal and the medial superior temporal regions. Superior temporal area projects heavily to the posterior parietal cortex.

In summary, there are at least two major streams of processing that begin at the ganglion cell layer and that are maintained at higher cortical areas. The M and P pathways are graphically depicted in Fig. 4.1. The P pathway begins with a class of ganglion cells that have small somas, dendritic fields and axons, that is more populated in foveal regions, and project to the dorsal parvocellular layers of the dorsal lateral geniculate nucleus. The P pathway continues through layer 4Cβ, blob and interblob regions of VI, through the pale and thin stripe region of VII, to the dorsal lateral cortical area, and ending in inferior temporal cortex. The M pathway begins with a class of ganglion cells that has large somas, dendritic fields, and axons, and is fairly evenly distributed across the retina. The

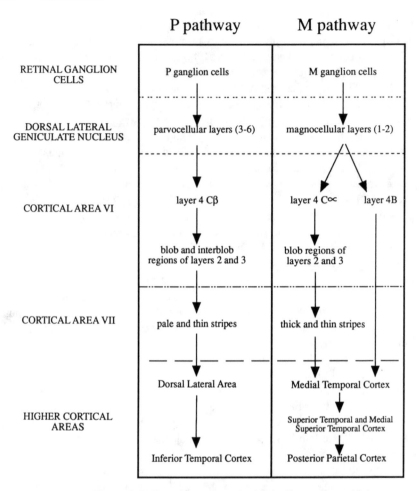

FIG. 4.1. The connections between retinal ganglion cells to higher cortical areas that distinguish the M and P pathways are summarized in this figure. The P pathway includes P ganglion cells through the inferior temporal cortex, and the M pathway includes M ganglion cells through the posterior parietal cortex. Please refer to the text for more discussion of the anatomical connections and for original references to the work that traced the connections of the M and P pathways.

M pathway projects to the magnocellular layers of the geniculate, then to layers 4c alpha and 4b. The M pathway projects from 4b to medial temporal cortical area, or to the blob regions of VI and then to the thick and thin stripes of VII. The thick stripe region also projects to the medial temporal area. Medial temporal cortex projects to the medial superior temporal region, which in turn projects to the posterior parietal cortex. In this chapter the P pathway refers to the P ganglion cell/temporal cortex stream, and the M pathway refers to the M ganglion cell/parietal cortex stream.

PHYSIOLOGICAL DIFFERENCES

The existence of two parallel, but retinally overlapping, streams through the visual system indicates that retinal information is sampled twice and processed in parallel. The next obvious step is to identify the information that is processed by and travels along each pathway. The physiological differences between the cells in the M and P pathways provide some clues about functional differences. In many instances the differences between the receptive fields of M and P ganglion and geniculate cells are simple physiological manifestations of the anatomical differences described earlier. The basic difference between the type of information processed by the M and P pathways originates in the connections between the photoreceptors and M and P ganglion cells (see Fig. 4.2). The present discussion about physiology focuses on response properties of M and P ganglion and geniculate cells.

M and P ganglion and geniculate cells have roughly circular receptive fields with a center and surround organization (Wiesel & Hubel, 1966). The sizes of the receptive fields, the interactions between center and surround, the nature of the cone input to the center and surround, and the temporal dynamics of the center response, all characterize the major physiological differences observed between M and P cells and give rise to the response differences observed between the two pathways to the spatial, temporal, and chromatic properties of the stimulus.

Spatial Response Differences

The size of the receptive field center and the strength of the surround are properties of the receptive field that can adequately explain the responses of M and P ganglion and geniculate cells to the spatial properties of the stimulus (Enroth-Cugell & Robson, 1966). The size of the receptive field center is determined by the extent of the dendritic field, which reflects the spatial extent over which the input from different photoreceptors are summed. On the average, the size of the center of the receptive field at corresponding retinal eccentricities is larger for M than for P cells. Second, the surrounds, which inhibit the response of the center, are stronger for P cells than for M cells. Therefore, the responses of P cells are more inhibited by surround stimulation than are M cells (Marroco, 1976; Schiller & Malpeli, 1987).

To characterize the differences between M and P cells, consider the hypothetical spot diameter/response functions depicted in Fig. 4.3. As the spot fills more of the center of the M and P cells the response increases until the entire center is filled by the spot. The receptive field center is smaller for P cells so the

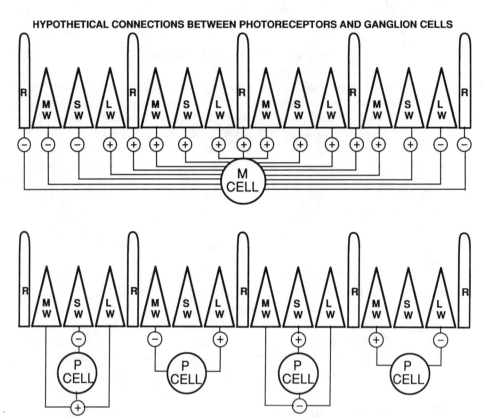

HYPOTHETICAL CONNECTIONS BETWEEN PHOTORECEPTORS AND GANGLION CELLS

FIG. 4.2. Schematic illustration of the hypothetical connections between rod and cone photoreceptors and M and P ganglion cells. The connections of an M ganglion cell is shown in the top half of the figure, and the connections for four different P ganglion cells are depicted in the bottom half. The purpose of this figure is to illustrate basic differences in the connections between the photoreceptors and M and P ganglion cells. M ganglion cells receive inputs from a larger number of receptors that span a larger retinal extent, which gives rise to receptive fields with a larger center (marked with a "+" connection) and surround (marked with a "−" connection). P ganglion cells receive inputs from a fewer number of receptors and have smaller receptive fields. M ganglion cells receive inputs from all cone types (short wavelength sensitive cones, SW; middle wavelength sensitive cones, MW; long wavelength sensitive cones, LW; and rods, R). P ganglion cells primarily receive input from specific combinations of cones, which produces the response property of color opponency. The P ganglion cells illustrated in the lower half of the figure, from left to right, have a yellow center/blue surround, a red center/green surround, a blue center/yellow surround, and a green center/red surround.

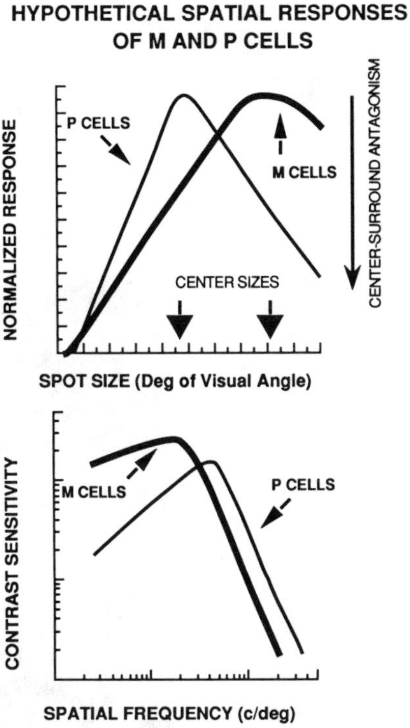

FIG. 4.3. Hypothetical spot size/response functions and spatial contrast sensitivity functions for M (thick lines) and P (thin lines) cells. The spot size/response functions illustrate two differences between M and P cells. First, P cells have smaller receptive field centers than M cells. This is illustrated by the observation that P cells have a peak response at a smaller spot size than M cells. A peak response indicates that a spot completely filled the center of the receptive field. Second, the center/surround antagonism is stronger for P cells. This is illustrated by the amount by which the response is reduced when large spots begin to effectively activate the surround to reveal its inhibitory influences over the response of the center. The most pronounced difference between M and P cells occurs for larger spot sizes. These two differences between M and P cells are also illustrated in the lower graph by the hypothetical spatial contrast sensitivity functions. Because P cells have smaller receptive field centers, the contrast sensitivity function peaks at a higher spatial frequency. Also because P cells have a stronger center/surround antagonism, the sensitivity of P cells falls off more than M cells at lower spatial frequencies. Absolute values have not been placed on the axes because the values depend on retinal eccentricity.

HYPOTHETICAL SPATIAL RESPONSES OF M AND P CELLS

response function reaches its peak at a smaller spot diameter. When the size of the spot begins to encroach the surround, the response of both M and P cells is reduced, but is reduced more for P cells because its surround is stronger. The largest difference between M and P cells occurs at larger spot sizes. Moreover, because P ganglion and geniculate cells are more dense in the foveal regions where receptor density is highest and receptor summation is the lowest, it is not surprising than these cells on the average tend to respond better to smaller spot sizes.

To translate the differences between the spot responses of M and P pathways to a more meaningful spatial continuum, representative spatial contrast sensitivity functions for M and P cells are also plotted in Fig. 4.3. The spatial contrast sensitivity functions follow directly from the spot/diameter response functions. The larger receptive field centers and weaker surrounds of M cells subserve the higher sensitivity of M ganglion and geniculate cells to low spatial frequencies (e.g., luminance changes that extend across a larger retinal area). The smaller receptive field centers, input from retinal areas with a high density of

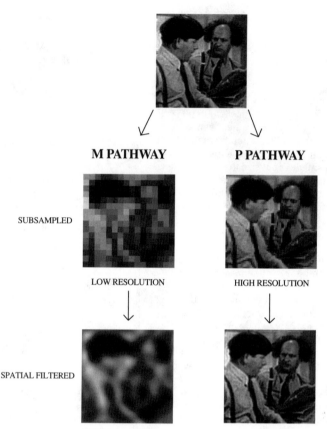

M PATHWAY **P PATHWAY**

SUBSAMPLED

LOW RESOLUTION HIGH RESOLUTION

SPATIAL FILTERED

LOW SPATIAL FREQUENCIES LOW + HIGH SPATIAL FREQUENCIES

FIG. 4.4.   This figure illustrates differences in the nature of the spatial information carried by the M and P pathways. An original picture is subsampled with low and high resolution. With subsampling, the average luminance is computed for prespecified blocked areas. The average luminance was computed within larger blocked areas for the low resolution subsampling, and the average luminance was computed within smaller blocked areas for the high resolution subsampling. The average luminance for each blocked area is then displayed in its appropriate position and produces the type of pictures shown in the middle row. The process of subsampling is similar to the way in which an array of receptive fields encode any luminance profile; any one cell will produce a response whose magnitude denotes the average luminance within the center of its receptive field. M cells subsample any image with low resolution because their receptive fields are relatively large (i.e., large blocks). P cells subsample with a higher resolution because their receptive fields are smaller (i.e., smaller blocks). Subsampling, however, produces artifactual edges formed by adjacent blocks that are not contained in the original image. This problem is obviated in the visual system because receptive fields, of both M and P pathways, overlap with each other. To remove the artifactual edges, one can simply blur their eyes. In doing so, one can visualize the

receptors, and the stronger surround of P cells subserves higher sensitivity to high spatial frequencies (e.g., luminance changes that extend across a smaller retinal area). The overall contrast sensitivity is higher for M cells. On the average, M cells are about 10 times more sensitive than P cells to spatial frequencies less than 1 c/deg (Derrington & Lennie, 1984; Kaplan & Shapley, 1982; Shapley, Kaplan, & Soodak, 1981).

To summarize, the M and P pathways sample the retinal image with different resolutions. The M pathway having larger receptive fields and being more sensitive to lower spatial frequencies, provides coarse spatial information that is important to identify the basic form and figure and ground relations. The P pathway having smaller receptive fields and being more sensitive to higher spatial frequencies, samples the retinal image with higher resolution and provides information about local, spatial detail. The difference between the spatial sampling of the M and P pathways is illustrated in Fig. 4.4.

Temporal Response Differences

The temporal response dynamics also differ between M and P cells. The conduction velocity of M cells is faster than P cells owing to the larger axonal diameter of M cells. The difference in conduction speed is probably insignificant because M cells are only 1 to 2 ms faster to the dorsal lateral geniculate and much of the temporal lead of M ganglion cells would be lost in the temporal variability of retinogeniculate synaptic transmission. The visual latency for optimal stimulation conditions, however, is about 10 to 15 ms shorter for M cells than P cells, which is physiologically significant (Kaplan & Shapley, 1982; Marroco, 1976).

Response transience is another response property that tends to distinguish M and P cells. Response transience refers to the brisk response observed following initial stimulus onset. M cells often elicit a more pronounced response transient than P cells (Hubel & Livingstone, 1991; Schiller & Malpeli, 1978). Response duration is a related temporal response property that does *not* per se clearly distinguish M and P cells. For example, cells would be classified as "sustained"

---

nature of the spatial information carried by each pathway. A spatial frequency filtered image allows one to visualize the types of information carried by each pathway without blurring their eyes to remove the artifactual edges. These images are shown in the bottom row. The M pathway provides information about basic form, and figure/ ground relationships. With low spatial frequencies only, one can localize borders and edges and extract some general information about the identity of objects (e.g., there are objects in the picture, vertically oriented, one on the left and right, and possibly are two people). The P pathway adds spatial detail. With the addition of high spatial frequency information, information contained in local luminance changes becomes available (two individuals with different hairstyles, they are wearing ties and suspenders, one seems to be talking, and etc.).

if the response continues throughout the duration of the stimulus. There does seem to be a tendency for M cells to produce larger response transients in relation to the sustained component of the response, whereas P cells produce weaker response transients in relation to the sustained response component.

Finally, it follows from the faster conduction times, shorter visual latencies, and larger response transience that M cells follow more rapidly moving stimuli than P cells. M ganglion and geniculate cells have a higher temporal resolution or critical flicker fusion than their P cell counterparts. For example, under certain stimulus conditions the temporal resolution of the M geniculate cells is about 50 Hz, where it is about 30 Hz for P geniculate cells (Derrington & Lennie, 1984; Marroco, 1976).

In summary, all aspects of temporal responsitivity of M cells are superior to P cells. Given this superior temporal response, it is not surprising that areas of visual cortex that receive M cell input, such as the medial temporal area, seem especially well suited to process motion information (Newsome, Wurtz, & Dursteler, 1985).

Chromatic Response Differences

The M pathway quickly, but coarsely, samples the retinal image and the P pathway samples more slowly but with higher resolution. The M and P ganglion and geniculate cells also respond differentially to the wavelength properties of the stimulus. The P cells receive inputs from specific combinations of cone types, whereas the M cells receive inputs from all cone types. The P cells arrange their cone inputs into spatially opponent color mechanisms. Some P cells have red centers and green surrounds or vice versa, and others have blue centers and yellow surrounds or vice versa. In other words, some P cells receive input from only long wavelength sensitive cones to generate the center response, and receive input from only middle wavelength sensitive cones to generate the surround response. Other P cells receive exclusive input from the short wavelength sensitive cones to produce center responses and from both the long and middle wavelength sensitive cones to produce surround responses. M cells receive inputs from the short, middle, and long wavelength sensitive cones to produce both center and surround responses (see Fig. 4.2). Because of these differences in cone inputs, P ganglion and geniculate cells are often referred to as color opponent cells and M ganglion and geniculate cells as nonopponent or broadband cells (DeMonasterio, 1978; De Valois & Jacobs, 1968; Wiesel & Hubel, 1966).

The color opponency of P cells is significant because these cells can distinguish wavelengths independent of the relative intensities of the wavelengths. That is, P cells have "color vision." Accordingly, M cells are "color blind" in that these cells respond only to the relative intensities of the center and surround stimulus, and not to wavelength per se. For example, an M cell would not respond to alternate stimulation by red and green lights if the relative intensities of the two lights were appropriately manipulated to equate the luminances of the red and green stimuli. A red/green color opponent P cell would respond to red/green alternations independent of the relative intensities of the two wavelengths (Livingstone & Hubel, 1988).

PSYCHOPHYSICAL INQUIRIES
INTO THE FUNCTIONS OF M AND P PATHWAYS

The anatomy and physiology indicate the existence of at least two parallel pathways that begin at the ganglion cell layer and travel to higher cortical areas. The two pathways respond differentially to the spatial, temporal, and chromatic properties of the stimulus. In this section, several animal experiments are described that attempt to isolate the relative contributions of the M and P pathways to spatial vision, temporal sensitivity, and color vision. The M and P cells are nicely segregated in the dorsal lateral geniculate nucleus, thus specific, localized lesions can be made in the parvocellular or magnocellular layers to remove the contributions of the M or P pathway for a particular range of retinal eccentricities. By controlling for fixation of the animal, the investigators can compare the performance of a lesioned area with a nonlesioned area by presenting the stimuli in appropriate retinal locations (Merigan, 1989; Merigan & Eskin, 1986; Schiller, Logothetis, & Charles, 1990).

Lesions to the parvocellular layers produce pronounced deficits in sensitivity at high spatial frequencies, but produce only small deficits at low spatial frequencies. The same lesions also produce profound deficits in color vision. When using the retinal area associated with the parvocellular lesion, the animal cannot discriminate between colors across all luminance combinations. There seems to be no effect of parvocellular lesions on temporal resolution or motion perception.

Magnocellular lesions produce small deficits in contrast sensitivity at any spatial frequency, which is surprising because the M pathway has overall a much higher contrast sensitivity. When these stimuli begin to move or flicker, however, the deficits associated with magnocellular lesions are revealed. There are pronounced deficits in temporal resolution when the gratings are low contrast. Not surprisingly, there were no deficits in color vision when the M pathway was compromised.

It is important to note that the results of these studies do not indicate that color vision and/or motion perception are the exclusive domains of the P and M pathways, respectively. Depending on the contrast, spatial frequency, and temporal frequency of the stimulus, rudimentary color, and motion percepts can be subserved by the "other" pathway (Schiller & Logothetis, 1990). It is clear from these studies, however, that the M and P pathways contribute differentially to color vision, spatial and temporal vision, and motion perception. It is also evident in these studies that one can strongly bias the relative contributions of the M and P pathways by controlling the contrast, spatial, temporal, and chromatic properties of the stimulus. Any high spatial, low temporal frequency stimulus that is composed of isoluminant colors will clearly activate the P pathway with little contribution from the M pathway. On the other hand, any low contrast, low spatial and high temporal frequency stimulus will preferentially excite the M pathway.

THE RELATION BETWEEN M AND P PATHWAYS
AND HUMAN PSYCHOPHYSICS

The physiological differences observed between the M and P pathways and the results of the magnocellular and parvocellular lesion experiments provide a data base against which one can interpret some common psychophysical observations made in humans. For example, in addition to changes in the optical quality of the retinal image, another reason why spatial resolution drops precipitously with increases in retinal eccentricity could be due to the reduction in the representation of the P cell pathway at more eccentric retinal locations. Temporal resolution for large stimuli remain relatively constant across a wide range of retinal eccentricities, which might simply reflect the relatively constant representation of the M pathway across the retina.

There are a number of spatiotemporal interactions that are observed in human psychophysics that can be explained by the functioning of the M and P cell pathways. For example, sensitivity to higher spatial frequencies is reduced at higher temporal rates (Kulikowski & Tolhurst, 1973). This could be explained by the weak response by the P pathway at higher temporal rates. Contrast sensitivity is enhanced at low spatial frequencies for moving stimuli (Kulikowski & Tolhurst, 1973). This could be explained by the higher sensitivity of the M pathway at low spatial and high temporal frequencies. In reaction time experiments and visual evoked potential experiments, human subjects respond quicker and evoked potentials are shorter to lower than to higher spatial frequencies (Harweth & Levi, 1978; Lupp, Hauske, & Wolf, 1976; Parker & Salzen, 1977; Vassilev & Strashimirov, 1979). This difference in processing speed is observed even when the different sensitivities to low and high spatial frequencies are controlled. The faster processing of low spatial frequencies can be explained by the shorter visual latencies observed for the M pathway, which responds preferentially at low spatial frequencies.

There are also chromotemporal interactions that can be understood within the context of the differential contributions of the P and M pathways to color vision and temporal resolution. When a stimulus alternates between two wavelengths, the temporal resolution or CFF is reduced when the component wavelengths are matched in brightness so only a chromatic difference remains. When the wavelengths are unbalanced for brightness, so there are both brightness and chromatic changes, temporal resolution improves (Ramachandran, 1987; Ramachandran & Gregory, 1978). The lower temporal resolution can be explained by the inferior temporal sensitivity of the P pathway, which would be the primary pathway to respond when the different wavelengths are balanced for brightness differences. When brightness differences exist, the superior temporal sensitivity of the M pathway contributes to the response.

The use of chromatic stimuli balanced for brightness differences, or better known as isoluminant stimuli, has recently been used as a technique to preferentially activate the P pathway in order to determine its contribution to many aspects of visual perception, such as motion, figure and ground, image segmentation and grouping, stereopsis, and so on (see Livingstone & Hubel, 1987). The results of these studies are still under considerable debate, which centers around several issues. One issue, mentioned earlier in this chapter, concerns the "exclusive domain" versus "relative contribution" of each pathway. The other issue focuses consideration on the entire stimulus ensemble. For example, motion perception is compromised at isoluminance, but under certain spatial and temporal conditions, the effect of isoluminance on motion perception is less than that expected if motion perception is the exclusive domain of the M pathway (Schiller, Logothetis, & Charles, 1991).

DISEASE AND M AND P PATHWAYS

Clinicians are becoming increasingly aware that in the beginning stages of certain diseases the M pathway is selectively compromised. For many years, standard visual exams included only visual acuity and color vision tests, which would selectively tap the sensitivity of the P pathway and entirely bypass the effects of the disease on the M pathway. However, a recent impetus to expand the regimen of visual exams to include tests of M pathway functioning comes from the work done in the areas of Alzheimer's disease and glaucoma.

At least in early stages of both diseases, anatomical findings suggest that the M pathway might be selectively compromised (Quigley, Dunkelberger, & Green, 1988; Quigley et al., 1987). It has been reported that the largest diameter axons were the first to be lost and the smallest diameter axons survived the longest in glaucomotous eyes. Electrodiagnostic studies indicate that both the electroretinograms and visual evoked potentials exhibited abnormally weak responses to low spatial, high temporal stimuli (Marx, Podos, Bodis-Wollner, Lee, & Wang, 1988; Trick, Barris, Bickler-Bluth, 1989). Taken together, these data point to early involvement of the M pathway in glaucoma.

In postmortem examination of the retinas and dorsal lateral geniculate nucleus of Alzheimer's patients, it was reported that there was a substantial dropout of retinal ganglion cells and axons, with a majority of these being large cells and large axons. It was also reported that there is more damage to the magnocellular layers of the geniculate nucleus (Bassi, Blanks, Sadun, & Johnson, 1987). The only electrodiagnostic deficit that has been reported for Alzheimer's patients was associated with fast temporal stimulation (Trick et al., 1989).

Livingstone, Rosen, Drislane, and Galaburda (1991) suggested that the M pathway may also be selectively compromised in dyslexia. In postmortem examination of the dorsal lateral geniculate nucleus of brains of dyslexics, there was a selective atrophy of cells in the magnocellular layers. It was also reported that the latencies of visual evoked potentials were longer for low contrast stimuli, and the potential did not follow fast rates of temporal modulation; all findings consistent with the notion that there is a selective deficit in the M pathway. Earlier psychophysical studies reported that sensitivity to low spatial frequencies was reduced, and temporal resolution was impaired, which again are findings that support the conclusion that the M pathway is selectively compromised in dyslexics (Lovegrove, Martin, Bowling, & Badcock, 1982; Martin & Lovegrove, 1987).

It is interesting to speculate why so diverse diseases seem to selectively compromise the M pathway. It may be that these diseases actually affect both pathways equally, but because a fewer number of neurones overall participate in the M pathway, visual deficits associated with this pathway are manifest first. Alternatively, it might be that the metabolic demands are greater for the larger soma and axonal processes of M cells, which makes the M pathway more susceptible if disease or injury affects the metabolic processes. On the other hand, the effects of each disease on the functioning of the M cell pathway may be completely unrelated.

M PATHWAY DEFICITS AND DYSLEXIA

Visual scientists learned much about the neurological bases of color vision by studying individuals with color deficiencies. Along these same lines, one might gain a better appreciation of the functional contributions of the M and P pathways to visual processing by studying vision of dyslexics. One way to pursue the relation between vision and M and P cell functioning is to develop a model that specifies the role of these two pathways in reading.

However, the first step in developing such a model is to demonstrate that the M pathway is involved in reading. The deficits in sensitivity at low spatial frequencies and higher temporal rates, together with the documented changes in geniculate anatomy support the contention that the M pathway is perturbed in dyslexics, but the results do not demonstrate that the M pathway is directly involved in the reading deficit. Because reading is a task that involves stationary stimuli composed of high spatial frequencies, stimulation best suited for the P pathway, one might argue that reading does not involve the M pathway.

The eye movements made during reading, however, make it a much more complex and dynamic process. Reading involves the rapid processing of high spatial frequencies in an independent fashion across successive fixations that are accurately programmed to direct the fovea to appropriate portions of text. When one considers both the spatial and temporal aspects of reading and the enormous visual processing demands that are imposed, reading must require the participation of both M and P pathways. Several chapters in this book model the participation and interaction between the M and P pathways during reading, and attempt to explain the type of reading problems experienced with a deficit in the M pathway.[1]

These visual models of reading deficits emphasize the importance of timing in the visual system. The anatomical and physiological studies of the M and P pathways indicate that retinal information is processed twice in a nonredundant fashion by the visual system. The M pathway quickly processes information about coarse form and the P pathway subsequently processes information about fine detail and color. The M pathway provides a quick primal glimpse of the stimulus that serves to indicate something about what the stimulus is and where it is in space. This coarse information serves to guide the processing of the P pathway by providing information about retinal position of the stimulus. This enables the oculomotor system to issue a command to place the stimulus on the fovea to permit further processing by the P pathway concerning the spatial detail and color of the stimulus. In parallel, the M pathway also provides information essential for figure ground segregation, so that information about local detail and color subsequently carried by the P pathway may be associated and segmented (Lehmkuhle, 1985; Sestokas & Lehmkuhle, 1986; Wong & Weisstein, 1983).

This global-to-local mode of visual processing, by definition, specifies that normal visual processing requires a specific temporal order in the processing of different stimulus attributes. If the normal order is disrupted, either by altering the relative contributions or processing speeds of the M and P pathways, visual deficits could be expected. Livingstone et al. (1991) reported that the latencies of evoked potentials in dyslexics are abnormally long to low contrast, low spatial frequency stimuli. This suggests that the normal timing of the visual system is perturbed in dyslexics, because the fast M pathway has been slowed. Many of the perceptual instabilities experienced by dyslexics that are exaggerated during and preclude normal reading may be due to the inability of the M pathway to appropriately direct foveation, and provide the figure-to-ground context necessary to associate visual details.

Some of the perceptual deficits associated with abnormal temporal sequencing might be corrected by restoring the appropriate order of information flow, without mending the absolute timing deficit. This notion is suggested by reports that reading in dyslexics can be facilitated by altering the visual characteristics of the text, which cannot restore absolute timing to normal, but may slow or reduce the

---

[1]In this book and elsewhere the P pathway may be referred to as "sustained" or "X cell"; whereas the M pathways may be referred to as "transient" or "Y cell." Although historically the different names refer to similar mechanisms in the different species, the intent on the part of the authors is to involve the participation of the mechanisms that have differential sensitivity to spatial, temporal, and chromatic properties of the stimulus, much like that described for the M and P pathways thus far in this chapter.

contribution of the P pathway relative to the deficient M pathway and restore the proper sequence and relative excitations of the two pathways. Colored overlays, tinted glasses, defocus, luminance reduction can facilitate reading in dyslexics and can be interpreted within a timing context (Irlen, 1983; Williams & Le Cluyse, 1989). Each stimulus manipulation reduces and slows the activity of the P pathway. The activity of the M pathway would be affected much less by these stimulus manipulations. Colored overlays and tinted glasses restrict the range of wavelengths reflected by the black-and-white text. Because the response of cells in the P pathway are more selective to different wavelengths, the fewer wavelengths contained in the filtered text will reduce the overall response of the P pathway. The response of the M pathway is less affected by the colored overlays or tinted filters because the response of this pathway is much less selective about the wavelength composition of the stimulus. There are reports that blue filters and overlays tend to be favored by dyslexics in removing some of the disturbing perceptual instabilities that make reading difficult. This is not surprising within the present context because a blue overlay would be most effective in reducing the relative contribution of the P pathway. Recall there is a paucity of short wavelength cones in the fovea, which is the region heavily populated by P cells. Defocus obviously reduces the contribution of the P pathway because the higher spatial frequencies are removed from the retinal image. A reduction in luminance to mesopic levels would favor the operation of the M pathway and reduce the relative contribution of the P pathway because the M pathway receives input from rods and cones, and the P pathway receives input primarily from cones.

In closing, the study of vision in dyslexics provides a unique opportunity to identify the perceptual instabilities associated with perturbations in the M pathway. In normal readers, vision is a unitary and stable experience with no vestige of the separate processes and the different rates at which visual information is processed to generate a percept. Yet when the separate processes are perturbed, by changing the relative strengths of each process and/or by altering the relative speeds of each process vision becomes unstable, and impedes reading. This is the scenario that seems to be emerging with many individuals who have reading problems and is one that will motivate both clinically and theoretically based studies on vision in dyslexics.

REFERENCES

Bassi, C. J., Blanks, J. C., Sadun, A. A., & Johnson, B. M. (1987). The retinal ganglion cell layer in Alzheimer's disease: A whole mount study. *Investigative Ophthalmology in Vision Science, 28* (Suppl.), 109.

DeMonasterio, F. M. (1978). Properties of concentrically organized X and Y ganglion cells of the macaque retina. *Journal of Neurophysiology, 41,* 1435–1449.

Derrington, A. M., & Lennie, P. (1984). Spatial and temporal contrast sensitivities of neurons in lateral geniculate nucleus of macaque. *Journal of Physiology 357,* 219–240.

De Valois, R. L., & Jacobs, G. H. (1968). Primate color vision. *Science, 152,* 533–540.

DeYoe, E. A., & Van Essen, D. C. (1988). Concurrent processing streams in monkey visual cortex. *Trends in NeuroScience, 11,* 219–226.

Enroth-Cugell, C., & Robson, J. G. (1966). The contrast sensitivity of retinal ganglion cells of the cat. *Journal of Physiology, 378,* 379–384.

Harwerth, R. S., & Levi, D. M. (1978). Reaction time as a measure of suprathreshold grating detection. *Vision Research, 18,* 1579–1586.

Hickey, T. L., & Guillery, R. W. (1979). Variability of laminar patterns in the human lateral geniculate nucleus. *Journal Comparative Neurology, 183,* 221–246.

Hubel, D. H., & Livingstone, M. S. (1991). A comment on "Perceptual correlates of magnocellular and parvocellular channels: Seeing form and depth in afterimages." *Vision Research, 31*(9), 1655–1656.

Hubel, D. H., & Wiesel, T. N. (1972). Laminar and columnar distribution of geniculo-cortical fibers in macaque monkey. *Journal of Comparative Neurology, 146,* 421–450.

Irlen, H. (1983). *Successful treatment of learning disabilities.* Paper presented at the 91st Annual Convention of the American Psychological Association, Anaheim, CA.

Kaas, J. H. (1986). The structural basis for information processing in the primate visual system. In J. D. Pettigrew, K. J. Sanderson, & W. R. Levick (Eds.), *Visual neuroscience,* (pp. 315–340). New York: Cambridge University Press.

Kaplan, E., & Shapley, R. M. (1982). X and Y cells in the lateral geniculate nucleus of macaque monkeys. *Journal of Physiology, 330,* 125–143.

Kulikowski, J. J., & Tolhurst, D. J. (1973). Psychophysical evidence for sustained and transient detectors in human vision. *Journal of Physiology, 232,* 149–162.

Lehmkuhle, S. (1985). Behavioral correlates of physiological deficits in visually deprived cats. In R. Aslin (Ed.), *Advances in neural and behavioral development* (Vol. 1, pp. 107–129). Norwood, NJ: Ablex.

Leventhal, A. G., Rodieck, R. W., & Dreher, B. (1981). Retinal ganglion cell classes in the Old World monkey: Morphology and central projections. *Science, 213,* 1139–1142.

Livingstone, M. S., & Hubel, D. H. (1982). Thalamic inputs to cytochrome oxidase-rich regions in monkey visual cortex. *Proceedings of the National Academy of Science USA, 79,* 6098–6101.

Livingstone, M. S., & Hubel, D. H. (1984). Specificity of intrinsic connections in primate primary visual cortex. *Journal of Neuroscience, 4,* 2830–2835.

Livingstone, M. S., & Hubel, D. H. (1987). Psychophysical evidence for separate channels for the perception of form, color, movement, and depth. *Journal of Neuroscience, 7,* 3416–3468.

Livingstone, M. S., & Hubel, D. H. (1988). Segregation of form, color, movement, and depth: Anatomy, physiology, and perception. *Science, 240,* 740–749.

Livingstone, M. S., Rosen, G. D., Drislane, F., & Galaburda, A. M. (1991). Physiological and anatomical evidence for a magnocellular defect in developmental dyslexia. *Proceedings of the National Academy of Science, 88,* 7943–7947.

Lovegrove, W. J., Martin, F., Bowling, A., & Badcock, D. (1982). Contrast sensitivity functions and specific reading disability. *Neuropsychologia, 20,* 309–315.

Lund, J. S., & Boothe, R. G. (1975). Intralaminar connections and pyramidal neuron organization in the visual cortex, area 17, of the Macaque monkey. *Journal of Comparative Neurology, 159,* 305–334.

Lupp, U., Hauske, G., & Wolf, W. (1976). Perceptual latencies to sinusoidal gratings. *Vision Research, 16,* 969–972.

Marroco, R. T. (1976). Sustained and transient cells in monkey lateral geniculate nucleus. Conduction velocities and response properties. *Journal of Neurophysiology, 39*(2), 340–353.

Martin, F., & Lovegrove, W. J. (1987). Flicker contrast sensitivity in normal and specifically disabled readers. *Perception, 16,* 215–221.

Marx, M. S., & Podos, S. M., Bodis-Wollner, I., Lee, P. Y., Wang, R. F., & Severin, C. (1988). Signs of early damage in glaucomatous monkey eyes: Low spatial frequency losses in the pattern ERG and VEP. *Experimental Eye Research, 24,* 173–184.

Merigan, W. H. (1989). Chromatic and achromatic vision of macaques: Role of the P pathway. *Journal of Neuroscience, 9,* 776–783.

Merigan, W. H., & Eskin, T. A. (1986). Spatio-temporal vision of macaques with severe loss of Pβ retinal ganglion cells. *Vision Research, 11,* 1751–1761.

Newsome, W. T., Wurtz, R. H., & Dursteler, M. A. (1985). Deficits in visual motion processing following ibotenic acid lesions of the middle temporal visual area of the macaque monkey. *Journal of Neuroscience, 5,* 825–840.

Parker, D. M., & Salzen, E. A. (1977). Latency changes in the human visual evoked response to sinusoidal gratings. *Vision Research, 17,* 1201–1204.

Perry, V. H., & Cowey, A. H. (1981). The morphological correlates of X- and Y-like retinal ganglion cells in the retina of monkeys. *Experimental Brain Research, 43,* 226–228.

Perry, V. H., Oehler, R., & Cowey, A. (1984). Retinal ganglion cells that project to the dorsal lateral geniculate nucleus in macaque monkey. *Neuroscience, 12,* 1101–1123.

Quigley, H. A., Dunkelberger, G. R., & Green, W. R. (1988). Chronic human glaucoma causing selectively greater loss of large optic nerve fibers. *Ophthalmology, 95,* 357–363.

Quigley, H. A., Sanchez, R. M., Dunkelberger, G. R., L'Hernault, N. L., & Baginski, T. A. (1987). Chronic glaucoma selectively damages large optic nerve fibers. *Investigative Ophthalmology Vision Science, 28,* 913–920.

Ramachandran, V. S. (1987). Interaction between colour and motion in human vision. *Nature, 328,* 645–647.

Ramachandran, V. S., & Gregory, R. L. (1978). Does colour provide an input to human motion perception. *Nature, 275,* 55–56.

Schiller, P. H., & Logothetis, N. K. (1990). The color-opponent and broad-band channels of the primate visual system. *Trends in Neuroscience, 13*(10), 392–398.

Schiller, P. H., Logothetis, N. K., & Charles, E. R. (1990). Role of color-opponent and broad-band channels in vision. *Vision Neuroscience, 5,* 321–346.

Schiller, P. H., Logothetis, N. K., & Charles, E. R. (1991). Parallel pathways in the visual system: Their role in perception at isoluminance. *Neuropsychologia, 29*(6), 433–441.

Schiller, P. H., & Malpeli, J. G. (1978). Functional specificity of lateral geniculate nucleus laminae of the rhesus monkey. *Journal of Neurophysiology, 41,* 788–797.

Sestokas, A. K., & Lehmkuhle, S. (1986). Visual latency of X- and Y-cells in the dorsal lateral geniculate nucleus of the cat. *Vision Research, 26*(7), 1041–1054.

Shapley, R. M., Kaplan, E., & Soodak, R. E. (1981). Spatial summation and contrast sensitivity of X and Y cells in the lateral geniculate nucleus of the macaque. *Nature, 292,* 543–545.

Sherman, S. M., & Koch, C. (1986). The control of retinogeniculate transmission in the mammalian lateral geniculate nucleus. *Experimental Brain Research, 63,* 1–20.

Trick, G. L. (1985). Retinal potentials in patients with primary open-angle glaucoma: Physiological evidence for temporal frequency tuning defects. *Investigative Ophthalmology Vision Science, 26,* 1750–1759.

Trick, G. L., Barris, M. C., & Bickler-Bluth, M. (1989). Abnormal pattern electroretinograms in patients with senile dementia of the Alzheimer's type. *Annuals of Neurology, 26,* 226–231.

Van Essen, D. C. (1979). Visual areas of the mammalian cerebral cortex. *Annual Review of Neuroscience, 2,* 227–263.

Vassilev, A., & Strashimirov, D. (1979). On the latency of human visually evoked response to sinusoidal gratings. *Vision Research, 19,* 843–845.

Wiesel, T. N., & Hubel, D. H. (1966). Spatial and chromatic interactions in the lateral geniculate body of the rhesus monkey. *Journal of Neurophysiology, 29,* 1115–1156.

Williams, M., & Le Cluyse, K. (1989). *Perceptual consequences of a transient system deficit in disabled readers.* Proceedings of the International Congress of Psychology, Sydney, Australia.

Wong, E., & Weisstein, N. (1983). Sharp targets are detected better against a figure, and blurred targets are detected better against a background. *Journal of Experimental Psychology, 9,* 194–202.

Sustained (P) and Transient (M) Channels in Vision: A Review and Implications for Reading

Bruno G. Breitmeyer
University of Houston

INTRODUCTION

The visual world is composed of surfaces, objects, and events, whose nearly endless varieties are based on a finite and relatively small set of distinct perceptual dimensions. One of the more evident trends in visual science has been to explore the existence of parallel visual streams, each of which seems to behave as a subsystem specialized to process one or a few of these dimensions. As pointed out by Stone (1983), the concept of parallel processing has had a relatively long history in modern visual science. As an obvious example, over the past century the existence of separate cone and rod systems and their respective relation to photopic and scotopic vision has been widely studied. In more recent years, separate chromatic and achromatic (luminance) channels (de Lange, 1958), direction, orientation, and spatial-frequency selective mechanisms (Blakemore & Campbell, 1969; Campbell & Kulikowski, 1966; Sekuler & Ganz, 1963), and pathways separately processing brightness and darkness (Jung, 1973) have been investigated psychophysically and, still more recently, anatomically (Schiller, 1982; Tootell, Silverman, Hamilton, DeValois, & Switkes, 1988b; Tootell, Silverman, Hamilton, Switkes, & DeValois, 1988c).

Whereas these and other developments pointed to the existence of various forms of parallel visual processing, it was the discovery of X and Y ganglion cells in cat retina by Enroth-Cugell and Robson (1966) that gave the impetus to visual neuroscientists to work out the physiological and anatomical details of these pathways (see Lennie, 1980a, and Sherman, 1985, for reviews) and to psychophysicists and perception psychologists to investigate analogues of these neural pathways in humans (see Breitmeyer, 1984, 1992, for reviews). Enroth-

Cugell and Robson's (1966) findings were corroborated and extended by Cleland, Dubin, and Levick (1971) in their study of optic tract fibers and lateral geniculate nucleus (LGN) cells of cat. Besides using Enroth-Cugell and Robson's (1966) classification procedure based on presence or absence of linear spatial summation across receptive fields, Cleland, Dubin, and Levick's (1971) classification criteria included neural responses to standing contrast, spatial frequency, and size and speed of target stimuli. One class of cells, termed *sustained* neurons, was characterized by presence of linear spatial summation, sustained response to standing contrast, small, slowly conducting axons, and a preference for high spatial frequency, slowly moving stimuli. The other class, termed *transient* neurons, was characterized by lack of linear spatial summation, transient response to on- and offset of standing contrast (with absence or attenuation of a sustained response component), larger and faster conducting axons, and preference for low spatial frequency, rapidly moving stimuli. According to Cleland et al. (1971), the sustained and transient cells corresponded in their response properties to Enroth-Cugell and Robson's X and Y cells, respectively. The sustained/transient terminology used by Cleland et al. (1971), despite its problems, was initially also adopted by psychophysicists investigating perceptual signs of these pathways. Tolhurst (1973) and Kulikowski and Tolhurst (1973) were among the first psychophysical investigators to adopt the sustained/transient distinction to describe pattern- or form-sensitive and flicker- or motion-sensitive channels in human vision. Based on their measurements of separate flicker/motion and form/pattern detection thresholds for moving sinusoidal gratings, these investigators concluded that sustained channels were characterized by preference for higher spatial frequencies but did not prefer temporally modulated stimuli over static ones. In contrast, transient channels preferred not only low spatial frequency stimuli but also temporally modulated or moving ones.

Other investigators adopted related approaches and interpretations based on the common feature among their diverse findings of consistent differences between the temporal response of the visual system at low and high spatial frequencies. Thus, besides showing greater sensitivity to motion and flicker, the low spatial frequency transient channels, relative to the high spatial frequency sustained ones, also show a shorter response latency to stimulus onset and offset (Breitmeyer, Levi, & Harwerth, 1981a), a higher sensitivity to abrupt as compared to gradual stimulus onset (Breitmeyer & Julesz, 1975; Wilson, 1978), briefer temporal summation (Breitmeyer & Ganz, 1977; Legge, 1978), broader orientational tuning (Kelly & Burbeck, 1987), and greater susceptibility to masking by onset and offset of uniform conditioning flashes of light or by uniform-field flicker (Badcock & Smith, 1989; Breitmeyer et al., 1981a; Green, 1981). Additional elaborations of the spatiotemporal response properties distinguishing transient from sustained channels have been noted elsewhere (Breitmeyer, 1984; Green, 1984; Kelly & Burbeck, 1984).

Although the parallels drawn for the distinctions between flicker/motion perception and form/pattern perception on the one hand and transient and sustained channels on the other continue to play an important role, they recently have met with several criticisms (Burbeck, 1981; Green, 1981, 1984; Kelly & Burbeck, 1984; Lennie, 1980b). Moreover, these parallels need to be revised and augmented by more recent distinctions drawn with respect to separate parvocellular (P) and magnocellular (M) pathways in primates and also with respect to color, texture, and depth perception (Cavanagh, 1991; DeYoe & Van Essen, 1988; Livingstone & Hubel, 1987, 1988; Logothetis, Schiller, Charles, & Hurlbert, 1990; Schiller, Logothetis, & Charles, 1990). The next section first discusses the controversies and criticisms and then the revisions and augmentations.

CONTROVERSIES AND CRITICISMS ATTENDING THE SUSTAINED TRANSIENT CHANNEL DISTINCTIONS

Controversies regarding the distinction between, and properties of, sustained and transient channels in humans arose shortly after the initial studies that supposedly demonstrated their existence. The disputes focus on three interrelated issues. One issue deals with problems of psychophysical method, another concerns the evidence supporting psychophysical distinctions between sustained and transient channels in humans, and a third concerns the linking hypotheses connecting the psychophysics and the neurophysiology of parallel pathways and the associated problems of identifying and classifying channels via psychophysical and physiological techniques. I have dealt with these issues, particularly the first two, elsewhere (Breitmeyer, 1992). For details of these two issues, the interested reader may go to this source, where they are discussed not only for their relevance to these problematic concerns but also for their theoretical and empirical significance. I only mention here that the existence of sustained and transient channels survives the methodological and evidential challenges, although the list of distinctive properties attributed to the two types of channels has had to be revised and updated. A more crucial issue, discussed more fully later, is the relationship of the psychophysics to the neurophysiology of parallel pathways.

The links between the psychophysics and neurophysiology of parallel channels are problematic and often not clearly specifiable (see Lee, 1991; Teller, 1984). Especially difficult is the determination of what Teller (1984) called the "bridge locus," that is, the site in the visual system at which a particular neural activity pattern is necessary for the occurrence of a particular perceptual state. Differences between sustained and transient channels and the perceptual states they give rise to have been defined in terms of spatiotemporal response properties of the visual system. However, we know from neurophysiological studies (Duysens, Gulyas, & Maes, 1991; Lee, Martin, & Valberg, 1989) that significant transformations of the spatiotemporal response of visual neurons occur from the retinal to the cortical levels of the visual system. Hence, making predictions on the basis of subcortical response properties of sustained and transient neurons may miss the mark relative to predictions based on cortical response properties (Lee, 1991; Lee et al., 1989; Peterhans & von der Heydt, 1991). Despite these and other difficulties, I share with Stone (1983) the view that proposing such links are useful to psychophysicist and physiologist alike, provided that one views them as tentative hypotheses in need of testing and correcting. Psychophysical phenomena can be viewed as tools for interpreting neuronal discharge patterns studied by physiologists (Peterhans & von der Heydt, 1991); in turn, neurophysiological properties suggest interesting hypotheses regarding neural mechanisms underlying perceptual effects.

Establishing such links rests on the main assumption that the neurophysiology of organisms like cat or monkey can be related to human psychophysics. For the sustained/transient approach this assumption in turn implies that two criteria be met. First, one must find psychophysical measures of sustained and transient activity in these organisms that resemble similar measures found in humans. Second, the animal psychophysics must relate to the physiology. The first criterion has been met in several convergent lines of behavioral study of cat and monkey. For instance, Blake and Casima (1977), in their study of cats, showed that temporal modulation of gratings increased visibility at low spatial frequencies but decreased it at high spatial frequencies. From these and related results it was concluded that shifts in the cat's contrast sensitivity function with temporal frequency reflects a relative shift in the involvement of X (sustained) and Y (transient) cells in grating detection. Similar conclusions were drawn by Harwerth, Boltz, and Smith (1980) in their study of monkeys. Using reaction time and contrast sensitivity measures, they found systematic differences in monkeys' visibility of low and high spatial frequency gratings as a function of their temporal modulation. Although consistent with existence of distinct sustained and transient channels, these animal studies, like their human counterparts, do require an inferential leap from psychophysical behavior to neurophysiology.

The justification of this leap rests on satisfying the second criterion stating that the psychophysics indeed relates to specifiable underlying neurophysiology. Satisfaction of this criterion, however, has been challenged recently by Lennie (1980b) and Frascella and Lehmkuhle (1984). On the basis of their physiological results, they argue that X and Y cells in cats do not subserve the distinct function of form/pattern and flicker/motion detection ascribed to the sustained and transient channels, respectively. One may need to revise the distinction to allow for a crude form of pattern analysis in transient channels and Y cells (Kelly & Burbeck, 1987; Lehmkuhle, Kratz, Mangel, & Sherman, 1980; Stone & Dreher, 1973) and for sensitivity to slow motion in sustained channels and X cells (Cleland & Harding, 1983; Green, 1984). However, an alternative consideration noted by Stone (1983; see also Breitmeyer, 1992) is based on the fact that these studies sampled cells, many of whose receptive fields fell outside the area centralis of the retina. This is important, because according to Stone (1983), it is in the area centralis that the spatial and temporal responses of X cells are most clearly differentiated from those of Y cells. Thus averaging over such a sample of cells in which many fall outside the area centralis would tend to eliminate response distinctions that would be found if the sample were restricted to cells falling in the area centralis. This point is particularly pertinent to links between animal psychophysics and neurophysiology, because cats (or monkeys) are typically trained in psychophysical tasks to direct their gaze and thus their area centralis (or fovea) to the relevant stimulus (Blake & Casima, 1977; Harwerth et al., 1980).

A more direct test of the links of psychophysics to underlying physiology relies on the selective suppression of the activity of the neural pathways thought to correspond to the sustained and transient channels. In the cat this has been done by pressure blocking of Y and X optic nerve fibers (Burke, 1986; Burke et al., 1987). With selective degenerative loss of Y fiber activity caused by pressure blocking, acuity, a function of sustained channels, is not impaired; however, discrimination of rapid motion, a function of the transient channels, is compromised. With additional pressure-block induced degeneration of a majority of X fibers, acuity is substantially reduced. Similarly, Merigan and Eskin (1986) found that neurotoxicant-induced selective loss of P activity in monkey results in impairment of vision at high spatial and low temporal frequencies, functions ascribed to sustained channels. As one would expect, sensitivity to high temporal and low spatial frequencies, functions ascribed to the unaffected transient M channels, was not impaired. Moreover, Merigan and Maunsell (1990) showed that chemical lesions in the transient M layers of monkey LGN cause severe reductions in the visibility of rapidly flickering or moving patterns but not of stationary ones. These selective impairments of visual functions caused by selective blocking of X or Y activity in cat or P and M activity in monkey provide a more direct link between the psychophysics and underlying neural activities ascribed to sustained and transient channels.

However, additional objections to linking the X/Y pathways to sustained/transient channels have been raised. For one, the temporal response characteristics of neurons such as transience and sustainedness are influenced by a number of stimulus variables (Kaplan & Shapley, 1982; Shapley & Victor, 1978) such as wavelength composition of the stimulus (DeMonasterio, 1978b; Marrocco, 1976), the retinal eccentricity of receptive fields (Cleland, 1983; Cleland & Levick, 1974), the state of adaptation (DeMonasterio, 1978a; Jakiela, Enroth-Cugell, & Shapley, 1976; Saito & Fukuda, 1986), and stimulus intensity relative to a fixed background (DeMonasterio, 1978a). In particular, with dark adaptation Y cell responses become more sluggish or sustained; in fact, at scotopic levels one cannot distinguish between X and Y cells on the basis of presence versus absence of a sustained response component (Jakiela et al., 1976; Saito & Fukuda, 1986). However, as noted by Saito and Fukuda (1986), at scotopic levels Y cells also show linear luminance summation across their receptive fields, a property whose absence at photopic levels (Saito & Fukuda, 1986) has been used as *the* distinguishing response characteristic of Y cells by Enroth-Cugell and Robson (1966). Hence, in Y cells, the absence and presence of response ·sustainedness seems to be positively correlated with the absence or presence of response nonlinearity. Besides raising obvious problems for classification schemes based on a single, essentialistic response criterion such as linear spatial summation, these results suggest a tighter link between the temporal (sustained-ness/transience) and spatial (linearity/nonlinearity) response characteristics of both X and Y cells than was previously thought.

Moreover, the problems associated with comparing response characteristics found at scotopic light adaptation levels to those found at photopic ones reoccur when responses for near-threshold stimuli are compared to those for su-prathreshold stimuli (DeMonasterio, 1978a). For instance, visual latency is an additional temporal response characteristic whose use in distinguishing between neural pathways has been criticized. Lennie (1980b) was able to eliminate re-sponse latency differences between X and Y cells when near-threshold stimuli were used. However, as noted by Maunsell (1987), although neither response latency nor transience or sustainedness provide absolutely reliable (i.e., essen-tialistic) classification criteria, the most severe deviations from such a classifica-tion scheme would be expected for near-threshold stimuli. In particular, Maun-sell (1987) reported that with clearly suprathreshold stimuli, the transient M-pathway cells have shorter visual response latency than the sustained P-path-way cells found not only in the LGN and cortical area V1 of macaque monkey but also at later stages of processing, for example, when comparing transient cells found in area MT to sustained cells found in area V4. Similar results with suprathreshold stimuli have been reported in extrastriate areas of owl monkey cortex (Petersen, Miezin, & Allman, 1988), as well as the retina (Bolz, Rosner, & Waessle, 1982; Sestokas, Lehmkuhle, & Kratz, 1987) and LGN (Sestokas & Lehmkuhle, 1986; Sestokas et al., 1987) of cats.

The early psychophysical models of sustained and transient channels (e.g., Breitmeyer & Ganz, 1976; Kulikowski & Tolhurst, 1973; Tolhurst, 1973) relied on the classes of cat X and Y cells as neural analogues; little was known of X- and Y-like pathways in primates. The human visual system, however, is more similar, anatomically, physiologically, and psychophysically, to that of monkey than to that of the cat. Earlier it was noted that the psychophysical performance of monkeys provides evidence for the existence of sustained and transient chan-nels that parallels similar evidence found in humans. Accordingly, it may be more appropriate to look to the monkey visual system for neural analogues of sustained and transient channels. However, recent studies of parallel pathways in the monkey that may be analogues of sustained and transient channels have been based on two classification schemes—the X/Y and the P/M distinctions—which do not always correspond to each other. For example, several studies (Dreher, Fukuda, & Rodieck, 1976; Maunsell, 1987; Schiller & Malpeli, 1978) report that the M and P cells in monkey LGN can be differentiated on the basis of greater transient and sustained response components, respectively. When response latency to electrical stimulation and absence or presence of a sustained response to standing contrast are used as classification criteria, Dreher et al. (1976) and Sherman, Wilson, Kaas, and Webb (1976) concluded that M and P cells were Y- and X-like, respectively. However, when, following Enroth-Cugell and Robson's (1966) method, linearity of spatial luminance summation across receptive fields is used to classify cells, not only are P cells X-like but so are many M cells (Blakemore & Vital-Durand, 1981; Kaplan & Shapley, 1982). With regard to these classification problems, Stone (1983) recommended use of multicriteria rather than single-criterion classification systems. Within a multicriteria system relying on a number of anatomical and physiological dimensions, the M and P cells of monkey are found to be largely transient and sustained, respectively (Livingstone & Hubel, 1987, 1988; Maunsell, 1987; Maunsell & Schiller, 1984; Schiller & Malpeli, 1978).

The geniculate P and M layers of cells in the LGN of monkey receive their inputs from the anatomically and physiologically distinct classes of B and A ganglion cells of the retina (Leventhal, Rodieck, & Dreher, 1981). In turn, the geniculate P and M pathways project to the cortex where they branch into three identifiable pathways with different laminar and tangential distributions as revealed by cytochrome oxidase and deoxyglucose staining patterns (Tootell, Hamilton, & Switkes, 1988a; Tootell et al., 1988b,c). In cortical area V1, the P pathway bifurcates into distinct P-blob sand P-interblob streams of processing that in turn project ventrally via the thin and pale stripes of area V2 to V4 and from there to inferotemporal cortex. The cortical M pathway originates in V1 and projects dorsally via V3 and the thick stripes of V2 to area MT and subsequently to the parietal cortex. Interactions exist between the cortical M and P pathways; besides projecting to MT, V3 also projects to V4; and, in addition to projecting to inferotemporal cortex, V4 is anatomically linked to MT and parietal areas (Desimone & Ungerleider, 1989; DeYoe & Van Essen, 1988). These three cortical processing streams and their cross-linkages are discussed more fully in several reviews and play a prominent role in current models of visual processing of form, color, motion, and depth information (Breitmeyer, 1992; Cavanagh, 1991; Desimone & Ungerleider, 1989; DeYoe & Van Essen, 1988; Lehmkuhle, chap. 4 this volume; Livingstone & Hubel, 1987, 1988; Ramachandran, 1990).

Although the various theoretical models and empirical findings generally agree that the P and M pathways are closely tied to the visual analyses of color and motion, respectively, there is disagreement regarding the specifics of this color/motion distinction and regarding the roles of these pathways in the analyses of form and depth. According to Livingstone and Hubel (1987, 1988), depth and motion are processed mainly by the M pathway, whereas form and color are processed predominantly the P pathway. However, DeYoe and Van Essen (1988) proposed an altered scheme: The P-blob pathway performs only analysis of color and the M pathway dominates motion perception. However, the M pathway does not enjoy an exclusive or dominant role in stereopsis, as proposed by Livingstone and Hubel (1987, 1988); rather, the P-interblob system, besides supporting color and form vision, also plays a crucial role in high-resolution stereopsis.

Evidence for DeYoe and Van Essen's (1988) scheme has recently been reported by Schiller and co-workers (Schiller & Logothetis, 1990; Schiller et al., 1990), who looked at the effects of selectively lesioning the P- or else the M-cell layers of the LGN on the disruption of visual function in monkeys. The P pathway was found to be essential for the perception of color, texture, and pattern detail as well as fine stereopsis; the M pathway was found to be crucial for the perception of fast flicker and motion. Coarse stereopsis and shape discrimination could be supported by either pathway. The P pathway was found additionally to support perception of slow flicker and motion. These results indicate that the M pathway does not dominate all aspects of stereopsis, nor does it dominate all aspects of motion or flicker perception.

These spatial and temporal response properties of the M and P pathways, listed in Table 5.1, agree remarkably well with the updated psychophysical distinctions between human transient and sustained channels noted earlier. The remainder of this chapter focuses on the relevance of the M and P pathways as neural analogues of human transient and sustained channels to the reading process.

TABLE 5.1
Response and Functional Properties of Neural Pathways

	Sustained/P	Transient/M
Receptive field size	small	large
Receptive field distribution	highest in fovea	highest in periphery
Response to standing contrast	sustained responses	onset/offset responses
Axonal conduction rate	medium	fast
Contrast sensitivity	low	high
Temporal frequency preference	low	high
Flicker/motion preference	slow	rapid
Spatial frequency preference	medium high	low medium
Pattern/texture discrimination	fine or coarse	coarse
Spatial resolution	high	low
Color coding	yes	no
Stereopsis/depth	fine or coarse	coarse

THE ROLE
OF SUSTAINED TRANSIENT CHANNELS
IN READING AND READING DISABILITY

The relevance of sustained and transient channels for our understanding of the reading process is clear once we consider how the aforementioned findings relate to theories of visual information processing and visual masking, particularly metacontrast masking. Metacontrast is a form of backward masking in which the contrast and contour visibility of a briefly flashed target stimulus is suppressed by a temporally following, spatially flanking, briefly flashed mask stimulus. Optimal masking occurs when the onset of the mask is delayed by about 50 to 100 ms relative to the target onset, with progressively less masking at progressively shorter or longer delays. One class of theories (see Breitmeyer, 1984, chap. 7) proposes that the U-shaped masking function relating the strength of metacontrast to the target-mask delay results from postretinal inhibitory interactions between the long-latency sustained channels activated by the target and the short-latency transient channels activated by the mask. Inhibitory interactions between X and Y cells have been investigated in the LGN and cortical area 17 of cat (Singer, 1976; Singer & Bedworth, 1973) and psychophysical analogues of inhibitory interactions between sustained and transient channels have been reported by Breitmeyer, Rudd, and Dunn (1981b). Up to now, such interactions have not been investigated in the monkey. Due to the anatomical segregation of P and M cells in the LGN, it is likely, as suggested by Lennie (1980a), that in the monkey they occur no earlier than the visual cortex.

According to Singer and Bedworth (1973), the inhibition of sustained by transient cells provides a mechanism of saccadic suppression when visual scanning of a spatially extensive scene is characterized by fixation-saccade sequences. They proposed that the slowly decaying, trailing activity in retinotopically organized sustained channels activated during a given fixation period is suppressed by the transient activity generated by abrupt image displacements accompanying a saccade at the end of the fixation. Hence, this prior sustained activity is prevented from persisting across the saccade interval (20–70 ms) as a form of noise to the sustained activity generated in the following fixation interval. In this way the afferent sustained channels are cleared of activity between fixations, resulting in a series of temporally segregated, retinotopic frames of sustained activity with each frame corresponding to the pattern information in a given fixation interval. This interpretation was adopted by Matin (1974) and Breitmeyer (1980, 1984; Breitmeyer & Ganz, 1976) to relate metacontrast to saccadic suppression. However, as I noted elsewhere (Breitmeyer, 1980, 1984), metacontrast is a spatially local mechanism of saccadic suppression that is weak in the fovea relative to the perifovea and periphery (Bridgeman & Leff, 1979; Kolers & Rosner, 1960). This would pose a problem because the sustained activity is most heavily concentrated at the fovea (see Breitmeyer, 1984, chap. 6), and thus one would want to have strong saccadic suppression there. This problem is solved by the jerk effect (Breitmeyer & Valberg, 1979) in which transient activity generated globally by the sudden saccadic image shifts in extrafoveal regions of the retina concenters on the fovea, where it additionally suppresses sustained activity.

Reading, like other visual scanning of the environment, relies on fixation-saccade sequences, so it is easy to see how the aforementioned notions apply to the reading process (Breitmeyer, 1980). Efficient pick-up of visual information during reading would depend, for one, on a properly functioning sustained system that processes the form or pattern content during a fixation. Additionally, it would depend on a properly functioning transient system whose saccade-produced activity provides a basis for saccadic suppression. Deficits in either system could thus contribute to visual problems with reading. With regard to such problems, the sustained/transient approach has proven useful in the study of dyslexia and specific reading disability (SRD). Psychophysical studies of phenomena such as visual persistence, flicker sensitivity, temporal order judgments, and metacontrast indicate that a transient-channel deficit characterizes about 70% to 80% of SRD children. These studies—many reviewed by Lovegrove, Martin, and Slaghuis (1986), Williams and LeCluyse (1990), and Lovegrove and Williams (chap. 14)—are important not only for their empirical contributions but also because they challenge past and prevailing views—for example, those of Benton (1975) and Vellutino (1987)—that visual deficits do not exist in SRD.

The transient-channel deficit found in SRD is important and intruiging. One important consequence of a transient deficit and, thus, of a deficit in transient-on-sustained inhibition in SRD would be a weakened saccadic suppression. This would result in at least a partial temporal overlap, rather than a clear temporal segregation, of successive frames of retinotopic sustained activity from successive fixations. This could comprise a primary, visually based impediment to the reading process. However, it could also contribute to secondary symptoms found in SRD. Besides clearing the sustained pattern-analyzing channels between fixations, saccadic suppression serves several other useful functions.

According to Matin (1974), it also prevents the perception of retinal image smear during saccades; and furthermore, it is important in maintaining constancy of visual direction and a stable visual world despite continual retinal image shifts while scanning the environment. Thus a transient deficit in SRD also could be associated with increased retinal image smear, loss of visual direction constancy, and instability of the visual world, symptoms that have been found in about 60% to 70% of the dyslexics investigated by Stein, Riddell, and Fowler (1989). It is intriguing and may be more than coincidental that the proportion of dyslexics noted by Stein et al. (1989; Stein, chap. 15 this volume) to show these latter symptoms closely approximates the proportion of SRD children noted by Lovegrove et al. (1986) to suffer from a transient-channel deficit.

Recent electrophysiological and anatomical findings reported by Livingstone, Rosen, Drislane, and Galaburda (1991) corroborated the previous theory of a transient-channel deficit in SRD. These investigators found that visually evoked scalp potentials to rapid, low contrast stimuli, which preferentially activate the M pathway, were diminished in dyslexic relative to normal subjects. However, the evoked potentials of the dyslexic subjects to slow, high contrast stimuli, which activate the P pathway, did not differ from those of the normal subjects. In line with this finding, the M layers in the LGN of dyslexic brains were found to be more disorganized and their cell sizes were found to be smaller and more variable than in nondyslexic brains. In contrast, the P layers of LGN of dyslexic brains did not differ from the P layers of nondyslexic brains. These electrophysiological and anatomical results accord well with the psychophysical results reviewed by Lovegrove et al. (1986), which indicate a deficit in the transient but not the sustained channels of SRD children.

Combined, these results suggest that the selective visual deficits in SRD are due to neural abnormalities that cannot be corrected and therefore may not be directly amenable to treatment. Even if the neural problems underlying the perceptual deficits cannot be treated, there is reason to be optimistic about devising treatment techniques that will alleviate the attendant perceptual deficits. A property of the transient M-pathway so far not mentioned is that its activity is suppressed by diffuse red light (DeMonasterio, 1978a; Dreher et al., 1976; Livingstone & Hubel, 1984; Wiesel & Hubel, 1966). As psychophysical analogues of this suppression, several collaborators and I showed that metacontrast is weaker for stimuli presented on red as compared to white or green backgrounds (Breitmeyer, May, & Heller, 1991; Breitmeyer & Williams, 1990; Williams, Breitmeyer, Lovegrove, & Gutierrez, 1991). An interesting and unexpected finding was that metacontrast was enhanced when stimuli were flashed on blue as compared to white or green backgrounds (Williams et al., 1991). These psychophysical results indicate not only that long wavelength, red backgrounds suppress transient activity but also that short wavelength, blue backgrounds enhance it when compared to white or medium wavelength, green backgrounds. On theoretical grounds one would expect that red backgrounds decrease the strength of saccadic suppression whereas blue backgrounds increase its strength.

Consequently, these findings have clear implications for the use of colored lenses or overlays in treating visual problems in SRD (Whiting, 1988). In particular, red overlays or glasses, by decreasing an already deficient transient activity, should exacerbate the transient deficit in dyslexics and thus lead to lowered reading performance. In contrast, blue overlays or glasses, by normalizing the temporal relation between sustained and transient channels and by increasing the strength of saccadic suppression, should alleviate the transient deficit and thus lead to increased reading performance. In fact, Williams, LeCluyse, and Faucheux (1992) recently showed that, whereas reading black-on-white material with red overlays decreases reading rate and comprehension scores in SRD children when compared to reading without such overlays, reading with blue overlays increases rate and comprehension scores significantly. These are intriguing and important findings and need to be replicated. Once they are firmly established, they could be used to develop theoretically motivated and empirically validated procedures for diagnosing and treating this class of visual deficits in SRD children.

Rather than speculating further about possible diagnosis and treatment, I would like to pursue other intriguing possibilities for empirical and theoretical research suggested by Livingstone et al. (1991). They noted that the abnormalities found in the M pathway of the visual system of dyslexics may also be found in similar fast responding pathways of the auditory and somatosensory systems. Deficits in the fast responding pathways of the auditory system could contribute to the deficiencies in processing rapidly presented acoustic information and the glissandolike frequency transitions characterizing the sound pattern of consonants (Tallal, 1976). Because analogues of metacontrast have been found in U-shaped backward masking functions with auditory (Porter, 1975; Studdert-Kennedy, Shankweiller, & Schulman, 1970) as well as tactile (Weisenberger & Craig, 1982) stimuli, such psychophysical phenomena provide ready tools for a closer look at possible deficits in the analogues of transient channels of the auditory and somatosensory systems of SRDs. Equally interesting and important, a deficit in the transientlike pathways across several sensory modalities may provide a basis for conceptually interrelating a diverse symptomatology that, up to now, has been taken as evidence for separate subtypes of dyslexia (Kinsbourne, 1986).

REFERENCES

Badcock, D. R., & Smith, D. (1989). Uniform field flicker: Masking and facilitation. *Vision Research, 29,* 803–808.

Benton, A. (1975). Developmental dyslexia: Neurological aspects. In W. J. Friedlander (Ed.), *Advances in neurology: Vol. 7. Current views of higher nervous system dysfunction* (pp. 1–47). New York: Raven.

Blake, R., & Casima, J. M. (1977). Temporal aspects of spatial vision in the cat. *Experimental Brain Research, 28,* 325–333.

Blakemore, C., & Campbell, F. W. (1969). On the existence of neurones in the human visual system selectively sensitive to orientation and size of retinal image. *Journal of Physiology, 203,* 237–260.

Blakemore, C. B., & Vital-Durand, F. (1981). Distribution of X- and Y-cells in monkey's lateral geniculate nucleus. *Journal of Physiology, 320,* 17–18P.

Bolz, J., Rosner, G., & Waessle, H. (1982). Response latency of brisk-sustained (X) and brisk-transient (Y) cells in the cat retina. *Journal of Physiology, 328,* 171–190.

Breitmeyer, B. G. (1980). Unmasking visual masking: A look at the "why" behind the veil of the "how." *Psychological Review, 87,* 52–69.

Breitmeyer, B. G. (1984). *Visual masking: An integrative approach.* New York: Oxford University Press.

Breitmeyer, B. G. (1992). Parallel processing in human vision: History, review, and critique. In J. R. Brannan (Ed.), *Applications of parallel processing in vision* (pp. 37–78). Amsterdam: Elsevier.

Breitmeyer, B. G., & Ganz, L. (1976). Implications of sustained and transient channels for theories of visual pattern masking, saccadic suppression, and information processing. *Psychological Review, 83,* 1–36.

Breitmeyer, B. G., & Ganz, L. (1977). Temporal studies with flashed gratings: Inferences about human transient and sustained channels. *Vision Research, 17,* 861–865.

Breitmeyer, B. G., & Julesz, B. (1975). The role of on and off transients in determining the psychophysical spatial frequency response. *Vision Research, 15,* 411–415.

Breitmeyer, B. G., Levi, D. M., & Harwerth, R. S. (1981a). Flicker masking in spatial vision. *Vision Research, 21,* 1377–1385.

Breitmeyer, B. G., May, J. G., & Heller, S. S. (1991). Metacontrast reveals asymmetries at red/green isoluminance. *Journal of the Optical Society of America A, 8,* 1324–1329.

Breitmeyer, B. G., Rudd, M., & Dunn, K. (1981b). Spatial and temporal parameters of meta-contrast disinhibition. *Journal of Experimental Psychology: Human Perception and Performance, 7,* 770–779.

Breitmeyer, B. G., & Valberg, A. (1979). Local, foveal inhibitory effects of global, peripheral excitation. *Science, 203,* 463–465.

Breitmeyer, B. G., & Williams, M. C. (1990). Effects of isoluminant-background color on meta-contrast and stroboscopic motion: Interactions between sustained (P) transient (M) channels. *Vision Research, 30,* 1069–1075.

Bridgeman, B., & Leff, S. (1979). Interaction of stimulus size and retinal eccentricity in meta-contrast masking. *Journal of Experimental Psychology: Human Perception and Performance, 5,* 101–109.

Burbeck, C. A. (1981). Criterion-free pattern and flicker thresholds. *Journal of the Optical Society of America, 71,* 1343–1350.

Burke, W. (1986). The function of optic nerve fibre groups in the cat studied by means of selective block. In J. D. Pettigrew, K. J. Sanderson, & W. R. Levick (Eds.), *Visual neuroscience* (pp. 97–110). Cambridge, England: Cambridge University Press.

Burke, W., Cottee, L. J., Hamilton, K., Kerr, L., Kyriacou, C., & Milosavljevic, M. (1987). Function of the Y optic nerve fibres in the cat: Do they contribute to acuity and the ability to discriminate fast motion? *Journal of Physiology, 392,* 35–50.

Campbell, F. W., & Kulikowski, J. J. (1966). Orientation selectivity of the human visual system. *Journal of Physiology, 187,* 437–445.

Cavanagh, P. (1991). The contribution of colour to motion. In A. Valberg & B. B. Lee (Eds.), *From pigments to perception* (pp. 151–164). New York: Plenum.

Cleland, B. G. (1983). Sensitivity to stationary flashing spots of the brisk classes of ganglion cells in the cat retina. *Journal of Physiology, 345,* 15–26.

Cleland, B. G., Dubin, M. W., & Levick, W. R. (1971). Sustained and transient neurones in the cat's retina and lateral geniculate nucleus. *Journal of Physiology, 217,* 473–496.

Cleland, B. G., & Harding, T. H. (1983). Response to the velocity of moving stimuli of the brisk classes of ganglion cells in the cat retina. *Journal of Physiology, 345,* 47–63.

Cleland, B. G., & Levick, W. R. (1974). Brisk and sluggish concentrically organized ganglion cells in the cat's retina. *Journal of Physiology, 240,* 421–456.

de Lange, H. (1958). Research into the dynamic nature of the human fovea-cortex systems with intermittent and modulated light. II. Phase shifts in brightness and delay in color perception. *Journal of the Optical Society of America, 48,* 784–789.

DeMonasterio, F. M. (1978a). Center and surround mechanisms of opponent-color X and Y ganglion cells of retina of macaques. *Journal of Neurophysiology, 41,* 1418–1434.

DeMonasterio, F. M. (1978b). Properties of concentrically organized X and Y ganglion cells in macaque retina. *Journal of Neurophysiology, 41,* 1394–1417.

Desimone, R., & Ungerleider, L. G. (1989). Neural mechanisms of visual processing in monkeys. In F. Boller & J. Grafman (Eds.), *Handbook of neuropsychology* (Vol. 2, pp. 267–299). Amsterdam: Elsevier.

DeYoe, E. A., & Van Essen, D. C. (1988). Concurrent processing streams in monkey visual cortex. *Trends in Neuroscience, 11,* 219–226.

Dreher, B., Fukuda, Y., & Rodieck, R. W. (1976). Identification, classification and anatomical segregation of cells with X-like and Y-like properties in the lateral geniculate nucleus of old-world primates. *Journal of Physiology, 258,* 433–452.

Duysens, J., Gulyas, B., & Maes, H. (1991). Temporal integration in cat visual cortex: A test of Bloch's law. *Vision Research, 31,* 1517–1528.

Enroth-Cugell, C., & Robson, J. G. (1966). The contrast sensitivity of retinal ganglion cells of the cat. *Journal of Physiology, 187,* 517–552.

Frascella, J., & Lehmkuhle, S. (1984). An electrophysiological assessment of X and Y cells as pattern and flicker detectors in the dorsal lateral geniculate nucleus of the cat. *Experimental Brain Research, 55,* 117–126.

Green, M. (1981). Spatial frequency effects in masking by light. *Vision Research, 21,* 861–866.

Green, M. (1984). Masking by light and the sustained-transient dichotomy. *Perception & Psychophysics, 35,* 519–535.

Harwerth, R. S., Boltz, R. L., & Smith, E. L. (1980). Psychophysical evidence for sustained and transient channels in the monkey visual system. *Vision Research, 20,* 15–22.

Jakiela, H. G., Enroth-Cugell, C., & Shapley, R. (1976). Adaptation and dynamics in X-cells and Y-cells of the cat retina. *Experimental Brain Research, 24,* 335–342.

Jung, R. (1973). Visual perception and neurophysiology. In R. Jung (Ed.), *Handbook of sensory physiology: Vol. VII/3A. Central processing of the visual system* (pp. 1–152). Berlin: Springer.

Kaplan, E., & Shapley, R. M. (1982). X and Y cells in the lateral geniculate nucleus of macaque monkeys. *Journal of Physiology, 330,* 125–143.

Kelly, D. H., & Burbeck, C. A. (1984). Critical problems in spatial vision. *CRC Critical Reviews in Biomedical Engineering, 10,* 125–177.

Kelly, D. H., & Burbeck, C. A. (1987). Further evidence for a broadband, isotropic mechanism sensitive to high-velocity stimuli. *Vision Research, 27,* 1527–1537.

Kinsbourne, M. (1986). Models of dyslexia and its subtypes. In G. Th. Pavlidis & D. F. Fisher (Eds.), *Dyslexia: Its neuropsychology and treatment* (pp. 165–180). New York: Wiley.

Kolers, P., & Rosner, B. S. (1960). On visual masking (metacontrast): Dichoptic observations. *American Journal of Psychology, 73,* 2–21.

Kulikowski, J. J., & Tolhurst, D. (1973). Psychophysical evidence for sustained and transient detectors in human vision. *Journal of Physiology, 232,* 149–162.

Lee, B. B. (1991). On the relation between cellular sensitivity and psychophysical detection. In A. Valberg & B. B. Lee (Eds.), *From pigments to perception* (pp. 105–115). New York: Plenum.

Lee, B. B., Martin, P. R., & Valberg, A. (1989). Sensitivity of macaque retinal ganglion cells to chromatic and luminance flicker. *Journal of Physiology, 414,* 223–243.

Legge, G. E. (1978). Sustained and transient mechanisms in human vision: Temporal and spatial properties. *Vision Research, 18,* 69–81.

Lehmkuhle, S., Kratz, K. E., Mangel, S. C., & Sherman, M. S. (1980). Spatial and temporal sensitivity of X- and Y-cells in dorsal lateral geniculate nucleus of the cat. *Journal of Neurophysiology, 43,* 520–541.

Lennie, P. (1980a). Parallel visual pathways: A review. *Vision Research, 20,* 561–594.

Lennie, P. (1980b). Perceptual signs of parallel pathways. *Philosophical Transactions of the Royal Society,* (Series B) *290,* 23–37.

Leventhal, A. G., Rodieck, R. W., & Dreher, B. (1981). Retinal ganglion cell classes in the Old World monkey: Morphology and central projections. *Science, 213,* 1139–1142.

Livingstone, M. S., & Hubel, D. H. (1984). Anatomy and physiology of a color system in the primate visual cortex. *Journal of Neuroscience, 4,* 309–356.

Livingstone, M. S., & Hubel, D. H. (1987). Psychophysical evidence for separate channels for the perception of form, color, movement, and depth. *Journal of Neuroscience, 7,* 3416–3468.

Livingstone, M., & Hubel, D. (1988). Segregation of form, color, movement, and depth: Anatomy, physiology, and perception. *Science, 240,* 740–749.

Livingstone, M. S., Rosen, G. D., Drislane, F. W., & Galaburda, A. M. (1991). Physiological and anatomical evidence for a magnocellular defect in developmental dyslexia. *Proceedings of the National Academy of Science, 88,* 7943–7947.

Logothetis, N. K., Schiller, P. H., Charles, E. R., & Hurlbert, A. C. (1990). Perceptual deficits and the activity of the color-opponent and broad-band pathways at isoluminance. *Science, 247,* 214–217.

Lovegrove, W., Martin, F., & Slaghuis, W. (1986). A theoretical and experimental case for a visual deficit in specific reading disability. *Cognitive Neuropsychology, 3,* 225–267.

Marrocco, R. T. (1976). Sustained and transient cells in monkey lateral geniculate nucleus: Conduction velocities and response properties. *Journal of Neurophysiology, 40,* 840–853.

Matin, E. (1974). Saccadic suppression: A review and analysis. *Psychological Bulletin, 81,* 899–917.

Maunsell, J. H. R. (1987). Physiological evidence for two visual subsystems. In L. Vaina (Ed.), *Matters of intelligence: Conceptual structures in cognitive neuroscience* (pp. 59–87). Amsterdam: Reidel.

Maunsell, J. H. R., & Schiller, P. H. (1984). Evidence for the segregation of parvo- and magnocellular channels in the visual cortex of the macaque monkey. *Neuroscience Abstracts, 10,* 520.

Merigan, W. H., & Eskin, T. A. (1986). Spatio-temporal vision of macaques with severe loss of P_β retinal ganglion cells. *Vision Research, 26,* 1751–1761.

Merigan, W. H., & Maunsell, J. H. R. (1990). Macaque vision after magnocellular lateral geniculate nucleus lesions. *Visual Neuroscience, 5,* 347–352.

Peterhans, E., & von der Heydt, R. (1991). Subjective contours—bridging the gap between psychophysics and physiology. *Trends in Neuroscience, 14,* 112–119.

Petersen, S. E., Miezin, F. M., & Allman, J. M. (1988). Transient and sustained responses in four extrastriate visual areas of the owl monkey. *Experimental Brain Research, 70,* 55–60.

Porter, R. J., Jr. (1975). Effect of delayed channel on the perception of dichotically presented speech and nonspeech sounds. *Journal of the Acoustical Society of America, 58,* 884–892.

Ramachandran, V. S. (1990). Visual perception in people and machines. In A. Blake & T. Troscianko (Eds.), *AI and the eye* (pp. 21–77). New York: Wiley.

Saito, H.-A., & Fukuda, Y. (1986). Gain control mechanisms in X- and Y-type retinal ganglion cells of the cat. *Vision Research, 26,* 391–408.

Schiller, P. H. (1982). Central connections of ON and OFF pathways. *Nature, 297,* 580–583.

Schiller, P. H., & Logothetis, N. K. (1990). The color-opponent and broad-band channels of the primate visual system. *Trends in Neuroscience, 10,* 392–398.

Schiller, P. H., Logothetis, N. K., & Charles, E. R. (1990). Functions of the color-opponent and broad-band channels of the visual system. *Nature, 343,* 68–70.

Schiller, P. H., & Malpeli, J. (1978). Functional specificity of lateral geniculate nucleus laminae of the rhesus monkey. *Journal of Neurophysiology, 41,* 788–797.

Sekuler, R. W., & Ganz, L. (1963). Aftereffect of seen motion with a stabilized retinal image. *Science, 139,* 419–420.

Sestokas, A. K., & Lehmkuhle, S. (1986). Visual response latency of X- and Y-cells in the dorsal lateral geniculate nucleus of the cat. *Vision Research, 26,* 1041–1054.

Sestokas, A. K., Lehmkuhle, S., & Kratz, K. E. (1987). Visual latency of ganglion X- and Y-cells: A comparison with geniculate X- and Y-cells. *Vision Research, 27,* 1399–1408.

Shapley, R. M., & Victor, J. D. (1978). The effect of contrast on the transfer properties of cat retinal ganglion cells. *Journal of Physiology, 285,* 275–298.

Sherman, M. S. (1985). Functional organization of the W-, X-, and Y-cell pathways in the cat: A review and hypothesis. In J. M. Sprague & A. N. Epstein (Eds.), *Progress in Psychobiology and Physiological Psychology* (Vol. 2, pp. 233–234). New York: Academic Press.

Sherman, M. S., Wilson, J. R., Kaas, J. H., & Webb, S. V. (1976). X- and Y-cells in the dorsal lateral geniculate nucleus of owl monkey (*Aotus trivirgatus*). *Science, 192*, 475–477.

Singer, W. (1976). Temporal aspects of subcortical contrast processing. *Neuroscience Research Program Bulletin, 15*, 358–369.

Singer, W., & Bedworth, N. (1973). Inhibitory interactions between X and Y units in cat lateral geniculate nucleus. *Brain Research, 49*, 291–307.

Stein, J., Riddell, P., & Fowler, S. (1989). Disordered right hemisphere function in developmental dyslexia. In C. von Euler, I. Lundberg, & G. Lennerstrand (Eds.), *Brain and reading* (pp. 139–157). New York: Stockton.

Stone, J. (1983). *Parallel processing in the visual system.* New York: Plenum.

Stone, J., & Dreher, B. (1973). Projection of X- and Y-cells of the cat's lateral geniculate nucleus to areas 17 and 18 of visual cortex. *Journal of Neurophysiology, 36*, 551–567.

Studdert-Kennedy, M., Shankweiler, D., & Schulman, S. (1970). Opposed effects of a delayed channel on perception of dichoptically and monoptically presented CV syllables. *Journal of the Acoustical Society of America, 48*, 599–602.

Tallal, P. (1976). Auditory perceptual factors in language and learning disabilities. In R. M. Knights & D. J. Bakker (Eds.), *The neuropsychology of learning disorders* (pp. 315–323). Baltimore: University Park Press.

Teller, D. Y. (1984). Linking propositions. *Vision Research, 24*, 1233–1246.

Tolhurst, D. J. (1973). Separate channels for the analysis of the shape and movement of a moving stimulus. *Journal of Physiology, 231*, 385–402.

Tootell, R. B. H., Hamilton, S. L., & Switkes, E. (1988a). Functional anatomy of macaque striate cortex. IV. Contrast and magno-parvo streams. *Journal of Neuroscience, 8*, 1594–1609.

Tootell, R. B. H., Silverman, M. S., Hamilton, S. L., De Valois, R. L., & Switkes, E. (1988b). Functional anatomy of macaque striate cortex. III. Color. *Journal of Neuroscience, 8*, 1569–1593.

Tootell, R. B. H., Silverman, M. S., Hamilton, S. L., Switkes, E., & De Valois, R. L. (1988c). Functional anatomy of macaque striate cortex. V. Spatial frequency. *Journal of Neuroscience, 8*, 1610–1624.

Vellutino, F. R. (1987). Dyslexia. *Scientific American, 256*, 34–41.

Weisenberger, J. M., & Craig, J. C. (1982). A tactile metacontrast effect. *Perception & Psychophysics, 31*, 530–536.

Whiting, P. R. (1988). Improvements in reading and other skills using Irlen coloured lenses. *Australian Journal of Remedial Education, 20*, 13–15.

Wiesel, T. N., & Hubel, D. H. (1966). Spatial and chromatic interactions in the lateral geniculate body of the rhesus monkey. *Journal of Neurophysiology, 29*, 1115–1156.

Williams, M. C., Breitmeyer, B. G., Lovegrove, W. L., & Gutierrez, C. (1991). Metacontrast with masks varying in spatial frequency and wavelength. *Vision Research, 31*, 2017–2023.

Williams, M. C., & LeCluyse, K. (1990). The perceptual consequences of a temporal processing deficit in reading disabled children. *Journal of the American Optometric Association, 61*, 111–121.

Williams, M. C., LeCluyse, K., & Faucheux, A. R. (1992). Effective intervention for reading disability. *Journal of the American Optometric Association, 63*, 411–417.

Wilson, H. R. (1978). Quantitative characterization of two types of line spread function near the fovea. *Vision Research, 18*, 971–982.

6 Visual Aspects of Neglect Dyslexia

M. Jane Riddoch
Glyn W. Humphreys
University of Birmingham, England

THE COGNITIVE NEUROPSYCHOLOGY OF READING

Following brain damage, reading processes can be severely disrupted even in people with previously well-established reading skills. Such acquired reading disorders can take several forms. In papers published in 1966 and 1973, Marshall and Newcombe distinguished between what have now come to be known as "surface" and "deep" dyslexic syndromes, both of which may involve "central" disorders of stored lexical knowledge, and/or of procedures for accessing phonology. For instance, the cardinal symptom of surface dyslexia, the "regularization" of a word with irregular spelling-to-sound correspondences (bread > breed), can occur in patients with poor visual access to word meaning (they have difficulty in understanding printed words) (Marshall & Newcombe, 1973; Schwartz, Saffran, & Marin, 1980; Shallice, Warrington, & McCarthy, 1983). The cardinal symptom of deep dyslexia, semantic errors in word reading, can reflect impaired semantic knowledge about words coupled with impaired procedures for translating between orthography and phonology (Coltheart, 1980; Marshall & Newcombe, 1980).

Such disorders have been well documented in relation to models of the normal reading process, and indeed have played an influential role in developing such models (Ellis & Young, 1988; Morton & Patterson, 1980). We may contrast such central disorders with more "peripheral" disorders of word recognition, concerned with generating prelexical representations of words. Included in such peripheral disorders are the syndromes of neglect dyslexia and letter-by-letter reading (see Riddoch, 1990). This chapter is concerned with neglect dyslexia. In it we attempt to discuss possible mechanisms underlying neglect dyslexia and their relations to normal reading processes.

WHAT IS NEGLECT DYSLEXIA?

Neglect dyslexia is typically classified as one of the peripheral dyslexias; meaning that the disorder results from an impairment in prelexical visual processing, rather than being a disorder in lexical knowledge. Cases of neglect dyslexia have been reported following both left (Caramazza & Hillis, 1990; Friedrich, Walker, & Posner, 1985; Patterson & Wilson, 1990; Warrington, 1991; Warrington & Zangwell, 1957) and right (Behrmann, Moscovitch, Black, & Mozer, 1990; Ellis, Flude, & Young, 1987; Riddoch, Humphreys, Cleton, & Fery, 1990) cerebral lesions in the region of either the middle or the posterior cerebral arteries. The disorder is characterized by particular kinds of reading errors; either areas of text on one side of the page are omitted or, within individual words, there are problems in reading the initial or final letters giving rise to substitution,

this   Will

~~Bill was not happy~~. He loved his animals ~~and~~ he was worried. Bill

before

~~had been~~ head keeper at the zoo for a long time. Things had

~~changed~~. People seemed to want to be amused by the animals. Bill

~~did not like that~~. He could remember ~~the~~ days when everyone

him

~~seemed happy~~ to admire them. But that was ~~not~~ enough. Bill

could

~~knew that the~~ animals should not be used to entertain people, but he

~~also knew he~~ had a job to do. He had to keep ~~the~~ crowds coming,

~~but Bill~~ did not want to hurt the animals.

FIG. 6.1. Examples of the typical pattern of errors produced by a patient with a right side lesion and a left neglect dyslexia in reading a passage of text. Striking out indicates word omissions. Italics indicates word errors. The typical errors made on single word reading are also illustrated here. For instance, substitutions (*Bill* → *Will*), omissions (*them* → *him*), and additions (*for* → *before*).

omission, and addition errors. Many patients show deficits both for single words and with reading text (Behrmann et al., 1990; Caramazza & Hillis, 1990; Ellis et al., 1987; Kinsbourne & Warrington, 1962; Riddoch et al., 1990; Young, New-combe, & Ellis, 1991; Warrington, 1991). These errors typically occur on the side contralateral to the lesion. Examples of both text and single word errors are shown in Fig. 6.1.

NEGLECT DYSLEXIA IN RELATION
TO THE WIDER NEGLECT SYNDROME

In the past, neglect in reading has been regarded as part of a wider syndrome where the patient may fail to respond to contralesional information, often inde-pendently of the modality of input and across a wide range of tasks. More recently, neglect has been shown to fractionate into a number of discrete syn-dromes, each of which may occur in isolation in a single patient. For instance, motor neglect has been described in the absence of sensory inattention or extinc-tion to double simultaneous stimulation. Patients with motor neglect show nor-mal sensation, strength, and muscle tone, and they show no neglect in drawing or line bisection; yet they will fail to use the contralesional limbs spontaneously even in response to painful stimuli (Laplane & Degos, 1983; Valenstein & Heilman, 1981). A double dissociation between "near" and "far" neglect has been demonstrated in lesion studies with monkeys by Rizzolatti and his associ-ates (Rizzolatti & Camarda, 1987; Rizzolatti, Gentilucci, & Mantelli, 1985) and "conjectural support" for equivalent dissociations in man has been presented by Bisiach and his co-workers (Bisiach, Perani, Vallar, & Berti, 1986). Such results suggest that the neglect syndrome may fractionate into a number of separate disorders. As far as neglect dyslexia is concerned, it is true that neglect in reading has been described in isolation from "generalized" neglect (i.e., neglect on other visual tasks; Baxter & Warrington, 1983; Patterson & Wilson, 1990; Riddoch, et al., 1990; Warrington, 1991). However, reading may be considered to be a particularly visually demanding task. It therefore remains possible that in all these cases, "general neglect" may have been elicited if performance had been assessed under more stringent conditions than those generally available clinically. For instance, M. O. (Riddoch et al., 1990) showed no neglect in everyday life nor on typical clinical tests (such as the Rivermead Star Cancella-tion Test). He also showed no clinical neglect in reading words or complex passages of text. However, under reduced exposure conditions (words being presented for a limited period) he showed the typical symptoms of a right hemi-sphere lesioned neglect dyslexic: That is, the initial part of the word was mis-read. It seems clear that more stringent tests of "general neglect" should be devised and applied before claims of a selective deficit (e.g., in reading) may be upheld.

THE FRACTIONATION
OF NEGLECT DYSLEXIA

Although neglect dyslexia is characterized by beginning or end position-specific errors in reading words and text, it is likely that several different "neglect dyslexic" errors exist. In some patients, single word reading may be selectively impaired although the reading of text may be intact (Costello & Warrington, 1987; Patterson & Wilson, 1990; Riddoch et al., 1990). The alternative impairment of intact reading of single words but impaired text reading, is reported by Kartsounis and Warrington (1989). Thus, there is a double dissociation between the neglect in reading text and the neglect with single words. Double dissociations such as this are typically taken to indicate the involvement of separate processes in tasks, in this case involving words and text. Only the processes involved in text reading are impaired in some patients, while others only have impaired word processing. Indeed, even more dramatic examples of dissociations between neglect for single words and neglect for text can be found in single cases who, surprisingly, neglect different sides of words and texts. Humphreys and Riddoch (in preparation) reported the case of a patient with a left parietal and right frontal lesions who made *left side* errors in single words reading but *right side* omissions of words in text and when required to read a number of words located randomly over a page. Such patients support the case for fractionation of the neglect syndrome. By studying the different types of neglect, for words and for text, we come to learn something about the different representations derived for these different stimuli.

Characteristics of Neglect Dyslexia
in Single Word Reading

Neglect errors produced in single word reading can be characterized in terms of their error type and rate; how the measures are affected when words are presented in different orientations, and whether the lexicality of the item affects performance.

As noted earlier, characteristic errors in single word reading are substitutions (HAND → LAND), additions (HAND → ISLAND) or omissions (HAND → AND). The nature of the error types varies across patients. In a number of reported cases, substitution errors predominate (see Behrmann et al., 1990; Case H. R.; Ellis et al., 1987; Kinsbourne & Warrington, 1962; Patterson & Wilson, 1990; Riddoch et al., 1990). Such cases have been used to support the idea that, while recognition of the identity of the target word may be impaired, appreciation of the *length* of the target word is not (Ellis et al., 1987; Kinsbourne & Warrington, 1962; Riddoch et al., 1990). However, intact coding of word length is not characteristic of all neglect dyslexics. For instance, gradient effects in single word reading (longer words are read less well than shorter words) are salient characteristics in the cases reported by Behrmann et al. (1990; Case A. H.), Caramazza and Hillis (1990), and Warrington (1991). All show a marked effect of word length with the probability of correct report decreasing for letters to the neglected side of the central letter position.

Manipulations in the rate of stimulus presentation can also affect error rate. For instance, one patient reported by Riddoch et al. (1990) showed error-free performance when items were presented in free vision. However, when words were presented for a limited duration, characteristic contralesional errors emerged for the initial letters of letter strings (particularly for pronounceable nonwords as opposed to words). The effect was exacerbated if stimulus exposure was further reduced (typically, the patient would report only the final two letters of four- or five-letter words). Note that this was not simply because the patient found it difficult to process briefly presented letters. The identification of ipsilesional letters remained good across exposure durations. Nor was the effect caused by the letters falling into blind areas of field when strings were presented for short durations, because that should not have produced further "shrinkage" of the correctly reported letters as the exposure duration decreased.

Performance on single word reading can improve if the words are presented in a vertical orientation (Behrmann et al., 1990; Young et al., 1991), although not always (Caramazza & Hillis, 1990). The differential sensitivity of patients to the orientation of words and letters strings has been used to support the idea that neglect dyslexia can result from an impairments to different underlying prelexical representations (Caramazza & Hillis, 1990). We return to this issue in a later section.

A further feature of single word reading is that performance is usually affected by the lexicality of the item, with word reading better than nonword reading (Case H. R., Behrmann et al., 1990; Caramazza & Hillis, 1990; Patterson & Wilson, 1990; Riddoch et al., 1990; Sieroff, 1990) although in one reported case reading of words and nonwords was equivalent (Ellis et al., 1987).

Characteristics of Neglect Dyslexia in Text Reading

In text reading, neglect patients often fail to attempt to read the words on one side of the text (the side contralateral to the lesion). The number of words omitted from this side will vary from line to line, and on some lines no omissions will be made. Text reading has not been as rigorously assessed as single word reading. However, similarities in performance between the two sorts of stimulus material have been reported. For instance, performance is characterized by contralesional omissions (of words rather than letters) (Young et al., 1991). Manipulation of the orientation of the text appears to improve performance in some cases of neglect dyslexia. Thus, Kinsbourne and Warrington (1962) and Ellis et al. (1987) reported reduced errors in reading when a passage of text was rotated clockwise through 90 degrees, so that the first line of text was to the right and the printed lines ran from the top downward.

We now turn to some explanatory accounts of neglect dyslexia. In order to have validity, the accounts must be able to accommodate the characteristic features outlined earlier.

ACCOUNTS OF NEGLECT DYSLEXIA

Two somewhat different accounts have been used to explain the pattern of performance in neglect dyslexics. The first considers neglect dyslexia in terms of a degraded prelexical representation (or representations). Any of a number of different representations could be affected. The impairment may be in an early sensory representation (due to some form of visual field deficit) or in a higher level abstract linguistic representation, specific to reading. A second account explains neglect dyslexia in terms of patients failing to attend appropriately to words, and so failing to derive appropriate information for word recognition (Humphreys & Riddoch, in press b; Riddoch et al., 1990).

Representational Accounts

Caramazza and his colleagues (Caramazza & Hillis, 1990; Rapp & Caramazza, 1991) argued that neglect dyslexia may result from a lesion at any one of a number of different representational levels. They proposed at least three prelexical representations (similar to the levels of analysis for object recognition defined by Marr, 1982). Processing will differ at each level as will the nature of the coordinate system involved. For instance, the representation said to be analogous to the primal sketch (the retino-centric feature level representation) is defined in terms of a retino-centric coordinate system. The representation said to be analogous to the $2\frac{1}{2}$-dimensional sketch (the stimulus-centered letter shape level representation) is defined in terms of a non-retino-centric viewer centered coordinate system, while the representation said to be analogous to the 3-dimensional sketch (the word-centered graphemic level representation) (see Fig. 6.2) is defined in terms of an object-centered coordinate system.

It should be possible to identify patients whose pattern of deficit conforms to an impairment of one or more of the different representational levels and they should accordingly generate different behaviors reflecting the nature of the underlying representation that is impaired. For instance, Warrington and Zangwill (1957) provided the first written report of a case of neglect dyslexia. They argued that the impairment observed in their patient may have been due to a failure to

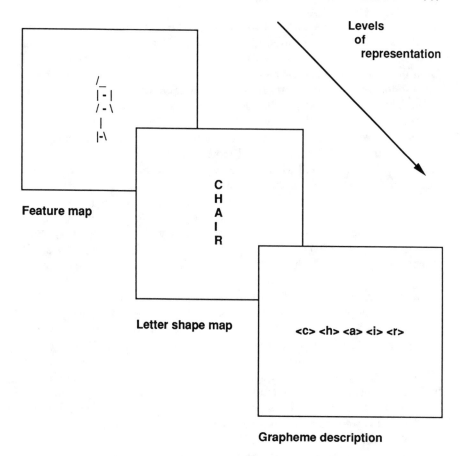

FIG. 6.2. A framework illustrating Caramazza and Hillis (1990) account of the different representations mediating word meaning.

compensate for a hemianopia (i.e., loss of one-half of the visual field): the impairment thus affecting a retino-centric level of representation.[1]

A number of cases may be described as having deficits at a stimulus-centered level of representation. The characteristic feature of these cases is that errors are

---

[1]Even in those cases of neglect dyslexia with field deficits the field deficit cannot totally account for the reading disorder. For instance, Ellis et al. (1987) presented words tachistoscopically to the intact right visual field of a patient with neglect dyslexia. Central fixation was monitored with a camera. Initial letter misreadings continued. Riddoch et al. (1990) compared identification of the initial letter of a word presented in isolation with that when the word was flanked by a # (LAND vs #LAND). In the first condition, report of the second letter in the string was nearly 100%. One would expect report of the L in the # condition to reach a similar level because both letters occupied the same position in the visual field. This was not the case. Report of the L in #LAND was significantly worse than the report of the A in LAND. Thus, although a visual field deficit may contribute to the impaired processing of contralesional letters in neglect dyslexia, other factors are also implicated.

made on the contralesional side of words even when words are projected into the intact visual field (Behrmann et al., 1990; Ellis et al., 1987; Kinsbourne & Warrington, 1962; Riddoch et al., 1990; Young et al., 1991). Caramazza and Hillis (1990) proposed that the problem cannot be retinally specific in these cases because for some patients, vertical presentation of words improves reading performance (Behrmann et al., 1990; Young et al., 1991). This improvement would rule out the possibility of a deficit both in a retinal-level representation (if the letters in the vertical array occupy the same position on the retina as letters in a horizontal array) and a word-centered representation, because even when presented vertically, letters fall within the same position within the *word* (first letters remain first letters whether presented horizontally or vertically). Neither retinal- nor word-centered impairments should be affected by this manipulation.

Only one patient has so far been described whose deficit would appear to conform with an impairment at a word-centered level of representation. Caramazza and Hillis (1990) described a patient with left hemisphere damage and a "right neglect dyslexia"; that is, she made errors with only the final letters of words. The same pattern of errors was apparent both in reading and in oral spelling. Caramazza and Hillis (1990) therefore proposed an impairment at a level of representation that specifies graphemes as primitives common to reading and writing processes, rather than a representation in which letters or visual features are specified. A characteristic feature of the patient's performance was the increase of errors as a function of the number of graphemes from the center of the word (i.e., a gradient effect); it appeared as if she was processing only about half of each centered representation. More interestingly, the same pattern of deficit was shown whatever the topographical arrangement of the stimulus (i.e., whether words were normally printed from left to right, vertically, or in mirror reversed print).

In sum, deficits at different representational levels are characterized in this way: Retinal level deficits can be claimed if visual field of presentation affects performance. String level deficits result in contralateral impairments in reading single words wherever the words are presented in the visual field; performance is improved with vertical presentation of words. Word level deficits are characterized by impairments both in reading and in oral spelling, the deficit is independent of field of presentation and it persists at the same locus in the word regardless of the topographic orientation of the stimulus.

We now consider how some of the phenomena of neglect dyslexia may be accommodated in a representational account of neglect dyslexia.

Text versus Single Word Reading.   As already indicated, dissociations have been observed in the reading of single words and text. This may be taken to imply that different mechanisms underlie the reading of the two forms of material. If we set this point aside for the moment and simply consider how a deficit in reading at the single word level may manifest in reading passages of text, it seems reasonable to assume that impairments at different representational levels in single word reading should manifest in a similar way in the reading of text. For instance, impairments at a retinal level of representation are tied to where words fall in the visual field. This should hold for words and texts. Hence the performance for words and texts should be similar: Stimuli that fall into an impaired region of the field should be neglected. Although "neglect effects" may not be so pronounced with texts, because context is likely to play a facilitatory role, the nature of the impairment should be the same.

This can be contrasted with impairments to the string- or word-based levels of representation. If either of these representations was impaired, errors would be expected to be individual words in the text, but the errors should be equally probable at any location within the text. This is because the representations are centered on the letter strings, not the text. *Omission of words* on the contralesional side of text would not necessarily be predicted. Consider now the patients described by Ellis et al. (1987) and Young et al. (1991), who we suggested earlier have deficits at a string-based level of representation. Both patients typically omitted large numbers of words on the contralesional side of text. A similar performance profile was shown by the patient described by Caramazza and Hillis (1990), who we suggested had a deficit at a graphemic-level representation. In all these instances, it appears that we need to posit an additional representational deficit at the retinocentric level in order to account for differences in performance between the reading of single words and the reading of passages of text. However, that then fails to explain why there is no effect of retinal position on single word reading in such cases. In these patients the problems in text reading contradict those in single word reading, presenting difficulties for a single representational account.

The Effects of Manipulating Stimulus Presentation.   Riddoch et al. (1990) demonstrated that reducing the exposure duration of single words or nonwords had the effect of "shrinking" the number of letters correctly reported in letters and words. When words were exposed for 400 ms, the patient was likely to make neglect errors (in particular omissions) to the first letter in the string. By reducing exposure to 250 ms, patient M. O. made neglect errors to the first two letters of a four-letter string and the first three letters of a five-letter string. Caramazza and Hillis (1990) argued M. O. had a retinal representation deficit because errors in single word reading were only made under tachistoscopic presentation conditions (as opposed to free viewing). They argued that this prevents compensation by eye movements for a problem affecting the processing the left half of a retino-centric representation. However, refixations were possible at the 400 ms exposure duration, yet first letters in words and letter strings were still neglected. All in all, the effects on performance under different exposure conditions are not easy to explain in terms of an impaired underlying representation.

Lexicality Effects.   Patients with neglect dyslexia can perform better with words than with nonwords. One possible account for the lexical effect is to propose that although the underlying representation is degraded, it nonetheless allows sufficient lexical activation for guessing to take place. Data from at least two cases suggests that this is not so. Sieroff, Pollatsek, and Posner (1988) presented patients with compound words and unrelated word *pairs* of equal length. They proposed that if performance was strongly influenced by guessing, compound words should produce a greater proportion of correct responses than unrelated word pairs. This was not found to be the case. Riddoch et al. (1990) compared compound words with single words of the same length. In this case guessing might benefit noncompounds, because the beginnings of single non-compound words tend to be more predictable from their end letters than those of compound words (this was shown with normal subjects who were asked to guess the identity of compound and noncompound words with their beginnings omit-ted). Again, no significant difference was found in neglect for compound and noncompound words. It therefore does not appear that "guessing" can account for the lexical effects observed in at least some patients.

Caramazza and Hillis (1990) used two of the assumptions about the structure of lexical access in current "activation" models of word recognition (cf. McClelland & Rumelhart, 1981) in order to account for the observed differences in levels of accuracy in reading single words and nonwords. The first assumption states that a word-centered graphemic representation activates all lexical repre-sentations in parallel in proportion to the degree of grapheme overlap between input and output lexical representations. The second assumption states that the lexical representation that receives the most activation, above a prespecified minimum level, or the one to reach threshold first, will be processed further and produced as a response. These assumptions imply that though the contralesional side of a particular representation of a word cannot be processed normally, the usable ipsilesional part may be sufficient to activate the correct lexical represen-tation resulting in a correct response. This procedure will not obtain for non-words. It is also possible that there is top-down feedback from lexical knowledge to benefit the degraded letter information, which is also consistent with activa-tion models of lexical access. This produces superior identification of letters in words in neglect just as it does for normal subjects when letters are degraded by pattern masking (see Johnston & McClelland, 1973). Thus reading accuracy for words should be expected to be superior to reading accuracy for nonwords.

The Effects of Manipulating the Orientation of Text.   Performance in reading single words at different orientations has been used as a diagnostic for deficits at different levels of representation (Caramazza & Hillis, 1990). For instance, consider a patient who shows neglect of the contralesional letters of horizontally presented words and no neglect for vertically presented words. Within Car-amazza and Hillis' (1990) scheme, this could be interpreted as indicating a problem within a string-centered representation. With horizontal letter strings, the first letters fall to the left of center in a string level representation. Within a vertical string, the same letters fall at the center of the representation. A problem due to a left-side degradation of a string-centered representation would impair the reading of horizontal but not vertical letter strings.

However, such an interpretation is by no means the only one that could be put forward. This is because processes in mapping to a putative grapheme-level description differ for horizontal and vertical arrays. For example, left-to-right scanning may be required for horizontal arrays, but top-to-bottom scanning for vertical arrays. Furthermore, whereas the reading of horizontally aligned words is little affected by word length, reading words set in unfamiliar configurations is affected by length (Seymour & Elder, 1986). Hence, scanning processes will differ not only in their direction but also in the extent to which they are used. Patients could have problems with horizontal but not with vertical arrays because:

1. Scanning is impaired along the horizontal but not the vertical meridian.
2. Their problem is due to initial fixation within a word. When forced to scan (with vertical but not with horizontal arrays), this problem may be overcome (more on this account later, when we discuss attentional accounts of neglect dyslexia).

In addition to this, reading words in unfamiliar orientations is affected by the degree of rotation from the horizontal (Koriat & Norman, 1985), suggesting additional processes such as mental rotation can come in. Such additional processes may lead to increased arousal and enhanced performance. Also, it may be that word recognition comes to depend on spelling processes with vertical arrays, and not normal reading processes at all. Patients with intact spelling "improve" (i.e., show no neglect). Patients with neglect in spelling as well as reading continue to show neglect (cf. Caramazza & Hillis, 1990).

For all these reasons, it may be difficult to relate the reading of normally oriented words to that of words placed in unfamiliar orientations.

Summary of the Representational Account.   It is clear that there are difficulties in accounting for a number of the characteristic features of neglect dyslexia solely in terms of a disorder to one or more underlying representations. For instance, it is difficult to account for why similar patterns of performance in the reading of single words and the reading of text are shown in some patients (or indeed, why different patterns occur in other patients, producing the double dissociation noted earlier). Although better performance with reading text relative to single words may be accounted for in terms of the facilitatory effects of context, it is not so easy to explain the apparently different representational impairments (i.e., a retinal-based representational deficit with text, a string- or word-level representational deficit with single words).

Representational accounts need also to be able to explain some other features

of the performance of patients with neglect dyslexia. For instance, cuing attention to the contralesional side has been shown to have facilitatory effects on the
degree of neglect shown in nonreading tasks such as line bisection (Riddoch &
Humphreys, 1983) and visual search (Riddoch & Humphreys, 1987). Cuing may
also improve performance in reading single words (Riddoch et al., 1990). In
order to account for cuing effects, representational theorists must hold that attention can operate on any given representation; if attention is deployed on the
degraded contralesional portion of a representation, processing is facilitated and
performance improves.

Attentional Accounts

We now consider an alternative position. Rather than arguing that a cerebral
lesion can have the effect of degrading underlying prelexical representations, it
may be that the characteristic performance on single word and text reading tasks
is the result of an impaired deployment of attention. Humphreys and Riddoch (in
press a) proposed that attentional allocation is based on interactions between
various components of an attentional network. These components serve either to
orient attention to salient visual targets, to maintain attention on objects of
current interest or to focus attention on a target. Orienting and maintenance
components are mutually inhibitory. When attention is engaged on an object,
there is an inhibition of the orienting component by the maintenance component.
Attention can be disengaged by the orienting component inhibiting the maintenance component. Within this scheme, clear distinctions can be made between
the role of attention in the reading of single words and in reading passages of
text. In the latter case, we rely on orienting processes, and subsequently saccades
(rapid eye movements) to move the eyes from one position to another; in contrast, the recognition of a single word (or the recognition of the words embedded
in the text) requires a fixation of attention to allow the detailed analysis of the
word in foveal vision. Eye movements and the allocation of attention appear to
be necessarily related for optimal performance in reading tasks. It may indeed
prove difficult to distinguish one from the other. The first two of the following
subsections consider some of the available evidence on the role of normal eye
movements in reading and how such movements may suffer as a result of brain
damage. An account of current attentional theories in neglect dyslexia follows in
the third subsection and emphasizes that impairments of both attentional and eye
movement systems may result in neglect dyslexia.

Eye Movements in Text Reading.   The primary function of eye movements is
to bring a new region of text into foveal vision for detailed analysis. There are
two factors that influence how far the eye is moved. First, textual variables and
second, word boundary information (K. Rayner & Pollatsek, 1987). A number
of studies have revealed that word information acquired parafoveally is used in

reading. These effects have been examined using "boundary techniques" where a moving window technique utilizes on-line eye movement recording systems to record subjects' eye movements in order to present text on a computer-controlled visual display contingent on where the reader is fixating (McConkie & Zola, 1979; Rayner, 1975). For instance, a single critical word in a sentence or paragraph is altered. When the readers saccade crosses over a prespecified boundary location in the text before the critical word location, the altered word is restored (K. Rayner, 1975). Using these sorts of techniques, Balota, Pollatsek, and K. Rayner (1985) varied the predictability of a target word and the availability of parafoveal information in order to examine the effects of parafoveal information on reading performance. They demonstrated that a predictable (predictability being gained from parafoveal information) target word is more likely to be skipped over than an unpredictable target word; furthermore, the gaze duration on the target word was shorter when the word was more predictable.

Word boundary information (conveyed mainly by the spaces between words) is also influential in determining the distance moved in a saccade. For instance, Pollatsek and K. Rayner (1982) showed that saccade length decreases markedly when the spaces between words were filled in.

One further characteristic of eye movements in normal reading is that about 10% to 15% of the saccades are regressions; that is, the eye moves back along the line of the text. It is generally believed that the two most common reasons for regressions are either that the reader has not understood some part of the text or that a saccade was overlong and the reader has to make a corrective saccade. This can occur when fixation falls too far into a single word (O'Regan & Lévy-Schoen, 1987).

To summarize, in normal reading, eye movements are determined both by textual and word boundary information and eye movements are made both forward and backward along the line of text. What might be the effects of brain damage on these characteristic features of normal reading? Let us first consider eye movements themselves. Reports on the effects of eye movements in the literature have largely focused on patients with right parietal lesions (with or without neglect). This is probably because left-sided neglect as a result of a right hemisphere lesion is far more common than right-sided neglect in patients with left hemisphere lesions. In patients with right parietal lesions, leftward eye movements have been found to be significantly slower to initiate and to have a slower scanning time than rightward eye movements (Girotti, Casazza, Musicco, & Avanzini, 1983; Heilman & Van Den Abel, 1980; Johnston, 1988). Patients with right-sided brain lesions and unilateral neglect are more likely to make multiple saccades than patients with either right- or left-sided lesions and no neglect (Girotti et al., 1983). The experiments described by Girotti et al. (1983) required subjects to detect visual targets situated to the right or left of fixation. It is unclear whether direct parallels may be drawn between performance requirements of this sort of task relative to the performance requirements in reading passages of text. However, the implication is that patients with right-sided lesions will be impaired in executing the regressive saccades characteristic of normal reading performance (Girotti et al., observed that on 25% of trials patients with unilateral neglect failed to shift their attention to a left-side target, even 10 s after its appearance). Rightward saccades also do not appear normal in cases of patients with right-sided lesions and unilateral neglect. For instance, control subjects were able to locate a right-side target with only 1 saccade on 60% of trials and with 2 saccades on 40% of trials. Patients with right-sided lesions and unilateral neglect were able to locate a right-side target with only 1 saccade on approximately 40% of trials, with 2 saccades on 40% of trials and on about 20% of trials 3 saccades were necessary (Girotti et al., 1983). If we consider word breaks in text to be somehow analogous to the targets in Girotti et al.'s experiments (both require saccadic eye movements in order to be correctly located and fixated), we might expect patients with neglect dyslexia to make mislocation errors when scanning lines of text from left to right.

The eye movement studies performed by Girotti et al. (1983) showed that the eye movement system in patients with unilateral neglect is impaired when patients are required to detect peripherally presented targets, whether the movement is in a left- or a rightward direction. Other studies have also shown that the pickup of parafoveal information contralesionally is impaired in the case of patients with right cerebral lesions. In a series of visual search tasks, Riddoch and Humphreys (1987) demonstrated that preattentive processing on the contralesional side of space was impaired. Detection of a target defined in terms of a defining feature (color) was poorer on the left relative to the right side of the search display. Discriminability of the target item was also a significant factor. Targets that were easy to discriminate from background/distracter items were neglected less than less easily discriminable targets (e.g., less neglect was shown for a red target item in an array of green distracter items than for a red target item in an array of green, blue, orange, and black distracter items) (see also Humphreys & Riddoch, in press b). Deficits in preattentive visual processing such as these may affect the normal reading of text, particularly in the case of patients with right cerebral lesions. For instance, the beginning of a line of text is signaled by a relatively large texture break (given by the distinction between the body of the text and the unfilled margin). If this distinction is not detected, reading may commence at a point *subsequent* to the actual beginning of the line. Such performance is often commented on anecdotally in cases of neglect. It has also been documented by Ellis et al. (1987) and Young et al. (1991).

The latter part of this section relates to visual processing rather than directly to reading. Nonetheless, the work of Girotti et al. (1983) and Riddoch and Humphreys (1987) suggested that patients with unilateral neglect may be impaired in performing regressive saccades, at accurately locating texture breaks when scanning from left to right, and in the detection of boundary information contralesionally, which has implications both for detecting the start of the line of text and for the execution of regressive saccades. The impaired performance of patients with neglect dyslexia in reading texts (omission of words on the contrale-sional side of the text, and the omission of single words at any location within the text) can be accounted for in terms of a defective attentional and/or eye move-ment system.

Eye Movements in Single Word Reading.   Typically, the region of visual field with the highest acuity (the fovea) is employed for single word recognition. Because there is a physical limit on the number of letters that can be clearly discriminated in the foveal region (see K. Rayner & Pollatsek, 1987, for a review), eye movements are therefore necessary in order to make fixations across a passage of text. With regard to neglect dyslexia we have indicated that there are possible differences in the reading of single words as opposed to the reading of passages of text. These differences may relate to two different components within the attentional/eye movement system. For instance, in the reading of single words there needs to be some consideration of the location of fixation within the word and whether this may vary with words of different lengths. When reading text, the actual eye movements themselves need to be considered in addition to the fixations within words. We should also note here that, in the reading of text, a word may receive no fixation, one fixation, or more than one fixation depending on the degree of contextual information available; furthermore, parafoveal as well as foveal information may be used in order to optimize fixation positions. (Inhoff, 1989; Lima & Inhoff, 1985).

If a word is initially fixated at what is known as the optimal viewing position (OVP) (near the center or slightly to the left of center for long words), recogni-tion will be faster than if the word is fixated anywhere else (O'Regan & Lévy-Schoen, 1987). This is due to the fact that there is a rapid drop in visual acuity with distance from the center of the fovea. The argument therefore runs that words are maximally identifiable when the eyes are near the word's center. O'Regan (1983) proposed that the farther the eyes initially fixate from the OVP, the greater the probability that a second eye fixation on the word will be required for identification. A further factor requiring consideration is the left–right asym-metry of the number of letters utilized during a fixation. To the left of fixation, only a few letters are used; to the right, however, the perceptual span may extend to 10 to 15 letters (McConkie & K. Rayner, 1976). Nazir, O'Regan, and Jacobs (1991) empirically assessed the probability of a single letter report when the letter occupied either the first or the last position in a nine-letter string. Initial fixation was either on the first or the last letter in the string. They were able to demonstrate that the probability of recognizing the successive letters going right-ward was greater than of those going leftward. In a second experiment, subjects were required to perform lexical decisions. The position of fixation location within the words was varied. Nazir et al. (1991) found that the probability of a correct lexical decision was a function of fixation location within the word. Thus, fixating at the OVP not only leads to a reduced probability of refixation, but also to faster lexical decisions and improved letter identification (Nazir et al., 1991).

Riddoch et al. (1990) argued that aspects of neglect dyslexia may be accounted for by postulating a shift in the OVP to the side ipsilateral to the lesion (thus, for a patient with a right-sided lesion, the OVP will be moved toward the right, the converse being true for a patient with a left-sided lesion). Shifts in the OVP may be more problematic for patients with right- than with left-sided lesions. We noted already that in normal subjects, the perceptual span is limited to 3 to 4 letters to the left of fixation (McConkie & K. Rayner, 1976; K. Rayner, Well, & Pollatsek, 1980), whereas it may extend to about 15 letter positions to the right of fixation (McConkie & K. Rayner, 1975; K. Rayner, 1986). Moving the OVP to the right (in left brain damaged subjects) may compromise identification of the initial letter(s) of a word, whereas moving the OVP to the left (in right brain damaged subjects) will not compromise identification to the same degree (except for very long words).

One further factor that should be considered is the ability to maintain fixation. Fixation stability performance has been assessed by Johnston (1984) in a group of patients with right cerebral lesions. The stimuli consisted of a 3 × 3 grid of 1 cm size crosses. Subjects were instructed to fixate the center of each cross for a period of 10s, and to attempt to maintain fixation as steadily as possible. Fixation stability was found to be worse for patients with right hemisphere damage with marked visual neglect than for control subjects whether fixating centrally, or to the left or right of center. A gradient of fixation stability performance could be observed in patients with right brain lesions (with marked visual neglect), being best centrally and worst to the left of fixation. This work suggests that following their initial fixation in a word, neglect dyslexics may find it hard to maintain that position, and the eyes will tend to drift in an ipsilesional direction.

Attentional Theories. The two previous subsections considered how the eye movement system operates during the reading of text and single words. The eye movement system is also likely to be closely linked to the visual attentional system. Saccade initiation may be linked to orienting responses, based on "preattentive" visual information such as word boundaries. Once fixated, there may be attentional focusing with an inhibitory effect on further orienting. For instance, Fischer and his colleagues (Fischer, 1986; Fischer & Breitmeyer, 1987) reported that the time to initiate a saccade to a peripheral target is increased when (non-brain-damaged) subjects fixate and attend to a central stimulus before the target's onset, relative to when there is no central stimulus present. Disorders of the visual attentional system may produce the characteristic features of neglect dyslexia, including impaired patterns of eye movements.

One of the earlier attentional accounts holds that, as a result of an abnormal distribution of attention, one side of the stimulus is attenuated with a resultant impairment in the registration of features on that side (Kinsbourne & Warrington, 1962). Shallice (1988) put forward the notion of a "visual attentional control subsystem," which determines the size and location of a "window." In cases of neglect dyslexia, Shallice suggested that the size of the attention window is unaffected, but that there is an uneven distribution of attention within the window resulting in attentional gradients. Patients with left-side brain lesions will apply attention maximally to the beginning of the word and patients with right-side brain lesions will apply attention maximally to the end of the word (see Fig. 6.3

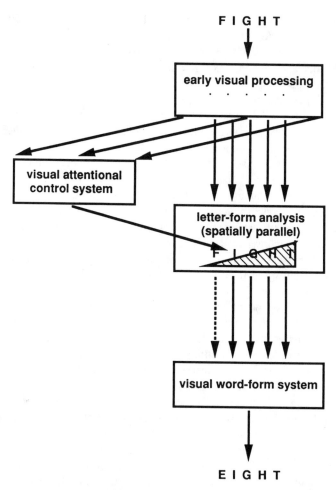

FIG. 6.3.   An attentional gradient produced by an uneven distribution of attention within an attentional window.

for an example of the attentional gradient in a patient with a right-sided brain lesion). The severity of the deficit may affect the attentional gradient. For instance, Behrmann et al. (1990) reported data on two patients with neglect dyslexia. On a bedside screening test one patient performed more poorly than the other (e.g., on line bisection, letter, and symbol detection tasks). In tests of reading single words, both patients were affected by manipulations of word length (either number of letters or horizontal extent). However, the performance of the more severely impaired patient was affected to a far greater degree than that of the patient with the lesser deficit. Behrmann et al. argued for different gradients of deficit in the two patients, with a steeper gradient of deficit in the more impaired patient.

In addition, the attention gradient may be affected by task conditions. For instance, where performance is time limited, the neglect gradient may be increased. As already noted, Riddoch et al. (1990) found that the number of letters neglected increased as the exposure duration of the words increased. The more stringent test conditions did not result in a general lowering of performance, but a more severe gradient effect was apparent.

The attentional window account provides a description of the pattern of performance of patients with neglect dyslexia, but fails to account for the relations between single word reading and the reading of text (e.g., are different attentional windows involved?), or why reducing the exposure duration of words induces a larger gradient. To progress further, we need to understand better the mechanisms involved in applying attention to visual stimuli. That is, we need to consider theories concerning attentional allocation. A gradient of performance could occur if patients are impaired at orienting contralesionally as a result of the brain lesion (Humphreys & Riddoch, in press b; Riddoch & Humphreys, 1983, 1987); if there is chronic ipsilesional orienting (Ladavas, 1990); or if there is a problem in disengaging from ipsilesional stimulation (due to over inhibition of contralateral orienting, Posner, Cohen, & Rafal, 1982). These three accounts are not necessarily independent: Orienting to the right and the left may depend on the relative strengths of the orienting systems responding to signals on the right and the left. A disorder of left-side orienting may result in chronic rightside orienting. A disorder of left-side orienting may also result in problems in disengaging from the right side in order to respond to stimulation on the left.

Normally, in reading text, attention may be directed ahead of where current fixation falls, and this attentional process helps direct the location of the next eye movement (Morrison, 1984). In reading English, this attentional process will be directionally specific, extending more to the right than the left, because reading proceeds left to right. This fits with evidence on the asymmetry of the perceptual span in English being longer to the right than the left (see the previous subsection). The location of fixation appears to be determined by factors such as word length, so that fixations tend to fall near the center of letter strings (O'Regan & Lévy-Schoen, 1987). According to the framework of a multicomponent attentional system (e.g., Humphreys & Riddoch, in press a; see earlier discussion of attentional accounts), information such as word length may be used to direct attentional orienting to an appropriate position within a word. Once engaged, attention may be maintained until subsequent signals from the orienting system inhibit attention maintenance so that either a word is re-fixated or new parts of the text are fixated. The probability of refixation is closely linked to where in a word the initial fixation falls. Re-fixation probability is least if fixation falls at the OVP, and it increases as the distance between the OVP and first fixation location increases (O'Regan & Lévy-Schoen, 1987).

Let us assume that a lesion impairs orienting to left-side cues. When faced with text, a patient may then tend to orient to the right, omitting words on the left. Also, when faced with single words, orienting may take place overly to the right of the OVP.[2] If this is coupled with a problem disengaging attention to reorient to the left, single word reading errors may be made. Consistent with the idea that patients may orient ipsilesionally is evidence on eye movements after brain lesions.

Text versus Single Word Reading.   Dissociations between text and single word reading may be explained by postulating impairments in different attentional processes. For instance, disorders in reading single words may be accounted for by proposing that the normal fixation position within the word has been shifted ipsilesionally resulting in a degradation of the contralesional letters. Disorders in text reading, on the other hand, may result from impaired contralesional orienting to preattentive visual cues. If there is a failure to process parafoveal information (such as gaps between words at text margins), words adjacent to the contralesional margin may be omitted because eye movements (and thus focused attention) have not been directed sufficiently far into the contralesional field. Words in the corpus of the text may also be omitted if word gaps are not

---

[2]Riddoch et al. (1990) proposed that length information is used to constrain attentional orienting in single words. In particular, word length information is used to compute the OVP in words, with the OVP being computed left-of-center in longer words. Left-side neglect dyslexia may be caused by chronic orienting to the right of the OVP. However, providing word length information is computed accurately, patients' performance may be determined by the position of letters-in-strings, and not their position-in-field, and substitution errors will predominate. In contrast, if there are conditions where word length is not accurately coded (e.g., under brief exposure conditions), various effects should result. First, substitution errors should not dominate. Second, if word length is underestimated, left-end letters should be detrimentally affected (due to increased orienting to the right, because the OVP is falsely computed). Third, if word length is overestimated, left-end letters may benefit (for the same reason as underestimation produces increased neglect). Fourth, when length is inaccurately coded, position-in-string may be less important than position-in-field. For instance, in cases where patients sometimes under- and sometimes overestimate word length, there will tend to be a gradual decrease in report moving from right-to-left in the string. This is because the attentional focus will shift across trials, but will on average be overly oriented to the right.

detected in a similar way. In almost all reported cases of neglect, when deficits in single word and text reading co-occur, the spatial location of errors is the same (i.e., a patient with a right-sided lesion, will make left-side errors in reading both text and words). The similarity in performance with the two sorts of material may suggest a single common underlying deficit (e.g., contralateral orienting). However, as mentioned in an earlier section the spatial location of impaired performance may differ for different types of material. Thus, cases reported by Humphreys et al. (in preparation) neglect the left side of single words and the right side of text. Such a case strengthens the claim that different attentional processes underlie the reading of single words and text. Similar deficits for words and texts may occur when there are similar impairments to the attentional processes underlying the reading of words and text.

Manipulations of Stimulus Presentation Rate. Manipulations of presentation conditions have been shown to affect performance in the case of at least one patient with neglect dyslexia (Riddoch et al., 1990). Decreasing the exposure time of a word appears to have the effect of reducing the span of available letters for report relative to free vision conditions. It also produces an increasing number of omission errors. One account of these results is that the patient, M. O., fixated further to the right as stimuli were presented more briefly. There seems little reason to propose that this should be so unless there was increased rightward orienting under reduced exposure conditions. Riddoch et al. (1990) proposed that this was what had occurred, and the increased rightward orienting was a function of M. O. tending to underestimate the length of briefly presented words.

Lexicality Effects. In many of the reported cases of neglect dyslexia, performance has been found to be better with words than with pronounceable nonwords (Behrmann et al., 1990; Caramazza & Hillis, 1990; Patterson & Wilson, 1990; Riddoch et al., 1990; Sieroff, 1991). There are fewer reported cases where performance was shown to be equivalent with the two sorts of stimulus material (Ellis et al., 1987). It has been argued that the visual recognition of words is less dependent on attention than the visual recognition of nonwords (Sieroff & Posner, 1988). This conclusion was based on the results of an experiment where subjects were required to report letters from either word or nonword letter strings under conditions where spatial attention had been cued either to the left or the right of the strings. Subjects made fewer errors in reporting the letters from the unattended side of words than nonwords. Sieroff et al. (1988) offered two attentional accounts for the lexicality effects observed in neglect dyslexia; attentional effects occur at different levels in the two accounts. First, at an early level, it may be argued that attention plays a role in affecting the efficiency of registration of letters. In an interactive word identification system (e.g., McClelland & Rumelhart, 1981), visual input activates stored lexical information that in turn, feeds back and enhances the visibility of letter input. Stored higher level information thus may support and improve the perception of the poorly registered contralesional letters. According to this account, words will be read better than nonwords because nonwords have no back-up from stored lexical knowledge and so cannot make up for poor registration due to impaired attentional processes. According to the second account, attention has no effect at a later stage where it produces a serial readout of identified letter information into phonological, articulatory, and semantic codes (Mewhort, A. J. Campbell, Marchetti, & J. I. D. Campbell, 1981). A word can be treated as a single item and requires relatively little attention to be read. However, nonwords will require the allocation of attention to all letter positions.

In line with this second account, Brunn and Farah (1991) demonstrated that not only are the contralesional sides of words reported more accurately than the contralesional sides of nonwords in patients with neglect, but that the report of nonorthographic contralesional information (such as letter color) is better with words than with nonwords. Brunn and Farah (1991) suggested that the reading of *words* is accompanied by a shift of visual attention to encompass the region of space subtended by the word. This notion receives support from the results of experiments with normal subjects. For instance, LaBerge (1983) investigated the spatial extent of attention to visually presented letters and words using a probe technique. In one condition of the experiment, subjects were asked to categorize five-letter words; in the other, they were asked to categorize the middle letter of five-letter word or nonword strings. In both conditions, the locus of attention was manipulated via probe trials that were randomly interspersed with stimulus trials. Probe trials consisted of four " + " signs and one critical item, a *7, T,* or *Z,* which appeared randomly in one of the five positions of the display string. On these trials, *7* was the positive item and *T* and *Z* were negative items. The effect of the probe trials was to produce a *V*-shaped function of reaction times across probe positions for the letter categorization condition. This contrasted with a relatively flat reaction time function for the word categorization condition. This suggests that the normal reading of words (as opposed to the categorization of letters within a word) is accompanied by an allocation of spatial attention that encompasses the whole word.

Effects of Manipulating the Orientation of the Text.   The performance of patients with neglect dyslexia often improves if the orientation of the single word of the passage of text is changed from the standard horizontal to a vertical format. We have noted that reading words in unfamiliar orientations is affected by the degree of rotation from the horizontal (Koriat & Norman, 1985), suggesting additional processes such as mental rotation can come in. Such additional processes may lead to increased arousal and enhanced performance (as discussed in an earlier section). We noted earlier that one reported case of neglect dyslexia made errors on locations that remained the same however the word was oriented (see Caramazza & Hillis, 1990). Similar effects were also observed in oral spelling. Are we able to account for this patient within an attentional framework? In some ways we can. For instance, in reading text she made contralesional omissions of words. In line bisection and letter cancellation tasks, contralesional information was neglected. Such a pattern of performance is consistent with an impairment in contralesional orienting. In single word reading, the errors were made with the final (contralesional) letters of the string whether the word was in a normal or mirror image orientation. This could reflect the particular scanning strategy selected by this patient (i.e., always scanning a word from left to right commencing with the initial letter of the word whatever its position in the visual field).

Summary of the Attentional Account.   We have argued that at least two attentional/eye movement processes are necessary for normal reading: Disorders in text reading may result from impaired contralesional orienting to preattentive visual cues, whereas disorders in single word reading may result from shifts in the normal optimal viewing position. The effect of this impairment on the reading of text is the omission of contralateral words. In single words, if word length information is computed accurately, there will be a degradation of contralesional information and substitution errors are likely to predominate. If word length is not accurately coded, fixation in the word will be displaced either to the right or left of the OVP. A variety of error types will result (addition, substitution, and omission errors).

The "shrinkage effects" observed when stimulus exposure duration is decreased may reflect an impairment in contralesional orienting. We have argued that there may be an underestimation of word length when experimental conditions are time forced, resulting in increased ipsilesional orienting.

In order to account for lexicality effects, it has been argued that the visual recognition of words is accompanied by an allocation of spatial attention that encompasses the whole word. In nonwords attention is more likely to be directed toward each individual letter.

Finally, we have accounted for the improved performance with vertical arrays of words or text by suggesting that the altered (and unusual) task demands may have an advantageous effect on arousal mechanisms and result in enhanced performance.

CONCLUSIONS

The neglect dyslexias are an interesting subset of the peripheral reading disorders that may be observed following brain damage. The reading of single words and/or text may be impaired. A number of patients have been reported with a material-specific impairment, so it is difficult to argue for a single underlying deficit. Two different theoretical approaches have been taken in order to explain performance. According to the representational account, one (or more) prelexical representations is impaired. There are problems with this interpretation because with a number of patients, the representational impairment appears to be different for different sorts of stimulus material. The alternative (attentional) account holds that impaired patterns of performance occur as a result of damage to one or more components of an attentional network. It is argued that different attentional/eye movement processes underlie the reading of text and single words. Both theories provide some explanation for some of the characteristic features of the performance of a patient with neglect dyslexia (e.g., the effects of different stimulus presentation rates, lexicality effects, and possible improvement in performance when the orientation of the test material is manipulated); however, it is easier to account for certain performance features in terms of the attentional account. For instance, the "shrinkage" of available letter report under forced performance conditions and the facilitatory effects of cuing attention to the (impaired) contralesional side of the stimulus. Given these effects, either we must propose that the deployment of attention can somehow reduce the noise in a degraded representation, or that an impairment (or impairments) within the attentional network are sufficient to account for all the available data without having to propose additional representational impairments. We tend to favor the latter view.

ACKNOWLEDGMENT

We gratefully acknowledge the support of the Medical Research Council of the United Kingdom in the production of this chapter.

REFERENCES

Balota, D. A., Pollatsek, A., & Rayner, K. (1985). The interaction of contextual constraints and parafoveal visual information in reading. *Cognitive Psychology, 17*, 364–390.

Baxter, D. M., & Warrington, E. K. (1983). Neglect dysgraphia. *Journal of Neurology, Neurosurgery and Psychiatry, 46*, 1073–1078.

Behrmann, M., Moscovitch, M., Black, S. E., & Mozer, M. (1990). Perceptual and conceptual mechanisms in neglect dyslexia: Two contrasting case studies. *Brain, 113*, 1163–1183.

Bisiach, E., Perani, D., Vallar, G., & Berti, A. (1986). Unilateral neglect: Personal and extrapersonal. *Neuropsychologia, 24*, 759–767.

Brunn, J. L., & Farah, M. J. (1991). The relation between spatial attention and reading: Evidence from the neglect syndrome. *Cognitive Neuropsychology, 8*, 59–75.

Caramazza, A., & Hillis, A. E. (1990). Levels of representation, co-ordinate frames, and unilateral neglect. *Cognitive Neuropsychology, 7*, 391–445.

Coltheart, M. (1980). Deep dyslexia: A review of the syndrome. In M. Coltheart, K. E. Patterson, & J. C. Marshall (Eds.), *Deep dyslexia* (pp. 22–47). London: Routledge & Kegan Paul.

Costello, A. de L., & Warrington, E. (1987). Word comprehension and word retrieval in patients with localised cerebral lesions. *Brain, 101*, 163–185.

Ellis, A. W., Flude, B. M., & Young, A. W. (1987). "Neglect dyslexia" and the early visual processing of letters in words and nonwords. *Cognitive Neuropsychology, 4*, 439–464.

Ellis, A. W., & Young, A. W. (1988). *Human cognitive neuropsychology*. London: Lawrence Erlbaum Associates.

Fischer, B. (1986). The role of attention in the preparation of visually guided eye movements in monkey and man. *Psychological Research, 48*, 251–257.

Fischer, B., & Breitmeyer, B. (1987). Mechanisms of visual attention revealed by saccadic eye movements. *Neuropsychologia, 25*, 73–83.

Friedrich, F. J., Walker, J. A., & Posner, M. I. (1985). Effects of parietal lesions on visual matching: Implications for reading errors. *Cognitive Neuropsychology, 2*, 253–264.

Girotti, F., Casazza, M., Musicco, M., & Avanzini, G. (1983). Occulomotor disorders in cortical lesions in man: The role of unilateral neglect. *Neuropsychologia, 21*, 543–553.

Heilman, K. M., & Van Den Abel, T. (1980). Right hemisphere dominance for attention: The mechanisms underlying hemispheric asymmetries of inattention (neglect). *Neurology, 30*, 327–330.

Humphreys, G. W., & Riddoch, M. J. (in press a). Interactions between object and space systems revealed through neuropsychology. In D. E. Meyer & S. Kornblum (Eds.), *Attention and performance XIV*. Hillsdale, NJ: Lawrence Erlbaum Associates.

Humphreys, G. W., & Riddoch, M. J. (in press b). Interactive attentional systems and unilateral visual neglect. In I. Robertson & J. C. Marshall (Eds.), *Unilateral neglect*. London: Taylor & Francis.

Humphreys, G. W., & Riddoch, M. J. (in prep.). *Neglect within and between-objects: Implications for spatial coding in the brain*.

Inhoff, A. W. (1989). Parafoveal processing of words and saccade computation during eye fixations in reading. *Journal of Experimental Psychology, Human Perception and Performance, 15*, 544–555.

Johnston, C. W. (1984). Visual hemi-inattention and occulomotor impersistence. In A. Gale & F. Johnson (Eds.), *Theoretical and applied aspects of eye movement research* (pp. 443–450). Amsterdam: Elsevier Science Publishers.

Johnston, C. W. (1988). Eye movements in visual hemi-neglect. In C. W. Johnston & F. J. Pirozzolo (Eds.), *Neuropsychology of eye movements* (pp. 235–263). Hillsdale, NJ: Lawrence Erlbaum Associates.

Johnston, J. C., & McClelland, J. L. (1973). Visual factors in word perception. *Perception and Psychophysics, 14*, 365–370.

Kartsounis, L. D., & Warrington, E. K. (1989). Unilateral neglect overcome by cues implicit in stimulus displays. *Journal of Neurology, Neurosurgery and Psychiatry, 52*, 1253–1259.

Kinsbourne, M., & Warrington, E. K. (1962). A variety of reading disability associated with right hemisphere lesions. *Journal of Neurology, Neurosurgery and Psychiatry, 25*, 339–344.

Koriat, A., & Norman, J. (1985). Reading rotated words. *Journal of Experimental Psychology, Human Perception and Performance, 111*, 490–508.

LaBerge, D. (1983). The spatial extent of attention to letters and words. *Journal of Experimental Psychology: Human Perception and Performance, 9*, 371–379.

Ladavas, E. (1990). Selective spatial attention in patients with visual extinction. *Brain, 113*, 1527–1538.

Laplane, D., & Degos, J. D. (1983). Motor neglect. *Journal of Neurology, Neurosurgery and Psychiatry, 46*, 152–158.

Lima, S. D., & Inhoff, A. W. (1985). Lexical access during eye fixations in reading: Effects of word-initial letter sequence. *Journal of Experimental Psychology: Human Perception and Performance, 11*, 272–285.

McClelland, J. L., & Rumelhart, D. E. (1981). An interactive activation model of context effects in letter perception: Part 1. An account of basic findings. *Psychological Review, 88*, 375–407.

McConkie, G. W., & Rayner, K. (1975). The span of an effective stimulus during a fixation in reading. *Perception and Psychophysics, 17,* 578–587.

McConkie, G. W., & Rayner, K. (1976). Asymmetry of the perceptual span in reading. *Bulletin of the Psychonomic Society, 8,* 365–368.

McConkie, G. W., & Zola, D. (1979). Is visual information integrated across successive fixations in reading? *Perception and Psychophysics, 25,* 221–224.

Marr, D. (1982). *Vision.* New York: W. H. Freeman.

Marshall, J. C., & Newcombe, F. (1966). Syntactic and semantic errors in paralexia. *Neuropsychologia, 4,* 169–176.

Marshall, J. C., & Newcombe, F. (1973). Patterns of paralexia: A psycholinguistic approach. *Journal of Psycholinguistic Research, 2,* 175–199.

Marshall, J. C., & Newcombe, F. (1980). The conceptual status of deep dyslexia: An historical perspective. In M. Coltheart, K. E. Patterson, & J. C. Marshall (Eds.), *Deep dyslexia* (pp. 1–23). London: Routledge & Kegan Paul.

Mewhort, D. J. K., Campbell, A. J., Marchetti, F. M., & Campbell, J. I. D. (1981). Identification, localisation, and "iconic memory": An evaluation of the bar probe task. *Memory and Cognition, 9,* 50–67.

Morrison, R. E. (1984). Manipulation of stimulus onset delay in reading: Evidence for parallel programming of saccades. *Journal of Experimental Psychology, Human Perception and Performance, 10,* 667–682.

Morton, J., & Patterson, K. E. (1980). A new attempt at an interpretation: or, an attempt at a new interpretation. In M. Coltheart, K. E. Patterson, & J. C. Marshall (Eds.). *Deep dyslexia* (pp. 91–118). London: Routledge & Kegan Paul.

Nazir, T. A., O'Regan, K., & Jacobs, A. M. (1991). On words and their letters. *Bulletin of the Psychonomic Society, 29,* 171–174.

O'Regan, J. K. (1983). Elementary perceptual and eye movement control processes in reading. In K. Rayner (Ed.), *Eye movements in reading: Perceptual and language processes.* New York: Academic Press.

O'Regan, J. K., & Lévy-Schoen, A. (1987). Eye-movement strategy and tactics in word recognition and reading. In Coltheart, M. (Ed.) *Attention and performance XII* (pp. 363–383). Hillsdale, NJ: Lawrence Erlbaum Associates.

Patterson, K. E., & Wilson, B. (1990). A ROSE is a ROSE or a NOSE: A deficit in initial letter identification. *Cognitive Neuropsychology, 7,* 447–477.

Pollatsek, A., & Rayner, K. (1982). Eye movement control in reading: The role of word boundaries. *Journal of Experimental Psychology, Human Perception and Performance, 8,* 817–833.

Posner, M. I., Cohen, Y., & Rafal, R. D. (1982). Neural systems control of spatial orienting. *Philosophical Transactions of the Royal Society, London, B298,* 60–70.

Rapp, B. C., & Caramazza, A. (1991). Spatially determined deficits in letter and word processing. *Cognitive Neuropsychology, 8,* 275–312.

Rayner, A. (1975). The perceptual span and peripheral cues in reading. *Cognitive Psychology, 7,* 65–81.

Rayner, K. (1986). Eye movements and perceptual span in beginning and skilled readers. *Journal of Experimental Child Psychology, 41,* 211–236.

Rayner, K., & Pollatsek, A. (1987). Eye movements in reading: A tutorial review. In M. Coltheart (Ed.), *Attention and performance XII* (pp. 327–361). London: Lawrence Erlbaum Associates.

Rayner, K., Well, A. D., & Pollatsek, A. (1980). Asymmetry of effective visual field in reading. *Perception and Psychophysics, 27,* 537–544.

Riddoch, M. J. (1990). Neglect and the peripheral dyslexias. *Cognitive Neuropsychology, 7,* 369–389.

Riddoch, M. J., & Humphreys, G. W. (1983). The effect of cuing on unilateral neglect. *Neuropsychologia, 21,* 589–599.

Riddoch, M. J., & Humphreys, G. W. (1987). Perceptual and action systems in unilateral neglect. In M. Jeanerrod (Ed.), *Neurophysiological and neuropsychological aspects of visual neglect* (pp. 151–181). North Holland: Elsevier Science Publishers.

Riddoch, M. J., Humphreys, G. W., Cleton, P., & Fery, P. (1990). Interaction of attentional and lexical processes in neglect dyslexia. *Cognitive Neuropsychology, 7,* 479–517.

Rizzolatti, G., & Camarda, R. (1987). Neural circuits for spatial attention and unilateral neglect. In M. Jeanerrod (Ed.), *Neurophysiological and neuropsychological aspects of visual neglect* (pp. 289–313). North Holland: Elsevier Science Publishers.

Rizzolatti, G., Gentilucci, M., & Matelli, M. (1985). Selective spatial attention: One centre, One circuit or many circuits? In M. I. Posner & O. Marin (Eds.), *Attention and performance XI* (pp. 251–265). Hillsdale, NJ: Lawrence Erlbaum Associates.

Schwartz, M. F., Saffran, E. M., & Marin, O. S. M. (1980). Fractionating the reading process in dementia: Evidence of word-specific print-to-sound associations. In M. Coltheart, K. E. Patterson, & J. C. Marshall (Eds.), *Deep dyslexia* (pp. 259–269). London: Routledge & Kegan Paul.

Seymour, P. H. K., & Elder, L. (1986). Beginning reading without phonology. *Cognitive Neuropsychology, 3,* 1–36.

Sieroff, E. (1990). Focusing on/in visual/verbal stimuli in patients with parietal lesions. *Cognitive Neuropsychology, 7,* 519–554.

Sieroff, E., Pollatsek, A., & Posner, M. I. (1988). Recognition of visual letter strings following injury to the posterior visual spatial attention system. *Cognitive Neuropsychology, 5,* 427–449.

Sieroff, E., & Posner, M. (1988). Cueing spatial attention during processing of words and letter strings in normals. *Cognitive Neuropsychology, 5,* 451–472.

Shallice, T. (1988). *From neuropsychology to mental structure.* New York: Cambridge University Press.

Shallice, T., Warrington, E. K., & McCarthy, R. (1983). Reading without semantics. *Quarterly Journal of Experimental Psychology, 35A,* 507–532.

Valenstein, E., & Heilman, K. M. (1981). Unilateral hypokinesia and motor extinction. *Neurology, 31,* 445–448.

Warrington, E. K. (1991). Right neglect dyslexia: A single case study. *Cognitive Neuropsychology, 8,* 193–212.

Warrington, E. K., & Zangwill, O. L. (1957). A study of dyslexia. *Journal of Neurology, Neurosurgery and Psychiatry, 20,* 208–215.

Young, A. W., Newcombe, F., & Ellis, A. W. (1991). Different impairments contribute to neglect dyslexia. *Cognitive Neuropsychology, 8,* 177–192.

III VISUAL PROCESSES IN READING

7 Visual Information Processing in Reading

Dominic W. Massaro
University of California, Santa Cruz

Thomas Sanocki
University of South Florida, Tampa

INTRODUCTION

The first half of the title of this book, *Visual Processes in Reading,* might seem redundant because reading is necessarily a visual act. However, reading is influenced by nonvisual information. Our concern is with visual processing, but nonvisual information (in many different forms) contributes to our perceptual experience of reading text. The goal of this chapter is to present a theoretical framework for visual information processing in reading and to sample relevant research. After presenting the model, we address the issue of what visual information is used in word identification. The results are consistent with the view that identification of a word depends on processing its component letters. Therefore, it is important to describe the visual information contributing to letter recognition. After considering letter recognition per se, we discuss a way of using visual information to increase the amount of orthographic and phonological information conveyed by letters. Then we return to the observed perceptual advantage for words and consider competing theoretical explanations. In particular, we focus on an account that emphasizes knowledge of spelling regularities (orthographic structure) and an account that utilizes specific words. We evaluate these accounts in terms of how they handle effects of processing time and other variables in word perception tasks. Finally, we close with consideration of effects of the discourse context on word recognition.

FUZZY LOGICAL MODEL
OF PERCEPTION (FLMP)

Within the framework of the Fuzzy Logical Model of Perception (FLMP), visual processing in reading can be conceptualized as a pattern recognition process. Well-learned patterns are recognized in accordance with a general algorithm, regardless of the modality or particular nature of the patterns (Massaro, 1987; Oden & Massaro, 1978). The model consists of three operations: feature evaluation, feature integration, and decision. Continuously valued features are evaluated, integrated, and matched against prototype descriptions in memory, and an identification decision is made on the basis of the relative goodness-of-match of the stimulus information with the relevant prototype descriptions. Prototypes are generated for the task at hand. The sensory systems transduce the physical event and make available various sources of information called *features*. During the first operation in the model, the features are evaluated in terms of the *prototypes* in memory. For each feature and for each prototype, feature evaluation provides information about the degree to which the feature in the signal matches the corresponding feature value of the prototype.

Feature evaluation provides the degree to which each feature in the stimulus matches the corresponding feature in each prototype in memory. The goal, of course, is to determine the overall goodness-of-match of each prototype with the stimulus. All of the features are capable of contributing to this process and the second operation of the model is called *feature integration*. That is, the features (actually the degrees of matches) corresponding to each prototype are combined (or conjoined in logical terms). The outcome of feature integration consists of the degree to which each prototype matches the stimulus. In the model, all features contribute to the final value, but with the property that the least ambiguous features have the most impact on the outcome.

The third operation is *decision*. During this stage, the merit of each relevant prototype is evaluated relative to the sum of the merits of the other relevant prototypes. This relative goodness-of-match gives the proportion of times the stimulus is identified as an instance of the prototype. The relative goodness-of-match could also be determined from a rating judgment indicating the degree to which the stimulus matches the category. The three operations between presentation of a pattern and its categorization can be formalized mathematically, but this is beyond the purview of this chapter (but see Massaro & Hary, 1986; Massaro, 1987). We begin with the study of the visual features that are functional in reading words.

WORD IDENTIFICATION

If the first psychologists from a century ago were to return to life and read our journals, they would be impressed by how much the fundamental questions they proposed remain at the center of research. Some of the first studies gave a surprising result. Subjects could read words under conditions that did not permit the identification of the component letters when they were presented in random letter strings. A great deal of excitement in psychological and educational circles was generated by this work. The research results convinced many people that word recognition was not dependent on the recognition of individual letters. Researchers and educators concluded that words are learned as patterns of unique shapes rather than as unique sequences of letters. If words have unique shapes, readers would learn words in terms of relatively gross properties that define their shape. We call these properties *supraletter features* because they supposedly are composed of multiletter patterns and even whole word patterns. This belief was responsible for the whole-word method of teaching reading.

As appealing as the concept of supraletter features might be, there is no evidence for this idea (Anderson & Dearborn, 1952; Gibson & Levin, 1975; Huey, 1968). One of the strongest arguments against the idea of supraletter features is their small potential contributions to reading. Overall word shape, for example, does not sufficiently differentiate among the words of a language (Groff, 1975). There is also experimental evidence against the idea of word recognition based on supraletter features. It has been shown that words with rare shapes are not more perceptible than those with more common shapes (Paap, Newsome, & Noel, 1984). A rare shape means that this shape specifies only one or a few words, whereas a common shape is consistent with many possible words. If word shape is functional in reading, words with rare shapes should have been easier to read.

The role of supraletter features has also been evaluated in a number of studies by determining whether mixing the case (McClelland, 1976) or type fonts (Adams, 1979) of letters eliminates the tachistoscopic identification advantage of word over nonword letter strings. For example, Adams (1979) studied the tachistoscopic recognition of words, pseudowords very high in orthographic structure, and nonwords very low in structure. The items were presented in a single type font or the items were constructed from a wide variety of fonts. Performance was more accurate for words than pseudowords and poorest for nonwords. Most importantly, the size of the differences among the three types of items did not change when the letters of the items were presented in a variety of type fonts. If supraletter features or whole-word cues contribute to the perceptual advantage of well-structured strings, the advantage of the word and pseudoword strings should have been drastically attenuated in the mixed-font presentation.

LETTER RECOGNITION

Although word recognition depends on identification of component letters, several sources of nonvisual information (i.e., orthographic, lexical, and syntactic and semantic) may contribute to letter identification. Therefore, in order to study letter recognition per se, it is necessary to strip away these nonvisual sources of information and study either single letters or strings of unrelated letters. A starting point in the study of letter recognition is the fact that instances of the same letter can vary markedly, depending on the font. In general, researchers have responded to differences between instances in either of two ways.

General Features

One approach is to assume that the features used in recognition are abstract, general features that apply to varying instances of the same letter. That is, prototype descriptions for letters would be in terms of general features. For example, Gibson's (1969) well-known feature list includes general binary contrasts such as the presence or absence of "straight-vertical" and "intersection." Intersection is present in instances of A and P, and absent in C and U. Such contrasts may be important in letter recognition because they are generally applicable and easy for the visual system to detect. However, there has not been much research in the last 20 years that directly tests these features, perhaps because of the very general level at which such features are (necessarily) specified. One exception is research examining fuzzy contrasts, in which features are present or absent to varying degrees (e.g., Massaro & Hary, 1986; Oden, 1979).

Recently, the importance of binary contrasts has taken on added meaning in models of object recognition (e.g., Biederman, 1987; Lowe, 1985). For example, Biederman (1987) proposed that objects are represented in terms of their parts, termed "geons," and geons are identified by detecting a limited number of easy-to-detect binary or trinary contrasts. Biederman referred to the features as "nonaccidental properties" because they have two important characteristics: They are unlikely to occur by accident, and they remain invariant across changes in viewpoint (see Lowe, 1985; Witkin & Tenenbaum, 1983). These characteristics are important because it is necessary in object recognition to distinguish between image properties that are valid indicators of object properties and image properties that may occur because of an accidental alignment of stimulus features. For example, parallel edges (over small visual angles) are nonaccidental properties because they are much more likely to be caused by parallel edges in the object rather than be caused by accident (e.g., by accident alignment of nonparallel edges when seen from a particular viewpoint).

Font-Specific Features

A second response to differences between instances of the category is to simply focus on a single font and to assume that features correspond to local parts or global properties within that font (e.g., Keren & Baggen, 1981; Townsend & Ashby, 1982). This approach has been used more often, and models have been fit with more precision, but it is not clear that a model fit to data from one font will fit data from another font (see Gilmore, 1985). Several different types of feature sets have been considered in this research. In one study, Keren and Baggen (1981) used features derived from a multidimensional scaling method. The features ranged from global ones (e.g., "facing right") to local ones (e.g., "horizontal line in center"). In a second study, Keren and Baggen used segments (of numerals, as on a calculator) as features, supplemented by two global features ("open-left" and "open-right"). Keren and Baggen showed that, when incorporated into Tversky's (1977) contrast model, such features predicted confusion data quite well. It is not clear, however, that Keren and Baggen's features would be easily detected by the visual system. For example, the feature "line in center" cannot be resolved until spatial relations within the pattern have been established. "Facing right" cannot be established until the parts of the figure that do the facing have been detected.

Font-Specific Tuning

One issue relevant to the two approaches already mentioned is the degree to which the processes underlying recognition become "tuned" to the details that characterize particular fonts. If features are only abstract and general, then varying the font should not matter. However, if tuning occurs, then letter prototypes could become modified for the current font. As a result, letter recognition should be more accurate with target sets of *n* letters of a single font than with *n* letters of two or more fonts because tuning can be more precise with a single font. Sanocki (1987, 1988) examined the recognition of strings of (typically) four unrelated letters in consistent and mixed-font conditions. Results from both a letter–nonletter reaction time task and a backward masking task indicated that tuning occurs. Advantages for consistent font conditions have been quite large in the letter–nonletter task, which requires explicit attention to visual structure (effects typically exceed 120 ms), but smaller in the masking task, which requires only identification (effects averaged about 3%). These results indicate that recognition can use features that are specific to particular fonts. However, the rather small effects in the masking task qualified the extent to which such features contribute to recognition; more general features may be more important.

Global Features

The assumption that recognition involves both specific and general features contrasts with a simpler assumption that features correspond to mutually exclusive segments of letters. In this simpler model, each segment is detected by an independent feature mechanism. Townsend and Ashby (1982) presented letters composed from line segments and obtained reports of letter identity and of the segments perceived. They found reasonably good fits for models that assumed segment features. However, a further prediction is that, if segment-features are detected independently, then the probabilities of detecting different segments should not be correlated. Townsend and Ashby found that the probability of detecting a given segment increased with the probability of detecting other segments in the letter (see also, Townsend, Hu, & Evans, 1984). These results appear to be inconsistent with the simple-segment model. One way to explain this result would be to assume that, in the initial stages of the letter recognition process, only global features (e.g., overall letter shape) have been extracted. Segments might then be perceived more accurately when they are contained within accurately perceived global features.

Townsend, Hu, and Kadlec (1988) replicated the intersegment correlations while finding moderately strong support for more detailed predictions of a global-to-local model of letter recognition. In that study, they also found evidence against explanations of the correlations in terms of a periodic waxing and waning of attention (i.e., more or fewer segments are perceived as alertness or attention gradually increases or decreases). However, their data do not rule out an explanation in terms of random trial-to-trial fluctuations in attention. That is, a subject's overall performance might fluctuate from trial to trial because of a variety of factors and this variability might be sufficient to produce a positive correlation among feature-detection probabilities. Further evidence against simple segment-feature models stems from the fact that when Keren and Baggen (1981) used segment features, they found it necessary to supplement the segment features with two global features. Unfortunately, they did not report results for a segment-features-only model. The importance of global features was demonstrated some time ago in Bouma's (1971) study of confusions between lowercase letters. Bouma found that letters with similar envelopes (enclosing outlines) were more likely to be confused.

Some global features may correspond to lower spatial frequency components of the stimulus. Gervais, Harvey, and Roberts (1984) analyzed letters into their spatial frequency components and then filtered the results to attenuate higher spatial frequency components (the filter was based on contrast sensitivity functions). The resultant "internal representations" were then used to predict confusions and did so with moderately high success (and with more success than a template or feature-based model). However, it is important to note that although models such as Gervais et al.'s have few free parameters, the internal representations assumed are quite complex. For example, the frequency analysis for each letter used as input a 50×45 cell array (2,250 cells in total) and the results of the analysis were represented in arrays of (apparently) similar complexity. In contrast, feature-based representations were simpler, consisting of trinary values on a small set of features.

Although global features in the low pass stimuli of Gervais et al. are not detailed, other global features could involve more detailed relations between parts of letters. Sanocki (1991a) studied the importance of relations between letter parts by measuring the perceptibility of backward-masked letters from four fonts. Sanocki used two different size "normal" fonts (one twice as large as the other), in which the relations between ascender or descender size and body size were typical of that found in most common text fonts (as established in a normative study). Two "abnormal" fonts were then created by interchanging ascenders or descenders and bodies between the two normal fonts. If letter perceptibility was determined by the discriminability of only segment features, then the average perceptibilities of the normal and abnormal pairs of fonts should be equal because they are composed of the same segments. On the other hand, if features more complex than segments are used in recognition, then there should be an advantage for the normal fonts, which have relations more typical of normal letters. Overall accuracy was higher with the normal fonts than with the abnormal fonts, consistent with the claim that relations between segments are important in letter recognition. There was an advantage for both the large and small normal fonts relative to the abnormal fonts (taken as a whole), so the results cannot be explained in terms of overall letter size or some other nonrelational feature.

Sanocki's (1991a) results are contrary to the impression of letter recognition given in many textbooks. Many texts contain a figure showing a wide variety of different font instances of a letter, all (or most) of which can be recognized. This demonstration is then taken as evidence that letter recognition is a general process than can handle a variety of instances. However, the differences obtained by Sanocki between normal and abnormal letters indicate that instances are not equally recognizable. Less typical patterns are more difficult to recognize, perhaps because they provide relatively poor matches for details of internal prototypes developed through years of experience.

The previous data indicate that to some extent recognition may rely on detailed feature information. This might seem contrary to models assuming general contrastive features such as those of Gibson and Biederman. However, further consideration of object recognition also implicates more specific features. Although Biederman (1987) emphasized simple nonaccidental contrasts such as "straight versus curved," such properties do not seem to provide sufficiently strong constraints for object recognition. Many objects have multiple geons and many edges, and any given edge can participate in many relations with neighboring edges. Simple contrasts such as "straight (vs. curved)" would not constrain the assignment of edges to geons, meaning that an edge may be wrongly combined with edges from other geons. On the other hand, somewhat more complex, relational properties such as vertice type (e.g., arrow vertice or fork vertice) put stronger constraints on geon identity because they can participate in only a limited number of relations with neighboring edges. Thus, in more recent computational work, vertice-types have played important roles (Hummel & Biederman, 1992). Consistent with the apparent importance of vertice-types, Enns and Rensink (1990, 1991) studied them in search tasks and obtained evidence that they are detected easily and in parallel ("pre-attentively visible"; Treisman &

Gormican, 1988). Furthermore, consistent with the importance of details of relations, Enns and Rensink found that vertices with less typical details (e.g., 60 rather than 90 degree angles) are not preattentively visible.

Further data on object recognition indicate that, as in reading, the perceptual system uses multiple sources of information, with the importance of a given type of information depending on its strength. In contrast to models in which only edge information is assumed to be used, Price and Humphreys (1989) found that surface details (e.g., color and shading) also contribute to recognition. The importance of such information increases with objects from categories with many visually similar members, because edge or shape information is less distinctive within such categories.

Integrating Features

In sum, letter recognition may involve a mixture of different features: Local features corresponding to specific letter parts and relations between parts, as well as both specific and more general global features. The type of features used may depend in part on visual conditions (e.g., length of eye fixation and quality of type). Also, many theorists believe that the type of features detected might vary during the process of recognition, with more general global features being detected first, followed by increasingly precise and more local features. Several types of evidence are consistent with this claim (e.g., Krueger & Chignell, 1985; Lupker, 1979; Townsend et al., 1988), but research has only begun to directly address the constancy or variance of information processed across the time course of recognition (Navon, 1991; Sanocki, 1991b). These features must be integrated together to achieve accurate letter recognition (see Oden, 1979, and Massaro & Hary, 1986, for an empirical and theoretical analysis of how features are integrated in letter recognition).

LETTERS AND SOUNDS

The process of recognizing letters in words appears to use multiple sources of information, including information about spellings and phonology (Venezky & Massaro, 1987). The extent to which a source of information will be used depends on its informativeness; in general, the least ambiguous source will have the largest effect. For skilled readers and familiar words, the extraction of visual letter information may be so quick that other types of information will not have an influence. However, with more difficult words or with beginning readers, nonvisual sources of information may become increasingly important. For example, phonological information resulting from the encoding of letter-to-sound correspondences may be useful for beginning readers.

Because of complexities of the English language, the spelling-to-sound translation of any given letter is often ambiguous. For example, *c* has a different sound in *cat* and *city*. Such ambiguities can be very troublesome for beginners. One way to reduce the ambiguity is to increase the amount of visual information associated with letters—that is, to modify the alphabet. For example, in the Initial Teaching Alphabet (i.t.a.; Pittman & St. John, 1969), new symbols were added to the alphabet so that each unique letter sound had its own symbol. Also, the spellings of many words were "regularized" by giving them new spellings. Although the i.t.a. was once widely used, it ran into serious problems. Most important was the fact that students who learned with the i.t.a. experienced great difficulty transferring to the traditional orthography (see, e.g., Downing, 1967).

However, it is important to note that alphabet modification follows from underlying assumptions about the reading process, and the assumptions underlying the i.t.a. are now known to be incorrect. In particular, Pittman subscribed to the aforementioned belief that words were recognized as whole units, and thus, that individual letters played little role in reading beyond preserving word shape (Pittman & St. John, 1969). Pittman allowed some sounds to be represented by new patterns that bore no resemblance to the old ones beyond shared envelope.

Quite different assumptions can be used to motivate alphabet modification. One example is the Graphophonic Alphabet (GP; Sanocki & Rose, 1989–90), in which different sounding versions of the same letter are distinguished by minor modifications of the letter's form. Because the more global properties of the letters remain unchanged, a modified letter should first be identified as an instance of the original letter. In addition, the modifications should become clear as the details of the instance are processed. The modifications correspond to how the appropriate sound is produced, and thereby provide cues to the letter's phonological status. As can be seen in Fig. 7.1, for example, the hard *c* sound is signified by a closure at the back of *c,* which corresponds to the closure in the throat used to make the sound. Soft *c* on the other hand is signified by *s*-like curls at the front of the letter, corresponding to the closure at the front of the mouth (as with *s*). Similarly, hard *g* has a closure at its back, whereas soft *g* is condensed and *j*-like.

The difficulty of transition to the traditional orthography should be minimized because the modified letters are similar to the traditional letters and because the

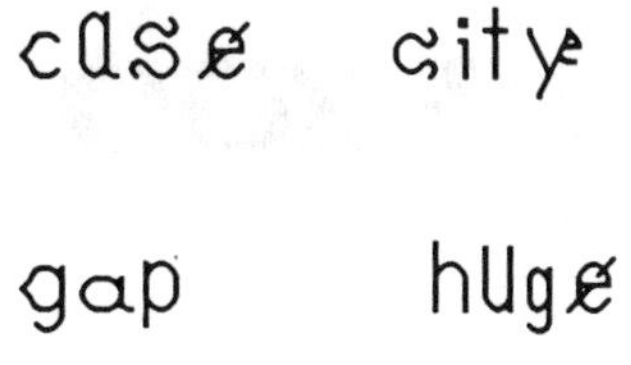

cɑsℯ   cityℯ

gɑp   hᴜgℯ

FIG. 7.1. Examples of Graphophonic Letters. In addition to the "c's" and "g's" mentioned in the text, note also the soft "s", the silent "e", the "y" on "city", and the short and long vowels (which are short or tall, respectively).

GP requires no new spellings. In addition, the modifications can be removed gradually in a fading-out process. The effectiveness of the alphabet remains to be seen (research is underway), and no claim is made that the current modifications are the best ones. The important point here is that the amount of visual information in letters can be increased to provide additional phonological and orthographic information. More generally, alphabet modification remains a potentially promising and relatively untested tool for teaching reading.

WORDS

Stimulus information about letters serves as the first source of information used in word recognition. The second is nonvisual information possessed by the sophisticated reader and stored in memory. There are three sources of nonvisual information that can aid the reader in decoding the written message. These sources are the orthographic, syntactic, and semantic structures that exist in English prose. The orthographic constraints define the valid spelling patterns in English. We know that words are separated by blank spaces and must have at least one vowel. Syntactic rules establish the permissible sequences of different parts of speech. For example, "The boy down fell the hill" is grammatically incorrect. Finally, semantic rules allow the reader to predict the word or words that make sense in a given sentence context. "The hill fell down the boy" is syntactically correct but semantically anomalous. All of these rules allow us to agree on the missing word in "Please clean the dirt from your s——s before walking inside."

In terms of the FLMP, the visual stimulus is transformed by the visual system, and letter features are evaluated. Recognition, or the interpretation of this information, depends on the integration of these features with the information possessed by the reader about the occurrences of spelling patterns in English. In Fig.

FIG. 7.2. The same visual configuration can be interpreted as two different letters, depending on the meaningful context.

7.2, although the visual information available about the last letter of the first word is the same as the first letter of the second word, the contribution of what one knows about the valid spelling patterns in English text demands that they be interpreted as different letters. (This knowledge is sometimes referred to as redundancy, because it reduces the number of valid alternatives a particular visual configuration can possess.) In reading, we would expect that this knowledge of English spelling would enable us to extract meaning from a page of text without analyzing all the visual information present or to identify words even when some of the visual information is incomplete or fuzzy.

Orthographic structure refers to the fact that a written language, such as English, follows certain rules of spelling. These regularities prohibit certain letter combinations and make some letters and combinations much more likely in certain positions of words than others. It is only natural that readers would use this information in letter and word perception. Concern for orthographic structure in reading has occurred only recently. An important question is the nature of a reader's knowledge about orthographic structure. It is possible to distinguish between two broad categories of orthographic structures: statistical redundancy and rule-governed regularity (Venezky & Massaro, 1987). The first category includes all descriptions derived solely from the frequency of letters and letter sequences in written texts. The second category includes all descriptions derived from the phonological constraints in English and scribal conventions for writing words as sequences of letters. Although these two descriptions are highly correlated in written English, it is possible to create letter strings that allow the descriptions to be orthogonally varied. Given these strings as test items, perceptual recognition tasks have been carried out to decide which general category seems to reflect the manner in which readers store and utilize knowledge of orthographic structure.

Massaro, Taylor, Venezky, Jastrzembski, and Lucas (1980) contrasted specific statistical-redundancy descriptions with specific rule-governed descriptions by comparing letter strings that varied orthogonally with respect to these descriptions. The statistical redundancy measures were summed token single-letter frequency, bigram frequency, and log bigram frequency. The rule-governed regularity measures were various sets of rules based on phonological and scribal constraints. In a typical experiment, six-letter words and anagrams of these words were used as test items. The anagrams were selected to give letter strings that represented the four combinations formed by a factorial arrangement of high or low frequency and regular or irregular orthographic structure. In a series of experiments utilizing a target-search task, subjects were asked to indicate whether or not a target letter was present in these letter strings. Both accuracy and reaction time measures indicated some psychological reality for both frequency and the regularity description of orthographic structure. The results of these studies provided evidence for the utilization of higher order knowledge in the perceptual processing of letter strings. Lexical status, orthographic regularity, and frequency appear to be important components of the higher order knowledge that is used (Massaro et al., 1980). In addition, Venezky and Massaro, in a reanalysis of the results of Waters and Siedenberg (1985), found that word frequency, spelling-to-sound correspondences, and orthographic regularity influence reaction time in naming and lexical decision performance.

Orthographic Knowledge versus Specific Words

There are two fundamentally different accounts of the word advantage. One type of explanation is that the subject can use knowledge of spelling during letter and word perception. In a typical trial, because of the brief duration of the display, there is only partial information about the letters in the display. However, the recognition process can use information about orthography to reduce the number of valid interpretations and arrive at a correct percept based on partial visual information. This information does not have to be consciously known or applied, and does not have to be perfect. That is, this information can still make a positive contribution to word recognition even if it provides only partial information. This explanation, within the context of the FLMP, states that readers have two sources of information given a word and only a single source given a nonword.

Another account of the word advantage dispenses with the idea of orthographic knowledge entirely, and explains the word advantage in terms of the contribution of the specific words in the reader's lexicon (Brooks, 1978; Glushko, 1979). The most complete model within this class is the interactive activation model (IAM). The model was designed to account for context effects in word perception and postulates three levels of units: features, letters, and words. Features activate letters that are consistent with the features and inhibit letters that are inconsistent; letters activate consistent words and inhibit inconsistent words; and most importantly, words activate consistent letters (top-down feedback). In addition, activated words inhibit other words. Interactive activation explains the word advantage over nonwords in terms of interactive activation from the word level to the letter level. The FLMP and IAM make very similar predictions and a more complex experiment is necessary to distinguish between them. We now describe an empirical test between these two accounts of the word advantage.

Context Effects and Backward Masking

It is possible to gradually transform the letter c into an e by extending the horizontal bar. To the extent the bar is long, there is good visual information for an e and poor visual information for a c. Now consider the letter presented as the first letter in the context -oin and the context -dit. Only c is orthographically admissible in the first context and only e is admissible in the second context. The context -oin favors c, whereas the context -dit favors e. The context -tsa and -ast can be considered to favor neither *e* or *c*. The first remains an inadmissible context whether *e* or *c* is present, and the second is orthographically admissible for both *e* and *c*. Four analogous contexts were used for presentations of the test letter in each of the other three positions of the four-letter string.

The experiment factorially combined six levels of visual information with these four levels of orthographic context, giving a total of 24 experimental conditions (Massaro, 1979). The bar length of the letter took on six values going from a prototypical *c* to a prototypical *e*. The test letter was presented at each of the four letter positions in each of the four contexts. The test string was presented for a short duration followed after some short interval by a masking stimulus composed of random letter features. Subjects were instructed to identify the test letter as *c* or *e* on the basis of what they saw. Figure 7.3 gives the probability of *e* judgments in the task. Both the test letter and the context influenced performance in the expected direction. Further, the effect of context was larger for the more ambiguous test letters along the stimulus continuum.

This study also evaluated context effects as a function of processing time

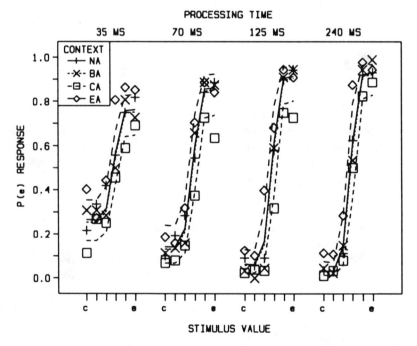

FIG. 7.3. Observed (points) and predicted (lines) probability of *e* identification as a function of the bar length of the test letter, the orthographic context, and the processing interval between the onset of the test stimulus and the onset of the masking stimulus for the dynamic FLMP model (results after Massaro, 1979; predictions from Massaro & Cohen, 1991).

controlled by the time between the test display and a backward masking stimulus. The masking stimulus was composed of nonsense letters created by selecting random feature strokes from the letters of the alphabet. Performance was more chaotic (in the sense of being more random and giving a more restricted range of response probabilities) at the short masking intervals. That is, less processing time leads to less orderly behavior—as expected from research on the time course of perceptual processing. Even for prototypical test letters, subjects did not make consistent identification judgments at short masking intervals. According to the FLMP, there was not sufficient time for feature evaluation and integration to take place before the onset of the masking stimulus.

Both the test letter and the context influenced performance at all masking intervals. The effect of test letter was attenuated at the short relative to the long processing time. That is, the identification functions covered a larger range across the $e-c$ continuum with increases in processing time. Context has a significant effect at all masking intervals. In fact, the context effect was larger for the prototypical test letters at the short than at the longer masking intervals. This result follows naturally from the trade-off between stimulus information and context in the FLMP. Context has a larger influence to the extent the stimulus information is ambiguous. We now discuss the tests of the FLMP and IAM against these results.

Tests of the FLMP and IAM

Massaro and Cohen (1991) extended the FLMP to account for the time course of perceptual processing. They assumed that feature evaluation would follow the same negatively accelerating growth function found in backward recognition masking tasks. The backward masking function can be described accurately by a negatively accelerated exponential growth function of processing time,

$$d' = \alpha(1 - e^{-\theta t}) \tag{1}$$

where d' is an index of resolution of the target. The parameter α is the asymptote of the function and θ is the rate of growth to the asymptote. The function putatively describes feature evaluation and can be conceptualized as representing a process that resolves some fixed proportion of the potential information that remains to be resolved per unit of time. The same increment in processing time results in a larger absolute improvement in performance early relative to late in the processing interval.

Early in featural evaluation, the perceiver would have some information about each feature (dimension), but the information would not be sufficient to inform the perceiver about the identity of the stimulus. Integration of the separate features (dimensions) would be continuous and would be based on the outputs of feature evaluation. Similarly, decision (and thus response selection) could occur at any time after the stimulus presentation. For example, a response could be initiated before sufficient information is accumulated—as might occur in speed accuracy experiments.

Following the theoretical analysis of backward masking, a masking stimulus would terminate any additional processing of the test stimulus. The dynamic model given by Equation 1 can be combined with the FLMP to describe how multiple sources of information are evaluated and integrated over time. The output from evaluation would be fed continuously to the integration process—which would operate as assumed in the FLMP. Integration outputs would be fed forward to the decision process, which would compute the relative goodness of match of the alternatives. In the backward masking task with unlimited response time, it seems reasonable to assume that the decision is not made until evaluation of the sources of information is near asymptote. That is, less processing time leads to less orderly behavior—as expected from research on the time course of perceptual processing.

This dynamic FLMP was tested against the results (Massaro & Cohen, 1991). Given the four masking intervals in the task, it is possible to describe performance in terms of the change in featural information and orthographic context across the four masking intervals. Eleven free parameters are required for the fit of the FLMP: the rate of growth of the functions and 10 asymptotic values for the 10 functions from the 6 levels of stimulus information and the four levels of context. The fit of the model was very good; the root mean square deviation (RMSD) between the observed and predicted points was .0501.

Massaro and Cohen (1991) also fit a variety of stochastic IAM models to the data (see McClelland, 1991). To bring the model in line with the empirical results of Massaro (1989), McClelland (1991) modified the original interactive activation model by allowing variability at the input and/or during each processing cycle and changing the decision rule from a relative goodness rule to a best one wins rule. The topology of the network tested by Massaro and Cohen (1991) is designed to account for the effects of both the target letter and the orthographic context in the Massaro (1979) study. The network assumes three layers of units: CONTEXT, TARGET, and WORD. There were two-way connections between the CONTEXT and WORD units and the TARGET and WORD units to reflect interactive activation. It was also assumed that the mask terminated further processing, as in the fit of the dynamic FLMP. This model also required 11 free parameters—10 for the inputs corresponding to the 6 levels of stimulus and 4 levels of context and 1 parameter that translates processing time in the number of processing cycles. The RMSD obtained for this model was .1135, about twice that found for the dynamic FLMP. Thus, the orthographic-knowledge account of the FLMP gives a much better description of the results than the specific-word account of interactive activation.

These results provide a dramatic falsification of the need for interactive activation in word recognition in reading. In the IAM, context modifies the representation of the target letter. As shown by the good description given by the

FLMP, however, the perceptual advantage for letters in words can be explained in terms of the word context functioning as an additional independent source of information. The IAM also falsely predicts that the influence of context must occur later during perceptual processing than the influence of stimulus information. Contrary to IAM, the FLMP accurately predicts that the influence of context does not necessarily lag behind the influence of stimulus information. These experimental results agree with our reading experience. In the IAM, slow reading means long processing times in which the context can overwhelm the stimulus information about the target letter. In contrast, we read slowly to detect spelling errors, which shows that information about the target letter can remain immune to the context. We recognize letters better in words than in nonwords simply because we recognize words better than nonwords, not because the letter is somehow modified differently in word and nonword contexts.

Word Superiority Effect (WSE)

We began this chapter with the early findings that words give an advantage to the letters that make them up. Psychologists were suspect of these results because post hoc guessing and memory are critical contributions to performance in tachistoscopic experiments, and these could be responsible for the results. In order to assess the perceptual effect, the experiments must account for both post hoc guessing and memory contributions to performance. This might be seen as an insurmountable obstacle, but some good solutions have been proposed. The most influential solution has been the Reicher–Wheeler task (Reicher, 1969; Wheeler, 1970). In this task, subjects see a short target display followed by two test alternatives for one letter position. For example, on one trial, the subject might see the target WORD. If the fourth letter position is tested, two alternatives would be presented after the display, D and K. The subject would have to choose one of these alternatives. In this task, then, the subject must make a choice only on the basis of the information processed during the visual display. Knowledge of the rules of English spelling will not help after the display because both alternatives D and K form words given the information WOR–. Of course, a different word is presented on each trial, and the subject does not know which letter position would be tested until the cue appears. Performance in this condition is compared with performance when the subject was presented with a single letter at any of the four letter positions defined by the word. For example, the subject could be presented with D alone and asked whether it was D or K. A third condition is a nonword that does not conform to the spelling rules of English: for example, OWRD or OWRK.

Performance in the task gives a word advantage over nonwords and sometimes over single letters. In Reicher's experiment, subjects picked the correct alternative 12% more often when faced with a word display than when tested with a single-letter display. The nonword display produced performance equivalent to the single-letter condition. The advantage of words over single letters and nonwords has been dubbed the Word Superiority Effect (WSE). Reicher's findings have been replicated repeatedly (e.g., Johnston & McClelland, 1973; Wheeler, 1970) and recent research has focused on the explanation of the findings.

Within the context of the FLMP, visual information and orthographic context are integrated during the perceptual processing of a letter string, and the resulting percept is influenced by both these sources of information. In the Reicher–Wheeler task, simple post hoc guessing is controlled by giving subjects two response alternatives, after the test presentation, but orthographic information can still be used during perception. As an example, suppose we are interested in comparing a word *WORD* with a test nonword *ORWD*. In both cases, the two test alternatives are *D* and *K* for the fourth position. If subjects have no visual information about the test string, they would have no advantage in the word relative to the nonword condition. However, if a curved feature from the fourth letter was derived from the visual information, then the candidates for this position might be *D, O,* or *Q*. If the first three letters *WOR* were also recognized in the test word, then orthographic context would eliminate the candidates *O* and *Q*, leaving *D* as the only perceptual alternative. Recognizing *ORW* in the nonword condition would not constrain the alternatives for the fourth position, thus making perception of any of the three alternatives equally likely. In the FLMP, the advantage of words over nonwords in the Reicher–Wheeler task results from this contextual difference. The Reicher–Wheeler control does not eliminate a possible influence of orthographic context during perception; the control only precludes a postperceptual guessing advantage for words.

In the IAM, a WSE occurs because top down connections from the word level to the letter level allow context to modify the representation at the letter level. Although the model can account for many of the existing results on the WSE, it is important to stress that interactive activation is not *necessary* to account for these results. The FLMP, for example, does so without interactive activation. In the FLMP, context operates independently of featural analyses, simply by providing an additional source of information (Massaro, 1984). We now describe a strong test of the FLMP's description of the WSE.

Backward Masking, Lateral Masking, and the WSE

Johnston and McClelland (1973) found a WSE over letters when the test display was followed by a mask, but not when no mask was presented, and offered three possible explanations. Massaro (1975) explained this effect in terms of the tradeoff between the positive contributions of orthographic context and the negative effect of lateral masking. To test this explanation, Massaro and Klitzke (1979) employed four types of display in the Reicher–Wheeler task: words, nonwords, letters, and letters flanked by dollar signs. On each trial, one of these test

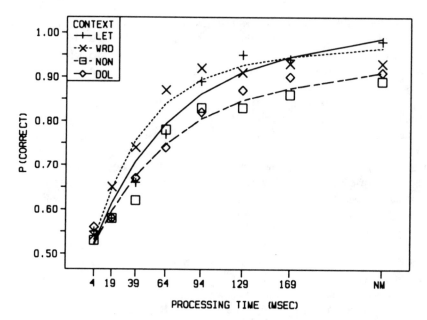

FIG. 7.4. Observed probability (points) of correct identification of the test letter as a function processing time for the letter alone (LET), word (WRD), nonword (NON), and letter-in-dollar-signs context (DOL) conditions. The lines are the predictions of the FLMP. The left-most line gives the predictions for the word context, the middle line for the letter-alone condition, and the right-most line for the nonword and letter-in-dollar-signs contexts. Note that both the observations and the predictions give a crossover between the word and letter-alone conditions (results after Massaro & Klitzke, 1979; predictions from Massaro & Cohen, 1991).

displays was presented alone or followed by a masking display after one of seven stimulus onset asynchronies (SOAs). Two choice-alternatives were presented ¼ s after the test display as in the standard Reicher–Wheeler control. The masking stimulus varied from trial to trial and was composed of nonsense letters created by selecting random feature strokes from the letters of the alphabet.

The results shown in Fig. 7.4 indicated that performance improved with increases in processing time. Performance was better for words relative to letters at short processing times, but not at long processing times. Performance for nonwords and letter-in-dollar-signs was poorer than for single letters at all processing times. Because of the lateral interference of adjacent letters on each other, the sensory information in the word, nonword, and letter-in-dollar-signs conditions must necessarily be less than the single-letter condition. Of course, the word condition still has the advantage of orthographic context, whereas the other three types of display do not. Lateral masking and orthographic context must necessarily counteract each other and only a quantitative model can be reasonably tested against the results.

The dynamic FLMP not only predicts a WSE, it predicts a subtle interaction between the WSE, backward masking, and lateral masking. In the FLMP, given a test letter alone, only a single source of information is evaluated. Given a test word, two sources of information are evaluated and integrated. Thus, the test word will tend to accumulate more information over time than the test letter, and a WSE should be observed. This instantiation of the FLMP can predict that two sources of information can lead to better performance than just one. If the visual information about the test letter is presented in a word or nonword context, an advantage for words over nonwords is predicted. This prediction is consistent with the observed results. At asymptote, the letter presented alone gave better performance than a letter presented in a word. The model also predicts a word advantage over single letters with a masking stimulus at short SOAs, but not at long SOAs and when no mask is presented.

Performance in the nonword and letter-in-dollar-signs conditions was poorer than in word and letter alone condition. Performance in the former displays suffers because of lateral masking and the lack of a benefit from orthographic context. These results were predicted using the same free parameters values that were used to describe the letter and word conditions.

The interaction of the WSE with SOA is an important result because it reflects the interaction of a contextual (cognitive) influence with two sensory influences (perceptual processing time and lateral masking). Massaro and Cohen (1991) showed that the dynamic FLMP captures the observed results in a direct and parsimonious manner by accounting for the influences at the appropriate levels of processing. The components of the FLMP reflect the contributions of lateral masking, backward masking, and orthographic context.

The research appears to support the reader's use of spelling regularities in word identification. A potentially problematical result was obtained by Johnston (1978), who found no effect of lexical constraint in test words in the Reicher–Wheeler task. Lexical constraint refers to extent three of the four letters reduces uncertainty about the fourth letter (e.g., the extent to which -hip constrains s--- versus the extent to which -ink contains s---). This result appears to question the assumption that the word context provides an additional source of information. Analogous to Paap, Newsome, McDonald, and Schvaneveldt (1982), we do not find Johnston's results troublesome. He calculated lexical constraint based on the assumption of complete knowledge of the three-letter context and no knowledge of the fourth letter. This analysis might not correlate with the actual constraints when only partial information about the test and context letters is available. Paap et al. provided evidence that the lexical constraint between Johnston's high and low constraint words does not differ when partial information is assumed to be available at each letter position. Paap et al. reanalyzed the results from the individual words in Johnston's experiment and found that lexical constraint had an effect when estimated under the assumption of partial information. In addition, we believe that sublexical constraints must also be included for a complete account of performance.

WORDS IN CONTEXT

Just as orthographic and lexical information can influence identification of letters, the identification of words can be influenced by syntactic and semantic information in the discourse context. However, the literature on context effects is conflicting; some experimenters have obtained large advantage for words in an appropriate context (e.g., Sanocki & Oden, 1984; Tulving & Gold, 1963) but others have not (e.g., Fischler & Bloom, 1979; Stanovich & West, 1983). However, these negative findings can be attributed to limitations in the methods used for measuring context effects. Often, the effects of information in a sentence context is gauged by presenting an incomplete sentence followed by a target word that completes the sentence appropriately or inappropriately. However, the occurrence of incongruous context-target relations invalidates the contextual information, with the result that subjects may use it less than otherwise (Sanocki & Oden, 1984). If only congruous context-target relations are used, advantages of an appropriate context increase, a result that obtains when word processing is measured with a lexical decision task (Sanocki & Oden, 1984) and with a naming task (Norris, 1987).

A more subtle problem with many context-effect studies is that the target word is presented in isolation and must be processed immediately. In contrast, during normal reading the processing of a word may be cascaded, beginning as parafoveal information is picked up and sometimes ending when the word's meaning is resolved, after fixation has moved beyond the word (see Sanocki et al., 1985). Therefore, it may be important to study context effects occurring when subjects can read whole sentences and phrases. In one such study, Sanocki et al. (1985, Experiment 3) compared the efficiency of processing words when either lexical, semantic, or both lexical and semantic information could be used. Subjects scanned word strings for violations, defined as either (a) a nonword within a scrambled sentence (in this case, only lexical information can be used), (b) an incongruous word in an otherwise meaningful sentence (semantic information only can be used), or (c) a nonword in a sentence (both lexical and semantic information can be used). Subjects were faster in the third condition when they could use both lexical and semantic information. More importantly, comparisons of the reaction time frequency distributions for the three conditions indicated that the advantage in this condition was greater than would be expected from a horse race in which the fastest of autonomous lexical and semantic processes was chosen (e.g., Forster, 1979). The results are consistent with the idea that lexical and semantic information were conjoined during the process, and with the general claim that two sources of information are better than one.

CONCLUSION

We have seen that visual processes are fundamental to reading letters and words. In addition, the perceptual processing of text is greatly facilitated by nonvisual information. The nonvisual information supplements the visual information and improves performance relative to the situation with just visual information. The IAM incorrectly predicts that nonvisual sources modify the representation of the visual sources rather than adding just an independent source. The results are nicely described by the FLMP, which predicts that two sources of information are more informative than just one. The FLMP is also able to account for the temporal course of perceptual processing of visual and nonvisual sources of information.

ACKNOWLEDGMENT

The research reported in this paper and the writing of the paper were supported, in part, by grants from the Public Health Service (PHS R01 NS 20314) and the National Science Foundation (BNS 8812728) to DWM.

REFERENCES

Adams, M. J. (1979). Models of word recognition. *Cognitive Psychology, 11,* 133–176.

Anderson, I. H., & Dearborn, W. F. (1952). *The psychology of teaching reading.* New York: Ronald Press.

Biederman, I. (1987). Recognition-by-components: A theory of human image understanding. *Psychological Review, 94,* 115–147.

Bouma, H. (1971). Visual recognition of isolated lower-case letters. *Vision Research, 11,* 459–474.

Brooks, L. (1978). Nonanalytic concept formation and memory for instances. In E. Rosch & B. B. Lloyd (Eds.), *Cognition and categorization* (pp. 169–211). Hillsdale, NJ: Lawrence Erlbaum Associates.

Downing, J. (1967). What's wrong with the i.t.a.? *Phi Delta Kappa, February,* 262–266.

Enns, J. T., & Rensink, R. A. (1990). Sensitivity to three-dimensional orientation in visual search. *Psychological Science, 1,* 323–326.

Enns, J. T., & Rensink, R. A. (1991). Preattentive recovery of three-dimensional orientation from line drawings. *Psychological Review, 98,* 335–351.

Fischler, I., & Bloom, P. A. (1979). Automatic and attentional processes in the effects of sentence contexts on word recognition. *Journal of Verbal Learning and Verbal Behavior, 5,* 1–20.

Forster, K. I. (1979). Levels of processing and the structure of the language processor. In W. E. Cooper & E. Walker (Eds.), *Sentence processing: Psycholinguistic studies presented to Merrill Garrett* (pp. 27–85). Hillsdale, NJ: Lawrence Erlbaum Associates.

Gervais, M. J., Harvey, L. O., & Roberts, J. O. (1984). Identification confusions among letters of the alphabet. *Journal of Experimental Psychology: Human Perception and Performance, 10,* 655–666.

Gibson, E. J. (1969). *Principles of perceptual learning and development.* New York: Appleton-Century-Crofts.

Gibson, E. J., & Levin, H. (1975). *The psychology of reading*. Cambridge, MA: MIT Press.

Gilmore, G. C. (1985). Letters are visual stimuli: A comment on the use of confusion matrices. *Perception and Psychophysics, 37,* 389–390.

Glushko, R. J. (1979) The organization and activation of orthographic knowledge in reading aloud. *Journal of Experimental Psychology: Human Perception and Performance, 5,* 674–691.

Groff, P. (1975). Research in brief: Shapes as cues to word recognition. *Visible Language, 9,* 67–71.

Huey, E. B. (1968). *The psychology and pedagogy of reading*. Cambridge, MA: MIT Press. (Original work published 1908)

Hummel, J. E., & Biederman, I. (1992). Dynamic binding in a neural network for shape recognition. *Psychological Review, 99,* 480–517.

Johnston, J. C. (1978). A test of the sophisticated guessing theory of word perception. *Cognitive Psychology, 10,* 123–153.

Johnston, J. C., & McClelland, J. L. (1973). Visual factors in word perception. *Perception & Psychophysics, 14,* 365–370.

Keren, G., & Baggen, S. (1981). Recognition models of alphanumeric characters. *Perception and Psychophysics, 29,* 234–246.

Krueger, L. E., & Chignell, M. H. (1985). Same-different judgments under high speed stress: Missing feature principle predominates in early processing. *Perception and Psychophysics, 38,* 188–193.

Lowe, D. G. (1985). *Perceptual organization and visual recognition*. Boston: Kluwer.

Lupker, S. J. (1979). On the nature of perceptual information during letter perception. *Perception and Psychophysics, 25,* 303–312.

Massaro, D. W. (1975). Primary and secondary recognition in reading. In D. W. Massaro (Ed.), *Understanding language: An information processing analysis of speech perception, reading, and psycholinguistics.* (pp. 241–289). New York: Academic Press.

Massaro, D. W. (1979). Letter information and orthographic context in word perception. *Journal of Experimental Psychology: Human Perception and Performance, 5,* 595–609.

Massaro, D. W. (1984). Building and testing models of reading processes. In P. D. Pearson (Ed.), *Handbook of reading research* (pp. 111–146). New York: Longman.

Massaro, D. W. (1987). *Speech perception by ear and eye: A paradigm for psychological inquiry.* Hillsdale, NJ: Lawrence Erlbaum Associates.

Massaro, D. W., & Cohen, M. M. (1991). Integration versus interactive activation: The joint influence of stimulus and context in perception. *Cognitive Psychology, 23,* 558–614.

Massaro, D. W., & Hary, J. M. (1986). Addressing issues in letter recognition. *Psychological Research, 48,* 123–132.

Massaro, D. W., & Klitzke, D. (1979). The role of lateral masking and orthographic structure in letter and word perception. *Acta Psychologica, 43,* 413–426.

Massaro, D. W., Taylor, G. A., Venezky, R. L., Jastrzembski, J. E., & Lucas, P.A. (1980). *Letter and word perception: Orthographic structure and visual processing in reading.* Amsterdam: North-Holland.

McClelland, J. L. (1976). Preliminary letter identification in the perception of words and nonwords. *Journal of Experimental Psychology: Human Perception and Performance, 2,* 80–91.

McClelland, J. L. (1991). Stochastic interactive processes and the effect of context on perception. *Cognitive Psychology, 23,* 1–44.

Navon, D. (1991). Testing a queue hypothesis for the processing of global and local information. *Journal of Experimental Psychology: General, 120,* 151–172.

Norris, D. (1987). Strategic control of sentence context effects in a naming task. *Quarterly Journal of Experimental Psychology, 39A,* 253–275.

Oden, G. C. (1979). A fuzzy logical model of letter identification. *Journal of Experimental Psychology: Human Perception and Performance, 5,* 336–352.

Oden, G. C., & Massaro, D. W. (1978). Integration of featural information in speech perception. *Psychological Review, 85,* 172–191.

Paap, K. R., Newsome, S. L., McDonald, J. E., & Schvaneveldt, R. W. (1982). The activation-verification model for letter and word recognition: The word-superiority effect. *Psychological Review, 89,* 573–594.

Paap, K. R., Newsome, S. L., & Noel, R. W. (1984). Word shape's in poor shape in the race to the lexicon. *Journal of Experimental Psychology: Human Perception and Performance, 10,* 413–428.

Pittman, J., & St. John, J. (1969). *Alphabets and reading.* New York: Pittman.

Price, C. J., & Humphreys, G. W. (1989). The effects óf surface detail on object categorization and naming. *Quarterly Journal of Experimental Psychology, 41A,* 797–828.

Reicher, G. M. (1969). Perceptual recognition as a function of meaningfulness of stimulus material. *Journal of Experimental Psychology, 81,* 275–281.

Sanocki, T. (1987). Visual knowledge underlying letter perception: Font-specific, schematic tuning. *Journal of Experimental Psychology: Human Perception and Performance, 13,* 267–278.

Sanocki, T. (1988). Font regularity constraints on the process of letter recognition. *Journal of Experimental Psychology: Human Perception and Performance, 14,* 472–480.

Sanocki, T. (1991a). Intra- and inter-pattern relations in letter recognition. *Journal of Experimental Psychology: Human Perception and Performance, 17,* 924–941.

Sanocki, T. (1991b). Effects of early common features on form recognition. *Perception and Psychophysics, 50,* 490–497.

Sanocki, T., Goldman, K., Walz, J., Cook, C., Epstein, W., & Oden, G. C. (1985). Interaction of stimulus and contextual information during reading: Identifying words within sentences. *Memory and Cognition, 13,* 145–157.

Sanocki, T., & Oden, G. C. (1984). Contextual validity and the effects of low-constraint sentence contexts on lexical decisions. *Quarterly Journal of Experimental Psychology, 36A,* 145–156.

Sanocki, T., & Rose V. (1989–90). Modifiable letterforms for teaching reading: The graphophonic alphabet. *Journal of Educational Technology Systems, 18,* 173–183.

Stanovich, K. E., & West, R. F. (1983). On priming by a sentence context. *Journal of Experimental Psychology: General, 112,* 1–36.

Townsend, J. T., & Ashby, F. G. (1982). Experimental test of contemporary mathematical models of visual letter recognition. *Journal of Experimental Psychology: Human Perception and Performance, 8,* 834–864.

Townsend, J. T., Hu, G. G., & Evans, R. J. (1984). Modeling feature perception in brief displays with evidence for positive interdependencies. *Perception and Psychophysics, 36,* 35–49.

Townsend, J. T., Hu, G. G., & Kadlec, H. (1988). Feature sensitivity, bias, and interdependencies as a function of energy and payoffs. *Perception and Psychophysics, 43,* 575–592.

Treisman, A., & Gormican, S. (1988). Feature analysis in early vision: Evidence from search asymmetries. *Psychological Review, 95,* 15–48.

Tulving, E., & Gold, C. (1963). Stimulus information and contextual information as determinants of tachistoscopic recognition of words. *Journal of Experimental Psychology, 66,* 319–327.

Tversky, A. (1977). Features of similarity. *Psychological Review, 84,* 327–352.

Waters, G. S., & Seidenberg, M. S. (1985). Spelling-sound effects in reading: Time-course and decision criteria. *Memory & Cognition, 13,* 557–572.

Venezky, R. L., & Massaro, D. W. (1987). Orthographic structure and spelling-sound regularity in reading English words. In D. A. Allport, D. G. MacKay, W. Prinz, & E. Scheerer (Eds.), *Language perception and production: Shared mechanisms in listening, speaking, reading and writing* (pp. 111–129). London: Academic Press.

Wheeler, D. D. (1970). Processes in word recognition. *Cognitive Psychology, 1,* 59–85.

Witkin, A. P., & Tenenbaum, J. M. (1983). On the role of structure in vision. In J. Beck, B. Hope, & A. Rosenfeld (Eds.). *Human and machine vision* (pp. 481–543). New York: Academic Press.

8 The Processing of Orthographic Information

Evelyne Corcos
Glendon College, York University

Dale M. Willows
Ontario Institute for Studies in Education

Orthographic information (OI) is found in the spelling patterns of written language and provides both readers and spellers with information regarding the probabilities of certain letter sequences and their spatial position within words. For this reason, OI is central to fast and accurate access to words from the lexicon, and, although this is likely achieved via a dual code—that is OI is encoded visually and phonemically—there is little doubt that OI is "knowledge particular to print" (Kolers, 1985). The focus of this chapter is on the visual rather than phonemic aspect of OI.

The chapter examines the literature dealing with the processing of orthographic information by adults, children, and readers of varying ability in an attempt to determine how readers acquire orthographic knowledge and how they utilize it in word recognition. The discussion attempts to identify the underlying mechanisms allowing some readers to make greater use of OI and the processes differentiating readers at different stages of reading acquisition.

This examination of OI usage includes only studies that promote the use of holistic rather than letter-by-letter processes because several researchers (e.g., Besner, Davelaar, Alcott, & Parry, 1984; Krueger, 1975, 1984) argue that tasks requiring subjects to name the stimuli (or collecting naming latencies) minimize the role of orthographic knowledge by directing attention to the letter level rather than clusters of letters. Hence, such studies (e.g., Francis, 1984; Olson, Wise, Conners, Rack, & Fulker, 1989; Rack, 1985; Rayner, 1988) are excluded from consideration.

The first section makes a case for conceptualizing OI in terms of visual and word familiarity. The next section, by examining the type and size of the perceptual unit as words increase in familiarity, strives to understand how OI may facilitate lexical access. This is followed by a discussion of the potential contribution of OI at different stages of information processing. The chapter then moves on to an analysis of the role of orthographic knowledge in early reading acquisition and a comparison of OI processing differences between good and poor readers. Finally, the closing section summarizes major research findings, points to some relevant questions concerning OI usage by elementary school children, and suggests a framework for investigating these questions.

THE NATURE
OF ORTHOGRAPHIC INFORMATION

The literature is not in agreement about the definition of orthographic information. Different definitions are implied by the term OI in various studies. Three definitions predominate—each with its own view regarding the processes involved in OI usage and each with its own method for operationalizing OI. There is sufficient evidence, however, to support a view of OI emphasizing the role of a visual code and this section attempts to make such a case.

In the literature OI has been characterized as:

1. information about the redundancy of the spatial frequency of letters in words (Mason, 1975);
2. information from the pronounceability of words (Gibson, Shurcliff, & Yonas, 1970);
3. information about the rules governing the phonemic and graphemic constraints in words (Massaro, Venezky, & Taylor, 1979).

Mason's (1975) definition highlights visual and spatial processes whereas other researchers have equated OI to an index of pronounceability that reinforces the relationship of print to spoken language (Bruder, 1978; Gibson et al., 1970). The definition of Massaro et al. (1979) introduced cognitive processes (in comparison with the more perceptual processes implied by the other two definitions) when they proposed that rules are generated as a result of the regularity present in the orthography.

Evaluating the Definitions

Spatial Frequency and Sequential Redundancy. Mason (1975) identified orthographic information as a form of redundancy that can be used to augment visual feature information. She initially isolated four possible sources of information in word recognition:

(a) direct visual information about the distinctive features of individual letters within a word;

(b) direct visual information about the spatial position of letters in a letter string;

(c) spatial frequency redundancy or the correlation of the two types of information cited in (a) and (b);

(d) sequential redundancy which is not perceptual in nature but is rather accessed from long term memory. It includes memory of the sequential dependencies between letters: valid spelling patterns and letter sequences. (p. 148)

According to Mason (1975), two of these different sources of information are central to orthographic information: spatial frequency, how often any one letter occurs in a particular position; and sequential redundancy, the successive order of letters within a string. The work of Healy (1974) in the information-processing literature parallel's Mason's conceptualization of OI. Healy focused on the processing of item information (information about letters) and order information (information about letter sequences) in multiletter strings rather than words. Healy's item information, therefore, is synonymous with Mason's idea that visual information is contained at the letter level and, order information (Healy, 1982) encompasses both the spatial frequency and sequential redundancy identified as OI by Mason.

Healy (1982) demonstrated that subjects required to remember letter sequences or the spatial location of certain letters were affected differently by an interpolated task. For example, subjects made a high proportion of phonemic confusion errors only when remembering letter sequences (Healy, 1982) and a significant number of visual confusions while retaining spatial information (Healy, 1978). This evidence implies that spatial frequency information may be tapping visual processes while sequential information draws on a phonemic component. Mason (1975) argued, however, that these two sources of information are difficult to isolate, presumably because they interact. None the less, both spatial frequency and sequential frequency are central to Mason's definition of orthographic structure and therefore visual processes may play an important role in the utilization of OI.

Pronounceability. Another conceptualization of OI is based on the degree of pronounceability contained in a word. Gibson et al. (1970) demonstrated that there was an observable speed advantage in identifying pronounceable versus unpronounceable pseudowords. Many experimenters support this view of OI each time they create their stimulus sets by taking words (e.g., BARE), generating anagrams (e.g., AREB, REAB, EABR) and then assigning each to a pseudoword (e.g., AREB, REAB) or nonword (e.g., EABR) category on the basis of pronounceability (Taylor, Miller, & Juola, 1977).

When Gibson et al. (1970) subjected letter strings, varying in their level of pronounceability, to frequency counts based on sequential dependencies, the kind drawn from Underwood and Schultz (1960), sequential redundancy was not correlated with pronounceability. This is unexpected because the findings of Healy (1982) would predict a positive correlation between sequential redundancy and pronounceability. Instead, Gibson et al. (1970) found that frequency ratings correlating most highly with pronounceability (.63) utilized "bigram" (two-letter) counts based on spatial position and word length: those available in tables produced by Mayzner and Tresselt (1965). Mason (1975) argued that pronounceability ratings in general actually reflect spatial frequency redundancy because the highest summed spatial bigram counts yield pronounceable letter strings. On the basis of this evidence, then, it can be concluded that the facilitating factor in the use of OI involves spatial redundancy rather than pronounceability (Krueger, 1975).

Rule-governed Regularity.   Massaro et al. (1979) proposed a rule-governed definition of OI based on their view that reading experience allows readers to extrapolate general rules based on the phonological and graphemic constraints of an orthography. These rules, in turn, can be applied to the decoding of new letter strings, perhaps by "analogy" (Goswami, 1990).

Massaro et al. (1979) compared their rule-governed definition to a frequency-governed definition, like the one proposed by Mason (1975). To evaluate the two definitions, Massaro et al. selected letter strings with high and low summed positional frequencies and letter strings that conformed to or violated rule-governed regularity. College students and sixth-grade readers were given a visual-search task. They were asked to look for letters embedded in four types of pseudowords containing letter sequences of high or low positional frequency and those conforming to or violating rule-governed regularity. Results indicated that both sets of stimuli (based on frequency and rule-governed regularity) affected reader performance in a similar manner. The authors explained this finding by noting that letter strings of high summed positional frequencies can also contain rule-governing information.

The frequency- and rule-governed definitions imply different processes when explaining how a reader learns to utilize OI to obtain the speed and accuracy advantages associated with its application. In the case of the frequency defini-tion, it follows that the reader requires repeated exposure to a particular letter string in order to acquire and utilize the OI contained in that string. Therefore each individual word is expected to acquire higher levels of OI as a function of repeated exposures. In contrast, a rule-governed definition focuses on the read-er's ability to extrapolate rules regarding phonemic and graphemic constraints as a result of repeated exposure to a variety of words. In this case, it is predicted that once readers isolate a particular rule, they can apply the rule to a new set of words whose structure conforms to the rule, and consequently obtain the OI speed and accuracy advantages. The findings of Samuels, Miller, and Eisenberg (1979) do not support this latter position. In their research, they presented words in a mirror-image orthography to a sample of college students. Subjects were shown a set of words presented only once and a set of words where each word was repeated four times. The latency for words displayed only once did not decrease across blocks and improvements in latency and accuracy were observed for those words displayed several times. The repeated exposure of certain items in one set had no effect on the words only seen once. This finding appears to support a frequency- rather than a rule-governed definition of OI although one could argue that four exposures to a target-word is insufficient to generate a rule.

More recently, the findings of Lovett, Ransby, and Barron (1988) further support a frequency definition of OI. In their study, Lovett et al. provided reading remediation to groups of reading-disabled students. In one of their conditions, instruction in recognizing regular words and exception words was provided to their subjects. The recognition of regular words was taught by presenting word families (*cat, mat, rat,* etc.) and the training of exception words was accomplished through repeated practice of individual words. In evaluating the final performance of their subjects, Lovett et al. discovered that exception words were acquired more easily than the regular words (those words containing the most regularity). Each exception word was presented to subjects and was practiced to a level of automaticity and regular words were only presented within the context of word families. Individual words in each set (regular and exception) did not receive equal amounts of exposure and the words receiving the most exposure (exception words) were remembered faster and more accurately although the regular words contained "rule-governed regularity."

None of the three definitions of orthographic information is entirely unique. The frequency (Mason, 1975), the rule-governed (Massaro et al., 1979), and the pronounceability (Gibson et al., 1970) factors in each definition have been used to construct stimuli in experiments exploring OI effects. Although none of the three definitions offers a method of constructing a set of stimuli that totally excludes the other two, it is apparent that Mason's (1975) spatial and sequential frequency factor can subsume the other two definitions and accommodate a visual familiarity effect because the number of times a letter-sequence is seen is the basis of a frequency definition.

There is additional evidence to support the argument that a visual component plays an important role in the processing of OI. Words are recognized more quickly and more accurately than pseudowords or nonwords. The speed and accuracy advantage typical of this word superiority effect (WSE) has been investigated in terms of visual familiarity, orthographic regularity, and word familiarity.

Visual Familiarity

To assess the effect of visual familiarity (the familiarity of the visual configuration of letter strings) in adult skilled reading, experimenters typically manipulate the visual configuration of words by mixing the case of the letters within words with the intention of disrupting the WSE. Pollatsek, Well, and Schindler (1975) demonstrated that the size of the familiarity effect (interfering with the WSE) was as large when differences involved a case change (e.g., LEAF-LEaF) or a letter change (e.g., SOWN-SEWN). These results were interpreted as evidence that subjects made visual rather than verbal comparisons. In addition, response times (RT) for different responses (in a same/different task) were unaffected when homophones (SOWN-SEWN) and nonhomophones (SOWN-SEEN) were compared. Krueger (1975) suggested that if name matches are being made, then responses to homophone items should be slower and, therefore, this RT data also supports a visual rather than a phonemic hypothesis.

Bruder (1978) examined the nature of the WSE to determine whether visual familiarity (case alteration) produces differences in RT when words and nonwords of varying length and orthographic structure are compared. She hypothesized that obtaining an interaction between visual familiarity and stimulus length would indicate that both factors were influencing the same stage of processing. More importantly, it would imply that visual familiarity determines the size of the unit of analysis.

Bruder (1978) conducted two experiments with adult subjects who were shown words and nonwords. Words were obtained from Thorndike and Lorge (1944) tables (frequency counts). Nonwords were constructed by generating unpronounceable anagrams of words equivalent to the set of words. Words and nonwords of three, four, five, and six letters were used. Half of the stimuli were presented in the same case and the rest were shown in a mixed case. Four different case-mixing patterns were used in order to vary levels of familiarity (with words presented in the same case representing the most visually familiar condition). A pair of letter strings, one above the other, was shown to subjects who were required to judge whether the letter strings were the same or different (i.e., ignoring the case of the stimuli). On the different trials, stimuli were varied by one letter. Median RTs were recorded and same and different latencies were analyzed separately.

In both experiments, performance with words was superior to performance with nonwords, case alternation was disruptive, and the length of the stimulus was found to be a significant factor. The RT for words presented in the same case (the highest level of visual familiarity) was faster than the other three case conditions, especially for the longer stimuli, and RT was less affected by stimulus length. Analyses of RTs on different trials indicated that RTs for words were significantly faster and that case mixing had a disruptive effect. Visual familiarity was found to be a significant factor and Bruder (1978) concluded that the word superiority effect (for same judgments) in Experiment 2 was a result of the familiarity of the visual characteristics of words. She then undertook a third experiment to determine whether the effects of word familiarity and orthographic regularity depended on the visual familiarity of the stimuli.

Word Familiarity and Orthographic Regularity

Word familiarity refers to the relative frequency of words used in written language. This differs slightly from the notion of visual familiarity which considers the familiarity of the visual configuration of letter strings rather than words. Some words, however, are encountered more often than others and, on the basis of a frequency definition of OI, these words are expected to be more familiar. Bruder (1978) defined orthographic regularity in terms of pronounceability and consequently constructed pseudowords of varying orthographic regularity by generating anagrams from words.

In Bruder's third experiment, words of high and low frequency represented different levels of word familiarity, and nonwords were constructed with high and low levels of orthographic structure. The high orthographic structure nonwords were constructed by replacing a single letter in words. The low items were unpronounceable anagrams of these words. Case changes were performed on the items. The results showed that words were processed faster when all the letters were in the same case. Case alternation was more disruptive in the processing of pseudowords of high and low orthographic structure than high and low frequency words although low frequency words were processed as quickly as high orthographically regular nonwords. In words varying in frequency, a greater effect was evident on high frequency words although the effect was also significant for low frequency words. This suggests that visual familiarity is a factor in the processing of pseudowords containing different levels of orthographic structure and also in words of high and low frequency. Visual familiarity also played a role in the processing of strings of increasing length. Bruder (1978) concluded that both word familiarity and orthographic regularity are dependent on visual familiarity. She explained that the facilitation in processing words and pseudowords may be related to the visual familiarity of letter clusters of various sizes.

Summary Regarding the Nature of OI

Visual familiarity (i.e., the degree of familiarity of the visual configuration of letter strings) is a significant factor in the word superiority effect (Bruder, 1978; Krueger, 1975; Pollatsek et al., 1975), in words of high frequency, and words that are orthographically regular and the processing of longer words (Bruder, 1978). This lends support to Mason's (1975) spatial frequency definition because it implies a strong visual factor in the nature of OI. The acquisition of orthographic knowledge may rely on a visual mechanism that processes information about the spatial and positional frequencies of letters by means of repeated exposure to words. This interpretation, however, does not preclude the observation that words and letter strings of varying orthographic structure also contain various levels of pronounceability or rule-governed regularity. It merely argues that the nature of orthographic information has a visual component regardless of the manner in which letter strings have been designed to resemble words.

The fact that nonwords are less pronounceable than words may be the result of disrupting the expected spatial and sequential location of letters. Words are pronounceable because letters (consonants and vowels) are sequenced and arranged to simulate the spoken word. Although sound to symbol relationships are a requisite to reading words, the movement away from letter-by-letter processing to the fluent reading of words in isolation is attributed to the usage of OI in word recognition (Taylor et al., 1977). Evidence from deaf readers (Hanson, 1986) confirms that OI can be utilized without recourse to phonology. Further support is provided by Venezky and Massaro (1987) who stated that "utilization of orthographic structure in perceptual recognition is assumed to occur independently of how the printed pattern is translated to sound" (p. 163).

It is more difficult to argue against a rule-governed conceptualization of OI because it does not contradict the contribution of a visual mechanism. Goswami (1990) presumably investigated rule-governed processes when the reading by analogy performance of 6- and 7-year-olds was assessed on a task presenting words of similar orthographic structure (*most-cost*), words of similar phonological/orthographic structure (*most-post*) and words of similar phonology only (*most-toast*). A strong orthographic effect was obtained with no effect of phonological similarity when subjects read words and identified words embedded in prose passages. This again supports the role of visual mechanisms in reading by analogy, a task encouraging a rule-governed strategy in word recognition.

A rule-governed hypothesis would imply that rules are generated on the basis of incoming information; rules that can be utilized in the processing of new words (words of low visual familiarity). This more conceptual (rather than perceptual) view of the OI mechanism generates the prediction that practice or exposure to a set of words should have transferability to nonpracticed words. That is, the OI information (the rules) acquired from a previously practiced set of words can benefit the reading of new or unfamiliar words. Samuels et al. (1979) found practice effects in adult subjects to be specific to words that were repeated with no transfer to the other "new" items in their stimulus set. Although Lovett et al. (1988) tested this notion indirectly with children and failed to find support for the rule-governed position, the possibility of transfer effects, an implicit assumption in the rule-governed definition, warrants direct examination with readers varying in age and reading ability.

HOW OI FACILITATES LEXICAL ACCESS

There is no dispute that the utilization of OI facilitates lexical access. Words are recognized faster than pseudowords and nonwords; high frequency words demonstrate a speed advantage over low frequency words. It is not clear, however, how OI facilitates this lexical access. It is possible that the visual familiarity associated with OI usage facilitates the processing of words by increasing the size of the unit of perception (Bruder, 1978). A word previously processed letter-by-letter would be processed in larger units when OI is applied. With this idea in mind, Taylor et al. (1977) attempted to determine whether readers attend to whole-word units, syllables, spelling patterns, or individual letters in order to speed up word recognition, and their findings identified spelling patterns as the functional units of analysis. Issues relating to whether the size of the perceptual unit contributes to the speed of word recognition are discussed in the next section. For example, is the same unit of perception used to process words, pseudowords, and nonwords? How does the size of the unit of perception develop?

The Unit of Perception

Taylor et al. (1977) attempted to isolate visual units involved in the perception of words and nonwords by using case alternation at different boundaries within words and nonwords to observe the resulting disruptions (longer latencies). These boundaries were selected to determine whether syllables and spelling patterns were the potential perceptual units in word recognition. Two experiments were conducted, each requiring subjects to make same/different judgments. Taylor et al. chose 48 common six-letter words from Kucera and Francis (1967). Twelve contained one syllable and the remaining words contained two syllables that differed in the location of their syllable boundary. Twelve words contained a boundary between the second and third letters, 12 words between the third and fourth letters, 12 words between the fourth and fifth letters. Another set of 48 words were similarly chosen to be used in the different trials. In addition, six case alternation conditions included:

1. intact, all letters were in upper- or lowercase (RIGHTS), (rights);
2. alternate, a case transition between every pair of letters (RiGhTs);
3. one case transition after the second letter (RIghts);
4. one case transition after the third letter (RIGhts);
5. one case transition after the fourth letter (RIGHts);
6. a case transition after every pair of letters (RIghTS).

Twelve undergraduate students were given 180 trials of the task. After viewing a fixation point for 200 ms, subjects were shown a target word whose case was always intact, for 500 ms. A masking field followed for 800 ms and then another word was displayed for 300 ms. When the second word belonged to the intact case condition, it was never shown in the same case as the target word. Latency data were collected. Results indicated that one-syllable words were judged faster than two-syllable words and that words presented in the intact case condition were faster than those containing one or two case transitions. Words containing one or two case transitions were processed faster than words presented in the alternate case transition. Case alternation did not interact with syllable structure. The authors concluded that their data identified two types of perceptual units: whole words and spelling patterns.

A second experiment compared the effects of case alternation on words and pseudowords because whole-word perceptual units cannot be applied to pseudowords. In addition, the authors were interested in seeing if different strategies are used to process words and pseudowords. The same word stimulus set as Experiment 1 was used. Pseudowords were constructed by changing a letter in the one-syllable words (*rights-bights*), and re-pairing the syllables of the two-syllable words. Four case alternation conditions were used: zero, one, two, and three case transitions. To determine strategy differences, three groups of undergraduate students, eight in each group, were given different proportions of filler trials to encourage word or pseudoword strategies if they existed. In this experiment, the stimulus exposure duration of target items was increased to 3 s. After an 800 ms masking field, the second item was presented for 1 s or until the subject responded. The data indicated a linear increase in reaction time with the number of case transitions for both words and pseudowords and the word superiority effect was found to be the same for all conditions. These findings were thought to demonstrate that spelling patterns were effective visual units for both words and pseudowords and both types of stimuli were processed in a similar fashion.

A third experiment included nonword stimuli to test whether nonwords were processed letter-by-letter (i.e., unaffected by case mixture). Taylor et al. (1977) used a simultaneous-matching task to minimize potential memory demands existing between words, pseudowords, and nonwords. The target and test items were presented simultaneously and subjects were immediately required to judge the two items as same or different. Three case alternation manipulations were made on the stimulus set: zero, two, and four case transitions. The results of the RT data indicated that words are judged faster than pseudowords, which in turn are judged faster than nonwords. A comparison of words and pseudowords to test the whole-word hypothesis indicated that the WSE was greater in the same case condition in comparison to the mixed case condition. Taylor et al. concluded that spelling patterns were the functional perceptual units in word recognition although the possibility that whole-word units are utilized in certain contexts could not be dismissed.

The finding that words are recognized faster and more accurately than pseudowords and nonwords suggests that groups of letters are processed simultaneously (i.e., larger units of perception) and perhaps knowledge of highly probable letter sequences in a written language enhances this perception. However, it is not evident which factors contribute to an increase in the unit of perception because the studies by both Taylor et al. (1977) and Bruder (1978) used adult subjects with an established lexicon.

Increasing the Unit of Perception

If OI usage effects are a consequence of processing larger units, can this process be shown experimentally? Is it possible to demonstrate a movement from component to holistic analysis? In investigating this issue, researchers have focused on the progress of adult subjects in learning a novel orthography (Kolers, 1975; Samuels et al., 1979) or have examined the development of word recognition in children of different ages (Samuels, Bremer, & LaBerge, 1978).

Adult Findings.   Samuels et al. (1979) investigated the size of the perceptual unit in relation to factors such as degree of reading fluency and word familiarity by testing the effect of practice on the size of the perceptual unit. To determine an increase in the size of the unit being processed, that is, the shift from letter-by-letter to larger letter groupings, they noted the effect of word length on reaction time. Component processing would be indicated by longer latencies as a function of word length, whereas more holistic processing would be inferred if word length had no significant effect on reaction time.

Thirty college students were asked to indicate whether a target word was a member of an animal or nonanimal category.[1] The target words were printed in a mirror image orthography that represented a visually unfamiliar configuration of the words. Some words were repeated during the experimental sequence and others were not. It was expected that the repeated words would gain visual familiarity. Word length was varied to include words of three, four, five, and six letters. The words were displayed on a CRT screen following the presentation of a fixation dot. Subjects were given feedback for error responses. Latencies were also collected.

Latency decreased across blocks but faster responses were obtained for the repeated words. Latency was generally found to increase across word length although the authors observed a tendency for responses to the set of repeated words to decrease in latency as word length increased and their error rate dropped from 12.4% to 2.1% across blocks. Samuels et al. (1979) concluded that skilled readers use a letter-by-letter strategy to process orthographically unfamiliar words and a more holistic process is used with familiar words. They found this effect to be specific to words that were repeated with no improvement in responses across the set of words only seen once.

Gernsbacher (1984) also supported the view that a subject's personal experience with a set of words (how often a particular set of words is seen) is crucial to

---

[1]In a previous investigation, this task had yielded no word length by reaction time interaction and therefore the investigators assumed that subjects were using holistic processing.

speed and accuracy advantages. Six studies conducted with adult subjects demonstrated that only experiential familiarity affected word recognition latencies.

Cross-sectional Findings.   Samuels et al. (1978) compared the performance of children in grades 2, 4, 6 and college students with the intention of investigating developmental changes in component versus whole-word processing across grade levels. Eighty subjects were given the same task reported by Samuels et al. (1979) with the exception that words were presented in standard orthography. Their results indicated significant effects of grade, word length, and a grade by word length interaction. An error analysis demonstrated no tradeoff between speed and accuracy.

Samuels et al. (1978) considered the slope information contained in their RT by word length data as being most descriptive of the word processing of their subjects because the absolute RT differences between groups are confounded by developmental factors. The steepest slope obtained by the second-graders was believed to indicate letter-by-letter processing because RT increased as word length increased. The flatter slopes typical of the sixth-graders and college students implied more holistic processing as RT was unaffected by word length. The fourth-grade curve suggested an intermediary stage explained in one of two ways: (a) a gradual increase in the size of the unit, or (b) a mixing of letter-by-letter and holistic strategies. Samuels et al.'s (1978) data did not differentiate between these two possibilities but Taylor et al. (1977) provided some support for strategy switching. This possibility is also strengthened if the role played by personal word familiarity (Gernsbacher, 1984) is considered. Subjects may use a component strategy for words that are least familiar and holistic strategies for words that are most familiar.

Unfortunately, Samuels et al.'s (1978) study did not examine the movement from letter-by-letter to holistic strategies by children of different ages. By comparing their performance on items seen once versus those seen several times, a central issue in the Samuels et al. (1979) study, the authors would have provided experimental evidence of processing differences. Instead, the effect of repeated exposure to a set of words was not tested and their findings are correlational.

STAGES OF PROCESSING

How does each stage of information processing accommodate the use of OI? This is another relevant issue relating to how OI usage facilitates lexical access. In his review of the visual familiarity literature, Krueger (1975) suggested that visual familiarity could affect several stages of processing. OI could facilitate lexical access at the prelexical stage of extraction, or the postlexical stages of interpretation, memory storage, or at the response level. The converging evidence, according to Krueger (1975), supports the use of OI in the extraction of visual features. Samuels et al. (1978) also believed that their flat curves representing whole-word processing, can be explained as long as it is assumed that information about item and position reaches the word code before individual letter codes complete their process. This view places the contribution of OI at the initial extraction stage.

Krueger (1975) also considered effects at the interpretation and storage stages, and different familiarity effects based on different processes or sets of processes, rather than a single effect at a single stage. Visual familiarity according to Krueger (1975) may:

1. aid in the extraction of visual features as Samuels et al. (1978) postulated.

2. facilitate at the interpretation level. Morton's logogen model predicted that the WSE does not result because more features are extracted but because less evidence is required to respond with the name of a high frequency word.

3. act at the storage level. The information that is extracted and interpreted is stored for brief periods before it is reported. The processing of nonwords may not survive storage.

4. affect the output level. Nonwords may be lost in the output by the interference produced by reporting letters one-by-one rather than by single units.

Corcos and Willows (1989) examined the effect of visual memory factors in the processing of OI by children in grades 2, 4, and 6. Memory load was increased by requiring subjects to retain each test item in memory for 1 s or 5 s before responding. No differences in accuracy of performance were obtained when subjects processed words containing high levels of OI at either response-delay, although letter-strings containing lower levels of OI were processed more accurately at the shorter response delay. This raises the possibility that unfamiliar words may not survive storage.

A recent line of inquiry relates to the potential benefit of OI usage at the interpretation level. The work of Logan (1985, 1988) points to the probability that the speed and accuracy benefits derived from OI usage are the result of a processing shift—from the bottom-up processing of a word that is time consuming and open to making errors to the direct retrieval of a word from the lexicon. Mason (1975) also proposed that sequential redundancy was directly accessed from long-term memory. This idea is further supported by Stanovich's (1990) application of the concept of modularity to the reading process. In essence, as a reader is continually exposed to a word, a modular representation of the word containing all the bottom-up mechanisms needed specifically to process that word is constructed. At the point when the word is to be processed, the module is retrieved rather than engaging in global processes. This new conceptualization circumvents an attentional explanation (Logan, 1988) of the benefits associated with OI usage and warrants further exploration of the mechanisms contributing to the construction of lexical "modules" and the role of word retrieval speed (Decker, 1989).

The evidence provided by Taylor et al. (1977) suggests that the unit of perception in word recognition is likely to be a spelling pattern rather than a syllable or word (although words may be unitized in special cases). This idea is further supported by the work of Olson, Wise, Conners, and Rack (1990), who measured the timed word recognition performance of reading-disabled subjects in grades 3 to 6. Stories and targeted words were displayed on a computer. Subjects were read these stories for 30 min a day and also saw target words presented as whole words, or words in syllable units, or spelling patterns with corresponding speech segments. Gains in both speed of word recognition and phonological measures were obtained for the group receiving the spelling pattern feedback. These findings reinforce the visual nature of OI because spelling patterns are particular to print. Furthermore, it dispels the prominence of a pronounceability definition of OI because syllables are not implicated as units in either studies.

The process by which readers learn to use OI and hence shift from letter-by-letter to more holistic processes is likely to involve repeated exposure to words (Samuels et al., 1979) to increase their visual familiarity. What remains unexplained is the relevance and the nature of a reader's personal lexicon in the processing of OI. The personal lexicon is presumed to contain the words to which a reader has been exposed. Gernsbacher (1984) suggested that the inconsistent findings in the OI literature may be the result of a confounded "experiential" familiarity factor. The amount of exposure of any individual word, then, reflects its level of visual familiarity, the method by which it can be processed (component versus holistic), and consequently, how quickly it can be recognized. This view argues against a rule-governed definition of OI and it restricts the level of familiarity of words in the reader's personal lexicon to the number of times a particular word has been encountered by the reader.

The next section summarizes the literature dealing with the role of OI in early reading acquisition. Issues of interest include when early readers begin to use OI in word recognition and whether OI usage is associated with reading ability.

ORTHOGRAPHIC KNOWLEDGE
IN EARLY READING ACQUISITION

To understand the role played by OI in the course of reading acquisition, it is important to determine when and how OI is utilized by the young reader. Readers, as early as the first grade, show sensitivity to OI, which increases rapidly to the third grade and develops further, possibly to the sixth grade. This increase in sensitivity to OI also appears to correlate with reading ability rather than other experiential factors relating to school.

Developmental Factors

Niles and Taylor (1978) undertook a longitudinal and cross-sectional study to determine the age or grade at which early readers develop sensitivity to orthographic structure. They examined the performance of first-, second-, and third-grade children on a lexical-decision task that presented eight letter strings of zero-, second-, and fourth-order approximations of English (the higher the approximation, the more like English). The students were required to make two judgments: first, which of the three letter strings looked most like a word; then, which of the remaining two strings looked more like a word. All children were administered a reading comprehension test and were tested on the experimental task three times: in the fall (Fall 1), in the spring (Spring), and the fall (Fall 2) of the following year.

A comparison of the performance means indicated a developmental trend between grade and time of testing within each grade. Formal analysis by the authors, however, indicated that only the first-grade children differed across all three testing sessions. Second-grade performance differed between Fall 1 and Spring and it is questionable whether the performance of third-grade children differed because these results were not reported. The authors also reported obtaining performance estimates from a group of adults on the same experimental task. Unfortunately, there were no comments comparing second- and third-grade performance to the adult data. This information would have been valuable in indicating whether the task was too easy or whether orthographic sensitivity involves simple processes that play a role only in the initial stage of reading acquisition, and have little impact in later stages.

In any case, Niles and Taylor (1978) concluded that orthographic sensitivity developed quickly in the first grade as children begin to read and then slowed down by the end of the third grade. This suggests that OI is fully available to readers at the end of the third grade. However, it is not clear which factors account for performance on this measure of OI sensitivity (lexical decision).

Orthographic sensitivity may develop in the manner described by Niles and Taylor (1978) because young readers receive increased exposure to reading material over the course of the first 3 years of reading acquisition. Allington (1978) attempted to examine the contribution of reading ability rather than mere experience by including a reading-match control group in his study.

Allington (1978) compared the performance of good and poor readers from grades 2 and 4 who were asked to determine whether zero-order and fourth-order approximations to English resembled words. Four groups of children (number of subjects was not provided) were matched on the basis of reading ability to yield good and poor reader groups in grades 2 and 4. All subjects were required to circle on a page, the letter string that looked more like a word. Only accuracy measures were recorded. An analysis of covariance indicated that means and standard deviations were similar for the grade 2 good readers and the grade 4 poor readers, thus allowing Allington to conclude that reading ability is the primary source of sensitivity to orthographic structure. Stanovich and West (1989), however, linked the processing of OI to exposure to print in adult subjects, finding that individual differences in reading and spelling are related to OI processing skills. The level of reading proficiency, then, may determine the role played by exposure to print.

Leslie and Shannon (1981) explored more fully the relationship of orthographic sensitivity to reading ability by constructing three tasks to examine how the development of orthographic knowledge is related to age, letter recognition, and word recognition.

Two kinds of redundancy facilitating the reading of text were identified: Interword redundancy allowing readers to recognize a word faster and more accurately when it is embedded in a sentence; and intraword redundancy, or orthographic structure, defined as the sequential probability of letters. Knowledge of OI was expected to affect word recognition at the feature analysis level (extraction) by reducing the number of features required to identify subsequent letters, and hence speed up word recognition. This study is particularly important because preschool and kindergarten children who have yet to receive formal reading instruction were included in the sample. OI was investigated at both the letter and word levels.

One hundred and forty-five children: 22 preschoolers, 36 from kindergarten, 44 from first grade, and 43 from second grade participated in the study and were tested twice, once in May and again in November. Two testing sessions were scheduled because this study was mainly correlational. All the elementary school children in the sample had been exposed exclusively to the Ginn 720 reading series and therefore, the authors designed a test of lowercase letter naming, and a word recognition test on the basis of words present at each level of this reading series. This manipulation insured to some degree that subjects had previous experience with the word set.

Three experimental tasks were constructed and required subjects to look at a pair of stimuli and point to the one that looked most like a word. The first task presented consonant trigrams (e.g., GSP) and trigrams containing a numeral in the medial position (e.g., G8P). The second task required that subjects differentiate three-letter consonant strings whose sequence is not found in English (e.g., RSD) from three-letter strings with the CVC (consonant-vowel-consonant) structure (e.g., WOC). The third task presented letter strings of four to six letters containing consonant clusters that either occur (e.g., grisp) or do not occur (e.g., tsacl) in English. Rule-governed regularity was applied to the construction of the stimuli.

Results of task 1 (e.g., GSP/G8P) indicated significant improvement in accuracy made by the first- and second-grade children at the second test sessions but no improvement made by the preschoolers and kindergarten children. The greatest gains were made by the children at the beginning of grade 2. Results of task 2 (e.g., RSD/WOC) and 3 (e.g., grisp/tsacl) produced significant main effects of group and time of administration. Task 3 also yielded a significant grade-by-time of testing interaction. Again, the source of improvement was a result of the performance of the grade 1 and 2 children.

Lowercase letter recognition correlated (.66) with task 1 performance. Word recognition was found to be the best single predictor of task 2 (.70) and task 3 (.80) performance. These correlations between reading achievement and orthographic knowledge were higher than those obtained by Niles and Taylor (1978) and Ryan, Miller, and Witt (1984). This is not a surprising outcome if one considers that Leslie and Shannon (1981) designed their own word recognition test, which utilized words from the children's own reading series instead of a comprehension subtest (Niles & Taylor, 1978) or a word recognition achievement test (WRAT) (Ryan et al., 1984).

Leslie and Shannon's (1981) results supported the findings of Allington (1978) by showing that orthographic knowledge is directly related to reading ability, because effects were found in grade 1 and 2 children who received formal reading instruction but not in kindergarten children. OI was also believed to contribute mostly at the word recognition level by aiding the process of extracting visual features.

Corcos and Willows (1993) collected a large battery of standardized measures of visual processing and memory, linguistic processing and memory, and reading and spelling achievement to determine which of these processes explained the performance of grade 2, 4, and 6 subjects on an orthographic task. On the basis of multiple regression analysis, the research demonstrated that the variance on the orthographic task was explained by different processes at each grade level. Visual processes explained a relatively large proportion of the variance associated with the processing of orthographic information by grade 2 and 4 readers and speed of retrieval related to grade 6 performance. Level of reading ability made some contribution to grade 4 performance on an easy task but mainly explained grade 6 performance. It would appear that reading ability has more direct relevance in explaining the OI usage of more proficient readers but individual cognitive measures, including visual processes, are more closely associated with OI usage in the less proficient reader.

OI and Word Recognition

The possibility that OI usage continues to develop past initial stages of reading acquisition suggests a process more directly associated with the lexicon. This is implied by the continuing development of OI usage as reading ability increases. Juola, Schadler, Chabot, and McCaughey (1978) and Stanovich, West, and Pollak (1978), however, found grade 2 and 3 readers able to match the performance of college students.

Juola et al. (1978) utilized a letter visual-search task with subjects in kindergarten, grade 2, grade 4, and college. They were asked to determine whether a target letter was present in words, pseudowords (pronounceable anagrams of the words), and nonwords (unpronounceable anagrams) of three, four, and five letters. The pattern of performance of the grade 2, 4, and college students was so similar that the authors concluded that all three groups processed letter strings in the same manner. Kindergarten children, however, were perceived as using different strategies and being insensitive to orthographic structure. Juola et al. (1978) believed that the WSE develops in children by the middle of grade 2 supporting earlier claims on the basis of lexical decision tasks. But, this would imply the acquisition of a general mechanism rather than one directly related to the lexicon.

The findings of this study can be challenged on several grounds. First, Stanovich et al. (1978) criticized studies making use of letter-search visual tasks, like the one used by Juola et al. (1978) because such tasks do not deal with the "unit of perception" or consider the effect of the unit (letter, word) being searched on the results. In addition, the visual search of a single letter does not have ecological validity because, presumably, it does not resemble an activity operative in the reading process (Rayner & Pollatsek, 1989).

Stanovich et al. (1978) conducted three experiments examining different age groups and they too found no indication that OI usage increases with age and reading ability. Normal readers from the third and sixth grades and adults were asked to search for a target word embedded in lists containing words, pseudowords, and nonwords. The words consisted of five-letter words of high frequency drawn from Kucera and Francis (1967). The pseudowords were created by making nonword anagrams of the words so that their summed bigram frequency on the basis of Mayzner and Tresselt (1965) tables was high. The nonwords were anagrams of low summed bigram frequency. In addition, 90% of the pseudowords and less than 25% of nonwords were pronounceable units. Subjects were given search sheets, each containing four columns of 20 five-letter stimuli and asked to put a line through the target item when it was found. Accuracy and latency measures were collected. Subjects were asked to search for the word "table" embedded in three different fields: words, pseudowords, and nonwords. The results indicated that the structure of the field did not effect the search time (RT) of any of the age groups.

A second experiment asked subjects to search for members of the category clothes ("shoes," "dress," "glove," "shirt," "pants") and again no group differences were found. Finally, a third study required subjects to search for three predesignated words to make the word search independent of semantic processes. It was expected that searching for the presence of three words, rather than one (Experiment 1) would insure that the search would not be limited to the use of global feature and initial letter information. Subjects were asked to identify instances of "house," "world," and "party." Main effects of age and field condition were significant and so was the age by field interaction. The search times for all three age groups were longer for the word condition than for pseudowords, as well as the nonword condition averages for all groups. Third-graders searched faster through nonwords than through pseudowords and the pseudoword/nonword difference between third-graders and adults approached significance. The authors suggested that adults may have greater access to auto-matized word recognition hence decreasing their field dependence. The authors concluded that all three age groups demonstrated the use of orthographic infor-mation with no indication that its usage increases with age.

Evidence from other studies and the limitations of their OI task seems to challenge the conclusions of Stanovich et al. (1978). Differences between readers in grades 2, 4, and 6 were found by Samuels et al. (1978) and more recently by Corcos and Willows (1989, 1993). On a task manipulating levels of OI contained in six-letter strings and requiring subjects to judge the similarity of a target-item and a test-item, Corcos and Willows found that grade 2 students were less accurate than grade 4 and 6 students, with no differences evident between grades 4 and 6. In contrast, grade 6 students were fastest in making these correct responses, with no RT differences emerging between grades 2 and 4.

Finally, their OI task may not be a test of OI usage (holistic processing). Besner et al. (1984) demonstrated that tasks measuring naming latencies eradi-cate the effect of case alternation on high frequency words because they encour-age letter-by-letter rather than holistic processes. Therefore, to search for a target-word embedded in lists of items may encourage subjects to remember the target words by verbal rehearsal and consequently adopt a letter-by-letter pro-cessing strategy. Such a practice renders the task inappropriate for measuring OI differences because the task is not a test of OI usage (i.e., holistic processing).

Summary of Evidence Relating to Early Reading Acquisition

Orthographic knowledge is highly correlated with reading ability (Allington, 1978; Leslie & Shannon, 1981; Niles & Taylor, 1978) and by the middle of grade 2, readers begin to use this source of information (Juola et al., 1978). But, according to Stanovich et al. (1978), when an ecologically valid word-search task is used, there is no indication that OI usage increases with age. This conclusion, however, is not supported by the results reported by Samuels et al. (1978), and Corcos and Willows (1989, 1993) whose findings support:

1. a stage of letter-by-letter processing (grade 2)
2. an intermediary stage typified by a mixture of letter-by-letter and holistic processing (grade 4), and
3. a final stage of holistic processing (grade 6 and adults).

A general conclusion from these studies is that young readers (as early as first grade) are sensitive to different approximations to English. Knowledge of orthographic information is available very early during reading acquisition and is strongly associated with the development of reading skills (Allington, 1978; Leslie & Shannon, 1981). The relationship existing between OI sensitivity and reading ability (Allington, 1978) may parallel stages of reading instruction. Chall (1983) describes Stage 2 (Confirmation, Fluency, Ungluing from Print) as the stage where increased familiarity and fluency with print develops. The reading fluency that is acquired as a result of practice during this stage may represent the establishment of a personal lexicon that grows to include more words processed holistically with increasing age. Transfer effects (the ability to apply known information to a new situation) may contribute to a speedier acquisition of new words sharing structural similarities with words already included in the reader's personal lexicon if a rule-governed definition of OI is plausible. But, such a hypothesis needs to be tested in this context.

OI DIFFERENCES BETWEEN GOOD AND POOR READERS

This section describes literature examining differences in OI usage by good and poor readers. Although these reader groups vary in reading ability and could have been included in the previous section, these two groups are highlighted because there is an implication that they are also qualitatively different. Differences between good and poor readers have been noted in their ability to use syntactical and morphological information and it is probable that differences in their orthographic knowledge also exist. Poor readers in grade 2 to 6 were found to be inefficient in their usage of OI when compared to normal readers in the same grade (Corcos & Willows, 1989, 1993; Ryan et al., 1984). By the same token, some studies (Horn & Manis, 1985; Stanovich & West, 1979) have suggested that poor readers demonstrate the greater orthographic sensitivity as they compensate for their syntactical and semantic difficulties. These two opposing views of OI usage by poor readers are the subject of the following section.

Poorer Readers Are More Sensitive to OI

Stanovich and West (1979) compared the performance of good and poor readers on the same type of word-search task as the one used in Experiment 3 of Stanovich et al. (1978). Subjects were asked to identify instances of "house," "world," and "party" embedded in fields of words, pseudowords, and nonwords.

No differences in search times were found between good and poor readers. But, the error rates of the poor readers were more affected by field condition.

There were two types of errors made: errors of omission (missing a target word); errors of commission (false alarms—identifying a string as a target word when it was not). In spite of these error differences, the authors concluded that poor readers showed the greater orthographic sensitivity because a comparison of performance between field conditions indicated that good readers differed across all three field conditions whereas poor readers differentiated the word and pseudoword conditions from the nonword condition but not from each other. Poor readers made many more errors in the word condition and the authors took this finding to represent a speed/accuracy tradeoff. The large number of commission errors made by poor readers was highly correlated with the field condition. As the field approximated words, the rate of commission errors increased. Stanovich and West (1979) suggested that poor readers made use of word shape and letter distribution (i.e., the more global features) rather than an analysis of the individual letters in the strings.

To look for a word embedded in a letter-string field is a variation of the lexical-decision task insofar that it encourages the subject the make a word/not-a-word decision when the target word is searched in a list of pseudowords and nonwords. When the target word, however, is searched in a field of words, orthographic information is no longer the locus of the judgment because it is contained in both the field and target items. Hence, the search for a target word in a field of words does not constitute a test of orthographic knowledge. Instead, it encourages a letter-by-letter visual comparison on the basis of target words held in memory. Krueger (1975) indicated that a target may not survive storage if a letter-by-letter comparison is being made and consequently a high rate of commission errors and false alarms is expected. This may be the case because these types of errors were typical of poor reader performance.

Leslie and Thimke (1986), however, used a similar word search task to assess young readers in grades 1 and 2 and grouped them on the basis of reading ability above and below the grade 2 level. Readers below grade 2 searched faster through nonword and pseudoword fields and readers above grade 2 searched faster through the nonword fields and hence, demonstrated the greater orthographic sensitivity. These findings question further the results of Stanovich and West (1979), who should have perhaps limited their comparison to pseudoword and nonword fields given that OI interference alone differentiates these fields.

Stanovich and West (1979) also suggested that poor readers were using configurational features rather than doing a letter-by-letter search. This conclusion does not consider the memory demand of the task and the subsequent effects. It is possible that all subjects were constrained to use a letter-by-letter search (Besner et al., 1984) and that good readers made a speed/accuracy tradeoff by focusing on accuracy and allowing their reaction time to decrease such that they approximated the performance of poor readers.

Despite finding significant differences in the performance of normal and disabled readers with a visual-search task, Horn and Manis (1985) conducted a second experiment using a lexical decision task. They predicted that, with this more externally valid task, disabled readers would make more errors and take a longer time to reject the regular and high frequency words if they are deficient in their use of orthographic knowledge.

Eighteen disabled readers (DR) were compared to two groups of normal readers: an age-matched group in grades 5 and 6 (AM) and a reading-matched group in grades 2 and 3 (RM). The six-letter words used as stimuli were high frequency words for grade 1 and 2 children. The nonword stimuli were anagrams. Subjects were shown a stimulus item and asked to judge whether the item spelled a word.

The accuracy data yielded facilitative effects of regularity and positional frequency for all subjects. All three groups made fewer errors on the regular-high positional frequency items at the expense of slower latencies. DR and RM subjects demonstrated a more pronounced speed and accuracy trade-off than AM subjects with DR showing the greater effect. The latency data revealed that disabled readers were slower than the AM but equal to the RM group. The DR group demonstrated a greater facilitative effect of regularity (478 ms vs. 98 ms) than the CA control. All subjects demonstrated weak positional frequency effects.

The authors concluded that disabled readers made greater use of regularity than their CA controls, younger readers (RM) made greater use than older readers (AM). These findings were interpreted as supporting Stanovich's (1980) interactive-compensatory model and demonstrating that the lexical-decision task is conducive to showing more consistent effects of orthographic sensitivity, at least in the time taken to reject nonwords by poor readers.

There are concerns with the data collected during the two experiments. The control groups were highly proficient on the tasks and there are also problems with the interpretation of the RT data. Inspection of Table 6 in Horn and Manis (1985, p. 156) indicates that AM controls were able to achieve accuracy levels of 95–99% on the experimental task. Similarly, Table 5 (p. 156) demonstrates a 98 ms difference between the conditions that the authors define as the easiest and the hardest. It appears that the AM control group was operating at a ceiling level and consequently the comparisons between AM, RM, and RD may not be meaningful. In addition, it is possible to interpret RT performance on the lexical decision task differently if subjects' RT performance on the visual search task is considered. In the visual search task, RD made more errors than AM or RM, and their reaction times were equivalent to AM and shorter than RM. This is the expected developmental pattern because RD and AM are the same age. In the lexical-decision task, however, RD's reaction times were slower than AM but equal to RM. Looking only at the performance of younger and disabled reader on the lexical-decision task, the latency differences between these two groups did not vary as in Experiment 1 although RT differences would be expected on the basis of developmental factors (Woodworth & Schlosberg, 1954). If the larger error rate demonstrated by RD is taken into account and assuming that younger readers were operating at the ceiling of the accuracy measure (92–98%), disabled readers with the poorer accuracy performance should show longer latencies if they equaled the reaction time of the younger readers. In fact, disabled readers, as a function of their age, should have produced faster reaction times than younger readers. Instead, disabled readers made more errors and performed more slowly and met Horn and Manis' (1985) original criteria (i.e., if disabled readers are deficient in their use of OI, they should make more errors and take a longer time to reject the regular high frequency words).

Poorer Readers Are Less Sensitive to OI

Ryan et al. (1984) studied differences in the orthographic knowledge of learning disabled (LD) and normal readers with the expectation that LDs would demonstrate poor use of OI.

They studied 90 children from grades 2, 3, and 4. Each group consisted of 15 LD and 15 normal readers. The LD children were identified by the school and depending on their grade placement were 1 to 2 years below in reading ability. The experimental task consisted of 20 word pairs. Words of 3, 4, 5 and 6 letters represented legal and illegal orthographic units. Two were presented on a card and subjects were required to point to the one that looked most like a word. Only accuracy measures were collected. Following the experiment, the Wide Range Achievement Test (WRAT) reading subtest was administered to all subjects.

Results indicated that between-grade and group-by-grade comparisons were not significant. Grade levels, therefore, were combined in the analysis and a significant group difference was obtained. Comparison of WRAT scores yielded significant differences in the normal reader group between grades 2 and 3, and grades 2 and 4. No between-grade comparisons were significant for the LD group. Correlations between experimental performance and WRAT scores for the normal reader group were $r = .51$, for the LD group $r = .54$, and for both groups combined $r = .67$.

Ryan et al. (1984) concluded that the LD children in grades 2, 3, and 4 had a limited knowledge of orthographic information in comparison to their normal counterparts in the same grade. They also proposed that normal readers had a larger reading vocabulary as reflected by their higher reading scores, and hence, had a greater pool of words from which to discover orthographic rules.

Corcos and Willows (1989, 1993) compared a total of 90 good and poor readers in grades 2, 4, and 6 on a task requiring a judgment of whether target-items containing different levels of OI were the "same" or "different" from test-items, identical or varying by one letter. Stimuli were manipulated to include a total of five levels of OI. Poor readers across all three grades demonstrated poorer accuracy performance on the most wordlike letter strings (those containing the highest levels of OI) with the greatest reader group discrepancy occurring on the accuracy performance at grade 2. No group differences were obtained on the response time measure for correct responses.

The expectation that poor readers may be more proficient in their use of OI than normal readers has roots in the assumption that phonemic and/or language factors are responsible for their reading difficulties rather than visual or spatial factors (Vellutino, 1979, 1987). Those who make this assumption postulate that poor readers invoke their intact visual processes to utilize OI in a compensatory manner. Poor readers are known to be deficient in their usage of morphographic and syntactical information and, similarly, they should be expected to be relatively insensitive to OI as well. In his review of the literature, Stanovich (1980) found poor readers to be more reliant on top-down strategies. They were more likely to use contextual clues and/or interword redundancy and they were relatively less successful reading words in isolation.

A final issue relates to the probability that poor readers do not constitute a homogeneous group with a single factor to account for their disability (Satz & Morris, 1981). In the past, Vellutino (1979, 1987) identified linguistic factors as the cause of reading disabilities and recently, Lovegrove and his associates (see chap. 14) reported finding basic visual processing deficits in the majority of LD readers. So, the possibility that only a subtype of poor readers is deficient in its usage of OI remains to be investigated. In the mean time, studies reporting OI advantages by poor readers (Horn & Manis, 1985; Rack, 1985; Stanovich & West, 1979) have not been supported as a result of the methodological and interpretive limitations previously discussed. In effect, such findings can be interpreted as supporting the position that good readers are more proficient than poor readers in OI stage.

CONCLUSIONS

Orthographic knowledge applied to word recognition yields certain benefits: more accurate recall and faster lexical access (Juel, 1983) and if a direct access model to word recognition is adopted, then OI represents a visual code based on the redundancy of letter sequences and their positions within words (Bruck, 1988, 1990; Chase & Tallal, 1990; Seidenberg & McLelland, 1989). Readers may initially process words letter-by-letter but continue to develop more holistic processes with spelling patterns as the most likely visual unit of analysis in OI (Prinzmetal, Treiman, & Rho, 1986; Taylor et al., 1977).

Readers begin to demonstrate a sensitivity to OI as soon as reading instruction begins (Juola et al., 1978; Leslie & Shannon, 1981) and at different ages, they vary in their ability to apply OI to word recognition (Corcos & Willows, 1989; Juel, 1983). In young readers, reading ability is highly correlated with orthographic knowledge (Massaro & Hestand, 1983; Zivian & Samuels, 1986) but as readers move from grade to grade, radical increases in exposure to print (Juel, 1988) progressively affect the processing of OI to the level of adult skilled reading (Stanovich & West, 1989).

Poor or disabled reader groups generally differ in their ability to use OI and this disparity continues into adulthood (Decker, 1989). In addition to phonological difficulties, disabled readers may have problems with visual processing (Lovegrove, Martin, & Slaghuis, 1986; Willows, 1991) and may not be able to directly access the lexicon (Bruck, 1988). Reader group differences may not simply reflect differential exposure to words but rather some strategy or skill difference. Corcos and Willows (1992) assessed the processing of words by good and poor readers in grade 6 and a reading-match control of grade 4 students. In spite of efforts to equate the familiarity of each subject's personal word list, group effects did not disappear and poor readers differed from their age- and reading-matched controls.

There remain methodological issues responsible for inconsistencies in research exploring the role of OI in word recognition. The first issue relates to the demands of the task and the second, to the type of stimuli. When there is an intent to compare the orthographic knowledge of various groups, the structure of the task must limit subjects to using only OI so that group differences cannot be attributed to other sources of information (e.g., phonological, phoneme-grapheme associations, morphological, etc.). Brown, Carr, and Chaderjan (1987) demonstrated with adult subjects that same–different tasks could be constructed to encourage the effects of visual or phonological information independently and interactively by manipulating attentional strategies. Marmurek and Briscoe (1982) illustrated that the temporal position of a target letter would affect the search speeds of words and pseudowords differently. They found that high levels of OI facilitated the search when the target letter was presented prior or simultaneously with the pseudoword. Words, however, were searched faster when the target letter was seen after the word. This relationship between task and findings identified by Krueger (1975) must be considered in our interpretation of the literature. Reading models generally agree about the existence of several routes to lexical access and studies should clarify their focus.

Finally, an issue of some importance in assessing children and adult performance is the personal familiarity of the stimuli. Gernsbacher (1984) suggested that this variable may account for the inconsistency of results obtained in OI studies. Thompson (1985) found that orthographic patterns of relatively high frequency words encountered in early reading have low frequency in adult text. Personal familiarity is a factor that requires more attention when adult–child familiarities with words (Chase & Tallal, 1990) and the personal familiarity of the lexicon existing between subjects (Corcos & Willows, 1992) is considered.

REFERENCES

Allington, R. L. (1978). Sensitivity to orthographic structure as a function of grade and reading ability. *Journal of Reading Behavior, 10,* 437–439.

Besner, D., Davelaar, E., Alcott, D., & Parry, P. (1984). Wholistic reading of alphabetic print: Evidence from the FDM and the FBI. In L. Henderson (Ed.), *Orthographies and reading: Perspectives from cognitive psychology, neuropsychology and linguistics* (pp. 121–135). London: Lawrence Erlbaum Associates.

Brown, T., Carr, T., & Chaderjan, M. (1987). Orthography, familiarity, and meaningfulness reconsidered: Attentional strategies may affect the lexical sensitivity of visual code information. *Journal of Experimental Psychology: Human Perception and Performance, 13*(1), 127–139.

Bruck, M. (1988). The word recognition and spelling of dyslexic children. *Reading Research Quarterly, 23*(1), 51–69.

Bruck, M. (1990). Word-recognition skills of adults with childhood diagnoses of dyslexia. *Developmental Psychology, 26*(3), 439–454.

Bruder, G. A. (1978). Role of visual familiarity in the word superiority effects obtained with the simultaneous-matching task. *Journal of Experimental Psychology: Human Perception and Performance, 4,* 88–100.

Chall, J. S. (1983). *Stages of reading development.* New York: McGraw-Hill.

Chase, C. H., & Tallal, P. (1990). A developmental, interactive activation model of the word superiority effect. *Journal of Experimental Child Psychology, 49,* 448–487.

Corcos, E., & Willows, D. M. (1989, November). *A developmental study of the processing of orthographic information in children with varying reading ability.* Paper presented at the Annual Meeting of the National Reading Conference, Austin, TX.

Corcos, E., & Willows, D. M. (1992, April). *The processing of words varying in personal familiarity by poor readers and their age-matched and reading-matched controls.* Paper presented at the Annual Meeting of the American Educational Research Association, San Francisco.

Corcos, E., & Willows, D. M. (1993). The role of visual processes in good and poor readers' utilization of orthographic information in letter strings. In S. Wright & R. Groner (Eds.), *Studies in visual information processing: Facets of dyslexia and its remediation* (pp. 95–106). Amsterdam: Elsevier North Holland.

Decker, S. N. (1989). Cognitive processing rates among disabled and normal reading young adults: A nine year follow-up study. *Reading and Writing: An Interdisciplinary Journal, 1,* 123–134.

Francis, H. (1984). Children's knowledge of orthography in learning to read. *British Journal of Educational Psychology, 54*(1), 8–23.

Gernsbacher, M. A. (1984). Resolving 20 years of inconsistent interactions between lexical familiarity and orthography, concreteness, and polysemy. *Journal of Experimental Psychology-General, 113*(2), 256–281.

Gibson, E. J., Shurcliff, A., & Yonas, A. (1970). Utilization patterns by deaf and hearing subjects. In H. Levin & J. P. Williams (Eds.), *Basic studies in reading* (pp. 57–73). New York: Basic Books.

Goswami, U. (1990). Phonological priming and orthographic analogies in reading. *Journal of Experimental Child Psychology, 49,* 323–340.

Hanson, V. (1986). Access to spoken language and the acquisition of orthographic structure: Evidence from deaf readers. *Quarterly Journal of Experimental Psychology, 38A,* 193–212.

Healy, A. F. (1974). Separating item and order information in short-term memory. *Journal of Verbal Learning and Verbal Behavior, 13,* 644–655.

Healy, A. F. (1978). A Markov model for the short-term retention of spatial location information. *Journal of Verbal Learning and Verbal Behavior, 17,* 295–308.

Healy, A. F. (1982). Short-term memory for order information. In G. H. Bower (Ed.), *The psychology of learning and motivation* (pp. 191–238). New York: Academic Press.

Horn, C., & Manis, F. R. (1985). Normal and disabled readers' use of orthographic structure in processing print. *Journal of Reading Behavior, 17*(2), 143–161.

Horn, C. C., & Manis, F. R. (1987). Development of automatic and speeded reading of printed words. *Journal of Experimental Child Psychology, 44,* 92–108.

Juel, C. (1983). The development and use of mediated word identification. *Reading Research Quarterly, 18*(3), 306–327.

Juola, J. F., Schadler, M., Chabot, R. J., & McCaughey, M. W. (1978). The development of visual 476.

Kolers, P. (1975). Memorial consequences of automatized encoding. *Journal of Experimental Psychology: Human Learning and Memory, 1,* 687–701.

Kolers, P. (1985). Phonology in reading. In D. R. Olson, N. Torrance & A. Hildyard (Eds.), *Literacy, language and learning: The nature and consequences of reading and writing* (pp. 404–411). Cambridge, England: Cambridge University Press.

Krueger, L. E. (1975). Familiarity effects in visual information processing. *Psychological Bulletin, 82,* 949–974.

Kruger, L. E. (1984). Multiletter comparisons with simultaneous and sequential presentation. *Journal of Experimental Psychology: Learning, Memory and Cognition, 10,* 271–284.

Kucera, H., & Francis, W. N. (1967). *Computational analysis of present-day American English.* Providence, RI: Brown University Press.

Leslie, L., & Shannon, A. J. (1981). Recognition of orthographic structure during beginning reading. *Journal of Reading Behavior, 13*(4), 313–324.

Leslie, L., & Thimke, B. (1986). The use of orthographic knowledge in beginning reading. *Journal of Reading Behavior, 18*(3), 229–241.

Logan, G. D. (1985). Skill and automaticity: Relations, implications, and future directions. *Canadian Journal of Psychology, 39*(2), 367–386.

Logan, G. D. (1988). Toward an instance theory of automatization. *Psychological Review, 4,* 492–527.

Lovegrove, W., Martin, F., & Slaghuis, W. (1986). A theoretical and experimental case for a visual deficit in specific reading disability. *Cognitive Neuropsychology, 3,* 225–267.

Lovett, M. W., Ransby, M. J., & Barron, R. W. (1988). Treatment subtype and word type effects in dyslexic children's response to remediation. *Brain and Language, 34,* 328–349.

Mamurek, H., & Briscoe, G. (1982). Orthographic and lexical processing of visual letter strings. *Canadian Journal of Psychology, 36*(3), 368–387.

Mason, M. (1975). Reading ability and letter search time: Effects of orthographic structure defined by single-letter positional frequency. *Journal of Experimental Psychology: General, 104,* 146–166.

edge of orthographic structure. *Contemporary Educational Psychology, 8*(2), 174–180.

Massaro, D. W., Venezky, R. L., & Taylor, G. A. (1979). Orthographic regularity, positional frequency and visual processing of letter strings. *Journal of Experimental Psychology: General, 108,* 107–124.

Mayzner, M. S., & Tresselt, M. E. (1965). Tables of single-letter and digram frequency counts of various word-length and letter-position combinations. *Psychonomic Monograph Supplements, 1,* 13–32.

Niles, J. A., & Taylor, B. M. (1978). The development of orthographic sensitivity during the school years by primary grade children. In P. D. Pearson & J. Hansen (Eds.), *Reading: Disciplined inquiry in process and practice* (pp. 41–44). Celmson, SC: National Reading Conference.

Olson, R., Wise, B., Conners, F., & Rack, J. (1990). Organization, heritability, and remediation of component word recognition and language skills in disabled readers. In T. H. Carr & B. A. Levy (Eds.), *Reading and its development: Component skills approaches* (pp. 261–322). San Diego: Academic Press.

Olson, R., Wise, B., Conners, F., Rack, J., & Fulker, D. (1989). Specific deficits in component reading and language skills: Genetic and environmental influences. *Journal of Learning Disabilities, 22*(6), 339–348.

Pollatsek, A., Well, A. D., & Schindler, R. M. (1975). Familiarity affects visual processing of words. *Journal of Experimental Psychology: Human Perception and Performance, 1,* 328–338.

Prinzmetal, W., Treiman, R., & Rho, S. H. (1986). How to see a reading unit. *Journal of Memory and Language, 25*(4), 461–475.

Rack, J. P. (1985). Orthographic and phonetic coding in developmental dyslexia. *British Journal of Psychology, 76*(3), 325–340.

Rayner, K. (1988). Word recognition cues in children: The relative use of graphemic cues, orthographic cues, and grapheme-phoneme correspondence rules. *Journal of Educational Psychology, 80*(4), 473–479.

Rayner, K., & Pollatsek, A. (1989). *The psychology of reading.* Englewood Cliffs, NJ: Prentice-Hall.

Ryan, M. C., Miller, C. D., & Witt, J. C. (1984). A comparison of the use of orthographic structure in word discrimination by learning disabled and normal children. *Journal of Learning Disabilities, 17*(1), 38–40.

Samuels, S. J., Bremer, C. D., & LaBerge, D. (1978). Units of word recognition: Evidence for developmental changes. *Journal of Verbal Learning and Verbal Behavior, 17,* 715–720.

Samuels, S. J., Miller, N., & Eisenberg, P. (1979). Practice effects on the unit of word recognition. *Journal of Educational Psychology, 71,* 524–530.

Satz, P., & Morris, R. (1981). Learning disability subtypes: A review. In F. J. Pirozzolo & M. C. Wittrock (Eds.), *Neuropsychological and Cognitive Processes in Reading* (pp. 109–141). New York: Academic Press.

Seidenberg, M. S., & McClelland, J. L. (1989). A distributed, developmental model of word recognition and naming. *Psychological Review, 96*(4), 523–568.

Stanovich, K. E. (1980). Toward an interactive-compensatory model of individual differences in the development of reading fluency. *Reading Research Quarterly, 16,* 32–71.

Stanovich, K. E. (1990). Concepts in developmental theories of reading skill: Cognitive resources, automaticity and modularity. *Developmental Review, 10,* 72–100.

Stanovich, K. E., & West, R. F. (1979). The effect of orthographic structure on the word search performance of good and poor readers. *Journal of Experimental Child Psychology, 28,* 258–267.

Stanovich, K. E., & West, R. F. (1989). Exposure to print and orthographic processing. *Reading Research Quarterly, 24*(4), 402–433.

Stanovich, K. E., West, R. F., & Pollak, D. (1978). The effect of orthographic structure on word recognition in a visual search task. *Journal of Experimental Child Psychology, 26,* 137–146.

Taylor, G. A., Miller, T. J., & Juola, J. F. (1977). Isolating the units of visual word perception. *Perception and Psychophysics, 21,* 377–386.

Thompson, G. B. (1985). Orthographic structures: Grapheme patterns in child and adult texts. *Journal of Research in Reading, 8*(1), 32–44.

Thorndike, E. L., & Lorge, I. (1944). *The teachers' wordbook of 30,000 words.* New York: Bureau of Publications, Teachers College, Columbia University.

Underwood, B. J., & Schultz, R. W. (1960). *Meaningfulness and verbal learning.* New York: Lippincott.

Vellutino, F. R. (1979). *Dyslexia: Theory and research.* Cambridge, MA: MIT Press.

Vellutino, F. (1987). Dyslexia. *Scientific American, 256*(3), 34–41.

Venezky, R. L., & Massaro, D. W. (1987). Orthographic structure and spelling-sound regularity in reading English words. In A. Allport, D. Mackay, W. Prinz, & E. Scheerer (Eds.), *Language perception and production: Relationship between listening, speaking, reading and writing* (pp. 159–179). London: Academic Press.

Willows, D. M. (1991). Visual processes in learning disabilities. In B.Y.L. Wong (Ed.), *Learning about learning disabilities* (pp. 163–193). New York: Academic Press.

Woodworth, R. S., & Schlosberg, H. (1954). *Experimental Psychology (rev. ed.).* New York: Holt, Rinehart & Winston.

Zivian, M. T., & Samuels, M. T. (1986). Performance on a word-likeness task by normal readers and reading-disabled children. *Reading Research Quarterly, 21*(2), 150–160.

9 Eye Movements in Reading

Alexander Pollatsek
University of Massachusetts

INTRODUCTION

This chapter can be no more that a brief introduction to the topic of "eye movements in reading," because roughly 250 pages of *The Psychology of Reading* (Rayner & Pollatsek, 1989) dealt with eye movements and reading, and our coverage of the topic is far from exhaustive. The first section is intended as background, and documents the assertion that the typical pattern of eye movements in reading is more-or-less word-by-word and that this pattern of movements is highly functional in reading rather than being a bad habit retained from childhood. The second section briefly reviews the literature to document those aspects of text that eye movements are sensitive to. The third section proposes a simple and elegant model of how eye movements are programmed in reading; however, the model is not fully adequate and its shortcomings (and possible modifications) are discussed. The last section discusses the use of eye movements to understand the processing of text. Two alternative approaches are compared.

NORMAL READING IS ESSENTIALLY WORD-BY-WORD

This section argues that the process of normal reading is a close approximation to a sequential encoding of the words in the text, with most words actually being fixated. A brief discussion of terms and some elementary facts about eye movements comes first.

Basic Facts About Eye Movements

When people view a static display (not necessarily text), the eyes are not continually moving. Instead, the eyes fixate (i.e., point at) a given location in space for a period of time (usually in the range of 200 ms–400 ms) and then execute a rapid eye movement (called a *saccade*) that lasts about 10 ms to 40 ms (depending on the size of the movement) to arrive at a new location. In normal viewing conditions, humans are functionally blind during the saccadic eye movement; hence all useful visual information is encoded during the stable periods called *fixations*. In reading, most saccades are forward through the text (rightward in English) and are typically seven to nine characters. In addition, of course, large leftward saccades, known as *return sweeps,* are needed to go from the end of one line of text to the beginning of the next. Somewhat less obviously, readers make other leftward movements in text (known as *regressions*) about 10% of the time. Some are large and may go back to the beginning of the line or paragraph, but many are small and go only several characters back (the reader is usually unaware of making the latter type of regression). This is a bit of an oversimplified picture of eye movements, but it is adequate for a discussion of reading. (See chap. 4 of Rayner & Pollatsek, 1989, for a more complete background on eye movements.)

Why Are the Eyes Continually Moving?

The acuity of the visual system is nonuniform. Information about fine detail is available only in a small region of central vision called the *fovea* that extends a degree of visual angle on either side of fixation. Acuity drops off even within the fovea and sharply drops off in the surrounding region of about 5 degrees on either side, termed the *parafovea,* and little detail is processed in the outer *peripheral* regions. (These figures apply to the horizontal direction; acuity falls off even faster in the vertical direction.) This suggests that the ability to perceive objects (or in the case of reading, words and letters) drops off rapidly from fixation and hence that a fixation must come close to a word in order for it to be processed.

There is abundant data indicating that fixations close to words are indeed necessary for them to be encoded (contrary to the lore about "speed reading"). The technique that demonstrates this most dramatically is the *moving window* technique developed by McConkie and Rayner (1975). In these experiments, a subject reads text from a cathode ray tube (CRT) display while the position of the eyes is being recorded and monitored by a computer. On each fixation, a "window" of normal text around the fixation point is presented with the text outside the window altered in some fashion. Each time the eye moves, the window is changed (see Fig. 9.1).

The basic logic of the method is as follows: If text can be read with normal speed and comprehension with vision being restricted to a window of a certain

```
By far the single most abundant substance in the biosphere


                   *
By far the single most abundXXXXXXXXXXXXXXXXXXXXXXXXXXXXXX   (1)

                       *
XXXXXr the single most abundant suXXXXXXXXXXXXXXXXXXXXXXXXX   (2)

                           *
XXXXXXXXXX single most abundant substancXXXXXXXXXXXXXXXXXXX   (3)

                                   *
XXXXXXXXXXXXXXXXXXXXXXXXXXbundant substance in the biosXXXXX   (4)


                           *
XXXXXXXXXXXXXXXXXXXXXXst abundaXXXXXXXXXXXXXXXXXXXXXXXXXXXXXX   (3a)


                           *
XXXXXXXXXXXXXXXXXXXXXXst abundant substanXXXXXXXXXXXXXXXXXXX   (3b)


                           *
XX XXX XXX XXXXXX XXst abundant substanXXXXX XXX XXXXXXXXX   (3c)


                           *
XX XXX XXX XXXXXX XXXX abundant XXXXXXXXX XX XXX XXXXXXXXX   (3d)


                           *
XX XXX XXX XXXXXX XXXX abundant substance XX XXX XXXXXXXXX   (3e)


                           *
XX XXX XXX XXXXXX XXXX abundant subXXXXXX XX XXX XXXXXXXXX   (3f)
```

FIG. 9.1. Illustration of a moving window. The top line represents a normal line of text. Lines 1–4 represent windows that a reader might see on four consecutive fixations in reading the line of text; the window area extends from 14 letter spaces to the left of fixation (indicated by the *) to 14 letter spaces to the right of fixation. Under this condition, reading rate and comprehension would be the same as if the text were presented without any window restrictions. The other lines illustrate other types of windows that have been used. In all cases, the fixation point is on the *b* in *abundant*. In line 3a, the region extends 4 character spaces on either side of the fixated letter, and reading would be substantially slower than normal. In contrast, in lines 3b and 3c, when the region is asymmetric, extending 4 character spaces to the left and 14 to the right, reading rate is normal. Lines 3d–3f illustrate windows defined by words rather than character spaces: a one-word window in 3d, a two-word window in 3e, and a hybrid one-word + 3 letter window in 3f. Reading in 3f is substantially faster than in 3d, indicating that information is integrated across fixations (see text for further details).

size, then one can infer that no useful information outside the window is being extracted by the reader. For example, suppose the window were constructed so that only the word fixated was normal (as in line 3d in Fig. 9.1) and reading was unimpaired. Then one would infer that the only useful information extracted from reading was the word fixated. In fact, however, when the window is constricted this much, reading is impaired. Comprehension is normal, but the speed goes down significantly: from about 300 to 350 words per minute (wpm) to about 200 wpm. Thus, we can infer that readers are processing more than the fixated word. However, when the window is expanded (as in lines 3b or 3c) to include 14 or 15 characters to the right of fixation, then reading is entirely unaffected by the window (McConkie & Rayner, 1975; Rayner, Well, Pollatsek, & Bertera, 1982). In normal reading, the reader is thus processing the fixated word and at most the two words to the right (Rayner et al., 1982).

Where do the limits of the perceptual span come from? The fact that no useful information is processed to the left of the fixated word in English (Rayner, Well, & Pollatsek, 1980) is due to attentional factors. When the order of the words in text runs from right-to-left as in Hebrew, the window of useful information then extends to the left of the fixated word (Pollatsek, Bolozky, Well, & Rayner, 1981). In contrast, the limit of 15 characters to the right of fixation (or about 5 degrees of visual angle in normal reading) appears to be due to visual acuity. When isolated words occur 5 degrees from fixation, no useful information can be extracted from them (Rayner, McConkie, & Ehrlich, 1978). Moreover, in a reading situation where the "window" is inverted and meaningful information is only available outside 5 degrees (a foveal "mask" covers the central 30 characters on each fixation), very little information about the text can be extracted (Rayner & Bertera, 1979). (In the typical experiment, three characters subtend a degree of visual angle; other experiments indicate that the character is the better metric and it will be used subsequently).

To summarize, the data from the contingent display experiments indicate that a fixation must be relatively near a word on a line of text (i.e., within 15 characters) in order for useful information to be extracted from that word. Moreover, a recent experiment (Pollatsek, Raney, LaGasse, & Rayner, in press) indicates that no useful information is extracted from text below the line fixated. The window appears to be no bigger for "speedreaders" (adults who successfully completed a commercial speedreading course). They needed to fixate on a key word (e.g., a name or date) in order to be above chance on a comprehension question that relied on correctly perceiving that word (Just & Carpenter, 1987).

Why Isn't It Necessary to Fixate Every Word?

The phenomenon of "speedreading" invites the question of what is in fact happening when people speedread. At present, there are little good data, but it is clear that people can skim fairly rapidly through text and extract *some* information. Although skimming is poorly understood, it is clear that for some materials (e.g., popular fiction that adhere to formulas, current affairs, or travel articles that largely rehash what the reader already knows), one does not have to read all the words to make some sense of what is said, and perhaps even to get the main point. An interesting and unsolved question is whether the typical skimmer samples the text randomly, or if not, what cues guide an "intelligent" sampling of text.

In the following, it will be assumed that the information in the text is nonredundant enough that the reader has to comprehend each sentence to be able to comprehend the text. If the reader is in this mode, the data are consistent with the hypothesis that the words in the text are comprehended sequentially, left to right, across a line of text and from top-to-bottom on the page. That does not mean, however, that all words need to be fixated. As the window experiments indicate, the effective visual span in reading extends beyond the word fixated and includes (on at least some fixations) the next word or two. Thus, just because a word is not fixated, it doesn't mean that it is not processed. This is a problem for interpretation of the eye movement record (to be discussed later).

There are several pieces of evidence indicating that at least some words that are skipped are processed. First, the word *the* was skipped more frequently than words equated on length in the same position in text (O'Regan, 1979). Second, a word that is highly predictable in text is skipped more often than a word that is not predictable (Balota, Pollatsek, & Rayner, 1985; Ehrlich & Rayner, 1981). For example, the word *cake* was skipped more often in a sentence about a wedding than the word *pies* in the same location (Balota et al., 1985). This phenomenon indicates that the skipped word was not merely guessed: If the subject merely used the context to guess the word *cake,* it would have been irrelevant whether *cake* or *pies* was actually present. Hence, visual information is being extracted on at least some fixations from the parafoveal location in order to decide whether or not to skip a word.

The processing of parafoveal information is even more complex, as a *preview* of a word to the right of fixation can also decrease fixation time when it is later fixated. For example, in a moving window experiment involving a two word window (the fixated word and the word to the right) fixation times on words are appreciably shorter than when the window is merely the fixated word (Rayner et al., 1982). Furthermore, this can be shown to reflect the presence or absence of a preview on a particular fixation (Blanchard, Pollatsek, & Rayner, 1989). Thus, it appears that words are often processed to some extent in the parafovea and processing completed when they are later fixated. (For further details on this integration process see Rayner & Pollatsek, 1989; Pollatsek & Rayner, 1992.)

What Are Eye Movements Sensitive To?

In the moving window studies discussed earlier, the pattern of eye movements changes as the window gets smaller: The average fixation duration gets longer, the average length of a forward saccade gets shorter, and the number of regressive eye movements increases. Thus, the system of eye control is sensitive to visual aspects of the display. The pattern of eye movements is similarly responsive to the meaning of the text. More difficult text (such as technical material) is read at a slower rate; this also translates into longer fixations, shorter saccades, and more regressive eye movements.

A central issue in reading is how the perceptual and cognitive processes involved in reading actually link up to the system that controls the eyes and allow the eyes to be sensitive to moment-to-moment changes in the text. The discussion of that issue is centered around the model of eye control introduced in the next section. That discussion is aided, however, if we first consider two extreme models of eye movement control.

At one extreme is the *global control* hypothesis, which is basically the null hypothesis. According to global control, the reader has no moment-to-moment control of the eyes. Instead, the eyes are set on an "automatic pilot": set to fixate a certain time, and set to move forward a fixed distance. The actual fixation times and saccade lengths would vary because of variability in the execution of motor commands. To explain differences in eye behavior due to varying window conditions or to varying text difficulty, one would need to add an assumption that there are "gain controls" that the reader can use globally to adjust the parameters of these processes (e.g., "this material is technical, so I'll make longer fixations and shorter saccades"). An obvious consequence of this view is that the pattern of eye movements in reading would reflect almost nothing about the underlying cognitive processes.

The opposite extreme is the "immediacy hypothesis" of Just and Carpenter (1980). They proposed that the fixation time on each word represents the time to complete all the psycholinguistic processing necessary in order for the word to be incorporated into the ongoing text structure. That is, on each fixation, a word is identified and then put into both the ongoing syntactic and discourse structures before the signal is sent out to move the eyes. Hence, if this hypothesis is true, the pattern of eye movements would be a very transparent record of the cognitive processes of reading; fixation times would merely be the time to do all psycholinguistic processing on a word plus a constant (the eye movement programming time).

As might be expected, eye movement control in reading is between these two extremes, although closer to the immediacy hypothesis. There are now abundant data against the global control hypothesis, indicating that both the duration of a fixation and the length of a saccade following that fixation can be affected by the extraction of visual information on that fixation. For example, an experiment by Rayner and Pollatsek (1981) employed a variant of the moving window technique in which the visual characteristics of the text varied randomly from fixation to fixation. Hence, any variation in eye movements related to the visual characteristics on fixation n had to be due to visual processing on that fixation. More specifically, Rayner and Pollatsek found that the size of the window of text visible on fixation n influenced the size of the subsequent saccade. In addition, they found that if the text in central vision was delayed after the beginning of a fixation (a meaningless pattern initially appeared instead of the letters), the fixation duration was delayed by almost that amount of time. Hence, both the decision about when to move the eyes to end a fixation and where to move the eyes can be affected by extraction of visual information on that fixation. Other data from these experiments indicated that characteristics of the window on the prior fixation (n-1) also had an effect on eye behavior. Consistent with this finding, subsequent work by Blanchard et al. (1989) indicated that when the size of windows varied from fixation to fixation, fixation time on a word was primarily influenced by the size of the window on fixation n-1 (i.e., by whether the fixated word had been previewed in the parafovea). In fact, in the Blanchard et al. experiment, there was little evidence for global control playing any part; fixation times and saccade sizes were almost totally predictable from the sizes of the windows on the two fixations immediately prior to an eye movement.

The virtue of the previous contingent display experiments is that one has control of the display and thus can state more precisely how immediate control is. On the other hand, they may be artificial and may not directly tap what readers are actually responding to when text is not changing. However, there are now a plethora of experiments using normal text that demonstrate that the reader's patterns of fixations and fixation times are responsive to the text right under the eye at the moment. In particular, a large amount of data indicate that fixation time on a word is primarily predicted by the frequency of that word in the language (e.g., Just & Carpenter, 1980). Of course, word frequency is confounded with word length (common words tend to be short), and a significant component of the frequency effect is explained by word length (Kliegl, Olson, & Davidson, 1982). However, even when length is controlled, common words are fixated for shorter periods of time than less common words (Inhoff & Rayner, 1986; Rayner & Duffy, 1986). (The two most common measures of fixation times are *gaze duration,* which is the total fixation time on a word before another word is fixated, and the *first fixation duration,* which is the duration of the first or only fixation on a word; except when otherwise specified, the following discussion assumes the measure is gaze duration.)

The correlation between word frequency and fixation duration in text, of course, has many possible interpretations. Even a global control model can explain the word length effect, because when saccade length is fixed, longer words would be more likely to receive multiple fixations and hence be fixated for a longer period of time. The fact that fixation times reflect word frequency even when length is controlled for, however, calls for a more "intelligent" mechanism. The simplest explanation for the relationship, of course, is that the frequency of a word determines lexical access time, or the time to look up a word in a "mental dictionary," and that the eye gets the signal to move when lexical access is completed. This, however, is not the only possible interpretation. An alternative is that higher frequency words have more common spelling patterns and the eye is sensitive to these spelling patterns (possibly in a very early stage of word identification). A second alternative is that more frequent words are not only easier to identify, but may also be more predictable and/or easier to integrate into the sentence structure.

The frequency effect on fixation times in reading may be due to all three of these factors: (a) "prelexical" effects such as orthographic contraints; (b) lexical access time; (c) "postlexical" effects such as predictability. Lima and Inhoff (1985) demonstrated that orthographic variables play a part; they found that words with common spelling patterns were fixated for shorter periods of time (even when frequency was held constant). Because high frequency words tend to have more common spelling patterns, the orthography effect is likely to be part of the effect of word frequency on fixation duration. In addition, the eye is responsive both to how predictable a word is and other aspects of how easily it is fit into sentence and discourse structures. Inhoff and Rayner (1986), however, demonstrated reliable frequency effects on fixation time even when the target words were not at all predictable. This indicates that postlexical effects do not explain all of the word frequency effect.

Eye movements, however, are quite sensitive to aspects of the text other than the time to access individual words. As indicated previously, words that are predictable from the prior text are both skipped more often and, when fixated, fixated for a shorter time than control words matched on word frequency and word length (Balota, Pollatsek, & Rayner, 1985; Ehrlich & Rayner, 1981; McConkie & Zola, 1981). In addition, the eyes reflect processing of syntax as illustrated by the following pair of sentences:

Since Jay always jogs a mile this seems like a short distance to him.

Since Jay always jogs a mile seems like a short distance to him.

The normal parsing strategy in these sentences ("late closure") is to incorporate "a mile" as the object of jogs (which is the correct interpretation of the first sentence). This strategy, however, is inappropriate for the second sentence, and thus the reader is "led down the garden path": at the "point of disambiguation" (the word "seems"), the verb cannot be incorporated into any sensible syntactic structure if "a mile" is taken as the object of "jogs" and the reader experiences processing difficulty. In fact, the eyes quickly register this difficulty; there are long fixation times on "seems" and many regressions back to earlier parts of the sentence both from the word "seems" and from the next fixation. Similar results have been obtained from a wide variety of sentences illustrating this and other types of syntactic parsing strategies (Frazier & Rayner, 1982).

Eye movements are not only sensitive to parsing of individual sentences, they are also sensitive to construction of discourse structures. The simplest illustration is anaphora, and in particular, the linking of a pronoun to its antecedent in discourse. One method for studying this process "on-line" is to vary the gender of a pronoun referring to a specific antecedent (e.g., a previously mentioned "doctor" is referred to by "he" or "she"). The basic idea is that cultural biases will make it harder to link "she" to "doctor" than to link "he" to "doctor" and this should be expressed in the eye movement record (e.g., Ehrlich & Rayner, 1983). Although there is some discrepancy between experiments, the usual finding is that there is some disruption in reading caused by the less "natural" pronoun. However, the disruption is often not immediate (on the fixation on which the pronoun is likely to be encoded), especially if the antecedent noun is either far back in the text and/or not the current topic of discourse. That is, the pattern of data suggests that search for the antecedent through the reader's working memory begins on the fixation when the pronoun is encoded. If the antecedent is easily accessible in memory, it may be found on that fixation, and if an anomaly is registered, may disrupt that fixation. However, if the antecedent is not easily accessible, the search may continue for several more fixations. These data thus provide one counterexample to the immediacy hypothesis, because the eyes appear to move on to the next word before the antecedent of a pronoun is accessed and hence before the pronoun is fully understood.

To summarize, the eyes appear to be sensitive to a variety of variables in the text: (a) prelexical variables such as the orthographic structure of words; (b) lexical variables such as word length and word frequency; (c) syntactic and discourse variables. However, progress through the text appears to be primarily determined by variables that appear to index lexical access. Even though these facts all seem plausible and intuitive, it is not at all clear how to explain them. The difficulty lies both in understanding how the cognitive system can process text rapidly enough to control the eyes, and how it uses the information from the text to exercise coherent control over the eyes. The next section presents one tentative approach toward understanding eye movement control.

HOW ARE THE EYES CONTROLLED IN READING?

To some, the task of constructing a model of eye movement control in reading would seem both Herculean and Quixotic because there are gaping holes in our knowledge of both text comprehension and eye control. As a result, the task might seem hopelessly open-ended, because hundreds of plausible models of eye movement control in reading could easily be constructed consistent with our present knowledge. I would like to argue, however, that the contrary is the case; given the general constraints imposed on the skilled reader and the data we already have, the difficulty is in constructing a single plausible theory that can explain the pattern of eye movements in reading.

First consider the time constraint. The typical eye fixation in reading is between about 200 ms to 300 ms. If, for example, lexical access influences fixation time, it means that (at least on some fixations) within 200 ms to 300 ms (a) a word is accessed; (b) this event communicated to the eye movement system; and (c) the eye movement is executed. There is a body of data that suggests that to do all this in 200 ms to 300 ms is no small feat. For example, when a subject is given a very simple task (e.g., fixating a series of fixation crosses in turn), the typical mean fixation time is around 175 ms (Rayner, Slowiaczek, Clifton, & Bertera, 1983). Thus, the programming and execution of an eye movement appear to take up an appreciable portion of the fixation time, not leaving much time for lexical access (or any other cognitive process) to be able to influence eye movements.

A second general constraint dictates that the mechanism for eye movement control should be relatively "dumb." That is, it seems quite unlikely that there is much intelligent, conscious control of eye movements during reading, as the process of comprehending the text appears to occupy virtually the full attention of the reader. To be sure, we occasionally go back to the beginning of a para- graph or page when we realize that we are completely lost in comprehending the text. Such incidents, however, are clearly the exception rather than the rule. Indeed, the striking thing about eye movements in reading (or in most normal perceptual situations) is that they are "automatic" and unplanned. For example, regressions usually account for about 10% of the saccades in reading, yet people are unaware of making most of them. Thus, any model that posits executive control to regulate the bulk of eye movements in reading is implausible.

The model outlined here satisfies these two constraints. It is a plausible account of how lexical access can drive the eyes through text. As such, it is at best incomplete, because it does not account for how either "prelexical" or discourse variables can influence eye movements. In addition, it primarily ac- counts for *when* eye movements are made, as it makes somewhat vague predic- tions about *where* eye movements actually land. In spite of these problems (and others to be introduced), the model is a promising start. It is also simple enough to provide a framework for discussing eye movement control in reading.

The essence of this model was developed by Morrison (1984) and has been adapted subsequently by Rayner and Pollatsek (1989; Pollatsek & Rayner, 1990). The basic idea comes from physiological work on spatial attention and eye movements (e.g., Wurtz, Goldberg, & Robinson, 1982) demonstrating that there are shifts of covert attention to a region of space (indicated by activity in the parietal regions of cortex) prior to actually making an eye movement. In Mor- rison's model, the basic engine driving eye movements are shifts of attention from word to word triggered by lexical access. That is, the reader is assumed to attend to each word in turn, and when word n is lexically encoded, attention is immediately shifted to the next word $(n+1)$. Crucially, this attention shift is assumed to automatically produce a "motor program" to move the eyes to word $n+1$. This motor program takes some time to execute, however, so that the reader has typically attended to word $n+1$ in the parafovea (and has done pro- cessing on it) before the eyes actually move to fixate it.

The mechanism described here successfully predicts that the fixation duration on a word is a function of word frequency (which influences the speed of lexical access) and information extracted from a word in the parafovea is used to help identify the word when it is later fixated. Without further modification, however, the model wrongly predicts that readers should fixate every word in turn. To take care of this problem, Morrison made an additional assumption that provides an elegant account of why readers skip certain words. He assumed that eye movements can be programmed in parallel: That is, there can be an attention shift to word $n+1$ (with a program created to move to word $n+1$) and a second attention shift to word $n+2$ (with a second motor program created to move to word $n+2$), such that both the second shift of attention and the creation of the second program occur before the execution of the first program (i.e., the saccade to word $n+1$).

What happens when two eye movement programs coexist? Morrison postulated three possibilities: (a) if the delay between the construction of programs 1 and 2 is long (more than 100 ms or so), there is no interaction—program 1 is executed with the eyes moving to location 1, and then program 2 is executed with the eyes moving to location 2; (b) if the delay between program 1 and 2 is very short, program 2 cancels program 1, with the eyes going directly to word $n+2$; (c) if the delay is intermediate, there is only one eye movement, but it will go to a location between the targets of programs 1 and 2. (These three possibilities were suggested by Becker & Jurgens', 1979, experiments, which involve subjects attempting to fixate a target that moves and moves again quickly.)

According to the model, the second and third alternatives are the primary causes of word skipping. The model predicts that a word will be skipped when attention shifts to it (when it is word $n+1$) and then shifts quickly to the succeeding word ($n+2$), causing the second motor program to "backwardly mask" the first. Consistent with the data (Balota et al., 1985; Ehrlich & Rayner, 1981; O'Regan, 1979), a rapid second attention shift (and skip of word $n+1$) would occur when lexical access of word $n+1$ is rapid, such as with high frequency words and words predictable from the prior context. This account of word skipping also accounts for another phenomenon: The fixation before the skip is longer than when the word is not skipped (Hogaboam, 1983; Pollatsek, Rayner, & Balota, 1986). This prediction follows because (a) a skip results only if a later program cancels an earlier one (b) skipping is unrelated to the time to make the first attention shift (to word $n+1$).

To summarize, according to Morrison's model, the reader encodes words one at a time, shifting attention each time a word is encoded, and eye movements are coupled to these attention shifts but lag behind them. These assumptions account for how the fixation duration on a word is influenced by word frequency. The model also assumes that if two eye movement programs are initiated close enough in time to each other, the second program has the potential to "backwardly mask" the first. This accounts for how "easy" words can be selectively skipped even though they are actually processed in the parafovea—an attractively "dumb" mechanism. In addition, the parallel programming assumption without backward masking (Morrison's first alternative) can explain why there are some very short (less than 150 ms) fixations in reading: These are presumably programmed on the prior fixation.

Morrison's model thus appears to be a promising start to explaining eye movements in reading. However, as indicated earlier, it is incomplete. In the first place, the model is not very precise about where an eye movement goes, because it merely predicts which word the eyes will land on. This deficit could be remedied by patching on the mechanism proposed by McConkie, Kerr, Reddix, and Zola (1988), based on the analysis of a large corpus of reading data. They posit that the reader always intends for a saccade to land on the center of a word, but that the eye movement system makes two kinds of errors. First, there is a bias to undershoot, so that the mean landing place tends to be to the left of center of a word (see also O'Regan, 1981; Rayner, 1979). McConkie et al. (1988) demonstrated that this bias is greater the further the prior fixation is from the center of the word. Second, there is random variability (roughly normally distributed) around this mean, with the variability greater the further the prior fixation is from the center of the target word.

This suggests that the decision of where to move is largely based on low level visual information (such as the location of word boundaries) and may be largely independent of the decision of when to move. There are data that support this hypothesis. For example, Rayner and Pollatsek (1981) found that the availability of parafoveal information on a fixation strongly influenced saccade length while having only minor effects on fixation duration. In contrast, delaying the onset of text in the fovea had strong effects on fixation duration but no effect on saccade length. In addition, work by Morris, Rayner, and Pollatsek (1990) and Pollatsek and Rayner (1982) suggested that the computation of where to move is usually made relatively early in a fixation.

There is a second hole in the model because it does not attempt a serious explanation of how text variables other than word frequency affect the pattern of eye movements. Earlier, I tacitly introduced an assumption that allows one text variable to influence fixation time: Lexical access was assumed to be more rapid if a word is predictable. This assumption is not sufficient to solve the problem, however, because in the "garden path" sentences discussed previously, processing difficulty is not plausibly associated with problems of lexical access; instead, the reader constructs a syntactic structure that does not "compute." The simplest way to modify Morrison's model to account for such effects is to assume that when the text processor registers that a syntactic structure does not compute (or that the semantic interpretation is nonsense), a signal is sent by an executive processor to Morrison's lexical processing module to stop and wait until the difficulty is cleared up. In fact, when readers encounter such difficulties, there are varying reactions: Sometimes the reader fixates near the point of disambiguation for a long time, sometimes a regression is made back in the region of the original ambiguity, and other times readers go back to the beginning of the sentence (Frazier & Rayner, 1982). It thus appears that on such occasions, the normal progress of the eyes is disrupted and some other process takes over.

These two mechanisms—top-down influences on lexical access and interruption when there are comprehension failures—may account in large part for how syntactic and discourse processing are reflected in the pattern of eye movements. Note that this account does not assume that syntactic and discourse processing take no time and effort; however, those processes could go on in parallel with lexical processing and they may usually lag far enough behind the eyes to be irrelevant to directing the normal forward progress of the eyes.

Although it would come as no great surprise that this account of the influence of higher order text processing on eye movements is incomplete, there are no compelling data that argue for its inadequacy. In contrast, there are three phenomena (related to the microstructure of eye movements) that are not easily explained by minor tinkering with the model. First, many words in text are refixated; moreover, the pattern is not random, because many refixations appear to be reflecting cognitive processing. Second (mentioned earlier), sublexical variables, notably the orthographic pattern of the word, appear to affect fixation time. Third, the amount of benefit derived from the preview of a word appears to be related to the difficulty of processing the fixated word. This section argues that the first two phenomena indicate that some event that precedes lexical access is also pushing the eye forward; however it is not clear what this event could be or how it moves the eye. The third phenomenon poses a different problem for Morrison's model, because it indicates that attention movements and eye movements are not as tightly coupled as the model assumes.

First consider the problem of refixations. Whereas the model outlined so far predicts that there will be some refixations on words due to random variability in saccade length, it does not predict that the probability of refixating a word increases when the word is more difficult to process. For example, Inhoff and Rayner (1986) showed that when there was no preview of a word, the first fixation duration on that word was unaffected by the frequency of the word, but the gaze duration (the total time spent on the word before moving on to the next word) was affected by word frequency. Thus, when there is no preview of a word, the duration of the first fixation on the word is unaffected by word frequency. Therefore, there must be circumstances where some event other than lexical access causes the eye to move. However, because gaze duration increased, slower lexical access to the word caused either a greater probability of refixating it, refixating it a longer period of time, or both. (The data indicated that both effects occur.) Similarly, Pollatsek et al., (1986) showed that when a word was approached by a long saccade (greater than eight characters) the benefit of the preview did not affect the first fixation duration on it but did affect gaze duration. The fact that first fixation duration is affected by word frequency when a word is previewed indicates that preview benefit is an important part of the explanation of how lexical access is fast enough to affect fixation duration.

But what moves the eye when lexical access does not? Henderson (1992) proposed a "deadline" mechanism: If no prior signal to move the eyes is given (e.g., by lexical access), a signal is given for the eyes to move when a certain amount of time has elapsed since the beginning of the fixation. Thus, on this view, lexical access only can have an effect if it is fast enough to beat this clock-imposed deadline. This deadline assumption not only explains that fixation duration may be unaffected by word frequency in some circumstances, it also explains the fact that the difficulty of a foveal word (word n) influences the size of the preview benefit from word $n+1$ (Henderson & Ferreira, 1990). (Rayner, 1986, similarly demonstrated that the effective window in reading was smaller for fourth-graders when they were reading difficult text than when they were reading age-appropriate text.) Although this "foveal difficulty effect" on preview benefit seems intuitively reasonable, it is contrary to Morrison's model, which predicts that preview benefit should be unaffected by foveal difficulty. This prediction follows because attention and eye movements are both locked to lexical access: Eye movements occur a fixed period of time after attention has moved (give or take random variation in the motor system). Hence if foveal word X takes 50 ms longer to access than foveal word Y, both the attention movement and eye movement will occur 50 ms later when processing X, and the time allotted for processing the parafoveal word is the same in both cases.

The deadline mechanism explains the foveal difficulty effect, because the deadline signal to move the eyes is assumed to be independent of both lexical access and the consequent shift of covert attention. Thus, for difficult foveal words, the shift of attention to word $n+1$ (produced by lexical access) occurs well after the clock signal to move the eyes (thus allowing little or no parafoveal processing), whereas for easy parafoveal words, the shift of attention may either be coincident with the signal to move the eyes or not long after it (thus allowing considerable parafoveal processing). Such a decoupling of attention and eye movements appears to be necessary to explain the foveal difficulty effect (see also Pollatsek & Rayner, 1990). However, there are data indicating that there are serious problems with assuming that a deadline clock is the primary engine moving the eyes when lexical access is not fast enough to do so.

First of all, when the text in the fovea is delayed, the fixation time is extended by almost an equal amount of time (Morrison, 1984; Rayner & Pollatsek, 1981). That is, whereas a relatively small fraction of the fixations in these studies did seem to be programmed "automatically" from the beginning of the fixation, most fixations appeared to be controlled by the presence of meaningful text. Thus, the clock cannot be starting, in general, at the beginning of the fixation. Although one can assume that the clock starts when meaningful text appears, this makes the clock mechanism much more sophisticated, because the trigger event "meaningful text has appeared" is a fairly complex decision. A second problem arises with the deadline model because it does not predict the distributions of fixation times very well. If the clock is the "last resort" signal to move the eyes, one would expect that cognitive variables such as word frequency would only affect the "lower end" of the fixation duration distribution. The upper end of the distribution should be primarily determined by the clock mechanism and hence the variability in this region should mainly reflect random variability in the clock and random variability in the eye movement system. However, lexical variables are reflected more heavily in the upper end of the distribution than the lower end (Inhoff & Rayner, 1986; McConkie, Underwood, Zola, & Wolverton, 1985).

A deadline mechanism probably accounts for some saccades in reading, but it does not seem like a convincing account of how most saccades are programmed before lexical access occurs. Instead, it seems more parsimonious to argue that these saccades are triggered by the successful completion of some "sublexical" process on the fixated word that wins a race with lexical access. Such a mechanism would explain why lexical access has a primary effect on the upper part of the fixation duration and why fixation durations were lengthened in the Morrison (1984) and Rayner and Pollatsek (1981) experiments when the text was delayed.

The work on sublexical effects (mentioned earlier) reinforces the conclusion that some sublexical mechanism is driving the eyes at least some of the time. Lima and Inhoff (1985) demonstrated that the first fixation on a word such as *clown* was shorter than that on a word such as *dwarf* even though the two words were equated on frequency and suitability in the passage (this was true even if there was no preview). O'Regan, Levy-Schoen, Pynte, and Brugaillere (1984) demonstrated that refixations on a word obey a similar pattern. That is, when the first part of a word is "less informative" (and hence a common pattern), it is fixated a shorter period of time before another fixation is made on the word. These findings indicate that the duration of fixations both before a refixation on the same word and before a saccade to the next word are influenced by some sort of event prior to lexical access.

My current belief is that the most promising approach toward resolving this puzzle is to view most eye movements in reading as resulting from a race between a sublexical identification process and lexical access. The sublexical process would determine something like "the letter cluster in a region around the center of attention has been encoded." If an eye movement is triggered by the sublexical process, then attention will remain on the same word and hence there will be "slippage" between an eye movement and an attention shift to the next word as in the deadline account. Using Morrison's cancellation mechanism, one can assume that if lexical access is rapid, the resulting attention shift and eye movement program will cancel the eye movement programmed by the sublexical event, and thus lexical access can affect the first fixation duration on a word. Analogously, if lexical access is not rapid, it will fail to cancel the sublexical process and not affect the first fixation duration on a word; however, it will affect the gaze duration on a word by affecting the duration of the second fixation.

Although in broad outline, this approach appears to be a successful "patch" on Morrison's model, there are significant problems with it. First, the sublexical mechanism is poorly specified. Although such a mechanism makes functional sense especially for longer words—one does not want to remain fixating the beginning of a 15-letter word long after all useful visual information has been extracted from that fixation—it is not at all clear what the computation would be to signal that the part of a word or object directly fixated is encoded in a satisfactory manner. Second, I have been vague about specifying the target of saccades that are programmed on the basis of these sublexical mechanisms. One possibility is that the target is somewhere else on the same word. If so, then one can account for refixations based on the sublexical mechanism but not fixations to the next word; however, a key assumption in much of this requires that sublexically programmed saccades account for a significant fraction of the saccades that go on to the next word. It thus seems safer to posit that the default location for the target of all saccades is the next word and only an explicit event (such as a covert attention movement to another place on the same word) will cause reprogramming of the target location. In addition, some refixations will be due to random variability in saccade length.

The previous paragraph indicates that we still have a long way to go before we have a model that can really account for the details of eye movements. Before moving on to discuss the use of eye movements in studying reading, I wish to caution against one type of explanation that seems attractive on the surface but is likely to be a delusion. That is, it is very natural to posit that the eyes refixate a word or a fixation is lengthened because the system records that the reader has not successfully completed some operation (e.g., has failed to access a lexical entry). The problem with postulating such mechanisms is that they are too slow, because one should only be able to detect failure to complete a process at a time when that process is usually complete. Thus, unless lexical access was patholog-ically slow (e.g., the fixated word has only been seen once before by the reader), it is likely that lexical access would be completed before the signal to stay on the word could be executed by the eye movement system. Hence, such signals would be nonfunctional. It is possible, of course, that there is some diagnostic event that occurs early in a fixation that could signal probable future failure of lexical access; it is far from clear, however, what such a diagnostic event would be.

USING EYE MOVEMENTS
TO UNDERSTAND READING

A good case can be made that eye movements are the most powerful tool we have for understanding the process of silent reading, because all the standard cognitive diagnostic tools (e.g., measuring naming time or lexical decision time) involve disrupting normal processing. The other on-line techniques (e.g., measuring evoked potentials, word-by-word self-paced reading) are slow and involve a substantial disruption of the normal reading process as well.

Difficulties in Using Fixation Times
As Literally Measuring Processing Time

The previous discussion indicates, however, that the eye movement record has to be interpreted judiciously because the relation between eye movements and cognitive processes is likely to be complex. In particular, one is on shaky ground for interpreting a single fixation time (or any combination of fixation times) as being equal to lexical access time. The argument initially focuses on using fixation time to measure lexical access time, but then is extended to use fixation time to measure the sum of processing stages (e.g., the multiple regression model of Just & Carpenter, 1980).

The main point, of course, is that the time spent fixating on a word is not equal to the time spent processing the word. In the first place, many words are skipped even though they are processed. Moreover, because skipping a word ($n+1$) tends to lengthen the fixation on the prior word (n), some of the fixation time on word n is used in processing the skipped word. Thus, at a minimum, the fixation time on word n should be apportioned into the lexical encoding time for word n and the lexical encoding time for word $n+1$. But how do we divide the time between the two? Clearly we do not know.

Word skipping, however, is just the tip of the iceberg. As we have seen, many words that are fixated are processed in the parafovea as well as the fovea. This would pose little problem if the simplest version of Morrison's model were true and if there were a constant amount of preprocessing on each fixation. Then there would be a tradeoff such that fixation n would contain preprocessing time for word $n+1$, but this preprocessing time would be the same as the preprocessing time for word n that occurred on the prior fixation. (For a fuller version of this argument, see Pollatsek & Rayner, 1990). Even if this assumption were true, however, there would still be problems with interpreting the duration of the first fixation on a line of text (where there is no preview benefit) and the duration of the last fixation on a line (often not on the last word of the line).

A major problem with assuming such a tradeoff between previews is that the foveal difficulty effect indicates that preview benefit is not constant. Thus one needs some independent measure of preview benefit (which does not exist) in order to make an appropriate adjustment to the fixation time. In addition, differential preview benefit will also be hard to estimate because it may produce nonlocal effects. That is, if word n is difficult to process, there may be no preview of word $n+1$; this in turn may make word $n+1$ difficult to process, which may mean that word $n+2$ receives little preview benefit and so forth.

So far, the argument has been in terms of attempting to infer lexical access time from fixation time on a word. What if one attempts to use fixation time on a word to measure the sum of putative processing times on a word? Just and Carpenter (1980), for example, invoked the "immediacy hypothesis"—that fixation time on a word was the sum of processing times on that word needed to fit it into the ongoing discourse structure—to claim that fixation time on a word was the sum of the time needed to lexically encode the word, fit it into the ongoing syntactic structure and into the ongoing discourse structure, together with processes related to fixing ideas in memory such as "sentence wrapup time." (It should be emphasized that subjecting fixation times to multiple regression analyses entails the assumption that the total time is literally the sum of these component times.)

None of the problems discussed here in using fixation time on a word to measure lexical encoding time go away when we instead use it to measure total processing time. That is, word skipping and parafoveal preview benefit imply (a) that at least part of the processing of words occurs before when they are fixated or when they are skipped, and (b) some of the processing time on word n is going into processing word $n+1$. There is a further problem in using fixation time on word n to infer the time taken for these higher order processes on word n: Many of these processes continue after a word is fixated. An example discussed earlier was anaphora, where processing difficultly related to unusual gender assignment is often registered at least several fixations "downstream" from the pronoun and may be distributed (on average) over a whole phrase. Another example is that when faced by syntactic ambiguity, such as "The desert trains" (which could be an adjective noun combination or a noun verb combination), readers tend to delay resolution of this ambiguity for a word or two (Frazier & Rayner, 1987).

These delayed effects do not necessarily argue against a decomposition of reading time into component times. That is, the time (for example) to make a pronoun assignment may be added to lexical encoding time, syntactic processing time, and so forth. However, they argue against a simple decomposition related to the text actually being fixated, because one does not know which delayed effect (if any) is going to show up on a particular fixation.

A Better Strategy—
Use Fixation Time As an Ordinal Measure

Given the aforementioned difficulties, how does one use eye movements to make inferences about cognitive processes? As has been argued elsewhere (Pollatsek & Rayner, 1990), one is on safer ground if fixation time is used as an ordinal measure. For example, an experimenter can employ two sentences that are identical except that one word is different—a high frequency word in one sentence and a low frequency word in the other sentence (Inhoff & Rayner, 1986). If one observes that the high frequency word is fixated for a shorter period of time, then one can safely infer that cognitive processing time was less for the high frequency word. Of course, it would not necessarily follow that either (a) the difference was due to the difference in frequency, or (b) the difference was in lexical encoding time. To make the former inference, one would have to control for the length of the word and other potential variables that could influence lexical processing (e.g., orthographic and phonological regularity). These precautions, of course, would have to be taken no matter what the measure. To make the latter inference, one would have to construct the sentences so that there was no other plausible explanation (e.g., the high frequency word fit into the sentence better). Again, this kind of control would be necessary regardless of the measure used. Even if all these precautions are taken, there is still no guarantee that the difference observed is due to lexical access. In this regard, fixation time is no worse than any other measure, because there is no guarantee that a difference in any other measure (e.g., naming time, lexical decision time) reflects lexical encoding rather than another stage of linguistic processing.

The previous paragraph is too negative because it suggests that fixation time is no worse than any other measure in making inferences about lexical encoding. However, there are reasons to think it is better. First, fixation times are much shorter than any manual or vocal response, so they should have less time to be contaminated by strategic effects. Second, the process one presumably wants to study is reading of text, so the other processes that may "contaminate" the fixation time besides lexical access are components of the reading process rather than components of an arbitrary laboratory task (such as lexical decision) whose generalizability to reading is questionable.

The logic applied to the word frequency example can obviously be extended to study syntactic and discourse processes. For example, in the "garden path" sentences discussed earlier, there are two sentences matched up to the point of disambiguation. One infers difficulty in syntactic processing when fixation times are much longer at the point of disambiguation (given that the difficulty is not plausibly related to difficulty in lexically encoding the word that disambiguates the sentence). The major problem with this approach is that it requires the use of controlled materials that are identical except for a key difference related to the manipulation of interest (e.g., the frequency of the critical word, the syntactic structure, the gender of a pronoun). This means that one uses materials constructed for the experiment and raises the possibility that these materials are "artificial" and not processed by the subjects as they would process ordinary discourse. Although this is a nontrivial problem, it can be minimized by exercising care in coming up with reasonable materials. In general it seems less of a problem than using less controlled correlational methods such as multiple regression, which, as argued earlier, rely on extremely dubious assumptions about fixation times.

To summarize, fixation time is virtually unassailable as a measure if it is used to make inferences of the form "X takes less time to process in reading than does Y." (X and Y could be words, phrases, clauses, etc.) That may sound insufficiently specific, because one generally wants to know which stages of processing are being affected. As indicated earlier, doing a stage analysis of eye movement data relies on similar logic to a stage analysis of other data. That is, if (for example) one wants to infer that lexical access has been affected, one varies only aspects of the text that would plausibly affect lexical access. There are other guidelines from the time course of processing, however, that should be of value. The simplest is that if a manipulation has its effect only after the eyes have left a word, then it is fairly safe to assume that the effect is postlexical. Note that a plausible mechanism was presented for how lexical effects could show up past the point of fixation: More difficult processing on fixation n could take away preview benefit on fixation $n+1$, which in turn could increase difficulty on fixation $n+2$, and so forth. However, it seems unlikely that such a mechanism could produce effects "downstream" without producing effects on fixation n.

According to a second reasonable rule of thumb, if a variable affects the amount of "preview benefit," then it is likely to be exerting at least some of its effect in the visual extraction stage of processing (which is presumably lexical or prelexical). For example, Balota, Pollatsek, and Rayner (1985), found that the predictability of a target word in a sentence determined the size of the preview benefit (more predictable words had a greater preview benefit) and inferred (using additive factors logic, Sternberg, 1969), that a visual process related to the visual manipulation (quality of preview) was being modulated by the predictability of the target word. Another way to state this is that the preview manipulation is early in the processing chain—it is an event that occurs before the word is fixated—and thus it only plausibly affects early stages of processing.

A final caution is in order. Fixation times are shorter than manual and vocal responses, but they do not only reveal early stages of processing, because (as argued earlier) they are sensitive to difficulties in syntactic and discourse processing. One way to determine the extent that they are reflecting lexical processing is to obtain converging validity using another measure of lexical access. The best such measure at present appears to be naming time. In this regard, it is worth noting that virtually all the preview effects we have reported show up in approximately equal magnitudes in fixation measures in reading and in naming times to individual words (see Rayner & Pollatsek, 1989, for a review and Pollatsek, Lesch, Morris, & Rayner, 1992, for a recent finding in this regard). Fixation times and naming times do not always converge, but their divergence can be illuminating. For example, Schustack, Ehrlich, and Rayner (1987) manipulated both the distance between a target word and its prior mention and the predictability of the target word. They found that both variables produced effects on the fixation time on the target word. In contrast, in a separate experiment in which subjects named the target word after reading the prior sentence context, only predictability had an effect on naming time. These data suggest that predictability had an effect on lexical access while the distance between the antecedent and the target word did not and only influenced the ease in making the anaphoric connection between the two. This interpretation was strengthened by the finding that the two manipulations had additive effects on fixation time. Of course, one cannot take as written in stone that naming time is a valid measure of lexical access (c.f. Balota & Chumbley, 1985), but this kind of convergent validity promises to add significant power to the inferences that can be drawn from the eye movement record.

REFERENCES

Balota, D. A., & Chumbley, J. I. (1985). The locus of word-frequency effects in the pronunciation task: Lexical access and/or production? *Journal of Memory and Language, 24,* 89–106.

Balota, D. A., Pollatsek, A., & Rayner, K. (1985). The interaction of contextual constraints and parafoveal visual information in reading. *Cognitive Psychology, 17,* 364–390.

Becker, W., & Jurgens, R. (1979). An analysis of the saccadic system by means of double-step stimuli. *Vision Research, 19,* 967–983.

Blanchard, H. E., Pollatsek, A., & Rayner, K. (1989). The acquisition of parafoveal word information in reading. *Perception & Psychophysics, 46,* 85–94.

Ehrlich, S. F., & Rayner, K. (1981). Contextual effects on word perception and eye movements during reading. *Journal of Verbal Learning and Verbal Behavior, 20,* 641–655.

Ehrlich, K., & Rayner, K. (1983). Pronoun assignment and semantic integration during reading: Eye movements and immediacy of processing. *Journal of Verbal Learning and Verbal Behavior, 22,* 75–87.

Frazier, L., & Rayner, K. (1982). Making and correcting errors during sentence comprehension: Eye movements in the analysis of structurally ambiguous sentences. *Cognitive Psychology, 14,* 178–210.

Frazier, L., & Rayner, K. (1987). Resolution of syntactic category ambiguities: Eye movements in parsing lexically ambiguous sentences. *Journal of Memory and Language, 26,* 505–526.

Henderson, J. M. (1992). Visual attention and eye movement control during reading and picture viewing. In K. Rayner (Ed.), *Eye movements and visual cognition: Scene perception and reading* (pp. 260–283). New York: Springer-Verlag.

Henderson, J. M., & Ferreira, F. (1990). Effects of foveal processing difficulty on the perceptual span in reading: Implications for attention and eye movement control. *Journal of Experimental Psychology: Learning, Memory and Cognition, 16,* 417–429.

Hogaboam, T. W. (1983). Reading patterns in eye movement data. In K. Rayner (Ed.), *Eye movements in reading* (pp. 309–332). New York: Academic Press.

Inhoff, A. W., & Rayner, K. (1986). Parafoveal word processing during eye fixations in reading: Effects of word frequency. *Perception & Psychophysics, 40,* 431–439.

Just, M. A., & Carpenter, P. A. (1980). A theory of reading: From eye fixations to comprehension. *Psychological Review, 87,* 329–354.

Just, M. A., & Carpenter, P. A. (1987). *The psychology of reading and language comprehension.* Newton, MA: Allyn & Bacon.

Kliegl, R., Olson, R. K., & Davidson, B. J. (1982). Regression analyses as a tool for studying reading processes: Comments on Just and Carpenter's eye fixation theory. *Memory & Cognition, 10,* 287–296.

Lima, S. D., & Inhoff, A. W. (1985). Lexical access during eye fixations in reading: Effects of word-initial letter sequence. *Journal of Experimental Psychology: Human Perception and Performance, 11,* 272–285.

McConkie, G. W., Kerr, P. W., Reddix, M. D., & Zola, D. (1988). Eye movement control during reading: 1. The location of initial fixations on word. *Vision Research, 28,* 1107–1118.

McConkie, G. W., & Rayner, K. (1975). The span of the effective stimulus during a fixation in reading. *Perception & Psychophysics, 17,* 578–586.

McConkie, G. W., Underwood, N. R., Zola, D., & Wolverton, G. S. (1985). Some temporal characteristics of processing during reading. *Journal of Experimental Psychology: Human Perception and Performance, 11,* 168–186.

McConkie, G. W., & Zola, D. (1981). Language constraints and the functional stimulus in reading. In A. M. Lesgold & C. A. Perfetti (Eds.), *Interactive processes in reading* (pp. 155–175). Hillsdale, NJ: Lawrence Erlbaum Associates.

Morris, R. K., Rayner, K., & Pollatsek, A. (1990). Eye movement guidance in reading: The role of parafoveal letter and space information. *Journal of Experimental Psychology: Human Perception and Performance, 16,* 268–281.

Morrison, R. E. (1984). Manipulation of stimulus onset delay in reading: Evidence for parallel programming of saccades. *Journal of Experimental Psychology: Human Perception and Performance, 10,* 667–682.

O'Regan, J. K. (1979). Eye guidance in reading: Evidence for linguistic control hypothesis. *Perception & Psychophysics, 25,* 501–509.

O'Regan, J. K. (1981). The convenient viewing position hypothesis. In D. F. Fisher, R. A. Monty, & J. W. Senders (Eds.), *Eye movements: Cognition and visual perception* (pp. 289–298). Hillsdale, NJ: Lawrence Erlbaum Associates.

O'Regan, J. K., Levy-Schoen, A., Pynte, J., & Brugaillere, B. (1984). Convenient fixation location within isolated words of different length and structures. *Journal of Experimental Psychology: Human Perception & Performance, 10,* 250–257.

Pollatsek, A., Bolozky, S., Well, A. D., & Rayner, K. (1981). Asymmetries in the perceptual span for Israeli readers. *Brain and Language, 14,* 174–180.

Pollatsek, A., Lesch, M., Morris, R. K., & Rayner, K. (1992). Phonological codes are used in integrating information across saccades in word identification and reading. *Journal of Experimental Psychology: Human Perception and Performance, 18,* 148–162.

Pollatsek, A., Raney, G. E., LaGasse, L. L., & Rayner, K. (in press). The effect on reading of information below the line. *Canadian Journal of Psychology.*

Pollatsek, A., & Rayner, K. (1982). Eye movement control in reading: The role of word boundaries. *Journal of Experimental Psychology: Human Perception and Performance, 8,* 817–833.

Pollatsek, A., & Rayner, K. (1990). Eye movements and lexical access in reading. In D. A. Balota, G. B. Flores d'Arcais, & K. Rayner (Eds.), *Comprehension processes in reading* (pp. 143–163). Hillsdale, NJ: Lawrence Erlbaum Associates.

Pollatsek, A., & Rayner, K. (1992). What is integrated across fixations? In K. Rayner (Ed.), *Eye movements and visual cognition: Scene perception and reading* (pp. 166–191). New York: Springer-Verlag.

Pollatsek, A., Rayner, K., & Balota, D. A. (1986). Inferences about eye movement control from the perceptual span in reading. *Perception & Psychophysics, 40,* 123–130.

Rayner, K. (1979). Eye guidance in reading: Fixation locations within words. *Perception, 8,* 21–30.

Rayner, K. (1986). Eye movements and the perceptual span in beginning and skilled readers. *Journal of Experimental Child Psychology, 41,* 211–236.

Rayner, K., & Bertera, J. H. (1979). Reading without a fovea. *Science, 206,* 468–469.

Rayner, K., & Duffy, S. A. (1986). Lexical complexity and fixation times in reading: Effects of word frequency, verb complexity, and lexical ambiguity. *Memory & Cognition, 14,* 191–201.

Rayner, K., McConkie, G. W., & Ehrlich, S. F. (1978). Eye movements and integrating information across fixations. *Journal of Experimental Psychology: Human Perception and Performance, 4,* 529–544.

Rayner, K., & Pollatsek, A. (1981). Eye movement control during reading: Evidence for direct control. *Quarterly Journal of Experimental Psychology, 33A,* 351–373.

Rayner, K., & Pollatsek, A. (1987). Eye movements in reading: A tutorial review. In M. Coltheart (Ed.), *Attention and Performance* (Vol. 12, pp. 327–362). London: Lawrence Erlbaum Associates.

Rayner, K., & Pollatsek, A. (1989). *The psychology of reading.* Englewood Cliffs, NJ: Prentice-Hall.

Rayner, K., Slowiaczek, M. L., Clifton, C., & Bertera, J. H. (1983). Latency of sequential eye movements: Implications for reading. *Journal of Experimental Psychology: Human Perception and Performance, 9,* 912–922.

Rayner, K., Well, A. D., & Pollatsek, A. (1980). Asymmetry of the effective visual field in reading. *Perception & Psychophysics, 27,* 537–544.

Rayner, K., Well, A. D., Pollatsek, A., & Bertera, J. H. (1982). The availability of useful information to the right of fixation in reading. *Perception & Psychophysics, 31,* 537–550.

Schustack, M. W., Ehrlich, S. F., & Rayner, K. (1987). The complexity of contextual facilitation in reading: Local and global influences. *Journal of Memory and Language, 26,* 322–340.

Sternberg, S. (1969). The discovery of processing stages: Extensions of Donders' method. In W. G. Koster (Ed.), *Attention and performance II, Acta Psychologica, 30,* 276–315.

Wurtz, R. H., Goldberg, M. E., & Robinson, D. L. (1982). Brain mechanisms of visual attention. *Scientific American, 246,* 124–135.

10 Eye Movement Control and Visual Display Units

Alan Kennedy
University of Dundee

INTRODUCTION

This chapter represents an attempt to account for the problems some readers encounter when they process text on a visual display unit (VDU) rather than as hard copy. The people most likely to complain are typists and other professionals who use VDUs for long periods. The symptoms reported include eye strain, headache, minor visual disturbances, and fatigue. The exact nature of the disadvantage that the screen as a presentation medium may represent, still remains something of a mystery, but on the assumption that this disadvantage is real, computer and screen manufacturers have devoted a great deal of design effort to the search for the ideal display terminal. Unfortunately, this effort has been, so far, in vain. The main purpose of this chapter is to offer an explanation as to why this should be so.

I wish to propose that visual fatigue arises, in a significant measure, from the effects of the pulsation of light characteristic of refreshed displays (which may or may not be seen as visible flicker). Pulsation of this kind may have several general effects and some of these are reviewed later, but one is particularly relevant to the skill of reading. Screen pulsation acts to disturb some of the processes of eye movement control. How this occurs is as yet obscure, but the nature of the effect is becoming more clear and I report on recent work from our laboratory (Kennedy & Murray, 1991) that has demonstrated a direct effect on saccade control, shortening the extent of some saccades and, as a consequence, changing their landing position in the to-be-fixated word. To appreciate the significance of this, it is necessary to consider in detail recent discoveries concerning eye movement control *within* the word. For a given word, there is a "best place" to which the eyes should be directed and deviations from this point will be paid for by slower and less efficient processing. The importance of the small changes in saccade length induced by screen pulsation now becomes evident: If there is an increase in nonoptimal landings within words, this will, in turn, exact a penalty in the form of increases in fixation duration and in the probability of additional within-word refixations. Whether or not these latter occur may depend on the reader's strategy: Subjects may be more or less tolerant of finding themselves inspecting a point other than that which was targeted within a word. Some typists in particular appear to be very intolerant of an inappropriate viewing position and it will be claimed that it is this subset of typists that has particular problems with screen displays.

The organization of the chapter takes the following form: The first section considers the rather scattered literature on processing differences between screen and paper. This is followed by an examination of subject differences, outlining the way in which the processing strategies of typists differ from those of other readers. Next, the effects of screen pulsation on reading are examined, with particular reference to eye movement control. Mechanisms that might underlie the obtained alterations in saccade length are discussed. This is followed by a brief discussion of the notion of the "Optimal Viewing Position" in both single word and continuous text processing. Finally, the results of some recent experimental work are presented, examining the eye movements of typists and non-typists as a function of screen refresh rate.

READING SPEED, COMPREHENSION AND DISPLAY FORMAT

Before attempting to answer the question as to what is it about visual display units that makes them difficult to read, it would be prudent to consider the evidence underlying its premise: Namely, the assertion that processing text from a VDU does, in fact, incur real penalties and, if this is the case, to examine what form they take. This preliminary work is necessary because an examination of the published literature reveals a somewhat confused picture. Table 10.1 is a summary of some of the more recent studies looking at the effects of mode of display on a variety of reading and comprehension measures. It is evident that research on this topic is not, as yet, in a settled state. There are several reasons for this. It has proved very difficult to compare like with like in experimental tasks. For example, text presented on a VDU screen may differ from its equivalent hard copy version in size, spacing, legibility, contrast, polarity, and density, and any of these factors could influence processing efficiency (Muter, Latremouille, & Treurniet, 1982). Similarly, restrictions on the size, orientation, and layout of VDU "pages" may influence processing speed (Kolers, Duchnicky, & Ferguson, 1981). In addition, the reading habits of the typical VDU

TABLE 10.1
Summary of Recent Studies Comparing Performance with Screen and Hard Copy

Author	Task	Measure	Outcome	Subjects
Askwall (1985)	Search/integration in short texts	Search time	VDU longer than hard copy	College students
Cushman (1986)	Reading from VDU and microfiche	Fatigue	Fatigue greater and reading time slower in negative polarity	Students
Haas & Hayes (1985, 1986)	Letter composition	Time	Time to compose; content and quality poorer with some screens	Expert writers; editors
Gould (1981)	Text composition	Time	Time to compose slower with VDU than paper	Writers; editors
Gould & Grischkowsky (1984)	Proofreading	Time accuracy	No difference in accuracy; slower with VDU than paper	Clerk-typists
Kennedy & Murray (1991)	Sentence reading and target	Eye movements	Saccades shorter and more variable in flicker	Students; typists
Kolers, Duchnicky, & Ferguson (1981)	Text processing	Eye movements	Processing from static "page" better than scrolled "page"	Students

(Continued)

TABLE 10.1
(Continued)

Author	Task	Measure	Outcome	Subjects
Kruk & Muter (1984)	Extended text processing	Reading time	VDU slower than hard copy	Students
Muter, Latremouille, & Treurniet (1982)	Extended text processing	Reading time	VDU slower than hard copy	Students
Newsted (1985)	Responding to questions	Accuracy	Performance better with VDU than hard copy	Students
Taptagaporn (1990)	Target detection and enumeration	Pupil size	Positive display polarity better than negative	Students
Wilkins (1986)	Fixating targets in text	Saccade size	Saccades larger in low frequency flicker	Women volunteers from subject panel volunteers
Wright & Lickorish (1988)	Finding items in extended text	Reading time	Time longer and accuracy worse with VDU	Subject panel volunteers
Askwall (1985)	Search/integration in short texts	Accuracy	No difference	College students
Cushman (1986)	Reading from VDU and microfiche	Comprehension Reading time	No difference No difference	Students
Kruk & Muter (1984)	Extended test processing	Viewing distance contrast	No difference	Students
Muter, Latremouille, & Treurniet (1982)	Extended text processing	Visual fatigue and nausea	No difference	Students
Oborne & Holton (1988)	Text processing	Comprehension	No difference	Students

user (i.e., professional typists) may differ systematically from those of the population at large (Inhoff, Morris, & Calabrese, 1986; Inhoff, 1991). Furthermore, as Oborne and Holton (1988) point out, the literature is extremely confused because the variables that have been considered relevant (posture, color, orientation, contrast, etc.) have rarely been manipulated systematically and the measures taken (reading time, time to comprehend, question accuracy, fixation duration, pupil size, visual fatigue, etc.) have not been comparable across studies. Thus for example, knowing that proofreading is slower on screen than on paper (Wright & Lickorish, 1983) but that responses to questions are apparently *more* accurate with screen presentation (Newsted, 1985) does little to clarify whether these differences relate to subject, task, or presentation variables.

Indeed, the situation has been made worse by the very flexibility of the VDU display itself, which has tempted experimenters into manipulations not possible with hard copy. For example, in "page scrolling" the screen position of words necessarily changes relative to the boundary defined by the screen border. It is possible that these dynamic characteristics of VDU displays act to disrupt spatial coding (see Kennedy, 1992, for a discussion) and this may underlie the observation that processing is easier when the displayed "page" mirrors a normal page and does not involve the reader in spatial mappings that overlap, as when two parts of a "virtual page" are viewed (Wright & Lickorish, 1983). The review of the literature carried out by Oborne and Holton (1988) led them to conclude that, in fact, no real differences could be demonstrated between screen and hard copy if adequate controls were employed. Unfortunately, this conclusion itself is less than convincing because their appeal to the null hypothesis rested on the use of very global measures of reading comprehension.

It is clear from an examination of Table 10.1 that at least one outcome is relatively ubiquitous, namely, processing times are longer when material is presented on a screen. For example, Zwahlen, Hartman, Rangarajula, and Escontrela (1985) examined the total time spent looking at screen or hard copy in matched tasks involving typing and data entry. The subjects (who were experienced typists) spent more time looking at a split screen (i.e., screen-to-screen) presentation than at the comparable page-to-page display. Zwahlen and Adams (1987) confirmed this outcome and demonstrated that similar effects obtain with both the familiar dark-on-light (positive polarity) presentation and with its reverse. Wright and Lickorish (1983), using nontypist subjects also found a VDU display disadvantage, with subjects slower to deal with questions relating to a previously read text. Although legibility was not controlled in this study, it is unlikely to have been a major factor, because the hard copy consisted of output from a dot-matrix printer. A number of other studies come to the same conclusion, suggesting that reading is, for some reason, slowed down when text is processed on a VDU screen. It is unfortunate that so much of the experimental work outlined in Table 10.1 is essentially atheoretical, because slower processing must relate in some way to the distribution of eye movements over the screen or page (involving, for example, changes in the frequency or duration of fixations, or possibly both), and a great deal of theoretical progress has been made in understanding the mechanisms of eye movement control in reading (Pollatsek, chap. 9; Rayner, 1983). Indeed, the position to be adopted here is that if the problem of visual fatigue is to be understood, principled hypotheses relating to eye movement control must be derived in three distinct domains: subject populations, task variables (in particular, the influence of screen pulsation), and the mechanisms underlying dysfunction.

SUBJECT VARIABLES

The subjects who complain of headache and visual disturbances of a more or less severe kind are mainly professional typists. The skill of typing has been examined in detail by Shaffer (1973, 1975) and two observations relevant to the present chapter can be made. First, between-word errors (e.g., spoonerisms) are extremely rare in the output of skilled typists, although letter transpositions and imports *within* a word may occur. Second, studies of typing under conditions where preview can be manipulated (using a contingent computer-controlled display) reveal advantages for preview up to the word boundary, but not much beyond. In other words, the skilled typist appears to act on words, converting letter strings into a series of patterned motor acts, without higher level relationships between words (e.g., syntactic or semantic relations) entering into this process. Thus, whereas typing may in a superficial sense appear to mimic speech production, there is no equivalent to the prosodic or suprasegmental level. As Shaffer (1975) remarks:

> There is an important and perhaps significant difference between typing on the one hand and speech and musical performance on the other: the more highly skilled the typist the more monotonous her performance becomes (Genest, 1965), whereas in fluent speech the intonation contour of the phrase conveys some of its meaning and music is interpreted by controlled variation in dynamics and timing. These 'suprasegmental' features provide a strong a priori reason for assuming hierarchic structure in response output while their absence as a task requirement argues for a simpler structure in typing. (p. 419)

An important question now arises. What influence on *normal* reading could these particular strategies have? Surprisingly, there appears to have been little or no systematic work on this topic. Studies comparing the eye movements of typists and nontypists on a normal reading task, that is, not specifically involving typing, are not available (although some preliminary data on the subject are reported later). It is clear, however, that when actually typing, the professional typist pays more attention to local orthography in text and exhibits an eye–hand span much shorter than the normal eye–voice span (Butch, 1932). Average fixation duration during transcription typing is longer than normal and saccade extent is shorter (Inhoff et al., 1986). If these patterns constitute a reading style that might carry over to nontyping tasks, this would have at least two important consequences. First, sensitivity to variation in landing position may be greater; and second, higher level influences (from syntax or from semantic context), which might normally act to support comprehension, may be engaged to a lesser degree.

SCREEN PULSATION

The experimental literature contrasting screen and page may be contentious, but there is no doubt that screen-based word processing does present problems to many users. The incidence of complaints of headache and short-term visual disturbance associated with VDU use is well-documented (see, for example, National Institute for Occupational Safety and Health [NIOSH], 1983, or House of Lords, 1988). The word of Wilkins and his colleagues (Neary & Wilkins, 1989; Wilkins, 1985, 1986, chap. 20 this volume) has gone a long way to explain some of these effects by demonstrating that the stimulus configuration provided by text, whether presented on a screen or as a printed page (that is, a high contrast striped surface with a spatial frequency typically of about three cycles per degree), is highly unacceptable to some subjects (Wilkins, 1991). In certain circumstances, and for some particularly susceptible individuals, looking at patterns of this kind can induce severe visual disturbance. There are advantages for readers in this category if all but a single line of text on a page is masked off (Wilkins & Nimmo-Smith, 1984, 1987). However, what is more important for the present argument is the observation that these problems are exacerbated if the stimulus itself flickers or is viewed under conditions of flickering illumination. Even the barely visible flicker produced by normal fluorescent strip-lighting may induce headaches.

The detailed neural effects of pulsating illumination of different frequencies would take us too far from the theme of this chapter (see Eysel & Burandt, 1984), but quite obviously they are relevant to the study of the VDU, where the screen must be continually refreshed. At the level of the pixels comprising each displayed letter, the surface of the VDU screen can be thought of as a light source undergoing rapid and continual pulsation. Whether or not this is perceived as visible flicker depends on a number of factors, including the brightness and size of the pulsating field, as well as the pulse frequency itself, and screen designers have attempted to solve the problem of perceived flicker by looking for a compromise between refresh rate and phosphor speed. With the right choice of phosphor, crisp screen displays can be produced that do not smear (that is, the phosphor decays very rapidly) and yet have virtually no visible flicker, particularly when refreshed at frequencies above the point of normal subjective fusion (i.e., above about 45 Hz). Unfortunately, this purely empirical approach to the problem has ignored other mechanisms that are certainly vulnerable to the effects of a pulsating display, whether or not the pulsation is visible.

Saccades are produced at high speed, involving spatial displacements at velocities up to 500 degrees per second (Fuchs, 1976). Bearing this in mind it is possible to reconsider the consequences of executing eye movements across a rapidly pulsating field. It is well known, of course, that visual input during the saccade is effectively suppressed, but relatively little of this suppression is truly "central": It is, in the main, the result of masking effects produced by successive superimposed foveal "snapshots" (Breitmeyer, 1980; Matin, 1974). In a number of papers, Breitmeyer and his colleagues (Breitmeyer, 1983, 1984, chap. 5 this volume) showed how the interaction between transient and sustained channels in the visual system can be used to account for saccadic suppression. Although not entirely uncontroversial (Breitmeyer, 1991), the psychophysical and physiological evidence in favor of a distinction between sustained and transient channels in the human visual system is impressive (see Legge, 1978, for a review). Breitmeyer's model assumes that as successive saccades are made, a series of overlapping sustained responses occur. This visual response persistence (or "iconic memory") means that the "contents" of each fixation have the potential to mask their successors through a process of stimulus integration. What needs explanation, therefore, is why this is not, in fact, the perceived outcome.

When reading (or viewing the world) we are conscious of a stable visual field that does not jump about and is not smeared as the eyes move. The explanation can be found by postulating a *transient* response also associated with the onset of each saccade and that has the effect of inhibiting the sustained response. That is, as Breitmeyer puts it, "normal vision is iconoclastic." The response of sustained neurones drops off at high velocities, but the transient neurones show little attenuation, even at the very high velocities found when images are displaced during a saccade. Unfortunately, the time course of the suppression that results from this rapid image displacement is, in fact, quite slow and would, other things being equal, appreciably outlast the duration of the saccade itself. The model must, therefore, be complicated a little. This can be done by considering that, in normal circumstances, the suppressive effect itself is curtailed by the central corollary discharges that accompany the control of directed saccades (that is, the intention to direct an eye movement to a particular location). Crucially, however, in the context of the present discussion, the orchestration of these saccade-produced inhibitory or facilitatory effects depends on whether the eyes are moving across a patterned or unpatterned surface (Adey & Noda, 1973, cited by Breitmeyer, 1984). The saccade-produced suppressive effect is found only when saccades are made across a patterned field. Obviously, when saccades are made across a pulsating surface, a proportion of them (depending on the rate of pulsation) will be executed wholly or partly across a blank field.

If the model proposed by Breitmeyer is correct, this will disrupt perception considerably, leading to a proportion of fixations being inadequately segregated. Unfortunately, there is little or no direct evidence on this from human subjects and for the time being the proposal must be seen as speculative. However, Becker, Kieffer, and Jurgens (1987) do provide indirect evidence, showing that a single transient event (either visual or auditory), which occurs after a saccade has been initiated will act to alter saccade velocity and end point. It is interesting to note in passing that there is increasing evidence implicating deficits in the transient system in reading-disabled subjects (Lovegrove, 1991; Lovegrove, Heddle, & Slaghuis, 1986; Lovegrove & Williams, chap. 14). What Lovegrove suggests, in effect, is that the mechanisms underlying transient-on-sustained channel inhibition are not fully effective in most (i.e., 60% to 65%) subjects characterized as reading disabled. Both Lovegrove (1991) and Breitmeyer (1991) are tempted to the conclusion that reading impairment stems from poor temporal segregation of successive fixations and a consequential ambiguity with regard to the spatial location of visual targets.

The possibility may also be entertained that saccades can be *triggered* by external events independent of the process of saccade computation itself. The stimulation produced by a pulsating peripheral field, in particular, may act as an external trigger of this kind. Thus, although in reading saccades are typically the result of voluntary attentional changes, taking the form of decision to fixate successive words, a pulsating display may act to engage event-triggered saccades typical of unplanned shifts of attention. In these circumstances, the eyes will be launched toward their destination on the basis of the current (but incomplete) state of computation regarding the next target location (i.e., the Optimal Viewing Point in the next word to be fixated). This target computation is continually updated on the basis of available visual information that becomes more refined with time and is modulated by attentional processes (Deubel, Wolf, & Hauske, 1984), with high spatial frequency information becoming available later than low frequency information. A premature saccade will be launched toward the visual center of gravity of the target region as a whole (Findlay, 1981, 1982). In principle, such an effect may lead both to an increased number of saccades falling short of their target and an overall increase in the variability of saccade end point.

It is possible, of course, that disruption to low level visual processes caused by stimulus pulsation may be quite global. For example, stimulation of the transient system may lead directly to anomalous visual effects (e.g., tilting or blurring of the image) and these may increase as the frequency of pulsation increases, regardless of their precise relation to saccade timing. It is perhaps more profitable to ask what are the *perceptual* consequences of the processes that screen pulsation may induce in the visual system? The most important is the possibility that the pulsating screen allows normally invisible suppressed images to become visible. Neary and Wilkins (1989) provide striking evidence in support of this proposition. They had subjects make saccades between two points displayed on a typical raster display, with a short persistence phosphor. Transient "ghost images" were seen in the vicinity of the target. If the saccades were made between pairs of lines, the effects were more dramatic, with the subject perceiving a momentary tilt in the target line. Neary and Wilkins account for these results by pointing to the fact that the raster scan "writes" the successive pixels comprising a line from top to bottom of the display screen and the perceived tilt can obviously be related to this process occurring as the eyes move across an otherwise blank field. The effects on the reader of manifestly visible events occurring *en saccade* could be significant, with illusory shifts in target location mimicking the effects of classical "double-step" experiments on saccade control (Becker & Jurgens, 1979). That is, the end point of the saccade will be modified as a result of uncertainty regarding the target position.

WITHIN-WORD EFFECTS
ON EYE MOVEMENT CONTROL

In a series of experiments, O'Regan and his colleagues (O'Regan, 1989, 1990; O'Regan & Levy-Schoen, 1987) examined the pattern of eye movements as single words are identified. Their work has led to the important conclusion that total processing time on a word is heavily influenced by the point of initial fixation. Under laboratory conditions it is possible to manipulate the point of initial fixation on a word systematically. The results of such experiments typically show that gaze duration (i.e., the sum of all fixations on the word up to the point when the eye first leaves the word boundary) is a function of the location of the point of initial fixation. This *Optimal Viewing Position* is located near the word's center. If the first fixation is located elsewhere, a penalty of about 20 ms is incurred for each character position of displacement. However, these increases in gaze duration are produced by changes in the probability of making more than one fixation on the word rather than by increases in fixation duration per se. In fact, considering the first fixation alone (when more than two are made) the relationship between initial viewing position and fixation duration takes an opposite form, with longer times at the Optimal Viewing Position. There are, in other words, trade-offs between fixation duration and the probability of making another within-word saccade (O'Regan & Levy-Schoen, 1987). An initial fixation in an inappropriate place will trigger one or more additional fixations and these will have the effect of increasing quite dramatically the total time spent inspecting a word.

The relationship between fixation duration and saccade extent (what might be termed the "when" and "where" decisions of eye movement control) is complex and depends crucially on the length of the fixated word. For short words, it is likely that lexical access can be secured in a single fixation, regardless of the initial fixation point. For longer words (which are unlikely to be processed in a single fixation) the picture can be summarized as follows (Pynte, Kennedy, & Murray, 1991): (a) the eye movement control system is intolerant of an initial landing position well to the right; if the eyes arrive in this position, there is an immediate correction, the locus of control for which is probably an oculomotor process sensitive only to relative landing position; (b) for initial landings near the beginning of long words, the duration of the very first fixation (in the case of multiple fixations) is influenced by sublexical properties of the word such as the familiarity of the letter sequences and by the "informativeness" of the region fixated (i.e., the degree to which the letters constrain possible "candidate" lexical entries); in this case there is a trade-off between fixation duration of the first fixation and the probability of making additional fixations; (c) whereas early processes associated with the first saccade-fixation-saccade event appear immune to the influence of high level factors such as lexical status and context, later fixations are influenced. Thus, a strong supporting context can act to reduce the duration of later fixations and alter the probability of making additional fixations. It may also influence the size of any additional within-word saccades.

These laboratory studies show quite clearly that there is an Optimal Viewing Position for words viewed singly, but it is important to ask whether, in normal reading, the reader directs saccades toward this point. Is the Optimal Viewing Position also the *Preferred Viewing Position?* McConkie, Kerr, Reddix, and Zola (1988) go some way toward an answer to this question by looking at the distribution of landing positions for very large samples of words of varying length in normal reading. Their results confirm that landing position is not randomly distributed, showing a marked preference for a point located somewhat to the left of the word center. Vitu, O'Regan, and Mittau (1990) provide additional evidence on the question, showing that the curvilinear relationship between gaze duration and initial fixation position obtains under conditions of text reading, although the function is very much flatter. However, the probability that a word will receive additional fixations shows a strong relationship with the point of initial fixation (McConkie, Kerr, Reddix, Zola, & Jacobs, 1989). In fact, for comparatively long words (seven or more letters), an initial fixation deviating by three characters from the word center increases the probability of a refixation from around zero to about 0.20.

Taken together, these findings suggest that eye movement control in reading is tightly coupled to properties of the inspected text. Each saccade must be considered as part of a pattern, reflecting a series of adjustments in launch position contingent on the appropriateness of a given landing point for efficient word identification. The most powerful influence over *between-word* saccades is the physical length of the word about to be fixated. More complex parafoveal processing may play a limited role, particularly for short words, but the acuity function of the eye and the density of the stimulus provided by printed letter strings set strong constraints on what is visible outside the current point of fixation (Anstis, 1974; O'Regan, 1990). In contrast, *within-word* saccades are triggered by the requirement to carry out additional processing. There is probably a point at which the decision to stay in a particular location is overtaken by the fact that word identification is not proceeding fast enough (e.g., that too many lexical candidates remain active). It should be appreciated that within-word saccades of this kind also act to shift the launch position of the next saccade, in the majority of cases taking it nearer to its target. However, there is no evidence, as yet, as to whether this is a primary effect or simply a by-product of the need to reinspect. That is, the possibility must remain open that readers could relocate within a word for no other reason than the fact that the current inspection site gives too little information on the length of the *next* word to allow the Optimal Viewing Position within it to be targeted.

It is possible to translate all these theoretical considerations into three broad hypotheses: (a) screen pulsation will interfere with saccade control, leading to systematic shifts in the intended within-word landing position; because the primary effect is a shortfall in saccade extent, this shift will be to the left; (b) as consequence of (a), screen pulsation will lead to alterations in fixation duration or in the probability of within-word refixations (or both); and (c) skilled typists will be less tolerant of deviations from the Optimal Landing Position and this will be reflected in the probability of refixation. The final section examines these hypotheses in the context of some recent experimental work from our laboratory.

EXPERIMENTAL STUDIES

The first experiment to be considered (Kennedy & Murray, 1991) was essentially a replication and extension of one of Wilkins' early studies (Wilkins, 1986). Wilkins asked subjects to make repeated saccades between two letters embedded in a line of text. The materials were presented as a photographic negative against a cathode ray tube (CRT) screen refreshed at either 50 Hz or 100 Hz. There was a statistically reliable difference between these two conditions, with an average saccade extent of 154 min of arc at 50 Hz and 139 at 100 Hz. These data can be considered as commenting on accuracy, but it is difficult to estimate the "flicker effect," because, if it is assumed that the subjects in fact managed to locate the targets, the average absolute saccade size is derived from both forward and backward saccades of varying size. Furthermore, the key question as to whether saccades should be seen as longer at 50 Hz or shorter at 100 Hz cannot really be addressed. We attempted to deal with this problem by carrying out a similar experiment, adding a third condition of steady DC illumination, controlled for brightness. Subjects read sentences displayed on a single horizontal line and then responded to the appearance of a stimulus word to the right of the sentence on the same line. The task was to indicate whether or not the word was present in the sentence. The materials were like the following:

1. The novels in the library had started to go mouldy with the damp.   novels
2. The workmen were leaning on their spades by the side of the road.   shovels

That is, when a "no" response was demanded, the stimulus word was a synonym of a word that had been presented. The position of the target in the sentence was varied systematically. The task is quite difficult and generates a number of saccades from the stimulus to its target equivalent in the sentence and back again (Kennedy & Murray, 1987), nonetheless, it is a reasonable analogue of some aspects of normal reading. The materials were presented under computer control using a back-projection system. The beam from the projector was interrupted by spinning sectored disks to produce pulsed illumination at either 50 Hz or 100 Hz. A third condition provided steady illumination, matched for brightness using neutral density filters.

Two groups of subjects were used: Thirty skilled typists, all of whom had responded to a questionnaire, reporting high levels of symptoms of visual discomfort; and 30 university students, of about the same age. The results are discussed in detail elsewhere (Kennedy & Murray, 1991), but some of the principal results are outlined here: (a) There were very pronounced differences in the reading style of the two groups of subjects: Saccades were significantly shorter in the group of typists (7.32 vs. 7.76 character positions); and their initial landing position (averaged over all word lengths) was further to the left (2.54 vs. 2.75 character positions from the word's beginning); (b) Figure 10.1 shows the extent of the first saccade into words of varying length for the group of typists. The data were taken from the initial reading of each sentence, before the target word was presented. There is a statistically reliable tendency for this to be shorter under conditions of pulsed illumination. (c) Typists showed a marked increase in the probability of making a second "corrective" saccade after landing on the target (see Fig. 10.2).

The results of this experiment can be taken in general terms to support the hypotheses outlined earlier: Screen pulsation appears to lead to shorter saccades and the consequent left shift in landing position leads to an increase in within-word refixations in the group of professional typists. However, there are some fairly obvious problems. First, the display conditions were far from being an exact replication of those found in the typical VDU. Phosphor persistence and rise time and the "frame flicker" induced by the vertical raster scan of the VDU were not effectively simulated by the pulsed white-light display. Second, the sample of words used was comparatively small—much too small, in fact, to achieve a satisfactory level of statistical power in a landing position analysis. Third, the experimental design was somewhat insensitive, because refresh rate was manipulated as a between-subjects variable, making it difficult to interpret the obtained differences between the responses of typists and nontypists. Finally, the task itself, although it had the advantage of producing above-average num-

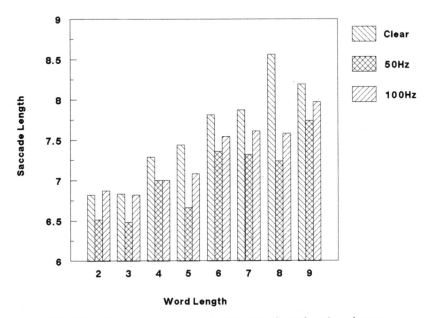

FIG. 10.1. Mean saccade length (in characters) as a function of screen pulsation. The data are taken from a sample of typists and are shown for words varying in length from two to nine letters. (Data from Kennedy & Murray, 1991).

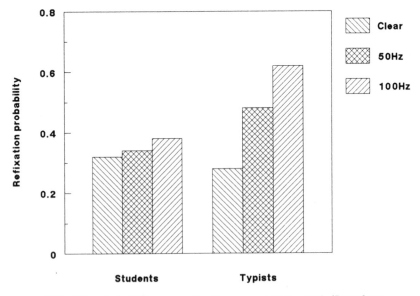

FIG. 10.2. Probability of a refixation on a target word. (Data from Kennedy & Murray, 1991).

bers of large saccades, did not necessarily demand reading for comprehension. The second experiment to be considered set out to remedy some of these defects.

The materials consisted of 60 sentence-question pairs. The sentences comprised an equal number of syntactically unambiguous constructions and more complex, temporarily ambiguous, structures (reduced relatives and reduced complements). Each sentence was paired with a comprehension question. The materials were presented on a variable frequency raster display set to operate, in different phases of the experiment, at 50 Hz, 75 Hz, and 100 Hz. Subjects received all three conditions of refresh rate, with order of presentation counterbalanced using a Latin Square. They were asked to read each sentence and press a button to see the question, which replaced the sentence on the screen. The questions were answered using button presses. Eye movements were recorded throughout the experiment. The subjects were 18 nontypist volunteers from a student subject pool and 18 typists. The latter group consisted of two subgroups: nine subjects with no symptoms of visual disturbance (using a self-report questionnaire), and 9 with a self-rating of at least three on a five-point scale of severity of symptoms of visual fatigue.

The results are discussed in two ways. First, in terms of comparisons between the two groups of subjects (typists and nontypists), in order to identify possible differences in reading strategy; and second, by examining, within the group of typists, differences between the "symptomatic" and "nonsymptomatic" subgroups. The data set consisted of measures, for each word length, of the length of the first saccade to enter a word; the landing position within a word (i.e., the saccade end point, measured in characters from the word beginning); and refixation probability, computed separately for left-going and right-going within-word saccades. Because the number of words of different lengths were not matched, the landing position analyses were restricted to those word lengths where a substantial number of landings took place (i.e., for these materials, words 4, 5, 7, and 8 characters in length).

Table 10.2 summarizes the results of a number of measures from typists and nontypists. The data confirm the findings of the first experiment: There are marked differences in reading style in the two groups. It is true that in this experiment there was a relatively large difference in the average age of the two groups (students = 20.4 years; typists = 30.6 years), but it is unlikely that the pattern of differences relates to this alone (or at all). The average fixation duration of typists was longer than that of nontypists. Typists also made significantly more fixations, associated both with more forward and more backward saccades and their average forward saccade length was somewhat shorter, although not significantly so. Perhaps the most important global outcome, however, is the significant relative shift to the left in landing position. It should be noted that the data on average landing position also show a marked interaction between subject group and word length. For short words, the groups did not differ (typists = 1.85; nontypists = 1.89), whereas for longer words there was a significant

TABLE 10.2
Comparisons Between Typists and Nontypists on a Number
of Parametric Eye Movement Measures (saccade length is
shown in character positions and landing position
in character positions from the left word boundary)

	Typist	Nontypist
No. of fixations	15.14	12.26
No. forward saccades	7.75	6.63
No. backward saccades	4.43	3.12
Saccade length	7.18	7.63
Landing position	2.29	2.50
Fixation duration (ms)	261	234

difference, with typists landing further to the left (typists = 2.73; nontypists = 3.12). It should be noted that these effects are to be seen in the absence of any differences in launch position: That is, on the average, both groups launched saccades from about the same distance from the target word. Obviously, this outcome implies that the two groups differ in the number of within-word adjustments in launch position. However, because these interacted strongly with refresh rate, their treatment will be taken up later in the context of the more detailed landing position analyses.

It will be recalled that the group of typists was made up of two subgroups consisting of symptomatic (S+) and asymptomatic (S−) subjects respectively. These were very closely matched for age (30.3 and 30.6 years respectively), but differed greatly on a five-point scale of rated eye strain, headache, visual discomfort, and minor visual disturbance associated with screen use. As far as possible, the two groups were also matched for hours of screen work per day, screen color, and handedness. The analyses that follow focus on differences between these two groups, using the data from the nontypists as a point of comparison.

The effect of refresh rate on the length of the first saccade into a word is shown in Fig. 10.3. Changes in refresh rate had similar (and statistically significant) effects on the two groups, with a reduction in saccade extent at higher frequencies. It is quite evident from Fig. 10.3 that the *overall* difference in saccade length between typists and nontypists is, in fact, solely the result of data contributed by the S+ group. From inspection, there appears to be no effect of refresh rate at all on saccade length for the group of nontypists. However, this conclusion is not entirely warranted: There were, in fact, highly significant interactions between refresh rate and condition order for this group, caused by strong asymmetric transfer effects. Obviously, given the Latin Square design, it is not possible to disentangle these, but a legitimate analysis can be carried out on the first phase of the experiment alone (i.e., with refresh rate as a between-subject variable). This revealed a significant effect, with saccade extent being

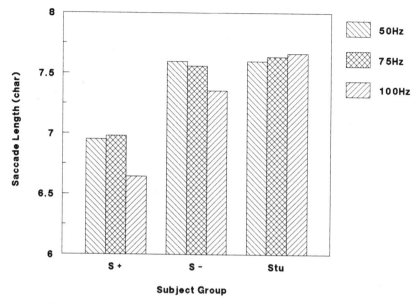

FIG. 10.3. Average saccade length as a function of refresh rate. Data are shown separately for a group of nontypists (Students) and groups of symptomatic (S+) and asymptomatic (S−) typists.

shorter at 75 Hz compared to both 50 Hz and 100 Hz. The most plausible interpretation of the obtained transfer effects is that *initial* experience at high refresh rates appears to carry over to later phases of the experiment for this group of subjects (who had relatively little experience of screen-based text processing). Further experiments are underway to examine this.

The landing position data are shown in Fig. 10.4. Again, there are no effects evident for the group of nontypists, although the same interactions were found with condition order. For the typists, there is a significant interaction between refresh rate and subject group. Variation in refresh rate has little effect on landing position for the S− group, whereas the S+ data show a mean shift to the left of approximately a third of a character over the range of refresh rates used.

Variation in refresh rate has very similar effects on saccade extent in the two groups of typists and quite distinct effects on landing position, which can only be accounted for by some systematic difference in within-word adjustments to position, arising as a consequence of an initially mislocated fixation. The group of nonsymptomatic typists appear to alter their within-word position so that the landing position on the following word is relatively constant. In contrast, the group of symptomatic subjects appear to make within-word saccades (to the right), holding the effective launch position toward the following word relatively constant. Clearly, these possibilities can be examined directly by analysis of the

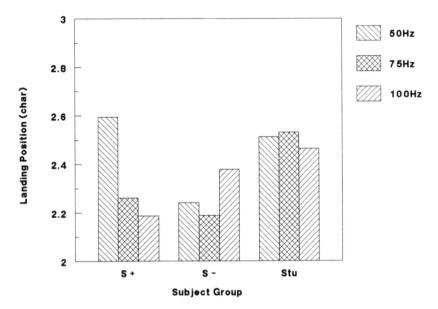

FIG. 10.4.   Average landing position as a function of refresh rate.

probability of making within-word saccades; the relevant data are shown in Fig. 10.5. The probability of left-going within-word saccades did not differ between groups (S+ = 0.046; S− = 0.033) and there were no effects of refresh rate and no interactions with this variable. In contrast, the probability of right-going within-word saccades (see Fig. 10.5) was greater in the symptomatic group (S+ = 0.104; S− = 0.058). Separate analyses for the two groups showed no effect of refresh rate for S− subjects, but a significant effect for the S+ Group.

CONCLUSION

The results presented here support the idea that typists, probably by virtue of their professional skill, adopt a particular reading strategy even when dealing with text they are not called on to type. However, the group of typists is not homogeneous: Symptomatic subjects appear particularly intolerant of relatively small shifts in intended viewing position. Although the link must be seen as speculative at present, it does seem plausible that the reports of visual fatigue in this group are related to the increased frequency of small within-word saccades they make in response to pulsation-induced mislocations. Keep in mind that eye movements are executed in the service of attentional demand: That is, the reader needs to examine (or reexamine) a particular location. There is, therefore, for the symptomatic group, a quite marked increase in cognitive load in comparison to

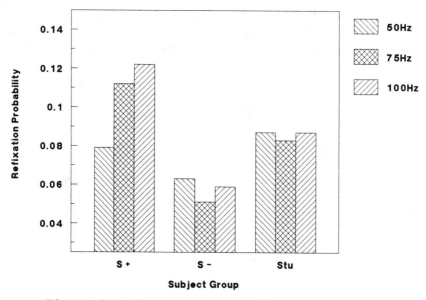

FIG. 10.5. Probability of a right-going within-word refixation as a function of refresh rate.

typical nontypists or to nonsymptomatic typists. What might be called a cautious reading style appears to conspire in some way with the effects of screen pulsation to make the task of text processing in this group much more demanding. Readers who are less cautious do not pay this price. In this context, caution has at least two interpretations: It may be that some readers are simply more efficient, for reasons not yet understood, at processing words from a sub-optimal position; it is also possible, however, that readers develop strategies that act to restrict the need for frequent fine adjustments in position. It is obviously important to identify what such strategies might be and recent research has identified at least one possibility. Supporting context may lead to a reduction in the probability of within-word refixations (Pynte & Kennedy, 1992). This is interesting, given the observation that typists typically do not process text at a syntactic or semantic level. It may be that the adverse effects of screen pulsation will need to be addressed on two fronts: obviously, by examining the properties of displays themselves, but also by looking with equal urgency at what it is about reading style that appears to lead to such large individual differences in tolerance of small mislocations in landing position.

The most striking outcome, however, is that effects of screen pulsation can be observed at frequencies well above estimates of normal fusion. Obviously, one route to eliminating perceptible flicker in display devices is to increase refresh rate. Indeed, there is evidence that some operators prefer displays refreshed at higher rates and report that they look more stable (Wilkins, 1985). The irony may be that the more proficient one becomes as a typist, that is, the more automatic the skill and the less dependent it is on the high level processes of contextual support, the more vulnerable one may become to the effects of misplaced fixations.

ACKNOWLEDGMENTS

The work reported here is supported by Grant No. G9006692N from the Medical Research Council (MRC) (UK) to A. Kennedy and W. S. Murray. The project is part of the program of work commissioned from MRC by the Health and Safety Executive. Thanks are due to K. O'Regan and B. Breitmeyer for helpful comments on an earlier version of the chapter.

REFERENCES

Adey, W. R., & Noda, H. (1973). Influence of eye movements on geniculostriate excitability in the cat. *Journal of Physiology, 235*, 805–821.

Anstis, S. M. (1974). A chart demonstrating variations in acuity with retinal position. *Vision Research, 14*, 589–592.

Askwall, S. (1985). Computer supported reading vs. reading text on paper: A comparison of two reading situations. *International Journal of Man-Machine Studies, 22*, 425–439.

Becker, W., & Jurgens, R. (1979). An analysis of the saccadic system by means of double step stimuli. *Vision Research, 19*, 967–983.

Becker, W., Kieffer, G., & Jurgens, R. (1987). Sensory stimuli can interrupt or perturb saccades in mid-flight. In G. Luer & U. Lass (Eds.), *Fourth European conference on eye movements* (pp. 103–105). New York: Academic Press.

Breitmeyer, B. G. (1980). Unmasking visual masking: A look at the "why" behind the veil of the "how." *Psychological Review, 87*, 52–69.

Breitmeyer, B. G. (1984). *Visual masking: An integrative approach*. New York: Oxford University Press.

Breitmeyer, B. G. (1983). Sensory masking, persistence, and enhancement in visual exploration and reading. In K. Rayner (Ed.), *Eye movements and reading: Perceptual and language processes* (pp. 3–30). New York: Academic Press.

Breitmeyer, B. G. (1991). Reality and relevance of sustained and transient channels in reading and reading disability. In R. Schmid & D. Zambarbieri (Eds.), *Oculomotor control and cognitive processes* (pp. 473–483). Amsterdam: North Holland.

Butch, R. L. (1932). Eye movements and the eye-hand span in typewriting. *Journal of Educational Psychology, 4*, 27–53.

Cushman, W. H. (1986). Reading from microfiche, a VDT, and the printed page: Subjective fatigue and performance. *Human Factors, 28*, 63–73.

Deubel, H., Wolf, W., & Hauske, G. (1984). The evaluation of the oculomotor error signal. In A. G. Gale & F. Johnson (Eds.), *Theoretical and applied aspects of eye movement research* (pp. 56–62). Amsterdam: North Holland.

Eysel, U. T., & Burandt, U. (1984). Fluorescent tube light evokes flicker responses in visual neurons. *Vision Research, 24*, 943–948.

Findlay, J. M. (1981). Local and global influences on saccadic eye movements. In D. F. Fisher, R. A. Monty, & J. W. Senders (Eds.), *Eye movements: Cognition and visual perception* (pp. 171–181). Hillsdale: Lawrence Erlbaum Associates.

Findlay, J. M. (1982). Global visual processing for saccadic eye movements. *Vision Research, 21,* 347–354.

Fuchs, A. F. (1976). The neurophysiology of saccades. In R. A. Monty & J. W. Senders (Eds.), *Eye movements and psychological processes* (pp. 39–53). Hillsdale: Lawrence Erlbaum Associates.

Genest, M. (1965). L'analyse temporelle du travail dactylographique. *Bulletin du Centre d'Etudes et Recherches Psychotechniques, 5,* 183–191.

Gould, J. (1981). Composing letters with computer-based text editors. *Human Factors, 23,* 593–606.

Gould, J., & Grischkowsky, N. (1984). Doing the same work with hard copy and with cathode-ray tube (CRT) computer terminals. *Human Factors, 26,* 323–337.

Haas, C., & Hayes, J. R. (1985). *Effects of text display variables on reading tasks: Computer screen vs. hard copy* (CDC Tech. Report No. 15) Carnegie-Mellon Communications Design Centre Technical Report Series.

Haas, C., & Hayes, J. R. (1986). *Pen and paper vs. the machine: Writers composing in hard copy and computer conditions.* (CDC Tech. Report No. 16) Carnegie-Mellon Communications Design Centre Technical Report Series.

House of Lords (1988). Select committee of the European Communities. Visual display units (HL paper 110). London: HMSO.

Inhoff, A. W. (1991). Word frequency during copytyping. *Journal of Experimental Psychology: Human Perception and Performance, 17,* 478–487.

Inhoff, A. W., Morris, R., & Calabrese, J. (1986). Eye movements in skilled transcription typing. *Bulletin of the Psychonomic Society, 24,* 113–114.

Kennedy, A. (1992). The spatial coding hypothesis. In K. Rayner (Ed.), *Eye movements and visual cognition: Scene perception and reading* (pp. 379–396). New York: Springer-Verlag.

Kennedy, A., & Murray, W. S. (1987). Spatial coordinates and reading: Comments on Monk (1985). *Quarterly Journal of Experimental Psychology, 39A,* 649–656.

Kennedy, A., & Murray, W. S. (1991). The effects of flicker on eye movement control. *Quarterly Journal of Experimental Psychology, 43A,* 79–99.

Kolers, P. A., Duchnicky, R. L., & Ferguson, D. C. (1981). Eye movement measurement of readability of CRT displays. *Human Factors, 23,* 517–527.

Kruk, R. S., & Muter, P. (1984). Reading of continuous text on video screens. *Human Factors, 26,* 339–345.

Legge, G. E. (1978). Sustained and transient mechanisms in human vision: Temporal and spatial properties. *Vision Research, 18,* 69–81.

Lovegrove, W. (1991). Mechanisms underlying saccadic suppression in dyslexics and controls. In R. Schmid & D. Zambarbieri (Eds.), *Oculomotor control and cognitive processes* (pp. 485–489). Amsterdam: North Holland.

Lovegrove, W., Heddle, M., & Slaghuis, W. (1986). Reading disability: Spatial frequency specific deficits in visual information store. *Neuropsychologia, 18,* 111–115.

Matin, E. (1974). Saccadic suppression: A review and analysis. *Psychological Bulletin, 81,* 899–917.

McConkie, G. W., Kerr, P. W., Reddix, M. D., & Zola, D. (1988). Eye movement control during reading: I. The location of initial eye fixations on words. *Vision Research, 28,* 1107–1118.

McConkie, G. W., Kerr, P. W., Reddix, M. D., Zola, D., & Jacobs, A. M. (1989). Eye movement control during reading: II. Frequency of refixating a word. *Perception and Psychophysics, 46,* 245–253.

Muter, P., Latremouille, S., & Treurniet, W. (1982). Extended reading of continuous text on television screens. *Human Factors, 24,* 501–508.

Neary, C., & Wilkins, A. J. (1989). Effects of phosphor persistence on perception and the control of eye movements. *Perception, 18,* 257–264.

Newsted, P. R. (1985). Paper versus on line presentations of subjective questionnaires. *International Journal of Man-Machine Studies, 23,* 231–247.

National Institute for Occupational Safety and Health (NIOSH). (1983). *Video display, work and vision.* National Academy Press.

Oborne, D. J., & Holton, D. (1988). Reading from screen versus paper: There is no difference. *International Journal of Man-Machine Studies, 28,* 1–9.

O'Regan, J. K. (1989). Visual acuity, lexical structure and eye movements in word recognition. In B. Elsendoorn & H. Bouma (Eds.), *Working models of human perception* (pp. 261–292). London: Academic Press.

O'Regan, J. K. (1990). Eye movements and reading. In E. Kowler (Ed.), *Reviews of oculomotor research: Vol 4. Eye movements and their role in visual and cognitive processes* (pp. 395–453). Amsterdam: Elsevier.

O'Regan, J. K., & Levy-Schoen, A. (1987). Eye movement strategy and tactics in word-recognition and reading. In M. Coltheart (Ed.), *Attention and performance XII:* The psychology of reading (pp. 363–383). Hillsdale, NJ: Lawrence Erlbaum Associates.

Pynte, J., & Kennedy, A. (1992). Referential context and within-word refixations: Evidence for 'weak interaction'. In J. Van Rensbergen & G. d'Ydewalle (Eds.), *Studies in visual information processing* (pp. 1–13). Amsterdam: North Holland.

Pynte, J., Kennedy, A., & Murray, W. S. (1991). Within-word inspection strategies in continuous reading: The time-course of perceptual, lexical and contextual processes. *Journal of Experimental Psychology: Human Perception and Performance, 17,* 458–470.

Rayner, K. (1983). *Eye movements and reading: Perceptual and language processes.* New York: Academic Press.

Shaffer, L. H. (1973). Latency mechanisms in transcription. In S. Kornblum (Ed.), *Attention and performance IV* (pp. 435–446). New York: Academic Press.

Shaffer, L. H. (1975). Control processes in typing. *Quarterly Journal of Experimental Psychology, 27,* 419–432.

Taptagaporn, S. (1990). How display polarity and lighting conditions affect the pupil size of VDT operators. *Ergonomics, 33,* 201–208.

Vitu, F., O'Regan, J. K., & Mittau, M. (1990). Optimal landing position in reading isolated words and continuous text. *Perception and Psychophysics, 47,* 583–600.

Wilkins, A. J. (1985). Discomfort and visual displays. *Displays,* 101–104.

Wilkins, A. J. (1986). Intermittent illumination from fluorescent lighting and visual display units affects movements of the eyes across text. *Human Factors, 28,* 75–81.

Wilkins, A. J. (1991). Visual discomfort and reading. In J. Stein (Ed.), *Vision and visual dysfunction: Vol 13. Visual Dyslexia.*

Wilkins, A. J., & Nimmo-Smith, I. (1984). On the reduction of eye-strain when reading. *Ophthalmic and Physiological Optics, 4,* 53–59.

Wilkins, A. J., & Nimmo-Smith, I. (1987). The clarity and comfort of printed text. *Ergonomics, 30,* 1705–1720.

Wright, P., & Lickorish, A. (1983). Proof-reading on screen and paper. *Behaviour and Information Technology, 2,* 227–235.

Zwahlen, H. T., & Adams, C. C. (1987). Eye scanning behavior of video display operators. In G. Luer & U. Lass (Eds.), *Fourth European conference on eye movements.* (Vol. 1, pp. 172–174). New York: Hogrefe.

Zwahlen, H. T., Hartmann, A. L., Rangarajula, S. L., & Escontrela, L. M. (1985). Eye scanning behavior when working on video display terminals. In R. Groner, G. W. McConkie, & C. Menz (Eds.), *Eye movements and human information processing* (pp. 385–402). Amsterdam: North Holland.

11

Bi-Alphabetism and the Design of a Reading Mechanism

Laurie Beth Feldman
State University of New York at Albany and Haskins Laboratories

The linguistic conditions in regions of Yugoslavia provide an ideal medium in which to investigate the role of a word's visual form in the process of word recognition. Specifically, two visually distinct alphabets, Roman and Cyrillic, are used interchangeably and with impressive fluency by most skilled readers in the Belgrade region. Consequently, words of Serbo-Croatian, the official language of Yugoslavia, can be written in either the Roman or the Cyrillic alphabet and, according to the educational policy in effect until recently, all school children are required to demonstrate and maintain proficiency in both alphabets. The implication of the foregoing is that skilled readers of Serbo-Croatian maintain two visually defined lexicons or at least, two visually defined descriptions for each word. And, because most of the phonemes are unique to one alphabet or another, the visual similarity of the two alphabetic transcriptions of a word is dramatically reduced relative to the experimental manipulations of visual form (e.g., case) that are possible in English. In addition, the writing system for Serbo-Croatian was reformed in the last century so that the mapping of letter to sound is consistent and regular. The implication of a phonologically regular writing system is that skilled readers of Serbo-Croatian need never rely on word-level knowledge in order to arrive at the correct phonemic form of a word.

This chapter summarizes six lines of investigation using variations on the lexical decision and naming methodologies that were conducted with bi-alphabetically fluent readers of Serbo-Croatian (see Table 11.1). Collectively, they investigate the role of an alphabetically defined (visual) level of description in word recognition. All of the studies exploit the particular relation between two alphabets that exists in Yugoslavia and all were conducted with first-year students at the University of Belgrade or with advanced high school students in the

TABLE 11.1
Summary of Lexical Decision (LD), Alphabet Decision (AD), and Naming (N) Studies

Study	Experimental Conditions	First Item	Example	Second Item	Example	Reference
1	alph alternated	LD	НОГОМ (C)	LD	NOGOM (R) "leg"	Feldman, unpublished
	alph preserved	LD	NOGOM (R)	LD	NOGOM (R)	
2	alph alternated	AD	НОГА (C)	LD	NOGA	Feldman, unpublished
	alph preserved	AD	NOGA (R)	LD	NOGA	
3	phon matched alph matched	No response	RAKUN (R)	LD/N	RAČUN (R) "bill"	Lukatela & Turvey, 1990a
	phon matched alph mismatched	No response	РАКУН (C)	LD/N	RAČUN (R)	Lukatela, Carello, & Turvey, 1990
	phon mismatched alph matched	No response	DUVAČ (R)	LD	RAČUN (R)	
	phon mismatched alph mismatched	No response	ДУВАЧ (C)	LD/N	RAČUN (R)	
4	phon ambiguous	None		LD/N	BEHA "vein"	Feldman & Turvey, 1983; Feldman, Kostić,
	phon unambiguous	None		LD/N	VENA "vein"	Lukatela, & Turvey, 1983; Feldman, 1991
5	alph. consistent sem. associated alph. inconsistent	No response	ОЛУЈА "storm" (C) OLUJA	LD/N	ВЕТАР (C) "wind"	Lukatela, Feldman, Turvey, Carello, & Katz, 1989

sem unassociated / alph consistent	No response	"storm" (R) ПАС	LD/N	BETAP (C)	Lukatela, Turvey, Feldman, Carello, & Katz, 1989
sem unassociated / alph inconsistent	No response	"dog" (C) PAS	LD/N	BETAP (C)	
sem associated / alph consistent	No response	"dog" (R) OLUJA	LD/N	BETAP (C)	
sem associated / alph inconsistent	No response	"storm" (R) ОЛУЈА	LD/N	VETAR (R) "wind"	
sem unassociated / alph consistent	No response	"storm" (C) PAS	LD/N	VETAR (R)	
sem unassociated / alph inconsistent	No response	"dog" (R) ПАС	LD/N	VETAR (R)	
sem. unassociated	No response	"dog" (C)	LD/N	VETAR (R)	
6					
alph consistent letters	No response	ЛДГ (C)	LD/N	BETAP (C)	Lukatela, Turvey & Todorović, 1991
alph inconsistent letters	No response	LDG (R)	LD/N	BETAP (C)	Lukatela & Turvey, 1990b
alph consistent letters	No response	LDG (R)	LD/N	VETAR (R)	
alph inconsistent letters	No response	ЛДГ (C)	LD/N	VETAR (R)	

TABLE 11.2

Letters Unique to the Roman and/or Cyrillic Alphabets and Letters Shared by the Roman and Cyrillic Alphabets

Roman Grapheme	Roman Phoneme	Cyrillic Phoneme	Classification	Cyrillic Grapheme	Cyrillic Phoneme	Roman Phoneme	Classification
A	/a/	/a/	common[1]	А	/a/	/a/	common
B	/b/	/v/	ambiguous[2]	Б	/b/		Cyrillic
C	/ts/	/s/	ambiguous	Ц	/ts/		Cyrillic
Ć	/tʃʲ/		Roman	Ћ	/tʃʲ/		Cyrillic
Č	/tʃ/		Roman	Ч	/tʃ/		Cyrillic
D	/d/		Roman	Д	/d/		Cyrillic
Đ	/dʒʲ/		Roman	Ђ	/dʒʲ/		Cyrillic
DŽ	/dʒ/		Roman	Џ	/dʒ/		Cyrillic
E	/e/	/e/	common	Е	/e/	/e/	common
F	/f/		Roman	Ф	/f/		Cyrillic
G	/g/		Roman	Г	/g/		Cyrillic
H	/x/	/n/	ambiguous	Х	/x/		Cyrillic
I	/i/		Roman	И	/i/		Cyrillic
J	/j/	/j/	common	Ј	/j/	/j/	common

Roman				Cyrillic			
K	/k/	/k/	common	К	/k/	/k/	common
L	/l/		Roman	Л	/l/		Cyrillic
LJ	/lj/		Roman	Љ	/lj/		Cyrillic
M	/m/	/m/	common	М	/m/	/m/	common
N	/n/		Roman	Н	/n/	/x/	ambiguous
NJ	/nj/		Roman	Њ	/nj/		Cyrillic
O	/o/	/o/	common	О	/o/	/o/	common
P	/p/	/r/	ambiguous	П	/p/		Cyrillic
R	/r/		Roman	Р	/r/	/p/	ambiguous
S	/s/		Roman	С	/s/	/ts/	ambiguous
Š	/ʃ/		Roman	Ш	/ʃ/		Cyrillic
T	/t/	/t/	common	Т	/t/	/t/	common
U	/u/		Roman	У	/u/		Cyrillic
V	/v/		Roman	В	/v/	/b/	ambiguous
Z	/z/		Roman	З	/z/		Cyrillic
Ž	/ʒ/		Roman	Ж	/ʒ/		Cyrillic

[1] Common letters have the same interpretation in Roman and Cyrillic.
[2] Ambiguous letters have different interpretations.

Belgrade region who are fluent in both alphabets. Studies 1 and 2 focus on the visual distinctiveness of orthographic forms. Specifically, most phonemes of Serbo-Croatian have two quite distinct visual forms, one Roman character and one Cyrillic character, and this variation provides a tool with which to ask whether multiple presentations that preserve alphabetically defined visual patterns facilitate performance relative to presentations that alternate alphabet. Study 3 examines facilitation due to visual and phonological similarity for words presented close in succession. The remaining three studies exploit properties of the subset of characters that are shared by the two alphabets. Specifically, there are a small number of phonemes where the mapping between letter and phoneme is complex because the same visual characters are shared by both alphabets. Of these shared characters, the *common* characters (i.e., *A, E, O, J, K, M, T*) receive the same phonemic interpretation in both alphabets, whereas the *ambiguous* characters (i.e., *B, C, H, P*) represent different phonemes in Cyrillic and in Roman (see Table 11.2). Comparisons between words composed exclusively of shared characters (i.e., words with two phonemic interpretations) and words that included at least one nonshared (i.e., alphabetically unique) character provided the basis of studies 4, 5, and 6 where the effect of alphabetic context on phonological processing is explored. To anticipate, this chapter reviews a series of studies that explores the graphemic and phonemic implications of reading in two alphabets and provides a model of word reading in Serbo-Croatian with its emphasis on phonology. Because the first two studies are not published and details are not easily obtained, they are described in more detail than subsequent studies.

STUDY 1: ALPHABETIC MANIPULATIONS ACROSS REPETITIONS OF A WORD

One way in which the bi-alphabetic fluency of readers of Serbo-Croatian has been exploited has been to investigate the role of alphabetically defined orthographic similarity of prime and target in repetition priming (Feldman & Moskovljević, 1987, Exp. 1). In this task, words and pseudowords are presented twice, with a lag of intervening items, and subjects are instructed to perform a lexical decision to each letter string as it appears (Stanners, Neiser, Hernon, & Hall, 1979). The critical experimental manipulation entailed repetitions in either the same or in different alphabets. In the *alphabet alternated* condition, prime and target were transcribed in different alphabets (e.g., ногом-NOGOM). In the *alphabet preserved* conditions, prime and target were in the same alphabet (e.g., NOGOM-NOGOM). Equal numbers of words and pseudowords were presented for durations of 750 ms. The interval between successive presentations of a word averaged 10 items with a range of 7 to 13. One group of subjects saw all items in Roman script (alphabet preserved) and the other saw primes in Cyrillic and targets in Roman (alphabet alternated). Results indicated that facilitation (i.e., reaction time to first minus second presentation) was numerically equivalent (viz., 90 ms) in the alphabet preserved and the alphabet alternated conditions. The authors interpreted this pattern of results as evidence that at lags of 7 to 13, visual similarity of prime and target alone did not provide a source of facilitation in the repetition priming task.

Because it is possible that the time course of activation of visual form varies with lag (Monsell, 1985; Ratcliff, Hockley, & McKoon, 1985), the first study attempted to replicate this finding. In addition, consistency of alphabet was systematically manipulated. Decision latencies to targets that were preceded by primes (where target and prime either alternated or preserved alphabet) were compared over lags of 10 and 20 (Experiment 1a) or lags of 3 and 10 (Experiment 1b) in an attempt to find evidence for facilitation based on repetitions of specific visual patterns. Materials consisted of 32 Serbo-Croatian words and 32 pseudowords. Words were familiar nouns in nominative case that contained three or four letters. Pseudowords were generated by changing one or two letters (vowel with vowel or consonant with consonant) and preserved orthographic and phonemic regularity.

Each word and pseudoword appeared two times, once as a target and once as a prime and, as noted earlier, the lag or interval between presentation of prime and its target was varied. Half of the targets were printed in uppercase Roman and half were printed in uppercase Cyrillic. And, at each lag, half of the prime target pairs alternated alphabet and half preserved it. Items were selected so that both alphabet transcriptions included at least one letter that uniquely specified alphabet (Feldman, Kostić, Lukatela, & Turvey, 1983). A small number of filler items were introduced to maintain the appropriate lags. Across test orders each target (word or pseudoword) was preceded by its prime at two different lags in both the alphabet alternated and alphabet preserved conditions. University students were tested individually in a lexical decision task. Each subject viewed one test order and a practice list of 10 items preceded the test list.

In addition to eliminating errors and extreme response times, responses were excluded when a subject responded incorrectly to one member of a prime target pair. Table 11.3 summarizes the mean recognition times over subjects for target words and pseudowords as a function of lag for alphabetically alternated and preserved pairs.

Analyses of variance on targets from Experiment 1a with lag (10, 20) and alphabet (alternated, preserved) as independent variables were performed separately for words and pseudowords using subjects ($F1$) and items ($F2$) as random variables. For pseudowords, no effects or interactions were significant. For words, the effect of alphabet was marginally significant in the analysis of latencies by subjects $F1$ (1, 35) = 4.08, MSe = 967, $p < .051$ but did not approach significance in the analysis by items. Neither the effect of lag nor the interaction of alphabet by lag was significant. Similarly with errors, no main effects or

TABLE 11.3
Mean Decision Latencies (ms) and Errors for Words and
Pseudowords in the Alphabet Preserved and Alphabet Alternated
Conditions of the Repetition Priming Task for Study 1

| | First Presentation | Lag | Repetition Alphabet | | Difference |
			Alternated	Preserved	
Experiment Ia					
Words	651	10	601	592	9
	12.7		6.6	7.3	−0.7
		20	607	595	12
			4.5	7.3	−2.8
Pseudowords	666	10	682	680	2
	5.7		5.2	5.9	−0.7
		20	672	661	11
			4.2	5.9	−1.7
Experiment Ib					
Words	628	3	562	562	0
	10.8		8.3	5.9	2.4
		10	567	573	−6
			7.9	7.9	0
Pseudowords	654	3	672	665	7
	5.7		6.9	7.6	−0.7
		10	648	629	19
			6.1	6.9	−0.8

interactions approached significance. Finally, the pattern observed with errors did not support the latency pattern.

When lags of 3 or 10 items separated prime and target, analyses performed on latencies for target items alone revealed no significant effect of alphabet, no effect of lag and no interaction. Analogously, the error scores were not sensitive to manipulations of lag or alphabet. The interaction of lag by alphabet was not significant for pseudowords.

The present study exploited the bi-alphabetic knowledge of Yugoslav readers in order to investigate the role of visually defined similarity as a source of facilitation in the repetition priming paradigm. In contrast to the design used in Feldman and Moskovljević (1987), the present design treats alphabet consistency of prime and target as a within-subjects variable. Two experiments were conducted and, across experiments, the average lag was manipulated. In neither experiment was the effect of lag significant for words. Neither at a lag of 3 nor at a lag of 20 did facilitation differ significantly from lag 10.

For both words and pseudowords, significant target facilitation occurred when primes appear in either the same alphabet or in a different alphabet from the target. Importantly, target facilitation was no greater in the alphabet preserved condition than in the alternating condition. Small numerical differences that were sometimes observed with the latency measure were not supported by the error measure. The intent of the alphabet decision study was to demonstrate an effect of prior experience with specific visual forms of words and pseudowords on subsequent lexical decision performance with those same materials. The experiment exploited a special characteristic of Serbo-Croatian, notably the multiple mapping from phoneme to graphemes that exist because readers are fluent in both the Roman and Cyrillic alphabets. Facilitation defined either in terms of the differences between first and second presentations or as a percent decrease in lexical decision latency (relative to the first presentation) were not significantly different for alphabet preserved and alphabet alternating conditions.

Words presented and represented in the same alphabet are more visually similar than are the Roman and Cyrillic transcriptions of a word. Yet, in the repetition priming task where several items intervened between first and second presentations, no significant increment to facilitation was observed on the alphabet preserved trials relative to the alphabet alternating trials. This outcome is not surprising if, as Masson and Freedman (1990, p. 356) claimed, visual analysis (e.g., improved perceptual sensitivity) is not responsible for the repetition effect but rather, the bases of facilitation for repeated items are more conceptual interpretive processes that are associated with a shift in decision bias. Perhaps, because of the nature of the experimental task, an analysis of the alphabet manipulation within a repetition priming task cannot provide compelling evidence for the role of visual analysis and orthographic representations in word recognition.

STUDY 2: ALPHABETIC MANIPULATIONS IN AN ALPHABET DECISION TASK

The pattern of facilitation in the repetition priming task with a within-subjects manipulation of alphabet provided no evidence that, in the course of visual word recognition, subjects are constrained by an orthographic representation based on the visual form of the letter string. Although the previous task did not foster a visual analysis, it is plausible that skilled readers of Serbo-Croatian who are fluent in two alphabets can, under the proper circumstances, engage in an analysis of a letter string that retains its visual characteristics and this is the focus of the second study. In the first phase of study 2, subjects were told to attend to the alphabetic characteristics of the letter strings they encountered. They were instructed to indicate the alphabet in which each letter string was printed by a key press. In a second phase, they were asked to make a lexical decision to those same letter strings. The goal was to try to induce subjects to attend to the visual attributes of the materials that they encountered in an attempt to demonstrate that skilled readers of Serbo-Croatian can attend to the visual characteristics of a letter string.

Forty-four first-year students from the Department of Psychology at the University of Belgrade participated in the experiment. Half of the subjects participated in an alphabet decision task and then in a lexical decision task. The remaining half participated only in the lexical decision task. Experimental targets consisted of 40 Serbo-Croatian words and 40 pseudowords. Words were familiar nouns in nominative case that contained three or four letters. As in the previous study, pseudowords were generated by changing one or two letters (vowel with vowel or consonant with consonant) and preserved orthographic and phonemic regularity. In both the alphabet decision and the lexical decision phases of Study 2, half of the words and half of the pseudowords were printed in Roman and half were printed in Cyrillic. Items were selected so that both alphabet transcriptions included at least one letter that uniquely specified alphabet.

As each letter string appeared on the CRT of an Apple II microcomputer in the alphabet decision task, subjects pressed either of two telegraph keys with both hands to indicate alphabet. In the second phase of the experiment, the same words and pseudowords were presented to subjects in a different order. Subjects performed a lexical decision to each letter string. The presentation format was identical to the alphabet decision phase described earlier. Reaction time was measured from the onset of the letter string.

In the lexical decision phase, as in the alphabet decision phase, half of the items were in Cyrillic and half were in Roman and words and pseudowords were equally represented in each alphabet. In the lexical decision phase, however, half of the words and half of the pseudowords preserved the alphabet of their earlier presentation and half alternated alphabet. In this study, alphabet (preserved or alternated) and lexicality (word or pseudoword) were manipulated within subjects and prior participation in the alphabet decision task was manipulated between subjects. Results revealed a significant effect of prior alphabet decision on performance in the lexical decision task. Subjects who participated in lexical decision following alphabet decision were significantly slower than subjects who participated only in the lexical decision task. This outcome is consistent with the observation that repetition effects are sensitive to the task at initial presentation and do not always reveal themselves as facilitation (Forster & Davies, 1984; Ratcliff et al., 1985; Bentin & Peled, 1990). Subsequent analyses were conducted on the lexical decision following alphabet decision data.

Mean latencies and error scores for the lexical decision phase are summarized in Table 11.4. (Scores greater than 1,200 ms or less than 400 ms were treated as errors and eliminated from the reaction time analyses.) An analysis of variance on latencies revealed a significant effect of lexicality $F1$ (1, 21) = 14.98, MSe = 1110, $p < .001$; $F2$ (1, 78) = 10.16, MSe = 3147, $p < .003$. Neither the effect of alphabet nor the interaction of lexicality by alphabet approached significance.

TABLE 11.4
Mean Decision Latencies (ms) and Errors for Words
and Pseudowords in the Lexical Decision Phase
of the Alphabet Decision Task

| | Alphabet | | |
	Alternated	Preserved	Difference
Words	712	702	10
	3.9	4.6	−0.7
Pseudowords	737	732	5
	2.3	3.9	−1.6

No effects were significant with errors as the dependent measure and the small numerical differences diverged in direction from the small latency differences.

The intent of the alphabet decision study was to demonstrate an effect of prior experience with specific visual forms of words and pseudowords on subsequent lexical decision performance with those same materials. By using both Roman and Cyrillic characters, orthographic form was either preserved or alternated across the alphabet and lexical decision phases of the study. The logic of the first phase of the study was to direct subjects to attend to alphabet and their accuracy levels proved that they could do this. The effect of attending to alphabet on subsequent word recognition was then examined.

Relative to performing a word level task in isolation, subjects were slower when they performed a letter level task such as alphabet decision prior to performing a word level task. The analysis of decision latencies in the second phase revealed a significant effect of lexicality on decision latency but no effect of alphabet. With respect to visual effects, viewing a word or a pseudoword twice in the same visual form (alphabet preserved) exerted no effect over and above the effect of viewing a word (or a pseudoword) once in its Roman form and once in its Cyrillic form (alphabet alternated). Moreover, the small numerical differences that were observed with the latency measure for the factor of alphabet were not supported by the accuracy measure. It appears that for recognition tasks at the level of the word, skilled readers of Serbo-Croatian, who tend to be equally fluent in both alphabets (Feldman & Moskovljević, 1987 fn 1), cannot benefit from multiple presentations of alphabet-specific orthographic forms.

In a repetition priming task (Study 1) and in an alphabet decision task that explicitly directed skilled readers to attend to alphabet (Study 2), no effects of orthographic repetition were observed. Although this is a null effect and it is possible that another task will be developed in which effects of alphabet-specific orthographic form can be demonstrated, it is evident that in two quite different word recognition tasks skilled readers do not appear to rely on a style of analysis that is primarily tied to the visual form of a word.

STUDY 3: MANIPULATIONS OF ALPHABETIC
AND PHONEMIC SIMILARITY

It is plausible that the experimental conditions in the first two studies where repetitions were separated by a number of intervening items could not reveal effects of preserving or alternating because the interval between successive presentations exceeded the duration over which alphabet effects can persist. Alternatively, or conjointly, it is possible that no alphabetic effects were evident because all target items included at least one letter that uniquely specifies alphabet and alphabet effects emerge only when alphabet context is not well-specified. Accordingly, in a third line of investigation using a priming paradigm (Lukatela & Turvey, 1990b), alphabetic effects at short lags are examined for target words that contain at least one unique letter.

In traditional priming paradigms, targets items are immediately preceded by a context or prime and in some experimental conditions, the context is related to the target along some dimension. Target latencies with and without related primes are compared. In contrast to the previous two studies where the first and second items were separated by other intervening items, in the third study, phonologically unambiguous targets were immediately preceded by contexts. Moreover, these contexts were related with respect to the dimensions of phonology, graphemic form, both or neither and subjects performed either a naming or a lexical decision task. Primes and targets were displayed serially, one immediately after the other in a presentation format that was likely to enhance similarity effects between prime and target.

The first item (prime) and the second item (target) consisted of either words or pseudowords. Items were phonemically matched or mismatched and were visually similar (alphabet preserved) or dissimilar (alphabet alternated). Primes appeared above the position of targets and disappeared 100 ms before the target was presented. Effects of phonological similarity were significant but direction varied with task. Visually similar primes had the same effect on target latencies as did visually dissimilar pairs in both the phonologically matched and the nonmatched conditions. For example, when primes and word targets differed in their initial phoneme and rhymed (i.e., phonologically similar condition), the difference between alternated (e.g., PAKYH-RAČUN) and preserved alphabet (e.g., RAKUN-RAČUN) latencies was 13 ms (0.22%) in lexical decision (Experiment 1; Lukatela & Turvey, 1990b) and 6 ms (0.43%) in naming (Experiment 5; Lukatela & Turvey, 1990b). Similar effects were observed for pseudoword targets. Effects of alphabet in the phonologically unmatched conditions of those experiments were even smaller. Stated generally, in Study 3, preservation or alternation of alphabet was used as a manipulation of visual similarity and no effect of alphabetic similarity was observed for target letter strings that, because of the presence of at least one unique letter, were well-specified with respect to alphabet. Under sequential presentation conditions at interstimulus intervals of

100 ms there was no effect of graphemic similarity over and above the effect of phonological similarity.

The present result contrasts to analogous experiments conducted with English materials where phonemic similarity effects are difficult to obtain (compare Martin & Jensen, 1988, with Hillinger, 1980, and Meyer, Schvaneveldt, & Ruddy, 1974, for example). With Serbo-Croatian materials, a robust effect of phonemic similarity was observed in the lexical decision task. Moreover, the direction of this effect depended on the position of the nonmatched letter and on the relative frequency of the context and target word. Relative to a phonologically dissimilar context, target context pairs that differed in their initial letter showed facilitation (+55 ms), whereas pairs that differed on a medial letter showed slowing (−27 ms) (Experiment 2; Lukatela & Turvey, 1990b). Pairs with low target familiarity (uncommon words and pseudoword targets) showed facilitation (+51 ms), whereas high familiarity (word) targets showed slowing (−21 ms) (Experiments 3–4; Lukatela & Turvey, 1990b).

In the naming task, in contrast to the lexical decision task, facilitation due to phonological similarity was observed for both words and pseudowords with both initial and medial letter differences between context word and target. As in the lexical decision task, alphabetically defined visual effects were never significant. Target familiarity had no effect (Experiments 5–6; Lukatela & Turvey, 1990b) although in naming, differences in word stress between context and target eliminated the effect of phonemic similarity (Experiment 9; Lukatela & Turvey, 1990b). When targets were highly familiar words and contexts were either real words or pseudowords, facilitatory effects of phonological similarity were observed in naming for both word and pseudoword contexts (Experiment 1; Lukatela, Carello & Turvey, 1990). In lexical decision, by contrast, phonemically similar word contexts produced inhibition whereas phonemically similar pseudoword contexts produced facilitation relative to dissimilar pairs (Experiment 2; Lukatela, Carello, & Turvey, 1990).

The effects of phonemic similarity of context and target were modeled as a network of letter, phoneme, and word units such that constraints on the lexical decision task arise primarily at the level of word units that are partially activated by the phonemic units activated by the context. In the course of partially activating word units similar to the target (which generate inhibition to the target), phonemically similar contexts will also enhance the activation of the letter and phoneme units that comprise the target (Lukatela & Turvey, 1990b). In general, the dependence of context target phonemic similarity on target familiarity in lexical decision reflects the balance between inhibitory effects at the word level and excitatory effects at the letter and phoneme levels.

By contrast, the primary source of constraint on the naming task arises at the level of phonemic units that are sensitive to inputs from both the letter and word levels. The states and inhibitory relations among word units partially activated by the context are essentially irrelevant although, it is important to point out that naming a word benefits from activation of a word unit (and subsequent reinforcement of its phonemic constituents) in a way in which naming a pseudoword cannot. For letter strings that are well-specified with respect to alphabet, in both the lexical decision and naming tasks, effects of phonemic similarity arise from the use of phonological information activated by the context in the course of processing the target but no distinct influence of letter level (i.e., alphabetic) activation on phonological activity is evident.

STUDY 4: ALPHABETIC MANIPULATIONS
WITH PHONOLOGICAL CONSEQUENCES

A fourth and very productive line of investigation into the consequences of two alphabetic systems probes the status, for the skilled reader, of words composed exclusively of letters shared by both alphabets. Results provide evidence of mandatory phonological processes prior to lexical access in word recognition tasks. As described in Table 11.2 (see also Turvey, Feldman, & Lukatela, 1980), some of these shared letters receive the same phonemic interpretation in both alphabets, whereas others are phonemically ambiguous in that they receive different interpretations in Roman and in Cyrillic. Words composed exclusively of shared letters with the same phonemic interpretation in both alphabets (e.g., MAMA, JAJE) are alphabetically ambiguous but well-specified phonologically. Words composed of shared letters with two phonemic interpretations (and no alphabetically unique letters) are phonologically as well as alphabetically ambiguous in that they can be pronounced according to the grapheme-phoneme correspondence rules of Roman or those of Cyrillic or by combination of the two.

Consider the word BEHA, which contains two phonologically ambiguous letters (viz., *B, H*) and two (alphabetically ambiguous but phonologically unique) common letters (viz., *E, A*). Interpreted as a Cyrillic letter string, it is pronounced /vena/, which means "vein." Interpreted as a Roman letter string, it is pronounced /bexa/, which is not a word in Serbo-Croatian, although it is a phonologically legal combination. A frequently replicated finding is that when skilled readers of Serbo-Croatian are presented with phonologically ambiguous letters strings in either the lexical decision or naming tasks, their responses are significantly slowed relative to their response latencies for phonologically unambiguous letter strings. In one study (Lukatela, Savić, Gligorijević, & Turvey, 1978), both the design of the experiment and the instructions to the subjects were created to restrict the task to the Roman alphabet: No letter strings contained uniquely Cyrillic letters, and subjects were asked to judge whether a letter string was a word by its Roman reading. In a following study (Lukatela, Popadić, Ognjenović, & Turvey, 1980), no alphabet restriction was imposed on lexical decision and the word interpretation could occur in either the Roman interpretation, the Cyrillic interpretation, both or neither. In both experiments, the prolonged decision times to all phonologically bivalent letter strings as compared to phonologically unambiguous letter strings suggested that subjects are unable to suppress multiple phonological interpretations when permitted by a letter string. Because phonologically unambiguous letter strings with and without alphabet ambiguity produced equivalent results (e.g., MAMA, which can be interpreted as either a Roman or a Cyrillic word was no slower than ЖАБА, which can only be interpreted as a Cyrillic string), this outcome was interpreted as evidence of phonological as contrasted with alphabetic ambiguity and it was concluded that lexical access always proceeds with reference to phonology.

In the two experiments cited earlier (Lukatela et al., 1978, 1980), different words appeared in phonologically unique and phonologically ambiguous conditions. That is, the effect of a letter string's phonological ambiguity was assessed by comparing recognition latencies of different words, some of which were phonologically ambiguous and some of which were not. Similarly, the effect of a letter string's alphabetic ambiguity was assessed by comparing recognition latencies of different (phonologically unambiguous) words, some of which were alphabetically ambiguous (e.g., MAMA, JAJE) and some of which were not (e.g., ЖАБА, ŽABA).

In a later experiment, the effect of phonological ambiguity was assessed by comparing decision (Feldman & Turvey, 1983) and naming (Feldman, 1981) latencies to the ambiguous and unique transcriptions of the same word. For example, the Serbo-Croatian word for "vein" is, as noted previously, written ВЕНА in Cyrillic characters but, in Roman characters, that word is written VENA. Both forms are meaningful and are equated with respect to variables such as frequency, meaning, and word length because they are forms of the same word. They differ, however, in that ВЕНА permits an alternative phonological interpretation (viz., /bexa/) and VENA does not. Comparisons between two alphabetic transcriptions of the same word, only one of which is phonologically ambiguous provide the basis of the within-word assessment of phonological complexity on word recognition in Serbo-Croatian known as the phonological ambiguity effect (PAE). Sometimes, differences as large as 300 ms have been observed between the ambiguous and unique alphabet transcriptions of a word although, among other factors, the magnitude of the PAE difference is sensitive to the number of ambiguous characters in the ambiguous form (Feldman, Kostić, Lukatela, & Turvey, 1983; Feldman & Turvey, 1983). PAE effects have also been observed for ambiguous letter strings where neither (Feldman & Turvey, 1983) or both of the readings are meaningful (Frost, Feldman, & Katz, 1990).

To state the PAE outcome in a general way, prolonged latencies in naming and lexical decision have been observed for ВЕНА type words as contrasted with VENA type word but not for MAMA type words as contrasted with ЖАБА or ŽABA type words. This outcome has been interpreted as reflecting activation of more phonemic units and competition among the word units to which they are linked (Feldman & Turvey, 1983; Feldman, Kostić, Lukatela, & Turvey, 1983). A model, foreshadowed in the preceding discussion of phonemic and alphabetic similarity effects, has been proposed (Lukatela, Turvey, Feldman, Carello, & Katz, 1989). It consists of three types of units, letter, phoneme, and word, and the linkages between them. At the level of the letter, the elements of the Cyrillic and Roman alphabets constitute functionally distinct sets. Shared letters with one phonemic interpretation (viz., *A, E, O, J, K, M, T*) are common to the two sets. Shared letters with two phonemic interpretation (viz., *B, C, H, P*) are represented in each alphabet set. That is, ambiguous letters are represented two times at the letter level.

At the level of the phoneme, by contrast, there is no duplication. Two grapheme units link to each phoneme unit (except for the shared letters that have the same phonemic interpretation in two alphabets.) For example, Φ and F both connect to /f/ and B and V both connect to /v/, whereas A—which is both a Cyrillic and a Roman character—is the only unit that connects to /a/. The pattern of linkages between letter and phoneme units captures the relatively simple relation between letter and phoneme that characterizes the Serbo-Croatian language relative to a language such as English.

In the proposed network, word units are activated from phonemic units in a two-way interactive process. Each word unit represents a particular ordering of phonemic units. When a word unit is activated, the units at the letter and phoneme levels for each letter position in that word are reinforced. It is also assumed that there are multiple inhibitory connections (in both directions) between the unique letters of one alphabet and the unique letters of the other. So, for example, when a unique Cyrillic letter is activated in one position, then the activity level of all Roman letters in complementary positions is reduced. The strength of inhibition varies as a function of the number of activated units that are unique to one alphabet. In a similar manner, the strength and pattern of activation that gives rise to PAE varies as a function of the number of ambiguous units present (Feldman et al., 1983; Feldman & Turvey, 1983).

Consider a word such as BEHA, which has phonemically ambiguous letters in the first and third positions. Each of these letters will activate two phonemic units (viz., B activates /b/ and /v/; H activates /x/ and /n/). Compare it with the Roman transcription of that same word, VENA, which has alphabetically unique letters in the first and third positions. The presence of unique Roman characters will decrease the activation of Cyrillic alphabet units and the phonemic units activated by them. (For the two versions of this word, the number and identity of shared unambiguous letters is the same). Activation at the phonemic level will feed to word level units where intralevel inhibitory influences will generate a complex pattern of excitatory and inhibitory influences. Generally, phonemic input from BEHA-type words will be enhanced relative to input from VENA-type words. (see Figs. 11.1a, b) And, in the terminology of interactive models such as McClelland and Rumelhart (1981), phonologically ambiguous BEHA-type words require more operational cycles to settle on a single word unit than

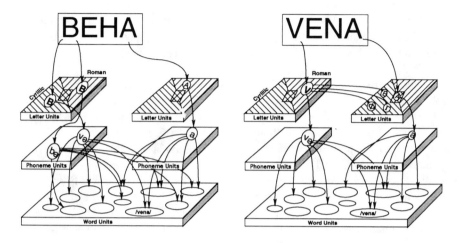

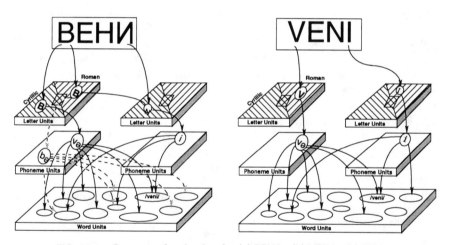

FIG. 11.1.   Patterns of activation for (a) BEHA-, (b) VENA-, (c) ВЕНИ-, and (d) VENI-type words.

do phonologically unambiguous VENA-type words (Lukatela, Turvey, & Todorović, 1991).

Strings that include a unique letter will, at the letter level, activate the alphabet of the unique letter and (partially) inhibit the letters of the complementary alphabet. Consequently, the composition of strings with ambiguous letters becomes less salient when the string includes a unique letter. For example, the Cyrillic word ВЕНИ, which is the dative case of the word meaning "vein," includes a unique letter as its affix in the word's final position as well as ambiguous letters in the first and third positions (the first three letters comprise the base morpheme). When activated, Cyrillic И will reduce the potential activation of Roman letters in other positions, that is, the Roman reading of B and H (see Fig. 11.1c).

In comparison with BEHA-type words where both the Roman and the Cyrillic phoneme units are activated in both the B and H letter positions, the presence of И in ВЕНИ type words will tend to excite the Cyrillic phoneme units of B and H and reduce activation of the analogous Roman units. Consequently, as activation spreads from the phoneme to the word level, the number of highly activated word units will be fewer for ВЕНИ-type words than for BEHA-type words. Accordingly, lexical decision latencies should be faster for ВЕНИ-type words than for BEHA-type words and, in fact, latencies for ВЕНИ words were not significantly different than those of VENI-type words (see Fig. 11.1d) in a lexical decision task (Feldman, 1991; Feldman et al., 1983). Similar effects were also observed in a naming task (Feldman, 1991).

Stated generally, the presence within an isolated letter string of a single character that unequivocally specifies alphabet can bias the activation from letter to phonemic units. This outcome is significant in consideration of the three previous studies where alphabetic manipulations exerted no influence on the processes of word recognition. In the present study, it is evident that an effect of alphabet ambiguity reveals itself when a letter string contains no unique letters to guide alphabet identification. That is, alphabetically defined visual effects are linked to the phonological characteristics of a word and reveal themselves when a word is phonologically complex. In the last two studies, the domain of alphabet bias is investigated by manipulating the temporal relation between a target and a

TABLE 11.5
Mean Decision and Naming Latencies (ms) and Errors for
Ambiguous and Unambiguous Base Morphemes with Ambiguous
and Unambiguous Affixes (modified from Feldman, 1991)

| | Base Morpheme | | |
Affix	Ambiguous	Unambiguous	Difference
Lexical decision			
Ambiguous	729	671	58
	28	14.3	13.7
Unambiguous	677	664	13
	9.2	6.6	2.6
Naming			
Ambiguous	616	588	28
	25.9	12.5	13.4
Unambiguous	626	613	13
	17.6	11.8	5.8

context that includes unique letters. Transient effects of alphabetically specified contexts on targets that are and are not comprised exclusively of letters that are shared by both alphabets are examined.

STUDY 5: ALPHABETIC MANIPULATIONS
ON PHONOLOGICAL AMBIGUITY

A fifth line of investigation into the effects of alphabetic bivalence on word recognition and hence a potential source of evidence for an alphabetically specified orthographic contribution to word recognition entailed primed lexical decision and naming tasks. For target words consisting of phonologically ambiguous strings, plausible related contexts include what the words mean (viz., a semantic associate) and which alphabet yields a word interpretation (viz., alphabetically consistent) as well as a combination of the two.

As already described, some words in Serbo-Croatian can be phonologically ambiguous in either their Cyrillic or their Roman form. For example, BETAP and PAJAC are both phonologically ambiguous because they are composed exclusively of letters that appear in both the Cyrillic and the Roman alphabet. BETAP is a word by its Cyrillic reading (viz., /vetar/, which means "wind") and is meaningless by its Roman reading (viz., /betap/). Conversely, PAJAC is a word by its Roman reading (viz., /pajats/, which means "clown") and is meaningless by its Cyrillic reading (viz., /rajas/). More typically, however, words contain at least one letter that is unique to one alphabet or the other so that a transcription is well-specified with respect to alphabet and phonology (for example, the bold letters of **VETAR** pronounced /vetar/ and ПАЈАЦ pronounced /pajats/ are unique to their respective alphabets).

In the one experiment (Experiment 2; Lukatela, Feldman, Turvey, Carello, & Katz, 1989), targets (either ambiguous or unambiguous) were preceded by a prime that was either alphabetically consistent with the word reading of the ambiguous word or was alphabetically inconsistent with the word reading of that target. Primes were presented for 700 ms with an ISI of 100 ms before the target appeared for 1,400 ms. All primes were semantically associated to the critical word targets. That is, BETAP (which means "wind" by its Cyrillic reading) was preceded either by the word "storm," written in Cyrillic characters (alphabetically consistent) or by the same word written in Roman characters (alphabetically inconsistent) and PAJAC (which means "clown" by its Roman reading) was preceded by the word for "circus," written in Roman characters or by the same word written in Cyrillic characters. Similarly, **VETAR** (which means "wind" by its Roman reading and cannot be read as Cyrillic) was preceded by the word for "storm," written either in Roman characters or in Cyrillic characters and ПАЈАЦ (which means "clown' by its Cyrillic reading and cannot be read as Roman) was preceded by the word for "circus," written either in Cyrillic characters or in Roman characters.

Min *F* analyses conducted on word latencies between 1,500 ms and 400 ms revealed significant effects of (consistent/inconsistent) alphabetic context and of ambiguity as well as a significant interaction between the two. Alphabet inconsistency of prime and target slowed lexical decision to phonologically ambiguous transcriptions of words by 63 ms and hurt accuracy by 15.9% relative to the consistent condition. That is, phonologically ambiguous BETAP following "storm" printed in Cyrillic characters was faster and more accurate than BETAP following "storm" printed in Roman characters. For phonologically unique transcriptions of those same words, however, alphabet consistency had a nonsignificant effect of 12 ms on latency and 0.2% on accuracy. For example, VETAR following "storm" printed in Roman characters was not significantly faster or more accurate than VETAR following "storm" printed in Cyrillic characters.

The significance of this outcome with respect to understanding the effect of alphabetic context on word recognition is the observation that latency (and errors) for phonologically ambiguous words is dramatically affected by consistency of alphabetic context whereas no analogous effect of alphabet consistency was observed for phonologically unambiguous words. A similar outcome was observed in a naming task (Experiment 4; Lukatela, Feldman, Turvey, Carello, & Katz, 1989) where alphabet consistency of prime with the word reading of the target reduced latencies for ambiguous target words by 52 ms and improved accuracy by 4.6% but, for unambiguous words, alphabet consistency had a nonsignificant effect of 8 ms on latencies and 1.6% on errors.

It is important to note that the specification of alphabet by a prior occurring context affects lexical decision and naming of phonologically ambiguous words not only when related word units appear as primes but also when unrelated words and nonwords appear. In fact, the reduction in recognition latencies to ambiguous words in alphabetically consistent contexts relative to alphabetically inconsistent contexts was 86 ms when contexts were defined by unrelated words and was 97 ms when context was defined by a meaningless string of predominantly unique consonants (Experiment 1: Lukatela, Turvey, Feldman, Carello, & Katz, 1989). As generally described, a context can bias but will not necessarily restrict processing to one alphabet. That is, all phonemic interpretations permitted by an orthographic string will be activated, at least partially. Finally, because words, both related and unrelated, as well as unpronounceable letter strings can serve as contexts, the effect of context on the activation of letter and associated phonemic units is unlikely to occur at the word level and more plausibly occurs at the linkage between letter and phonemic units.

It is interesting to note that lexical effects can sometimes override the consistent biasing toward one alphabet over another. For example, the word meaning "harem" can be written as either XAPEM, which is a Cyrillic form, or as HAREM, which is a Roman form—but the combination HAPEM is meaningless. If the Roman and Cyrillic interpretations are assigned independently for each of the two ambiguous graphemes, this meaningless string can be pronounced in four different ways. One combination is of particular interest: By treating the H grapheme as Roman and the P grapheme as Cyrillic, the word meaning "harem" can be produced from HAPEM. This response constitutes a virtual word. In a lexical decision task, error rates for pseudowords with this structure (i.e., virtual word responses) averaged 42% when they were presented in the context of an unassociated word and increased significantly to 60% in the context of a word that was associated (e.g., the word for "sultan") to the mixed alphabet reading of this string. And, in the context of an associated prime, correct rejection latencies were slowed by 23 ms relative to the unassociated context (Experiment 4; Lukatela, Turvey, Feldman, Carello, & Katz, 1989). In the naming task, 43% of responses to these strings were interpreted as words in the unassociated context and that percentage increased to 63% in the associated context. Similarly, latencies for virtual words named as words were 32 ms faster in the associated context than in the unassociated context (Experiment 5; Lukatela, Turvey, Feldman, Carello, & Katz, 1989). Evidently, influences of word level activation on activation at the phonemic level can offset the inhibition of letters belonging to the alphabet not specified by context. That is, in both the lexical decision and the naming task, word level processes can contribute to the pattern of activation in that under some circumstances skilled readers will activate both alphabets in order to interpret a pseudoword as a word.

Alphabet contexts that are consistent across prime and target facilitate recognition of ambiguous target words and sometimes they have a numerically small and statistically nonsignificant effect on unambiguous target words (Experiment 3: Lukatela, Turvey, Feldman, Carello, & Katz, 1989). The proposed interpretation of this finding is that the effect of context is to help disambiguate the mapping between letter and phoneme levels. An alternative interpretation is that context could serve to facilitate some later postlexical process. Accordingly, as processing of the context becomes progressively less complete, either in terms of the number of levels stimulated or in terms of the number of elements processed at one level, then strategic and postlexical processing suffers most. By this reasoning, if alphabet biasing is automatic and prelexical, then effects should not vary under experimental conditions that encourage incomplete as contrasted with relatively complete processing of alphabetic information. Alternatively, if alphabet biasing is subject to postlexical strategies and checks then the effect of alphabet may not be evident under conditions that render the context less available.

STUDY 6: MANIPULATIONS
OF ALPHABETIC ACCESSIBILITY

In principle, alphabetic contexts could exert their influence either early or late in the recognition process. A final methodology for examining the locus of influence of alphabetic context entailed visual presentation conditions in which the availability for processing of alphabetic context was varied by following it with a mask (Lukatela et al., 1991). As in the studies described earlier, subjects were required to name phonologically ambiguous target words in either Roman or Cyrillic alphabet prime contexts. In one experiment, contexts consisted of 3 to 5 unique letters presented for 70 ms and followed after an ISI of 30 ms by a target. In this nonmasked condition, results replicated the typical effect of alphabet consistency on naming whereby subjects were 131 ms faster (and 32% more accurate) when both the context and the prime were in the same alphabet than when they were in different alphabets (Experiment 1; Lukatela et al., 1991). Similar results were obtained both when the context duration was reduced to 18 ms and was preceded at an ISI of 0 ms by a masking pattern (Experiment 2) and when the context consisted of a single unique letter (Experiment 4). Evidently, it is not the lexical property of the prime that governs its ability to influence the activation of graphemic and phonemic units.

Effects of alphabetic context have also been observed when the context follows the ambiguous target, and is itself masked so that identifying the alphabetic context and working from there to the target is highly implausible. It is claimed that if processing of the target is disrupted differentially according to linguistic properties of the masked context (and figural properties are held constant), then properties of the masked context must contribute to lexical access for the target and cannot simply influence postlexical processes. In one experiment (Experiment 5; Lukatela et al., 1991), targets consisted of phonologically ambiguous letter strings and their unambiguous alphabet controls and contexts consisted of strings of unique consonants (some of which were repeated) printed in the alphabet that was either consistent or inconsistent with the word reading of the ambiguous letter string. Phonologically, all alphabetically consistent and inconsistent contexts were equivalent. Targets appeared for 40 ms and were followed at an ISI of 0 ms by a context letter string. The context was presented for 40 ms and was followed by a series of hash marks that remained until the onset of the next trial. In that experiment, consistent with previous studies, the difference between correct target identification with alphabetically consistent and inconsistent contexts was 6.98% for ambiguous targets and 1.46% for unambiguous targets. This interaction was statistically significant and was interpreted as evidence that alphabet congruity between target and masked context reduces (and alphabet incongruity augments) the disruption to processing caused by the mask. Because backward pattern masks are assumed to interfere with lexical access, these results were interpreted as prelexical in locus. That is, the benefit associated with alphabetically consistent contexts and targets arises at the level of letter as contrasted with word units.

An interesting prediction that follows from the claim that alphabet effects arise as inhibition at the level of letter units is that when target and subsequent pseudoword mask differ with respect to alphabet, the letters of the mask will be activated relatively slowly because they must overcome prior inhibition from the target. As a consequence, the phoneme units of the target will have more time to activate possible word units. Of course, the effect of masked pseudowords will also be affected by the phonemic similarity of target and mask.

Phonology and alphabet of target and masked prime were manipulated in a backward priming paradigm in which a phonologically unambiguous word target (20 ms) was followed by a pseudowords mask (20 ms) and then by a pattern mask (Lukatela & Turvey, 1990a). Effects of phonological similarity were replicated. Moreover, a significant interaction of phonology and alphabet was obtained. As anticipated, for phonologically dissimilar pairs, alphabetically mismatched targets and masks were identified significantly more accurately than matched pairs. For phonologically similar pairs, there was a nonsignificant trend in the opposite direction. The effect of phonological properties of the mask on target identification suggests enhanced activation of phonemic units activated while processing the target. The interaction suggests a transient inhibition of letter units due to alphabetic status of the mask. That is, under very restricted viewing conditions, alphabetic context can influence the identification of unambiguous letter strings in a manner not unlike its influence on ambiguous letter strings.

CONCLUSIONS

In six word recognition studies using variations of the lexical decision and naming tasks evidence for alphabetically defined visual effects was examined. The experimental manipulation common to all studies exploited the bi-alphabetic fluency of skilled readers of Serbo-Croatian and entailed a comparison of presenting context and target strings (or successive presentations of word or pseudoword letter strings) in either the same or in different alphabets. It was observed that relative to alternating alphabet, the preservation of alphabet over successive presentations of a word had no significant effect on recognition. Effects of alphabetic context were evident for target strings that were phonologically ambiguous and were typically slow in both the lexical decision and naming tasks, however. The presence of a letter unique to one alphabet, either in the target string itself or in a prior or later occurring context was sufficient to diminish and sometimes to eliminate any significant effect of phonological ambiguity. This series of results was interpreted as evidence of mandatory phonological processing in Serbo-Croatian word recognition and suggested a processing architecture efficient at handling two sets of mappings between letter and phoneme.

In the experimental literature, phonological effects are sometimes interpreted as postlexical effects and sometimes interpreted as occurring prior to lexical access. Phonological effects in Serbo-Croatian have been interpreted as reflecting early processes for several reasons, including the findings that they occur for both real word and orthographically legal but meaningless pseudoword targets and that the alphabetic context need not be fully processed in order to influence processing of the target. That is, unmasked as well as masked alphabetic contexts have similar effects on phonologically ambiguous letter strings and alphabetic contexts can be words, pseudowords, or a single letter. For phonologically unambiguous letter strings, effects of alphabetic context are rare. Finally, rates of target identification under alphabetically matched and mismatched conditions with phonologically mismatched masks suggest that the time course for effects of alphabetic context on unambiguous strings exist but may be quite transient.

The proposed model of a reading mechanism for the skilled reader of two alphabets entails letter, phoneme, and word units. Effects in lexical decision are constrained primarily by activity at the word level and naming is constrained primarily by activity at the phonemic level. Effects of alphabet arise relatively early in the model and tend to be graded in nature. For example, inhibitory connections between alphabets exist at the letter level so that within a word, activation of a letter unique to one alphabet will tend to reduce the level of activity of letter units in the alternative alphabet. Similarity. the influence of a context that specifies alphabet is to bias the connections between letter and phoneme toward the designated alphabet. In sum, the processing microstructure for word recognition in Serbo-Croatian includes principles whereby inhibitory connections exist between the letter units of the two alphabets and the systematic covariation of letters and phonemes within each alphabet is realized. Evidence for alphabet effects at the word level are not typically observed.

ACKNOWLEDGMENTS

This research was supported by grant HD 01994 to Haskins Laboratories and grant HD 08495 to the University of Belgrade from the National Institutes of Child Health and Human Development. Results of Study 1 were presented to the 1989 meeting of the Psychonomic Society in Atlanta, GA.

REFERENCES

Bentin, S., & Peled, B-S. (1990). The contribution of task-related factors to the repetition effect at short and long lags. *Memory & Cognition, 18,* 359–366.

Feldman, L. B. (1981). Visual word recognition in Serbo-Croatian is necessarily phonological. *Haskins Laboratories Status Report on Speech Research, SR-66.*

Feldman, L. B. (1989, November). *Morphological priming in lexical decision and naming.* Paper presented at the Psychonomic Society, Atlanta, GA.

Feldman, L. B. (1991). The contribution of morphology to word recognition. *Psychological Research, 53.*

Feldman, L. B., Kostić, A., Lukatela, G., & Turvey, M. T. (1983). An evaluation of the "Basic Orthographic Syllabic Structure" in a phonologically shallow orthography. *Psychological Research*, *45*, 55–72.

Feldman, L. B., & Moskovljević, J. (1987). Repetition priming is not purely episodic in origin. *Journal of Experimental Psychology: Learning, Memory, and Cognition*, *13*, 573–581.

Feldman, L. B., & Turvey, M. T. (1983). Visual word recognition in Serbo-Croatian is phonologically analytic. *Journal of Experimental Psychology: Human Perception and Performance*, *9*, 288–298.

Forster, K. I., & Davies, C. (1984). Repetition priming and frequency attenuation in lexical access. *Journal of Experimental Psychology: Learning, Memory and Cognition*, *10*, 680–698.

Frost, R., Feldman, L. B., & Katz, L. (1990). Phonological ambiguity and lexical ambiguity: Effects on visual and auditory word recognition. *Journal of Experimental Psychology: Learning, Memory and Cognition*, *80*, 569–580.

Hillinger, M. L. (1980). Priming effects with phonemically similar words: The encoding bias hypothesis reconsidered. *Memory & Cognition*, *8*, 115–123.

Lukatela, G., Carello, C., & Turvey, M. T. (1990). Phonemic priming with words and pseudowords. *European Journal of Cognitive Psychology*, *2*, 373–394.

Lukatela, G., Feldman, L. B., Turvey, M. T., Carello, C., & Katz, L. (1989). Context effects in bi-alphabetical word perception. *Journal of Memory & Language*, *28*, 214–236.

Lukatela, G., Popadić, D., Ognjenović, P., & Turvey, M. T. (1980). Lexical decision in a phonologically shallow orthography. *Memory & Cognition*, *8*, 124–132.

Lukatela, G., Savić, M., Gligorijević, B., Ognjenović, P., & Turvey, M. T. (1978). Bi-alphabetic lexical decision. *Language & Speech*, *21*, 142–165.

Lukatela, G., & Turvey, M. T. (1990a). Automatic and pre-lexical computation of phonology in visual word identification. *European Journal of Cognitive Psychology*, *2*, 325–343.

Lukatela, G., & Turvey, M. T. (1990b). Phonemic similarity effects and prelexical phonology. *Memory & Cognition*, *18*, 128–152.

Lukatela, G., Turvey, M. T., Feldman, L. B., Carello, C., & Katz, L. (1989). Alphabetic priming in bi-alphabetical word perception. *Journal of Memory & Language*, *28*, 237–254.

Lukatela, G., Turvey, M. T., & Todorović, D. (1991). Is alphabet biasing in bialphabetic word perception automatic and prelexical? *Journal of Experimental Psychology: Learning, Memory and Cognition*, *17*, 653–663.

Martin, R. C., & Jensen, C. R. (1988). Phonological priming in the lexical decision task: A failure to replicate. *Memory & Cognition*, *17*, 505–521.

Masson, M.E.J., & Freedman, L. (1990). Fluent identification of words. *Journal of Experimental Psychology: Learning, Memory and Cognition*, *16*, 355–373.

McClelland, J. L., & Rumelhart, D. E. (1981). An interactive activation model of context effects in letter perception: Part I. An account of basic findings. *Psychological Review*, *88*, 357–407.

Meyer, D. E., Schvaneveldt, R. W., & Ruddy, M. G. (1974). Functions of graphemic and phonemic codes in visual word recognition. *Memory & Cognition*, *2*, 309–321.

Monsell, S. (1985). Repetition and the lexicon. In A. W. Ellis (Ed.), *Progress in the psychology of language* (pp. 147–195). London: Lawrence Erlbaum Associates.

Ratcliff, R., Hockley, W., & McKoon, G. (1985). Components of activation: Repetition and priming effects in lexical decision and recognition. *Journal of Experimental Psychology: General*, *114*, 435–450.

Stanners, R. F., Neiser, J. J., Hernon, W. P., & Hall, R. (1979). Memory representation for morphologically related words. *Journal of Verbal Learning and Verbal Behavior*, *18*, 399–412.

Turvey, M. T., Feldman, L. B., & Lukatela, G. (1984). The Serbo-Croatian orthography constrains the reader to a phonologically analytic strategy. In L. Henderson (Ed.), *Orthographies and reading* (pp. 81–90). Hillsdale, NJ: Lawrence Erlbaum Associates.

IV VISUAL FACTORS IN READING DISABILITIES

12

Are There Differences Between Disabled and Normal Readers in Their Processing of Visual Information?

Dale M. Willows
Ontario Institute for Studies in Education

Richard Kruk
University of Wollongong

Evelyne Corcos
Glendon College, York University

INTRODUCTION

Disabled–normal reader comparisons have represented a major research approach to investigating the possible involvement of visual processing deficits in reading disabilities. Studies using this approach have normally tested the performance of disabled and normal readers on one or more tasks thought to be tapping some aspect of visual processing to determine whether the disabled readers have significantly more difficulty. Conclusions about whether or not there is evidence of visual processing differences between disabled and normal readers are mixed: Some researchers and theoreticians have contended that the evidence shows disabled readers do not differ from normal readers in their processing of visual information (e.g., Calfee, 1983; Stanovich, 1985; Vellutino, 1979, 1987), whereas others have concluded the contrary (e.g., Di Lollo, Hansen, & MacIntyre, 1983; Lovegrove, Martin, & Slaghuis, 1986; Willows, Kershner, & Corcos, 1986). The conclusion drawn may depend on the stage of processing under investigation.

To understand the current status of our knowledge about visual processing differences between disabled and normal readers, it is important to consider the research within the context of the types of methodologies involved. The visual processing demands vary from one study to another. A fundamental dimension that differentiates most of the studies is the level of visual processing assessed. From the instant a visual stimulus reaches the eye, the visual information begins to undergo processing, proceeding from the retina to the visual cortex, to various association areas of the brain. It is possible that deficits in any or all of the levels of visual processing might have some role in reading, spelling, and writing

265

disabilities. Some researchers have focused their efforts on understanding the earlier levels of visual processing, immediately after the information has entered the visual system, and others have been more interested in later levels of processing in which higher cognitive processing may play a greater role. Some studies simply require that subjects indicate when they see a stimulus on a screen; others may require that subjects correctly recognize what they saw at some later point or even that they be able to reproduce what they saw.

This chapter reviews studies that have examined disabled and normal readers' processing of visual information at various stages in the system to determine whether disabled readers appear to manifest any sort of deficit. It is not the objective of the chapter to determine whether or not visual processing deficits have a *causal* role in explaining reading disabilities, although that ultimately is the crucial issue. Because the view that disabled readers do not differ from normal readers in their visual perception or visual memory processes has been widely promoted in the literature, it is simply our intention here to bring together the evidence. If the evidence of differences is sufficiently persuasive, we hope that others will be motivated to investigate the mechanisms accounting for them and their role, if any, in reading disabilities.

The interpretation of any particular study depends on the level of processing demanded in the experimental task, consequently the studies reviewed in the following sections are roughly organized from earlier to later levels of visual processing. Before moving on to review studies examining the early and later visual processes of disabled and normal readers, we begin with some basic methodological considerations fundamental to the later discussion.

METHODOLOGICAL CONSIDERATIONS

A primary problem in the literature on visual processing is the potential for confounds. Although intuitively it might seem that the most direct way of assessing for visual processing differences between disabled and normal readers would be to test them with letters and words, there are serious problems with such an approach. In view of the fact that linguistic processing deficits undoubtedly play a very significant role in reading disabilities (e.g., Mann, 1991; Vellutino, 1987), an important factor to consider in defining experimental tasks thought to be assessing visual processes is whether performance on the task may involve the use of linguistic processes confounded with the visual processes of interest. Some studies attempting to assess visual processes in reading disability may inadvertently have been assessing verbal as well as visual factors. Most studies in which the goal has been to assess visual factors free of linguistic/verbal confounds have avoided this pitfall by employing stimuli that are very difficult to label verbally, or by using procedures in which performance could not be affected by verbal labeling, or by taking precautions of both types. The review that follows includes only studies that have attempted to rule out the possibility that the "visual" task could have been performed by labeling the stimuli.

Another important factor to consider in examining research using disabled–normal reader comparisons is the operational definition used in the research. Throughout this chapter the term *reading disability* is defined by the conventional definition,[1] which requires that subjects have normal general intellectual ability, educational opportunity, and social/emotional functioning but below normal reading achievement. For children at or above the age of 8, a lag of 2 or more years below grade level in reading achievement is defined as a reading disability. For children who are below the age of 8, and therefore cannot be more than 2 years below grade level, an individual who is at least 1 year below age/grade at age 7 or at least 6 months below age/grade expectation at age 6 is designated as reading disabled.

Virtually all of the studies examining the role of visual processes in reading disabilities have compared the performance of a group of disabled readers with that of normally achieving readers. Not all researchers have adopted an acceptable definition of reading disability. Because the operational definition of the groups of readers is key to the interpretation of the data produced by research, this review focuses on studies that provide evidence of having met the conventional discrepancy definition for selecting the reading-disabled group and also of having employed an appropriate comparison group of nondisabled "normal" readers that differs from the disabled on measures of written language (e.g., reading, spelling) but that is similar to them on factors such as age and general cognitive ability.

EARLY VISUAL PROCESSES

Clinical observations that disabled readers seem to confuse similar-looking letters and words in their reading and writing (see Willows & Terepocki, chap. 2) suggest that in comparison with normal readers, they may have some underlying difficulty in basic visual perception. A large number of studies have been undertaken to investigate this possibility. These studies have attempted to determine whether disabled and normal readers differ in their perception of visual stimuli in the early stages of processing before higher level cognitive processes have had time to come into play.

---

[1]There has been extensive discussion in the literature of the inadequacy of the discrepancy approach for defining reading disabilities (Stanovich, 1991). Although we are in agreement with this literature that IQ test scores are of questionable relevance in defining groups of reading-disabled children, until very recently the standard in the literature has been the discrepancy definition. There has been no systematic use of any other definition of reading disability in the disabled–normal reader literature examining visual processes.

Much of the research comparing the early stages of visual information processing of disabled and normal readers has involved two main paradigms: temporal integration and backward masking. These techniques are used to determine whether disabled and normal readers differ in how quickly they can perceive and extract information from a visual stimulus. Tachistoscopes, oscilloscopes, and computer presentation technologies are used to control the time intervals, which are measured in milliseconds.

Temporal Integration

A given piece of information, read during one fixational pause, can still be perceived for a period of time after the eye has moved to read another section of text (Coltheart, 1980). The duration of this "visible persistence" can be measured by presenting two stimuli in very close temporal sequence and assessing whether the stimuli have been perceived as two separate stimuli or as a single stimulus. There are two main types of temporal integration task that have been used to compare the initial stages of visual information processing in disabled and normal readers. One type involves the presentation of two different stimuli with a variable time interval, the interstimulus interval (ISI), between them. The minimum length of ISI required for a person to perceive the two stimuli as separate is considered to reflect the duration of the visible persistence of the first stimulus. This is often referred to as the "separation threshold." In a well-known study by Stanley and Hall (1973), groups of disabled readers and normal readers were shown pairs of stimuli. To begin with, each pair of stimuli was presented simultaneously so that they would be perceived as a single image. If each pair of stimuli were displayed simultaneously in the same location they would combine to make the word "NO," a cross, and a cross within a square, respectively. Next the procedure involved increasing, by very small steps (20 ms), the time interval between each pair of stimuli until the children reported that they saw two shapes instead of one. The results of Stanley and Hall's research indicated that the disabled readers' separation threshold before they reported seeing two separate images were significantly longer than that of the normal readers. This pattern of results showing longer visible persistence among the reading disabled has been confirmed in other studies using similar procedures (Lovegrove & Brown, 1978; Stanley, 1975).

A second type of temporal integration task has involved the presentation of two identical stimuli (such as two identical straight lines or sets of parallel lines called "gratings") in close temporal sequence, also to assess the visible persistence of the first stimulus. The task begins by presenting the two stimuli simultaneously and then the ISI is increased by very small steps until the subject reports that the stimulus is flashing rather than constant. Using this type of temporal integration task, researchers have amassed considerable evidence also indicating that disabled readers have longer visible persistence than normal readers (Di Lollo et al., 1983; Lovegrove, Billing, & Slaghuis, 1978; O'Neill & Stanley, 1976). Based on evidence of this kind it has also been suggested that the processing deficit is not at the level of the retina but occurs later in processing, at the level of the visual cortex (Slaghuis & Lovegrove, 1985, 1986). Moreover, it has been reported that 75% of disabled readers in a series of studies of early visual processing exhibited evidence of such deficits (Lovegrove et al., 1986). An extensive program of research is now ongoing to examine the nature of the processing mechanisms involved in these early visual processing deficits among disabled readers (for a review of this research, see Lovegrove and Williams, chap. 14).

Backward Masking

When the onset of one visual stimulus (the target) is followed almost immediately by the onset of another visual stimulus (the mask), the second stimulus interferes with the processing of the first. This effect is known as backward masking. Whereas the temporal integration tasks described earlier are thought to provide an index of the visible persistence of a stimulus after its termination, backward masking tasks are thought to provide a measure of the rate of information pick up in the initial stages of visual information processing (Di Lollo et al., 1983; Rayner & Pollatsek, 1989). In a typical backward masking experiment, a target stimulus (e.g., a figure or letter) is briefly presented, then a mask is presented, and then a test stimulus is presented. The task involves a same–different paradigm such that one key is pressed to indicate that the test stimulus is the same as the target or another key is pressed to indicate that it is different. On every trial there is a 50/50 chance of a "same" or "different" response being correct. Typically, the time interval between the onset of the target and the mask, the stimulus onset asynchrony (SOA), is varied until a performance level of 75% accuracy is achieved. The SOA at which a subject is able to perform at 75% accuracy is referred to as the critical SOA. The results of several experiments comparing performance on backward masking tasks have shown that disabled readers process visual information more slowly (their critical SOA is longer) than normal readers (Di Lollo et al., 1983; Lovegrove & Brown, 1978; Mazer, McIntyre, Murray, Till, & Blackwell, 1983; O'Neill & Stanley, 1976; Stanley & Hall, 1973).

Consistency of Findings

Not all studies using temporal integration and backward masking tasks have produced the same patterns of early visual processing differences between disabled and normal readers reported previously. A few studies have been repeatedly cited in the literature as sources of contrary evidence (e.g., Arnett & Di Lollo, 1979; Fisher & Frankfurter, 1977; Morrison, Giordani, & Nagy, 1977).

Although the existence of studies reporting conflicting evidence suggests that caution is certainly warranted in drawing conclusions, the evidence in support of early visual processing differences between disabled and normal readers is almost overwhelming. Moreover, careful review of the research articles reporting conflicting findings has usually uncovered possible explanatory factors, often involving inadequacy of the operational definition of reading disability employed in the studies. For example, Di Lollo et al. (1983) pointed out that in the earlier study by Arnett and Di Lollo (1979), the fact that there was only a 1-year discrepancy between the "disabled" and normal reader groups may account for the lack of significant difference between those two groups. Also, the very unusual finding by Fisher and Frankfurter (1977) of a disabled reader superiority in early visual processes, may be the result of these authors having failed to control for general cognitive ability of their disabled and normal groups (who were selected from different school settings). The disabled readers in their sample may, in fact, have been superior in IQ to the age- and reading-level matched normal groups with which they were compared. Perhaps brighter children process visual information faster, or perform laboratory tasks more efficiently. Another often-cited source of contrary evidence is Morrison et al. (1977) in which no early visual processing differences were found between disabled and normal readers. Like Fisher and Frankfurter (1977), however, these authors failed to match their disabled and normal groups on measures of general intelligence. In addition, the Morrison et al. (1977) study had a small sample size, with only 9 disabled and 9 normal readers. Their failure to find reading group differences in early visual processes may have resulted from their having tested too few children.

Virtually all of the studies cited here that have found early visual processing deficits among disabled readers have employed the conventional operational definition of reading disability and an age- and IQ-matched normal reader group. Also, the sample sizes in the studies reporting differences have been quite large, with most of the studies having a minimum 15 subjects per group, and many having sample sizes substantially greater. Thus, although this type of post hoc explanation of conflicting findings cannot be considered definitive, it does cast doubt on the reliability of the results of the studies. If the conflicting findings prove in the future to be replicable, then they should be considered more seriously. At this point, however, the evidence of early visual processing deficits among disabled readers is very persuasive. There is also some suggestive evidence that this visual processing deficit may diminish with age (Badcock & Lovegrove, 1981; Di Lollo et al., 1983; Lovegrove & Brown, 1978).

Relation of Early Visual Processing Deficits to Reading

There are some researchers who contend that the types of methodologies used to assess early visual processing differences between disabled and normal readers "are remote from the perceptual conditions facing a child learning to read" (Hulme, 1988, p. 373), but there are others who argue just as persuasively that the types of measures of visual perception described here are more sensitive and powerful approaches to comparing the visual-perceptual functioning of disabled and normal readers (Di Lollo et al., 1983; Gross & Rothenberg, 1979; Lovegrove et al., 1986). Other types of procedures may be confounded with higher cognitive processes (e.g., verbal labeling, rehearsal, cognitive strategies, etc.). Moreover, there is evidence from studies of letter, number, and word perception, stimuli more closely related to reading, that seems to confirm that disabled readers require stimuli to be exposed for a longer duration than normal readers in order to produce a given level of correct responding (e.g., Allegretti & Puglisi, 1986; Gross, Rothenberg, Schottenfeld, & Drake, 1978; Kruk & Willows, 1993; Stanley, 1976). These findings appear to confirm that when brief visual presentations are used to measure adequacy of visual perceptual functioning disabled readers show deficits relative to normal readers.

Just what role, if any, these deficits might have in reading disabilities is not yet clear. Early visual processes undoubtedly play an important role in eye movements and information intake in reading. Visible persistence, which can last for about one-quarter second beyond the fixational pause, raises a problem for reading. If there is visible persistence, how can text be read without successive visual input overlapping with previously read material, making the text appear like a jumble of letters and words? Researchers have answered this question by showing that, at the onset of each new eye movement, the input from the last fixational pause is erased or inhibited (Breitmeyer, 1984; Breitmeyer, chap. 5) by the activity of the "transient" visual system.

The evidence that visible persistence often lasts longer in reading-disabled children than in normal readers has prompted some researchers to speculate that the visual transient system of reading-disabled children does not operate properly (Lovegrove et al., 1986; Lovegrove & Williams, chap. 14). They maintain that disabled readers' difficulties are a result of a slowing down of the process of erasure of previous input—reflecting a "sluggish" transient visual system (Williams & LeCluyse, 1990). Without the inhibiting activity that takes place with eye movements, words read on the page would appear unclear and jumbled, at least for the duration of the persisting image from the last fixational pause. Furthermore, there would be an impairment in the accuracy of eye movements as words are read across a line of text. These potential effects have, however, only begun to be investigated in controlled reading contexts with disabled readers.

The possibility that a deficit in the visual transient system, discussed by Breitmeyer (chap. 5) and Lovegrove and Williams (chap. 14), might explain the visual processing differences demonstrated in the studies comparing the early visual processes of disabled and normal readers has been explored in the work of Kruk (Kruk, 1991; Kruk & Willows, 1993), using a backward masking paradigm. Most of the research demonstrating early visual processing differences between normal and disabled readers—using both temporal integration and backward masking tasks—has involved the methods and materials of traditional psychophysical analysis, which bear little resemblance to reading. In Kruk's research the extent to which these findings can be extrapolated to more reading-like tasks has been explored. Three main experiments, involving gradual approximations toward more normal reading demands, examined how visual processing differences might be manifested between normal and disabled readers. These studies also investigated whether a deficit in the transient visual system might account for the differences. The first two studies focused specifically on visible persistence, and the third on eye movements as well as visible persistence in reading. All three experiments involved visual form discrimination in a pattern masking task. The time interval between the onset of a stimulus item and a mask item (SOA) was varied to provide a measure of visible persistence, as reflected by accuracy of performance and response time. In the context of a "computer game" the child's task was to press a key to indicate whether a target and test item, which followed the mask, were the same or different.

The studies involved 8- to 11-year-old disabled and normal readers selected according to a conventional discrepancy definition. The general hypothesis suggested that if a deficit in the transient visual system accounts for differences in visual processing between disabled and normal readers, then disabled readers should experience different rates of release from the effects of masking than normal readers. This would be indicated by a significant interaction effect between reader group and SOA, showing faster improvement by normal readers than disabled readers as the SOA interval increased.

In Experiment 1, pairs of unfamiliar visual stimuli, Japanese letters with spatial frequency characteristics similar to English letters, were shown in rapid succession, with a mask presented after the first stimulus. Significant group differences were found in overall accuracy of performance, with normal readers scoring higher than disabled readers. These data add further support to the extensive evidence of visual processing differences between normal and disabled readers. However, as there was no indication of a reader group by SOA interval interaction, the "sluggish" transient system interpretation of the mechanism involved in visual processing deficit in disabled readers was not supported.

The second experiment involved familiar materials, English letters and words, as well as unfamiliar nonwords made up of English letters. Like the first experiment, the SOA was varied. Results similar to those of Experiment 1 were found with the letter data of Experiment 2, again indicating visual processing differences. In Experiment 2 as well, however, there was no reader group by SOA interaction, arguing against a transient system deficit interpretation. Furthermore, the involvement of the word superiority effect (WSE) was evident in the word/nonword data. This supported the view that visual processing factors alone are not sufficient to explain the results.

Experiment 3 introduced complete sentences, with target words embedded, to provide a closer approximation to "natural" reading. Sentences were presented in one of two modes in order to examine possible differences in eye movement efficiency. Rapid serial visual presentation (RSVP), displaying words sequentially at a fixed location, which has been cited as a potential tool for improving reading in disabled readers (Potter, 1984), was used as a reading condition that did not require eye movements. The moving window mode presented words at different locations moving across the screen from left to right, thus requiring eye movements. The time interval between the target word and the next word in the sentence was varied in order to produce backward masking. Significant group differences were again obtained, but like the first two experiments no significant reader group by SOA effect was found, indicating visual processing differences, but not in accordance with a transient system deficit interpretation. Furthermore, there was no effect of mode of presentation, showing that the requirement for eye movements was not an important factor in mediating performance.

The results of Kruk's (1991; Kruk & Willows, 1993) investigation have shown that visual processing differences between the two groups of readers are manifested within the context of more natural reading; using materials like those encountered in actual reading. However, although a transient system deficit was not ruled out, it did not provide an adequate explanation of the mechanism that mediates differences in performance in the research.

Conclusions Concerning Early Visual Processes

Returning to the question of whether disabled readers differ from normal readers in their early visual processes, the answer seems to be in the affirmative. There have been many well-controlled studies employing temporal integration and backward masking tasks to compare the early visual information-processing abilities of disabled and normal readers. Most of them have resulted in similar patterns of results. In general, it seems that the early visual processes of disabled readers are different from those of nondisabled normal readers.

In answer to the more fundamental question of whether early visual processing deficits are one of the causes of reading disability, the answer is much less clear at this point. The role of these early visual processing differences in reading disabilities is not yet well understood. They may have some direct causal role in the perception, discrimination, and analysis of the visual features of letters and words. On the other hand, they may be reflecting some more basic underlying processing differences between disabled and normal readers, such as speed of information processing (Di Lollo et al., 1983) or attentional processes, which in turn may have some causal role in reading disability. It has even been suggested that disabled–normal reader differences could be a result of reading experience, although evidence argues against this interpretation (Di Lollo et al., 1983; Lovegrove et al., 1986). Whatever the case, the performance differences between disabled and normal readers on tasks designed to assess early visual processes appear to be real and whatever their explanation, theories, and models of reading disability must take them into account.

LATER VISUAL PROCESSES

In order to remember the letters and groups of letters that characterize the orthographic patterns and words of the language—to recognize them for reading and to recall them for writing and spelling—an individual must be able to retain a record of them in memory and have easy access to that stored information.

After visual information has passed from the very brief visible persistence level to a short-term memory storage level, the information must be processed further in long-term memory if it is to be retained for later recognition and recall (Rayner & Pollatsek, 1989). A variety of experimental procedures have been used to determine whether there are differences between disabled and normal readers at these later processing stages. Most of the studies designed to investigate visual memory differences between disabled and normal readers have employed one of four main types of task, involving visual recognition memory, reproduction from visual memory, visual-visual paired-associate learning, and serial learning of visual designs. All of these types of tasks are designed to investigate how well individuals remember visual information they have perceived, in order to recognize or reproduce it from memory later.

Visual Recognition Memory

In order to recognize words with speed and accuracy, a reader must be able to make use of information such as the overall shape of words. A series of investigations by Lyle and Goyen was designed to examine how accurately disabled readers and normal readers recognize unfamiliar visual stimuli that resemble "word contours" or "word shapes." In five experiments Lyle and Goyen, using tachistoscopic procedures, presented a series of different word shapes to disabled and normal readers (Goyen & Lyle, 1971a, b, 1973; Lyle & Goyen, 1968, 1975). Shortly after the presentation of each word shape target, one of two test formats was used. In one test situation a set of several test word shapes was presented and the children's task was to select the target stimulus they had just seen. In the other test format, involving a same–different paradigm, the children had to press one key to indicate whether they thought the test letter was the same as the target or another key if they thought it was different. Lyle and Goyen were interested not only in determining whether disabled readers differed from normal readers in their visual recognition of the word shapes, but also in whether younger children (age 6 to 8 years) in the two reading groups differed from older (age 8 to 10). In addition they wanted to know whether the exposure duration of a word shape (ranging from .10 s to 5.0 s) and the degree of similarity among the set of test alternatives affected accuracy of responding.

The results of Lyle and Goyen's research showed clearly that, at the younger age level, disabled readers were less accurate in recognizing word shapes than were normal readers. Such differences were not found at the older age level.

These differences between disabled and normal readers were found at the shorter stimulus duration rates (.10 s and 1.0 s) but not at longer ones (5.0 s). Consistent with the findings of the studies described in the previous sections on early visual processes, Lyle and Goyen (1975) concluded from their research that

> the perceptual deficit manifested by young [disabled] readers on tachistoscopic tasks involves the input or processing of visual information at rapid exposures. The relative deficit of young [disabled] readers appears to arise not through short-term memory deficits or difficulty in discriminating between alternatives on response cards but through incomplete analysis of the tachistoscopically presented stimulus, so that certain distinctive features or their interrelationships are not taken into account. (pp. 675–676)

Willows, Corcos, and Kershner (1988, 1993) conducted a study of children's visual recognition memory for unfamiliar visual symbols (letters from the Hebrew alphabet), using a same–different paradigm in a computer game format. Disabled and normal readers at three age levels (6, 7, and 8 years) were tested. On each trial in the computer game the child was shown a target stimulus selected randomly from a pool of 18 Hebrew letters. After a brief interval they were shown the test stimulus; either the same letter again or a different, but similar looking, letter from the same set. The child had to press one key to indicate that the test item was the same as the target and another if it was different. The delay between the target and test stimuli was varied to determine whether disabled readers' visual processing difficulty was at the level of initial input or whether it was a result of memory difficulty. The results of this research were consistent with Lyle and Goyen's findings: Reading-disabled children were less accurate and slower in their visual recognition performance. Moreover, there was a developmental pattern, with the effect being greater among younger than older disabled readers, and the deficit appeared to be at the level of initial visual perception rather than visual memory because the disabled/normal reader difference was consistent across the three delay intervals (500, 1,500, and 3,000 ms).

Taken together then, the pattern of results from studies of visual recognition that involve rapid stimulus presentation is consistent. Younger disabled readers make more errors and are slower at responding than normal readers of similar age and IQ. The disabled readers' difficulty seems to occur at the initial input stage rather than at a later storage stage. In other words, the findings of these studies that assessed both early and later stages of information processing add to the evidence of early visual processing differences between disabled and normal readers.

Reproduction from Visual Memory

In learning to read and write the child must attend to and remember the visual information in the symbols (i.e., in letters, numbers, and words) in order to recognize them for reading and reproduce them for writing. A widely cited series of studies was undertaken by Vellutino and his colleagues to investigate the possibility of visual memory differences between disabled and normal readers. These studies involved having children view difficult-to-label visual stimuli, and then after the stimuli had been removed, to "copy" them from memory (in two of the studies), or recognize them from a list (in a third study). Because these studies have been considered by many researchers as presenting key evidence demonstrating that there are no visual processing differences between disabled and normal readers—despite the fact that they have been repeatedly criticized on methodological and statistical grounds in the literature—they are reviewed here in some detail.

Hebrew Studies.   The three experiments (Vellutino, Pruzek, Steger, & Meshoulam, 1973b; Vellutino, Steger, Kaman, & DeSetto, 1975c; Vellutino, Steger, DeSetto, & Phillips, 1975b) all used the unfamiliar orthography of Hebrew as a source of novel visual stimuli. Groups of non-Hebrew and Hebrew-speaking subjects were compared on measures of visual recognition and recall. Non-Hebrew children were chosen from the public school system in a middle-class suburban area. Hebrew-speaking subjects were drawn from a private, all-day Hebrew school. All subjects were initially screened for hearing, vision, emotional problems and truancy. Students included in the sample pool had either a verbal or performance Wechsler Intelligence Scale for Children-Revised (WISC-R) IQ of 90 or above and their reading achievement levels were determined by the Gilmore Oral Reading Test. The subjects were subdivided into disabled and normal readers solely on the basis of the reading achievement measure. Children whose grade equivalent scores were 2 or more years below their grade placement were selected for the disabled reader group and those whose scores were at or above grade level were chosen for the normal reader group. In the initial study (Vellutino et al., 1973b) subjects were also administered the Bender Visual Motor Gestalt Test. In each study there were three groups per grade tested—a disabled reader and a normal reader group of non-Hebrew children differentiated on the Gilmore Oral Reading Test and a Hebrew group (who were substantially higher in IQ, reading achievement, and phonic skill than either of the non-Hebrew groups in every study).

Similar stimulus sets were used in all three experiments. Three sets of consonant groupings made up the nine Hebrew stimulus words projected on a screen. The first two experiments (Vellutino et al., 1973b, 1975c), involved immediate visual recall measures. Subjects were instructed to look at each item (three-, four-, five-consonant groupings) for the duration of the exposure and then "copy" them from memory. The consonant strings were exposed for the number of seconds that there were letters in the string. The third experiment (Vellutino et al., 1975b) was designed to investigate immediate and delayed visual recognition of Hebrew letter strings.

The first experiment in the series (Vellutino et al., 1973b) involved a sample of older children, ages 10 to 13 years (grades 4, 5, and 6), and the second experiment (Vellutino et al., 1975c) included second- and sixth-graders, in order to generalize the findings to younger populations. To further extend the findings, the third experiment (Vellutino et al., 1975b) involved recognition memory of subjects from grades 2, 4, and 6.

Based on the findings of these key studies involving the ability to recognize and/or reproduce unfamiliar visual shapes from memory, Vellutino and his colleagues (Vellutino, Steger, Moyer, Harding, & Niles, 1977) concluded that "in all these investigations, disabled readers performed as well as normals in short- and long-term memory of Hebrew letters and words—symbols unfamiliar to both groups" (p. 57).

Limitations of the Hebrew Studies. Although, on the surface, this series of experiments appeared to represent an experimentally tight and thorough test for possible differences in disabled and normal readers' later visual processes, methodological and statistical weaknesses have been raised in the literature (Doehring, 1978; Fletcher & Satz, 1979a; Gross & Rothenberg, 1979; Satz & Fletcher, 1980; Singer, 1979). These problems seriously limit the conclusions that can be drawn from the studies.

After finding an almost identical pattern of results for disabled and normal readers in the first experiment involving older children (5 fourth-graders, 12 fifth-graders, and 4 sixth-graders), Vellutino et al. (1973b) recognized that visual processing deficits might play a more important role in the reading problems of younger children. Thus, they included second-graders in the other two experiments as well as older children.

In the second experiment (Vellutino et al., 1975c), there were 11 children in each of the disabled, non-Hebrew normal, and Hebrew normal reader groups at each grade (grades 2 and 6), and the second-graders averaged about 8 years of age. Thus, the sample size was relatively small and the subjects were at the high end of the "younger" range. The results of the experiment are reported as having shown that there is no difference between disabled and normal readers in visual perception and memory. An examination of the tables in the article, however, raises questions about this conclusion from the data. For one thing, the task was clearly difficult for second-graders. Even the very bright Hebrew second-graders (whose average full scale WISC-R score was 122, contrasting with 104 for the non-Hebrew disabled readers) omitted 40% of the items in the three-letter strings. Over all string lengths, the non-Hebrew disabled readers omitted 33% of the items and the normal readers omitted 23%. Thus, there was a 10% difference in errors of omission between the two groups of 11 subjects. In addition, of the items they completed, the normal readers reproduced 14% of the items in the three-letter strings, and 14% of the items in the five-letter strings more accurately than the disabled readers (scores on the four-letter strings were also low and essentially identical for disabled and normal readers). Whether or not these findings are statistically significant with such a small sample and given the great difficulty of the task (the disabled readers were less than 45% accurate on the 67% of the items they did respond to), it seems inappropriate to draw any strong conclusions from these null (not negative) findings.

The comparison of younger disabled and normal readers in the third study (Vellutino et al., 1975b) is vulnerable to the same type of criticism. The groups that would fit into a "young" age range were the disabled and normal readers in second grade (average age about 7.9). The fourth-graders, who averaged over 10 years would be considered "older" in a developmental framework. The sample was larger than in the other study with 14 children per group. The results were interpreted as showing that "poor readers sustain *no basic dysfunction* in visual perception and immediate visual recall" (p. 229). An examination of the results again raises questions about this interpretation of the data, however. The task was also extremely difficult, with the disabled readers achieving less than 30% accuracy on the immediate recognition task in which 15% accuracy could be expected on the basis of chance alone. Although the comparison with the performance of second-grade normal readers may not have been statistically significant, the direction of the means, 2.59 (29%) versus 4.28 (48%) for the disabled and normal readers respectively, supports rather than refutes a visual processing/memory difference between these two groups. A floor effect is clearly in evidence, especially for the disabled readers, so a "no difference" interpretation of these null findings is definitely unjustified.

The third experiment (Vellutino et al., 1975b), which was intended as a test of long-term memory, differed procedurally from the other two experiments. After viewing 9 cards for 5 s each (with one-, two- and three-symbol strings on them), the child's task was to select (recognize) those letter strings in 3 lists of 20 items. The same procedure was followed 24 hours later and again, 6 months later. It is evident from the results that the task was very difficult for all children (both non-Hebrew and Hebrew, poor and normal readers at grades 2, 4, and 6). Even on immediate recall the second-grade poor readers were less than 30% accurate, only slightly above the guessing rate. (They averaged fewer than 1 item correct per list of 20). Thus, the long-term-memory tests at 24 hours and 6 months were essentially meaningless: The children had almost nothing to remember because they did not get the items correct immediately after seeing them. This floor effect invalidates disabled–normal reader comparisons of long-term memory in the study.

Taken together then, the findings from the studies that have often been cited in the literature as representing a "clean" experimental test (Calfee, 1977) of disabled–normal reader differences in visual perception and memory cannot be interpreted as conclusive. The comparisons of the young non-Hebrew disabled and normal readers in this series of experiments do not provide an adequate test of the role of visual processing and visual memory factors in the reading disabilities of young children, in the age rage (6 to 8 years) where some other authors might predict such differences (e.g., Lyle & Goyen, 1975; Willows et al., 1993). Given the relatively small samples in each group, the extreme task difficulty, and the pattern of results suggesting that (despite floors) there may be differences, further research at this age range is clearly warranted. Moreover, the test of long-term memory was very weak. Fletcher and Satz (1979a, b) argued strongly that this series of studies does not adequately assess the role of visual processing deficits among younger children. Our review of the three key experiments involving the use of Hebrew orthography concurs with Fletcher and Satz's position. Across the series of experiments, every comparison that was intended to test for disabled–normal reader differences in visual memory among younger children showed that such differences may well exist. In any case, there is no basis in the research for concluding otherwise.

Other Evidence.   The findings from other research indicates that disabled and normal readers may perform differently on a draw-from-memory task. Lyle (1968) and Willows et al. (1988), for example, compared the abilities of disabled and normal readers to draw unfamiliar visual patterns from memory using the memory-for-designs test. The results showed that disabled were significantly inferior to normal readers in their reproductions of designs. Moreover, the previously mentioned findings by Willows et al. (1993) showing disabled–normal reader differences in visual recognition of Hebrew letters (a less demanding task than reproduction from visual memory), suggest that caution is warranted in drawing definitive conclusions at this point.

Thus, the three experiments involving Hebrew orthography reported by Vellutino and his colleagues, although representing a serious attempt at a clean experimental test for differences in disabled and normal readers' perception and memory for unfamiliar visual stimuli, fell short, especially with respect to the younger disabled–normal reader comparisons. The failure to find differences between disabled and normal readers in reproduction from visual memory in the older groups (above 8 years of age) in the first and second experiments where there was no statistical floor, suggest that in the older age range there may not be differences. These findings involving reproduction from visual memory (and visual recognition) do not, however, contradict evidence from research on early stages of processing, because all of the studies by Vellutino and his colleagues involved "long" stimulus exposures. The Hebrew letter strings were presented for 3 to 5 s. These are exposure durations that are longer than those at which the research on early visual processes found disabled–normal reader differences in performance.

Visual-Visual Paired-Associate Learning

In the context of attempting to compare disabled and normal readers' ability to associate unfamiliar visual shapes with sounds and words, as the child must do in learning to read, Vellutino and his colleagues undertook another line of research in which they had disabled and normal readers learn to associate pairs of unfamiliar visual designs with each other. These studies also involved having the children associate visual designs with verbal responses, but this visual-verbal association aspect of the research is concerned with the children's ability to use verbal labels, and is essentially irrelevant to questions about visual perception and memory processes. Thus, only the visual-visual paired-associate tasks are discussed here. In these tasks the child was shown pairs of difficult-to-label shapes, and told "to try to remember what two designs go together" (Vellutino, Steger, & Pruzek, 1973a, p. 117). On test trials the children were shown one of each stimulus pair and required to select its mate from a set of five choices. In both experiments Vellutino and his colleagues (Vellutino, Harding, Phillips, & Steger, 1975a; Vellutino, et al., 1973a) found no differences between disabled and normal readers' ability to associate visual designs with each other.

These results have been interpreted as additional evidence that there are no visual processing differences between disabled and normal readers, and this conclusion seems warranted with respect to later visual processes in the older age range. The disabled and normal readers in these studies were in an older age range, between about 9.5 and 12.5 years of age, and the stimulus presentation rates were relatively slow. Again, the results do not contradict the evidence on early visual processes.

Serial Learning of Visual Designs

Following from the work of Vellutino and his colleagues, Swanson also undertook a series of studies designed to compare disabled and normal readers' abilities to remember difficult-to-label visual shapes under conditions in which verbal labels were either excluded or included. Swanson used a probe-type serial memory task in which he presented six nonsense shapes. Again, the task involving the use of verbal labels, although interesting, is not relevant to the present discussion about visual memory processes. Only the unnamed condition is discussed here. In the unnamed condition a set of six cards, each with a different shape printed on it, was placed face down in front of the child. From left to right, each of the cards was then turned up for a few seconds and then turned down again. A probe (one of the six shapes) was then shown and the children had to point to the card in the row in front of them that matched the probe. Their task was essentially a visual-spatial task, because they were shown a probe and they had to remember where they had seen it. In three experiments involving children from 7 to 12 years of age, Swanson consistently found no differences between disabled and normal readers in serial memory for unnamed stimuli (Swanson, 1978, 1982, 1983).

Other research examining visual-spatial memory has produced a different pattern of results, however. Willows et al. (1993) presented strings of Hebrew letters to 6- to 8-year-old disabled and normal readers in a computer game. After each string of three visually distinct letters, one of the same three letters was shown in one of the three spatial positions that the original string had occupied. The children's task was simply to press one of two keys to indicate whether the letter was in the same or different position from the one they had just seen it in. The results on both accuracy and response speed measures indicated that disabled readers were less able than normal readers to remember visual-spatial information. The disabled–normal reader differences were greater at the younger age levels.

Conclusions Concerning Later Visual Processes

The answer to the question of whether there are differences in later visual processes between disabled and normal readers is still uncertain. The evidence with respect to older children is fairly consistent. It seems quite unlikely that there are visual memory differences between older (over age 8) disabled and normal readers on the types of tasks reviewed here. At the younger age level, however, the possibility of some sort of developmental lag in visual memory still exists. There is evidence to suggest that younger disabled readers have difficulty in remembering visual information in a variety of task types. It may be that these difficulties are due to differences in early perceptual processes, because most of the studies that have found differences in visual memory tasks have involved brief stimulus presentation rates whereas studies that have failed to find such differences have usually presented stimuli at slower rates. Further carefully done research is required to clarify the relation between later visual processes and reading disability, particularly in the younger age range (up to age 8).

CONCLUSIONS AND FUTURE DIRECTIONS

Research Directions

Taking the high degree of consistency of the early visual processing evidence together with the inconclusiveness of the later visual processing evidence, it appears that visual perceptual and visual memory deficits may be implicated in reading disabilities. The conclusion by some theorists that disabled readers have no visual processing difficulties appears to be premature. There may be more to reading disabilities than the verbal labeling (or, phonological coding) and verbal memory problems that have been widely identified. It is incumbent on researchers to explore all factors that may contribute to reading disabilities and not to limit themselves to those that may seem to fit with currently popular models.

Ultimately the goal of research examining the visual processing of readers of different ability levels is to determine the role that visual processes might play in learning to read and in reading failure. However, establishing whether a weakness in any particular processing ability is causal in reading acquisition or reading failure is a difficult problem. Nearly all of the research examining the strengths and weaknesses of children who differ in reading ability is correlational in nature. Very little research on reading disabilities can validly be interpreted as demonstrating a causal link between a particular processing deficit and reading failure. Deficits in some well-documented correlates of reading ability, such as phonemic awareness, have been suggested as causes of reading disability, but even these have not always passed crucial experimental tests (Bryant & Goswami, 1987; Hulme, 1987) demonstrating causation.

Future research examining the relation between visual processing deficits and reading disability should focus particular attention on the possibility of visual memory deficits among reading-disabled children in the age range from 6 to 8 years. In addition, future research should attempt to explore the underlying causal factors that are responsible for the relation between visual deficits and reading disabilities. Perhaps, for example, poor performance on tasks attempting to assess visual and/or linguistic deficits may reflect general weaknesses in attention or working memory. The challenge for future researchers is not to demonstrate whether reading disabilities are related to visual, linguistic, or other types of processing factors, but to explain how basic processing weaknesses of various types may be related to each other or may interact in causing reading disabilities.

Practical Implications

If some disabled readers have delays or deficits in their visual processing abilities, such weaknesses could be a factor in their apparent difficulties in differentiating between similar looking letters and words; especially in analyzing and remembering the orthographic patterns in words and in processing letters and words at a rapid rates in text. Clinical observations and case reports (Willows & Terepocki, chap. 2), correlational evidence from studies using standardized psychometric instruments (Willows, 1991), and visual deficit subtypes from clinical and neuropsychological studies (Watson & Willows, chap. 13) all point to some role of visual processing deficits in reading disabilities. Evidence from information-processing research involving basic visual perception and visual memory also suggests that there is some relation between visual processing deficits and reading disabilities. At this point, however, the potential role of visual processing weaknesses in written language problems is not well enough understood to draw confident conclusions about practice.

Clinicians and educators in the field of learning disabilities should certainly keep an open mind about the possibility that visual processing deficits contribute in some way to reading disabilities. Prudence would dictate that both assessment approaches and teaching techniques should be devised on the assumption that the reading-disabled child may have some difficulty in coping with the visual demands of the task.

ACKNOWLEDGMENT

Portions of this chapter have appeared previously in Willows (1991).

REFERENCES

Allegretti, C. L., & Puglisi, J. T. (1986). Disabled vs. nondisabled readers: Perceptual vs. higher-order processing of one vs. three letters. *Perceptual and Motor Skills, 63,* 463–469.

Arnett, J. L., & Di Lollo, V. (1979). Visual information processing in relation to age and to reading ability. *Journal of Experimental Child Psychology, 27,* 143–152.

Badcock, D., & Lovegrove, W. (1981). The effects of contrast, stimulus duration, and spatial frequency on visible persistence in normal and specifically disabled readers. *Journal of Experimental Psychology: Human Perception and Performance, 7,* 495–505.

Bryant, P. E., & Goswami, U. (1987). Phonological awareness and learning to read. In J. Beech & A. Colley (Eds.), *Cognitive approaches to reading* (pp. 213–244). Chichester, England: Wiley.

Breitmeyer, B. G. (1984). *Visual masking: An integrative approach.* New York: Clarendon Press.

Calfee, R. (1977). Assessment of independent reading skills: Basic research and practical applications. In A. S. Reber & D. Scarborough (Eds.), *Towards a psychology of reading: Proceedings of the CUNY Conference* (pp. 289–324). Hillsdale, NJ: Lawrence Erlbaum Associates.

Calfee, R. (1983). The mind of the dyslexic. *Annals of Dyslexia, 33,* 9–28.

Coltheart, M. (1980). Iconic memory and visible persistence. *Perception and Psychophysics, 27,* 183–228.

Di Lollo, V., Hansen, D., & McIntyre, J. S. (1983). Initial stages of visual information processing in dyslexia. *Journal of Experimental Psychology: Human Perception and Performance, 9,* 923–935.

Doehring, D. G. (1978). The tangled web of behavioral research on developmental dyslexia. In A. L. Benton & D. Pearl (Eds.), *Dyslexia: An appraisal of current knowledge* (pp. 123–138). New York: Oxford University Press.

Fisher, D. F., & Frankfurter, A. (1977). Normal and disabled readers can locate and identify letters: Where's the perceptual deficit? *Journal of Reading Behavior, 9,* 31–43.

Fletcher, J. M., & Satz, P. (1979a). Unitary deficit hypotheses of reading disabilities: Has Vellutino led us astray? *Journal of Learning Disabilities, 12*(3), 155–159.

Fletcher, J. M., & Satz, P. (1979b). Has Vellutino led us astray? A rejoinder to a reply. *Journal of Learning Disabilities, 12*(3), 168–171.

Goyen, J. D., & Lyle, J. G. (1971a). Effect of incentives and age on the visual recognition of retarded readers. *Journal of Experimental Child Psychology, 11,* 226–273.

Goyen, J. D., & Lyle, J. G. (1971b). Effect of incentives upon retarded and normal readers on a visual-associate learning task. *Journal of Experimental Child Psychology, 11,* 274–280.

Goyen, J. D., & Lyle, J. G. (1973). Short-term memory and visual discrimination in retarded readers. *Perceptual and Motor Skills, 36,* 403–408.

Gross, K., & Rothenberg, S. (1979). An examination of methods used to test the visual perceptual deficit hypothesis of dyslexia. *Journal of Learning Disabilities, 12,* 670–677.

Gross, K., Rothenberg, S., Schottenfeld, S., & Drake, C. (1978). Duration threshold for letter identification in left and right visual fields for normal and reading-disabled children. *Neuropsychologia, 16,* 709–715.

Hulme, C. (1987). Reading retardation. In J. Beech and A. Colley (Eds.), *Cognitive approaches to reading* (pp. 245–270). Chichester, England: Wiley.

Hulme, C. (1988). The implausibility of low-level visual deficits as a cause of children's reading difficulties. *Cognitive Neuropsychology, 5,* 369–374.

Kruk, R. (1991). *Functional consequences of a transient visual processing deficit in reading disabled children*. Unpublished doctoral dissertation, OISE, University of Toronto.

Kruk, R., & Willows, D. M. (1993). Toward an ecologically valid analysis of visual processes in dyslexic readers. In S. Wright & R. Groner (Eds.), *Studies in visual information processing: Facets of dyslexia and its remediation* (pp. 193–206). Amsterdam: Elsevier North Holland.

Lovegrove, W., & Brown, C. (1978). Development of information processing in normal and disabled readers. *Perceptual and Motor Skills, 46*, 1047–1054.

Lovegrove, W., Billing, G., & Slaghuis, W. (1978). Processing of visual contour orientation information in normal and disabled reading children. *Cortex, 14*, 268–278.

Lovegrove, W., Martin, F., & Slaghuis, W. (1986). A theoretical and experimental case for a visual deficit in specific reading disability. *Cognitive Neuropsychology, 3*, 225–267.

Lyle, J. G. (1968). Performance of retarded readers on the memory-for-designs test. *Perceptual and Motor Skills, 26*, 851–854.

Lyle, J. G., & Goyen, J. D. (1968). Visual recognition, developmental lag, and strephosymbolia in reading retardation. *Journal of Abnormal Psychology, 73*, 25–29.

Lyle, J. G., & Goyen, J. D. (1975). Effect of speed of exposure and difficulty of discrimination on visual recognition of retarded readers. *Journal of Abnormal Psychology, 84*, 673–676.

Mann, V. (1991). Language problems: A key to early reading problems. In B.Y.L. Wong (Ed.), *Learning about learning disabilities* (pp. 129–162). New York: Academic Press.

Mazer, S. R., McIntyre, C. W., Murray, M. E., Till, R. E., & Blackwell, S. L. (1983). Visual persistence and information pick up in learning disabled children. *Journal of Learning Disabilities, 16*(4), 221–225.

Morrison, F. J., Giordani, B., & Nagy, J. (1977). Reading disability: An information-processing analysis. *Science, 19*, 77–79.

O'Neill, G., & Stanley, G. (1976). Visual processing of straight lines in dyslexic and normal children. *British Journal of Educational Psychology, 46*, 323–327.

Potter, M. C. (1984). Rapid serial visual presentation (RSVP): A method of studying language processing. In D. E. Kieras & M. A. Just (Eds.), *New methods in reading comprehension research* (pp. 91–118). Hillsdale, NJ: Lawrence Erlbaum Associates.

Rayner, K., & Pollatsek, A. (1989). *The psychology of reading*. Englewood Cliffs, NJ: Prentice-Hall.

Satz, P., & Fletcher, J. M. (1980). Minimal brain dysfunctions: An appraisal of research concepts and methods. In H. E. Rie & E. D. Rie (Eds.), *Handbook of minimal brain dysfunctions: A critical view* (pp. 669–715). New York: Wiley.

Singer. H. (1979). On reading, language and learning. *Harvard Educational Review, 49*, 125–128.

Slaghuis, W. L., & Lovegrove, W. J. (1985). Spatial-frequency-dependent visible persistence and specific reading disability. *Brain and Cognition, 4*, 219–240.

Slaghuis, W. L., & Lovegrove, W. J. (1986). The effect of physical flicker on visible persistence in normal and specifically disabled readers. *Australian Journal of Psychology, 38*, 1–11.

Stanley, G. (1975). Two-part stimulus integration and specific reading disability. *Perceptual and Motor Skills, 41*, 873–874.

Stanley, G. (1976). The processing of digits by children with specific reading disability (dyslexia). *British Journal of Educational Psychology, 46*, 81–84.

Stanley, G., & Hall, R. (1973). Short-term visual information processing in dyslexics. *Child Development, 44*, 841–844.

Stanovich, K. E. (1985). Explaining the variance in terms of psychological processes: What have we learned? *Annals of Dyslexia, 35*, 67–96.

Stanovich, K. E. (1991). Discrepancy definitions of reading disability: Has intelligence led us astray? *Reading Research Quarterly, 26*, 7–29.

Swanson, L. (1978). Verbal encoding effects on the visual short-term memory of learning disabled and normal readers. *Journal of Educational Psychology, 70*(4), 539–544.

Swanson, L. (1982). Verbal short-term memory encoding of learning disabled, deaf, and normal children. *Learning Disability Quarterly, 5,* 21–28.

Swanson, L. (1983). A study of nonstrategic linguistic coding on visual recall of learning disabled readers. *Journal of Learning Disabilities, 16*(4), 209–216.

Vellutino, F. R. (1979). *Dyslexia: Theory and research.* Cambridge, MA: MIT Press.

Vellutino, F. R. (1987). Dyslexia. *Scientific American, 256*(3), 34–41.

Vellutino, F. R., Harding, C. J., Phillips, F., & Steger, J. A. (1975a). Differential transfer in poor and normal readers. *Journal of Genetic Psychology, 126,* 3–18.

Vellutino, F. R., Pruzek, R., Steger, J. A., & Meshoulam, U. (1973b). Immediate visual recall in poor and normal readers as a function of orthographic-linguistic familiarity. *Cortex, 9,* 368–384.

Vellutino, F. R., Steger, J. A., DeSetto, L., & Phillips, F. (1975b). Immediate and delayed recognition of visual stimuli in poor and normal readers. *Journal of Experimental Child Psychology, 19,* 223–232.

Vellutino, F. R., Steger, J. A., Kaman, M., & DeSetto, L. (1975c). Visual form perception in deficient and normal readers as function of age and orthographic linguistic familiarity. *Cortex, 11,* 22–30.

Vellutino, F. R., Steger, J. A., Moyer, B. M., Harding, S. C., & Niles, C. J. (1977). Has the perceptual deficit hypothesis led us astray? *Journal of Learning Disabilities, 10,* 54–64.

Vellutino, F. R., Steger, J. A., & Pruzek, R. (1973a). Inter- versus intra-sensory deficiency in paired-associate learning in poor and normal readers. *Canadian Journal of Behavioral Science, 5,* 111–123.

Williams, M. C., & LeCluyse, K. (1990). The perceptual consequences of a temporal processing deficit in reading disabled children. *Journal of the American Optometric Association, 61,* 111–121.

Willows, D. M. (1991). Visual processes in learning disabilities. In B.Y.L. Wong (Ed.), *Learning about learning disabilities* (pp. 163–193). New York: Academic Press.

Willows, D. M., Corcos, E., & Kershner, J. R. (1988, August). *Disabled and normal readers' visual processing and visual memory of item and spatial-order information in unfamiliar symbol strings.* Paper presented as part of the symposium, "Visual factors in learning disabilities," at the XXIV International Congress of Psychology, Sydney, Australia.

Willows, D. M., Corcos, E., & Kershner, J. R. (1993). Perceptual and cognitive factors in disabled readers' perception and memory of unfamiliar visual symbols. In S. Wright & R. Groner (Eds.), *Studies in visual information processing: Facets of dyslexia and its remediation* (pp. 163–178). Amsterdam: Elsevier North Holland.

Willows, D. M., Kershner, J. R., & Corcos, E. (1986, April). *Visual processing and visual memory in reading and writing disabilities: A rationale for reopening a "closed case."* Paper presented as part of the symposium, "The role of visual processing and visual memory in reading and writing," at the annual meeting of the American Educational Research Association, San Francisco.

13 Evidence for a Visual-Processing-Deficit Subtype Among Disabled Readers

Catherine Watson
Dale M. Willows
Ontario Institute for Studies in Education

A major source of contention between present-day theorists concerns the issue of whether reading disabilities are the result of one, or more than one, type of processing problem. There are those who argue strongly that all developmental reading disabilities are a result of subtle and not-so-subtle verbal/linguistic processing deficits (e.g., Liberman, 1983; Mann, 1991; Swanson, 1984; Vellutino, 1987). Others, however, believe that there may be a variety of factors contributing to reading disabilities (e.g., Doehring, Trites, Patel, & Fiedorowicz, 1981; Malatesha & Dougan, 1982; Satz, Morris, & Fletcher, 1985), with different reading-disabled individuals being more or less affected by linguistic, visual, and other types of processing deficits.

Those who contend that there is only one type of developmental reading disability, and that it involves a deficit in verbal/linguistic processes, use as the basis for their argument the massive literature relating language processing problems in phonemic awareness (e.g., Bryant & Goswami, 1987), grammatical sensitivity (e.g., Siegel & Ryan, 1984), and lexical access (e.g., Denckla & Rudel, 1976) to reading disabilities. They also suggest that there is a large body of evidence indicating that there are no visual processing differences between disabled and normal readers (e.g., Calfee, 1983; Stanovich, 1985; Vellutino, 1979, 1987). Those who question this unitary causation position, on the other hand, adopt a multiple causation position, proposing either that there are different subtypes among reading-disabled individuals (e.g., Feagans & McKinney, 1991; also see extensive review by Hooper and Willis, 1989), or that individual differences in two or more areas of processing in combination may underlie reading disabilities (e.g., Rayner & Pollatsek, 1989; Willows, 1991). Those who hold a multiple causation view agree with the unitary causation theorists that research evidence clearly demonstrates that linguistic processing deficits are related to some, if not all cases of reading disability, but they question the validity of the conclusion that there are no visual processing differences between disabled and normal readers (see Willows, Kruk, & Corcos, chap. 12). Rather, on the basis of findings demonstrating the existence of basic visual processing deficits among disabled readers, they hypothesize that, in addition to linguistic factors, visual perceptual and/or visual memory deficits may also play some role in reading disabilities. The purpose of this chapter is to bring together evidence from the subtyping literature demonstrating that a substantial subgroup of disabled readers seem to exhibit visual processing deficiency.

HISTORY OF THE SINGLE VERSUS MULTIPLE CAUSATION DEBATE

An historical perspective on reports dealing with the nature of reading disability chronicles debate and controversy. Inherent in this ongoing argument is the role played by visual factors in accounting for underlying causes of both developmental and acquired dyslexia.

At the same time that Pringle Morgan (1896) was describing a clinical case of severe developmental reading disability that he attributed to the unitary cause of underdevelopment of the left angular gyrus, Charcot (reported in Freud, 1953) was proposing the duality of language learning that he denoted as visile and audile typologies. Hinshelwood (1917) defined what he considered to be a single disorder as congenital word blindness while Orton (1937) later suggested the problem was one of faulty or incomplete cerebral dominance; both emphasized the visual features associated with word difficulty. Bronner (1917), on the other hand, explained the reading disability of one teenaged subject as deficient visual memory and that of another as deficient auditory discrimination and memory. Fildes (1921) reported that, in comparison with normal readers, poor readers had inferior ability in visual form discrimination, memory, and spatial orientation. In contrast to these findings, Gates (1922) found no differences in visual discrimination of nonlinguistic stimuli between good and poor readers. However, each of Schelder (1944), Drew (1956), and Hermann (1959) attributed reading disability to a general disorder of visual perception manifested as inability to learn words as gestalts.

Benton (1962) expressed the opinion that, although defective visuoperceptive skills were involved in slow reading development among younger children, this was a transient problem and the visual factor "accounts, I think, for only a very small proportion of cases of developmental dyslexia in older school children (i.e., above the age of ten)" (p. 95). Barrett (1965) conducted an extensive review of the research relating visual discrimination abilities and first-grade reading achievement. He began his paper with the rationale that visual discrimination had been identified as important for study "evidenced by the fact that all available readiness tests devote attention to it" (p. 53).

In order to explore the possibility that different processing deficits might account for the reading disabilities of different groups of individuals, a number of major studies have been undertaken. These studies were designed to search for subgroups or *subtypes* among the reading disabled. A majority of them have uncovered a grouping in which some sort of visual deficiency is implicated.

PATTERNS OF DIFFICULTIES
AMONG DISABLED READERS:
THE CONCEPT OF SUBTYPES

Based on the notion that there may be differences among individuals in the causes of their reading disabilities, clinicians and researchers have attempted to determine whether there are relatively homogeneous subgroups among the reading disabled. A variety of approaches have been used to explore this possibility, ranging from subjective clinical judgments to more objective multivariate statistical techniques. Taken together, the subtyping studies have produced considerable evidence that disabled readers differ among themselves with respect to their visual processing abilities.

Clinical Subtyping Studies

The clinical approach has involved examining disabled readers' performance—at times arbitrarily and subjectively—on a variety of measures in an attempt to partial the variance into relatively similar patterns. Table 13.1 summarizes the characteristics of the visual-processing-deficit subtypes reported in major clinical subtyping studies. These efforts by clinicians to systematically categorize disabled readers according to their performance on both achievement and more basic cognitive/linguistic variables began what has become a growing body of subtyping literature. This literature suggests that it is neither the case that all reading problems are of the same etiological origin nor that all reading problems are completely individualized. Rather, commonalities among problem readers, in dealing with both language and visual processes, continue to be documented.

In a study often cited for its historical significance Kinsbourne and Warrington (1966) divided subjects into a language-impaired group as defined by a large discrepancy between Wechsler Intelligence Scale for Children (WISC) Verbal and Performance IQ scores in favor of Performance, and a group in which the opposite discrepancy was found, labeled the Gerstmann group because of pronounced difficulties in sequential ordering on finger differentiation tests. Although this study must be criticized on methodological grounds (e.g., only 13 subjects were used and these ranged in age from 8 to 31 with no control for sex;

TABLE 13.1
Visual-Processing-Deficit Subtypes from Clinical Subtyping Studies

Kinsbourne & Warrington (1966)	−Gerstmann group; difficulties in sequential ordering −54% of sample of 13 patients −8–14 years with 1 subject 31 years old −verbal score 20–35 pts. > performance −low block design & object assembly −no language impairment −weak handwriting −all failed finger differentiation tests −no systematic reversals
Ingram, Mason, & Blackburn (1970)	−Visuo-spatial difficulties; confusions involving letters/words but not auditory-phonic capacity −21% of sample of 62 children that met criteria for specific dyslexia −Scottish students −satisfactory performance in school subjects independent of reading and spelling, particularly mechanical arithmetic
Boder (1968, 1971); Boder & Jarrico (1984)	−Dyseidetic dyslexia; primary deficit in ability to perceive letters and words as configurations/visual gestalts −10% of sample of 107 subjects −grade 3 or above −reading ≥ 2 years below grade level −normal IQ (> 90 on S-B or WISC) verbal or performance −low sight vocabulary −can recite alphabet but may not recognize or write letters until grade 4–5 −visuospatial letter and word reversals
Mattis, French, & Rapin (1975)	−Visuo-spatial perceptual disorder; poor visual patterning and memory −16% of sample of 113 subjects −31 brain-damaged normal readers; 53 brain-damaged dyslexics; 29 non-brain-damaged dyslexics −verbal IQ > 10 pts. above performance −weak on Raven's matrices & Benton's test of visual retention −language skills and blending intact
Bayliss & Livesey (1985)	−Dyseidetic readers; defined as having above 65% phonetic-equivalent errors on a screening test −58% of sample of 19 reading-disabled subjects −9–11 years; 11 dyseidetic, 8 dysphonetic, 11 normal readers

(*continued*)

TABLE 13.1
(*Continued*)

―weak performance on memory for hard-to-label
  drawings requiring holistic strategy
―nondifferentiated performance on memory for easy-
  to-label drawings where analytic strategy could be
  used
―recalled items according to serial order of
  presentation rather than according to spatial gestalt
  pattern formed by items

there was no comparison group of normal readers; children with mixed verbal and spatial patterns were excluded in the analysis), it did offer some data to suggest that each of the two syndromes was associated with a characteristic delay in reading and writing development. Johnson and Myklebust (1967), and Ingram, Mason, and Blackburn (1970) also proposed both auditory and visual types of dyslexia.

About the same time, Boder (1968) introduced an approach to clinical identification of reading-disabled subgroups on the basis of comparisons of reading and spelling patterns. By analyzing patterns in the spelling errors disabled readers made on words they could read by sight and words they could not read, Boder (1971) concluded that some disabled readers were less able to process the visual gestalts of words (the "dyseidetics") and others were less able to make use of the phonological patterns in words (the "dysphonetics"). In a study involving 107 children who were in third grade or above but who were achieving two or more years below their grade placement in reading, Boder classified 94% of the sample into one of the following diagnostic subtypes: (a) dysphonetic readers/spellers (67%) who showed deficits in word analysis skills and relied on global features of words because they were unable to segment and blend component letter sounds; (b) dyseidetic readers/spellers (10%) who lacked facility with whole word visual gestalts and relied totally on phonetic analysis; and (c) mixed dysphonetic-dyseidetic readers/spellers (23%) who were handicapped in both phonetic analysis and visual discrimination. Boder's approach to subtyping has been sufficiently popular among both clinicians and researchers that the standardized form of the test (Boder & Jarrico, 1984) has been used fairly extensively in research.[1]

―――――――――
[1]Although the Boder test has now been widely used as a research instrument (e.g., van den Bos, 1984; Dorman, 1987; Freebody & Byrne, 1988; Hooper & Hynd, 1985; Nockleby & Galbraith, 1984), serious questions have been raised about its reliability and validity (e.g., Alexander, 1984; Reynolds, 1984; Willows & Jackson, 1992).

Another widely cited approach that involved clinical-inferential methods of defining subtypes was employed by Mattis and associates (Mattis, 1978, 1981; Mattis, French, & Rapin, 1975). There was an underlying assumption that separate subgroups of dyslexic children characterized by different clusters of deficiencies should exist because if "the development of fluency in reading requires the complex integration of several input, output, and mediating processes, then a deficit in any given process would impair the learning of this complex skill" (1975, p. 151). In recognizing that reading disability can be associated with both brain damage and with family history involving no brain damage Mattis et al. (1975) divided their 113 clinic sample into brain-damaged normal readers, brain-damaged dyslexic readers, and non-brain-damaged dyslexic readers. The results of their analysis, involving a wide variety of language, perceptual, and motor tasks for each subject, produced three distinct, nonoverlapping subgroups: (a) language deficit, (b) articulatory and graphomotor dyscoordination, and (c) visual-spatial-perceptual disorder. It was significant that the developmental dyslexics and the brain-damaged dyslexics differed little; disorders in language development and in motor-speech abilities occurred with similar frequency whereas the visuospatial-perceptual problem affected a smaller proportion of the population. Seventeen percent of the brain damaged dyslexic group and 14% of the developmental dyslexic group displayed visual problems.

Bayliss and Livesey (1985) investigated visual memory strategies used by 33 Australian boys, ages 9 to 11 years, who were categorized as dysphonetic, dyseidetic, or normal readers on the basis of performance as defined by Boder. The dyseidetic group performed less well than the dysphonetic group on the hard-to-label items (drawings of abstract forms) but the groups did not differ on the easy-to-label items (drawings of common objects/animals). When the results of the two dyslexic groups were combined there were no differences between the disabled and normal readers. In a second experiment involving 18 normal and 18 reading-disabled children where memory for order of easy-to-label items could be processed either spatially (left to right) or serially (first to last), it was found that dysphonetics recalled the display as a gestalt whole whereas dyseidetics recalled the display according to the serial order in which the items had been presented. That is to say, the dysphonetics chose the response that corresponded to the visual array that resulted after the three pictures had been presented on a computer screen one at a time and the dyseidetics chose the response that corresponded to the specific sequence in which the three pictures had appeared on the screen. Again, when the differentiated dyslexic groups were combined, there was no difference between the responses of disabled and normal readers. Thus the distinctive cognitive strategies only emerged when the poor readers were separated into the two subtypes.

Satz and Morris (1981), in discussing the traditional clinical-inferential approach to classifying heterogeneous learning-disabled children into more homogeneous groupings, raised some concerns and suggested an alternative approach.

Although they viewed the results of studies such as those by Kinsbourne and Warrington, Boder, and Mattis and his colleagues as having heuristic value regarding the nature of specific subtypes, Satz and Morris cautioned that "visual inspection of complex data sets is limited and may not generate optimal and valid subgroups. What is additionally needed is the application of more powerful statistical methods that may allow one to validate these clinical models" (p. 122).

Statistical Subtyping Studies

To reduce subjectivity and to deal with multidimensional data several research groups have attempted to apply complex mathematical techniques to more objectively categorize reading-disabled individuals into relatively homogeneous subtypes based on different patterns of processing difficulties. Table 13.2 summarizes the characteristics of the visual-processing-deficit subgroups reported in major statistical subtyping studies in the literature. In trying to circumvent the heavy reliance on visual inspection of complex data that characterized the clinical-inferential approach, these researchers have applied multivariate statistical techniques such as Q-type factor analysis and cluster analysis. These techniques, however, although having good promise, are still considered controversial (Adams, 1985; Satz & Morris, 1981).

A study by Doehring and Hoshko (1977) is reported to be one of the first major attempts to adopt the statistical Q-technique of factor analysis in the search for learning disability subtypes. One group of children ranging in age from 8 to 17 years represented primarily reading problems ($n = 34$) while a second group ranging in age from 8 to 12 years represented learning problems that included language and mental deficits ($n = 31$). A battery of tests requiring rapid responses to sets of letters, syllables, words, and sentences was administered; these measures were developed by the researchers. Among the reading-disabled subjects three subgroups resulted, described as (a) poor oral word reading ($n = 12$), (b) weakness in associating printed and spoken letters ($n = 11$), and (c) deficient auditory-visual matching of syllables and words ($n = 8$). This latter subgroup was interpreted as conforming to auditory dyslexia and dysphonetic dyslexia as discussed by Johnson and Myklebust and Boder, respectively. Among the subjects having mixed learning disabilities Subtypes b and c were preserved while a third subtype reflected a visual perception deficit. This grouping included 7 of the 26 subjects classified and was likened to similar syndromes discussed by Johnson and Myklebust, Boder, and Mattis et al. In a follow-up investigation Doehring, Hoshko, and Bryans (1979) replicated the subtypes using cluster analysis and found that performance of normal readers from grades 1 through 11 on the same criterion measures did not sort into these discrete groupings.

Doehring et al. (1981) described another large-scale research project in which they combined the battery of reading measures from the earlier work with a set of nonreading measures (language and neuropsychological tests) to determine "how

TABLE 13.2
Visual-Processing-Deficit Subtypes from Statistical Subtyping Studies

Doehring & Hoshko (1977)	−Visual perception deficit
Doehring, Hoshko, & Bryans (1979)	−27% of sample of 26 children with mixed learning problems −8 years & older −poor visual and auditory-visual matching −this subgroup was not preserved when sample with mixed learning problems was combined with a reading-disabled sample
Doehring, Trites, Patel, & Fiedorowicz (1981)	−Sequence deficit; difficulty in responding to sequences of letters as units −74% of sample of 72 subjects classified −age range of 8 to 27 years −majority of IQ scores 90−110 −WRAT arithmetic less impaired than reading −spelling was most impaired
Rourke & Finlayson (1978)	−3 subtypes identified based on WRAT scores −one group showed weakness on criterion measures of visual-perceptual & visual-spatial skills −33.3% of sample of 45 LD subjects −9 to 14 years, IQ range of 86−114 −verbal & auditory-perceptual strength −deficient arithmetic
Petrauskas & Rourke (1979)	−79 of 133 retarded readers fit into stable subtypes where auditory-linguistic difficulty was basis of groupings −29 others fit into less stable subtypes where visual perceptual/spatial functioning was more variable
Satz & Morris (1981)	−Visual-perceptual-motor impaired type −27% of sample of 86 LD subjects −mean age 11 years, grade 5 boys −selectively impaired on only the nonlinguistic perceptual tests −performance on language tests within normal range
Lyon & Watson (1981)	−Deficient visuoperceptive capacity −34% of 94 reading-disabled subjects −age range 11 to 12.5 years −membership of 32 was unexpected at this age level; was largest of the 6 subtypes identified −mean WISC-R FS score of 105.7

(continued)

TABLE 13.2
(Continued)

Lyon, Stewart, & Freedman (1982)	−Visual deficit subtype
	−28% of 64 LD readers who were classified
	−mean age of 7.6 years
	−youngest mean age of the 5 groups; subjects ranged from 6–5 to 9–9 years
	−supports Satz' finding that visuo-perceptive deficits affect younger chilren while verbal/conceptual affect older
Watson, Goldgar, & Ryschon (1983)	−visual processing deficit
	−31% of sample of 65 LD children
	−age range from 7–0 to 14–11
	−average scores across all language tests
	−weak short-term auditory memory
	−severely impaired reading/spelling despite normal phonic skills (sound analysis & blending)
Van der Vlugt & Satz (1985)	−visual-perceptual-motor deficit
	−results similar to Satz' Florida Longitudinal Study
	−18% of 83 LD Dutch children
	−no impairment in language
McKinney, Short, & Feagans (1985)	−severe perceptual deficit
	−7% of Carolina longitudinal sample of 63 grade 1 & 2 LD children
	−declining pattern of academic outcomes across subsequent 3 years
Korhonen (1988, 1991)	−visuo-motor; specific problems on Bender Gestalt Test & Motor-Free Visual Perception Test
	−25% of sample of 143 grade 3 Finnish students
	−18 LD & 18 Controls
	−twice number of boys to girls
	−no linguistic problems
	−high longitudinal stability at grade 6
	−problems in Arithmetic increased with age
Feagans & Merriwether (1990)	−perceptual discrimination problems; defined as high error pattern on line-to-curve transformation (Gibson letterlike task)
	−27% of 127 LD and control children tested at ages 6/7 & 12 years
	−23 LD & 12 Controls
	−particularly weak letter identification & word attack but performed more poorly than group with low error perceptual pattern on all achievement measures across time (reading & math)

(continued)

TABLE 13.2
(*Continued*)

Watson (1990)	−visual processing problems in combination with symbolic processing/memory problems
	−52% of sample of 50 high-risk & older-disabled readers aged 6 to 10 years
	−low scores on visual memory, visual sequential memory, digit span, reading of symbols, spelling
	−2 of 25 successful readers aged 6/7 years also clustered in this subtype

patterns of reading skill deficits interact with patterns of cognitive and linguistic deficits in different types of reading problems" (p. 60). This comprehensive test battery was assembled in recognition of the theoretical significance of the complex organization and interaction of language and cognition and reading, operating in different types of reading problems. Eighty-eight subjects, the majority of whom were from 8 to 14 years of age and delayed by at least 2 years on standardized reading tests, were selected from referrals to a neuropsychological clinic; as in most cases of reading disability there was a higher proportion of males than females in the sample. Analysis of scores on the reading tests used— Wide Range Achievement Test (WRAT) and Durrell Analysis of Reading Difficulty—as well as 39 informal tests of reading-related skills (visual matching, auditory-visual matching, oral reading, visual scanning used previously, plus naming of nonverbal stimuli, sentence comprehension, spelling), resulted in the detection of three major subtypes. These were (a) oral reading deficit, (b) association (intermodal) deficit where auditory-visual letter association was even poorer than oral reading, and (c) sequence deficit where abilities involving letters and numbers were consistently better than those involving syllables and words. The basic premise was that covariance from the linguistic and neuropsychological variables would interact with covariance from the reading variables so that it could be demonstrated how the reading subtypes related to corresponding differences in the more general cognitive/linguistic processes. There were 37 neuropsychological tests and 22 language tests including the WISC, Raven's Progressive matrices, Peabody Picture Vocabulary Test, phonemic segmentation, and sentence repetition tasks. Results did not reveal that each type of reading skill deficit was associated with particular types of neurological and linguistic dysfunctions but some interpretations of characteristics were attempted. The neuropsychological test profiles showed that all three reading disability subtypes tended to have lower verbal skills than nonverbal skills, with the oral reading deficit type exhibiting least impairment and the association deficit type exhibiting most impairment overall; the sequence deficit type tended to be most impaired on a visual nonverbal test and on finger localization. This latter visual subtype accounted for 19% (17 of 88) of the sample.

In their study known as the Florida Longitudinal Project, Satz and his co-workers used the statistical technique of cluster analysis in the identification of learning disability subgroups in a relatively unselected sample of school children who were followed from kindergarten through grade 5 (Darby, 1978; Morris & Satz, 1984; Satz & Morris, 1981). During the first phase the WRAT scores of 230 of 236 subjects (averaging 11 years of age in grade 5) sorted into nine clusters, each cluster exhibiting a unique pattern in terms of reading, spelling, and arithmetic performance scores. Because subgroups 8 and 9 showed 2-year depressed achievement, these 89 boys were labeled as learning disabled. During the second phase their performance on four neuropsychological tests that had high loadings on a language factor and a perceptual factor was subjected to further classification analysis. This resulted in the following subtype impairments: (a) global language, (b) specific language/naming, (c) global language and perceptual, (d) visual-perceptual-motor, (e) unexpected—that is, average to superior performance on all neuropsychological measures despite their low WRAT achievement. Satz and Morris commented that the first four subtypes confirmed the clinical findings that language problems, some type of visual problem, as well as mixed problems, can be associated with learning disability. Twenty-six percent of these disabled readers clustered in subtype d, the visual-perceptual-motor subtype.

In a cross-cultural replication study Van der Vlugt and Satz (1985) reported similar findings with Dutch children. Of the 83 learning-disabled students 18% exhibited visual-perceptual-motor difficulty with no impairment in language and some type of linguistic/verbal deficit characterized 82% of the sample. In commenting on the comparable results obtained with disabled learners from both the United States and Holland (82% similarity across studies) the researchers observed that most subtyping studies identify a subgroup having deficiency in processing visual information. They went on to state that "to ignore this subtype of learning-disabled children could retard progress in the search for differential causes, as well as subject these children to inappropriate methods of remediation" (pp. 224–225).

Other support for the application of cluster analysis as a reliable and valid technology in the identification of homogeneous subtypes within learning-disabled populations is found in work by Lyon (Lyon, 1983; Lyon, Stewart, & Freedman, 1982; Lyon & Watson, 1981). One hundred children of average general intelligence, who were designated as reading disabled in terms of both scores on the Peabody Individual Achievement Test and their school placement, were compared with 50 normal readers (all between 11.0 and 12.5 years of age) with respect to performance on a battery of what could be categorized as psycholinguistic (e.g., sentence repetition, sound blending, auditory discrimination), neuropsychological (e.g., nonverbal reasoning, visual-motor integration), and reading tasks. Raw scores were transformed to standard scores and both the raw and standard scores were analyzed by a cluster analysis algorithm to control for the effect of solution as a function of data input type (see Lyon & Watson, 1981, p. 257). These procedures yielded the same six homogeneous SLD/R subgroups (specific learning disability/reading) in the form of raw and standard score profile patterns. These were described as exhibiting the following deficiencies: (a) language comprehension, auditory memory, sound blending, visual-motor integration, visual-spatial and visual memory, word analysis skills; (b) language comprehension, auditory memory, visual-motor integration; (c) language comprehension, sound blending, all phonetic skills; (d) visuoperceptive capacity; (e) auditory sequence; (f) normal language and perceptual skills although reading disabled.

Deficient visuoperceptive capacity affected 34% of the disabled readers and had the largest membership of the six subtypes: This was reported as an unexpected finding given that these problems are frequently associated with younger children. The results were similar to those of other researchers in that both linguistic and perceptual processes and a mixture of each are implicated in reading disorders. These researchers did go beyond many of their predecessors, though, in discussing the consequences of applying knowledge of specific reading disability subtypes to the selection of appropriate teaching materials and methods, noting the importance of "time-and-cost-efficient" (Lyon & Watson, 1981, p. 261) procedures in educational remediation.

Another major series of studies using neuropsychological tests and objective statistical classification methods to uncover differential subgroups among reading disorders was conducted by Rourke and colleagues (Fisk & Rourke, 1979; Petrauskas & Rourke, 1979; Rourke, 1978; Rourke & Finlayson, 1978). Although a clear visual processing subtype did not emerge among their clinical samples some implications about such a subgroup did arise. Rourke and Finlayson first divided 45 learning-disabled children into three groups based on their reading, spelling, and arithmetic achievement. Group 1 was delayed in all three areas, Group 2 was delayed in reading-spelling relative to arithmetic, and Group 3 was delayed on arithmetic relative to reading-spelling. A test battery consisting of 16 dependent measures classed as verbal/auditory-perceptual and visual-perceptual/visual-spatial was administered and the patterns of performance of each group on these measures was plotted in graph form. Group 3 performed significantly better than Groups 1 and 2 on the verbal/auditory-perceptual tests and significantly poorer on the visual-perceptual/visual-spatial tests. Group 3 upheld the hypothesis that pattern of performance was consistent with relative dysfunction of right cerebral hemisphere and, according to these researchers, confirmed the necessity of specifying profiles of strengths and weaknesses attained by subtypes of learning disabilities. Findings supported the concept of subtyping and highlighted the fact that true differences across these subgroups would have been distorted and/or masked by collapsing Groups 2 and 3 into a single group that attained low arithmetic scores.

In the work of Petrauskas and Rourke, a sample of 160 children 7 and 8 years old was used, consisting of 133 disabled readers and 27 normal readers. Twenty measures of tactile-perceptual, sequencing, motoric, visual-spatial, auditory-verbal, and abstract-conceptual skills were selected from a larger battery according to their value as discriminative and clinically significant criteria. The subjects were divided into two equal subsamples and the resulting data matrices were subjected to Q-factor analysis. Results with the two subsamples corresponded to those with the entire sample, including reliable subtypes. The retarded readers showed much more scatter among scores than did the normal readers; three reliable and two less-well defined subtypes of disabled readers emerged in addition to the normal reading factor. The largest group showed clear verbal deficits with large discrepancy between verbal and performance IQs, was composed of an approximate ratio of three males to one female, and had higher arithmetic scores than reading and spelling scores on the WRAT. This is clearly similar to the language deficient group shown in all other studies discussed previously. A second group showed poorest results on tasks involving sequencing and represented an approximate ratio of 12 males to 1 female with the so-called ACID pattern on the WISC-R evident. This is clearly similar to the group deficient in memory for sequences discussed by others (e.g., Bakker, 1983; Doehring et al., 1981). Petrauskas and Rourke compared the types of problems exhibited by children in the third group to those described by Mattis et al. as displaying articulation and grapho-motor dyscoordination. An interesting observation was that in the most reliable subgroupings (1, 2) language skills were poor while visual skills were age-appropriate. However, this discrepancy decreased across the sequence of less reliable subgroupings (3, 4, 5), indicating the presence of nonlinguistic deficiencies.

Fisk and Rourke used Q-factor analysis to statistically classify learning-disabled students of three different age levels (9–10, 11–12, 13–14 years) using a battery of 21 neuropsychological tests. Although a visual-perceptual deficit subgroup did not emerge it was noted that across all three stable subtypes performance on the short-term visual memory measure (target test) was weak. These researchers referred to the utility of this task in predicting reading performance across their research projects. They raised the possibility, as have others (e.g., Vellutino, Scanlon, & Tanzman, 1991; Watson, 1990), that a verbal labeling or coding strategy may be operative in remembering visual sequences. However, because in past studies visual sequential memory measures have typically been categorized through both task analysis and factor analysis as tapping visual processing, further investigation is needed.

Another aspect of the Rourke series of investigations that has significance here is the qualitative analysis of spelling errors with regard to phonetic accuracy.

An example is given of two types of retarded spellers, a group of phonetically accurate spellers who wrote *nacher* for nature versus a group of phonetically inaccurate spellers who wrote the word as *diltum* or *qpwo*. Differences on measures of psycholinguistic abilities between the two groups of spellers were found at grade 8 but not at grade 4. In other words, this distinction in spelling behavior appears during middle school years. Within a conceptualization of reading disability that allows for both linguistic and visual processing components, phonetically accurate spellings would be explained by the presence of a type of reading disability in beginning readers that is not characterized by inferior phonological development. If such a possibility is supported, disabled readers should exhibit phonetically accurate spelling errors (at least at later ages after initial difficulty with single letter-sound relationships has been overcome through instruction). This observation of phonetically accurate versus inaccurate spelling appears to be a phenomenon commonly reported by clinicians and is perhaps evidence in itself that not all reading/writing disability is accompanied by poor phonological processing (Freebody & Byrne, 1988).

Watson, Goldgar, and Ryschon (1983) applied cluster analysis to the scores of 65 reading-disabled children on a test battery consisting of 23 achievement/linguistic/cognitive tasks. Three subtypes resulted; the one designated as visual processing deficiency accounted for 31% of this sample. Reading and spelling were severely impaired but language and phonic skills, including sound analysis and sound blending, were normal. Weak scores on auditory short-term memory (Digit Span) as well as on all three visual processing subtests (Spatial Relations, Visual Matching, Coding) were apparent. These researchers likened this subtype to the one involving visual processing identified in past studies by Doehring, Lyon, Mattis, and Satz.

McKinney, Short, and Feagans (1985) identified six subtypes using a battery of six perceptual, problem-solving, and linguistic measures in a longitudinal investigation referred to as the North Carolina Study. Each of 63 learning-disabled first- and second-graders was matched to a normally achieving child and followed over a 3-year period. Cluster analysis of profiles isolated the following: normal subtype (11%), severe perceptual deficit (7%), severe language comprehension deficit (27%), a second normal subtype (22%), mixed perceptual-linguistic deficit (14%), marginal perceptual/semantic problems (18%). The low incidence of severe perceptual deficits compared to severe language deficits was reported as unexpected. It was also surprising to find that, whereas 63% of the control subjects clustered in the normal subtype, 29% of them clustered in the perceptual deficit subtype. The implications of this are discussed later.

In a large-scale longitudinal study of Finnish children, Korhonen (1988, 1991) extracted through cluster analysis six subgroups from among 82 learning-disabled and 84 control students in grade 3. One of these subgroups was labeled as visuo-motor. The eight neurological tests used tapped language, memory, naming, and visuo-motor-spatial skills. It was found that an equal number of control subjects (18 LD, 18 control) also clustered in this visuo-motor deficit group. Korhonen remarked that no previous subtype studies report this finding; he speculated that a lag in the visual-motor area may not by itself result in school difficulties. Rather, it may be only in combination with some other weakness that learning is adversely affected. This hypothesis was made in light of the observation that within this subtype the LD subjects tended to have more attentional immaturity than the control subjects. In a follow-up study 3 years later, the visuo-motor group was marked by particularly weak achievement in mathematics along with poor writing (from dictation) and relatively better reading. Although Korhonen concludes that the restricted visuo-motor-spatial performances do not seem closely related to poor reading, it is possible that this is a consequence of the particular tests selected to assess these performances. The measures used were Bender Gestalt (copying figures), Auditory-Visual Integration Test (matching auditory tap patterns to printed dot patterns), Auditory-Motor Integration (tapping sound patterns), and the Motor-Free Visual Perception Test. It might be said that these measures emphasize motor and spatial skills over visual perception and memory.

Feagans and Merriwether (1990) used tasks that required processing of letterlike forms in which subjects had to match to a standard form from among choices that involved features being transformed (straight lines and curves interchanged), rotated/reversed, and/or inserted. They hypothesized that there would be a subtype, among the 66 learning-disabled (defined as reading 6 months below grade level) and 66 control subjects 6 to 7 years old, who displayed problems specifically measured by these tasks. This hypothesis was confirmed as subjects were followed through elementary school. Although the study by Feagans and Merriwether was not intended to be a full subtyping study because they were investigating performance on a single type of task they found, as did Korhonen, that visual processing difficulties were not always associated with reading disability. Both the disabled ($n = 23$) and control ($n = 12$) readers with visual weaknesses had lower perceptual motor scores on the WISC-R than either the LD low error group ($n = 38$) or the control low error group ($n = 54$), whereas the control readers with weak visual processing had higher overall nonverbal scores on the WISC-R than their learning-disabled counterparts. (It was noted that weak mathematics achievement accompanied weak reading achievement at age 12.) These results are congruent with Korhonen's theory that visual processing weakness may impact adversely on reading only when it occurs in combination with one or more other deficits.

Watson (1990) conducted a study involving the use of both Q-factor and cluster analysis that further confirmed the existence of a subtype marked by visual processing weakness among reading-disabled children. Watson's research investigated developmental reading difficulty among children who had average or above-average oral language and nonverbal reasoning ability. Thus, she explicitly excluded those reading-disabled subjects from her sample who had blatant oral language processing problems.[2] Three groups consisting of 25 high-risk first-grade readers, 25 successful first-grade readers, and 25 older-disabled readers, as classified by both teacher nomination and scores on the GMRT-Comprehension subtest, were matched according to performance on the Peabody Picture Vocabulary Test-Revised, WISC-R Vocabulary, and Raven's Colored Progressive Matrices. A test battery, comprised of 19 cognitive/linguistic/achievement measures identified in past studies as important correlates of reading, was individually administered to these 75 subjects.

When their standard score profiles were submitted to R-factor analysis, three factors emerged that were interpreted as symbolic processing/memory, rapid automatized naming, and visual processing. Examination of individual differences across the three a priori groupings of subjects using analysis of variance (ANOVA) with planned comparisons and discriminant analysis revealed that the younger and older problem readers had very similar information-processing patterns while collectively they differed significantly from the successful readers in terms of the first factor, specifically on short-term auditory memory and decoding/encoding. When compared separately to the controls, the age-matched high-risk group showed additional weakness in rapid automatized naming and the reading-level-matched older-disabled group showed additional weakness in phonological coding and visual sequential memory. Multiple regression analysis yielded a prediction equation in which reading symbols (decoding), spelling (encoding), and rapid automatized naming of numbers accounted for 77% of the reading variance. In these analyses that involved the heterogeneous a priori groups, symbolic processing/memory was the most significant of the three factors, even though all had some effect. However, in the next set of analyses—those involving the use of Q-factor analysis and cluster analysis to search for homogeneous subtypes within the heterogeneous a prior groups—a visual processing factor assumed more importance.

Examination of the second-level classifications using cluster and Q-factor analyses suggested the presence of three potential subtypes among the 50 poor readers. All were characterized by weak short-term auditory memory and sound-symbol knowledge (Subtype 1, $n = 16$), which occurred in combination with visual processing/memory deficiencies (Subtype 2, $n = 26$) and deficits in visual processing as well as rapid automatized naming (Subtype 3, $n = 8$). The critical variables that defined these clusters were: Reading of Symbols from the Goldman-Fristoe-Woodcock Sound-Symbol Tests, WISC-R Digit Span, and WRAT Spelling (subtype 1); Visual Memory and Visual Sequential Memory from the Test of Visual Perceptual Skills (subtype 2); Rapid Automatized Naming—Num-

---

[2]By including only those problem learners who reveal a specific type of achievement deficit (i.e., contextual reading difficulty with intact oral language), the focus was on refined information-processing differences between control and problem readers and among problem readers. This perspective exemplifies an attempt to adopt a sufficiently rigorous operational definition of reading dysfunction to permit more precise exploration of its properties than has occurred in many preceding studies.

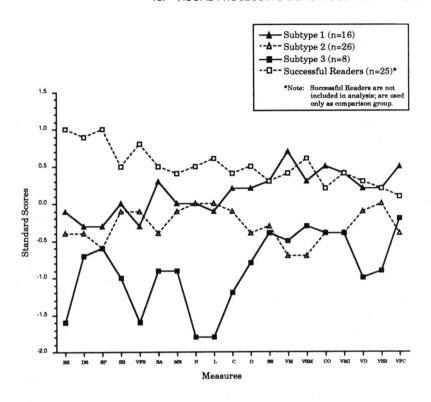

FIG. 13.1. Score profiles of the three statistically determined subtypes in Watson's (1990) study.

Measures:

RS	= Reading Symbols	SS	= Sound Symbol
DS	= Digit Span	VM	= TVPS-VM
SP	= Spelling	VSM	= TVPS-VSM
SB	= Sound Blending	CO	= Coding
VFS	= Visual Form of	VMI	= VMI
	Sounds	VD	= TVPS-VD
SA	= Sound Analysis	VSR	= TVPS-VSR
MS	= Model Sentences	VFC	= TVPS-VFC
N	= RAN-N		
L	= RAN-L		
C	= RAN-C		
O	= RAN-O		

bers and Letters (subtype 3). The profiles are displayed graphically in Fig. 13.1.
Thus, when differences within the combined group of younger and older weak
readers were examined, the largest subgroup to emerge (52%) experienced problems in visual processing, in conjunction with the symbol processing/memory
weakness. This reinforces the observation made by Feagans and Merriwether that
a subgroup with visual deficits may be masked if investigators document only

group differences between disabled and nondisabled readers; rather variability among disabled readers must be examined.

CONCLUSIONS FROM SUBTYPING STUDIES

Taken together, the foregoing summary of research would seem to provide compelling documentation that, despite long-standing disagreement as to the function of visual processing deficits in reading disabilities, a subgroup manifesting deficits in some aspect of visual perception, visual memory, or visuo-spatial-motor skills, has repeatedly emerged in both clinical and statistical classification research. There are, however, clear limitations associated with these subtyping studies that must be acknowledged. Two of these limitations are (a) the wide variability among both tests and subjects across investigations, and (b) the complexity in mathematical properties that may need to be satisfied before application of statistical classification techniques to educational data can be justified (Gorsuch, 1983; Lorr, 1983; Watson, 1990). Conclusions must be cautious, then, because there is not a high level of comparability across subtyping investigations due to differences in their methodological approaches, and analytical procedures and assumptions; the scenario in which "the method or measure will drive the science" (Feagans & McKinney, 1991, p. 26) must be avoided. Nonetheless, although the subtyping studies have strongly confirmed the involvement of linguistic deficits in reading disabilities, they have also fairly consistently pointed to visual processing differences within groups of disabled readers, as well. Moreover, when children who have blatant and obvious oral language processing deficits are excluded from samples of reading-disabled individuals, the proportion of subjects exhibiting characteristics of a visual processing deficit is considerably higher. Based on all of this evidence it would seem prudent, at this point, for both scientists and clinicians to keep an open mind about the possibility that visual processing deficits might contribute in some way to reading disabilities.

Three main possibilities exist with respect to the role of visual processing in reading disability. First, it may be that deficient visual analysis skills characterize a true subgroup of individuals whose reading difficulties are, in part, caused by this deficit. Second, it may be that visual processing differences within learning-disabled groups reflect individual variation in these processes within the normal population and have little or no role in causing reading disabilities. This possibility was highlighted in the studies reported by McKinney et al. (1985) and Korhonen (1988, 1991) in which fairly significant numbers of control subjects clustered with the subgroup involving visual processing deficits. Not all subtyping research has included a comparison group of normal readers and this omission is a serious impediment to drawing meaningful conclusions with respect to the potential role of visual processing deficits in causing reading disabilities. Third, it may be that it is only when visual processing weakness occurs in combination with another processing deficit (or deficits) that it is of consequence. Vellutino et al. (1991) theorized that different subtypes of poor readers may be defined by the weighting associated with the processing deficit or deficits occurring. Although a single processing deficiency of sufficient magnitude by itself may interfere with reading performance, another processing deficiency less critical to reading performance may be tolerated until it occurs in combination with a second deficiency or multiple deficiencies. This interpretation of reading disability, which has been raised previously by researchers such as Jorm and Share (1983), may account for the visual processing problems that characterized some normal readers in several of the subtyping studies cited in this chapter. The possibility that, either a certain minimal level of visual processing deficit or visual processing deficit in the absence of any additional cognitive/linguistic weakness can be compensated for, needs to be more directly examined.

It would seem that there is growing agreement among researchers and clinicians that reading disability is analogous to obesity rather than measles (Ellis, 1985). In other words, reading disability is not an all-or-nothing condition but instead is arbitrarily defined depending "entirely upon where the line is drawn" (p. 172) between normal and abnormal performance. If one subscribes to a heterogeneity theory of reading disability (adopted by a subtyping perspective) then it is probable that the various processing components also represent continua, along which readers display differing patterns of individual strengths and weaknesses. The many subtyping studies reviewed here establish that visual processing of some type comprises one of these components; researchers must now proceed to the next stage of studying *if* and *how* it operates as a causative factor in reading dysfunction.

IMPLICATIONS FOR FUTURE RESEARCH

The objective of identifying meaningful subtypes is to develop differential treatment programs that will provide effective remediation for the specific problem areas. Reports of attempts to test the efficacy of subtype-treatment interactions (e.g., Aaron, Grantham, & Campbell, 1982; Doehring, 1984; Lyon, 1985) reveal varying degrees of success and tentative findings. What they do underscore is the need for creative, carefully designed research projects because "success in the treatment arena for a specific subtype model may be among the best tests for determining the ecological validity of that classification model" (Hooper & Willis, 1989, p. 201).

REFERENCES

Aaron, P. G., Grantham, S. L., & Campbell, N. (1982). Differential treatment of reading disability of diverse etiologies. In R. N. Malateha & P. G. Aaron (Eds.), *Reading disorders: Varieties and treatments* (pp. 449–452). New York: Academic Press.

Adams, K. M. (1985). Theoretical, methodological, and statistical issues. In B. P. Rourke (Ed.), *Neuropsychology of learning disabilities: Essentials of subtype analysis* (pp. 17–39). New York: Guilford Press.

Alexander, P. A. (1984). Enlarging the gap between theory and practice: A review of the Boder Test of Reading-Spelling Patterns. *School Psychology Review, 13,* 529–533.

Bakker, D. J. (1983). Hemispheric specialization and specific reading retardation. In M. Rutter (Ed.), *Developmental neuropsychiatry* (pp. 498–506). New York: Guilford Press.

Barrett, T. C. (1965). The relationship between measures of pre-reading visual discrimination and first grade reading achievement: A review of the literature. *Reading Research Quarterly, 1,* 51–76.

Bayliss, J., & Livesey, P. J. (1985). Cognitive strategies of children with reading disability and normal readers in visual sequential memory. *Journal of Learning Disabilities, 18,* 326–332.

Benton, A. L. (1962). Dyslexia in relation to form perception and directional sense. In J. Money (Ed.), *Reading disability: Progress and research needs in dyslexia* (pp. 81–102). Baltimore: Johns Hopkins Press.

Boder, E. (1968). Developmental dyslexia: A diagnostic screening procedure based on three characteristic patterns of reading and spelling. A preliminary report. In M. Douglass (Ed.), *Claremont reading conference, 32nd yearbook* (pp. 173–187). CA: Claremont University Center.

Boder, E. (1971). Developmental dyslexia: Prevailing diagnostic concepts and a new diagnostic approach. In H. R. Myklebust (Ed.), *Progress in learning disabilities* (Vol. 2, pp. 293–321). New York: Grune & Stratton.

Boder, E., & Jarrico, S. (1984). A diagnostic screening test for subtypes of dyslexia: The Boder test of reading-spelling patterns. In R. N. Malatesha & H. A. Whitaker (Eds.), *Dyslexia: A global issue* (pp. 405–418). The Hague: Nijhoff Publishers.

Bronner, A. F. (1917). *The psychology of special abilities and disabilities.* Boston: Little, Brown.

Bryant, P. E., and Goswami, U. (1987). Phonological awareness and learning to read. In J. Beech & A. Colley (Eds.), *Cognitive approaches to reading* (pp. 213–244). Chichester, England: Wiley.

Calfee, R. (1983). The mind of the dyslexic. *Annals of Dyslexia, 33,* 9–28.

Darby, R. O. (1978). *Learning disabilities: A multivariate search for subtypes* (doctoral dissertation, University of Florida, 1978) *Dissertation Abstracts International, 39,* 6113–6114.

Denckla, M. B., & Rudel, R. G. (1976). Rapid "automatized" naming (R.A.N.): Dyslexia differentiated from other learning disabilities. *Neuropsychologia, 14,* 471–479.

Doehring, D. G. (1984). Subtyping of reading disorders: Implications for remediation. *Annals of Dyslexia, 34,* 205–216.

Doehring, D. G., & Hoshko, I. M. (1977). Classification of reading problems by the Q-technique of factor analysis. *Cortex, 13,* 281–294.

Doehring, D. G., Hoshko, I. M., & Bryans, B. N. (1979). Statistical classification of children with reading problems. *Journal of Clinical Neuropsychology, 1,* 5–16.

Doehring, D. G., Trites, R. L., Patel, P. G., & Fiedorowicz, C.A.M. (1981). *Reading disabilities: The interaction of reading, language and neuropsychological deficits.* New York: Academic Press.

Dorman, C. (1987). Reading disability: Subtypes in neurologically-impaired students. *Annals of Dyslexia, 37,* 166–168.

Drew, A. L. (1956). A neurological appraisal of familial congenital word blindness. *Brain, 79,* 440–60.

Ellis, A. W. (1985). A cognitive neuropsychology of developmental (and acquired) dyslexia: A critical survey. *Cognitive Neuropsychology, 2*(2), 169–205.

Feagans, L. V., & McKinney, J. D. (1991). Subtypes of learning disabilities: A review. In L. V. Feagans, E. J. Short, & L. J. Meltzer (Eds.), *Subtypes of learning disabilities: Theoretical perspectives and research* (pp. 3–31). Hillsdale, NJ: Lawrence Erlbaum Associates.

Feagans, L. V., & Merriwether, A. (1990). Visual discrimination of letter-like forms and its relationship to achievement over time in children with learning disabilities. *Journal of Learning Disabilities, 23,* 417–425.

Fildes, L. G. (1921). A psychological inquiry into the nature of the condition known as congenital word blindness. *Brain, 44,* 286–307.

Fisk, J. L., & Rourke, B. P. (1979). Identification of subtypes of learning disabled children at three age levels: A neuropsychological, multivariate approach. *Journal of Clinical Neuropsychology, 1,* 289–310.

Freebody, P., & Byrne, B. (1988). Word-reading strategies in elementary school children: Relations to comprehension, reading time, and phonemic awareness. *Reading Research Quarterly, 23,* 441–453.

Freud, S. (1953). *On aphasia.* New York: International Universities Press.

Gates, A. I. (1922). *The psychology of reading and spelling with special reference to disability.* New York: Teachers College, Columbia University.

Gorsuch, R. (1983). *Factor analysis.* Hillsdale, NJ: Lawrence Erlbaum Associates.

Hermann, K. (1959). *Reading disability.* Springfield, IL: Charles C Thomas.

Hinshelwood, J. (1917). *Congenital word-blindness.* London: Lewis.

Hooper, S. R., & Hynd, G. W. (1985). Differential diagnosis of subtypes of developmental dyslexia with the Kaufman Assessment Battery for Children (K-ABC). *Journal of Clinical Child Psychology, 14*(2), 145–152.

Hooper, S. R., & Willis, W. G. (1989). *Learning disability subtyping.* New York: Springer-Verlag.

Ingram, T.T.S., Mason, A. W., & Blackburn, I. (1970). A retrospective study of 82 children with reading disability. *Developmental Medicine and Child Neurology, 12,* 271–281.

Johnson, D. J., & Myklebust, H. R. (1967). *Learning disabilities.* New York: Grune & Stratton.

Jorm, A., & Share, D. (1983). Phonological recoding and reading acquisition. *Applied Psycholinguistics, 4,* 103–147.

Kinsbourne, M., & Warrington, E. K. (1966). Developmental factors in reading and writing backwardness. In J. Money & G. Schiffman (Eds.), *The disabled reader: Education of the dyslexic child* (pp. 59–71). Baltimore: Johns Hopkins Press.

Korhonen, T. (1988). *Learning disabilities in children: An empirical subgrouping and follow-up.* Annales Universitatis Turkuensis, Turku, Finland.

Korhonen, T. (1991). Neuropsychological stability and prognosis of subgroups of children with learning disabilities. *Journal of Learning Disabilities, 24,* 48–57.

Liberman, I. Y. (1983). A language-oriented view of reading and its disabilities. In H. R. Myklebust (Ed.), *Progress in learning disabilities* (pp. 81–101). New York: Grune & Stratton.

Lorr, M. (1983). *Cluster analysis for social scientists.* San Francisco: Jossey-Bass.

Lyon, G. R. (1983). Learning-disabled readers: Identification of subgroups. In H. R. Myklebust (Ed.), *Progress in learning disabilities* (pp. 103–133). New York: Grune & Stratton.

Lyon, G. R. (1985). Educational validation studies of learning disability subtypes. In B. P. Rourke (Ed.), *Neuropsychology of learning disabilities: Essentials of subtype analysis* (pp. 228–253). New York: Guilford Press.

Lyon, G. R., & Watson, B. (1981). Empirically derived subgroups of learning disabled readers: Diagnostic characteristics. *Journal of Learning Disabilities, 14,* 256–261.

Lyon, R., Stewart, N., & Freedman, D. (1982). Neuropsychological characteristics of empirically derived subgroups of learning disabled readers. *Journal of Clinical Neuropsychology, 4,* 343–365.

Malatesha, R. N., & Dougan, D. R. (1982). Clinical subtypes of developmental dyslexia: Resolution of an irresolute problem. In R. N. Malatesha & P. G. Aaron (Eds.), (1982). *Reading disorders: Varieties and treatments* (pp. 69–92). Toronto: Academic Press.

Mann, V. (1984). Reading skill and language skill. *Developmental Review, 4,* 1–15.

Mann, V. (1991). Language problems: A key to early reading problems. In B.Y.L. Wong (Ed.), *Learning about learning disabilities* (pp. 129–162). New York: Academic Press.

Mattis, S. (1978). Dyslexia syndromes: A working hypothesis that works. In A. L. Benton & D. Pearl (Eds.), *Dyslexia: An appraisal of current knowledge* (pp. 45–58). New York: Oxford University Press.

Mattis, S. (1981). Dyslexia syndromes in children: Toward the development of syndrome-specific treatment programs. In F. J. Pirozzolo & M. C. Wittrock (Eds.), *Neuropsychological and cognitive processes in reading* (pp. 93–107). New York: Academic Press.

Mattis, S., French, J., & Rapin, I. (1975). Dyslexia in children and young adults: Three independent neuropsychological syndromes. *Developmental Medicine and Child Neurology, 17,* 150–163.

McKinney, J. D., Short, E. J., & Feagans, L. (1985). Academic consequences of perceptual-linguistic subtypes of learning disabled children. *Learning Disabilities Research, 1,* 6–17.

Morris, R., & Satz, P. (1984). Classification issues in subtype research: An application of some methods and concepts. In R. N. Malatesha & H. A. Whitaker (Eds.), *Dyslexia: A global issue* (pp. 59–82). The Hague: Nijhoff.

Nockleby, D. M., & Galbraith, G. G. (1984). Developmental dyslexia subtypes and the Boder Test of Reading-Spelling Patterns. *Journal of Psychoeducational Assessment, 2,* 91–100.

Orton, S. T. (1937). *Reading, writing and speech problems in children.* New York: Norton.

Petrauskas, R. J., & Rourke, B. P. (1979). Identification of subtypes of retarded readers: A neuropsychological, multivariate approach. *Journal of Clinical Neuropsychology, 1,* 17–37.

Pringle Morgan, W. (1896). A case of congenital word blindness. *British Medical Journal, 2,* 1378.

Rayner, K., & Pollatsek, A. (1989). *The psychology of reading.* Englewood Cliffs, NJ: Prentice-Hall.

Reynolds, C. R. (1984). Psychometric characteristics of the Boder Test of Reading-Spelling Patterns: Take one giant step backwards. *School Psychology Review, 13*(4), 526–529.

Rourke, B. P. (1978). Reading, spelling, arithmetic disabilities: A neuropsychologic perspective. In H. R. Myklebust (Ed.), *Progress in learning disabilities* (pp. 97–120). New York: Grune & Stratton.

Rourke, B. P., & Finlayson, M.A.J. (1978). Neuropsychological significance of variations in patterns of academic performance: Verbal and visual-spatial abilities. *Journal of Abnormal Child Psychology, 6,* 121–133.

Satz, P., & Morris, R. (1981). Learning disability subtypes: A review. In F. J. Pirozzolo & M. C. Wittrock (Eds.), *Neuropsychological and cognitive processes in reading* (pp. 109–141). New York: Academic Press.

Satz, P., Morris, R., & Fletcher, J. M. (1985). Hypotheses, subtypes, and individual differences in dyslexia: Some reflections. In D. B. Gray & J. F. Kavanagh (Eds.), *Biobehavioral measures of dyslexia* (pp. 25–40). Parkton, MD: New York Press.

Schelder, P. (1944). Congenital alexia and its relation to optic perception. *Journal of Genetic Psychology, 65,* 67–88.

Siegel, L. S., & Ryan, E. B. (1984). Development of grammatical-sensitivity, phonological, and short-term memory skills in normally achieving and learning disabled children. *Developmental Psychology, 24,* 28–37.

Stanovich, K. E. (1985). Explaining the variance in reading ability in terms of psychological processes: What have we learned? *Annals of Dyslexia, 35,* 67–96.

Swanson, L. (1984). Semantic and visual memory codes in learning disabled readers. *Journal of Experimental Child Psychology, 37,* 124–140.

van den Bos, K. P. (1984). Letter processing in dyslexic subgroups. *Annals of Dyslexia, 34,* 170–193.

Van der Vlugt, H., & Satz, P. (1985). Subgroups and subtypes of learning-disabled and normal children: A cross-cultural replication. In B. P. Rourke (Ed.), *Neuropsychology of learning disabilities: Essential of subtype analysis* (pp. 212–227). New York: Guilford Press.

Vellutino, F. R. (1979). *Dyslexia: Theory and research.* Cambridge, MA: MIT Press.

Vellutino, F. R. (1987). Dyslexia. *Scientific American, 256*(3), 34–41.

Vellutino, F. R., Scanlon, D. M., & Tanzman, M. S. (1991). Bridging the gap between cognitive and neuropsychological conceptualizations of reading disability. *Learning and Individual Differences, 3,* 181–203.

Watson, B. U., Goldgar, D. E., & Ryschon, K. L. (1983). Subtypes of reading disability. *Journal of Clinical Neuropsychology, 5,* 377–399.

Watson, C. (1990). *Specific processing difficulties in developmental reading disability among elementary school children.* Unpublished doctoral dissertation, OISE, University of Toronto.

Willows, D. M. (1991). Visual processes in learning disabilities. In B.Y.L. Wong (Ed.), *Learning about learning disabilities* (pp. 163–193). New York: Academic Press.

Willows, D. M., & Jackson, G. (1992, April). *Differential diagnosis of reading disability subtypes based on the Boder Reading-Spelling Test: Issues of reliability and validity.* Paper presented at the American Educational Research Association, San Francisco.

14 Visual Temporal Processing Deficits in Specific Reading Disability

William J. Lovegrove
University of Wollongong

Mary C. Williams
University of New Orleans

Specific reading disability is a broad term encompassing reading disabilities that may arise from a number of sources. A *specific-reading-disabled child* (SRD) is defined here as one of normal or better intelligence with no known behavioral or organic disorders who, despite normal schooling and average progress in other subjects, has a reading disability of at least 1.5 years. Because reading is a dynamic visual processing task requiring the analysis and integration of visual pattern information across fixation-saccade sequences, studies in the area of reading disability have explored the possibility that visual processing abnormalities contribute to reading difficulties. A number of studies have provided evidence for basic visual processing differences between normal and disabled readers, especially at early stages of visual processing (Lovegrove & Brown, 1978; Stanley, 1975). These results indicate that some disabled readers process information more slowly and have a more limited processing capacity than normal readers. Studies that used tasks relying less on dynamic visual processing and temporal resolution, and more on pattern-formation processes and long-term visual memory, however, have failed to show visual processing differences between normal and disabled readers (Benton, 1975; Vellutino, 1979), although the validity of some of these studies has been called into question (Fletcher & Satz, 1979). Thus the long-standing debate as to whether visual factors play a significant role in reading disabilities has been complicated by the differences in methodological factors and the failure to distinguish between the measurement of temporal versus pattern-formation processes. In the following section an approach to vision that considers different mechanisms for the processing of temporal and pattern information is outlined.

SPATIAL FREQUENCY ANALYSIS

One approach to vision research (Campbell, 1974; Graham, 1980) indicates that information is transmitted from the eye to the brain via a number of separate parallel pathways (see Lehmkuhle, chap. 4). The separate pathways are frequently referred to as channels. Each channel is specialized to process information about particular features of visual stimuli.

The properties of channels often have been investigated using patterns composed of black-and-white bars with fuzzy edges. These patterns are usually called sine-wave gratings. Two properties of these patterns are of interest here:

1. Spatial frequency, which refers to the number of cycles (one dark plus one light bar) per degree of visual angle (c/deg). High spatial frequency information conveys information about stimulus detail whereas low spatial frequency information carries information about general shape. Spatial frequency can be thought of in terms of stimulus size.

2. Contrast, which refers to the difference between the maximum and minimum luminances of the grating. It is a measure of the ratio of the brightest to the darkest section of the pattern.

Spatial frequency or size-sensitive channels are relevant to reading because when we read we process both general (low spatial frequency) and detailed (high spatial frequency) information in each fixation. We extract detailed information from an area approximately 5 to 6 letter spaces to the right of fixation. Beyond this we also extract visual information but only of a general nature such as word shape (Rayner, 1975). These two types of size information must in some way be combined.

It has also been shown that the different spatial channels transmit their information at different rates and respond differently to different rates of temporal change. Some channels are sensitive to very rapidly changing stimuli and others to stationary or slowly moving stimuli. Such results have led to the proposal of two subsystems within the visual system. This division is believed to be important in combining the two types of size information involved in reading.

THE SUSTAINED
AND TRANSIENT SUBSYSTEMS

It has been shown that spatial frequency channels differ in their temporal properties. In a typical experiment subjects are shown sine-wave gratings flickering at various rates. Subjects are required to set contrast levels so that they just can see either flicker or pattern. When low spatial frequency gratings flicker quickly, we see flicker at lower contrasts than we see pattern but we experience the reverse at high spatial frequencies. Separate measures can be taken of our sensitivity to flicker and pattern with a range of different size stimuli (spatial frequencies) flickering at different speeds. Thus we can plot sensitivity functions for pattern and flicker thresholds at a range of spatial frequencies. With large stimuli (low spatial frequencies) we are more sensitive to rapidly changing stimuli but with small stimuli (high spatial frequencies) we are more sensitive to stationary or slowly moving stimuli. The two functions obtained from such experiments are believed to measure the functioning of two subsystems in the visual system, the transient and sustained subsystems. An extensive discussion of the properties of these systems and how they are identified can be found in Breitmeyer's chapter (5). Breitmeyer also discusses the evidence indicating the physiological basis of these two systems.

The properties of these two subsystems have been identified and are shown in Table 5.1 in Breitmeyer's chapter. It has been demonstrated physiologically (Singer & Bedworth, 1973) and psychophysically that the two systems may inhibit each other. In particular if the sustained system is responding when the transient system is stimulated, the transient will terminate the sustained activity. An example of how this may occur is as follows. If we are fixating on the detail of an object and a stimulus moves into the periphery of our vision, the transient system is likely to inhibit or override the sustained system until we know what is in our peripheral vision. How this may have evolved is easier to imagine if we consider not a human reading but a rabbit eating and a predator appearing to the side. There would be survival value for the rabbit in having the transient system inhibit the sustained system until the nature of the threat could be determined. These two subsystems and the interactions between them may serve a number of functions essential to the reading process. A fuller discussion of this may be found in Chapter 5.

SUSTAINED AND TRANSIENT SUBSYSTEMS AND READING

When reading, the eyes move through a series of rapid eye movements called *saccades*. These are separated by fixation intervals when the eyes are stationary. Saccadic eye movements are generally in the direction of reading, that is, from left to right when reading English. Sometimes the eyes also move from right to left in what are called *regressive eye movements* or *regressions*. The average fixation duration is approximately 200 ms to 250 ms for normal readers and it is during these stationary periods that information from the printed page is seen. The average saccade length is 6 to 8 characters or about 2 degrees of visual angle (Rayner & McConkie, 1976). Saccadic eye movements function to bring unidentified regions of text into foveal vision for detailed analysis during fixations (Pollatsek, chap. 9). Foveal vision is the area of high acuity in the center of vision extending approximately 2 degrees (6 to 8 letters) around the fixation point on a line of text. Beyond the fovea acuity drops off rather dramatically.

The role of transient and sustained subsystems in reading has been considered by Breitmeyer (1980; chap. 5 this volume). Breitmeyer covered the main points in detail so there is little else to say here: Successful reading requires normal processing in both the transient and sustained systems and normal interactions between them. This dual processing system has recently been reconceptualized in terms of the magnocellular and parvocellular systems of the primate visual system, differing in color, acuity, speed, and contrast sensitivity (Livingstone & Hubel, 1987, 1988). The magnocellular and parvocellular systems are closely analogous to the previously proposed transient and sustained systems, respectively. Although the transient/sustained distinction is still quite schematic and requires additional work for confirmation, it has provided a useful organizing hypothesis in the study of reading disability, and has been found to be a good predictor of the visual processing characteristics of the reading disabled. The usefulness of the transient/sustained analysis as an organizing tool thus seems to warrant its continued use at the present time.

Although these two subsystems operate in parallel, it is believed that the transient system has temporal precedence: It operates preattentively and functions as an early warning system. It performs a global analysis of the incoming stimulus, parsing the field into units and regions and coding the position and movement of objects in space. The transient system may function to direct the sustained system to particularly salient areas where it might be most efficacious in performing a more detailed analysis of the shape and color of objects. The functioning of the sustained system, then, would depend to a degree on the prior output of the transient systems.

Transient and Sustained Channels and Specific Reading Disability

There is evidence that this transient-sustained relationship is different in normal and disabled readers. Lovegrove and co-workers have shown that visual processing differences between normal and disabled readers are evident when transient system processing is involved, but these differences fail to surface under sustained processing conditions. For example, several studies have compared SRDs and controls on measures of visible persistence. Visible persistence is one measure of temporal processing in spatial frequency channels and refers to the continued perception of a stimulus after it has been physically removed. Visible persistence is assumed to reflect ongoing neural activity initiated by the stimulus presentation.

In a series of experiments, Badcock and Lovegrove (1981) and Slaghuis and Lovegrove (1985) compared visible persistence in SRD and normal readers aged 8 to 15 years. The duration of visible persistence was determined by measuring the temporal separation required for the detection of a blank interval between two successively presented gratings. In normal readers, the duration of visible persistence increased monotonically with the spatial frequency of the test grating. The SRDs had a significantly smaller increase in visible persistence duration with increasing spatial frequency than did controls. In the SRD group, visible persistence was longer for low spatial frequencies and shorter for the higher spatial frequencies compared with controls.

This difference in visible persistence as a function of spatial frequency between controls and SRDs can be explained by suggesting a disparate type of transient-sustained interaction present in those with specific reading disability. This is argued to be the case because a manipulation known to reduce transient system activity, uniform field flicker masking (Breitmeyer, Levi, & Harwerth, 1981), has a much greater effect on visible persistence at low spatial frequencies in controls than in SRDs. Furthermore, uniform field flicker masking reduces the persistence differences between the two groups.

Other evidence for a transient system deficit in specific reading disability has been advanced by the study of contrast sensitivity. Contrast sensitivity is the minimum amount of contrast needed to perceive a grating pattern. Sensitivity is greatest for patterns of intermediate spatial frequency and decreases for patterns that are of lower or higher spatial frequency. Contrast sensitivity plotted as a function of stimulus spatial frequency is referred to as the contrast sensitivity function (CSF).

CSFs have been measured in five separate samples of disabled and normal readers 8 to 14 years of age (Lovegrove, Bowling, Badcock, & Blackwood, 1980a; Lovegrove et al., 1982; Martin & Lovegrove, 1984). SRDs showed a consistent pattern of lower sensitivity to low spatial frequencies (1–4 c/deg) than did controls. The pattern of differences at the high spatial frequencies (12–16 c/deg) is less exact. In some studies, the two groups did not differ in sensitivity and in others the SRDs were slightly more sensitive than controls in that range. The differences between the groups were greatest with stimulus durations ranging from 150 ms to 500 ms.

It should be noted that the magnitude of the differences between the groups on measures of pattern CSF are not as great as those found on measures of visible persistence (see Lovegrove, Martin, & Slaghuis, 1986). The finding of a small but consistent sensitivity loss at low spatial frequencies in SRDs is consistent with the proposal of a transient system deficit as argued by Lovegrove et al. (1982).

Transient system functioning can be investigated more directly by the measurement of flicker contrast sensitivity where, instead of a static display of a stimulus, a test grating is counterphased or moved leftward and rightward the width of one cycle. It has been argued that flicker thresholds are mediated by the transient system (Kulikowski & Tolhurst, 1973). A transient system deficit, then, should result in decreased sensitivity to flicker in SRDs, and this decrement should increase as temporal frequency increases.

Martin and Lovegrove (1987) required 13-year-old subjects to detect a 2 c/deg sine wave grating that counterphased at 5, 10, 15, 20, and 25 cycles per second. On the average, controls were found to be more sensitive than SRDs across the range of temporal frequencies tested. The sensitivity difference between the two groups increased with increasing temporal frequency. Similar results were obtained by Brannan and Williams (1988a) using uniform field flicker. These results add further to the argument that a difference in transient system function exists between SRDs and normal readers.

In another experiment (Martin & Lovegrove, 1987), the flicker contrast sensitivity function was determined for the same two groups using spatial frequencies from 1 c/deg to 12 c/deg counterphasing at 20 cycles per second. These results also indicated that these controls were more sensitive than SRDs across all spatial frequencies, the differences being larger at the higher spatial frequencies.

A further series of experiments has been conducted comparing sustained system processing in controls and SRDs (Lovegrove et al., 1986). Using similar procedures, equipment, and subjects as the experiments outlined earlier, this series failed to show any significant differences between the two groups in orientation or spatial frequency tuning. This implies that either there are no differences between the groups in the functioning of their sustained systems, or that such differences are small compared to the transient system differences demonstrated.

Additional support for differences between the groups in terms of transient system processing comes from a series of recent visual evoked potential studies (May, Lovegrove, Martin, & Nelson, 1991; May, Dunlap, & Lovegrove, 1992; Livingstone, Rosen, Drislane, & Galaburda, 1991). Finally Livingstone, Rosen, Drislane, and Galaburda (1991) conducted postmortem studies on SRDs and controls. They investigated cell size and organization in the magno- and parvo-cellular layers of the lateral geniculate nucleus in both groups. They found that the groups did not differ in terms of cell size in the parvocellular layers. On the other hand, SRDs appeared to have smaller cells in the magnocellular layers. In addition these layers in SRDs showed less of the typical laminar organization than did controls.

In summary, six converging lines of evidence suggest a visual system deficit in SRDs. The results are internally consistent and consistent with the proposal of a transient system deficit. The differences between the groups are quite large and discriminate well between individuals in the different groups, with approximately 75% of SRDs showing reduced transient system sensitivity (Slaghuis & Lovegrove, 1985). At the same time, evidence to date suggests that the two groups do not differ in sustained system functioning. The two findings taken together may help to explain some of the confusion reported in the literature over many years. In these terms whether or not differences are found will depend on which system is investigated.

Support for this position has recently been provided by Meca (1985), who has conducted a meta-analysis on a large number of studies investigating vision and reading. He plotted effect size as a function of spatial frequency. As would be expected if SRDs had a transient system problem but not a sustained system problem, effect size was greatest at low spatial frequencies and decreased with increasing spatial frequency.

Perceptual Consequences of a Transient Deficit

The studies reported here demonstrate that a large subgroup of disabled readers do have visual deficits. Given what is known of the perceptual functions that the transient system performs, it is reasonable to expect that SRDs with transient system difficulties would show deficits in global, preattentive processing operations and on tasks requiring fine temporal resolution.

A number of studies by Williams and her colleagues expanded on Lovegrove's work by studying the perceptual consequences of a transient deficit in reading-disabled children. These studies employed subject populations consisting of children reading at least 1 year below grade level (disabled readers), and children reading at or above grade level (normal readers). Because normal performance on standardized reading tests includes a range of scores +/− one standard deviation from the mean, this classification criterion would theoretically designate 84% of a normally distributed population as normal readers, and 16% as disabled readers, which is only slightly higher than any estimates of the prevalence of reading disability in the general population (e.g., Critchley, 1964). These selection criteria may have led to a slightly different sample from the subjects selected by Lovegrove and his colleagues. This possibility is currently being investigated. All children in these studies were 8 to 12 years old, of normal or above normal intelligence, had normal color vision and normal or corrected-to-normal visual acuity, and scored within the normal range on tests of auditory discrimination. The normal and disabled reader groups were matched for age and IQ.

Visual Masking Studies

Direct measures of the time course of visual processing in normal and disabled readers have been obtained in recent visual masking studies (Williams et al., 1989; Williams & LeCluyse, 1990). In visual masking, two temporally separated visual stimuli are presented, and one stimulus, called the mask, interferes with the processing of the other stimulus, called the target. Williams, LeCluyse, and Bologna (1990) employed a masking of pattern by light paradigm to measure visual integration and persistence characteristics of normal and disabled readers. Masking of pattern by light is a special case of visual masking where the visibility of the target pattern is reduced by a spatially uniform luminance mask flash that overlaps the target. It is assumed that target visibility is degraded to the extent that the sensory activity of the target and mask persist and overlap in time or are integrated during a brief temporal interval. Thus masking by light constitutes a measure of the temporal resolution limits of the visual system imposed by either response persistence or response integration.

Disabled readers showed more prolonged masking as compared with normal subjects, suggesting that visual processing is characterized by a longer integration time and/or longer visible persistence. Disabled readers also showed enhancement effects (where the mask made the target easier rather than harder to see) rather than masking effects when stimuli were presented in the peripheral retina, suggesting that peripheral visual processing is characterized by a disinhibition or enhancement of sustained pattern information due to a diminished inhibitory effect imposed by peripheral transient channels. This facilitation effect provides evidence for the proposal that sustained pattern formation processes are affected by the temporal processing characteristics of disabled readers through an abnormal pattern of interactions over time.

The finding of facilitation in peripheral vision is consistent with the recent finding (Grosser & Spafford, 1989, 1990) showing that SRDs discriminate color in the periphery better than controls. Grosser and Spafford (1989) interpreted their data as showing differences between the groups in the distribution of cones and rods. More specifically SRDs have a broader distribution of cones than do controls. Even though there are problems with Grosser and Spafford's interpretation of their data (see Stuart & Lovegrove, 1992 for a discussion of this point), the basic data are consistent with the finding of facilitation reported here. A neutral interpretation of both sets of results is that a weak transient system may be accompanied by a stronger sustained system in SRDs. This issue is discussed more fully later.

Additional measures of the time course of visual processing in normal and disabled readers have been obtained by Williams et al. (1989). In this study a metacontrast masking paradigm was used to index processing rate in both foveal and peripheral vision. In metacontrast, a target is briefly presented, and is followed at various delays by a spatially adjacent masking stimulus. Accuracy for the target is measured as a function of the delay between the target and the mask. The time course of the accuracy function is thought to reveal the time course of the processing of the target and mask. The accuracy functions typically obtained in metacontrast experiments are U-shaped, much like the schematic one shown in Figure 14.1a. Accuracy first decreases, reaches a low point at an intermediate delay, and then increases again to baseline level. Two-component metacontrast theories (Breitmeyer & Ganz, 1976; Matin, 1975; Weisstein, 1968, 1972; Weisstein, Ozog, & Szoc, 1975) attribute U-shaped metacontrast functions to the interaction of transient and sustained components of visual response. These models posit metacontrast masking as the result of the transient response to the later occurring mask catching up with, and inhibiting, the slower sustained response to the target. For this to occur, the mask must be delayed in time relative to the target. Figure 14.1b illustrates these timing assumptions. The dip, or

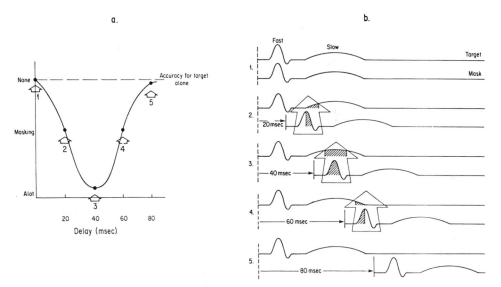

FIG. 14.1.   A schematic U-shaped metacontrast function together with hypothetical visual response to a target and to a mask. (a) Schematic U-shaped metacontrast function: Accuracy is plotted against delay. (b) Hypothetical visual responses. (1) simultaneous onset of target and mask. Transient responses do not overlap with sustained responses, and there is no masking, as shown by the arrow labeled 1 on the left. (2) Target leads the mask by 20 ms. The transient response to the mask slightly overlaps the beginning of the sustained response to the target and some interference occurs. There is a small amount of masking, as shown by arrow 2 on the left. (3) Difference in onsets of target and mask produce maximum overlap of transient and sustained components, and thus, the greatest amount of interference. As shown by arrow 3 on the left, this is the point of maximum masking. (4) Target leads mask by 60 ms. The transient response to the mask again only slightly overlaps the sustained response to the target, and the amount of interference is again small. Masking begins to decrease, as shown by arrow 4 on the left. (5) Target leads mask by a long delay. No interference occurs, and from this point on, no masking occurs either. From "The Effect of Perceived Depth and Connectedness on Metacontrast Functions" by M. Williams and N. Weisstein 1984; *Vision Research, 24*(10), pp. 1279–1288. Copyright by Pergamon Press. Reprinted with permission.

lowest accuracy point in the function, is the point of maximum inhibition. As the dip shifts rightward toward longer delays, it could be assumed that some aspect of the transient (inhibitory) response to the mask is traveling faster. This is simply because something that occurs later has to travel faster to catch up. Thus, according to these models, dips at long delays between the target and mask imply fast processing, and dips at short delays imply slower processing.

Williams et al. (1989), using diagonal line segments as targets and a surrounding outlined square as a masking stimulus, measured metacontrast functions in adults, young normal readers, and disabled readers. The differences in dip location in the functions obtained from adults, normal readers, and disabled readers indicated that the rate of foveal visual processing was fastest in normal adults, slowest in reading-disabled children, and intermediate in normal reading children. These findings are consistent with previous reports of increased temporal resolution with age (Brannan & Williams, 1988a, b), and sluggish temporal processing in disabled readers, as described earlier.

The magnitude of metacontrast masking increased in the peripheral retina in adults and normal readers, which is consistent with previous reports of increased masking effects in the periphery (Williams & Weisstein, 1981). There was, however, an absence of metacontrast masking in disabled readers with peripheral presentations, a finding that is compatible with Geiger and Lettvin's (1987) finding that dyslexic subjects show a smaller magnitude of simultaneous lateral masking in the periphery. Geiger and Lettvin attributed the reduced masking effect to an attentional strategy of dyslexic subjects to allocate more processing capacity to peripheral as compared to foveal areas of the visual field. An alternate explanation can be derived from the two-component masking theories described previously, which attribute metacontrast masking to the inhibition of relatively slow pattern formation processes by short latency temporal processing channels. These theories would predict that a temporal processing deficit would lead to an attenuation or elimination of metacontrast. A stronger sustained system in SRDs as discussed earlier would also produce this result.

The masking studies described provide additional evidence that the visual processing differences observed between normal and disabled readers are related to the relative timing of low and high spatial frequency channels in disabled readers. The results of these studies suggest that a sluggish transient system in disabled readers may result in a lack of temporal separation between transient and sustained processes. The functioning of the sustained system is affected through a different pattern of interactions over time. An important issue is whether there is any way to change the relative timing of the transient and sustained systems in SRDs. The next section considers one method that has been attempted.

The Effect of Wavelength on the Time Course of Visual Processing.   Recent psychophysical and physiological data indicate that color or wavelength differentially affect the response characteristics of transient and sustained processing channels, and that wavelength can affect the relative contributions of transient and sustained channels to the processing of a stimulus. Physiological observations of the primate visual system indicate that there are differences in the color selectivity of these systems (Livingstone & Hubel, 1988), and that a steady red background light attenuates the response of transient channels (Dreher, Fukuda,

& Rodieck, 1976; Kruger, 1977; Schiller & Malpeli, 1978). A recent investigation by Breitmeyer and Williams (1990) provided evidence that variations in wavelength produce similar effects in the human visual system. They found that the magnitude of both metacontrast and stroboscopic motion was decreased when red as compared with equiluminant green or white backgrounds were used. According to transient-sustained theories of metacontrast and stroboscopic motion, these results indicate that the activity of transient channels is attenuated by red backgrounds. Williams, Breitmeyer, Lovegrove, and Gutierrez (1991), using a metacontrast paradigm, additionally found that the rate of processing in transient channels increases as wavelength decreases, and red light enhances the activity of sustained channels. Other human psychophysical studies have shown that transient channels are not sensitive to changes in hue when luminance transients are not also present (Bowen, Pokorny, & Cacciato, 1977), and, that the time course of visual processing is wavelength-specific (Walters, 1970).

Williams, Faucheux, and LeCluyse (in press) utilized a metacontrast paradigm to obtain direct measures of the effects of color on temporal visual processing in normal and disabled readers. Using white diagonal lines as targets, and a white, red, or blue 12 c/deg flanking grating as a mask, Williams et al. obtained the metacontrast functions shown in Figs. 14.2 and 14.3. Normal readers showed differences in both enhancement and dip location with the different colored masks (Fig. 14.3). The fact that the delay of maximum masking occurred at a

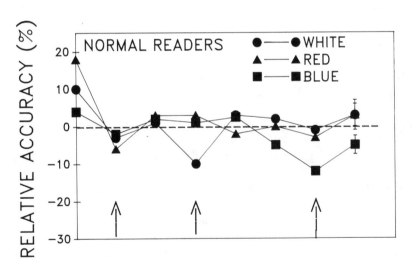

FIG. 14.2. Metacontrast functions collected on normal readers with masks varying in wavelength. Accuracy for the target lines when followed by a flanking grating mask is plotted relative to accuracy for the target lines-alone (horizontal line). Positive accuracy indicates that the mask enhanced the visibility of the target, and negative accuracy indicates that the mask impaired the visibility of the target.

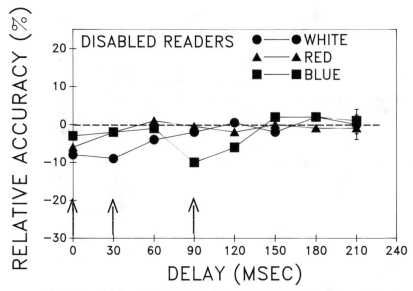

FIG. 14.3.   Metacontrast functions collected on disabled readers with masks varying in wavelength. Accuracy for the target lines when followed by a flanking grating mask is plotted relative to accuracy for the target lines-alone (horizontal line). Positive accuracy indicates that the mask enhanced the visibility of the target, and negative accuracy indicates that the mask impaired the visibility of the target.

shorter delay for the red compared with the other masks suggests that the processing rate in transient channels is slowest for the red masks. This finding may be related to previous findings that red light inhibits the activity of transient channels (Breitmeyer & Williams, 1990; Dreher, Fukuda, & Rodieck, 1976). Along the same lines, the fact that the delay of maximum masking occurred at a longer delay for the blue as compared with the other masks suggests that blue light may enhance the processing rate in transient channels.

Next, consider the differences found in the magnitude of masking at the dips in the functions. Again, this is the point in the metacontrast function where the transient response to the target maximally overlaps with, and inhibits, the sustained response to the target. The target was always the same, so differences in the magnitude of masking at the dip can be attributed to differences in the response magnitude of transient channel activity generated by the mask. The fact that there was a smaller magnitude of masking with the red as compared with the longest wavelength masks suggests that transient channels respond less vigorously to short wavelength stimuli.

At simultaneous presentation of the target and mask, target identification accuracy was enhanced over the accuracy level for the targets when they were presented alone. This finding is consistent with previous reports of contextual information enhancing the detectability of briefly presented targets (Weisstein & Harris, 1974; Williams & Weisstein, 1981, 1984). According to masking models based on transient/sustained theory, this is the part of the function where the sustained components of response to the target and mask can interact. Because the enhancement effect varied with the wavelength of the mask, it appears that the sustained component of visual response is sensitive to variations in wavelength. The results indicate that the sustained channels respond with greater sensitivity to red light as compared with blue and white light.

Disabled readers also showed differences in dip location and magnitude of masking with the wavelength of the mask (Fig. 14.3). Overall, dip locations occurred at shorter delays for disabled as compared with normal readers, suggesting that the processing rate in transient channels is slower in disabled readers. As with the normal readers, however, the processing rate in transient channels appears to be slowest with the red mask and fastest with the blue mask. Disabled readers generally showed a smaller magnitude of masking than normal readers, again suggesting that, overall, transient channels respond less vigorously to short wavelength stimuli. Finally, it is interesting to note that the function produced by the blue mask in disabled readers is similar in time course to the function produced by the white mask in normal readers. This finding suggests that blue light produces a normal time course of processing in disabled readers, and is consistent with the contention that blue light may enhance the processing rate in transient channels.

The Effect of Wavelength on Reading Performance.   Given the systematic effects of color on the perceptual performance of the reading disabled, and the fact that this manipulation can render their performance comparable to that of normal readers, Williams et al. (in press) investigated the effects of color on actual reading performance. This is crucial in asking whether or not there is a causal link between transient system deficits and reading disability. To assess reading performance, reading comprehension was measured for standardized reading passages under three temporal presentation conditions. In all cases the children read silently. In the first condition, the passages were presented one word at a time, each word being centered on a computer monitor. In this reading condition, eye movements were not required for successful reading. In the second condition, the passages were presented one word at a time, with the words painted from left to right in a moving window fashion. In this condition, eye movements were required, but were guided by the presentation of the text. In the third condition, the passages were presented one line at a time, with all of the words in each line being painted simultaneously. This was a free eye movement condition; eye movements were required and were under each subject's control. The grade level and presentation rate of the passages were determined by each subject's performance on a standardized reading test. The passages were presented with white, red, and blue text on a black background in separate blocks.

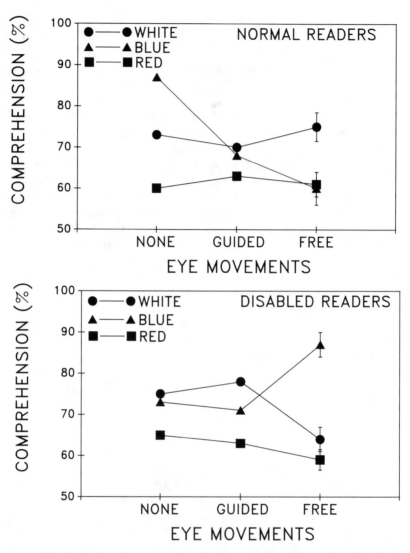

FIG. 14.4. Reading comprehension (measured as % correct on literal recall questions) for clear white text (circles), blue text (triangles), and red text (squares) under three temporal presentation conditions for normal readers and disabled readers.

Figure 14.4 shows the reading comprehension scores obtained with the white as compared with colored text. When the passages were presented in white, the three presentation conditions did not have differential effects on the reading comprehension of normal readers. Disabled readers, on the other hand, performed more poorly in the free eye movement condition than in the other conditions.

The red text had a detrimental effect on the reading performance of both normal and disabled readers. On the other hand the blue text improved reading in the SRD group especially in the free eye-movement condition.

These results can best be interpreted within the model of fixation-saccade processes in reading described earlier (Breitmeyer, 1980; Breitmeyer & Ganz, 1976; E. Matin, Clymer, & L. Matin, 1972). The reading performance of normal readers may improve in the no eye movement condition when blue text is used if the use of a short wavelength stimulus results in a faster, more vigorous response from the transient channels, resulting in improved transient-on-sustained inhibition (Williams et al., in press). The deterioration of the reading performance of normal readers in this condition when red text is used may be due to an increased masking by integration effect. This increased masking by integration effect would be the result of an increase in sustained channel activity and weaker transient-on-sustained inhibition produced by a long wavelength stimulus (Williams et al., in press). When eye movements *are* involved, color may disrupt the normal pattern of transient-sustained interactions due to the fact that the timing and sensitivity of transient and sustained channel response are altered. Thus a decrement in performance is observed in the no eye movement condition with the color manipulation.

Disabled readers performed poorly in the free eye movement condition when clear, white text was used, but performed better in the conditions requiring no eye movements or guided eye movements. In the latter conditions it could be assumed that transient activity was minimized. When red text was used, disabled readers showed a smaller decrement in performance in the no eye movement condition than normal readers showed. This result may be related to the finding that disabled readers do not show the increase in sustained channel sensitivity that normal readers show with red stimuli (as indexed by an enhancement effect in the metacontrast function), although they do show a less vigorous response from transient channel activity (as indexed by a smaller magnitude of masking). The increased masking by integration effect, therefore, in disabled readers may be smaller in this condition, resulting in a smaller decrement in performance. When blue text was used, reading performance in SRDs improved significantly suggesting that the use of the short wavelength stimulus stimulates a normal pattern of visual processing during reading.

It should be noted that in the studies just outlined what was being measured was reading comprehension. The evidence shows clearly that manipulations shown to have clear effects on visual functioning (metacontrast) also have a direct effect on comprehension. This implies (but does not prove) that comprehension in poor readers is normally adversely affected by deficient low level visual processes modified by color.

In a related study, Lovegrove and Macfarlane (1990) measured the number of errors, comprehension, and reading rate under the same three temporal presentation conditions. Here it was found that disabled readers made fewer errors in the no eye movement condition than controls, and more errors in the free eye movement condition. Furthermore, reading rate increased in the no eye movement condition as compared with the free eye movement condition in disabled readers, and there was a trend, although insignificant, toward higher comprehension scores in the no eye movement condition. Lovegrove and Macfarlane interpreted their results within the framework of a central-peripheral processing dichotomy. The no eye movement condition required the processing of only central (foveal) information, whereas the free eye movement condition required the integration of central and peripheral information from successive fixations. When disabled readers only have to process central information, which requires little transient system involvement, they make fewer errors and read at a faster rate than in the condition that approximates normal reading.

There were several differences between Williams et al.'s and Lovegrove and Macfarlane's studies that may account for the fact that normal and disabled readers did not show differences in comprehension scores in the latter study. Most importantly, in Lovegrove and Macfarlane's study reading rate was increased on each trial that subjects correctly answered 80% of the comprehension questions posed, whereas in Williams et al.'s study reading rate remained constant. Thus, improvement in comprehension may have been obscured by a speed-accuracy tradeoff in the former study.

Is there only a Transient System Deficit?   Although there is considerable evidence that the visual processing of disabled readers is characterized by poor temporal processing as measured by transient system processing, it may be misleading to consider that all visual processing abnormalities can be explained this way. Although Lovegrove and co-workers failed to find evidence of sustained system differences, this is not true for all the work reported by Williams. A number of studies have found that the functioning of sustained pattern formation processes are affected by the poor temporal processing of disabled readers. Williams, Brannan, and Lartigue (1987) investigated detail processing operations in normal and disabled readers using a visual search task, where subjects were required to search for a target letter embedded in a list of distractor letters. This task requires scrutiny of local differences in detail between target and distractor items and should involve the sustained system. Brannan and Lartigue found that search times were much longer in disabled readers than in either normal readers or adults. This suggests that although the primary visual deficit of disabled readers seems to involve temporal, or transient, processing operations, the sustained pattern formation processes are necessarily affected through a different pattern of interactions over time. It is likely that tasks involving transient-sustained systems interacting will show differences between the groups.

CONCLUSIONS

Research conducted over a number of years has demonstrated a transient system deficit in a majority of specifically disabled readers tested. Differences have been found between normal and disabled readers in measurements of visible persistence, pattern contrast sensitivity, and temporal or flicker contrast sensitivity. The foveal temporal processing of disabled readers has been found to be sluggish compared to that of normal readers. Peripheral visual processing has been found to be characterized by a lack of inhibitory processes. Differences in the temporal processing of normal and disabled readers surface in the processing of a range of stimuli. The primary deficit appears to be in the response properties of the transient subsystem of the visual system, although the response of the sustained system may be affected through a different pattern of interactions with the transient system over time. Measures of sustained system function that presumably do not involve a dynamic interaction between transient and sustained systems fail to demonstrate visual processing differences between normal and disabled readers. The use of color appears to have the effect of reestablishing a normal pattern of visual processing in disabled readers. These effects are potentially important and replication and extension of them is now in progress. Of particular interest is whether these effects are found with most SRDs or whether they are restricted to a particular subset of SRDs.

REFERENCES

Badcock, D., & Lovegrove, W. (1981). The effects of contrast, stimulus duration, and spatial frequency on visible persistence in normal and specifically disabled readers. *Journal of Experimental Psychology. Human Perception and Performance, 7,* 495–505.

Benton, A. (1975). Developmental dyslexia: Neurological aspects. In W. J. Friedlander (Ed.), *Advances in neurology: Vol. 1. Current reviews of higher order nervous system dysfunction* (pp. 1–47). New York: Raven Press.

Bowen, R., Pokorney, J., & Cacciato, D. (1977). Metacontrast masking depends on luminance transients. *Vision Research, 17,* 971–975.

Brannan, J., & Williams, M. (1988a). The effects of age and reading ability on flicker thresholds. *Clinical Vision Sciences, 3*(2), 137–142.

Brannan, J., & Williams, M. (1988b). Developmental versus sensory deficit effects on perceptual processing in the reading disabled. *Perception and Psychophysics, 44*(5), 437–444.

Breitmeyer, B. (1980). Unmasking visual masking: A look at the "why" behind the veil of the "how." *Psychological Review, 87,* 52–69.

Breitmeyer, B., & Ganz, L. (1976). Implications of sustained and transient channels for theories of visual pattern masking saccadic suppression and information processing. *Psychological Review, 83,* 1–36.

Breitmeyer, B., Levi, D., & Harwerth, R. (1981). Flicker masking in spatial vision. *Vision Research, 21,* 1377–1386.

Breitmeyer, B., & Williams, M. (1990). Effects of isoluminant-background color on metacontrast and stroboscopic motion: Interactions between sustained (P) and transient (M) channels. *Vision Research, 25,* 1595–1601.

Campbell, F. W. (1974). The transmission of spatial information through the visual system. In F. O. Schmidt & F. S. Worden (Eds.), *The neurosciences third study program* (pp. 95–103). Cambridge, MA: MIT Press.

Critchley, M. (1964). *Developmental dyslexia.* London: Heinemann.

Dreher, B., Fukuda, Y., & Rodieck, R. (1976). Identification, classification and anatomical segregation of cells with X-like and Y-like properties in the lateral geniculate nucleus of old-world primates. *Journal of Physiology, 258,* 433–452.

Fletcher, J., & Satz, P. (1979). Unitary deficits hypothesis of reading disability: Has Vellutino led us astray? *Journal of Learning Disabilities, 12*(3), 155–159.

Geiger, G., & Lettvin, J. (1987). Peripheral vision in persons with dyslexia. *New England Journal of Medicine, 316,* 1238–1243.

Graham, N. (1980). Spatial frequency channels in human vision. Detecting edges without edges detectors. In C. S. Harris (Ed.), *Visual coding and adaptability* (pp. 215–262). Hillsdale, NJ: Lawrence Erlbaum Associates.

Grosser, G., & Spafford, C. (1989). Perceptual evidence for an anomolous distribution of rods and cones in the retinas of dyslexics: A new hypothesis. *Perceptual and Motor Skills, 68,* 683–698.

Grosser, G., & Spafford, C. (1990). Light sensitivity in the peripheral retinal fields of dyslexics and proficient readers. *Perceptual and Motor Skills, 71,* 467–477.

Kruger, J. (1977). Stimulus dependent color specificity of monkey lateral geniculate neurones. *Experimental Brain Research, 30,* 297–311.

Kulikowski, J. J., & Tolhurst, D. J. (1973). Psychophysical evidence for sustained and transient detectors in human vision. *Journal of Physiology, 232,* 149–162.

Livingstone, M., Rosen, G., Drislane, F., & Galaburda, A. (1991). Physiological and anatomical evidence for a magnocellular defect in developmental dyslexia. *Proceedings of the National Academy of Science, 88,* 7943–7947.

Livingstone, M. S., & Hubel, D. H. (1987). Psychophysical evidence for separate channels for the perception of form, color, movement and depth. *Journal of the Neurosciences, 7,* 3416–3468.

Livingstone, M. S., & Hubel, D. H. (1988). Segregation of form, color, movement and depth: Anatomy, physiology and perception. *Science, 240,* 740–749.

Lovegrove, W., Bowling, A., Badcock, D., & Blackwood, M. (1980). Specific reading disability: Differences in contrast sensitivity as a function of spatial frequency. *Science, 210,* 439–440.

Lovegrove, W., & Brown, C. (1978). Development of information processing in normal and disabled readers. *Perceptual and Motor Skills, 46,* 1047–1054.

Lovegrove, W., & Macfarlane, T. (1990). The effect of text presentation on reading in dyslexic and normal readers. *Perception, 19,* A 46.

Lovegrove, W., Martin, F., Bowling, A., Blackwood, M., Badcock, D., & Paxton, S. (1982). Contrast sensitivity functions and specific reading disability. *Neuropsychologia 20,* 309–315.

Lovegrove, W., Martin, F., & Slaghuis, W. (1986). A theoretical and experimental case for a visual deficit in specific reading disability. *Cognitive Neuropsychology, 3,* 225–267.

Martin, F., & Lovegrove, W. (1984). The effects of field size and luminance on contrast sensitivity differences between specifically reading disabled and normal children. *Neuropsychologia, 22,* 73–77.

Martin, F., & Lovegrove, W. (1987). Flicker contrast sensitivity in normal and specifically disabled readers. *Perception, 16,* 215–221.

Matin, E. (1975). The two-transient (masking) paradigm. *Psychological Review, 82,* 451–461.

Matin, E., Clymer, A., & Matin, L. (1972). Metacontrast and saccadic suppression. *Science, 178,* 179–182.

May, J., Dunlap, W., & Lovegrove, W. (1992). Factor scores derived from visual evoked potential latencies differentiate good and poor readers. *Clinical Vision Sciences, 7,* 67–70.

May, J., Lovegrove, W., Martin, F., & Nelson, W. (1991). Pattern-elicited visual evoked potentials in good and poor readers. *Clinical Vision Sciences, 2,* 131–136.

Meca, J. (1985). La hipotesis del deficit perceptivo del retraso especifico en lectura: un estudio meta-analitico. *Anales de Psicologia, 2,* 75–91.

Rayner, K. (1975). The perceptual span and peripheral cues in reading. *Cognitive Psychology, 7,* 65–81.

Rayner, K., & McConkie, B. (1976). What guides a reader's eye movements? *Vision Research, 16,* 829–837.

Schiller, P., & Malpeli, J. (1978). Functional specificity of lateral geniculate nucleus laminae of the rhesus monkey. *Journal of Neurophysiology, 41,* 788–797.

Singer. W., & Bedworth, N. (1973). Inhibitory interaction between X and Y units in cat lateral geniculate nucleus. *Brain Research, 49,* 291–307.

Slaghuis, W., & Lovegrove, W. (1985). Spatial-frequency mediated visible persistence and specific reading disability. *Brain and Cognition, 4,* 219–240.

Stanley, G. (1975) Two-part stimulus integration and specific reading disability. *Perceptual and Motor Skills, 41,* 873–874.

Stuart, G., & Lovegrove, W. (1992). Visual processing deficits in dyslexia: Receptors or neural mechanisms? *Perceptual and Motor Skills, 74,* 187–192.

Vellutino, F. (1979). *Dyslexia: Theory and research.* London: MIT Press.

Walters, J. (1970). Metacontrast: The effects obtained with consecutively presented concentric disks and rings of different wavelengths. *American Journal of Optometry, 45,* 634–639.

Weisstein, N. (1968). A Rashevsky–Landahl neural net: Simulation of metacontrast. *Psychological Review, 75,* 494–521.

Weisstein, N., & Harris, C. (1974). Visual detection of line segments: An object-superiority effect. *Science, 186,* 752–755.

Weisstein, N., Ozog, G., & Szoc, R. (1975). A comparison and elaboration of two models of metacontrast. *Psychological Review, 82,* 325–342.

Williams, M., Brannan, J., & Lartigue, E. (1987). Visual search in good and poor readers. *Clinical Vision Sciences, 1*(4), 367–371.

Williams, M., Breitmeyer, B., Lovegrove, W., & Gutierrez, C. (1991). Metacontrast with masks varying in spatial frequency and wavelength. *Vision Research, 31,* 2017–2023.

Williams, M., Faucheux, A., & LeCluyse, K. (in press). The time course of the processing of stimuli with different wavelengths in normal and disabled readers. *Clinical Vision Sciences.*

Williams, M., LeCluyse, K., & Bologna, N. (1990). Masking by light as a measure of visual integration time and persistence in normal and disabled readers. *Clinical Vision Sciences, 5,* 335–343.

Williams, M., & LeCluyse, K. (1990). Perceptual consequences of a temporal processing deficit in reading disabled children. *Journal of the American Optometric Association, 61,* 111–121.

Williams, M., LeCluyse, K., & Faucheux, A. (in press). Effects of image blurring and color on reading performance in normal and disabled readers. *Journal of the American Optometric Association.*

Williams, M., Molinet, K., & LeCluyse, K. (1989). Visual masking as a measure of temporal processing in normal and disabled readers. *Clinical Vision Sciences, 4*(2), 137–144.

Williams, M., & Weisstein, N. (1981). Spatial frequency response and perceived depth in the time-course of object-superiority. *Vision Research, 21,* 631–646.

Williams, M., & Weisstein, N. (1984). The effect of perceived depth on metacontrast functions. *Vision Research, 24*(10), 1279–1288.

15 Visuospatial Perception in Disabled Readers

John F. Stein
Oxford University

Many children who have difficulties with learning to read complain that their vision is abnormal. They say that words and letters seem to move around, jump over each other, merge, or seem blurred. These are the children whom their teachers tend to call "visual dyslexics" (Stein, 1991). Following are some of the illusions that such children describe:

"The letters go all blurry."
"T's and d's sort of get the wrong way round."
"The letters move over each other."
"The 'e' moved over the 'r', so it looked like a 'c.' "
"Things go double and drift away from each other."
"The letters hang over the page."

What these children report appears to be the result of inability to localize visual targets stably. This suggested to me that their reading difficulties may be the result of deficient ocular motor control. "Oscillopsia" is the word used by neurologists to describe patients' illusions that their visual world appears to move around. It is a more severe form of what these children describe; it is usually a consequence of uncontrolled movements of the two eyes. So Sue Fowler and I began to study the binocular control of children with reading disorders.

UNSTABLE BINOCULAR CONTROL

The main test that we have used was introduced by P. Dunlop (1972) to identify the "reference" or dominant eye under fully binocular conditions. It is based on

331

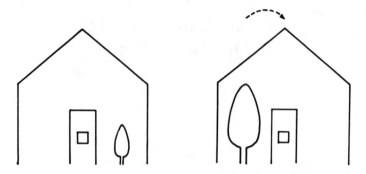

FIG. 15.1.   Slides viewed in synoptophore. When the eyepiece tubes are diverged one of the trees appears to move toward the door just before fusion breaks.

the phenomenon first reported by Ogle (1962) that when the eyes are made to point toward (converge) or away from each other (diverge) fused stationary images may appear to move just before fusion breaks down and double vision (diplopia) ensues. The child is asked to look at the slides shown in Fig. 15.1 through a stereoscope with eye pieces that can be converged or diverged (a synoptophore). Initially the eye pieces are set parallel, so that the child can fuse the slides. Then they are slowly diverged, which causes the eyes to do likewise in order to maintain fusion. Normal children can diverge by up to 5 degrees. After this one eye (the dominant or reference eye) continues to track the slide it sees; the other "breaks" and swings to be parallel with the reference. Hence fusion breaks; and the child begins to see two houses (diplopia). Just before fusion breaks the target tree seen by the nondominant eye appears to move toward the door, and then over it, as the two images separate. If the test is repeated 10 times the reference eye in normal children is found to be on the same slide on every occasion. But after we had been using this test for some time with children with reading problems it became clear to us that many of them show not the crossed laterality often attributed to dyslexics, but inconsistently lateralized responses when the Dunlop test is repeated many times. Most reading-disabled children appear to change their reference eye from trial to trial (Fowler & Stein, 1980). The dominant or reference eye is known to provide important directional cues under conditions of vergence (Ogle, 1962), so it seemed possible that confusion between the varying directional cues resulting from alternating the reference eye might contribute to these children's reading difficulties.

It is worth emphasising that what we found using the Dunlop Test (DT) suggested that unstable binocular control rather than crossed laterality is what is significant; crossed laterality is when the dominant eye and the hand preferred for writing are on opposite sides (P. Dunlop, 1972). We have compared the results of the DT with monocular and binocular tests for eye dominance. We found a clear relationship between unstable vergence responses in the DT and reading retardation, but like many others (see A. L. Benton, 1991) we have been unable to find any clear association between stable crossed laterality and reading retardation (P. Riddell, Fowler, & Stein, 1987).

Clearly it is not enough merely to show an association between unstable responses in the Dunlop Test and reading retardation; we also needed to show the corollary that normal readers do not have unstable responses in the test. We studied a group of children, who were defined as dyslexic because despite having a normal IQ (Wechsler Intelligence Scale for Children, WISC > 90) their reading age (RA) was more than 18 months behind their chronological age (CA); and we compared these with age-matched good readers (whose RA was greater than their CA). We found that whereas 63% of the dyslexics had unstable DT responses, only 1% of the good readers showed such instability (Stein & Fowler, 1982).

We also compared the DT responses of another group of dyslexics, (now defined as RA > 2 SDs behind that expected from their CA and IQ), with those of younger normal readers matched for reading age (Stein, P. Riddell, & Fowler, 1987). The purpose of this reading, rather than chronological, age match was to see whether learning to read might cause children to gain binocular stability rather than vice versa. All the younger normal readers showed stable responses in the text, whereas 67% of the older dyslexics reading at the same standard did not. If learning to read had been the cause of the younger normals developing binocular stability, the dyslexics should have had as stable eye control as the normals, as they were reading as well as the latter. But they did not. Hence we concluded that gaining binocular stability helps children to learn to read, rather than vice versa.

In addition we administered the DT to a large number of unselected primary school children (451), most of whom were "normal" readers. We were able to show that the reading of those who showed unstable responses in the DT was on average 6.3 months behind that of their peers with stable control. Thus, having unstable binocular vergence control as revealed by failing the DT significantly impedes children's reading (Stein, P. Riddell, & Fowler, 1986). So good readers seldom fail it; about 20% of low average readers fail it; and 60% to 70% of very poor readers fail it. It should be noted however that the fact that some children who are not dyslexic show unstable responses in the test means that it cannot be used as the sole diagnostic criterion for dyslexia. It is a test for unstable binocular control, not dyslexia per se.

Very young children do not possess stable binocular control. They develop it as they grow older. Only 52% of 159 5- to 6-year-olds tested had achieved stable binocular control in the DT (Stein et al., 1986). Also, 59% of 7-year-olds had developed it; 63% of 8-year-olds; 69% of 9-year-olds; 78% of 10-year-olds; and 90% of 11-year-olds. But, as mentioned earlier, those who failed the DT were usually worse readers than those who passed it. This developmental trend means that the age of the child must always be taken into account when interpreting the results of the Dunlop Test. Again it emphasises that unstable binocular control does not automatically lead to dyslexia; it just makes it more likely.

Although several groups have replicated our results (Bigelow & MacKenzie, 1985; Bishop, Jancey, & Steel, 1979; Masters, 1988) there has been much criticism of the Dunlop Test and of its reliability (Bishop, 1989; Newman et al., 1985). The test requires children to report their perceptual responses in a complicated situation. Often they try to second guess what the examiner is expecting. Thus, although it is fairly reliable in a clinical situation in experienced hands, it has turned out not to be ideal in experimental situations in which a rigid protocol is used; and the examiner is not free to interpret the responses in the light of the child's behavior. We therefore decided to record children's eye movements during the DT to see if we could obtain more reliable and objective measures of binocular instability.

VERGENCE EYE MOVEMENTS

Our eye movement recordings have shown that children who fail the Dunlop Test have more unstable eye movements in the test; they are unable to converge or diverge as much as normals (Stein, P. Riddell, & Fowler, 1988); and the eye that "breaks" when diplopia arises in the test varies from trial to trial. In normals it is always the eye on the same side (that opposite to the reference eye) that breaks. Thus the DT appears to identify the eye that is dominant for vergence tracking of a visual target, just before vergence breaks down and diplopia intervenes.

When reading at the normal reading distance of about 30 cms the eyes take up a position of about 12 degrees convergence pointing in an arrowhead at the text. The important consequences of the vergence instability that we record in children who fail the DT is that their eyes may wobble by as much as ± 1 degree. This movement would cover three to four letter spaces. Hence it is not surprising that for them letters seem to move around and change places. Neither of the eyes of normals who pass the DT deviate by more than 0.2 degree; this is less than one letter's worth (Cornelissen, 1993; C. Riddell, P. Riddell, & Stein, 1990a). The fixation wobble of those who pass the DT is small; because it does not exceed one letters' worth they do not experience illusions that letters appear to move around.

Interestingly we also found that the tendency for these dyslexics' eyes to wobble is considerably worse in their left eye, whereas in normals the left eye is the more steady.

The results discussed so far indicate that many dyslexics, together with some low average readers, have impaired binocular vergence control, which causes their eyes to wander more around a fixation point than in normals, particularly when the child's eyes are converged in order to view small targets close by, such as letters when reading. It is natural therefore to ask why this state of affairs arises. What mechanisms underlie normal stable fixation; and how do they go wrong in these children?

THE TRANSIENT SYSTEM
AND OCULAR MOTOR CONTROL

As described in other chapters in this volume, visual processing can to some extent be subdivided into two subprocesses, which are variously known as the "transient" and "sustained" systems, the magnocellular and parvocellular, or the "where" and "what" systems. The highest level of the magnocellular, transient, or where system is the posterior parietal cortex, particularly that in the right hemisphere in humans (Andersen, 1989; Stein, 1989a, 1992). The magnocellular transient system is achromatic, but more responsive than the parvocellular to low spatial frequencies, low contrasts, and high temporal frequencies. Its output is known to play an important part in the control of eye movements. Reflex eye movements are mainly controlled by the superior colliculus, which receives most of its retinal input from the magnocellular system; but those that are voluntary responses to the interest of visual targets are mediated by the posterior parietal cortex (Andersen, 1989; Elkington, Kerr, & Stein, 1991; Stein, 1989a, 1992).

Lovegrove and colleagues (see Lovegrove & Williams, chap. 14) have gathered much evidence in favor of the hypothesis that many dyslexics (up to 75%) exhibit a developmental impairment of their transient system. This is revealed in dyslexics by a slight impairment of their contrast sensitivity at low spatial frequencies; these coarse patterns are dealt with almost exclusively by the transient system. Also the critical fusion frequency of these dyslexics is somewhat lower than normal; again this suggests poorer temporal performance of their transient systems. Moreover they exhibit a significantly smaller increase in the duration of visual persistence with increasing spatial frequency. Again this is consistent with a diminished transient response. Finally because low contrast, low spatial frequency stimuli are thought to stimulate the transient system selectively, the visual evoked responses to such stimuli have been compared in dyslexics and normal controls. They were clearly reduced in the dyslexics, as would be expected if their transient system is deficient (Livingstone, Rosen, Drislane, & Galaburda, 1991; Mecacci, Sechi, & Levi, 1983). Livingstone, et al. went on to demonstrate that the magnocellular layers of the lateral geniculate nucleus, which relay transient visual signals to the cerebral cortex, were abnormally small in the brains of five dyslexics examined postmortem. Thus there is now a fairly convincing body of evidence to suggest that most dyslexics have a mild disorder of their magnocellular, transient, stream of visual processing.

The magnocellular division of the visual system is known to play a dominant role in the control of eye movements. So it was natural to ask whether the children that we have shown to have unstable binocular control in the Dunlop and other tests exhibit evidence of specific impairment of their transient system. Using the Vistech clinical test for contrast sensitivity we found that children who failed the DT did indeed demonstrate reduced contrast sensitivity at low spatial frequencies (Stein et al., 1987). However the Vistech test has been criticized for its lack of sensitivity and reliability; so Cornelissen, Mason, and I (Cornelissen, 1993) measured the contrast sensitivity of 20 reading retarded children who failed the DT in a four alternative, forced choice procedure; we compared their contrast sensitivity with 20 reading age and IQ-matched poor readers who passed it. We have been able to show that children who fail the DT have the same pattern of contrast sensitivity changes as the dyslexics studied by Lovegrove et al. Our children who failed the DT showed a mild impairment at low spatial frequencies, together with increased sensitivity at high spatial frequencies (Fig. 15.2). There was a bigger effect of flicker on these children. Those who failed the DT were nearly 5 dB more sensitive to 20-Hz flicker than the reading age and IQ-matched children who passed it. Thus it seems clear that children who fail the DT do indeed have a mild disorder of their transient systems; and therefore that the children we have been seeing are similar to those reported by Lovegrove et al.

So we now believe that poor performance in the DT is associated with unstable vergence control, in particular poor fixation; and we speculate that this may be caused by abnormal development of the transient system. We have therefore begun to investigate whether 20-Hz flicker, which is known to fatigue the transient system, and to impair ocularmotor control in normals, has any greater effects in our dyslexic children with already unstable binocular control. Our preliminary results suggest that this procedure may indeed have an especially deleterious effect on these subjects, particularly as regards their binocular vergence control. If confirmed, these results will further support the hypothesis that in these dyslexics the transient system's input to their ocular motor control centers is compromised.

VISUAL DIRECTION SENSE

Our hypothesis is that dyslexic children have impaired vergence control that prevents them from being able to fixate letters stably and therefore to locate them reliably; this in turn leads letters to appear to move around for them. However the ocular deviations that we measured amounted to no more than 1 degree. So they probably only affect accurate localization of small visual targets such as letters. Objects larger than 1 degree would not be covered by such eye movements. Hence they may be more easily stabilized by higher order perceptual processes; and indeed we find that these children's vergence control is much better for large targets (Stein et al., 1988).

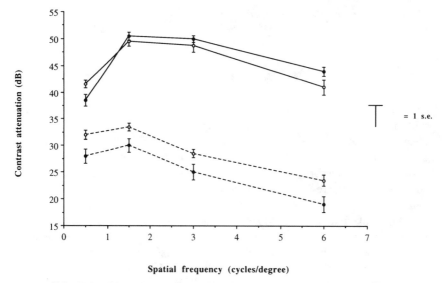

FIG. 15.2. Contrast sensitivity (plotted as mean contrast attenuation in decibels, db, as a function of spatial frequency). Open circles are children who passed the DT. Filled circles are children who failed the DT. The solid lines are the contrast sensitivity functions for static gratings presented for 1 s. Dashed lines are the contrast sensitivity functions for gratings presented for 1 s whose contrast was counterphase modulated at 20 Hz (flickered).

To support our hypothesis it was important to show that children with unstable binocular control demonstrate poor visual direction sense for small targets. We therefore developed a computer game to assess children's ability to localize dots visually. The subject was given a long time (2 s) to fixate a small target spot that could appear anywhere on the screen, so that any uncontrolled eye movements that might occur would show up. After a blank delay of half a second, a second test spot was displayed slightly to the left or right of the first for 200 ms. The child's task was to point whether the second spot had appeared to the left or right of the first. By adjusting the distance between first and second spots we could determine the accuracy of their localization of them. In full support of our hypothesis we found that those who failed the DT were significantly less accurate at localizing the dots in this task than either age- or reading age-matched controls (P. Riddell, Fowler, & Stein, 1990b).

It was also particularly interesting that whereas normal subjects were somewhat better at localizing dots on their left sides, our children with unstable binocular control were considerably worse when the second test spot was presented on the left side of the first; but they were almost as good as the normals when it appeared on the right. Recall also that these children's left eyes tended to wobble most when their eyes were converged, whereas in normal children it is the right eye that wobbles most.

PARIETAL NEGLECT

These results call to mind the left "neglect," which is so characteristic of patients with damage to the right posterior parietal cortex (see Riddoch & Humphreys, chap. 6, for more on this topic). Routinely we ask all the children we see to draw a clock, because this is a standard test used by neurologists to indicate whether a patient has visuospatial problems. Right parietal patients characteristically squeeze all the figures of the clock into the right-hand side leaving the left-hand side empty. Fig. 15.3 shows a clock drawn by a 7-year-old dyslexic boy. In a 65-year-old stroke patient it would be pathognomic of a right parietal lesion. Hence in this 7-year-old it suggests some abnormality there also. Such marked left neglect is admittedly comparatively rare in dyslexic children. Nevertheless we have found that a high proportion of children with unstable binocular control do draw poorly proportioned clocks, with the figures crammed into the right hand side. Eden (Eden, Stein, & Wood, 1991) showed that the tendency of reading-disabled children to draw clocks showing signs of left-sided distortion is much more common than in normal readers.

Another commonly used test for neglect is *symbol cancellation*. In such tests the subject has to cross out all of one type of symbol on a sheet containing a random mixture of small and large symbols, letters, and/or words. Eden et al. (1991) gave dyslexic children five different kinds of symbol cancellation charts. They found that in these relatively easy tasks, although the dyslexics did not make significantly more errors overall than normal controls, again what errors they did make tended to be on the left side, whereas normals were better on the left side.

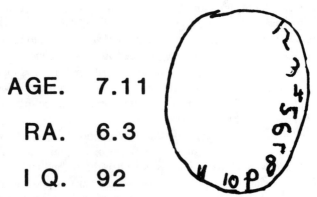

AGE.   7.11

RA.   6.3

I Q.   92

FIG. 15.3   Clock showing left neglect drawn by a 7-year-old dyslexic with unstable binocular control.

Eden et al. also found in a variety of other visuospatial tests that the number of errors the subjects made on their left sides was a good predictor of their reading ability. In 38 reading-disabled and normal children the correlation between left-sided errors and reading ability reached 0.45. The tests included immediate recall of the Rey figure, dividing errors into those made on the left and right of the figure; judgment of the orientation of lines on the left; dot localization on the left; and the stability of fixation with the left eye in the binocular fixation test mentioned earlier.

We have thus assembled a fairly convincing body of evidence suggesting that a mild disorder of the transient system in many dyslexics may cause unstable binocular control. This instability particularly affects fixation when the eyes are converged to look at small targets such as letters at the reading distance. Because the right posterior parietal cortex is the highest level for visuospatial perception, we were not surprised to find that children with poor vergence control showed evidence of impaired right posterior parietal function (Stein, P. Riddell, & Fowler, 1989). Indeed we have recently been able to show the converse; patients with a damaged right posterior parietal cortex show markedly impaired vergence control (Fowler, Munro, Richardson, & Stein, 1989).

VISUAL IMPAIRMENT: CAUSE OR EFFECT?

So far, however, nothing described here proves unequivocally that the visual imperfections we find in these children are a cause of their reading disability. It would be possible, though I believe perverse, to argue that visual abnormalities are either irrelevant, or merely a consequence of failing to learn to read. It has been suggested that learning to read may be what tunes up binocular stabilization, rather than vice versa (Bishop, 1989). Our reading age matches demonstrated that dyslexic children have worse binocular control than normal children reading at the same level as the dyslexics; this makes it highly unlikely that reading skill determines binocular stability.

Nevertheless we needed more direct evidence to convince the sceptics. First we wished to show that unstable eye fixation leads to particular kinds of reading error that are predictable from our theory. Next we needed to show that poor binocular control predicts future reading problems. But the strongest evidence that unstable binocular fixation causes reading problems came from being able to demonstrate that if we stabilize a child's binocular control then we improve reading.

NONSENSE WORD READING ERRORS

The unstable binocular fixation shown in dyslexic children enables us to make predictions about the types of reading error that might result from the visual confusion engendered by this instability. We have shown that the lines of sight of their two eyes may wander by as much as a degree of visual angle, so that up to four or five letters may move over each other, or merge. These confusions may give rise to disorders of the sequencing of letters and the generation of false ones, particularly if two merged ones are visually similar. Hence we would expect children with unstable binocular fixation to make bizarre letter order errors when trying to read. Their mind's eye presents them with merged and missequenced letters so we would expect them to tend to misread real words as nonsense words that are visually but not phonologically related to the target, rather than phonologically plausible real word alternatives.

So Cornelissen began to analyze the errors made by children who failed the DT in single word reading tests. He quickly found that the errors made by children who failed the DT did indeed tend to be nonsense words. The proportion of such nonword errors made by DT failures was significantly higher than that made by children who passed the DT (Cornelissen, 1991; Cornelissen, Bradley, Fowler, & Stein, 1991).

PHONOLOGICAL ERRORS

It has become clear, however, that most dyslexic children experience not only the visuospatial problems described here, but also the phonological ones that are better documented. It is well known that there are purely phonological reasons for making nonword errors, and these become more frequent the better a child's phonological skills. So it was important to rule out the possibility that the high nonword error rate observed in children who failed the DT was merely the result of impaired phonological rather than visual processing. Cornelissen therefore gave 45 children who failed the DT and 45 children matched for reading age and IQ but who passed the DT three identical word lists that were chosen to elicit about 50% errors. The three lists were printed in different size type: large, medium, or small. He found that when the print size was reduced the children who failed the DT made a larger proportion of nonword errors than those who passed it. This difference remained significant even after the fact that children of higher reading ability tend to make more nonword errors had been allowed for (Cornelissen et al., 1991). Thus a purely visual manipulation, reducing print size, increased the proportion of nonword errors made by the children who failed the DT; but small print did not affect the children who passed the DT. Because phonological factors had been kept rigorously constant the increased nonword error rate of those who failed the DT suggests that small print caused them visual confusion whereas it had no such effect on the controls. Therefore this result supports our hypothesis that children with unstable binocular control (DT failures) experience visual confusion when reading small print because the letters appear to move around; this unsteadiness generates nonwords visually, instead of the correct words they are trying to read.

Cornelissen found converse results, as would be expected, when he asked the children to read the word lists using only one eye. Those who failed the DT when they viewed the words monocularly made a significantly smaller proportion of nonword errors; whereas reading with one eye made no difference to those with stable binocular control (Cornelissen, Bradley, Fowler, & Stein, 1992). Thus again a purely visual manipulation was able to improve the reading of those with unstable binocular control, even when phonological factors were held completely constant.

These effects of print size and monocular viewing in children with unstable binocular control strongly imply that their ocular motor instability contributes causally to their reading difficulties. It is difficult to see how such results could be obtained if the development of stable binocular control were a consequence of learning to read. The children with stable binocular control who had the same IQ and reading ability as those with unstable binocular control failed to show them.

Another way of demonstrating a causal connection between acquisition of stable binocular control and reading progress is to show that in a cohort of children the former predicts the latter. We have followed a small group of children for their first 3 years in a primary school; and we have been able to show that this is indeed the case. Early acquisition of stable binocular control, as assessed by the DT, predicted more rapid progress in reading (Riddell, 1988). We are currently undertaking a larger study to confirm this result.

MONOCULAR OCCLUSION

Much of the confusion experienced by children with unstable binocular control probably arises because the two eyes are not working properly together, thus viewing print monocularly assists these children to read, as mentioned earlier. We also found that wearing monocular occlusion for 6 months for all reading and close work often has a permanently beneficial effect on these children's binocular control. In a pilot study carried out over 10 years ago we compared 15 children who failed the DT and were given monocularly occluding glasses to wear for 6 months, with 15 children of similar age, reading age, and IQ who were not given the glasses. The former not only improved their binocular control in the DT; but also their reading improved by nearly 12 months in the 6 months we observed them, whereas those who were not treated improved by less than 6 months, that is, their reading fell behind their chronological age still further (Stein & Fowler, 1981). In a subsequent placebo controlled trial we confirmed this result in a larger group of 98 dyslexic children who failed the DT and 47 who passed it. They were randomly assigned glasses that were either placebo or had the left lens occluded by opaque tape. Neither we nor the children knew who had been wearing the spectacles that were meant to help. They wore them only for reading, writing, and number work for a period of 6 months.

This study confirmed that monocular occlusion does indeed encourage the development of stable binocular control. Fifty-four percent of the treated children developed stable responses in the DT, compared with 24% of children who went stable spontaneously, a highly significant difference. But the study also warned us about the effect of occlusion on children who had already achieved stable binocular control. Occlusion did not help these; if anything it slowed down their progress.

The children who did achieve binocular stability by whatever means, whether spontaneously or with the help of occlusion, improved their reading by 11.5 months in the 6 months of observation. But the children who remained unstable improved by less than 6 months, as before. Bishop (1989) objected that the magnitude of the children's reading improvement depended on their initial reading age; but even after allowing for this, overall their improvements were much greater if their binocular control stabilized (Stein, 1989b).

We believe that monocular occlusion helps children to develop stable binocular control by simplifying the visuomotor problems imposed by binocular vision when reading. These arise from the fact that fine binocular control requires that the eye seeing a target be able to route its foveal signals to the ocular muscles moving it. This is known as "utrocular" control; it is absolutely required for accurate fixation. But the visual pathways beyond the striate cortex are mainly binocular; so information about which eye provides a given retinal signal is obscured. Occlusion of one eye may simplify the problem because only the retina of the seeing eye can now contribute to ocular motor control. If such monocular occlusion is carried out between the ages of 6 and 10 it seems to help a child to sort out the difficulties of utrocular routing, and permanent binocular stability often develops. After the age of 10 however we find that monocular occlusion seldom has a permanent effect, although reading with one eye can still help those with binocular instability to make less errors. In subjects over the age of 10 we have preliminary evidence that exercises designed to improve their vergence control, and in particular to promote stable fixation under conditions of convergence, may help them considerably.

It must be admitted however that our claims for monocular occlusion are still very controversial (Bishop, 1989). Nevertheless many other groups have found that occluding one eye can help dyslexic children's reading (C. D. Benton & McCann, 1969; D. B. Dunlop & P. Dunlop, 1975; Masters, 1988). We are now completing a third trial of monocular occlusion, which is producing much the same results as the previous two, namely that if the eye control of children with unstable binocular fixation stabilizes then their reading improves significantly, and sometimes dramatically; and this effect is independent of initial IQ or reading age.

PHONOLOGICAL SEGMENTATION
AND VISUOSPATIAL SKILLS

A major problem militating against the acceptance of the idea that reading problems are ever the result of a visual disorder is the very large body of evidence that demonstrates that most dyslexics have problems with phonological segmentation (Liberman, 1989). They are remarkably bad at reading nonwords (Snowling, 1987), rhyming and alliteration (Bradley & Bryant, 1983), and other phonological tasks. It is therefore widely agreed that the main problem faced by dyslexics is deficient phonological processing, probably associated with disordered development of the left temporal association cortex. Indeed it is often accepted without further argument that dyslexic children have no other impairments. However this is by no means a logical conclusion.

None of the evidence emphasizing dyslexics' phonological problems excludes the possibility that they may also suffer visual impairments. In 1985 (Stein & Fowler, 1985) we presented evidence that many of the children whom we found to have unstable binocular control on the DT were also poor at a phonological test (rhyming). More recently Eden et al. (1991) studied 38 children from the Bowman Gray Learning Disability Project (Winston Salem, NC, USA). We were able to make use of the large set of phonological and visuospatial test results that are available for these children, and to add to these the visuospatial and ocular-motor tests that we have been developing in Oxford.

Visual tasks testing children's ability to localize and orientate small targets, particularly on the left-hand side, together with those that indexed binocular stability, were almost as useful at discriminating between good and bad readers as phonological tests. This was because visual and phonological scores often correlated very highly with each other, and both were good predictors of reading ability. We were able to show that a statistical model that took into account chronological age, verbal IQ, the shared variance between a phonological task and our visual localization test, together with our binocular stability score, accounted for an extremely high proportion (65%) of the total variance in reading ability of our sample (Eden et al., 1991). These results therefore support the idea that children with reading problems often suffer disordered development of the specialized processing functions of both the left temporal association cortex, which is probably responsible for phonological segmentation, and of the right posterior parietal cortex, which organizes visuospatial skills.

A MAGNOCELLULAR DISORDER?

Possibly a common developmental disorder underlies both the phonological and visuospatial deficiencies. The large cells and heavily myelinated axons found in the magnocellular division of the visual system are not confined to vision. They are found in all sensory and motor pathways. Their most important function is to mediate fast transmission of signals coding rapid temporal modulations. Latest to mature (indeed some are not fully myelinated until the late teens), they are also the most vulnerable to disease. So it is possible that in dyslexic children a genetically controlled, or congenitally acquired, disorder of development of all magnocellular systems underlies the abnormal processing of visuospatial information and of ocularmotor control signals by the right hemisphere, and of phonological information by the left hemisphere.

CONCLUSION

There is now good evidence that many dyslexics suffer impaired operation of the transient, magnocellular division of their visual systems. The highest level of this pathway is the right posterior parietal cortex. Its functioning appears to be abnormal in many dyslexics because they show impaired localization on the left and mild signs of left neglect. In particular right posterior parietal malfunction leads to unstable binocular vergence control and inability to fixate stably on small targets such as letters, which need to be viewed with the eyes reliably converged at a close distance. This unstable binocular fixation gives rise to visual confusion, because the images seen by the two eyes may appear to move around independently and merge. Thus children with this problem have poor visual direction sense. Because their mind's eye presents them with a visual jumble, they make a high proportion of nonsense word errors when attempting to read. These visual problems of reading may be alleviated by monocular viewing. Moreover, 6 months' monocular occlusion for all reading and close work often improves their binocular stability permanently. If their binocular control stabilizes, then very often their reading progresses much faster thereafter. We have found that most children who suffer unstable binocular control are also poor at segmenting words phonologically. Thus phonological and visuospatial error rates are correlated in dyslexics, suggesting that both are a consequence of a common developmental abnormality. Possibly at the cellular level this disorder is the result of impaired development of the magnocellular neural systems responsible for signaling rapidly changing, transient, events; and whose highest cortical levels are the right posterior parietal and the left temporal association cortices.

REFERENCES

Andersen, R. (1989). Visual and eye movement functions of the posterior parietal cortex. *Annual Review of Neuroscience, 12,* 377–404.

Benton, A. L. (1991). Dyslexia and visual dyslexia. In J. F. Stein (Ed.), *Vision and visual dysfunction: Vol. 13. Vision and visual dyslexia* (pp. 113–120). London: Macmillan.

Benton, C. D., & McCann, J. W. (1969). Dyslexia and dominance. *Journal of Pediatric Ophthalmology, 6,* 220–222.

Bigelow, E. R., & MacKenzie, B. E. (1985). Unstable ocular dominance and reading ability. *Perception, 14,* 329–335.

Bishop, D.V.M. (1989). Unstable vergence control and dyslexia—a critique. *British Journal of Ophthalmology, 73,* 223–245.

Bishop, D.V.M., Jancey, C., & Steel, A. McP. (1979). Orthoptic status and reading disability. *Cortex, 15,* 659–666.

Bradley, L., & Bryant, P. (1983). Categorising sounds and learning to read—a causal connection. *Nature, 301,* 419–421.

Cornelissen, P. (1993). Fixation, contrast sensitivity and children's reading. In S. Wright & R. Groner (Eds.), *Studies in visual information processing: Facets of dyslexia and its remediation* (pp. 139–162). Amsterdam: Elsevier North Holland.

Cornelissen, P., Bradley, L., Fowler, S., & Stein, J. F. (1991). What children see affects how they read. *Developmental Medicine and Child Neurology, 33,* 755–762.

Cornelissen, P., Bradley, L., Fowler, S., & Stein, J. F. (1992). Covering one eye affects how some children read. *Developmental Medicine and Child Neurology, 34,* 296–304.

Dunlop, P. (1972). Dyslexia: The orthoptic approach. *Australian Journal of Orthoptics, 12,* 16–20.

Dunlop, D. B., & Dunlop, P. (1975). New concepts of visual laterality in relation to dyslexia. *Australian Journal of Ophthalmology, 2,* 101–112.

Eden, G., Stein, J. F., & Wood, F. B. (1991). *Visuospatial ability and language processing in reading disabled children.* Paper presented at 18th Rodin Conference, Berne, Switzerland.

Elkington, P., Kerr, G. K., & Stein, J. F. (1991). The effect of electromagnetic stimulation of posterior parietal cortex on saccadic eye movements. *European Journal of Neuroscience, Suppl. 4,* 4346.

Fowler, M. S., Munro, N., Richardson, A., & Stein, J. F. (1989). Vergence control in patients with posterior parietal lesions. *Journal of Physiology, 417,* 92P.

Fowler, M. S., & Stein, J. F. (1980). Visual dyslexia. *British Orthoptic Journal, 37,* 11–18.

Liberman, I. Y. (1989). Phonology and the beginning reader. In C. von Euler (Ed.), *Brain and reading* (Wenner Gren Symposium, No. 54). London: Macmillan.

Livingstone, M. S., Rosen, G. D., Drislane, F. W., & Galaburda, A. M. (1991). Physiological and anatomical evidence for a magnocellular defect in developmental dyslexia. *Proceedings of the National Academy of Sciences, USA, 88,* 7943–7947.

Masters, M. C. (1988). Orthoptic management of visual dyslexia. *British Orthoptic Journal, 45,* 40–48.

Mecacci, I., Sechi, E., & Levi, S. (1983). Abnormal visual evoked potentials in children with specific reading disability. *Brain and Cognition, 2,* 135–143.

Newman, S. P., Karle, H., Wadsworth, J. F., Archer, R., Hockly, R., & Rogers, P. (1985). Ocular dominance, reading and spelling: A reassessment of a measure associated with specific reading difficulties. *Journal of Research in Reading, 8,* 127–138.

Ogle, K. (1962). The optical space sense. In H. Davson (Ed.), *The eye* (Vol. 4, pp. 242–356). New York and London: Academic Press.

Riddell, P. (1988). Vergence eye movements and dyslexia. Unpublished doctoral dissertation, Oxford University.

Riddell, P., Fowler, M. S., & Stein, J. F. (1987). A comparison of sighting dominance and the Dunlop Test reference eye in reading disabled children. *British Orthoptic Journal, 44,* 64–69.

Riddell, C., Riddell, P., & Stein, J. F. (1990, April). Binocular instability in dyslexic children. Association for Research in Vision and Ophthalmology ARVO Meeting reports, Sarasota.

Riddell, P., Fowler, M. S., & Stein, J. F. (1990). Spatial discrimination in children with poor vergence control. *Perceptual and Motor Skills, 70,* 707–718.

Snowling, M. (1987). *Dyslexia: A cognitive developmental perspective.* Oxford: Blackwell.

Stein, J. F. (1989a). Representation of egocentric space in the posterior parietal cortex. *Quarterly Journal of Experimental Physiology, 14,* 583–606.

Stein, J. F. (1989b). Unstable vergence control and dyslexia. *British Journal of Ophthalmology, 73,* 319.

Stein, J. F. (1991). (Ed.). *Vision and visual dysfunction: Vol. 13. Visual dyslexia.* London: Macmillan.

Stein, J. F. (1992). Egocentric space and the posterior parietal cortex. *Behav. & Brain Sciences, 15,* 691–703.

Stein, J. F., & Fowler, M. S. (1981). Visual dyslexia. *Trends in Neurosciences, 4,* 77–80.

Stein, J. F., & Fowler, M. S. (1982). Diagnosis of dyslexia by means of a new indicator of eye dominance. *British Journal of Ophthalmology, 66,* 332–336.

Stein, J. F., & Fowler, M. S. (1985, July 13). Effect of monocular occlusion on visuomotor perception and reading in dyslexic children. *The Lancet,* 69–73.

Stein, J. F., Riddell, P., & Fowler, M. S. (1986). The Dunlop Test and reading in primary school children. *British Journal of Ophthalmology, 70,* 317.

Stein, J. F., Riddell, P., & Fowler, M. S. (1987). Fine binocular control in dyslexic children. *Eye, 1,* 433–438.

Stein, J. F., Riddell, P., & Fowler, M. S. (1988). Disordered vergence eye movement control in dyslexic children. *British Journal of Ophthalmology, 72,* 162–166.

Stein, J. F., Riddell, P., & Fowler, M. S. (1989). Disordered right hemisphere function in developmental dyslexics. In C. von Euler (Ed.), *Brain and reading* (Wenner Gren Symposium No. 54, pp. 139–159). London: Macmillan.

16 The Visual (Orthographic) Processor and Developmental Dyslexia

Philip H. K. Seymour
Henryka M. Evans
University of Dundee

INTRODUCTION

In recent years a "cognitive neuropsychological" approach has been successfully applied to the analysis of acquired disorders of reading and writing in adult neurological patients (see Ellis & Young, 1988; McCarthy & Warrington, 1990; Shallice, 1988). This approach, which derives from the innovative psycholinguistic studies of "deep" and "surface" dyslexia by Marshall and Newcombe (1973), emphasizes the importance of a model specifying the overall "cognitive architecture" of the reading and spelling systems. A key assumption has been that the appropriate unit for analysis is the *single patient* rather than the patient group (Caramazza & McCloskey, 1988).

Is there a place for a cognitive neuropsychological approach in the study of developmental disorders of reading and spelling? There have been a few examples of case study approaches, including Boder's (1973) studies of dysphonetic and dyseidetic patterns, and, more recently, investigations of adults or adolescents who display distinctive reading patterns that correspond broadly to the acquired conditions of "phonological dyslexia" or "surface dyslexia" (Campbell & Butterworth, 1985; Coltheart, Masterson, Byng, Prior, & Riddoch, 1983; Goulandris & Snowling, 1991; Seymour, 1986; Seymour & MacGregor, 1984; Temple & Marshall, 1983). However, there is currently a lack of consensus on the way in which such studies should be interpreted (see Bryant & Impey, 1986). This is in part an issue of whether or not dyslexic cases are functionally different from younger children at the same level of reading competence. The more fundamental point is whether studies of individual cases can provide information about *types* of reading disability or about the *causes* of the problem.

VISUAL PROCESSING AND DYSLEXIA:
IS THERE A CONNECTION?

If one looks at 'cognitive architecture' models (e.g., Ellis & Young, 1988) it becomes evident that the new systems (modules) specifically required for reading lie within a visual domain. They consist of procedures for visual analysis of print, recognition of words and graphemes, and pathways that transmit from a visual level to central processes concerned with meaning, speech, or phonological assembly. In this light, it may seem surprising that the prevailing wisdom is that the cause of dyslexia lies in the area of phonology rather than in the area of vision (Stanovich, 1988).

Visual explanations of dyslexia are typically stated in terms of a *peripheral* dysfunction, such as the "transient system" deficit discussed by Lovegrove, Martin, and Slaghuis (1986; Lovegrove & Williams, chap. 14), which somehow affects the efficiency of *central* reading processes. The problem for such accounts is one of establishing a bridge between a peripheralist (physiological) explanation and a higher level, cognitive explanation. In Fig. 16.1 this difficulty is approached by incorporating a peripheral component into a simple "cognitive architecture." Essentially, this proposes a distinction between the peripheral component, which is involved in the visual processing of all incoming information, and more central components consisting of specialized analyzers, one for the processing of print, and others for objects or other visual categories. The hypothetical print analyzer is referred to as the *visual (orthographic) processor*. General arguments for the separation of this system from other aspects of visual object processing have been considered by Seymour (1973, 1979) and by Warren and Morton (1982). In neuropsychology, the modularity of the systems is suggested by dissociations between pure alexia and agnosia for objects (Farah, 1991).

The model allows different ways in which a "visual deficit" could impair reading. The points at issue concern the locus of the primary deficit and the causal mechanism involved. Possible loci are: (a) the peripheral component; (b) an adjacent analyzer (e.g., object recognition); or (c) an impairment intrinsic to the orthographic processor itself. For the first two locations to be effective, a causal link extending into the orthographic processor would seem to be required [marked (a) and (b) in Fig. 16.1]. If so, a visually based dyslexia should always be marked by evidence of impaired functioning in the visual (orthographic) processor. The impairment at this level might then be expected to produce adverse effects on the higher, more central components of the reading process, such as word recognition or grapheme-phoneme translation [link (c) in Fig. 16.1].

The force of this analysis is to suggest that the correct place to look for visual deficits in dyslexia is in the visual (orthographic) processor. Such deficits might or might not be consequent on more peripherally defined disorders. The critical

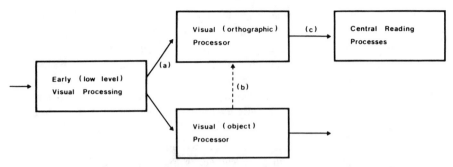

FIG. 16.1. Causal model for visually based reading impairments in which adverse influences located in peripheral (low level) processes affect the functions of a specialized visual (orthographic) processor, link (a), which in turn affects more central reading processes, link (c).

question is whether a visual orthographic impairment, however determined, produces consistent adverse effects on higher level, central reading functions.

MEASUREMENT OF VISUAL (ORTHOGRAPHIC) PROCESSOR FUNCTIONS

A large amount of work in experimental cognitive psychology has been directed at the analysis of visual orthographic processes. This includes tachistoscopic studies of word or nonword perception and various reaction time methods involving same–different judgments of letter arrays or effects of "format distortions," such as zigzag or vertical arrangement of letters (Seymour, 1987).

The matching procedures involve comparisons of letters at a physical identity (PI) level or above (Posner & Mitchell, 1967). Nominal identity (NI, cross case) matching was originally thought to involve a name code but is now seen as tapping a level of "abstract letter identities" (ALIs) (see Bigsby, 1988; Coltheart, 1982; Howard, 1987). In many theories of word recognition, the abstract letter code is viewed as the input to a word recognition (logogen) system.

In the present study two matching procedures were used as indicators of visual orthographic functions:

1. *Identity Matching*. This is a modification of Posner and Mitchell's (1967) letter matching task introduced by Beller (1970). A row of letters of varying length is displayed and the subject is instructed to indicate (by key press) whether or not all the letters are "same" according to a PI or NI criterion. In normal subjects RT is independent of array size. This is taken to reflect an early parallel

stage of the orthographic processor, which is sensitive to global identity or discrepancy.

The task involved the presentation on a VDU of 54 arrays of length 3, 5, or 7 letters. These were equally divided between upper, lower, and mixed case arrays. Half of the displays contained one different letter that occurred equally often in a left, central, or right position. Subjects were instructed to press the "Yes" key if all letters were physically or nominally the same, and the "No" key if a different letter was present.

2. *Array Comparison.* In this procedure two arrays of letters are presented simultaneously on the VDU and the subject is instructed to indicate, by key press, whether or not they are the same. The position of a single difference can be varied. The task appears to require an analytic point-by-point comparison. In normal subjects evidence of serial self-terminating processing is given by effects on reaction time of variations in array size and the number or position of differences.

The array comparison task was run as two subexperiments, each of 40 trials. A trial involved a warning signal followed by two horizontal arrays of five lowercase letters, aligned one above the other. Half the arrays consisted of legal letter sequences, and half illegal. The different letter was equally distributed across positions 1–5. Subjects were instructed to press a "Yes" key if the arrays were identical and a "No" key if a difference was present.

Previous studies using these methods have produced somewhat inconsistent results. N. Ellis (1981) found no reaction time difference between dyslexic and control groups in PI letter matching though there was an effect on NI matching. Bigsby (1990) conducted four experiments involving PI and NI letter matching. Individual analyses indicated that some, but not all, dyslexics showed marked impairments on these tasks. Similar results were obtained by Seymour (1986). Performance of adolescent and young adult cases was compared with controls on tests of identity matching, array comparison, and reading distorted words. Some cases showed large response delays in matching and an exaggeration of the length effect when reading distorted words.

There is, therefore, reason to argue that visual orthographic disturbances are present in a proportion of dyslexic cases. The present study aims to verify this conclusion for a new sample of younger cases. The question of whether or not visual orthographic impairments can be related to central reading disturbances is then addressed.

Method

Subjects. The dyslexic sample was recruited from various sources, including contacts with schools and referrals from educational, medical, and voluntary agencies. No exclusionary criteria were applied. The Appendix identifies the children by their initials and gives information on reading and spelling ages, chronological age, and verbal and performance IQ as estimated from a reduced WISC-R. The cases were treated as individuals in all subsequent data analyses. Note that they are arranged as four series in the Appendix, according to a scheme developed in the next two main sections of this chapter, and that the general information is given in Tables I.1, II.1, III.1, and IV.1 of the Appendix.

Control samples were drawn from a study of all members of the primary 3, 4, and 5 classes in schools located in Fife and Dundee. A few children who presented with evidence of reading difficulties were transferred to the dyslexic sample. This included occasional subjects who read words accurately but who had unexpectedly high error rates when attempting to read nonwords. The remaining children were placed into groupings defined by 1-year intervals according to (a) chronological age, and (b) Schonell reading age. Results obtained from this sample were used to define a normal range for each chronological and reading age represented in the dyslexic sample.

Procedure.   All subjects completed an identity matching experiment and an array matching experiment. An Apple II microcomputer was used to present the stimuli and to record reaction times and errors. The displays were created using a set of large clear upper- and lowercase letters and appeared at the center of a VDU driven by the computer. Each trial consisted of a warning signal (an array of asterisks), which was presented for 500 ms followed by a blank period of 1,500 ms followed by onset of the display that remained in view until one of two keys (designated "Yes" and "No") was pressed. The software determined whether or not the correct key had been pressed and measured the reaction time (RT), in ms, from onset of the display to closure of the switch. Advance to the next trial was controlled by the experimenter.

Results and Conclusion

The Appendix presents the mean reaction times and error rates in identity matching and array comparison for the individual dyslexic cases (Tables I.2, II.2, III.2, IV.2). Also shown are the ranges of scores obtained from the samples of normal readers at each chronological age level.

A dyslexic case was classified as having normal visual (orthographic) functions (V+) if both sets of reaction time and error scores fell within the range of the appropriate chronological age control group. It can be seen that approximately 50% of the sample had normal functions according to this criterion.

This investigation tends to confirm the results reported for older age groups by Seymour (1986) and Bigsby (1990). Although some dyslexic cases appeared impaired on visual (orthographic) tasks others were seemingly quite normal. These latter cases exhibit a *dissociation* between reading impairment and visual orthographic function. According to the arguments presented earlier, a peripherally defined impairment might be expected to affect central reading systems via the mediation of the visual (orthographic) processor [causal links (a) and (c) in Fig. 16.1]. The existence of cases whose visual orthographic functions are apparently unimpaired weakens the generality of this mechanism.

What of those cases who do show evidence of an impairment? One possibility is that the effects are functionally unrelated to the reading difficulty. On the other hand, given a cognitive architecture in which visual orthographic processing appears to provide input data to higher level functions, such as word recognition or grapheme-phoneme translation, it appears almost inevitable that a processor disturbance will produce damaging effects. This was the position adopted by Bigsby (1990):

> No subject who showed an impairment in ALI coding was a competent word reader. And, conversely, no normally competent reader showed an impairment of ALI coding. Since any reader who displayed an impairment of ALI coding also had problems with word recognition . . . results were taken to be consistent with a model which incorporates some measure of modular interdependence and which represents ALI coding as a necessary precursor of word recognition. (p. 261)

According to this account, a disturbance of visual (orthographic) processing is one factor that, if present, can produce problems in higher level functions (word recognition, grapheme-phoneme translation). Because not all cases show the effect, it must be concluded that there is some other factor, located elsewhere in the cognitive system, which can disturb central processing in other instances. It seems reasonable to suppose that adverse factors having different cognitive locations will result in different patterns of disturbance in the central systems. If so, "cognitive descriptions" of central reading functions formulated for cases without a visual orthographic disturbance will differ from descriptions constructed for cases with a visual orthographic disturbance.

The verification of this suggestion requires that we should have a method of describing dyslexic reading systems that will reveal functionally distinct patterns. This is the issue of *heterogeneity* in the dyslexic population, which is addressed in the next two sections.

DISTRIBUTION OF DYSLEXIC CASES

The possibility that the dyslexic population may be internally heterogeneous has been extensively if inconclusively discussed. Many researchers make group comparisons between undifferentiated dyslexic and control samples,   thus implying support for a homogeneous (single pattern) model. Others take the view that a few distinctive subtypes can be identified (e.g., the dysphonetic, dyseidetic, and mixed patterns of Boder, 1973) though a reliable procedure for identification has proved elusive.

A. W. Ellis (1985) contributed a helpful discussion. He distinguished between *extrinsic* and *intrinsic* typologies, and considered that the latter, which are formulated in terms of characteristics of the reading process itself, might be expressed categorically or dimensionally. He proposed that the most important dimensions reflected *lexical* (whole word) reading on the one hand, and *nonlexical* (phonic) reading on the other. He suggested that the distinction between the categorical and dimensional models could be discussed in terms of the *regional distribution* of cases on a two-dimensional surface defined by (a) success in whole word reading and (b) success in phonic (nonword) reading. Cases might be scattered continuously over such a surface, or, in the event that a categorical model was correct, might might fall into regionally localized clusters ("galaxies in multi-dimensional space," p. 191).

The definition of heterogeneity within the present sample was based on A. W. Ellis' (1985) approach. Assessments of word reading and nonword reading were used to locate each case on a two-dimensional surface. Individual analyses were then applied with the aim of determining the detailed patterns that occurred in different regions.

Method

Subjects

The normal and dyslexic cases who contributed the results on the visual matching tests also completed a cognitive investigation of their reading functions.

Tasks and Materials

Three principal tasks were employed, referred to as: (a) word vocalization; (b) nonword vocalization; and (c) semantic decision. It was assumed that they related to the three central processing pathways identified in the standard cognitive architecture of the reading system (e.g., Morton & Patterson, 1980; Seymour, 1986; A. W. Ellis & Young, 1988). These are (a) the lexical (morphemic) route to phonology, associated with the word vocalization task; (b) the nonlexical route to phonology (associated with the nonword vocalization task); and (c) the lexical (morphemic) route to semantics (associated with the semantic decision task).

Word Vocalization. The vocabulary was selected following a psycholinguistic analysis of a list of words used by 5- to 7-year-old children compiled by Edwards and Gibbon (1973). Three lists, each of 40 items, incorporating a variation in frequency of usage and length, were constructed to represent three levels of orthographic complexity, referred to as: (a) Regular, containing items pronounceable by simple letter-sound associations; (b) Rule, requiring a knowledge of pronunciations assigned to letter groups; and (c) Irregular, containing low frequency or unique correspondences. Examples of the lists appear in Seymour, Bunce, and Evans (1992).

Nonword Vocalization.   The nonwords were constructed by rearrangement of the orthographic components of the words. There was, therefore, a set of three nonword lists, derived respectively from the regular, rule, and irregular word lists, which paralleled the word lists in orthographic content and complexity.

Semantic Decision.   In these experiments a category name was presented on the screen followed by a blank period of 1,500 ms followed by presentation of a word. The subject was instructed to press the "Yes" key if the word was a member of the category and the "No" key if it was not. Items were equally divided between positive and negative instances and also varied in length and relatedness to the categories.

Procedure

Stimuli were presented via a VDU driven by an Apple II computer using large clear lowercase letters. In the vocalization tasks a voice-switch was used to detect the onset of speech and to measure vocal reaction times. Response information was entered by the experimenter on the keyboard.

Results and Conclusion

The distribution of the cases was determined by locating each subject on a two-dimensional surface defined by: (a) percentage of error in reading lower frequency words (y-axis); and (b) percentage of error in reading nonwords (x-axis). These values were treated as indices of Ellis' lexical (whole word) and nonlexical (phonic) dimensions. The resulting scatter of cases has been displayed in Fig. 16.2. It can be seen that, contrary to A. W. Ellis' (1985) expectations (see Figs. 1A and 1B of Ellis' article), the cases are not scattered over the full extent of the surface but tend to fall in the lower half of the space. This outcome is, of course, dependent on the difficulty of the lists (word frequency, orthographic complexity) and the use of actual scores (rather than standardized deviations from a control group mean). It does, however, agree broadly with the finding from the earlier study of adolescent cases (Seymour, 1990a). The indication is that error rates on nonwords are, in general, higher than error rates on low frequency words. (FH was the one exception in the present sample.) Within the lower segment the cases appear to be quite widely scattered. Obviously a much bigger sample would be needed in order to determine the actual distribution in the population at large.

The regions occupied by the normal controls at reading ages of 7, 8, and 9 years are shown in Fig. 16.2 as rectangles defining the upper and lower limits of the range on each measure. Although some cases fall beyond the control range

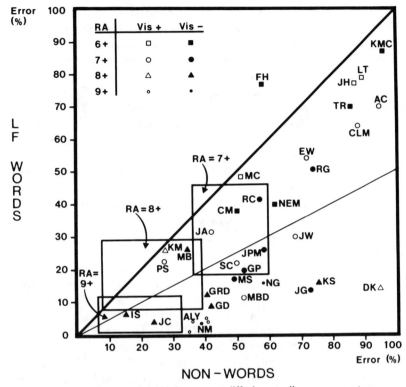

FIG. 16.2. Scatter of dyslexic cases at differing reading ages on a two-dimensional surface defined by: (a) percentage error in reading low frequency words; and (b) percentage error in reading nonwords. Cases with normal visual (orthographic) functions are marked by un-filled symbols. Rectangles indicate ranges of values for reading age controls. The lower part of the graph has been bisected into the upper and lower quadrants discussed in the text.

for errors on nonwords this is by no means true for all of them, indicating that a special difficulty with nonwords is probably not a fully general feature of dyslexia (see Olson, Wise, Conners, & Rack, 1990, for a discussion of this point).

CHARACTERISTICS OF CASES

The distribution displayed in Fig. 16.2 suggests a substantial measure of heterogeneity in the dyslexic sample. This is expressed in terms of error liability in word reading, error liability in nonword reading, and in the degree of discrepancy between the two measures. The cases who lie close to the diagonal of the graph demonstrate a small word–nonword discrepancy, whereas those who lie close to the base show a large discrepancy. These latter cases are instances of *phonological dyslexia* (nonword reading disproportionately poor relative to word reading). The previous studies with older children (Seymour, 1986, 1990a) suggest that the cases lying close to the diagonal are likely to show the features of *surface* or *morphemic dyslexia*.

On these grounds, the scatter of cases was divided into two regions, which are referred to as the upper quadrant and the lower quadrant (see Fig. 16.2). The previous studies suggest that the upper quadrant will contain cases showing the properties of morphemic or surface dyslexia while the lower quadrant will contain cases showing properties of phonological dyslexia. If this proposition can be verified, it will become possible to determine whether or not a visual (orthographic) impairment can be related to a particular class of central dyslexic impairment. In essence, this position will be discounted if any region of the graph that contains cases with similar properties includes cases who show no visual effect. The cases who do not show an effect have been indicated by unfilled symbols in Fig. 16.2.

The analysis of each individual involved a consideration of a number of key indicators. These included error and reaction time levels for high and low frequency words and nonwords. More specific reaction time indicators were (a) the effect of word length, that is, a processing rate in ms/letter; and (b) the form of the reaction time distribution, defined by a three category system, where A refers to "efficient" distributions in which almost all responses are bunched into a narrow range below 2,000 ms; C refers to "inefficient" dispersed distributions in which only a minority of responses fall below 2,000 ms; and B refers to intermediate distributions that include both a set of fast times (below 2,000 ms) and an extended tail of slower responses (see Seymour and Evans, 1992, for a definition of the categories). The other indicators were the error scores (%) for the Regular, Rule, and Irregular word lists, the number of error responses classed as "regularizations," and the error pattern (proportions of word and nonword responses to word or nonword targets). The values of these indicators are set out for the individual cases in the third and fourth tables of each section in the Appendix.

Upper Quadrant

The cases located in the upper quadrant were ranked according to distance from the origin of graph and were then examined individually. For purposes of presentation an arbitrary division was made between the most severely impaired cases (EW, RG, and beyond) and the remainder.

Very Impaired Cases

The results for the first subset of cases have been summarized in Section I of the Appendix. These subjects exhibited a severe "dual impairment," with the effect on the word recognition process indexed by (a) numerous errors on high frequency words; (b) a further increment in errors on low frequency words; and (c) slow response times (Category B or C distributions). An impairment of letter-sound translation is suggested by the high error rates and slow response times in nonword reading (B or C distributions). In some instances errors were mainly refusals (case JH) or word substitutions (EW, AC, LT, KMC), suggesting a lexical or logographic bias in reading. However, there was evidence of a compensatory use of phonological processing in the regularity effects, which were significant for all cases other than RG and FH, in the production of occasional regularized error responses, and in the production of appreciable numbers of nonword error responses (especially FH, CLM, and TR).

The results for the semantic categorization task (mean reaction time and error rate) were compared with the appropriate reading age control ranges. Two cases, RG and TR, had very high error rates (above 40%), probably reflecting an impoverished semantic system associated with a low verbal IQ (see Table I.1 of the Appendix). FH had extremely slow response times (C-distribution), which can be viewed as part of the morphemic dyslexia (word recognition impairment affecting both semantic and phonological access). The other cases performed within the range of their reading age controls on the categorization task.

Does a visual (orthographic) impairment dissociate from a severe and pervasive central dyslexia of this kind? In Fig. 16.2 cases who did not show an impairment on the visual matching tests (Vis+) are marked by unfilled symbols (see also Table I.2 of the Appendix). It can be seen that four severely impaired cases (EW, CLM, JH, AC) were within the range of their CA controls on the reaction time and error level measures for these tasks. We can conclude that visual orthographic processing efficiency *dissociates* from a severe dual reading impairment and cannot be assigned an essential causal role. The visual effects were restricted to FH, who had a high rate of error on the array comparison task, and to the low IQ cases (RG, TR, and KMC).

Stable Morphemic Cases

The Appendix provides a summary of the key data points for the remaining upper quadrant cases. As has already been noted these cases are expected to display a surface or morphemic pattern in which difficulty with irregular words and a tendency to produce regularized responses are dominant features (Coltheart et al., 1983). Theoretically, it is supposed that the primary feature in such cases is an impairment of the word recognition process. The positive indications of this are (a) a strong effect of word frequency; (b) a slow, dispersed reaction time distribution; and (c) a consistent (linear) effect of word length. This pattern is broadly present in the sample (see Table II.3 of the Appendix). All of the cases showed large word length effects (between 200 and 800+ ms/letter) and gave significant outcomes at $p < .05$ or better on an F test for linear trend. Error rate for low frequency words was often double the rate for high frequency words. Vocal reaction times in word reading were elevated and the distribution always included a tail of slow responses (B or C pattern). Evidence of compensatory processing via the nonlexical (phonological) process was provided by the large regularity effects and the production of regularized error responses (see Table II.4 of the Appendix). All cases produced regularized responses and all were significantly affected by regularity (contrast between regular and irregular words). Errors included large numbers of nonword responses and reflected a consistent antilexical bias in some instances (KM, CM, RC, MC). An additional feature, noted in a previous study of RC (Seymour, 1990a; Seymour & Bunce, in press), was that nonword reading tended to be somewhat less accurate than word reading but to have a very similar reaction time distribution. In Table II.3 the distribution patterns were the same or different by no more than one step on the category scale for six of the eight subjects. Three of the cases (CM, RC, NEM) were very slow on the semantic categorization task, with dispersed (type C) distributions and mean latencies above 5,000 ms, falling well outside the range of the appropriate reading age control.

A visual (orthographic) impairment might be expected in cases of morphemic dyslexia. The difficulty in recognition of whole words and the commitment to slow serial processing suggest an impaired recognition of groups of letters—a form of orthographic simultanagnosia. Results consistent with this view are provided by errors (MB) or delays in identity matching (CM, RC, NEM), a task that arguably requires parallel apprehension of sameness of letter forms. However, the proposal receives no general support because four of the cases (PS, KM, JA, MC) fell within the range of their CA controls on the measures of letter matching. On these grounds, we have to conclude that visual orthographic functions may dissociate from the morphemic dyslexic pattern.

Lower Quadrant

The cases in the lower quadrant were successful in word reading but disproportionately liable to error in nonword reading (phonological dyslexia). The most extreme case, DK, made errors on only 14% of low frequency words but on 95% of nonwords (see Seymour, 1990a, and Seymour & Bunce, in press, for earlier accounts of this case). A review of the lower quadrant cases suggested that a significant point of differentiation was the level of reaction time for correct responses to nonwords. Some subjects made fast but inaccurate responses to nonwords whereas others read nonwords by a slow and laborious process. In recognition of this point, the lower quadrant cases were divided into two subsets for purposes of presentation, referred to as Fast Nonword readers and Slow Nonword readers.

Fast Nonword Readers

Section III of the Appendix gives results on the key indicators for the cases who appeared to be inaccurate but fast in nonword reading. These subjects were all efficient in word reading, indexed by fast responses (A or B+ distributions), low error rates on high and low frequency words, and, GP excepted, absence of a substantial (> 100 ms/letter) effect of word length (see Table III.3 of the Appendix). Effects of regularity were generally small (Table III.4). Error rates in nonword reading were high, often exceeding 30% to 40%, but were associated with fast (A or B) distributions (Table III.3). Despite the inefficiency of letter-sound translation, use of a phonological strategy was suggested by (a) production of occasional regularizations; and (b) an appreciable incidence of nonword error responses, especially on the nonword lists (Table III.4).

This group might also be expected to give evidence of a visual (orthographic) impairment. The overcommitment to fast global responses could reflect a disorder of *analytic* orthographic processing, affecting the capacity to make detailed, point-by-point comparisons of letter arrays. Inspection of Table III.2 of the Appendix offers some support for this position. All but one of the cases aged 9 years or above (KF) showed a visual effect, usually a raised error rate on the array comparison task, but sometimes including identity matching. The two 8-year-old cases, DK and KEVM, were not affected. It is not possible, therefore, to assert that visual orthographic functions never dissociate from a central dyslexic pattern involving fast inaccurate responses to unfamiliar forms. However, the dissociation is evident in only 3 out of 11 cases and is restricted to younger subjects. The possible link with age does, of course, raise the possibility that the inaccurate matching is a consequence rather than a cause of the global strategy that has been adopted in reading.

Slow Nonword Readers

Results for the second set of lower quadrant cases are included in the Appendix. These cases also had low error rates for both high and low frequency words combined with disproportionately high error rates on nonwords (see Table IV.3). The word–nonword dissociation also appeared in the reaction time data. Responses to words, although somewhat slowed relative to the normal range, contained a preponderance of times below 2,000 ms (A-, B+, or B distributions). Responses to nonwords were much slower, often with mean latencies above 3,000 to 5,000 ms, and formed a widely dispersed distribution (C or B-pattern). Word length effects were small in some instances, but substantial effects, with a significant linear trend, occurred in other cases (RF, GRD, JPM, JW). This could indicate a partial involvement of phonological processing in word reading. Additional evidence is provided by the regularity effects and the production of regularized and nonword error responses (see Table IV.4).

If this pattern of phonological dyslexia was similar to the one found in the fast nonword readers we would expect to see evidence of a visual orthographic impairment affecting analytic processing (i.e., a difficulty with the array comparison task). However, this occurred for only one of the 10-year-old cases (GRD). Two (GD and JPM) were delayed on the identity matching task. The remainder (5/8 cases) performed within the range of their CA controls. A dissociation between phonological dyslexia and visual orthographic functioning is suggested.

GENERAL DISCUSSION

In this chapter, we have been concerned with two fundamental issues in the study of dyslexia: (a) the question of heterogeneity and (b) the question of causation. The problem is one of determining whether the dyslexic population is internally heterogeneous in a theoretically significant way, and, if so, to find a method of describing the heterogeneity. If heterogeneity is admitted, then the question of causation is complicated, because differing patterns of dyslexia may require differing causal explanations.

Heterogeneity

As already noted, heterogeneity may be discussed by reference to extrinsic or intrinsic criteria (A. W. Ellis, 1985). In our view, extrinsic criteria are not of theoretical interest unless a causal link exists between (a) a process external to the reading system; and (b) one or more components of the reading system itself. The critical issue, therefore, is whether or not dyslexic reading systems are heterogeneous.

Our position, following the work of Ellis and many others, was that the location of cases on a two-dimensional surface defined by scores on tests of word and nonword reading might be an appropriate indication of intrinsic heterogeneity. The degree of scatter exhibited in Fig. 16.2 seems sufficient to establish a *regional heterogeneity* of this kind, reflecting variations in degree of impairment (distance from the origin) and the word–nonword discrepancy (upper vs. lower quadrant). The method appears to offer a relatively straightforward way of revealing heterogeneity. This is encouraged by the apparent correspondence between regional location and functional characteristics uncovered by the review of the individual cases. The upper quadrant contained cases who displayed a severe dual impairment or a classic surface dyslexic (morphemic) pattern. Lower quadrant cases presented with the characteristics of phonological dyslexia (disproportionately poor nonword reading, sometimes associated with slow and laborious processing).

The lower quadrant (phonological) cases tend to be older and more competent on a standardized word recognition test than the upper quadrant cases. They are theoretically important because they have developed a (more or less) effective word recognition system despite the absence of normal letter-sound translation, processes. As such, they provide evidence of a *dissociation* between lexical and nonlexical processes in reading. This is most readily interpreted in terms of a traditional two-route model, because the results suggest that the nonlexical process may be operationally distinct, in terms of error liability and timing, from the lexical process, and that a lexical process can develop successfully even if the nonlexical process is severely impaired. The distinction between the fast and slow nonword readers may be one of teaching. Seymour and Bunce (in press) reported a longitudinal intervention study of subject DK from the present sample. Instruction designed to highlight elements of orthographic structure appeared to produce a shift from fast nonword reading to slow and laborious reading.

The upper quadrant cases have been presented as exhibiting a primary impairment of the word recognition process (morphemic dyslexia), which is indexed by the errors and the effects of frequency, regularity, and word length. These cases are most obviously described in terms of a single process model of the kind developed by Seidenberg and McClelland (1989). In such models, the effect of training is to elaborate a network that encodes both general and specific aspects of the correspondence between orthography and phonology. This network is involved in assigning pronunciation to unfamiliar forms (nonwords) as well as previously encountered words. The results from the simulations indicate that words have an advantage over nonwords and there are effects of frequency and regularity. Degradation of the system, by elimination of units or connections, tends to exaggerate these effects. Possibly the performance of the morphemic cases can be interpreted as reflecting partial learning in a single impoverished network of this kind. The suggestion in favor of a single network is supported by the striking similarity of the reaction time distributions for word and nonword reading. Seymour and Bunce (in press) monitored the progress of case RC in a longitudinal intervention study and found that changes in the reaction time pattern for words were consistently tracked by equivalent changes for nonwords.

These comments suggest a need for a reconsideration of the significance of impaired nonword reading in dyslexia. A standard view has been that poor nonword reading is a signal of a fundamental phonological problem (the "core deficit" of Stanovich, 1988). However, our results suggest that a difficulty in nonword reading might arise in at least three functionally distinct ways:

1. The fourth group of cases (slow nonword readers) exhibited a clear selective impairment of phonological assembly that was shown by their laborious and inaccurate attempts at reading unfamiliar forms. Further cases were described by Seymour (1986). It seems almost certain that a central problem in phonological working memory is implicated in these cases.

2. In the third group (fast nonword readers) the errors on the nonword lists

appeared to result from the adoption of an inappropriate fast global strategy. Although this could derive from a central phonological difficulty it is also arguable that it has a visual basis (an impaired analytic function).

3. For the upper quadrant morphemic cases difficulty with nonwords seemed to be conditional on the primary impairment of word reading and could reflect a central difficulty in internalizing orthographic structure or a visual disturbance (orthographic simultanagnosia).

On these grounds, it may be premature to treat difficulties in nonword reading as a unifying feature of dyslexia that implies the generality of a phonological cause.

Causation

The introduction to this chapter proposed a simple model (Fig. 16.1) by which a visual factor might function as a cause of dyslexia. The problem appeared to be one of bridging a gap between a cognitive description of the reading system and a cause defined at another level (anatomical, physiological). According to the proposal, a peripheral cause, such as a visual anomaly, might be expected to intrude into the cognitive component closest to the relevant sensory channel. This component was identified with a *visual (orthographic) processor,* a system specialized for the analysis and identification of printed forms [link (a) in Fig. 16.1]. Disruption of this system might, as suggested by Bigsby (1990), be expected to produce more central effects, giving rise to a particular pattern of developmental dyslexia [link (c)]. More specifically, we suggested two possible orthographic dysfunctions:

1. An impairment of a global, wholistic function, indexed by the identity matching task, might damage word recognition and give rise to a morphemic (surface) dyslexia.
2. An impaired analytic process, indexed by array comparison, might discourage the graphemic parsing necessary for nonlexical letter-sound translation and produce an apparent phonological dyslexia.

In this chapter we have not examined link (a) but have attempted to explore the validity of link (c).

The causal hypothesis can be assessed using either an *association* methodology or a *dissociation* methodology. In practice, dyslexia research has tended to favor an association method, such that:

$$\text{Dyslexia} = \text{Reading disability} + \begin{array}{c}\text{Causal} \\ \text{factor } X\end{array} + \begin{array}{c}\text{Other} \\ \text{factors}\end{array}$$

as in Stanovich's (1988) "phonological-core variable-difference" model. A theory of this kind is said to be supported if group studies reveal a correlation between reading disability and causal factor X, or if individuals are found who display the association (e.g., the phonological difficulties shown by Campbell & Butterworth's [1985] case, RE). According to this approach dyslexia appears analogous to a neurological *syndrome*, which is defined, minimally, by the co-occurrence of a reading problem (or a particular type of reading problem) and the proposed causal factor.

Using an association approach we might wish to claim that a role for visual (orthographic) factors in dyslexia had been demonstrated. A substantial number of cases performed outside the range of their chronological age controls on the matching tasks. Most of the cases in the lower quadrant fast nonword series (group 3) made errors on array comparison, consistent with the presence of an impaired analytic function. Three very clear morphemic cases—CM, RC, and NEM—showed effects in identity matching, possibly reflecting an impaired global function.

The position is less secure if a dissociation method is applied. The point here is that dissociations have more powerful theoretical implications than associations (Shallice, 1988). For example, Goulandris and Snowling (1991) reported a developmental case in whom surface dyslexia was accompanied by deficits in visual memory and viewed these as a probable cause of the dyslexia. However, Hanley, Hastie, and Kay (1992) described a further case who displays features of surface dyslexia and dysgraphia without an accompanying visual memory deficit. The discovery of negative instances of this kind effectively weakens confidence in the causal hypothesis.

Similar conclusions apply in the present study. Many children with reading difficulties, including some of the most severely impaired cases (upper quadrant, group 1) and clear cases of phonological dyslexia (lower quadrant, group 4), apparently had normal visual orthographic functions. Within the morphemic set (group 2), cases MC, JA, PS, MB, and KM did not show effects in identity matching although the dyslexic features (frequency effect, length effect, regularity effect, regularizations) were clearly present. Three cases in the fast nonword series (group 3), KEVM, KF and DK, were inaccurate in nonword reading but performed well within the control range on the array comparison task.

Strict application of a dissociation method therefore suggests that an essential causal role for a visual orthographic dysfunction has not been demonstrated for any of the subvarieties of dyslexia considered here. However, this conclusion could change following a fuller and more refined differentiation among the cases. For example, efforts to teach DK to read nonwords established clearly that his difficulties were phonological rather than visual (Seymour & Bunce, in press).

Role of the Visual (Orthographic) Processor

Our results appear problematic for theories asserting either: (a) that dyslexia has a visual cause (Lovegrove et al., 1986), or (b) that visual orthographic processing is critical for central reading functions (Bigsby, 1990). However, these conclusions are obviously critically dependent on the validity of the particular measures of visual orthographic functioning that we have used. In some process models (e.g., Newcombe & Marshall, 1980, or Seymour & MacGregor, 1984), a direct pathway to word recognition is postulated in addition to an orthographic procedure that operates on abstract letter identities. It is possible that procedures such as format distortion (Seymour, 1986, 1987) or visual matching tap only a subset of operations within the visual analysis stage of reading, perhaps those concerned with parsing and grouping of letter arrays and the normalizing of distortions. The situation could be analogous to the one found in neuropsychological studies of object recognition. Reviews by McCarthy and Warrington (1990) and Humphreys and Riddoch (1987) suggested the existence of a particular condition, referred to as "transformational agnosia," which damages the capacity to recognize objects which are degraded or presented from unusual views, even though recognition of normally presented objects may remain more or less intact.

According to this view, our results suggest that some cases exhibit an impairment of a transformational function of the visual orthographic processor but that this is not a critical factor in the production of a central (morphemic or phonological) dyslexia. This would not exclude the possibility that the impairment is of significance in other areas. The series studied by Seymour (1986) included three cases—RO, MF, and CE—in whom a visual orthographic impairment appeared to be the most obvious feature. These three subjects had difficulties, marked by reaction time delays, in same–different matching and in reading distorted words, particularly when the vertical format was used. In all three cases reading processes were reasonably efficient. There was, however, a suggestion of special difficulties in spelling, mainly of the surface dysgraphic type, that is, a lack of knowledge of word specific information, and a tendency to produce phonetically plausible spellings.

Conclusion

These results are somewhat inconclusive regarding the possible role of visual factors in the production of reading disorders. Visual orthographic impairments, as indexed by the matching tasks, appear not to be necessarily implicated in *phonological dyslexia* (laborious nonword reading) or in *morphemic dyslexia* (impaired word recognition). On the other hand, morphemic dyslexia is consistently associated with serial length dependent reading that may have a visual origin (orthographic simultagnosia). The possibility that an impaired analytic function and/or overcommitment to fast global processing may be related to inaccurate nonword reading remains open and deserves further investigation.

At a more general level, the study reinforces the conclusion that the dyslexic population is internally heterogeneous. This heterogeneity may conveniently be described by locating cases on a two-dimensional surface defined by success in word and nonword reading and by then undertaking more detailed analyses of individuals occupying particular regions of the surface. It appears likely that the scatter of cases will be found to be continuous but that reliable associations between regions and characteristics, broadly corresponding to the morphemic and phonological patterns, can be demonstrated.

With respect to causation, our argument has been that candidate causes need to be evaluated with due regard to the regional distribution and individual characteristics of the cases, and that greater weight should be given to dissociations than to associations. The general method outlined here can readily be applied to an assessment of the effects of a range of possible causes.

ACKNOWLEDGMENTS

The research described in this chapter was supported by a grant from the Medical Research Council of the UK. The cooperation of our subjects and their parents and teachers is gratefully acknowledged.

REFERENCES

Beller, H. K. (1970). Parallel and serial stages in matching. *Journal of Experimental Psychology, 84*, 213–219.

Bigsby, P. (1988). The visual processor module and normal adult readers. *British Journal of Psychology, 79*, 455–469.

Bigsby, P. (1990). Abstract letter identities and developmental dyslexia. *British Journal of Psychology, 81*, 227–263.

Boder, E. (1973). Developmental dyslexia: A diagnostic approach based on three atypical reading-spelling patterns. *Developmental Medicine and Child Neurology, 21*, 504–514.

Bryant, P., & Impey, L. (1986). The similarities between normal readers and developmental and acquired dyslexics. *Cognition, 24*, 121–137.

Campbell, R., & Butterworth, B. (1985). Phonological dyslexia and dysgraphia in a highly literate subject: A developmental case with associated deficits in phonemic processing and awareness. *Quarterly Journal of Experimental Psychology, 37A*, 435–476.

Caramazza, A., & McCloskey, M. (1988). The case for single-patient studies. *Cognitive Neuropsychology, 5*, 517–528.

Coltheart, M. (1981). Disorders of reading and their implications for models of reading. *Visible Language, 15*, 245–286.

Coltheart, M., Masterson, J., Byng, S., Prior, M., & Riddoch, J. (1983). Surface dyslexia. *Quarterly Journal of Experimental Psychology, 35A*, 469–495.

Edwards, R.P.A., & Gibbon, V. (1973). *Words your children use.* London: Burke Books.

Ellis, A. W. (1985). The cognitive neuropsychology of developmental (and acquired) dyslexia: A critical survey. *Cognitive Neuropsychology, 2*, 169–205.

Ellis, A. W., & Young, A. W. (1988). *Human cognitive neuropsychology.* London: Lawrence Erlbaum Associates.

Ellis, N. (1981). Visual and name coding in dyslexic children. *Psychological Research, 43*, 201–218.

Farah, M. (1991). Patterns of co-occurrence among the associative agnosias: Implications for visual object representation. *Cognitive Neuropsychology, 8,* 1–19.

Goulandris, N., & Snowling, M. (1991). Visual memory deficits: A plausible cause of developmental dyslexia? Evidence from a single case study. *Cognitive Neuropsychology, 8,* 127–154.

Hanley, J. R., Hastie, K., & Kay, J. (1992). Developmental surface dyslexia and dysgraphia: An orthographic processing impairment. *Quarterly Journal of Experimental Psychology, 44A,* 285–319.

Howard, D. (1987). Reading without letters? In M. Coltheart, G. Sartori, & R. Job (Eds.), *The cognitive neuropsychology of language* (pp. 27–58). London: Lawrence Erlbaum Associates.

Humphreys, G. W., & Riddoch, M. J. (1987). The fractionation of visual agnosia. In G. W. Humphreys & M. J. Riddoch (Eds.), *Visual object processing: A cognitive neuropsychological approach* (pp. 281–306). London: Lawrence Erlbaum Associates.

Lovegrove, W., Martin, F., & Slaghuis, W. (1986). A theoretical and experimental case for a visual deficit in specific reading disability. *Cognitive Neuropsychology, 2,* 225–267.

Marshall, J. C., & Newcombe, F. (1973). Patterns of paralexia: A psycholinguistic approach. *Journal of Psycholinguistic Research, 2,* 175–199.

McCarthy, R. A., & Warrington, E. K. (1990). *Cognitive neuropsychology: A clinical introduction.* London: Academic Press.

Morton, J., & Patterson, K. E. (1980). A new attempt at an interpretation, or, an attempt at a new interpretation. In M. Coltheart, K. E. Patterson, & J. C. Marshall (Eds.), *Deep dyslexia* (pp. 91–118). London: Routledge & Kegan Paul.

Newcombe, F., & Marshall, J. C. (1980). Transcoding and lexical stabilisation in deep dyslexia. In M. Coltheart, K. E. Patterson, & J. C. Marshall (Eds.), *Deep dyslexia* (pp. 176–188). London: Routledge & Kegan Paul.

Olson, R., Wise, B., Connors, F., & Rack, J. (1990). Organisation, heritability, and remediation of component word recognition and language skills in disabled readers. In T. H. Carr & B. A. Levy (Eds.), *Reading and its development: Component skills approaches* (pp. 261–322). London: Academic Press.

Posner, M. I., & Mitchell, R. F. (1967). Chronometric analysis of classification. *Psychological Review, 74,* 392–409.

Seidenberg, M. S., & McClelland, J. L. (1989). A distributed developmental model of word recognition and naming. *Psychological Review, 96,* 523–568.

Seymour, P.H.K. (1973). A model for reading, naming and comparison. *British Journal of Psychology, 64,* 35–49.

Seymour, P.H.K. (1979). *Human visual cognition: A study in experimental cognitive psychology.* West Drayton: Collier Macmillan.

Seymour, P.H.K. (1986). *Cognitive analysis of dyslexia.* London: Routledge & Kegan Paul.

Seymour, P.H.K. (1987). Word recognition processes: An analysis based on format distortion effects. In J. Beech & A. Colley (Eds.), *Cognitive approaches to reading* (pp. 31–55). Chichester, England: Wiley.

Seymour, P.H.K. (1990a). Developmental dyslexia. In M. W. Eysenck (Ed.), *Cognitive psychology: An international review,* (pp. 135–196). Chichester, England: Wiley.

Seymour, P.H.K. (1990b). Semantic processing in dyslexia. In D. A. Balota & G. B. Flores d'Arcais (Eds.), *Comprehension processes in reading* (pp. 581–602). Hillsdale, NJ: Lawrence Erlbaum Associates.

Seymour, P.H.K., & Bunce, F. (in press). Application of developmental models to remediation in cases of developmental dyslexia. In M. J. Riddoch & G. W. Humphreys (Eds.), *Cognitive neuropsychology and cognitive rehabilitation.* London: Lawrence Erlbaum Associates.

Seymour, P.H.K., Bunce, F., & Evans, H. M. (1992). A framework for orthographic assessment and remediation. In C. Sterling & C. Robson (Eds.), *Psychology, spelling and education* (pp. 224–249). Clevedon: Multilingual Matters.

Seymour, P.H.K., & Evans, H. M. (1992). Beginning reading without semantics: A cognitive study of hyperlexia. *Cognitive Neuropsychology, 9,* 89–122.

Seymour, P.H.K., & MacGregor, C. J. (1984). Developmental dyslexia: A cognitive experimental analysis of phonological, morphemic and visual impairments. *Cognitive Neuropsychology, 1,* 43–82.

Shallice, T. (1988). *From neuropsychology to mental structure.* Cambridge: Cambridge University Press.

Stanovich, K. E. (1988). Explaining the differences between the dyslexic and the garden variety poor reader: The phonological-core variable-difference model. *Journal of Learning Disabilities, 21,* 590–612.

Temple, C. M., & Marshall, J. C. (1983). A case study of developmental phonological dyslexia. *British Journal of Psychology, 74,* 517–533.

Warren, C., & Morton, J. (1982). The effects of priming on picture recognition. *British Journal of Psychology, 73,* 117–129.

APPENDIX

The appendix is organized into four sections, each referring to a series of cases, and provides information about: (a) psychometric details; (b) results on the visual orthographic tests; (c) characteristics of word and nonword reading; and (d) effects of regularity and error patterns.

I. First Series (Upper Quadrant: Very Impaired)

TABLE I.1

Chronological Ages, Schonell Reading and Spelling Ages, and Verbal and Performance IQs for Very Impaired Upper Quadrant Cases
(Ages in Years)

			Schonell		Wechsler	
Case	*Sex*	*CA*	*RA*	*SA*	*VIQ*	*PIQ*
RG	M	10.5	7.4	7.3	74	70
EW	F	8.1	7.2	6.3	87	81
FH	M	8.7	6.2	6.7	108	92
CLM	M	11.6	7.0	6.8	109	105
TR	F	8.5	6.5	6.6	66	70
JH	M	9.1	6.9	6.8	94	117
AC	F	8.8	7.0	6.2	108	100
LT	F	8.8	5.8	6.7	75	92
KMC	M	8.8	6.1	6.4	75	80

TABLE I.2
Control Ranges and Individual RT and Error Scores on the Identity
Matching and Array Comparison Tasks by Very Impaired Upper
Quadrant Cases (Visual Processor Status is Designated Normal (+)
If All Scores Fall Within the Chronological Age Control Range.)

	Visual Processor Status	Identity Matching		Array Comparison	
		RT (ms)	Error (%)	RT (ms)	Error (%)
8+ Control		942–2063	0–17	1509–3808	0–32
EW	+	1964	2	3103	4
TR	−	1864	0	4215	18
FH	−	1162	11	1932	40
KMC	−	2063	4	4916	5
AC	+	1283	13	2717	2
LT	?	—	—	—	—
9+ Control		900–1789	0–6	1243–3007	1–14
JH	+	—	—	2878	8
10+ Control		880–1593	2–6	1313–2740	0–5
RG	−	2068	4	2925	11
CLM	+	1217	0	2643	1

TABLE I.3
Mean Vocal Reaction Times (ms), Error Rates (%), Word Length
Effects (ms/letter), and Distribution Types in Word and Nonword
Reading, by Upper Quadrant Very Impaired Cases

		Words		Nonwords	Length Effect	Distribution Type	
		HF	LF			Words	Nonwords
RG	RT	2512	2906	3549	509**	B−	C
	E%	22	51	73			
EW	RT	2059	2970	3551	377*	B	B−
	E%	31	54	72			
FH	RT	4502	4261	5856	1139**	C	C−
	E%	50	77	58			
CLM	RT	1618	2264	2391	278*	B	B−
	E%	40	64	88			
TR	RT	1911	2672	2105	93	B	B
	E%	51	70	86			
JH	RT	2626	3423	3840	511	B−	C
	E%	71	80	87			
AC	RT	2748	2040	2868	−327	B	C
	E%	38	70	95			
LT	RT	5407	5991	5520	1850**	C−	C−
	E%	71	80	89			
KMC	RT	5540	9480	5143	438	C−	C−
	E%	67	87	96			

*, **Linear trend significant at $p < .05$ or $.01$

TABLE I.4
Error Rates (%) On Regular, Rule, and Irregular Lists, Number
of Regularized Error Responses, and Incidence of Word
and Nonword Responses to Word or Nonword Targets
(As % of All Errors, Refusals Included)

| | List | | | | Error Pattern | | | |
| | | | | | Words | | Nonwords | |
	Regular	Rule	Irregular	Regularizations	W	NW	W	NW
RG	43	15	40	2	88	12	45	55
EW	38	40	58**	4	80	14	53	38
FH	64	54	73	8	61	39	40	60
CLM	38	52	66***	2	52	47	40	60
TR	59	53	76*	3	57	43	56	44
JH	68	67	94**	0	26	3	20	29
AC	52	38	69*	2	89	5	85	13
LT	52	82	94***	2	44	12	54	11
KMC	75	—	89**	1	77	17	79	21

*, **, *** Regularity effect (regular vs. irregular) significant at $p < .05, .01$ or $.001$ by chi-square test.

II. Second Series (Upper Quadrant: Stable Morphemic)

TABLE II.1
Chronological Ages, Schonell Reading and Spelling Ages, and Verbal
and Performance IQs for Stable Morphemic Upper Quadrant Cases
(Ages in Years)

| | | | Schonell | | Wechsler | |
Case	Sex	CA	RA	SA	VIQ	PIQ
PS	M	8.7	7.5	7.7	84	117
KM	F	10.9	8.5	7.5	98	98
MB	F	9.2	8.2	7.6	81	73
JA	M	8.6	7.5	7.1	114	109
CM	F	7.6	6.8	6.3	107	108
RC	M	8.4	7.1	7.0	94	102
MC	M	7.7	6.8	7.3	87	106
NEM	M	8.2	6.9	6.1	117	98

TABLE II.2

Control Ranges and Individual RT and Error Scores on the Identity
Matching and Array Comparison Tasks by Stable Morphemic Upper
Quadrant Cases (Visual Processor Status Is Designated Normal (+) If
All Scores Fall Within the Chronological Age Control Range.)

	Visual Processor Status	Identity Matching		Array Comparison	
		RT (ms)	Error (%)	RT (ms)	Error (%)
7+ Control		1173–2251	0–18	1584–3653	1–19
MC	+	1647	6	3422	8
8+ Control		942–2063	0–17	1509–3808	0–32
CM	–	2109	2	4170	0
RC	–	2123	7	3477	8
JA	+	1230	2	3071	5
PS	+	974	9	2418	18
9+ Control		900–1789	0–6	1243–3007	1–14
NEM	–	2057	4	4317	2
MB	–	1126	15	2132	25
10+ Control		880–1593	2–6	1313–2740	0–5
KM	+	1233	4	2152	5

TABLE II.3

Mean Vocal Reaction Times (ms), Error Rates (%), Word Length
Effects (ms/letter), and Distribution Types in Word and Nonword
Reading, by Upper Quadrant Stable Morphemic Cases

		Words		Nonwords	Length Effect	Distribution Type	
		HF	LF			Words	Nonwords
PS	RT	1795	2456	3699	547**	B	C
	E%	7	23	27			
KM	RT	1475	1865	2672	231**	B+	B–
	E%	5	26	27			
MB	RT	1456	2137	2664	231*	B	B–
	E%	6	26	36			
JA	RT	1895	1611	1684	463**	B+	B+
	E%	15	32	42			
CM	RT	2160	2457	3084	496**	B–	B–
	E%	19	38	50			
RC	RT	3568	3809	3788	711**	C	C
	E%	32	42	57			
MC	RT	2029	3739	3542	873**	B–	C
	E%	22	49	51			
NEM	RT	2658	3126	2790	418**	B–	B–
	E%	21	40	62			

*, **Linear trend significant at $p < .05$ or $.01$

TABLE II.4

Error Rates (%) On Regular, Rule, and Irregular Lists, Number
of Regularized Error Responses, and Incidence of
Word and Nonword Responses to Word or Nonword Targets
(As % of All Errors, Refusals Included)

| | List | | | | Error Pattern | | | |
| | | | | | Words | | Nonwords | |
	Regular	Rule	Irregular	Regularizations	W	NW	W	NW
PS	8	0	28**	5	52	44	24	76
KM	7	8	28***	13	40	60	32	68
MB	5	14	33***	9	50	50	35	65
JA	11	24	32*	6	—	—	21	79
CM	15	18	49***	10	47	53	25	75
RC	28	25	50*	4	31	60	29	71
MC	20	30	61***	13	37	55	24	59
NEM	18	23	48***	7	72	28	32	68

*, **, *** Regularity effect significant at $p < .05, .01$ or $.001$

III. Third Series (Lower Quadrant: Fast Nonword)

TABLE III.1

Chronological Ages, Schonell Reading and Spelling Ages, and Verbal
and Performance IQs for Lower Quadrant Fast Nonword Cases
(Ages in Years)

| | | | Schonell | | Wechsler | |
Case	Sex	CA	RA	SA	VIQ	PIQ
IS	M	9.2	8.2	7.1	95	115
JC	F	9.8	8.6	7.4	98	113
NM	M	9.6	9.5	8.4	95	91
KEVM	M	8.2	9.2	10.3	100	68
KF	F	9.4	9.6	8.5	103	95
MS	M	10.1	7.9	7.8	82	90
GP	M	9.4	7.9	7.5	66	82
NG	M	10.0	9.2	8.3	87	90
JG	M	9.3	7.9	6.8	84	90
KS	F	8.7	8.1	7.9	94	88
DK	M	8.7	8.3	7.2	96	149

TABLE III.2

Control Ranges and Individual RT and Error Scores on the Identity
Matching and Array Comparison Tasks by Lower Quadrant Fast
Nonword Cases (Visual Processor Status is Designated Normal (+)
If All Scores Fall Within the Chronological Age Control Range.)

	Visual Processor Status	Identity Matching		Array Comparison	
		RT (ms)	Error (%)	RT (ms)	Error (%)
8+ Control		942–2063	0–17	1509–3808	0–32
KEVM	+	1687	2	2447	0
DK	+	1453	2	2972	2
9+ Control		900–1789	0–6	1243–3007	1–14
GP	−	1639	7	3393	1
KF	+	1061	2	1794	4
KS	−	1033	7	2054	15
10+ Control		880–1593	2–6	1313–2740	0–5
NG	−	1078	2	2040	10
JC	−	1221	0	2602	9
JG	−	1499	10	2489	25
NM	−	807	20	1728	9
IS	−	938	0	1415	6
MS	−	1368	7	2766	19

TABLE III.3
Mean Vocal Reaction Times (ms), Error Rates (%), Word Length
Effects (ms/letter), and Distribution Types in Word and Nonword
Reading, by Lower Quadrant Fast Nonword Readers

		Words		Nonwords	Length Effect	Distribution Type	
		HF	LF			Words	Nonwords
IS	RT	886	940	1275	15	A	A−
	E%	2	7	15			
JC	RT	1132	1335	1645	88*	B+	B+
	E%	3	4	24			
NM	RT	791	790	1764	20	A	B+
	E%	2	4	39			
KEVM	RT	821	924	1101	−20	A−	A−
	E%	1	5	41			
KF	RT	995	1109	1307	25	A−	B+
	E%	1	1	35			
MS	RT	1042	1115	1598	9	A−	B+
	E%	5	18	49			
GP	RT	1055	1280	1743	141**	B+	B
	E%	5	19	52			
NG	RT	1193	1342	1763	75*	B+	B
	E%	11	16	58			
JG	RT	1386	1324	2117	38	B+	B
	E%	6	14	73			
KS	RT	1086	1133	1596	8	A−	B+
	E%	4	16	75			
DK	RT	1250	1300	1799	−2	B+	B+
	E%	11	14	95			

*, ** Linear trend significant at $p < .05$ or .01

TABLE III.4
Error Rates (%) on Regular, Rule, and Irregular Lists, Number
of Regularized Error Responses, and Incidence of Word
and Nonword Responses to Word or Nonword Targets
(As % of All Errors, Refusals Included)

| | List | | | | Error Pattern | | | |
| | | | | | Words | | Nonwords | |
	Regular	Rule	Irregular	Regularizations	W	NW	W	NW
IS	3	1	5	1	—	—	32	61
JC	2	3	5	0	—	—	29	71
NM	3	3	2	3	—	—	23	77
KEVM	0	2	8	5	—	—	49	51
KF	2	0	3	1	—	—	29	71
MS	6	9	15*	8	59	41	54	46
GP	9	5	24*	4	50	50	47	52
NG	7	13	20*	5	64	36	31	69
JG	7	10	18*	3	63	37	44	56
KS	8	10	12	0	93	7	40	60
DK	14	9	16	0	—	—	25	75

*, **, *** Regularity effect significant at $p < .05$, .01, or .001

IV. Fourth Series (Lower Quadrant: Slow Nonword)

TABLE IV.1
Chronological Ages, Schonell Reading and Spelling Ages,
and Verbal and Performance IQs for Lower Quadrant
Cases with Slow Nonword Reading (Ages in Years)

| | | | Schonell | | Wechsler | |
Case	Sex	CA	RA	SA	VIQ	PIQ
ALY	F	8.2	9.5	9.0	131	131
RF	F	11.3	9.1	9.4	79	86
GD	M	8.8	8.7	7.5	115	118
GRD	M	11.8	8.5	7.8	67	96
MBD	M	8.5	7.7	7.5	94	104
SC	M	9.7	7.9	7.5	88	105
JPM	M	8.1	7.3	6.8	113	106
JW	F	9.0	7.8	7.2	87	115

TABLE IV.2
Control Ranges and Individual RT and Error Scores on the Identity
Matching and Array Comparison Tasks By Lower Quadrant Slow
Nonword Cases (Visual Processor Status is Designated Normal (+)
If All Scores Fall Within the Chronological Age Control Range.)

	Visual Processor Status	Identity Matching		Array Comparison	
		RT (ms)	Error (%)	RT (ms)	Error (%)
8+ Control		942–2063	0–17	1509–3808	0–32
ALY	+	1449	6	3702	2
MBD	+	1189	9	2791	13
9+ Control		900–1789	0–6	1243–3007	1–14
JW	+	1158	4	2597	4
GD	−	2111	6	2496	5
SC	+	1374	4	2131	5
JPM	−	2121	9	2455	10
10+ Control		880–1593	2–6	1313–2740	0–5
RF	+	957	0	1735	5
GRD	−	1498	0	3427	10

TABLE IV.3
Mean Vocal Reaction Times (ms), Error Rates (%), Word Length
Effects (ms/letter), and Distribution Types in Word and Nonword
Reading, by Lower Quadrant Slow Nonword Cases

		Words		Nonwords	Length Effect	Distribution Type	
		HF	LF			Words	Nonwords
ALY	RT	1090	976	5288	63*	A−	C+
	E%	0	5	36			
RF	RT	1242	1543	3863	123**	B+	C+
	E%	7	4	42			
GD	RT	1104	1299	2723	107	A−	B−
	E%	7	9	42			
GRD	RT	2085	2615	5914	234*	B	C−
	E%	9	12	41			
MBD	RT	1794	2129	3779	68	B+	C
	E%	2	12	52			
SC	RT	1087	1270	3856	55	A−	C
	E%	8	22	50			
JPM	RT	1631	2053	2964	210**	B	C+
	E%	10	26	59			
JW	RT	1798	2728	4060	515**	B	C
	E%	12	30	68			

*, **Linear trend significant at p < .05 or .01

TABLE IV.4

Error Rates (%) on Regular, Rule, and Irregular Lists, Number
of Regularized Error Responses, and Incidence of Word
and Nonword Responses to Word or Nonword Targets
(as % of All Errors, Refusals Included)

| | List | | | | Error Pattern | | | |
| | | | | | Words | | Nonwords | |
	Regular	Rule	Irregular	Regularizations	W	NW	W	NW
ALY	0	0	7	2	—	—	17	78
RF	3	8	4	1	—	—	27	43
GD	3	6	12	4	—	—	33	67
GRD	4	15	11	2	—	—	26	64
MBD	3	8	14*	6	65	35	37	63
SC	38	55	42	7	44	56	31	69
JPM	10	18	21*	2	69	31	26	74
JW	14	15	36***	2	90	8	49	50

*, **, *** Regularity effect significant at p < .05, .01, or .001

376

17 Disabled and Normal Readers' Eye Movements in Reading and Nonreading Tasks

Richard K. Olson
Helen Forsberg
University of Colorado

INTRODUCTION

Differences between disabled and normal readers' eye movements were first observed during the 1930s through the painstaking analysis of photographic records (for review, see Tinker, 1946). A number of these early studies reported that when disabled readers read text that was appropriate for their age level, they made more frequent fixations, shorter saccades, and proportionally more regressive saccades than normal readers. This discovery led many researchers and practitioners to argue that erratic eye movements were a primary cause of reading problems, and disabled readers could be helped through training in eye movement exercises. This idea achieved some popularity in the 1940s and 1950s. Many eye movement monitoring and training devices were sold to the schools and optometrists often prescribed eye movement training for their reading-disabled patients. However, careful studies with appropriate control groups revealed that eye movement training yielded no unique improvement in reading skills (Taylor, 1965; Tinker, 1958). Nevertheless, a number of practitioners continue to recommend eye movement training with disabled readers (cf. Cohen, 1988). In support of their approach, they cited studies by Pavlidis (1981a, b) reporting disabled readers' erratic eye movements in both reading and nonreading tasks.

There has been a resurgence of studies on eye movements in disabled readers, partly due to the recent development of more efficient computer-based techniques for monitoring eye movements and analyzing the resulting voluminous data. The purpose of this chapter is to provide an overview of this recent research with particular attention to studies in our own laboratory. We have been monitoring eye movements in disabled and normal readers since 1979 within an NIH-sponsored program project titled "Differential Diagnosis in Reading Disability." The first section briefly discusses the subject sampling procedures, general research strategies, and major results in other parts of the program project that are important for interpreting the group comparisons of disabled and normal readers' eye movements. The remainder of the chapter is presented in two main sections, one dealing with studies of eye movements in reading, the other with eye movements in nonreading tasks.

PROGRAM PROJECT:
DIFFERENTIAL DIAGNOSIS
IN READING DISABILITY

It is widely recognized that reading disability is a heterogeneous disorder and that sampling procedures may have a significant impact on the results from comparisons of disabled and normal readers. The Colorado Reading Project was formed to conduct an epidemiological and behavioral-genetic study of specific reading disability in children from grade 3 through high school. Our early studies were based on samples of disabled and normal readers referred from the Boulder schools. Later studies of genetic influence were based on samples of identical and fraternal twins ascertained from records of their reading behavior in 27 Colorado school districts (DeFries, Olson, Pennington, & Smith, 1991). To be considered reading disabled, children had to have a history of reading problems in their school and they had to score below the tenth percentile, by local norms, on a composite score that included the word recognition, spelling, and comprehension subtests of the Peabody Individual Achievement Test (PIAT; Dunn & Markwardt, 1970). A normal comparison group had no indication of reading disability in their school records and generally scored above the 40th percentile on the PIAT. Other traditional inclusionary criteria for the disabled and normal groups included a score of 90 or above on the verbal or performance subscale of the Wechsler Intelligence Scale for Children, Revised (WISC-R, Wechsler, 1974), no uncorrected sensory deficits, no overt evidence of neurological disorder such as seizures, normal school attendance, and English as their first language.

Several of the studies obtained subjects from clinic referrals or from small and expensive special schools for learning-disabled children. It is uncertain how representative these children are of disabled readers in the public schools. Even referrals by teachers from public schools can result in a strong gender bias for males that is much reduced when the samples are ascertained directly from school records of reading performance. A valid epidemiological study of the varieties of reading disability requires direct ascertainment from school records followed by extensive testing in the laboratory. We used this selection procedure to provide an unbiased estimate of the frequency of unique eye movement patterns and other problems in disabled and normal readers.

The subjects were administered a wide variety of tests in 2 ½-hour morning and afternoon sessions. The standardized WISC-R IQ and PIAT tests along with several other widely used psychometric tests of memory and naming speed were administered in a session at John DeFries' laboratory. The other session in our laboratory included a number of experimental measures developed to assess component reading, language, and visual processing skills, including the eye movement measures discussed in this chapter. The broad range of measures was selected at the beginning of the project to be sensitive to the varieties of visual and auditory deficits proposed in the literature. We are in the process of adding new visual-temporal processing measures recommended by Breitmeyer and Lovegrove and Williams (Chaps. 5 and 14, respectively).

Before turning to our studies of eye movements, it is important to document the differences we have found between disabled and normal readers in other domains. Although all of the children in the disabled group met the minimum IQ criterion described above and they averaged about 101 on the performance scale versus 97 on the verbal scale, the average full-scale IQ for the normal sample was about 10 points higher with no significant difference between the verbal and performance subscales. The normal readers' higher scores are consistent with the mean level of performance in the school districts used for the sample. Instead of matching disabled and normal groups on IQ, we have observed the relations between various components on the IQ test and performance in other measures of reading, language, and perceptual skills. After all, at least some aspects of IQ must be reciprocally related to reading ability (Stanovich, 1986).

When our same-age groups of disabled and normal readers are compared on reading and other language-based tasks such as those in the WISC-R verbal subtests, there are significant differences between the groups. However, the magnitudes of differences between age-matched groups vary with different reading and language subskills. This could be because some skills, such as oral vocabulary, are partly constrained by the lower exposure to print attained by most disabled readers (Stanovich, 1986). Larger deficits in other skills suggest their causal role in reading disability. To better understand the etiology of reading disabilities it is helpful to know which reading and related skills are actually lower than expected for the disabled readers' level of reading skill (Bryant & Goswami, 1986).

In several studies we have matched older disabled readers (mean age about 15) with younger normal readers (mean age about 10) on a reliable measure of word recognition and then ascertained that there were no significant regression effects on a second measure of word recognition (Conners & Olson, 1990; Olson, 1985; Olson, Wise, Conners, & Rack, 1990; Olson, Wise, Conners, Rack, & Fulker, 1989). When so matched, the older disabled group was significantly better in their raw scores on the different subtests of the WISC-R, including verbal measures such as oral vocabulary. They were also significantly better on measures of both reading and listening comprehension, perhaps aided by their higher level of general knowledge. However, the older disabled readers were significantly and substantially worse in a task that required them to read non-words such as "tegwop" aloud (phonological coding). Most studies from other laboratories have found a similar result (Rack, Snowling, & Olson, 1992). The other measures that have shown deficits greater than expected from level of word recognition include oral language tasks that require subjects to segment and manipulate a spoken word's phonemic components. For example, the disabled group was significantly worse in a "pig latin" task that required subjects to segment the initial phoneme, place it at the end of the word, and add the sound "ay" (e.g., pig = igpay) (Olson et al., 1989). Our attempts to find deficits in the *same* disabled readers' eye movements should be viewed with these results in mind.

EYE MOVEMENTS IN READING

Eye movement monitoring during disabled and normal subjects' reading of stories was initially introduced in the program project to address two basic questions. First, are there group differences in reading eye movements that cannot be accounted for by word-decoding problems in texts that are too difficult for the disabled readers? Second, are there important within-group individual differences in eye movement reading style that might be related to differences in children's profiles of component reading and related cognitive skills? This section addresses these questions following a brief description of our general methods in the eye movement studies. Research from other laboratories is reviewed where relevant.

Reading Materials and Methods
for Monitoring Eye Movements

Children in the program project read stories aloud from a computer screen while their eye movements were recorded (see Olson, Kliegl, & Davidson, 1983a; Olson, Kliegl, Davidson, & Foltz, 1985, for details). The stories were selected from the Spache (1963) diagnostic reading scales based on the subjects' word-recognition level. The story grade levels assigned to subjects were selected to be difficult enough to produce a number of word recognition errors but easy enough so that they could understand the stories. All subjects above the seventh-grade level in word recognition read the highest available eighth-grade level Spache stories. Eight comprehension questions were asked at the end of each story. The stories ranged in length from about 200 words at the higher grade levels to about 100 words at the lower grade levels. The stories were presented in a 60-character, 11 double-spaced line format, 3 character spaces per degree of visual angle, in white characters on a black background.

The eye tracker was an Applied Science Laboratories model 1996. It measured eye position 60 times per second with an absolute position accuracy of plus or minus one character. The system tolerated sufficient head movement to allow subjects to read the paragraphs aloud. Subjects were initially calibrated as they fixated a 9-point grid prior to reading each story. The 60-Hz samples, including information about pupil diameter, horizontal, and vertical position, were reduced off line to fixation positions by character and line position, sequence, and duration. From these data we computed a large number of eye movement variables, including average forward saccade length and percentage of forward saccades that are the primary measures discussed in this chapter. Forward saccade length was computed in character spaces for left-to-right movements along a line. The percent of forward saccades was computed from all eye movements larger than the system's movement resolution of about ⅓ degree of visual angle, excluding return sweeps to the beginning of the next line. Thus, 100 minus the percentage of forward saccades equals the percentage of regressive eye movements.

Between-Group Comparisons of Reading Eye Movements

The first analyses compared groups of same-age normal and disabled readers on eye movements in the Spache stories (Olson, Kliegl, & Davidson, 1983b). The disabled subjects from the referred Boulder school sample were matched on age to normal children from the same schools. In spite of the disabled subjects' very substantial deficit in reading level, there were only minor differences between the two groups' eye movements, probably because the reading material was adjusted for the subjects' level of word recognition. The disabled group's slightly shorter average saccade length was associated with the generally shorter words in their stories.

A second age-matched group comparison was recently reported on data from a large sample of identical and fraternal twins (Olson, Conners, & Rack, 1991). The reading disabled group ($N = 118$), compared to a same-age normal group ($N = 112$), had significantly shorter forward saccade length in character spaces (5.36, sd .83 vs. 6.34, sd .74), and a lower percentage of forward saccades (77%, sd .05 vs. 81%, sd .05). However, this comparison included reading-disabled children at the very low text levels who made a very large number of decoding errors. No normal readers were in these very low reading levels. In addition, those older disabled readers who were assigned to the eighth-grade level stories were substantially lower in reading ability and made more word-recognition errors than the older normal subjects who read these stories.

Olson et al. (1991) used the large twin sample to match 72 older disabled and younger normal subject pairs on level of word recognition and their Spache stories. The matched pairs excluded the younger disabled readers and older normal readers for whom a match could not be found. There were no significant differences between the disabled and normal groups respectively in forward saccade length (5.82, sd .93 vs. 5.63, sd .78), or percentage of forward saccades (78%, sd .06 vs. 77%, sd .05). It is apparent from these results that the small but statistically significant differences found for the age-match groups were due to the difference in word decoding problems. From this we conclude that the frequently reported abnormal eye movements in text for disabled readers are predominantly a consequence rather than a cause of their reading difficulty.

The opposite view has been presented by Pavlidis (1981b). He informally reported results for disabled readers with normal IQ, "retarded" readers with low IQ, normal readers, and advanced readers. The groups were given reading material at or near their level of reading skill. Pavlidis reported that his fourteen disabled readers were particularly distinguished from the other groups by their much higher percentage of regressive saccades, which we estimated from Pavlidis' work (1981b, fig. 6.5, p. 132) to be 30% for the disabled group and less than 10% for the other three groups. (This regression rate for normal subjects is about half the average rate found in our studies.) In a recent review of this work, Pavlidis (1991, p. 265) stated that the disabled readers' "abnormal eye movements may have caused their reading problems." However, we found it difficult to evaluate Pavlidis' (1981b) brief report because of conflicts between data reported in his tables and figures. In addition, the 14 disabled readers who met his lengthy list of exclusionary criteria were selected from 49 children referred from clinics and special schools for learning-disabled children in England. Pavlidis was well known through a BBC television program for his work on eye movements and it seems possible that there might have been some referral bias toward children with eye movement problems (Pollatsek, 1983). In any case, this sample is not likely to be representative of specific reading disability in the general population.

We are not aware of any other large group studies using reading-level-match comparisons or text that has been carefully adjusted for the subjects' reading level. A recent study by Fletcher (1991) compared the eye movements of 10 normal and 10 reading-disabled 15-year-old adolescents while they read sentences that were syntactically ambiguous or semantically anomalous. The word-difficulty level was at about the fourth grade so that word decoding would not be a problem for the disabled readers. Fletcher presented a detailed evaluation of different eye movement patterns associated with different error recovery strategies. General eye movement parameters, including saccade length and frequency of regressions, were also evaluated. There were no significant differences between the disabled and normal groups in either the error recovery patterns or basic eye movement parameters.

There have been case studies reported by Ciuffreda, Bahill, Kenyon, and Stark (1976), Elterman, Abel, Daroff, Dell'Osso, and Bornstein (1980), Pirozzolo and Rayner (1979), and by Zangwill and Blakemore (1972) of disabled readers whose eye movements in easy text were clearly abnormal and dominated by regressive saccades. Morris and Rayner (1991) labeled these subjects "visual-spatial dyslexics," and argued that they were rare compared to "language deficit dyslexics" whose abnormal eye movements were due to word decoding problems. Our research suggests that the "visual-spatial" cases are rare indeed. No subjects in our current program project sample of 223 disabled readers expressed such extreme abnormalities. (The combined sample of 223 disabled readers consists of 105 subjects referred from the Boulder schools and 118 twins ascertained from school records). However, the range of "normal" behavior is quite broad in measures such as the percentage of forward saccades.

Within-Group Individual Differences in Reading Eye Movements

Recall that the standard deviations were quite large for forward saccade length and the percent of forward saccades within our reading level-matched samples of disabled and normal readers (Olson et al., 1991). These eye movement variables were normally distributed within both groups. There was an equally wide range of performance within the groups and the distributions were almost perfectly overlapped. For example, the wide range of performance on the percent of forward saccades is indicated by a few disabled and normal readers who had less than 65% forward saccades and by a few disabled and normal readers with more than 85% forward saccades.

Several lines of evidence indicated that the within-group variability in eye movement behavior was not simply due to error variance. In our most recent analyses (Olson et al., 1991), the split-half reliability was .95 for forward-saccade length and .88 for percentage of forward saccades. In addition, after adjustment for subjects' level of word recognition, there was a significant negative correlation of $r = -.47$ between forward-saccade length and the percentage of forward saccades, that is, subjects who made longer forward saccades tended to make more frequent regressive eye movements.

Earlier studies of the referred Boulder school sample found modest but significant correlations between the within-group variance in disabled readers' eye movements and several measures of component reading skills and verbal IQ (Olson, 1985; Olson et al., 1985). Those analyses were based on locating fixations at the word level and calculating a combined measure of forward and regressive movements that skipped words. Disabled readers who were high on this normally distributed dimension tended to have higher verbal IQ scores. Eye movement data from the twin sample have not yet been subjected to this type of analysis. Instead, we have focused on another interesting issue.

Data from identical and same-sex fraternal twin pairs has allowed us to assess the relative influence of genetic and environmental factors on individual differences in eye movements (Berry & Olson, in press; Olson et al., 1991). Both types of twin pairs are assumed to have the same degree of shared environment in their homes and schools, but monozygotic (MZ) twins share the same genes whereas dizygotic (DZ) twins share only half their segregating genes on average. Therefore, evidence for genetic etiology is provided if the MZ twins are significantly more similar than the DZ twins. The sizes of the MZ and DZ twin intraclass correlations can be used to estimate the degree of genetic (h^2), shared environment (c^2), and specific environment influence (e^2) (Plomin, DeFries, & McClearn, 1990). In the traditional procedure of comparing within-group intraclass correlations for MZ and DZ twin pairs, h^2 (the proportion of variance due to genetic factors) is estimated by doubling the difference between the MZ and DZ correlations. The difference between the MZ correlation and 1.0 represents the proportion of variance due to test error and environmental influences not shared within families (e^2). The proportion of shared within-family environmental influence (c^2) is the MZ correlation minus h^2.

Because the distributions for disabled and normal readers' eye movement variables were similar and the heritability estimates were not significantly different for the two groups, the samples were combined for a more statistically powerful analysis. The most recent analysis by Berry and Olson (1991) was based on data from 124 MZ and 129 DZ twin pairs. After adjusting the eye movement variables for their very small relation to subjects' level of word recognition, the heritability for forward saccade length was $h^2 = .53$, SE $= .23$. The heritability for the percent of forward saccades was $h^2 = .66$, SE $= .23$. As indicated by the standard errors, both heritability estimates were significantly greater than zero. The estimates for shared environment influence (c^2) were near zero and not significant, indicating that the environmental influence, which includes test error, is not shared between members of twin pairs.

It is important to note that the significant heritability found for disabled and normal readers' eye movements was present after adjusting the subjects' eye movement scores for their relations to level of word recognition. Therefore, the heritability of individual differences in eye movements was completely orthogonal to the same subjects' significant heritability for individual differences in word recognition reported by Olson, Gillis, Rack, DeFries, and Fulker (1991).

Summary of Results for Reading Eye Movements

We found no significant group differences in eye movements between the reading level-matched disabled and normal groups and only small differences for the age-matched groups. Our results are in conflict with the extreme differences reported by Pavlidis (1981b) for his select group of 14 disabled readers, and with the results of a few case studies of disabled readers. On the other hand, our results are consistent with the recent study by Fletcher (1991) and with the earlier conclusion of Tinker (1958) that disabled readers' abnormal eye movements are a consequence of their reading problems.

The analyses of twin data indicated significant heritability for eye movement patterns in reading that was independent from the same subjects' substantial heritability for individual differences in word recognition. We speculate later about the meaning of the significant genetic influence on eye movements after considering a similar genetic influence on nonreading eye movements described in the next section.

EYE MOVEMENTS IN NONREADING TASKS

The program project included two nonreading tasks. As in the preceding review of disabled and normal children's eye movements in reading, we begin with our group comparisons and discuss similar studies in other laboratories. Then we turn to the within-group individual differences and heritability analyses for nonreading eye movements.

Group Comparisons of Nonreading Eye Movements

The "Pavlidis Test" and Related Studies. Our exploration of nonreading eye movements was stimulated by Pavlidis' (1981a) report that a group of 12 disabled readers was extremely different from normal group in a simple tracking task. He had his subjects sequentially fixate a series of five small LED lights as they were illuminated from left-to-right and right-to-left. The lights were separated by 5 degrees of visual angle. The two end lights were illuminated for 2 s and the middle three lights for 1 s each. Pavlidis' results were striking. His disabled group averaged 26 fixations in each left-to-right sweep across the five lights. Normal subjects averaged only 8 fixations and there was no overlap for the normal and disabled distributions. In addition, there was no overlap in the group distributions for the mean percentage of regressive eye movements (disabled mean = 35%; normal mean = 12%).

Olson, Kliegl, and Davidson (1983b) attempted a replication of Pavlidis' (1981a) study, except that lights were replaced by black dots against the white background on a computer monitor. (Pavlidis', 1991, current version of the "Pavlidis Test" uses a similar computer display.) We compared the eye movements of 34 reading-disabled children with 36 normal children in the referred sample from the Boulder schools. We found no significant group differences for the mean number of eye movements in each sweep across the five positions (disabled = 9.24; normal = 9.28). Moreover, the range for the disabled group was 4.8 to 13.8 fixations, similar to the normal group. None of our disabled subjects had as many fixations in this task as reported by Pavlidis for all 12 of his disabled subjects. In addition, there were no group differences in the mean percentage of regressive eye movements (disabled = 19%; normal = 20%). Note that the percent of regressive movements in our normal sample was nearly twice as large as that reported by Pavlidis. This may be because our eye monitor was more sensitive to subjects' small corrective saccades.

Two other laboratories concurrently attempted similar but less exact replications of Pavlidis' (1981a) study (Brown et al., 1983; Stanley, Smith, & Howell, 1983). Neither study found significant group differences although Stanley et al. mentioned that one of their disabled subjects seemed distinctly abnormal in their tracking task. Pavlidis (1991) responded that none of the replication failures are valid because they did not use exactly the same task and the subjects were not true dyslexics who would fit his detailed selection criteria. As in his previously discussed study of reading eye movements, the disabled subjects in his tracking study were selected from a larger group of children referred from clinics and special schools in England. It was not clear if the same subjects were used in both the reading and tracking studies.

Pavlidis (1991) reported a new study of 62 normal readers and 87 disabled readers from special schools for learning-disabled children in the United States. Highly significant group differences were reported for "off target" fixations and number of fixations although no means and standard deviations were presented. The tracking task was claimed to have correctly classified 90.5% of the disabled readers but the classification rate for the normal subjects was not given. Based on this study and his earlier work, Pavlidis strongly promoted his test and related equipment for diagnostic screening in the schools, even for preschoolers. He also recommended the use of computer displays that present one word at a time in the same location to circumvent disabled readers' problematic eye movements.

We are aware of only one similar tracking study that has been published since the initial flurry of activity during the early 1980s. A recent study of Spanish children by Martos and Vila (1990) included a tracking task that was nearly identical to the "Pavlidis Test." The study is quite interesting because of its epidemiological nature with solid design and statistical analyses. Teachers initially referred 209 children who they thought were "dyslexic" out of a total population of 3,500. Forty of these children, 1.1% of the school sample, met the authors' selection criteria. Thirty of these children participated in the study. It seems likely that this lowest 1% of the population was much more extremely reading disabled than the average in our studies, but only the minimum criterion of 2 years behind chronological age was mentioned. The study compared 30 disabled readers with IQ greater than 95, 30 equally poor readers with an IQ between 75 and 90, and 30 normal readers. The disabled readers' mean number of saccades (58, sd 10) was significantly greater than the low IQ poor readers (50, sd 11), but not significantly different from the normal group (50, sd 12). The disabled readers' mean percent of regressive movements (22%, sd 8) was significantly greater than for both the poor readers (19%, sd 9) and the normal readers (16%, sd 9). However, it should be noted that the disabled group differed from the normal group by only about two-thirds standard deviation. This substantial overlap between the groups is radically different from the completely nonoverlapping and widely separated distributions reported by Pavlidis (1981a). In addition, there were significant interactions between the subjects' three age groups (7–9, 10–11, > 12) and reading group for differences in percent regressions and number of saccades. It was only the oldest disabled group ($N = 10$) that was significantly different from the other groups, and it may have been only a few subjects in this group that contributed to the difference. Therefore, it appears that whereas the present group results are quite different from those of Pavlidis, there may have been a small minority of older children in this apparently severe reading-disabled sample that had distinctly abnormal eye movements.

Group Differences in Target Search Eye Movements.   After failing to replicate Pavlidis' (1981a) results we decided to design a target-search task that would be more difficult, would require subjects to scan essentially the same distributions of spatial frequencies as in reading, and would be nonverbal (Olson, Conners, & Rack, 1991). In addition to monitoring subjects' eye movements, we were interested in their absolute level of accuracy in the task. The task required subjects to decide if a target string of two symbols (e.g., <?) presented for 2 s at the left side of the screen was present in the same order and orientation once, twice, or not at all in a subsequently displayed character string:

$$/)@[@ \ !=\backslash= \ [@ \ \{*+*><+\}\}>@] -\$ \ ][\} \ \#\%?([\$+/ -<!\$ @?- \\ \&<?\#\backslash\%$$

For the previous example, the correct answer is "one." The search string was displayed for 6 s or until the subject responded. All strings contained either one target, two targets, a mirror image foil but no target, or a transposition foil but no target. There were 10 strings of each type.

Comparisons of the age-matched disabled ($N = 129$) and normal ($N = 146$) groups showed that the normal group was significantly more accurate in the target-present (61% vs. 52%) and foil conditions (71% vs. 58%). There was a .75 standard deviation difference between the groups in combined accuracy, in contrast to a much larger 2.73 sd group difference in word recognition. At least part of the group difference may have been due to the normal readers' greater familiarity with the symbols even though they were not letters. For eye movements, the normal group displayed significantly shorter forward saccades (6.1, sd 1.1 vs. 6.6, sd 1.3), and a significantly larger percent of forward saccades (78%, sd 7, vs. 74%, sd 7). However, the group distributions overlapped to a great extent.

Analyses were also performed on 101 reading level-matched pairs. On the target present trials, the disabled group scored 55% vs. the younger normals' 45%, a significant difference, but the older disabled subjects were nonsignificantly worse on the foil trials (59% vs. 63%). There were *no* significant differences in eye movements and the distributions for the groups were completely overlapping.

Within-Group Individual Differences in Nonreading Eye Movements

In spite of the high split-half reliabilities for forward saccade length (.91) and percent of forward saccades (.94) in the target search task, there was substantial within-group variance. The two eye movement variables were negatively correlated ($r = -.78$), more strongly than in reading. Between reading and target search, partial correlations for subjects' forward saccade length and percent forward saccades were $r = .33$ and $r = .44$ respectively, after controlling for age and word recognition. Thus, there were modest but significant similarities between subjects' reading and target search eye movements that were independent of reading ability and age.

Heritabilities for the target search, eye movement variables were not significantly different between the disabled and normal groups so the samples were combined for a total sample of 152 MZ pairs and 96 DZ pairs. The heritability estimates were $h^2 = .36$, SE $= .26$, for positive saccade length and $h^2 = .79$, SE $= .24$, for percent of forward saccades after adjusting the variables for age and word recognition. Only the heritability for the percent of forward saccades was significantly greater than zero.

SUMMARY AND CONCLUSIONS

The two main questions of the program project study were: (a) Are there significant differences between disabled and normal readers' eye movements in school ascertained samples? (b) Are there significant within-group individual differences? The answer to the first question was clear. For the large sample of disabled readers ascertained in the Colorado schools, there were no significant group differences for both reading and nonreading eye movements when compared to reading level-matched normal subjects. The minor differences between the age-matched groups could be attributed to their difference in word decoding problems and/or reading experience.

Results from the program project epidemiological study were contrasted with those reported by Pavlidis for his smaller samples of disabled readers referred from clinics and special schools for learning-disabled children (1981a,b, 1991). His report that disabled readers had distinctly abnormal eye movements and there was no overlap with the distributions for normal readers is difficult to reconcile with our results. We suggested the likely possibility of a referral bias toward children with eye movement problems. In addition, there were inconsistencies in the reported results for the earlier studies and a vagueness in the most recent report that made Pavlidis' studies very difficult to evaluate.

Also in apparent conflict with our results for disabled readers ascertained in the schools, a number of case studies have been published on disabled readers with distinctly abnormal eye movements that did not seem to be a direct result of their difficulty in reading. The small epidemiological study of Martos and Vila

(1990) also indicated that there are a few severe disabled readers with abnormal eye movements. However, the absence of *any* clearly abnormal eye movement patterns in our sample of over 200 disabled readers indicates that the abnormal pattern must be extremely rare. The results of our epidemiological study strongly argue against Pavlidis' (1991) recommendations that children should be screened for eye movement problems for the diagnosis of reading disability or that they should use special technology to read without eye movements. Our results also provide no support for programs that attempt to train disabled readers' eye movements.

Regarding the second main question of within-group individual differences, we found that there was a wide range of "normal" eye movement behavior, and there were significant correlations between subjects' reading and nonreading eye movements. We explored the relations between individual differences in eye movements, performance in various visual and language tasks, and genetic influence. Some modest within-group correlations have been found between disabled readers' word-skipping eye movements and verbal IQ (Olson et al., 1985), but most of the reliable within-group variance in both reading and nonreading eye movements was unrelated to any of our broad range of reading, language, and perceptual processing measures.

Analyses of identical and fraternal twin data provided significant evidence of genetic influence on individual differences in both reading and nonreading eye movements, but we have no evidence regarding the mechanistic pathway for this genetic influence. George McConkie (personal communication) suggested that individuals might vary in their peripheral acuity and this might lead to differences in saccade length and regressive fixations.

Finally, it appears at first glance that our eye movement results are out of step with a dominant theme of this volume. In particular, Breitmeyer (chap. 5), and Lovegrove and Williams' (chap. 14) findings of transient channel deficits in vision have been linked in theory to disabled readers' problems in saccadic suppression of iconic images from earlier fixations. It seems plausible but not necessary that this type of deficit would produce differences between disabled and normal readers' eye movements. Of course it is possible that for some reason disabled readers in our school sample have more language-based deficits and fewer visual deficits than the disabled readers in studies of transient channel function. It is also possible that phonological processing and transient-channel deficits coexist in disabled readers because of some common underlying neurological deficiency. We plan to address these questions by adding measures of transient channel sensitivity to the program project test battery.

ACKNOWLEDGMENTS

The research was supported in part by NICHD Grant Nos. HD 11683, HD 22223, and HD 27802.

REFERENCES

Berry, C., & Olson, R. K. (in press). Heritability of eye movements in normal and reading-disabled individuals. *Behavior Genetics.*

Brown, B., Haegerstrom-Portnoy, G., Adams, A. J., Yingling, C. D., Galin, D., Herron, J., & Marcus, M. (1983). Predictive eye movements do not discriminate between dyslexic and control children. *Neuropsychologia, 21,* 121–128.

Bryant, P. E., & Goswami, U. C. (1986). Strengths and weaknesses of the reading level design: A comment on Backman, Mamen, and Ferguson. *Psychological Bulletin, 100,* 101–103.

Ciuffreda, K., Bahill, A. T., Kenyon, R. V., & Stark, L. (1976). Eye movements during reading: Case reports. *American Journal of Optometry and Physiological Optics, 53,* 389–395.

Cohen, A. H. (1988). The efficacy of optometric vision therapy. *Journal of the American Optometric Association, 59,* 95–105.

Conners, F., & Olson, R. (1990). Reading comprehension in dyslexic and normal readers: A component skills analysis. In D. A. Balota, G. B. Flores d'Arcais, & K. Rayner (Eds.), *Comprehension processes in reading* (pp. 557–579). Hillsdale, NJ: Lawrence Erlbaum Associates.

DeFries, J. C., Olson, R. K., Pennington, B. F., & Smith, S. D. (1991). Colorado reading project: An update. In D. Duane & D. Gray (Eds.), *The reading brain: The biological basis of dyslexia* (pp. 53–87). Parkton, MD: York.

Dunn, L. M., & Markwardt, F. C. (1970). *Examiner's manual: Peabody Individual Achievement Test,* Circle Pines, MN: American Guidance Service.

Elterman, R. D., Abel, L. A., Daroff, R. B., Dell'Osso, L. F., & Bornstein, J. L. (1980). Eye movement patterns in dyslexic children. *Journal of Learning Disabilities, 13,* 312–317.

Fletcher, J. (1991). Qualitative descriptions of error recovery patterns across reading level and sentence type: An eye movement analysis. *Journal of Learning Disabilities, 24,* 568–574.

Martos, F. J., & Vila, J. (1990). Differences in eye movements control among dyslexic, retarded and normal readers in the Spanish population. *Reading and Writing: An Interdisciplinary Journal, 2,* 175–188.

Morris, R. K., & Rayner, K. (1991). Eye movements in skilled reading: implications for developmental dyslexia. In J. F. Stein (Ed.), *Vision and visual dyslexia* (pp. 233–242). London: Macmillan.

Olson, R. K. (1985). Disabled reading processes and cognitive profiles. In D. Gray & J. Kavanagh (Eds.), *Biobehavioral measures of dyslexia* (pp. 215–244). Parkton, MD: York Press.

Olson, R. K., Conners, F. A., & Rack, J. P. (1991). Eye movements in dyslexic and normal readers. In J. F. Stein (Ed.), *Vision and visual dyslexia* (pp. 243–250). London: Macmillan.

Olson, R. K., Gillis, J. J., Rack, J. P., DeFries, J. C., & Fulker, D. W. (1991). Confirmatory factor analysis of word recognition and process measures in the Colorado Reading Project. *Reading the Writing: An Interdisciplinary Journal, 4,* 43–56.

Olson, R. K., Kliegl, R., & Davidson, B. J. (1983a). Dyslexic and normal readers' eye movements. *Journal of Experimental Psychology: Human Perception and Performance, 9,* 816–825.

Olson, R. K., Kliegl, R., & Davidson, B. J. (1983b). Eye movements in reading disability. In K. Rayner (Ed.), *Eye movements in reading: Perceptual and language processes* (pp. 467–479). New York: Academic Press.

Olson, R. K., Kliegl, R., Davidson, B., & Foltz, G. (1985). Individual and developmental differences in reading disability. In G. E. MacKinnon & T. G. Waller (Eds.), *Reading research: Advances in theory and practice* (Vol. 4, pp. 1–64). New York: Academic Press.

Olson, R. K., Wise, B., Conners, F., & Rack, J. (1990). Organization, heritability, and remediation of component word recognition and language skills in disabled readers. In T. H. Carr & B. A. Levy (Eds.), *Reading and its development: Component skills approaches* (pp. 261–322). New York: Academic Press.

Olson, R. K., Wise, B., Conners, F., Rack, J., & Fulker, D. (1989). Specific deficits in component reading and language skills: Genetic and environmental influences. *Journal of Learning Disabilities, 22,* 339–348.

Pavlidis, G. Th. (1981a). Do eye movements hold the key to dyslexia? *Neuropsychologia, 19,* 57–64.

Pavlidis, G. Th. (1981b). Sequencing, eye movements and the early objective diagnosis of dyslexia. In G. Th. Pavlidis & T. R. Miles (Eds.), *Dyslexia research and its applications to education.* Chichester, England: Wiley.

Pavlidis, G. Th. (1991). Diagnostic significance and relationship between dyslexia and erratic eye movements. In J. F. Stein (Ed.), *Vision and visual dyslexia* (pp. 263–270). London: Macmillan.

Pirozzolo, F. J., & Rayner, K. (1978). The neural control of eye movements in acquired and developmental reading disorders. In H. Avakian-Whitaker & H. A. Whitaker (Eds.), *Advances in neurolinguistics and psycholinguistics.* New York: Academic Press.

Plomin, R., DeFries, J. C., & McClearn, G. E. (1990). *Behavior genetics: A primer;* San Francisco: W. H. Freeman.

Pollatsek, A. (1983). What can eye movements tell us about dyslexia? In K. Rayner (Ed.), *Eye movements in reading: Perceptual and language processes* (pp. 511–521). New York: Academic Press.

Rack, J. P., Snowling, M. J., & Olson, R. K. (1992). The nonword reading deficit in developmental dyslexia: A review. *Reading Research Quarterly, 27,* 29–53.

Spache, G. D. (1963). *Diagnostic reading scales.* New York: McGraw-Hill.

Stanley, G., Smith, G. A., & Howell, E. A. (1983). Eye movements and sequential tracking in dyslexic and control children. *British Journal of Psychology, 74,* 181–191.

Stanovich, K. E. (1986). Matthew effects in reading: Some consequences of individual differences in the acquisition of literacy. *Reading Research Quarterly, 21,* 360–407.

Taylor, S. (1965). Eye movements while reading: Facts and fallacies. *American Educational Research Journal, 2,* 187–202.

Tinker, M. A. (1946). The study of eye movements in reading. *Psychological Bulletin, 43,* 93–120.

Tinker, M. A. (1958). Recent studies of eye movements in reading. *Psychological Bulletin, 55,* 215–231.

Wechsler, D. (1974). *Wechsler intelligence scale for children* (rev. ed.). New York: Psychological Corp.

Zangwill, O. L., & Blakemore, C. (1972). Dyslexia: Reversal of eye movements during reading. *Neuropsychologia, 10,* 371–373.

18 Artists as Dyslexics

P. G. Aaron
Indiana State University

Jean-Claude Guillemard
International School Psychology Association
Dourdan, France

INTRODUCTION

Even though it is true that not all individuals with developmental dyslexia are artistically talented and not all artists have reading disability, there appears to be an above-chance relationship between artistic skill and specific reading disability. In our experience, a disproportionately large number of dyslexic college students choose to major in subject matter areas such as art, drafting, or engineering technology, which require well-developed visual skills. In this chapter, we raise the following two questions and try to answer them: What is the relationship between developmental dyslexia and visual processes? Did some historically famous artists have developmental dyslexia? These questions, in light of the resurgence of interest in visual processes as etiological factors of dyslexia, are significant. The implication is that because artists presumably have good visual skills, dyslexic symptoms, if detected, cannot be attributed to poor visual processes. Could extraordinary visual skills be responsible for these artists having adopted a strategy that is incompatible with efficient reading and correct spelling?

WHAT IS THE RELATIONSHIP BETWEEN DEVELOPMENTAL DYSLEXIA AND VISUAL PROCESSES?

The Nature of Developmental Dyslexia

Reading is a complex skill made up of several components. To be considered a component, a process should be functionally distinct from other processes (Carr

& Levy, 1990). Evidence from experimental psychology (Hunt, Lunneborg, & Lewis, 1975; Jackson & McClelland, 1979), neuropsychology (Marshall & Newcombe, 1973; Patterson, Marshall, & Coltheart, 1985), as well as genetic studies of reading disabilities (Olson, Wise, Conners, Rack, & Fulker, 1989), show that comprehension and word recognition are two major components of reading. Developmental studies also show that dyslexic children are relatively more impaired in their word recognition skills than in comprehension (Frith & Snowling 1983), whereas children diagnosed as hyperlexics are proficient in decoding the written language but impaired in comprehension (Aaron, Franz, & Manges, 1990; Healy, 1982).

Comprehension is used in this chapter as a generic term to encompass both reading and listening comprehension. Beyond the differences that arise due to the variation in the modalities of input in reading and listening, the same cognitive processes appear to mediate both forms of comprehension.

Word recognition, as used here, refers to the process of converting graphemes into their phonemic representations; it is also commonly referred to as "decoding skill." Even though there is some disagreement about the need for decoding in skilled reading, it is believed that when reading, propositions are to be retained in primary memory for the realization of the meaning of sentences and this is best accomplished when propositions are stored in the form of phonological representations.

Research conducted during the past 20 years shows that phonology-related deficiencies are causally associated with developmental dyslexia (specific reading disability). Complimenting this conclusion is the finding that comprehension ability of dyslexic individuals, as assessed by tests of listening comprehension, tends to be within normal range (Aaron, 1989; Frith & Snowling, 1983). In addition to impeding word recognition processes, phonological deficiency also manifests itself in several reading-related symptoms. These include difficulty in correctly reading uncommon words, poor spelling, errors of syntax in oral reading and writing, and a weakness of processing sequentially presented verbal material. These symptoms constitute the *syndrome* of developmental dyslexia.

Even though with prolonged reading experience, dyslexic individuals can develop a reasonably good sight vocabulary and thus become adequate readers, poor spelling and slow reading continue to be persistent problems (Joshi & Aaron, 1991). We want to emphasize the observation that many children with dyslexia eventually grow up to be adequate readers, not because their phonology-related problems have been resolved but probably because they have learned to recognize words by utilizing alternate strategies such as sight reading and use of context.

A majority of researchers treat word recognition skill as a single component— the ability to decode the phonology of the written word. However, the possibility that word recognition itself may be composed of two separate subskills has been considered by some researchers. The proposed two subskills of word recognition involve phonological and visual processing of the written word. The tendency to implicate visual processes in developmental dyslexia is not new but can even be detected in the writings of Hinshelwood and Orton. Although our understanding of visual processes has undergone considerable modification since the days of Hinshelwood and Orton, the relationship between visual processes and reading and spelling remains unclear.

Visual Processes and Dyslexia

Research in dyslexia has considered three different types of visual processes: (a) vision-related processes, (b) visuospatial processes, and (c) visual memory.

Vision-related processes focus on physiological and optical aspects of visual information. It is reasonable to expect that defects in the physiology of vision would affect not only processing of the written language but the perception of all objects in the environment. Furthermore, by definition, reading difficulty arising from sensory deficits is excluded from the category of developmental dyslexia. To be sure, vision-related deficits such as myopia can adversely affect reading achievement; but this form of reading problem is not considered dyslexia. More-over, as indicated earlier, developmental dyslexia is a syndrome that includes poor word recognition skill as well as erratic spelling. Any vision-related hypoth-esis of dyslexia should be able to account for not only input problems (i.e., poor word recognition) but also output problems (i.e., poor spelling). It is hard to see how vision-based hypotheses of dyslexia can satisfy this requirement.

Visuospatial domain is thought to be made up of four separate but correlated abilities: spatial rotation ability (e.g., the ability to rotate figures in mind), spatial visualization (e.g., the ability to assemble jig-saw puzzles), orientation of self in space, and judgment about moving bodies (Hunt, 1990). Of these four abilities, the latter two are unlikely to be essential for the reading process. In this chapter, we refer to the first two abilities collectively as visual-spatial ability. Clinical studies have relied on children's inability to successfully reproduce geometrical figures, errors of written spelling, and errors of reversal in writing as indices of poor visual-spatial ability. If poor visual-spatial ability can, by itself, lead to reading problems, two forms of disabilities can be postulated: phonological dyslexia and visual dyslexia.

Johnson and Myklebust (1967) were among the first to propose the existence of a putative "visual dyslexia" and thus introduce a two-way classification of dyslexia (i.e., visual dyslexia and auditory dyslexia). Evidence for visual dyslex-ia, however, was based on the results of tests such as the Bender Gestalt, which are only remotely related to the reading process and, therefore, open to different interpretations. For instance, it can be argued that reproduction of Bender figures is not a purely visual task but involves language skills as well. Yet another subtyping system of dyslexia based on reading and spelling errors was introduced by Boder (1973) and standardized by Boder and Jarrico (1982). According to this classification system, children who made phonologically acceptable spelling errors (*girl—gal; blue—bloo*) were thought to be weak in some visual process and labeled as *dyseidetic;* children whose spelling was phonologically unacceptable (*girl—gril; stop—spot*) were thought to be weak in phonological skills and were labeled as *dysphonetic*. The occurrence of two types of spelling errors is, however, open to another interpretation. Instead of representing two subtypes of dyslexia, these errors may represent two stages in reading acquisition. Evidence for this interpretation was obtained by Phillips, Taylor, and Aaron (1985) in a study of 41 normal readers and 26 poor readers from grades 2 through 6. Analysis of the spelling errors committed by poor readers showed that the types of errors they committed changed from being predominantly dysphonetic in grades 2 and 3 to being mostly dyseidetic in grade 4 and above.

Visual dyslexia as a subtype of developmental dyslexia has been proposed also by Gjessing and Karlsen (1989). They reached this conclusion on the basis of their investigation of 195 poor readers. According to these researchers, the predominant characteristics displayed by visual dyslexics were an extreme dependence on phonetic analysis, as revealed by a tendency to spell irregular words phonetically and a tendency to commit errors of reversals in reading and writing. The tendency to spell words phonetically, as noted earlier, may be due to the possibility that these disabled readers were able to make use of simple grapheme-phoneme correspondence rules but not the more complex rules. As for reversal errors, it is documented that such errors do not constitute a reliable symptom of developmental dyslexia (Liberman, Mann, Shankweiler, & Werfelman, 1982). Nor does it appear to be a sign of a weakness of the visual-spatial processing system. As a matter of fact, reversals may be indicative of a biased tendency to process print in a visuospatial rather than a phonological format. This conclusion is based on the following rationale. Experimental studies show that pictures are processed by adults without much regard to their left–right orientation (Blount, Holmes, Rodger, & Coltheart, 1975; Nickerson & Adam, 1979). For instance, most people cannot tell with certainty whether the face of Abraham Lincoln on the U.S. penny is facing left or right. Nevertheless, people have no difficulty in distinguishing a penny from a dime. When the written word is processed as a logogram rather than a sequence of graphemes, it probably is processed visuospatially. Under such circumstances, the left–right orientation is disregarded resulting in randomly occurring reversals. Thus, reversals in the reading and writings of children may be an indication that these children are relying on visual-spatial skills rather than on phonology for reading and spelling.

For these reasons, we do not further consider vision processes and visual spatial skills in our discussion of developmental dyslexia but focus on visual memory for which, a stronger case can be made.

That *visual memory* plays a role in the reading process can be supported by rational arguments and empirical data. For instance, homophones (*meat—meet; sea—see*) could be correctly spelled only by relying on visual memory. It has also been shown that visually stored information about words has a priming effect on language processing. For instance, Seidenberg and Tanenhaus (1979) found that in an aurally presented rhyme detection task, words that were visually similar (e.g., *pie—tie*) were identified faster as rhymes than visually dissimilar words (*tye—pie*). The ability to spell homophones correctly and the priming effect of visually similar morphemes may be facilitated by visual memory for *small units* of spelling patterns. Such small but redundant units of spelling are considered an orthographic feature of words; the ability to remember such units is orthographic memory. Recently orthographic memory has been implicated in reading disability by several investigators (e.g., Berninger, 1990; Ehri & Wilce, 1982). But, is orthographic memory the same as visual memory, or does it involve phonologic as well as semantic memories?

Orthographic memory, in general, refers to the retention and recall of information about spelling patterns. Orthography itself is defined as "the graphemic patterns of a written language and their mapping onto phonology, morphology, and meaning" (Henderson, 1984, p. 1). This definition implies that accurate reproduction of spelling patterns or the utilization of spelling patterns in the process of reading involves phonology and semantics, in addition to visual memory. This statement can be supported by rational and empirical evidence. Thus, there is no compelling reason to consider orthographic memory as a synonym of visual memory. There is, however, the possibility that visual memory is one aspect of orthographic memory.

In word recognition, does visual memory operate independent of phonology and semantics so that it can be assigned a componential status? In their analysis of the component processes of reading, Levy and Carr (1990) concluded that "deficits in phonological processing are major contributors to reading failure . . . orthographic deficits also contribute in some cases, but they are rarer or less severe difficulties and they may be secondary to phonological difficulty" (p. 424). In a recent study (Aaron, Wills, & Wleklinski, in press) the recognition memory of children from grade 2 through 5 was assessed by using several lists of words that differed on dimensions of meaning, phonology, and visual memory. Stepwise regression analysis showed that phonology contributed the most to word recognition skills and visual memory the least, almost nothing. Among the children studied, there were some poor readers with weak visual memory, but they also had low IQ suggesting that visual memory may not operate as an independent factor in word recognition.

There is a possibility, as Ehri (1987) pointed out, that as children progressively acquire reading skills, visual images for spelling patterns can become amalgamated with phonological and semantic features of words. The view that experience plays a major role in the development of orthographic memory is supported by empirical as well as genetic studies. In two studies involving a large number of dyslexic twins, Olson and his associates (Olson, Wise, & Rack, 1989) found that about 40% of the probands' deficit was due to heritable influences, primarily for phonological coding. Although the genetic correlation between word recognition and phonological coding deficits was quite large, the correlation between word recognition and orthographic coding was small, which led them to conclude that orthographic coding is predominantly influenced by environmental factors. A study by Stanovich and West (1989) revealed similar findings leading to the conclusion that exposure to print and reading experience contribute significantly to orthographic coding skill. Developmental dyslexia is defined in such a way as to exclude any environmental influence as an etiological factor. Consequently, an environmentally induced reading deficit cannot be considered dyslexia.

In summary, the status of visual memory as an *independent component* of reading remains to be established. The role of visual memory as an independent factor of reading and spelling can be addressed in yet another way by asking the question whether accurate word recognition and correct spelling could be accomplished by superior visual memory alone and whether superior visual memory also means an equally superior orthographic memory. A study of famous visual artists who appear to have had developmental dyslexia follows this approach.

DID SOME FAMOUS ARTISTS HAVE DEVELOPMENTAL DYSLEXIA?

Visual Memory and Artistic Talent

It is not unreasonable to expect individuals talented in visual arts to have superior visual memory. This expectation, in addition to being intuitively appealing, is supported by empirical studies (Getzels & Csikszentimihalyi, 1976; Rosenblatt & Winner 1988). Artistic skill certainly is more than the ability to remember visual images. Schweiger (1988) cited neuropsychological evidence suggesting that superior artistic skill involves two abilities: (a) an ability to conceptualize a visual production by attaching meaning to it and (b) the skill to reproduce details and execute the conceptualization. Neurological impairment can affect one skill and leave the other intact. In a discussion of visual memory, Schwartz and Reisberg (1991), concluded that available experimental evidence indicates that pictures are remembered better when they are processed deeply by encoding their meaning as compared to pictures that are devoid of meaning and, therefore, processed in a shallow manner. This led them to recommend the identification of two forms of visual memory, *schematic memory* and *detail memory*. In these respects, memory processes involved in artistic production appear to be similar to processes involved in orthographic memory. Similar to orthographic skill, talent in art depends on the conceptualization of an idea as well as the successful portrayal of visual details. Great artists such as Leonardo da Vinci, Charles Russell, and Auguste Rodin appear to have been abundantly endowed with these two skills.

In this chapter, the case histories of these three men, namely, Leonardo da Vinci, Auguste Rodin, and Charles Russell are presented. Although the artistic caliber of these men is indisputable, questions can be raised about them having had developmental dyslexia. The remainder of this chapter is devoted to this issue.

Rationale for Decision Making in Regard to Reading Disability in Historic Persons

One of the earliest efforts to investigate the possibility that some historically famous persons might have had learning disability was made by Thompson (1969). His conclusions, however, are open to criticism because he relied almost exclusively on biographers who have a tendency to dramatize trivial events and embellish minor details. The progress made within the last three decades in the areas of cognitive psychology and neuropsychology has increased our understanding of reading disabilities and has provided reliable tools to carry out a more objective investigation.

Inferences made about developmental dyslexia in historic persons are based on information obtained from the four sources shown in Table 18.1. A detailed description of the rationale is presented by Aaron, Phillips, and Larsen (1988).

Individually, each one of these factors may not provide unequivocal evidence for the presence of reading disability in historic persons, but collectively they can strengthen inferences drawn regarding dyslexia.

TABLE 18.1
The Four Sources of Information on Which
Inferences About Dyslexia in
Historic Persons are Based

Biographical information
    1. Descriptive accounts by biographers
    2. School records
    3. Self-reports
Cognitive characteristics
    1. Written spelling errors
    2. Errors of syntax in written language
    3. Deficits in sequential processing of information
    4. Superior ability in simultaneous processing of information
Neuropsychological characteristics
    1. Evidence of incomplete cerebral lateralization
    2. Handedness
Biological characteristics
    1. Genetic predisposition in the family
    2. Immune system disorders

CASE HISTORIES
OF THREE FAMOUS ARTISTS

Leonardo da Vinci (1452–1519)

Leonardo was born out of wedlock on April 15, 1452 in the small village of Vinci, which lies in the Tuscan hill country of modern Italy about 20 miles away from Florence. His family had a number of notaries over many generations. Later on, one of his step brothers continued the family tradition by becoming a notary. In many respects, notaries of Renaissance Italy functioned as lawyers and also acted as agents and legal advisers to ecclesiastical institutions, guilds, and wealthy citizens. In contrast, artists of that period, unless they have proved to have extraordinary talents, were considered as craftspersons. In view of these observations, it is reasonable to raise the question why Leonardo did not choose to become a notary.

Biographical Information

Descriptive Accounts.   That Leonardo was an illegitimate child is sometimes advanced to explain the fact that he did not pursue formal education. Although illegitimacy carried a stain of some sort in Italian Renaissance society, men could be made to overlook it by force of power and position or by means of money and special dispensation (Martines, 1968). A more plausible reason is the one advanced by Payne (1978): "He (Leonardo) had difficulty in learning languages; it was not that he could not apply himself to the task, for at one time he made a serious attempt to learn Latin" (p. 238). It is also known that curriculum pursued in medieval grammar schools placed heavy emphasis on the learning of languages and required a great deal of reading and memorization of Italian and Latin. A lack of aptitude for learning languages, therefore, emerges as a possible reason for Leonardo's not choosing to become a notary.

Self-reports.   Starting from about the age of 37, Leonardo recorded most of his thoughts by writing them down. A good many of his ideas were jotted down on loose sheets of paper in a haphazard, unsystematic fashion. Hidden among this jumble, self-deprecating remarks such as, "I being not a man of letters"; "having a lack of literary training" (Reti, 1974, p. 293), could be seen. Marioni (1974), who has translated the two manuscripts discovered in Madrid in 1965 (Codex Madrid, I and II), quotes additional examples: "They will say that being without letters I cannot say properly what I want to say" (p. 77); "the painter is a man without letters who does not possess to the full the contemporary linguistic instruments." (p. 80).

Cognitive Characteristics

Errors in Written Spelling.   Compared to English, Italian orthography is shallow; no complex rules are involved in phoneme-grapheme conversion, and

400

TABLE 18.2
Written Spelling Errors of Leonardo and Those of
a Fifteen-year-old Dyslexic Subject

Type of Error	Leonardo	Correct Spelling	Dyslexic Subject	Correct Spelling
Blending	cicommette	chi commette (who makes)	pergliamici	per gli amici (for the friend)
Segmenting	muta tionj	mutationj (mutations)	in chiostro	inchiostro (ink)
	lumj nosa	lumjnosa (luminous)	i nizio	inizio (beginning)
	aritro vare	a rit rovare (at finding again)	a dogni	ad ogni (at every)
	ino ccidente	in occidente (in the west)	lanno scorso	l'anno scorso (the last year)
Consonant errors	quelglj	queglj (those)	tacquini	taccuini (notebook)
	sciatta	schiatta (sons)	lanno	l'hanno (have)
	tottare	toccare (touch)	socquadro	soqquadro (topsy-turvy)

words are spelled the way they are pronounced. Such a highly regular orthography minimizes the opportunities for making spelling errors. There exists, however, a possibility for committing errors of parsing, segmentation, and blending in written Italian.

Leonardo often "wrote haphazardly . . . spelling arbitrarily, skipping words and phrases" (Marinoni, 1974, p. 60). Sartori (1987), who examined Leonardo's writings from the perspective of dyslexia, noted that his orthography can be described as "capricciosa e singolarissima; inconsueta e incoerente" (capricious and peculiar; inconsistent and unusual). Sartori also points out that no normal reader, living or historical, is known to commit such errors. In contrast, the errors committed by Leonardo are similar to those committed by a 15-year-old dyslexia boy studied by Sartori (Table 18.2).

Alternate hypotheses could be advanced to account for the idiosyncracies of Leonardo's orthography and these deserve to be examined. It is possible that, during the Renaissance period, firm rules of spelling were not laid down and the spelling of Italian was inconsistent. Or perhaps spelling varied from region to region within Italy; Tuscany, the region Leonardo came from, could have had its own peculiarities of spelling. According to another hypothesis, having had no formal schooling, Leonardo was not acquainted with many words. Even though all these could have contributed to Leonardo's erratic spelling, none of these seems to be a major factor. Sartori (1987), after examining the spontaneous writings of Michaelangelo Buonarroti and Francesco Melzi—both of whom came from Tuscany and were Leonardo's contemporaries— reported that he could not find errors similar to those committed by Leonardo in their writings. Melzi, who inherited Leonardo's manuscripts, corrected all the spelling and punctuation errors found in Leonardo's original manuscript. It is obvious, therefore, that even at the time of Renaissance, the errors committed by Leonardo were considered unusual. The incorrect word segmentation and blending could not be explained by the fact that Leonardo lacked formal schooling because they resulted in nonwords. Furthermore, even when he copied other manuscripts, Leonardo committed the errors similar to those seen in his spontaneous writing.

Deficits in Sequential Processing of Information.   Difficulties in processing sequences of words and phrases, remembering days and dates, and in carrying out arithmetic operations could be seen in Leonardo's writings. Among Leonardo's errors of sequence, two in particular are of relevance in the present context. He recorded Caterina's (his mother?) arrival by writing "On the 16th day of July Caterina came on the 16th day of July 1493" (MacCurdy, 1958, p. 1156). His diary entry of his father's death reads: "On the ninth day of July 1504, on Wednesday at seven o'clock, died, at the Palace of Podesta, Ser Piero da Vinci, notary, my father, at seven o'clock; he was eighty years old, he left ten sons and two daughters" (MacCurdy, 1958, p. 1159). In addition to the repetition of the phrase "7 o'clock," several other errors can be detected. The day of death was Tuesday and not Wednesday as he had written; his father's age was 77 instead of 80; it is also possible that the number of children is incorrect because Payne (1978) stated that Ser Piero had three daughters. It may be noted that all these errors involve information that is sequential in nature.

Superior Ability in Simultaneous Processing of Information.   Leonardo relied a great deal on drawings and sketches to communicate his ideas; his diaries and notebooks are filled with rebuses, sketches, and drawings. When copying Euclid's theorems, Leonardo did not transcribe the Latin text word for word, but often translated and recorded the theorems in an unusual form, in a series of drawings. For him, drawings and sketches constituted another medium of expression, a form of communication in which he excelled.

Leonardo's painting of the Virgin and Child with St. Anne provides further evidence of his superior visualization ability. Portraying the personal relationship among the three figures (Christ, Mary, and Mary's mother St. Anne) without violating the importance attributed to each one of them by religious tradition, had, for artists, posed a tremendous problem in composition. Leonardo solved it through a gestaltlike fusion of the figures into a "pyramidal arrangement." A similar fusion of figures is also seen in the *Last Supper*. Leonardo's manuscripts from 1496 through 1499 devote more space to geometry than to any other subject, an indication of his preoccupation with the field during those years. Leonardo's illustrations of complex three-dimensional designs in solid geometry are extraordinary for their depth and accuracy.

Neuropsychological Characteristics

Cerebral Lateralization.   There appears to exist some association between diffuse cerebral organization, incomplete lateralization, and specific reading disability (Corballis & Beale, chap. 3). During the last year of his life, when he was the resident artist at the court of the French king Francis I at Amboise, Leonardo suffered a stroke. Evidence of this illness comes from a record made by Antonio de' Beatis, secretary of the Cardinal of Aragon who visited Leonardo on October 10, 1517. The secretary's observation that Leonardo's right arm was paralyzed indicates that the lesion was localized in the left cerebral hemisphere. In right-handed persons, a lesion in the left cerebral hemisphere that causes paralysis of the right arm is usually accompanied by aphasic symptoms. The Cardinal's secretary had conversations with Leonardo but still does not make any reference to any speech problems, so it has to be inferred that Leonardo, in spite of a left hemisphere stroke, was free from aphasic symptoms. Furthermore, on April 23, 1518, about 6 months after the Cardinal's visit, Leonardo went to the chambers of the royal notary at Amboise and made his last will. It was made in the presence of five witnesses and was an intricate document with 18 separate clauses. The information contained in the will is private for the most part, which indicates that Leonardo was able to communicate to the panel of witnesses his intent and describe his relatives as well as details regarding his personal possessions and properties. The fact that Leonardo was able to make a deposition of a complex nature suggests that his language remained relatively unimpaired in spite of the left-sided cerebral lesion.

Handedness.   Analysis of his handwriting as well as sketches reveals that Leonardo wrote, drew, and painted with his left hand (Marinoni, 1974). A well-known characteristic of Leonardo was his tendency to write in the mirror-reversed form. According to Vasari (1959), his biographer, Leonardo wrote backward, in rude characters, and with his left hand. A plausible explanation of this tendency to mirror-write is that Leonardo processed written words holistically as gestalts; the directional orientation of the word, right to left or left to right, was, therefore, not important. Such a cognitive strategy is also associated with a diffuse cerebral organization and specific reading disability (Corballis, 1980).

Auguste Rodin (1840–1917)

Arguably, Rodin is the greatest sculptor since Michaelangelo. Although some of his sculptures such as the *The Thinker* and the *The Kiss* have gained universal acclaim, others such as *Balzac* and *The Burghers of Calais* have aroused a good deal of controversy and criticism. As far as *impressionism* applies to sculpture, Rodin is considered to have introduced impressionism into the field. In this sense, he can be compared to the painter Claude Monet, who was his contemporary. According to Descharnes and Chabrun (1967), whose book on Rodin is based on substantial research, he is the last of the great classical sculptors and the first of the great modern sculptors.

Rodin's parents were of humble origin; his father was a clerk in a police precinct in Paris and his mother was a housewife. At the age of 8, Rodin started attending a school run by the *Brothers of the Christian Doctrine.* Three years later, he was sent to a boarding school in Beauvais where his uncle Hippolyte Rodin was the headmaster. The decision to send young Rodin to a boarding school 100 miles away from home and not to a school in Paris may not be unrelated to his performance at the local school. After about 2 years, at the age of 14, Rodin returned to Paris and entered the *Petite Ecole* in Paris, where he started to learn drawing, painting, and sculpting. Thus, Rodin had received 6 or 7 years of education, which was more than most ordinary children had in those days. When he was about 22, Maria, his older sister with whom Rodin was very close, died. Depressed over this tragic event, Rodin entered the noviatiate in the *Order of the Fathers of the Very Holy Sacrament,* but returned to sculpting and painting a year later. It can therefore be surmised that Rodin had ample opportunity to read and write.

When he was 24 years old, Rodin met Rose Beuret who, a year later, bore a son for him. Even though Rodin's liaison with Rose remained unsolemnized by marriage almost his entire life, the two were eventually married a few months before his death. Other important people in his life were Camille Claudel, who was his student and an associate in more than one sense; Judith Cladell, who was a faithful companion, particularly during Rodin's last days, and the best informed of his biographers; and Marcelle Tirel, "the most patient and the longest-lasting of his secretaries" (Descharnes & Chabrun, 1967, p. 192), who also has written an informal but intimate account of the sculptor.

Biographical Information

Descriptive Accounts.   Rodin's biographers are consistent in describing him as a poor student, uninterested in reading and writing, but preoccupied with drawing. According to Cladell (1917), at the boarding school "he found the scholar's life dreary and dull . . . certain studies were repugnant to him, mathematics and *solfeggio.* Near-sighted, without being aware of it, he could not make out the figures and the notes the masters wrote on the blackboard; he understood nothing and was almost bored to death" (p. 17). Even though myopia could have interfered with his education, it is doubtful if Rodin's reading and spelling problems could be attributed to nearsightedness because his paintings done at the age of 20 reveal astonishing details, indicating that he could perceive details remarkably well if he wanted to.

According to Descharnes and Chabrun (1967), "The brothers of the Christian Doctrine vainly tried to drill a minimum of knowledge into the little red-head's skull. It appears that their task, to say the least, was far from easy" (p. 13). Even though it is uncertain how much of the material is gleaned from original sources, Champigneulle (1967) provided a dramatic description of Rodin's school days:

> He attended the Ecoles Chretiennes in the Rue du Val-de-Grace but had great difficulty in learning to read and write despite the Brothers' noted achievements in the field of primary education. At the age of nine, he was packed off to his paternal uncle Alexandre who ran a boys' boarding school at Beauvais. . . . As for his studies, he seemed to be genuinely retarded. His dictation was riddled with crass spelling mistakes. He never succeeded in learning Latin like the others, and his mathematics were non-existent. He drove his teachers to despair. . . . When he was thirteen, his uncle decided that there was nothing more to be done with him and sent him back to Paris. (pp. 11, 12)

Truman Bartlett, who was an art critic and teacher of modeling at the Massachusetts Institute of Technology, met Rodin in 1887 and published an account of him in 1889. This was republished in 1965 as part of a book edited by Albert Elsen. He noted that "at an early age he was sent to a little boarding school at Beauvais, of which his uncle was the principal, and where he pursued only the simplest studies. Neither the master, the school, nor the lessons attracted him" (p. 16). According to Elsen, who wrote several books about Rodin as an artist, Rodin did have problems with grammar and punctuation, and contented himself with writing mostly short notes, well over 100,000. Rodin, however, was an avid reader all his life, even when desperately poor (personal communication, 1988).

From 1906, until Rodin's death in 1917, Marcelle Tirel was his secretary and a compassionate companion. In *The Last Years of Rodin* (1925), Tirel gives some intimate accounts of the talents and foibles of Rodin. This book shows a deep respect for Rodin and is set in a tone of adulation. Statements in this book could, therefore, be considered objective and reliable. According to Tirel, Rodin had doubts about his own literary ability and many a time would say: "I shall never be able to write well." He would write "areoplane" for *aeroplane,* "cariathide" for *cariatide.* When told that *cariatide* does not have the letter *h,* he was most astonished but remarked "those are trifles for a man like myself " (pp. 99, 103). When Tirel pointed out errors in his writings, he would say "My French? that means nothing" (p. 103). Tirel continued, "He wrote and wrote, scribbled, rather, and for the most part what he produced was valueless but the snobs applauded, saying it was wonderful. . . . Why should people want to make of a sculptor of genius what he could never be, a man of letters?" (pp. 112, 114). About his reading habits, Tirel said: "I never saw Rodin open any books other than those he bought for their binding from the antique dealers in Versailles. The great library at the Hotel Biron (where Rodin stayed part of the time) was full of them. Now and again he would take one from its shelf, open it, and chant, deciphering the text then he would replace the volume on its shelf" (p. 116).

These biographical accounts indicate two things: Rodin had a number of years of schooling and he had difficulty with academic subjects.

Self-reports.   In his edited book on Rodin, Elsen (1965) included a mono-logue by Rodin that was originally published by Dujardin-Beaumetz in 1913 under the title *Entretiens avec Rodin.* Dujardin-Beaumetz was the undersecretary of state for fine arts in France and the report was based on notes made by him during his numerous conversations with Rodin. About his education, Rodin said: "When I was about fourteen, I boarded at Beauvais, at my uncle's. The students there studied Latin. I don't know why, but I didn't like Latin. I've often regretted (it)" (p. 145).

The Musée Rodin in Paris has published four volumes of *Correspondance de Rodin,* which contains the following statement in a letter by Rodin to Helene Wahl dated October 1895: "You know that I am not a scholar and that writing and speaking turn me to confusion. My natural means of expression are clay and pencil" (Vol. 1, p. 7).

Cognitive Characteristics

Errors in Written Spelling and Syntax.   By about 1900, Rodin became afflu-ent enough to hire secretaries. As a result, he himself wrote few letters after this date. It appears that Rodin did not read even personal letters but relied on his secretary to read for him. For instance, Tirel wrote, "often when I read a passage over to him" (p. 98); "the next day, I read the article over again to him" (p. 112); "he sat in silence, holding his beard, while I read them (the letters)" (p. 122).

After commenting on Rodin's writings, Tirel wrote, "I have before me an unpublished fragment of those *Thoughts,* scrawled in pencil on the back of a letter from a model; the letters are badly formed, the words stumble and trip, the sentences are incomplete" (p. 115). The sample writing Tirel wrote about is reproduced here:

> Ces nuages frisés blancs, cette crême fouettée. Ils sont dans le perspective anonyme quand ils passent au-dessus de vastes arbres . . . entre les arbres on voit comme des terres de géographies immenses sur les cieux découpé. La majesté des arbres réunis en bouquet ose se composer au ciel. Ily a pour les bêtes la joie d' aimer la beaute. Nous, on nous forme au malheur . . . les gens intelligents ne savent plus ce que les bêtes savent . . . nos mauvaises éducations entretènues avec soin nous cachent la lumiere. Toute une vie de suicides, dont on sourira . . . les nations neurastheniques . . . Bourrée - Pendant qu' elle danse elle est inondé de lumi-ère . . . ma lumière; les pulsations de mon coeur qui bat aussi la mesure.

It could be argued that errors found in Rodin's writings could be due to a lack of formal education and insufficient reading experience. This, however, does not appear to be the case. According to a biography written by Butler (in press), Rodin and his friend Leon Fourquet from the Petite Ecole corresponded with each other as teenagers. Fourquet's letters to Rodin that survive indicate that both of them shared much enthusiasm for literature. These letters indicate they both read *Notre Dame de Paris* by Victor Hugo and *Gil Blas,* a romantic novel by Lesage. Leon did not own the second volume of *Gil Blas* and wrote to Rodin, "When will you write me the rest of the story?" Thus errors seen in Rodin's writings cannot be attributed entirely to limited education or lack of reading experience.

The following samples are selected from Rodin's writings, mostly letters, published by *Musèe Rodin* (1985) under the title *Correspondences of Rodin.*

Aug. 11, 1860

la locomotive qui vous emportaient [noun-verb disagreement]; comme corespondance [awkward style; spelling error]; toutes ces choses réunis avec un peu d'inquiétude [subject verb disagreement]; les ennuies [spelling]; tu me racontera [syntax error]; une soeur éloignée est doublement aimé [subject gender disagreement]; la distance qui nous sépare les rendraient tres importantes [subject-verb disagreement]; que tu pense a nous, tu mette cette pensée sur ton papier; tu sèra la secrétaire aussi des pensees [wrong verb endings]; les souvenirs qu'elle a eu a etaim [spelling and capitalization errors]; que ta lettre soit chargé, bouré, compilé [syntax errors]; ces colis chargé ou non cest toujours le meme prix 20 centimes [wrong form of adjective]. (Vol. 1, p. 21)

Rodin's disregard for punctuation and grammar is evident from one of his letters.

October 1871 to Rose.

Mon petit Ange je suis heureux que vous êtes sains et saufs seulement quand je suis avide de nouvelles tu ne m'en met pas bien long tu ne réponds pas à toutes les questions que je te fais donne moi des détails que je sache ce que tu as fait pendant ces jours lugubres je te console d'avance en te disant que je vais vous envoyer de l'argent dans quelques jours car j'en toucherai bientot je crois que mes affaires vont marcher esperance mon ange et si je suis pour rester â Bruxelles je te ferai venir car je m'ennuie après toi. tu ne me parle pas de Monsieur Garnier de Monsieur Bernard a qui j enverrai de l'argent bientot tu iras le voir et ira aussi a i'atelier rien n'est-il casse

J'ai eu figure toi ma petite Rose beaucoup d'ennuies il y a près de trois mois que je ne travaille pas tu pense comme je l'ai passe dure nous sommes fâchés avec monsieur Carrier cependant ca va marcher. (Vol. 1, p. 30)

The fact that Rodin's writing did not improve over the years is evident from the following letter he wrote to Helene de Nostiz in 1908.

noble et cher amie

J'ai recu votre belle lettre la comparaison de ceux qui travaillent et tout à coup appercoivent la nature la vallée admirable est bien vrai . . . et comme par tradition le Chef d'oeuvre de la femme et l'enfant a ete souvent compris non pas trop du temps des Grecs, ou l'enfant etait l'amour, et Venus; mais du temps des Egyptiens ou la femme et l'enfant est de toutes les deesses et dieux, la plus grande. Reprise par la tradition chrétienne elle reposait cette gloire, des Raphaels madones si sévères a l'epoque Espagnole des 12 siècle. (Vol. 2, p. 162)

Deficits in Sequential Processing of Information and Superior Ability in Simultaneous Processing.   Rodin was not good in remembering dates and events. Often he would make appointments with models only to forget until they showed up. Nor was he good at remembering the sequence and dates and places of his exhibitions. His poor memory for dates is revealed by an anecdote recorded by Tirel. One day he hurriedly got dressed to attend the funeral of his old friend Dr. Bigot. When he reached the grave site, he recognized nobody and no one knew who he was. When he returned home and reread the telegram, he realized that the funeral service was seven days before and he was late by one week.

Charles Marion Russell (1864–1926)

In the introduction to *Good Medicine* (Russell, 1929), which contains a collection of Charles Russell's letters adorned with water color illustrations, Will Rogers wrote, "He wasn't just Another Artist. He wasn't 'just another' anything. . . . He was a philosopher. He was a great humorist. . . . If he had devoted the same time to writing that he had to his brush, he would have left a tremendous impression in that line" (pp. 13–15). Along with the well-known artists Karl Bodmer and George Catlin, Russell is also considered to be a great chronicler of the history of the West. Russell, unlike Western artists such as Frederick Remington, seldom portrayed Indians and the U.S. cavalry as antagonists. The Indian maids he painted were tender, independent, and self-assured; they were portrayed not as serfs but as fulfilling roles of domestic and social responsibility (G. Renner, 1984). Russell was also a great story teller and as Frederick Renner (1984) put it, he has "a gorgeous darting wit which tickled but never stung" (p. 31). He wrote in the same style as he told his tales and *Trails Plowed Under* (1927) is notable for its great humor and earthly wit. Appropriately, the people from Montana call their territory *Russell Country*.

Charles Russell was born in St. Louis in 1864 into a family prominent in business and public affairs. His father had attended Yale University and was later involved in the Russell Mining and Manufacturing Company, a family-owned business. He was also on the board of the Oak Hill school, which young Charlie attended as a child. Russell's mother also came from an illustrious family and was an artist herself. Before entering school, Russell, along with his brothers and sisters, appears to have been tutored at home.

Russell started attending Oak Hill school during the 1870–1871 school year and continued there till 1879 when he was sent to the Burlington Military Academy in New Jersey. Based on information from some of Russell's relatives,

Woodcock (1982) wrote that when at Oak Hill school, young Russell had the habit of skipping school; when he did attend school, he would fill his lunch box with beeswax and spend a good deal of his time modeling figures for his class-mates. The decision to send Russell to the military academy might have been a desperate effort by his parents to salvage his education by placing him in a structured environment where academics were stressed. The academy, however, also failed to prod him into taking his studies seriously. Nor did it succeed in thwarting his preoccupation with art and "he was made to walk guard for hours because book study was not in his mind" (Nancy Russell, in Russell, 1929, p. 18). A sketchbook he maintained while at the academy contains several drawings of cowboys and Indians, a reflection of his abiding interest in the West and a premonition of things to come. After one term in the Burlington academy, Russell was presented by his parents with a trip to the West, perhaps in the hope the harsh realities of the West would impress on him the hardships of life there and force him to return to school; they were mistaken. By now Charlie was almost 16 years old and had had about 9 years of formal education.

After about 2 years of sheep-herding and trapping in Montana, Russell spent the following 11 years in tending saddle horses and herding cattle. During this time, he continued to sketch and draw with whatever material that was available to him. During one year, Russell was obliged to spend a winter with Blood Indians, an experience that increased his admiration for the natives, whom he frequently referred to as his "red brothers." Eventually his paintings found their way into towns such as Great Falls and Helena, as well as cities outside Mon-tana, which ultimately captured the attention of the art world.

Biographical information

Descriptive Accounts. The unimpressive school accomplishment of Charles Russell is well documented not only by his biographers but also by his wife Nancy. As she put it, "School had no charm for Russell, and he spent a consider-able amount of time on Guard duty for inattention while at the Burlington Military Academy. His teachers gave him up because he could not be made to read books" (Russell, 1929, p. 18).

School Records. We were not able to locate any school records because, according to Woodcock (personal communication), all school records were damaged in the tornado of 1927 and rather than try to salvage those records, everything remaining in the wreckage was thrown away. The Burlington Acade-my no longer exists.

Self-reports. Charles Russell made occasional remarks about his own writing skill. Some of these are taken from his letters and are reproduced here without correcting the spelling errors. He wrote to Senator Paris Gibson: "As I am verry poor writer I will make a kind of Injun letter mostly pictures" (Russell, 1929, p. 70). To W. M. Armstrong, he wrote in 1922, "Im better than a green hand with talk but with a pen Im plenty lame so Im limping in with my thanks" (Russell, 1929, p. 111). To "Mr. Hart" he wrote, "I am average on talk but hand me this tools (i.e., pen and ink) an Im deaf an dum" (Russell, 1929, p. 30). In one of his illustrated letters to a former schoolmate, he wrote, "Dear Charley . . . I guess you remember old Smith our teacher and the lickinges he gave us it has been maney years ago but he is still fresh in my memory" (Montana State Historical Society).

Cognitive Characteristics

Errors of Spelling and Syntax.   One need not search too far to locate errors of spelling and syntax in Russell's writings. Practically every other word is misspelled. Sometimes it is claimed that he meant to be theatrical and followed an oral style and misspelled words deliberately in order to inject a sense of humor into his writings (e.g., McDowell, 1986). These errors, creative as they may be, are too numerous to be considered deliberate and humorous. In fact, they hinder easy reading and distract the reader from enjoying the wit and humor of Russell's artful writing. Russell also misspelled people's names, a slip that may not be considered amusing even by close friends (see. Fig. 18.1). In one of his letters, he wrote, "To Harry Cary Bill Hart Douglass Farbancks Afreal Hart Bill Rodgers ore aney other moovey man" (Montana Historical Society). When he wrote a letter to Senator Paris Gibson, he addressed the letter to "Senitor Paris Gibson" (Russell, 1929, p. 70). He spelled the name of the town *Havre* variously as "Haver," "Havrre," and "Havre."

The type of spelling errors Russell committed in his adult writing are also seen in his *Sketchbook* from his school days at the Burlington Military Academy when he was 15 years old (Warden, 1972). A sample of misspellings from the *Sketchbook* includes the following: "mooving" (moving), "miners" (miner's), "braking" (breaking), "bars hole" (bear's hole), "secine" (scene), "mountians" (mountains), "Colradoe" (Colorado), "Bufalow Bill" (Buffalo Bill). These "phonologically acceptable spelling errors" suggest that visual memory may not play an important role in spelling.

According to Ginger Renner, a Russell scholar and art historian (personal communication), Russell was a voracious reader and built up an extensive library during his life. Russell's letters indicate that he periodically received books from his friends, read them, and was interested in discussing their contents (Russell, 1929): "Im sending you a book which I hope you enjoy" (p. 74); "thank yu for the book you sent me I ingoyed the book verry much" (p. 77); "I enjoyed your book Let Her Buck very much" (p. 102); "To make sketeches in Francis Parkman's books has been a pleasure to me When I read his work I seem to live in his time and travel the trails with him" (p. 105); "I just received your gift the books by Will James which I like verry much" (p. 160).

There is evidence that Russell was aware of his own misspellings, but paid

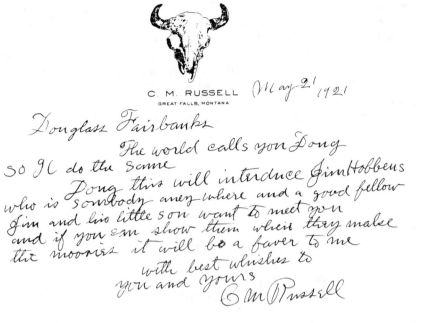

FIG. 18.1.   Russell's letter to Douglas Fairbanks.

little heed to it. For instance, in a letter to Ed. Neitzling he wrote, "the old rumitism I dont know wheter that the way to spll it or not but it is still with me" (Russell, 1929, p. 90); to "Friend Joe" he wrote, "Youd have don better with a hay knife It would give more teck neque maby that aint spelt right but you savvy" (Russell, 1929, p. 126).

Not only the sheer number of Russell's spelling errors is striking but considering the fact that he had had several years of formal schooling, carried on extensive correspondence, and was in the habit of reading books, these errors defy ordinary explanation. Perhaps, Russell's thinking was more visual than verbal and he tended to process written words as ideograms. In fact, he described written work as "word pictures" and remarked that there are two kinds of men, those who paint with their brush and those who paint with their pen. Russell's superb use of metaphors lends credence to this hypothesis. For him, the historical past of the West was "days before the wires," milk was "cow juice," New York was "the big camp," New Yorkers were "cliff dwellers," writing was "paper talk," and "life is a trail and a birthday is a p(l)ace where one stops to look back."

CONCLUSIONS

An analysis of the life history of three famous artists and an examination of their cognitive characteristics suggest that superior visual information-processing skills can coexist with developmental dyslexia. The writing samples of these famous men contain indisputable signs of errors of spelling, punctuation, and syntax. These symptoms suggest that visual memory may not be entirely relied on to produce correct spelling but that a weakness in phonological processing is responsible for errors of spelling and syntax. The study of the lives of these men has another important message. That is, developmental dyslexia does not necessarily mean a life sentence of reading failure. By probably utilizing alternative strategies of word recognition, these artists have eventually become adequate readers. The utilization of alternative strategies to compensate for a weakness in phonological processing skills has been documented by several investigators (e.g., Aaron, 1978; Kershner, 1977; Stanovich, 1980).

ACKNOWLEDGMENTS

Research reported in this chapter has been supported by a grant from the *Research Committee,* Indiana State University. We wish to thank the following scholars and organizations for providing us with valuable information regarding the lives of artists described in this chapter:

Musèe Rodin, 77, rue de varenne, 75007 Paris
Russell Museum, Great Falls, MT
Montana Historical Society, Helena, MT
Albert Elsen, Walter A. Haas Professor of Art History, Stanford University
Ruth Butler, Boston, MA, Rodin Scholar
Ginger Renner, Lyle Woodcock, both Russell Scholars and art historians
Janet Postler, Registrar, Russell Museum
Bart McDowell, Assistant Editor, *National Geographic*

REFERENCES

Aaron, P. G. (1978). Dyslexia, an imbalance in cerebral information processing strategies. *Perceptual and Motor Skills. 47,* 699–706.

Aaron, P. G. (1989). *Dyslexia and hyperlexia.* Boston: Kluwer Academic Publishers.

Aaron, P. G., Franz, S., & Manges, A. (1990). Dissociation between comprehension and pronunciation in dyslexic and hyperlexic children. *Reading and Writing: An Interdisciplinary Journal, 2,* 243–264.

Aaron, P. G., Phillips, S., & Larsen, S. (1988). Specific reading disability in historical men of eminence. *Journal of Learning Disabilities, 21,* 523–538.

Aaron, P. G., Wills, C., & Wleklinski, M. (in press). Visual memory and dyslexia. In R. M. Joshi and C. K. Leong (Eds.), *Reading and writing disorders: Diagnosis and treatments.* Boston: Kluwer Academic Publishers.

Berninger, V. W. (1990). Multiple orthographic codes: Key to alternative instructional methodologies for developing the orthographic-phonological connections underlying word identification. *School Psychology Review, 19* (4), 518–533.

Blount, P., Holmes, J., Rodger, J., & Coltheart, M. (1975). On the ability to discriminate original from mirror-image reproductions of works of art. *Perception, 4,* 385–389.

Boder, E. (1973). A diagnostic approach based on three atypical reading-spelling patterns. *Developmental Medicine and Child Neurology, 15,* 663–887.

Boder, E., & Jarrico, S. (1982). *Boder reading and spelling pattern test: A diagnostic screening test for developmental dyslexia.* New York: Grune & Stratton.

Butler, R. (in press). *Auguste Rodin.*

Carr, T. H., & Levy, B. A. (1990). *Reading and its development: Component skills approaches.* New York: Academic Press.

Champigneulle, B. (1967). *Rodin.* New York: Harry N. Abrams.

Cladell, J. (1917). *Rodin: The man and his art.* New York: Century.

Corballis, M. (1980). Laterality and myth. *American Psychology, 35.* 284–285.

Decharnes, R., & Chabrun, J. G. (1967). *Auguste Rodin.* New York: Viking.

Ehri, L. C. (1987). Learning to read and spell words. *Journal of Reading Behavior, 19,* 5–31.

Ehri, L. C., & Wilce, L. S. (1982). Recognition of spellings printed in lower and mixed case: Evidence for orthographic images. *Journal of Reading Behavior, 14,* 219–230.

Elsen, A. (Ed.). (1965). *Auguste Rodin: Readings on his life and work.* Englewood Cliffs, NJ: Prentice-Hall.

Frith, U., & Snowling, M. (1983). Reading for meaning and reading for sound in autistic and dyslexic children. *British Journal of Developmental Psychology, 1,* 329–342.

Getzels, J., & Csikszentimihalyi, M. (1976). *The creative vision: A longitudinal study of problem finding in art.* New York: Wiley.

Gjessing, H. J., & Karlsen, B. (1989). *A longitudinal study of dyslexia.* New York: Springer-Verlag.

Healy, J. (1982). The enigma of hyperlexia. *Reading Research Quarterly, 17,* 319–338.

Henderson, L. (1984). Introduction. In L. Henderson (Ed.), *Orthographies and reading* (pp. 1–5). Hillsdale, NJ: Lawrence Erlbaum Associates.

Hunt, E. (1990). A modern arsenal for mental assessment. *Educational Psychologist, 25* (3–4), 223–241.

Hunt, E., Lunneborg, C., & Lewis, J. (1975). What does it mean to be high verbal? *Cognitive Psychology, 7,* 194–227.

Jackson, M. D., & McClelland, J. L. (1979). Processing determinants of reading speed. *Journal of Experimental Psychology, General. 108* (2), 151–181.

Johnson, D., & Myklebust, H. R. (1967). *Learning disabilities.* New York: Grune & Stratton.

Joshi, R. M., & Aaron, P. G. (1991). Developmental reading and spelling disabilities: Are these dissociable? In R. M. Joshi (Ed.), *Written language disorders* (pp. 1–19). Boston: Kluwer Academic Publishers.

Kershner, J. R. (1977). Cerebral dominance in disabled readers, good readers, and gifted children: Search for a model. *Child Development, 48,* 61–67.

Levy, B. A., & Carr, T. H. (1990). Component process analyses: Conclusions and challenges. In T. H. Carr & B. A. Levy (Eds.). *Reading and its development: Component skills approaches* (pp. 320–328). New York: Academic Press.

Liberman, I. Y., Mann, V., Shankweiler, D., & Werfelman, M. (1982). Children's memory for recurring linguistic and non-linguistic materials in relation to reading ability. *Cortex, 18,* 367–378.

MacCurdy, E. (1958). *The notebooks of Leonardo da Vinci.* New York: Braziller.

Marioni, A. (1974). Leonardo the writer. In L. Reti (Ed.), *The unknown Leonardo* (pp. 125–146). New York: McGraw-Hill.

Marshall, J. C., & Newcombe, F. (1973). Patterns of paralexia. *Journal of Psycholinguistic Research, 2,* 179–199.

Martines, L. (1968). *Lawyers and statecraft in Renaissance Florence.* Princeton, NJ: Princeton University Press.

McDowell, B. (1986). C. M. Russell, Cowboy artist. *National Geographic, 169,* 60–94.

Nickerson, R. C., & Adam, M. J. (1979). Long-term memory for a common object. *Cognitive Psychology, 11,* 287–307.

Olson, R. K., Wise, B. W., Conners, F. A., Rack, J., & Fulker, D. (1989). Specific deficits in component reading and language skills: Genetic and environmental influences. *Journal of Learning Disabilities, 22,* 339–348.

Olson, R. K., Wise, B. W., & Rack, J. P. (1989). Dyslexia: Deficits, genetic aetiology, and computer-based remediation. *Irish Journal of Psychology, 10,* (4), 494–508.

Patterson, K. E., Marshal, J. C., & Coltheart, M. (1985). *Surface dyslexia.* Hillsdale, NJ: Lawrence Erlbaum Associates.

Payne, R. (1978). *Leonardo.* Garden City, NY: Doubleday.

Phillips, S., Taylor, B., & Aaron, P. G. (1985, April). *Developmental dyslexia: Subtypes or substages?* Paper presented at the Indiana Psychological Association, Indianapolis, IN.

Renner, F. (1984). *Charles M. Russell.* New York: Harry N. Abrams.

Renner, G. (1984). Charlie Russell and the ladies in his life. *Montana, the Magazine of Western Society* (Montana Historical Society) Autumn, 34–61.

Reti, L. (1974). *The unknown Leonardo.* New York: McGraw-Hill.

Rosenblatt, E., & Winner, E. (1988). Is superior visual memory a component of superior drawing ability? In L. K. Obler & D. Fein (Eds.), *The exceptional brain: Neuropsychology of talent and special abilities* (pp. 280–296). New York: Guilford Press.

Russell, C. M. (1927). *Trails plowed under.* Garden City, NY: Doubleday.

Russell, C. M. (1929). *Good medicine.* Garden City, NY: Doubleday.

Sartori, G. (1987). Leonardo da Vinci: Omo sanza lettere. A case of surface dyslexia. *Cognitive Neuropsychology, 4,* (1), 1–10.

Schwartz, B., & Reisberg, D. (1991). *Learning and memory.* New York: Norton.

Schweiger, A. (1988). A portrait of the artist as a brain-damaged patient In L. K. Obler & D. Fein (Eds.), *The exceptional brain: Neuropsychology of talent and special abilities* (pp. 170–177). New York: Guilford Press.

Seidenberg, M. S. & Tanenhaus, M. K. (1979). Orthographic effects on rhyme monitoring. *Journal of Experimental Psychology: Human Learning and Memory, 5* (6), 546–554.

Stanovich, K. (1980). Toward an interactive-compensatory model of individual differences in the development of reading fluency. *Reading Research Quarterly, 16,* 32–71.

Stanovich, K., & West, R. F. (1989). Exposure to print and orthographic processing. *Reading Research Quarterly, 23,* 402–433.

Thompson, L. J. (1969). Language disabilities in men of eminence. *Bulletin of the Orton Society, 14,* 113–120.

Tirel, M. (1925). *The last years of Rodin.* New York: Robert M. McBride.

Vasari, G. (1959). *Lives of the most eminent painters, sculptors, and architects.* New York: Modern Library.

Warden, R. D. (1972). *C. M. Russell Boyhood Sketchbook.* Bozeman, MT: Treasure Products.

Woodcock, L. (1982). The St. Louis Heritage of Charles Marion Russell. *Gateway Heritage, 2* (4), 2–15.

V
PARAMETERS AFFECTING
VISUAL PROCESSING

19 Optometric Factors in Reading Disability

Ralph P. Garzia
University of Missouri-St. Louis

INTRODUCTION

Educators and clinicians have been interested in the relationship between vision and reading for more than half a century. Although vision is not a requirement for reading (e.g., braille reading), in those individuals with normal vision, vision is more than merely coincidental to the reading process. At worst, it can cause certain types of reading difficulties or at least be an impediment to reading efficiency or an obstacle to remediation. The presence of reduced visual acuity, uncorrected refractive error, poor oculomotor control, or binocular vision dysfunction may contribute to reading difficulties by creating blurred or diplopic (double vision) text, or discomfort during reading.

An understanding of the reading-disabled child is important for clinicians because of the frequency of questions from parents and educators about the visual status of the child. Clinicians are often the first health care professionals consulted when a child is having difficulty making expected progress in reading. On other occasions, a vision examination is included in a comprehensive multi-disciplinary assessment of the child.

This chapter discusses the association between clinical vision function and reading, and the difficulties in determining this association.

VISUAL FUNCTIONS RELATED TO THE READING PROCESS

A number of visual functions are required for normal, efficient reading. Visual acuity and visual field are important determinants of reading performance (Krischer, Stein-Arsic, Meissen, & Zihl, 1985; Legge, Pelli, Rubin, & Schleske,

1985; Sloan & Habel, 1973). In visually impaired individuals, reading performance can be severely affected. Reading rate and accuracy are inversely related to the size of a central scotoma (an area of reduced sensitivity in the visual field corresponding to the fovea) (Cummings, Whittaker, Watson, & Budd, 1985) and directly related to visual acuity (Krischer et al., 1985).

For individuals with normal vision, creation of an artificial central scotoma by masking makes reading nearly impossible when the central 11 to 17 characters around the fixation point are occluded (Rayner & Bertera, 1979).

Efficient reading also requires sufficient central visual field, particularly to the right of the fixation point. Normal readers can extract information about 15 characters to the right of the fixation point (McConkie & Rayner, 1975). This perceptual span of the right visual field is necessary to preview upcoming text, assisting word identification during subsequent fixation (McConkie & Rayner, 1975; Pollatsek, chap.9).

Sufficient oculomotor control is required to move the eyes to appropriate locations in the reading text. The oculomotor system must find the preferred viewing location for timely word recognition (McConkie, Kerr, Reddix, & Zola, 1988; O'Regan & Levy-Schoen, 1987), and return sweep to the next line of text. Disabled reading occurs in the presence of oculomotor control difficulties (Jones & Stark, 1983; Pirozzolo, 1983; Rayner & Pollatsek, 1989). Individuals with frank oculomotor dysfunctions, such as congenital nystagmus (repetitive, rhythmic, involuntary movement of the eyes), or those caused by neurological disorders often have severe difficulties with reading. The presence of saccadic intrusions, hypometric saccades, or dynamic overshoots create obstacles for smooth and continuous reading (Ciuffreda, Kenyon, & Stark, 1983, 1985).

Accurate accommodation and convergence responses are necessary for efficient reading. This ensures that the reading text is perceived as neither blurred nor diplopic. Although most of the research on accommodation has been done with optical gratings (Ciuffreda, 1991), accommodation has been found to be very accurate for reading text, usually within 0.50 diopter (Ciuffreda, Rosenfield, Rosen, Azimi, & Ong, 1990). The presence of higher order odd harmonic spatial components in letters and words produces a steep contrast gradient for accommodative control. When the text is defocused, or when first attended, its retinal image contrast gradient and contrast amplitude decreases. This elicits a reflex increase (or decrease) in accommodation to maximize foveal retinal image contrast.

Similarly, high contrast letters and words on a printed page present a rich texture of retinal disparity stimuli for convergence. The convergence response is usually quite accurate, within the central limits of Panum's fusional area (areas in the retinas of both eyes, if stimulated simultaneously by a single stimulus will give rise to a single fused percept). Even the peripheral edge of the reading material serves as a stabilizing fusion lock.

Assuming a reading distance of 33 cm and an interpupillary distance of 60

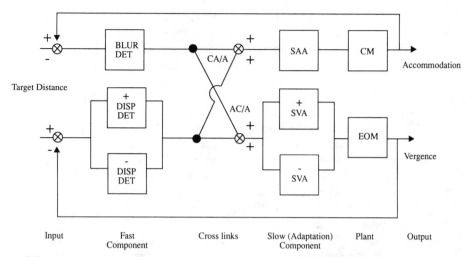

FIG. 19.1   Control systems model for the accommodative (top) and disparity vergence (bottom) mechanisms. The two motor systems are synkinetically interconnected at points between their phasic and tonic mechanisms. BLUR DET, blue detector; DISP DET, disparity detector; SAA, slow accommodative adaptation mechanism; SVA, slow vergence adaptation mechanism; CM, ciliary muscle; EOM, extraocular muscles.

mm, the overall demand of accommodation is 3.00 diopters, and for convergence 15 prism diopters. A significant function for these systems is the maintenance of these levels throughout the duration of reading.

Accommodation and vergence are both error-controlled systems requiring negative feedback for proper operation (Carroll, 1982) (Fig. 19.1). Examining reaction times, disturbing the input, reversing the sign, and the effects of opening the feedback loop substantiate the operation of feedback control (Toates, 1972, 1974).

Each has two components that operate serially, a phasic (fast) mechanism that initiates the response, and a tonic (slow) or maintaining mechanism. For the purposes of this chapter, only vergence system function is described. Input to the vergence system is a change in fixation distance, creating retinal image disparity (the images of an object to not stimulate exactly corresponding retinal points in the two eyes). A large disparity is present in the first instant when beginning reading or changing fixation from some relatively distant object to the text.

The resulting error signal drives the fast disparity vergence controller to initiate a vergence response. This is fed forward to the extraocular muscles producing the convergence required to eliminate the disparity.

Subsequently, vergence output is compared to, and subtracted from stimulus demand levels through feedback processes. Disparity vergence has a response time of less than 1 s.

If necessary, a small, purposeful steady-state error (fixation disparity) persists as a stimulus to maintain the vergence response (Schor, 1980). This steady-state error drives the fast vergence controller to compensate for any decay of its response. The magnitude of the steady-state error depends on the gain and decay time constant of the vergence controller and is directly related to the output of fast disparity vergence.

The vergence system has a slow disparity vergence controller in parallel with the output of the fast disparity vergence controller. Their outputs are summed. As reading continues, the slow disparity vergence controller assumes a greater proportion of the response and reduces the output of fast disparity vergence. Tonic accommodation and tonic vergence increase with sustained reading (Wolf, Ciuffreda, & Jacobs, 1987). This substitution of tonic control for phasic control is the basis for oculomotor adaptation to sustained reading. This is commonly referred to as *prism adaptation*. This myopic shift in tonic accommodation and convergent shift in tonic vergence reduce the magnitude of the fast disparity vergence response. This is significant because it is the magnitude of fast disparity vergence response that determines the level of visual comfort during sustained reading (Ehrlich, 1987). Low levels of sustained fast disparity vergence are related to maintained visual comfort during reading.

Dual mutual interactions between accommodation and vergence systems by cross links exist in the form of accommodation-induced convergence and disparity-induced accommodation (Schor, 1985). The slope of the relationship between accommodative response and resultant convergence is the amount of convergence stimulated per unit of accommodation change (AC/A) ratio. Conversely, the slope of the relationship between disparity vergence response and induced accommodation is the amount of accommodation stimulated per unit of convergence change (CA/C) ratio. The magnitude of these ratios have important clinical relevance in the genesis of binocular vision anomalies. For example, an unusually high AC/A ratio creates significant esophoria and demand for divergent disparity vergence activation to maintain motor fusion. These ratios are influenced by adaptational changes in phasic and tonic levels and undergo modification during fatigue of accommodation and convergence (Schor & Tsuetaki, 1987).

One of the most overlooked sources of influence on reading efficiency are the impacts of letter size, illumination, contrast, and glare. Adult reading rates are generally fastest for moderate letter sizes (0.3–2.0 deg) (Legge et al., 1985). The Illuminating Engineering Society recommends illumination levels of 25 to 50 foot-candles with sustained reading of standard printed materials (Kaufman & Hayes, 1981). As many as 200 foot-candles are recommended for sustained reading of low contrast materials or very small letter sizes. The critical level of illumination for reading newsprint is 7 foot-candles. Beyond this level, no further increase in reading efficiency occurs as illumination increases (Tinker, 1951).

For commonly used print sizes, reading rate is very tolerant to reduced contrast. For smaller text size, however, the size commonly found in scientific journals and newspapers, contrast has a more critical role in reading efficiency (Legge, Rubin, & Luebker, 1987). However, there are important individual differences in sensitivity to contrast. Contrast polarity (black-on-white vs. white-on-black) has little effect on reading rate (Legge et al., 1985).

There are also interactions between contrast and illumination. For high contrast reading materials, increasing illumination beyond 5 foot-candles has no effect on reading speed. For lower contrast materials, reading speed increases with increased illumination (Tinker, 1959).

Light sources produce direct glare. Reflected glare are reflections of light from surfaces in the field of view. They are often uncomfortable and distracting, and when they are near the reading material, reduce visibility of the text. Veiling reflections are reflections directly from the reading surface. These reflections act as if a luminous overlay were superimposed over the reading surface. An example of this is text printed on glossy paper. Light is scattered over the retinal image, effectively reducing its contrast gradient. The text may be entirely obscured under the right viewing conditions (Kaufman & Hayes, 1981).

Combined, these types of glare can produce visual discomfort and reduced reading efficiency. Discomfort glare is a sensation of annoyance or pain by high or nonuniform distributions of light in the field of view. It has been related to pupillary activity (King, 1972). Discomfort glare is based on the size, luminance, number, and location of glare sources in the field of view and the background luminance. When reading performance is reduced, the glare effect is referred to as disability glare (Kaufman & Hayes, 1981).

VISUAL ABNORMALITIES NOTED
DURING READING

Visual Symptoms

Common visual symptoms noted during reading are blur and/or diplopia of the text. Associated with these symptoms may be complaints of headaches or eye discomfort (asthenopia) or generalized feelings of fatigue and drowsiness. In children, parents may notice squinting, eye rubbing, or the adoption of an unusually close reading distance. Symptoms can occur almost immediately after reading is initiated, or more frequently, after 15 or 20 min.

These symptoms can be caused by uncorrected refractive errors or breakdowns in accommodation and convergence control related to the demands of reading. Reading under conditions of demanding productivity and efficiency goals creates an environment for visual stress. Prolonged and cognitively exacting reading tasks are more likely to produce visual symptoms than more casual reading. Sustained reading under stressful conditions has deleterious effects on binocular vision function observed by monitoring changes in heterophoria (latent tendency of one eye to deviate; esophoria, inward deviation; exophoria, outward deviation) (Pickwell, Jenkins, & Yetka, 1987) and fixation disparity (Garzia & Dyer, 1986). Accommodative and vergence anomalies associated with reading are thought to originate from an overloading or fatiguing of their central control mechanisms. The fatigue is not at the level of the extraocular or ciliary muscles because these do not easily fatigue.

Uncorrected hyperopia creates a situation of increased stimulus demand on accommodation for reading and a tendency to create esophoria, through cross-link interaction with vergence (AC/A ratio) requiring divergent disparity vergence for compensation to maintain fusion. There is a common misconception about uncorrected hyperopia in children. Although most children have an amplitude of accommodation large enough to optically neutralize uncorrected hyperopia, this does not translate to symptom-free operation for sustained periods of reading.

Clinical accommodative and vergence anomalies include difficulty rapidly changing responses, reduced gain or amplitude, and reduced sustainability. Based on these parameters, a number of binocular vision anomalies have been identified (Table 19.1).

Recently developed models suggest that the nature of these binocular vision disorders may actually represent anomalies of visual system adaptation during reading (Schor & Horner, 1989). In effect, poor prism adaptors have an increased likelihood of visual discomfort with reading. The capacity of adaptational mechanisms (North & Henson, 1981) and rate of adaptational changes (Fisher, Ciuffreda, Levine, & Wolf-Kelly, 1987) distinguish symptomatic from asymptomatic readers. There are also individuals with hyperreactive adaptational mechanisms, producing significant visual after-effects. Symptom ratings have

TABLE 19.1
List of Common Clinical Accommodative
and Vergence Disorders

ANOMALIES OF ACCOMMODATION
  excess of accommodation
  insufficiency of accommodation
  infacility of accommodation
  ill-sustained accommodation
  spasm of accommodation
ANOMALIES OF VERGENCE
  basic esophoria
  basic exophoria
  convergence excess
  convergence insufficiency
  divergence excess
  divergence insufficiency

been found to be more significantly correlated with vergence adaptation than accommodative adaptation (Owens & Wolf-Kelly, 1987).

From a biobehavioral perspective, binocular vision dysfunctions related to reading may be considered the result of reduced efficiency of feedback control (Schwartz, 1979). As discussed earlier, accommodation and convergence operate in a closed-loop, negative feedback system. An individual is not usually aware of these complex, normally self-regulatory processes. They can become disordered when feedback is disrupted. Sustained reading tasks produce stress on binocular function promoting a functional disconnection or attenuation in which negative feedback signals are ignored. This disconnection of negative feedback short-circuits self-regulatory behavior and can result in disregulation of binocular functions. The effects of disregulation are observable as a less stable or disordered system, which cannot respond properly or consistently to the stimulus. Over a period of time, an individual may attempt voluntary control as a substitute. However, such voluntary methods are not nearly as effective and can produce significant visual discomfort (Ciuffreda, 1991; Garzia & Nicholson, 1988).

Vision anomalies are not thought to affect reading directly. Uncorrected refractive error or binocular vision dysfunction may make reading uncomfortable, reducing actual time spent reading. Blurred or diplopic reading may decrease reading speed and efficiency. Also these conditions may divert attention needed to support cognitive processing for reading toward voluntary control of those visual functions (Neisser, 1967; Sperling & Melchner, 1978). Inducing vision disorders in normal adult readers has led to loss of reading accuracy (Brod & Hamilton, 1973) and comprehension (W. M. Ludlam & D. E. Ludlam, 1988).

Reading Behavior Abnormalities

Some readers experience loss of place, skipping words or lines, or general confusion within a line of text. Some of these phenomena may be related to poor oculomotor control (Ciuffreda, Kenyon, & Stark, 1983, 1985).

Disabled readers have particular difficulty with return sweeps (Pirozzollo, 1983). At the end of a return sweep, there are uncertainties about the location of the next line of print. Some report momentary diplopia. This results in delays and loss of continuity in reading. Frequently, the appropriate text line is missed entirely or previously read lines are reacquired. One explanation for this may be the particular nature of binocular saccadic eye movements. During the return sweep, binocular saccades show an abduction–adduction asymmetry (Collewijn, Erkelens, & Steinman, 1988). This represents a dynamic violation of Hering's Law (Bahill, Ciuffreda, Kenyon, & Stark, 1977). During abduction, saccades are larger, with a higher peak velocity and shorter duration. As a result, the eyes converge transiently during saccades creating esophoria (Clark, 1935). A transient loss of the vergence signal during saccades has been suggested as an explanation for this phenomenon (Collewijn et al., 1988). Disabled readers may have difficulty reestablishing binocular alignment because of slower than normal disparity vergence responses (Hung, 1989) and reduced vergence ranges (Stein, Riddell, & Fowler, 1988).

Perceptual Abnormalities

There are disabled readers who describe unusual disturbances of visual perception during reading, many similar to those reported in amblyopia (Pugh, 1958). These perceptual anomalies range from illusory movements of the text to spatial distortions. These individuals report uncontrolled text movement in the form of oscillations or even words bouncing from one point to another. Letters are described as vibrating, flickering, wobbling, or having a scintillating appearance. Individual letters or words may be seen as misshaped, deformed, or ill-proportioned to the point of hindering their identification. It is not uncommon to report variation in text contrast. Letters or words may be seen as dull or smudged. These individuals may report that the printed page appears too bright or the white background draws their attention away from the text. This is akin to the annoyance and distraction experienced from disability glare. These observations are not noted by all disabled readers, nor are all of these particular perceptions noted in the same individual. But, when present create severe impediments to efficient reading.

These perceptual abnormalities are reminiscent of the scotopic sensitivity syndrome (SSS) of Irlen (1991). The name was derived from the scotopic sensitivity function of the human eye and the similar range of wavelength transmission qualities of colored filters used to symptomatically treat patients with SSS. The use of the term *scotopic* is unfortunate and inconsistent with the usual understanding of reading occurring under photopic luminance conditions. Irlen proposed that persons with SSS have difficulty processing full-spectrum light efficiently. SSS has five components: light sensitivity, inadequate background accommodation (attention drawn away from the text to the white background), poor print resolution, restricted span of recognition, and lack of sustained attention. Individuals with SSS experience one or all of these components. In treating SSS, after ascertaining the level of perceptual abnormality, a colored filter, selected from many dozens with slightly different spectral transmission qualities (considered "specifically adapted" to the patient) is chosen based on subjective criteria. There is no reason to believe that the visual system is so sensitive to wavelength distribution on the retina, let alone during reading. The treatment of SSS with colored filters has not undergone controlled clinical trial at this time and reports of its effectiveness are largely anecdotal. Symptomatic relief of perceptual disturbances related to the attenuation of background luminance is more likely than improved reading efficiency per se. The effect of colored filters on chromatic aberration of the eye is also an important element for consideration.

The exact nature of these perceptual abnormalities is poorly understood at this time. They have been associated with clinical anomalies of binocular vision (Scheiman et al., 1990) and oculomotor dysfunctions (Ciuffreda et al., 1983). In fact, Scheiman et al. (1990) showed that a large majority of patients tested positively for SSS have common binocular vision disorders (Table 19.1). Perceptual symptom elimination can be obtained with conventional optometric therapy (Blaskey et al., 1991).

Another interpretation for the perception of instability of text with reading may be derived from the framework of parallel visual channels and their interactions (Breitmeyer, 1989; Breitmeyer, chap. 5; Lehmkuhle, chap. 4). Lovegrove and colleagues identified a transient channel deficit in a majority of specific reading disabled tested (Lovegrove, Garzia, & Nicholson, 1990; Lovegrove, Martin, & Slaghuis, 1986). As a consequence, transient inhibition of sustained channels is reduced, weakening saccadic suppression and increasing visible persistence. Defective saccadic suppression would lead to a loss of visual direction constancy with instability of the visual world (Matin, 1974). Increased visible persistence interrupts the normal flow of information across successive fixations during reading, contributing to the confusion (Breitmeyer, 1989).

Others have suggested that these disturbances are caused by the lack of development of a dominant eye necessary for singular control and registration of eye position and movements of the eye during reading (Stein, chap. 15; Stein & Fowler, 1982; Stein, Riddell, & Fowler, 1987). These authors speculate that without a dominant eye, reading-disabled individuals are unable to associate the retinal and oculomotor signals relating to each eye independently. This creates difficulty in correctly localizing letters on a page of print.

RELATIONSHIP BETWEEN VISUAL SKILLS AND READING

Difficulties

Throughout the last half century there have been innumerable attempts to determine the oculomotor, refractive, and binocular correlates of disabled reading. Because reading involves vision, vision was an obvious place to search for the singular underlying etiology. These investigations were intended to determine the degree of association between vision anomalies and reading disorders, with the view to uncovering the etiology of reading disability. The persistent question was the prevalence of vision anomalies among the reading disabled compared to normal readers. Vision disorders were thought to be a potential biological marker for reading disability, in much the same way as eye movement disorders are emerging as a biological marker for schizophrenia (Clementz & Sweeney, 1990). At this time, vision disorders meet none of the requirements of a biological marker.

Despite many attempts, there remains considerable confusion and misunderstanding. Confusion arises from the nature of the research itself and the complexities of both vision and reading.

Some studies have used nonvalid measures of visual functions, small or inappropriate samples, or measurement of visual functions by nonprofessionals. Others have used arbitrary nonuniform criteria for designating normal and abnormal visual function. Few studies have used comprehensive clinical testing or complete diagnostic classification.

There has been an overreliance on inadequate tests of visual function; for example, brief assessments of visual function usually obtained on vision screenings. By their very nature, these assessments have questionable relevance to sustained reading. There is also the tendency to view each visual function as separate and isolated and not interrelated or grouped together as a syndrome or a cluster of skills, as is commonly done clinically.

There are dilemmas associated with cursory classification of vision anomalies. For example, although intuition predicts that a higher amount of hyperopia should be more disruptive, clinical experience dictates that lower amounts are just as likely to create difficulties with binocular vision and visual comfort. Analogous to this is the conundrum associated with strabismus (frank deviation of one of the eyes). The individual with constant strabismus will suppress the vision of one eye, and perform reading monocularly. In contrast, the individual with an intermittent strabismus or significant lateral heterophoria would most likely experience diplopia or visual discomfort as the disparity vergence system fatigues. The constant strabismic is judged the more abnormal; whereas the individual with the lesser form of binocular vision anomaly, albeit more significant to reading efficiency is judged more normal.

Other uncontrolled variables are the presence of compensatory factors such as intrinsic motivation (Gottfried, 1985). Children may learn to compensate by utilizing alternative learning strategies that militate a significant visual dysfunction. There are also the uncontrolled effects of pedagogy. Effective teaching or matching teacher–student styles may mask the effects of a visual dysfunction.

Because of the muddle created in answering the fundamental question, many clinicians have underestimated the potential effects of a vision dysfunction on reading, practicing therapeutic inaction.

Correlates

A careful analysis of the existing literature does provide credible evidence that some visual functions are correlated with reading performance. The literature regarding refractive status indicates that hyperopia and anisometropia (unequal refractive errors between the two eyes) are associated with poor reading performance, whereas myopia and distance visual acuity are not (Grisham & Simons, 1986). There is some evidence supporting a relationship between poor reading and reduced nearpoint visual acuity, particularly binocularly. Relative to specific binocular anomalies, there is consistent evidence that exophoria at near, reduced disparity vergence ranges, aniseikonia (a relative difference in ocular image sizes between the eyes), convergence insufficiency and presence of fixation disparity are related to reading problems (Simons & Grisham, 1987). A meta-analysis of 34 studies of vision anomalies and reading skills reached very similar conclusions (Simons & Gassler, 1988). Furthermore, prescribing needed refractive corrective can improve reading skills (Farris, 1936; Grisham & Simons, 1986).

These correlations are not robust, however. There is considerable overlap in the distribution of vision dysfunctions among readers. Some reading-disabled individuals have normal visual functions and some good readers have very poor visual function. Many individuals learn to read well despite the presence of vision anomalies. One reason for this is that in the vast majority of studies, reading skill was the independent variable, and the vision anomaly the dependent variable. Because of the generally low number of vision dysfunctions identified, a sample of disabled readers should include a significant proportion of subjects with normal visual function (Simons & Gassler, 1988). Only a few studies have been designed with vision anomalies as the independent variable, in which case, a significant proportion of subjects with vision disorders would probably have reading disability (Simons & Gassler, 1988).

One also has to consider the onset and duration of vision anomalies. They may have been present for a considerable period of time, influencing reading efficiency for that time or may have developed only recently, with less severe impact.

Developmental Aspects

The potential impact of vision dysfunctions on reading performance is dependent on reading demands. Compared to beginning readers, older children or adults read text with smaller print with longer words and sentences. Lines of text are more closely spaced. This requires greater precision of binocular vision and oculomotor function. Longer periods of reading are required. More complex comprehension and higher order inferences are necessary. These more sophisticated reading situations are much more likely to be disrupted by a vision disorder than beginning reading (Flax, 1968).

Reading Level Considerations

Using a classification scheme of disabled readers from Rayner and Pollatsek (1989), poor readers (IQ scores in the normal range, 1–2 years below reading), would be more vulnerable to a visual dysfunction than either backward readers (IQ dependent reading problems) or dyslexic readers (more than 2 years below in reading), who have a more profound type of reading disability. Another way of stating this, the correction of a vision dysfunction is more likely to have an impact on the less disabled readers. Clinicians should also be wary of recent decline in reading performance, recent decreased interest in reading, and difficulty sustaining attention during reading. These may be due to the effects of a vision disorder.

Reading Disability Subtypes

Reading disabilities have been classified into two broad syndromal categories, auditory-linguistic and visual-spatial based on discrete reading, spelling, and neuropsychological performance patterns. Of particular interest in this discussion is the visual-spatial subtype (Watson & Willows, chap. 13). Disabled readers of the visual-spatial subtype are identified by average to above-average verbal IQ, lower performance IQ relative to verbal IQ, poor handwriting, reading errors involving the visual aspects of text, faulty eye movements during reading, right–left disorientation, and use of phonetic decoding strategies (Pirozzolo, 1983). Clinicians would expect that these individuals with relatively intact language skill development would be at greater risk for a vision disorder contributing to the reading disability.

VISUAL ASSESSMENT
OF THE READING DISABLED

Any visual assessment of the reading disabled must include not only tests of visual acuity and refractive status but also tests of nearpoint visual skills associated with reading. The functions of ocular motility, accommodation, and vergence should be investigated in detail for the presence of any anomaly that may induce visual symptoms or discomfort. Reading-disabled children can have difficulty describing their symptoms and must be questioned carefully. Particular attention should be directed at the hyperopic individual because of its correlation with poor reading.

Refractive anomalies may be corrected with a spectacle correction. For children, these are usually worn in school and for all reading activities. The lenses should be designed to enable the individual adequate vision for both distance viewing and reading.

Other visual conditions may require vision therapy (orthoptics). Vision therapy, like biofeedback, reestablishes the normal operation of feedback mechanisms. These new feedback loops, through repetition, become established, internalized, and automatized. Various techniques and instruments provide controlled stimuli and sequential experiences for learning. The importance of vision therapy can be observed in the enhancement of binocular adaptational processes during reading (North & Henson, 1982).

Others have advocated occlusion therapy to promote the ocular dominance of the nonoccluded eye (Stein & Fowler, 1985). Occlusion would also be effective in any individual suffering from binocular vision-related deficits.

Masks or optotypes may assist some disabled readers with oculomotor deficiencies. Masks are also effective for individuals experiencing discomfort or disability glare. One option for individuals who experience severe perceptual disturbances with reading is the use of attenuating filters, either colored or neutral density, to reduce illumination and contrast. This filtering may alter the relationship between sustained and transient channels, reestablishing a more normal transient and sustained interaction (Lovegrove & Williams, chap. 14).

SCREENING FOR VISUAL DEFICITS

A discussion of the relationship between vision and reading has implications for school vision screening programs. These are nominally intended to identify children with potentially troublesome vision deficits. Based on what is known about visual functions that may be correlated with reading disability, the traditional screening of distance visual acuity falls short of identifying at risk individuals. Distance visual acuity measures are only sensitive to the presence of myopia. Myopia is clearly not related to poor reading.

For this reason, vision screening programs must be more comprehensive in nature. Screening goals should include identifying hyperopia, particularly low or moderate amounts, anisometropia, and binocular vision disorders.

REFERENCES

Bahill, A. T., Ciuffreda, K. J., Kenyon, R., & Stark, L. (1977). Dynamic and static violations of Hering's law of equal innervation. *American Journal of Optometry and Physiological Optics, 53,* 786–796.

Blaskey, P., Scheiman, M., Parisi, M., Ciner, E. B., Gallaway, M., & Selznick, R. (1991). The effectiveness of Irlen filters for improving reading performance: A pilot study. *Journal of Learning Disability, 23,* 604–612.

Breitmeyer, B. G. (1989). A visually based deficit in specific reading disability. *Irish Journal of Psychology, 10,* 534–541.

Brod, N., & Hamilton, D. (1973). Binocularity and reading. *Journal of Learning Disability, 6,* 574–576.

Carroll, J. P. (1982). Control theory approach to accommodation and vergence. *American Journal of Optometry and Physiological Optics, 59,* 658–669.

Ciuffreda, K. J. (1991). Accommodation to gratings and more naturalistic stimuli. *Optometry and Vision Science, 68,* 243–260.

Ciuffreda, K. J., Kenyon, R. V., & Stark, L. (1983). Saccadic intrusions contributing to reading disability. *American Journal of Optometry and Physiological Optics, 60,* 242–249.

Ciuffreda, K. J., Kenyon, R. V., & Stark, L. (1985). Eye movements during reading: Further case reports. *American Journal of Optometry and Physiological Optics, 62,* 844–852.

Ciuffreda, K. J., Rosenfield, M., Rosen, J., Azimi, A., & Ong, E. (1990). Accommodative responses to naturalistic stimuli. *Ophthalmic and Physiological Optics, 10,* 168–174.

Clark, B. (1935). The effect of binocular imbalance on the behavior of the eyes during reading. *Journal of Educational Psychology, 26,* 530–538.

Clementz, B. A., & Sweeney, J. A. (1990). Is eye movement dysfunction a biological marker for schizophrenia? A methodological review. *Psychological Bulletin, 108,* 77–92.

Collewijn, H., Erkelens, C. J., & Steinman, R. M. (1988). Binocular coordination of human horizontal saccadic eye movements. *Journal of Physiology, 404,* 157–182.

Cummings, R. W., Whittaker, S. G., Watson, G. R., & Budd, J. M. (1985). Scanning characters and reading with a central scotoma. *American Journal of Optometry and Physiological Optics, 62,* 833–843.

Ehrlich, D. L. (1987). Near vision stress: Vergence adaptation and accommodative fatigue. *Ophthalmic and Physiological Optics, 7,* 353–357.

Farris, L. P. (1936). *Visual defects as factors influencing achievement in reading.* Unpublished doctoral dissertation, Berkeley, University of California.

Fisher, S. K., Ciuffreda, K. J., Levine, S., & Wolf-Kelly, K. S. (1987). Tonic adaptation in symptomatic and asymptomatic subjects. *American Journal of Optometry and Physiological Optics, 64,* 333–343.

Flax, N. (1968). Visual function in dyslexia. *American Journal of Optometry and Archives of the American Academy of Optometry, 45,* 574–586.

Garzia, R. P., & Dyer, G. (1986). Effect of nearpoint stress on the horizontal forced vergence fixation disparity curve. *American Journal of Optometry and Physiological Optics, 63,* 901–907.

Garzia, R. P., & Nicholson, S. B. (1988). The effect of volition on the horizontal forced-vergence fixation disparity curve. *American Journal of Optometry and Physiological Optics, 65,* 61–63.

Gottfried, A. E. (1985). Academic intrinsic motivation in elementary and high school students. *Journal of Educational Psychology, 77,* 631–645.

Grisham, J. D., & Simons, H. D. (1986). Refractive error and the reading process: A literature analysis. *Journal of the American Optometric Association, 57,* 44–55.

Hung, G. K. (1989). Reduced vergence response velocities in dyslexics: A preliminary report. *Ophthalmic and Physiological Optics, 9,* 420–423.

Irlen, H. (1991). *Reading by the colors.* Garden City Park: Avery.

Jones, A., & Stark, L. (1983). Abnormal patterns of normal eye movements in specific dyslexia. In K. Rayner. (Ed.), *Eye movements in reading* (pp. 481–498). New York: Academic Press.

Kaufman, J. E., & Hayes, H. (1981). *IES Lighting Handbook.* New York: Illuminating Engineering Society of North America.

King, V. (1972). Discomfort glare from flashing sources. *Journal of the American Optometric Association, 43,* 53–56.

Krischer, C. C., Stein-Arsic, M., Meissen, R., & Zihl, J. (1985). Visual performance and reading capacity of partially sighted persons in a rehabilitation center. *American Journal of Optometry and Physiological Optics, 62,* 52–58.

Legge, G. E., Pelli, D. G., Rubin, G. S., & Schleske, M. M. (1985). Psychophysics of reading—I. Normal vision. *Vision Research, 25,* 239–252.

Legge, G. E., Rubin, G. S., & Luebker, A. (1987). Psychophysics of reading—V. The role of contrast in normal vision. *Vision Research, 27,* 1165–1177.

Lovegrove, W., Martin, F., & Slaghuis, W. A. (1986). A theoretical and experimental case for a vision deficit in specific reading disability. *Cognitive Neuropsychology, 3,* 225–267.

Lovegrove, W. J., Garzia, R. P., & Nicholson, S. B. (1990). Experimental evidence for a transient system deficit in specific reading disability. *Journal of the American Optometric Association, 61,* 137–146.

Ludlam, W. M., & Ludlam, D. E. (1988). Effects of prism induced accommodative convergence stress on reading comprehension test scores. *Journal of the American Optometric Association, 59,* 440–445.

Matin, E. (1974). Saccadic suppression—a review and analysis. *Psychological Bulletin, 81,* 899–917.

McConkie, G. W., & Rayner, K. (1975). The span of the effective stimulus during a fixation in reading. *Perception and Psychophysics, 17,* 578–586.

McConkie, G. W., Kerr, P. W., Reddix, M. D., & Zola, D. (1988). Eye movement control during reading: I. The location of initial eye fixations on words. *Vision Research, 28,* 1107–1118.

Neisser, U. (1967). *Cognitive psychology.* New York: Appleton-Century-Crofts.

North, R. V., & Henson, D. B. (1981). Adaptation to prism-induced heterophoria in subjects with abnormal binocular vision or asthenopia. *American Journal of Optometry and Physiological Optics, 58,* 746–752.

North, R. V., & Henson, D. B. (1982). Effect of orthoptics upon the ability of patients to adapt to prism-induced heterophoria. *American Journal of Optometry and Physiological Optics, 59,* 983–986.

O'Regan, J. K., & Levy-Schoen, A. (1987). Eye movement strategy and tactics in word recognition and reading. In M. Coltheart. (Ed.), *Attention and performance: XII. The psychology of reading* (pp. 363–383). Hillsdale, NJ: Lawrence Erlbaum Associates.

Owens, D. A., & Wolf-Kelly, K. (1987). Near work, visual fatigue, and variations of oculomotor tonus. *Investigative Ophthalmology and Vision Science, 28,* 743–749.

Pickwell, L. D., Jenkins, T.C.A., & Yetka, A. A. (1987). The effect on fixation disparity and associated heterophoria of reading at an abnormally close distance. *Ophthalmic and Physiological Optics, 7,* 345–347.

Pirozzolo, F. J. (1979). *The neuropsychology of developmental reading disorders.* New York: Praeger.

Pirozzolo, F. J. (1983). Eye movements and reading disability. In K. Rayner. (Ed.), *Eye movements in reading.* (pp. 499–521). New York: Academic Press.

Pugh, M. (1958). Visual distortion in amblyopia. *British Journal of Ophthalmology, 42,* 449–460.

Rayner, K., & Bertera, J. H. (1979). Reading without a fovea. *Science, 206,* 468–469.

Rayner, K., & Pollatsek, A. (1989). *The psychology of reading.* Englewood Cliffs, NJ: Prentice-Hall.

Scheiman, M., Blaskey, P., Ciner, E. B., Gallaway, M., Parisi, M., Pollack, K., & Selznick, R. (1990). Vision characteristics of individuals identified as Irlen filter candidates. *Journal of the American Optometric Association, 61,* 600–606.

Schor, C. M. (1980). Fixation disparity: A steady state error of disparity-induced vergence. *American Journal of Optometry and Physiological Optics, 57,* 618–631.

Schor, C. M. (1985). Models of mutual interactions between accommodation and convergence. *American Journal of Optometry and Physiological Optics, 62,* 369–374.

Schor, C. M., & Horner, D. (1989). Adaptive disorders of accommodation and vergence in binocular dysfunction. *Ophthalmic and Physiological Optics, 9,* 264–268.

Schor, C. M., & Tsuetaki, T. K. (1987). Fatigue of accommodation and vergence modifies their mutual interactions. *Investigative Ophthalmology and Vision Science, 28,* 1250–1259.

Schwartz, G. E. (1979). Disregulation and systems theory: A biobehavioral framework for biofeedback and behavioral medicine. In N. Birbaumer & H. D. Kimmel (Eds.), *Biofeedback and self-regulation,* (pp. 27–56). Hillsdale, NJ: Lawrence Erlbaum Associates.

Simons, H. D., & Grisham, J. D. (1987). Binocular anomalies and reading problems. *Journal of the American Optometric Association, 58,* 578–587.

Simons H. D., & Gassler, P. A. (1988). Vision anomalies and reading skill: A meta-analysis of the literature. *American Journal of Optometry and Physiological Optics, 65,* 893–904.

Sloan, L. L., & Habel, A. (1973). Reading speed—with textbooks in large and in standard print. *Sight Saving Review, 43,* 107–111.

Sperling, G., & Melchner, M. J. (1978). The attention operating characteristic. Examples from visual search. *Science, 202,* 315–318.

Stein, J. F., & Fowler, S. (1982). Diagnosis of dyslexia by means of a new indicator of eye dominance. *British Journal of Ophthalmology, 66,* 332–336.

Stein, J., & Fowler, S. (1985, July 13). Effect of monocular occlusion in visuomotor perception and reading in dyslexic children. *The Lancet,* 69–73.

Stein, J. F., Riddell, P. M., & Fowler, S. (1987). Fine binocular control in dyslexic children. *Eye,*
1, 433–438.

Stein, J. F., Riddell, P. M., & Fowler, S. (1988). Disordered vergence control in dyslexic children.
British Journal of Ophthalmology, 72, 162–166.

Tinker, M. A. (1951). Derived illumination specifications. *Journal of Applied Psychology, 35,*
377–380.

Tinker, M. A. (1959). Brightness contrast, illumination intensity and visual efficiency. *American*
Journal of Optometry and Archives of the American Academy of Optometry, 36, 221–236.

Toates, F. M. (1972). Accommodation function of the human eye. *Physiological Review, 1972,*
828–863.

Toates, F. M. (1974). Vergence eye movements. *Documenta Ophthalmologica, 37,* 153–214.

Wolf, K. S., Ciuffreda, K. J., & Jacobs, S. E. (1987). Time course and decay of effects of near
work on tonic accommodation and tonic vergence. *Ophthalmic and Physiological Optics, 7,*
131–135.

20 Reading and Visual Discomfort

Arnold Wilkins
Medical Research Council Applied Psychology Unit
Cambridge, England

Reading can provoke perceptual distortion, eye strain, headaches, and seizures. In this chapter it is argued that these adverse effects occur because the successive lines of printed text resemble a pattern of stripes. The stripelike pattern can have spatial characteristics within a critical range for which adverse effects are possible. The striped properties vary considerably from one text to another and depend in part on the horizontal and vertical spacing of the words. There are large individual differences in susceptibility to the effects of stripes. It is shown that in persons who are susceptible, text can usually be made clearer and more comfortable by covering the lines that are not being read, thereby attenuating the striped pattern. Some people find that tinted glasses reduce the anomalous perceptual effects provoked by text. The appropriate tint varies from one individual to another and may be very specific. It can be selected using a colorimeter and associated tinted trial lenses. The physiological basis for efficacy of the tints is uncertain but may relate to a selective impairment of achromatic or color-opponent channels. It may be possible to change the spatial characteristics of conventional text slightly and improve clarity without increasing costs.

PATTERNS CAN BE HARMFUL

About 4% of patients with epilepsy are photosensitive and liable to seizures induced by flickering light. About half these patients are sensitive not only to flickering light but also to geometric patterns, particularly stripes with certain specific characteristics. It can be inferred that the seizures arise in the visual cortex when normal physiological excitation involves more than a critical

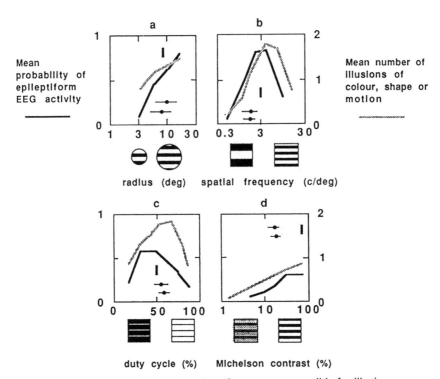

Mean probability of epileptiform EEG activity

Mean number of illusions of colour, shape or motion

a radius (deg)

b spatial frequency (c/deg)

c duty cycle (%)

d Michelson contrast (%)

FIG. 20.1. Spatial characteristics of patterns responsible for illusions and seizures. The solid lines show the probability of epileptiform EEG activity in patients with photosensitive epilepsy. The probability was estimated from repeated randomized presentations of the pattern. The values for a group of patients were averaged. The gray lines show the average number of illusions of color, shape, or motion reported by normal observers. (a) Effects of the field size (angular subtense of the radius of the pattern at the eye). (b) Effects of the spatial frequency of a square-wave grating (number of spatial cycles of the pattern in one degree subtended at the eye). (c) Effects of the duty cycle (proportion of spatial cycle occupied by bright bars). (d) Effects of the Michelson contrast (difference in the luminance of the bright and dark sections of the pattern expressed as a proportion of their sum). Icons beneath each x-axis demonstrate variations in the parameter. The patterns in these icons are shown with horizontal stripes, although some of the data were collected using different orientations. In general, pattern orientation had little effect. The curves were obtained by manipulating each parameter independently, the values of the other parameters being chosen arbitrarily. As data were acquired it transpired that the values chosen were close to those for which illusions and epileptiform EEG activity were maximally likely (after Wilkins et al., 1984). The solid points and horizontal bars indicate the mean +/− 1 sd of the value of the parameter for text, when text is considered as stripes. The upper and lower bars refer to "less clear" and "clear" text, respectively. In (a), central fixation of the page is assumed and half the width of the page is taken as the radius of the pattern. In (b), the observer's choice of a comfortable reading distance is used. In (c), the estimate is based

number of cortical neurons (Wilkins, Binnie, Darby, & Kasteleijn-Nolst Trenité, 1990).

The patterns that provoke epileptiform activity in patients with photosensitive epilepsy are judged unpleasant by people who do not have epilepsy. The patterns induce a variety of anomalous visual effects that may be cortical in origin. People who suffer headaches and eye strain are particularly susceptible to the illusions (Khalil, 1991; Marcus & Soso, 1989; Wilkins et al., 1984). Susceptibility is increased up to 24 hours before a headache (Neary & Wilkins, unpublished data). In persons with migraine who have a consistently lateralized visual aura, the susceptibility (between headaches) is greater in the affected visual field (Khalil, 1991).

It is only when they have certain very specific spatial characteristics that patterns become aversive and induce anomalous visual effects and unpleasant neurological sequelae. The worst patterns are those of black-and-white stripes, particularly (a) when the pattern is large; (b) when each stripe subtends about 10 min of arc at the eye (i.e., the spatial frequency of the pattern is about 3 cycles/degree); (c) when the stripes have an even width and spacing (a duty cycle close to 50%); and (d) when the stripes are bright and strongly contrasting. The effects of these pattern characteristics are shown in Fig. 20.1. Figure 20.2 provides an example of an aversive pattern with spatial characteristics for which illusions and seizures are likely. The pattern is yet more aversive if it vibrates or changes phase (black-white, white-black) repeatedly at a frequency close to 20 Hz. Warning: Do not look at fig. 20.2 if you have epilepsy or migraine.

Text As a Striped Pattern

The successive lines of text form a pattern rather like that of stripes. If you look at the text in this paragraph and almost close your eyes so that you can no longer see detail, the stripes will become more apparent. You may find the text in this paragraph more difficult to read than on neighboring paragraphs, and that it becomes clearer when the lines above and below those you are reading are covered up. The text in this paragraph has been altered so that the spacing of lines and letters increases the effect of the stripes, as is described.

---

on the ratio of x-height to interline spacing. In (d) the estimates are based on the space-averaged reflectance of a rectangular section of the page, with width similar to that of the line and height less than the x-height of the letters (after Wilkins & Nimmo-Smith, 1987). Note that the parameter ranges for text are close to the peak of the functions for spatial frequency and duty cycle. The short vertical bars represent the values for the pattern shown in Fig. 20.2 when viewed from a distance of 0.4 m.

FIG. 20.2. An example of a pattern with characteristics likely to induce anomalous visual effects, discomfort, eye strain, headaches, and seizures. *Cover this pattern if you have epilepsy or migraine.*

Measuring the Stripes

The angular size of the grating-like pattern that text provides is determined by the size of the page (less the margins) and the distance from which the text is read. The reading distance and the interline spacing combine to determine the spatial frequency of the grating (the number of spatial cycles of the pattern in one degree of angle subtended at the eye). The ascenders and descenders of letters contribute little to the mean line density profile of a line of text (Wilkins & Nimmo-Smith, 1987). If, for the sake of simplicity they are ignored, the width of the stripes depends on the height of the central body of the letters, or x-*height,* and the x-height and interline spacing combine to provide an estimate of the ratio of bar width to bar separation (duty cycle) of the grating. (Note that in accordance with convention the duty cycle refers to the ratio of the width of the bright bar to the period of the grating, so that in the present context the duty cycle would be estimated from the difference between the interline spacing and the x-height expressed as a ratio of the interline spacing). The contrast of the grating is determined by the contrast of the ink on the paper and the width and spacing of the letter strokes and can be estimated from the space-averaged reflectance of a line of text, measured using simple photometric methods described by Wilkins and Nimmo-Smith (1987).

The horizontal bars in Fig. 20.1 show, for text printed on paper, the range of values of each pattern characteristic. These values were obtained in the study by Wilkins and Nimmo-Smith (1987), who asked volunteers to select books from their personal libraries, choosing those with "clear" and "less clear" text. The upper bars show the values for "less clear" text.

Extending the Measurements to Two Dimensions

Text is a two-dimensional pattern and the stripelike quality depends on the variation in character density within a line, and the extent to which such variations change from one line to another, as shown in Fig. 20.3.

Consider the two samples of text shown in Fig. 20.3a. Both have similar line spacing and character spacing, but in the sample on the left the spaces between neighboring words are rather small.

Figure 20.1b shows that spatial frequencies in the range 1 to 8 cycles/degree are most likely to be harmful, at least for gratings with sharp edges, or more correctly, those with a square wave luminance profile. (The narrow spatial tuning of the function suggests that the higher frequency harmonics of the square wave gratings have only a small effect). Watt and Wilkins (unpublished observations) *filtered* samples of text so that only these midrange spatial frequencies were visible, see Fig. 20.3.

Figures 20.3b and 20.3c show the filtered images. In Fig. 20.3c the standard deviation of the filter is twice as large as in Fig. 20.3b, in other words more of the details (high spatial frequencies) have been removed. Note that the sample on the left is striped and remains so for a wide range of filter settings. In the sample of text on the left the words in a line easily blur together to form a stripe, whereas in the sample on the right the words tend to remain separate. As the standard deviation of the filter is increased, increasing the blur, the words in the sample on the right tend to coalesce with those on lines above and below as much as with those on the same line. In Figs. 20.3d and 20.3e the contrast of the filtered image has been exaggerated by setting all luminance values below the mean to black and those above to white. This serves to make the stripes more visible. Those readers who are susceptible to the effects of stripes may see illusions in the patterns on the left, but are less likely to do so in the patterns on the right, which have shorter line segments (see Fig. 20.1e). The text on the right may appear easier to read. For further examples of the effects of filtering see Watt, Bock, Thimbleby, and Wilkins (1990).

VISUAL AND CLINICAL EFFECTS OF THE "STRIPES" IN TEXT

In the previous section it has been shown that text is theoretically appropriate for the induction of illusions, eye strain, headaches, and seizures. In the following sections it is shown that text does indeed provoke these unfortunate effects in people who are visually sensitive: those who suffer photophobia or photosensitive epilepsy. The anomalous visual effects and eye strain are considered first. The evidence concerning seizures is discussed later.

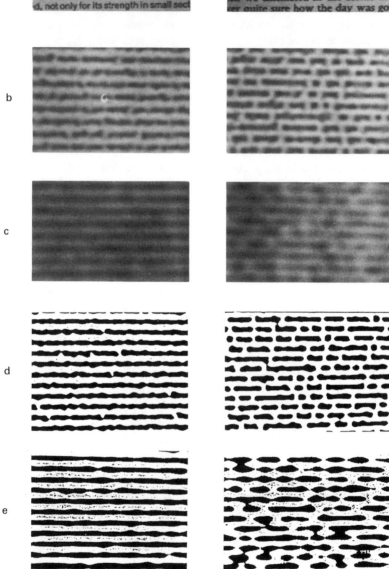

440

Anomalous Visual Effects

Wilkins and Nimmo-Smith (1987) asked normal observers to look at a letter in the center of a page of text for 30s. Various anomalous visual effects were reported, covering the range of illusions commonly seen in striped patterns, and including a lattice of faint rhomboid shapes: an illusion sometimes reported after prolonged observation of a striped pattern. When text with a larger typeface was used, so that the spatial frequency of the grating was reduced, the size of the rhomboid lattice increased in just the same way as when the spatial frequency of a grating is reduced.

The 3rd paragraph on page 437 has been typeset in such a way as to render illusions likely. The height of the central body of the letters (x-height) has been reduced so that at a typical reading distance of 0.4 m it subtends 10 min of arc at the eye; the lines of text have been separated by spaces of similar height so that the duty cycle of the "grating" is close to 50%; the contrast of the lines has been increased by reducing the spaces between adjacent letters and words. The spatial characteristics formed by the text are close to those for which illusions are maximally likely. When you look at the paragraph in a strong light the lines may seem to shimmer. If you gaze at a letter in the center of the paragraph for a while, a faint rhomboid lattice may appear. Compare the illusions you see in this paragraph with those seen in the grating in Fig. 20.2. They will be less intense but are probably similar in nature.

Eye Strain

The samples of text shown in Fig. 20.3 were selected by a 41-year-old woman who was unable to read for more than about 20 min before she suffered disorientation (which she described as feeling "disconcerted"). She selected the sample on the left of Fig. 20.3a as being particularly difficult to read: The other sample gave her no problems.

The degree to which the lines of text form stripes when blurred in this way

---

FIG. 20.3.   Two samples of printed text (a) before and (b-e) after spatial filtering. Both samples have similar line spacing and character spacing but the sample on the left has greater interword spacing. These samples were selected by a 41-year-old woman who suffered an inability to read for periods of more than about 20 min without feeling "disconcerted." She selected the sample on the left as being particularly difficult to read: The sample on the right have her no problems. In (b) the samples of text above have been filtered by convolution with a Mexican hat filter, which has the effect of removing the high spatial frequency components. In (c) the filter has a standard deviation twice that in (b). In (d) and (e) the filtered images in (b) and (c) respectively have been altered to make the "stripes" more apparent by setting all luminance values above the mean to white and all those below to black.

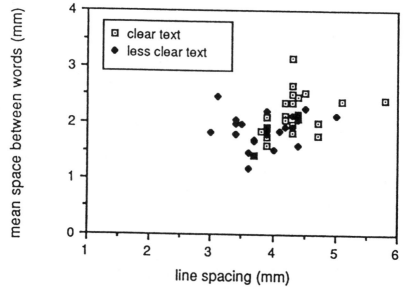

FIG. 20.4. The mean horizontal spacing between words plotted as a function of the vertical spacing between lines for samples of "clear" and "less clear" text selected by undergraduates. The samples of clear text tend to have a relatively large spacing between words and between lines (Wilkins, unpublished data).

depends in part on the relationship between the horizontal spacing between words and the vertical spacing between lines. Figure 20.4 shows these variables for samples of text selected as "clear" or "less clear" by undergraduates. As can be seen, "clear" text tends to have larger spaces between the words and between the lines.

PREVENTING EYE STRAIN, HEADACHES, AND SEIZURES

Reading Masks

In 1897 Prentice described a device that he christened the "Typoscope." It consisted simply of a card in which was cut a rectangular slot sufficient to reveal one line of text when the card was placed on the page of a book (see Mehr, 1969). The front surface of the card was matt black and was thought to reduce the effects of scattered light in patients with cataract and those with amblyopia (lazy eye) who wore lenses with strong magnification. The devise has been reinvented (and different versions patented) several times since then. Figure 20.5 provides a demonstration of the effects of a reading mask.

A demonstration of the effects of a reading mask. The text in this figure has been set in 12pt Times on a Macintosh computer using Aldus PageMaker (R) with default values for letter spacing, word spacing and line spacing. There are two passages of text, both identical, the lower one "covered" by a reading mask so as to reveal just three central lines. Compare the clarity of these lines in the top passage with their clarity in the the bottom passage. These are the central lines. Some people perceive these lines to have a greater clarity when the surrounding lines are masked. They report that the letters appear more contrasted, or that the lines appear further apart. You may perceive these improvements in clarity if you also see illusions of colour, shape or movement in the pattern of stripes shown in Figure 2. It is argued that the perceptual distortions you see in Figure 2 measure your susceptibility to stripes, that the successive lines of text resemble stripes, and that covering the unnecessary lines with a mask removes their deleterious effects, improving the clarity of the text that remains.

A demonstration of the effects of a reading mask. The text in this figure has been set in 12pt Times on a Macintosh computer using Aldus PageMaker (R) with default values for letter spacing, word spacing and line spacing. There are two passages of text, both identical, the lower one "covered" by a reading mask so as to reveal just three central lines. Compare the clarity of these lines in the top passage with their clarity in the the bottom passage. These are the central lines. Some people perceive these lines to have a greater clarity when the surrounding lines are masked. They report that the letters appear more contrasted, or that the lines appear further apart. You may perceive these improvements in clarity if you also see illusions of colour, shape or movement in the pattern of stripes shown in Figure 2. It is argued that the perceptual distortions you see in Figure 2 measure your susceptibility to stripes, that the successive lines of text resemble stripes, and that covering the unnecessary lines with a mask removes their deleterious effects, improving the clarity of the text that remains.

FIG. 20.5.   Demonstration of the effects of a reading mask. For many readers, the text in the window appears clearer than the identical text in the unmasked paragraph above.

A reading mask such as that in Fig. 20.5 reduces the effects of the striped pattern by covering the stripes above and below those being read. In a study by Wilkins and Nimmo-Smith (1984) about 70% of normal observers noticed that the text in the "window" of such a mask appeared clearer. The observers who noticed the improvement in clarity tended to be those who reported many illusions in a pattern of striped lines (see Fig. 20.2). In the same study about one-third of a sample of people who suffered eye strain or headaches from reading reported that a reading mask was of sufficient benefit to be worth the nuisance of using it. No benefits were reported from "placebo" aids that did not cover the lines both above and below those being read. These studies helped with the design of an inexpensive reading aid now marketed as the "Cambridge Easy

TABLE 20.1

Incidence of epileptiform EEG activity (discharges/min) in three patients with photosensitive epilepsy and pattern sensitivity. The EEG was recorded whilst the patients were at rest and when they read a book with and without a mask that darkened and blurred the lines of text above and below those being read.
(After Wilkins & Lindsay, 1985.)

	Patient MN	Patient IJ	Patient RB
At rest	0.70	0.00	Not tested
Reading without mask	1.48	2.67	8.52
Reading with mask	0.73	0.58	2.50

Reader" by Engineering and Design Plastics, 84 High Street, Cherry Hinton, Cambridge, UK. The device consists simply of two rectangular pieces of grey matt translucent plastic joined along one shorter edge by a magnetic slide.

Wilkins and Lindsay (1985) reported that the reading aid reduced liability to seizures in patients with epileptic pattern sensitivity. The electroencephalogram (EEG) was recorded during periods of rest, and also during randomly interleaved periods when the patient read a book in the usual way, and when the book was read using the reading mask. The mask darkened and blurred the lines of text above and below those being read, and was adjusted so that it left three lines unobscured. Table 20.1 shows the rate of epileptiform EEG discharges during the three conditions, for the two patients reported by Wilkins and Lindsay and for a third patient subsequently recorded by Darby (personal communication). The incidence of epileptiform discharges was significantly increased by reading, and significantly reduced by the use of the reading mask.

OVERLOAD OF THE VISUAL SYSTEM

The findings described so far have been interpreted from a theory of visual discomfort originally outlined by Wilkins et al. (1984). According to the theory, visual discomfort is a reflection of an "overload" of the visual system. The overload can be understood from several different but mutually consistent points of view. (a) The visual system is particularly sensitive to the stimuli that give rise to discomfort; (b) the stimuli that cause discomfort give a greater aggregate neurological response than others; (c) uncomfortable stimuli are difficult to process computationally.

Sensory Thresholds

Generally speaking, the patterns that evoke aversive effects are those for which sensory thresholds are low. In their classical work, Campbell and Robson (1968) demonstrated that, at low contrast, gratings can most readily be seen when their spatial frequency is close to 3 cycles/degree and when the bars of the grating have an even width and spacing (50% duty cycle). The low sensory thresholds suggest that, in some way, the physiological response to patterns with aversive characteristics is greater than that to other patterns.

Further evidence for a large physiological response is obtained at high contrasts. At high contrasts, aversive patterns interfere with perception, masking lower contrast stimuli. Ruddock and co-workers (Barbur & Ruddock, 1980; Holliday & Ruddock, 1983; Grounds, Holliday, & Ruddock, 1983) measured thresholds for the detection of a small dim circular target moving across a background modulated in space, in time, or in both. The background could be made to resemble the patterns that have aversive properties, and when it was, the moving target became more difficult to see. The background could also be made to flicker, and when the brightness and frequency were such as would provoke seizures in patients with photosensitive epilepsy, the target again became more difficult to see. The threshold functions showed subtle spatiotemporal interactions and had properties more complex than those implied by the limitations of Fig. 20.1, nevertheless they were generally consistent with the notion that the greater the physiological excitation induced by a visual stimulus, the greater its interference with the perception of other stimuli.

Aggregate Response

Aversive patterns tend to be those that give rise to high amplitude electrical responses from the brain (measured on the scalp as a visual evoked potential). For example, Plant, Zimmern, and Durden (1983) measured the amplitude of the evoked potential in response to (sinusoidal) gratings as a function of their spatial frequency and contrast. The functions were in broad agreement with those in Fig. 20.1.

As already mentioned, stimuli that are aversive are those that evoke seizure activity in patients with primary generalized epilepsy, suggesting that they can compromise cortical inhibitory processes. Recordings from single units and staining techniques have revealed that the visual cortex is organized into columns of cells responsive to bars and edges with similar orientation. A visual stimulus such as a grating is likely to result in patches of localized excitation of pyramidal neurons, those that respond to the grating orientation. Certain interneurons inhibit the firing of pyramidal neurons making them selectively sensitive to particular orientations (Sillito, 1979). The operation of these interneurons may be compromised if the local availability of inhibitory neurotransmitters is depleted by a strong localized excitation. This depletion may result in a spread of activation that gives rise to illusions. In patients whose cortex is hyperexcitable, the activation may spread further, inducing seizures (Meldrum & Wilkins, 1984; Wilkins et al., 1984). As already mentioned, aversive patterns are those that give rise to seizures in patients with photosensitive epilepsy.

Computational Vision

The brain's computational algorithms may analyze the visual scene at different spatial scales, the smaller scales responsible for analysis of the fine detail, and larger scales for the analysis of spatial position (Watt, 1988, 1991). Any repetitive image content may make it difficult to analyze spatial position. Consider the image of a piano keyboard. The white keys form a repetitive pattern. If only the white keys are visible, it is difficult to identify the position of any one particular key, such as middle C: The spatial scales that resolve the individual keys give an ambiguous output because one key is very much like another. The black keys differ from the white keys in that they are grouped, and although they have a repetitive structure, the structure differs at a variety of spatial scales. The structure of the finer scales that resolve the individual keys differs from the structure of the coarser scales that fail to resolve the keys but resolve instead only the gaps between the groups of two or three keys. In other words, the coarser scales can provide unambiguous information as to the position of each black key, perhaps in a hierarchy as suggested by Watt (1991, p. 181).

Aversive patterns have repetitive spatial content at all spatial scales: There is no grouping of the image that can facilitate the computation of position; this may make for greater computational complexity, and hence computational "overload."

CONTROL OF EYE MOVEMENTS

The notion of visual overload is undoubtedly simplistic, but it may have heuristic value. It is attractive when one considers not only pattern glare such as already discussed, but the ocular motor control that reading demands. When the eyes move from one point of regard to another they do so in a series of high velocity jerks known as *saccades*. Findlay (1982) and Ottes, van Gisbergen, and Eggermont (1984) asked observers to make an eye movement to one of two spots, both of which could easily be seen in the periphery of vision. When the spots were close together, the eyes landed at a point in space between the two spots, and then made a subsequent small corrective movement toward the appropriate target. It was difficult, if not impossible, for subjects to learn to move their eyes directly to one of the targets, even though they could distinguish them in peripheral vision before they began the eye movement. It was as if the part of the visual system controlling the first fast movement was unable to distinguish the two spots, but used instead some more global representation. Text in which the words coalesce to form stripes in the midrange spatial frequencies (e.g., the text on the left in Fig. 20.3) should place greater computational demands on the saccadic system, increasing the likelihood of overload, but see O'Regan (in press) for review.

TINTED GLASSES

Irlen Institute

Helen Irlen founded the Irlen Institute, which supplies tinted glasses for people with a sensitivity to light that she called "scotopic sensitivity." The term implies an undue sensitivity of the rod receptors and there is, as yet, little scientific evidence to justify its use. On the other hand, the clinical condition Irlen described overlaps with photophobia and involves many symptoms of visual discomfort. Opticians have long prescribed tinted glasses for those with photophobia, although with little to support the practice.

Wilkins and Neary (1991) examined 20 volunteers with a history of reading difficulty selected by the Irlen Institute as having benefited from the use of their tinted glasses. Fourteen were from different families. All had a history of reading problems and only one wore refractive correction. Many had migraine in the family. Nearly all had good acuity, contrast sensitivity, and stereopsis (in other words they were well able to see small detail and faint contours, and they were able use differences between the images in the two eyes to form a perception of depth). Ten had poor muscle balance (when the two eyes were not constrained to look at the same object, the axes of the eyes did not remain directed at the same point in space).

Vision with the tinted glasses was compared with vision using (a) dark (neutral density) glasses having the same (photopic) transmission and (b) untinted lenses that corrected any residual refractive error. In a few subjects acuity and muscle balance were significantly improved when the tints were worn. For the group as a whole there was a modest increase in the speed of visual search. The subjects were asked to report the illusions they saw in a pattern of stripes. Fewer illusions were reported when the tinted glasses were worn, irrespective of whether illusions of color were included.

Some of the beneficial effects could have been due to changes in motivation, although it is difficult to see how muscle balance could be affected in this way, given that subjects were unaware as to what the test was measuring and how the measurements were made.

This study, and other similar studies reviewed by Evans and Drasdo (1991), have the disadvantage that subjects are aware of the color of the lens placed in front of their eyes before they look through it and adapt to its color. It is difficult to obtain a genuine placebo. An "intuitive colorimeter" was designed to overcome some of these problems, and to provide a continuously variable source of colored light.

Intuitive Colorimeter

The colorimeter is a variant of the Burnham (1952) colorimeter. It enables hue and saturation to be varied independently and continuously, keeping luminance constant. It thus allows a wide range of color space to be explored thoroughly and quickly (Wilkins, Nimmo-Smith, & Jansons, 1992). For example, hue can be varied, keeping saturation and brightness more or less constant. The color-imeter has a wheel divided into three sectors, each sector transmitting light of a different color. A collimated cylindrical beam of white light passes through the wheel, and is colored as a result. The colored light is then mixed by multiple reflection and illuminates a page of print. When the wheel is concentric with the beam, the three sectors have equal proportion and, given the appropriate filters, the mixed light is white. The wheel is free to translate so that the beam can pass eccentrically through it. The filters then no longer have similar area. The mixture becomes progressively more saturated as eccentricity increases. The wheel is also free to rotate. This changes the hue. In terms of the CIE 1976 Uniform Chromaticity Scale Diagram, rotating the wheel moves the coordinates of the mixed light in a near-circular locus centered on white. Changing its eccentricity moves the coordinates along radii from white.

A series of children has been examined using the apparatus. For most chil-dren—but not all—there is a region of color space within which the perceptual distortions of text reportedly abate. When asked to vary the color until the distortions disappear, some children produce a very consistent setting. There appears to be a patch of color space within which the distortions disappear, but the location of that patch varies from one observer to another. For children with reading difficulties there is a tendency for the symptom-free area of color space to be within the left-hand half of the CIE 1976 Uniform Chromaticity Scale Diagram (u' < 0.25). Some children find no consistent area. They report a reduction in distortions but for colors that vary over time.

Those observers who consistently report a benefit from certain colors usually also find a region of color space in which the distortions become worse and text may become painful. The signs of discomfort are obvious: Observers wince or avert their gaze. The colors with which this discomfort occurs are usually com-plementary to those with which distortions abate. When adults with migraine are asked to mix colors that make text *un*comfortable they tend to choose shades of red (Chronicle & Wilkins, 1991). When using the colorimeter, these colors are rarely chosen by children who have reading disorders and report perceptual distortions. As already mentioned, many of these children have parents with migraine.

Subjective Precision Tinting

A set of tinted trial lenses has been developed using plastic (CR39 resin) lenses dyed with progressively increasing deposition of each of seven chemically stable dyes, avoiding composite dyes where possible. The dyes chosen have the follow-ing appearance: rose, orange, yellow, green, turquoise, blue, and purple. They have CIE 1976 hue angles about 50 degrees apart. There are five levels of deposition of each dye. The levels range from a very light tint to a very strong tint, the dye deposition doubling from one level to the next. The set of trial lenses has two trial lenses at each level (one for each eye). Thirty-one ($2^5 - 1$)levels of dye deposition can be obtained for each dye by superimposing the five trial lenses. To obtain a given color of tint, trial lenses from two dyes with similar hue angle are combined. To obtain orangey red, for example, orange and rose trial lenses would be combined. A total of 961 (31 × 31) combinations of orange and rose are possible. There are 7 combinations of neighboring colors: rose with orange, orange with yellow, yellow with green, and so forth making 7 × 961 = 6,727 combinations of dyes with similar hue. Any desired color within a large gamut can therefore be very closely approximated using only two dyes at a time.

Individuals usually report a reduction in discomfort and distortion when viewing a natural scene through the combination of lenses that matches the visible appearance of the colorimeter setting. When the setting has a strong saturation, however, lenses with the same hue angle but lower saturation are sometimes preferred, perhaps because these interfere less with color constancy and leave white surfaces remaining white in appearance.

In open trials, patients with reading disorders, eye strain, headaches, or photosensitive epilepsy have reported a reduction of symptoms when wearing glasses tinted using the aforementioned techniques (Maclachlan, Yale, & Wilkins, in press). Double-blind placebo-controlled clinical trials are now under way.

Possible Mechanisms

There are many alternative explanations for any beneficial effects of tinted glasses and more than one mechanism may be involved.

Explanations can be divided into those that are peripheral and those that are central. The peripheral explanations might involve (a) chromatic aberration contributing constructively or destructively to the control of accommodation; (b) the role of rods in controlling pupil size at photopic luminance levels (Berman, Fein, Jewett, Saika, & Ashford, 1992), with secondary effects on accommodation and vergence; or even (c) a contribution from fluorescence of intraocular structures. Possible central mechanisms include (a) the reduction of pattern glare (Wilkins & Neary, 1991) or (b) the restoration of optimal signal transmission over selectively impaired pathways. In the present context, the last two explanations merit further consideration.

The signals from the cones are thought to be combined early in visual processing so as to give a luminance signal (a combination of signals from the three cone types) and two color difference signals, one red-green, and the other yellow-blue, the latter obtained by an opposition of a signal from the short wavelength cones with signals from the other two types. Buchsbaum and Gottschalk (1983) showed that these three signals are precisely what might be anticipated if the information transmission were optimized. The signals from the cones are redundant (their spectral sensitivities overlap), and by summing the cone outputs to give a luminance signal, and by subtracting their outputs to derive two color difference signals, information can be transmitted more efficiently.

Suppose that the visual pathways are impaired by disease in such a way as to change the relative information capacity of the channels carrying the luminance and color difference signals. It follows from the mathematics outlined by Buchsbaum and Gottschalk that the information transmission could be optimized for the damaged system by changing the spectral composition of light captured by the cones. In other words, there may be some colored lens that will affect the signaling from the three cone types in such a way as to optimize the signal transmission over the damaged pathways. The color would need to be sufficiently saturated to overcome the adaptation that would undoubtedly occur.

There is evidence that the visual pathways may indeed be affected. In children with specific reading disability there exists a selective deficit on psychophysical tasks that measure transient system function, but not on those that measure the sustained system (see Lovegrove & Williams, chap. 14). The transient system is thought to signal luminance rather than information about color differences. The selective deficits, therefore, suggest an imbalance of function between achromatic and chromatic channels, although it would be inappropriate to equate the achromatic channel of Buchsbaum and Gottschalk with magnocellular pathways and transient system function (see Breitmeyer, chap. 5).

People with migraine show deficits in contrast sensitivity that are greater the longer the duration of the disease (Khalil, 1991). These deficits suggest that repeated attacks of migraine may damage the visual system. Since migraine affects the circulation of blood in the brain, the visual deficits may result from a transient insufficiency of blood supply. This might be expected to have a greater effect on cells with a high metabolic turnover. There are blob-like regions of layers 2 and 3 of the primary visual cortex of monkeys that are labeled preferentially with radioactive 2-deoxyglucose because of their heightened metabolic activity (Horton & Hubel, 1981; Humphrey & Hendrickson, 1983). These blobs are also revealed by cytochrome oxidase staining. They receive inputs from both magnocellular and parvocellular pathways. Within the blobs the cells show poor orientation tuning but a color opponency (Livingstone & Hubel, 1988). The surrounding inter-blob cells show no color opponency. The blob cells project to striped areas of V2 that are also concerned with the processing of color. Interference with the activity of cells in the blobs and stripes might be expected to affect the processing of color, given that cells in the blobs are color-opponent, whereas those in the surrounding tissue are not. Perhaps this is one mechanism for the selective color preferences shown by people with migraine (Chronicle & Wilkins, 1991).

An impairment of channel function may place a greater computational burden on the signal processing capabilities of the visual cortex, contributing in some quite nonspecific way to a processing overload similar to that described in the previous section. This may give rise to symptoms of visual discomfort by a breakdown of intracortical inhibitory mechanisms similar to those already hypothesized for the visual induction of migraine headache by Wilkins et al (1984). Interpretations of this kind are admittedly highly speculative and far from complete, but they may in time provide an explanation for the reduction of perceptual distortions and associated visual discomfort that is sometimes reportedly brought about by the wearing of tinted glasses.

If children find text aversive, and their visual orientation is compromised by anomalous visual effects, then the process of learning to read may be made yet more difficult. Any relationship between visual discomfort and visual dyslexia may not, however, be causal but due to shared brain mechanisms. The argument for a causal link is weakened by the fact that the text used in early readers differs from adult text in having large letters and few words, often on a single line. It is therefore less likely to give rise to anomalous visual effects and to discomfort. Anecdotally, however, the visual problems experienced by dyslexic children often arise as they progress to adult text. And sometimes even children's text is far from ideal. The text may be printed in a bold typeface, and the letters and words closely spaced. The appropriate grouping of the image then becomes difficult, particularly for an observer unfamiliar with letter shapes. Children with dyslexia can be more susceptible than others to the effects of crowding (Atkinson, 1991). Willows (1974) showed that poor readers read single-spaced text more slowly and less accurately than double-spaced, regardless of content. No such differences emerged for good readers.

TEMPORAL FACTORS

So far, we have considered only the spatial characteristics of text, although the visual stimulus it provides can vary in both space and time. The page is often illuminated by fluorescent light, or presented on the surface of a visual display terminal and under these conditions the luminance is varying continuously. Fluorescent light is generated by a gas discharge that occurs twice with each cycle of the AC electricity supply. On a visual display terminal the text is lit once each time the cathode ray refreshes the screen. The resulting pulsations of light are usually too rapid to be seen as flicker but they affect the visual system nevertheless. As reviewed by Kennedy (chap. 10), Eysel and Burandt (1984) recorded from the lateral geniculate nucleus of the cat and showed that under fluorescent lighting the cells fired more strongly than under daylight or incandescent light, and they fired at a certain interval after each light pulsation. Berman, Greenhouse, Bailey, Clear, and Raasch (1991) recorded electrical signals from the human retina (electroretinogram) in response to the pulsation from fluorescent lighting and Wilkins (1986) and Neary and Wilkins (1989) demonstrated small effects of the pulsation on the control of saccades across text and other patterns.

Wilkins, Nimmo-Smith, Slater, and Bedocs (1989) monitored the incidence of eye strain and headaches in office workers when the rooms were lit with conventional fluorescent lighting or with a new type, outwardly identical, from which the pulsations were electronically removed (i.e., lighting with electronic high frequency ballast). The incidence of eye strain and headache was halved under the new lighting.

The pulsation from fluorescent lighting depends on a coating of phosphor on the inner surface of the lamp. The phosphor fluoresces, converting the ultraviolet energy from the gas discharge into visible light. The most common (and cheapest) lamps use a halophosphate coating. This fluoresces at the long wavelength (red) end of the visible spectrum and exhibits phosphorescence, holding much of the long wavelength light from one discharge to the next (Wilkins & Clark, 1990). This means that most of the light pulsation is at the short wavelength end of the spectrum. Spectacles that reduce short wavelength light (e.g., amber, yellow, or rose tints) can therefore reduce the overall pulsation from fluorescent lighting. Wilkins and Wilkinson (1991) designed an ophthalmic tint (now commercially available) that reduces the pulsation of light from halophosphate lamps. In a double-blind study it has been shown to reduce migraine in children (Good, Taylor, & Mortimer, 1991). People with migraine often complain of fluorescent lighting: They can show a high amplitude steady-state evoked potential in response to intermittent light (Golla & Winter, 1959; Lehtonen, 1974; Jonkman & Lelieveld, 1981; Marsters, Good, & Mortimer, 1988), particularly at high frequencies (Brundrett, 1974).

On a visual display terminal with a cathode ray tube the screen is usually scanned by a spot of light that zig-zags down the screen varying in brightness so as to create the image. The phosphor on the screen usually loses most of its light from one scan to the next, so the picture is lit only very briefly, though at high frequency. When the eyes make a saccade, for example, from the left of the screen to the right, the eyes move extremely rapidly so that the image appears on the screen only once or maybe twice during the flight of the eye. The top part of the image is drawn earlier and therefore to the left of the image relative to the bottom of the screen. The visual image painted during the flight of the eye is therefore brief and distorted and can sometimes evade the saccadic suppression that normally makes it difficult to see the retinal image created whilst the eye is in flight. The intra-saccadic stimulation appears as a momentary image that can interfere with the perceptual stability of the visual world as the eyes come to rest. The small corrective saccades that normally follow the larger saccades are increased in number, perhaps as a result (Neary & Wilkins, 1989). As reviewed elsewhere in this volume, Kennedy and Murray (1991) showed that for typists (who read with attention to orthography and who complain of visual discomfort) there is a two-fold increase in the number of corrective saccades during reading when the display is lit intermittently, even when it is lit 100 times per second. The increase occurs with displays that scan in a raster and also with those that have no directional component to the flicker (Kennedy, personal communication).

IMPROVING TEXT
WITHOUT INCREASING COSTS

In the first three sections it has been shown that the pattern from text can provoke illusions, headaches, eye strain, and even seizures in those who are susceptible. The pattern can be reduced by covering the lines with a reading mask, but according to the theory outlined by Wilkins et al. (1984), the mask should not be necessary: It should be possible to reduce the effects of the pattern in other ways. One obvious way is to increase the spacing between the lines. As can be seen from Fig. 20.1, this has two effects: It increases the duty cycle and decreases the spatial frequency of the "grating." Both changes are in a direction appropriate for a reduction in the adverse effects of the pattern. The clarity of text has long been known to depend on the spacing of the lines (see, for example, Tinker, 1963), and this might be one reason why.

Increasing the spacing of the lines is likely to increase the costs of printing, because these costs depend partly on the amount of paper used. Can line spacing be increased without increasing costs?

The amount of paper used depends in part on the average area of paper occupied by a character. The average area is the product of the separation of the lines and the mean horizontal distance from one character to the next. Wilkins and Nimmo-Smith (1987) asked volunteers to select books from their own libraries that had "clear" or "less clear" print. They showed that subjects' judgments of clarity were strongly associated with the spacing between the lines, but not so strongly associated with the area of paper used per character. Interline spacing accounted for 33.7% and 37.7% of the variance associated with judgments of clarity in the two studies. The average area occupied by a letter explained 6.6% and 30.3% respectively. In other words there were books with text judged as "clear" that cost no more to print than books with text judged as "less clear." Evidently printing convention does not specify the spatial characteristics of text appropriately for the maximization of clarity at a given cost.

It should therefore be possible to improve the clarity of text without making it more expensive. One way of doing so might be to increase the spacing between lines while reducing the average spacing between characters. Both these changes would only need to be extremely slight, and both the line spacing and character spacing could remain within the limits set by conventional typographic practice. It would be important to ensure that the decrease in the average horizontal spacing between characters occurred within words, and maintained an appropriate relationship between horizontal word spacing and vertical line spacing.

CONCLUSION

The theory of visual discomfort outlined here explains why small changes in the layout of the words on a page can have large effects on the clarity of text. The theory provides some guidance as to how the clarity of text might be improved without making it more expensive. The theory provides an explanation for the visual discomfort with which the use of cathode ray tube displays has been associated. It links the anomalous visual effects reported in text by some children with visual dyslexia to those reported in response to more stressful stimuli by normal observers (particularly those with migraine). The theory suggests possible physiological mechanisms in common. It also suggests ways in which the visual stimulation can be altered so as to make the anomalous effects less likely. Finally, the theory provides one explanation (among many) for the beneficial effects of tinted glasses.

According to the theory, we need to think of the visual problems involved in reading as arising from a combination of factors, including those relating to the spatial and temporal characteristics of the stimulus, and those relating to the reader's difficulties with visual processing. The former we can do something about, for the benefit not only of those with reading difficulties, but of a broad cross-section of the population as well. The latter may ultimately be traceable to brain mechanisms in posterior areas that sustain the links between visual and linguistic information. It may be these mechanisms that are jointly responsible for anomalous visual effects and language difficulties.

ACKNOWLEDGMENT

This chapter is a revision of a chapter published in J. F. Stein (Ed.), *Vision and Visual Dyslexia: Vision and Visual Dysfunction* (Vol. 13). London: MacMillan Press.

REFERENCES

Atkinson, J. (1991). Review of human visual development: crowding and dyslexia. In J. F. Stein (Ed.), *Vision and visual dyslexia: Vision and visual dysfunction* (Vol 13., pp. 44–57). London: MacMillan.

Barbur, J. L., Ruddock, K. H. (1980). Spatial characteristics of movement detection mechanisms in human vision: I. Achromatic vision. *Biological Cybernetics, 37,* 77–92.

Berman, S. M., Fein, G., Jewett, D. L., Saika, G., & Ashford, F. (1992). Spectral determinants of steady-state pupil size with full field of view. Manuscript in preparation.

Berman, S. M., Greenhouse, D. S., Bailey, I. L., Clear, R. D., & Raasch, T. W. (1991). Human electroretinogram responses to video displays, fluorescent lighting, and other high frequency sources. *Optometry and Vision Science, 68*(8), 645–662.

Burnham, R. W. (1952). A colorimeter for research in colour perception. *American Journal of Psychology, 65,* 603–608.

Buchsbaum, G., & Gottschalk, A. (1983). Trichromacy, opponent colours coding and optimum colour information transmission in the retina. *Proceedings of the Royal Society of London, B 220*, 89–113.

Brundrett, G. W. (1974). Human sensitivity to flicker. *Lighting Research and Technology, 6*(3), 127–143.

Campbell, F. W., & Robson, J. G. (1986). Application of Fourier analysis to the visibility of gratings. *Journal of Physiology (London), 197*, 551–566.

Chronicle, E. P., & Wilkins, A. J. (1991, October). Colour and visual discomfort in migraineurs. *The Lancet, 338*, 890.

Evans, B.J.W., & Drasdo, N. (1991). Tinted lenses and related therapies for learning disabilities—a review. *Ophthalmic and Physiological Optics, 11*, 206–217.

Eysel, U. T., & Burandt, U. (1984). Fluorescent tube light evokes flicker responses in visual neurons. *Vision Research, 24*, 943–948.

Findlay, J. M. (1982). Global processing for saccadic eye movements. *Vision Research, 22*, 1033–1045.

Golla, F. L., & Winter, A. L. (1959). Analysis of cerebral responses to flicker in patients complaining of episodic headache. *Electroencephalography and Clinical Neurophysiology, 11*, 539–549.

Good, P. A., Taylor, R. H., & Mortimer, M. I. (1991). The use of tinted glasses in childhood migraine. *Headache, 31*, 533–536.

Grounds, A. R., Holliday, I. E., & Ruddock, K. H. (1983). Two spatio-temporal filters in human vision: II. Selective modification in amblyopia, albinism and hemianopia. *Biological Cybernetics, 47*, 191–201.

Holliday, I. E., & Ruddock, K. H. (1983). Two spatio-temporal filters in human vision: I. Temporal and spatial frequency response characteristics. *Biological Cybernetics, 47*, 173–190.

Horton, J. C., & Hubel, D. H. (1981). A regular patchy distribution of cytochrome-oxidase staining in primary visual cortex of the macaque monkey. *Nature, 292*, 762–764.

Humphrey, A. L., & Hendrickson, A. E. (1983). Background and stimulus-induced patterns of high metabolic activity in the visual cortex (area 17) of the squirrel and macaque monkey. *Journal of Neuroscience, 3*, 345–358.

Jonkman, E. J., & Lelieveld, M. H. (1981). EEG computer analysis in patients with migraine. *Electroencephalography and Clinical Neurophysiology, 52*, 652–655.

Kennedy, A., & Murray, W. S. (1991). The effects of flicker on eye movement control. *Quarterly Journal of Experimental Psychology, 43A*(1), 79–99.

Khalil, N. (1991). *Investigations of visual function in migraine by visual evoked potentials and visual psychophysical tests.* Unpublished doctoral dissertation, University of London.

Lehtonen, J. (1974). Visual evoked cortical potentials for single flashes and flickering light in migraine. *Headache, 14*, 1–12.

Livingstone, M., & Hubel, D. (1988). Segregation of form, color, movement, and depth: Anatomy, physiology and perception. *Science, 240*, 740–749.

Maclachlan, A., Yale, S., & Wilkins, A. (in press). Open trial of subjective precision tinting: A follow-up of 55 patients. *Ophthalmic and Physiological Optics.*

Marcus, D. A., & Soso, M. J. (1989). Migraine and stripe-induced discomfort. *Archives of Neurology, 46*, 1129–1132.

Marsters, J. B., Good, P. A., & Mortimer, M. J. (1988). A diagnostic test for migraine using the visual evoked potential. *Headache, 28*, 526–530.

Mehr, E. B. (1969). The typoscope by Charles Prentice. *American Journal of Optometry, 46*, 885–887.

Meldrum, B. S., & Wilkins, A. J. (1984). Photosensitive epilepsy in man and the baboon: Integration of pharmacological and psychophysical evidence. In P. A. Schwartzkroin & H. V. Wheal (Eds.), *Electrophysiology of Epilepsy* (pp. 51–77). Academic Press: London.

Neary, C., & Wilkins, A. J. (1989). Effects of phosphor persistence on perception and the control of eye movements. *Perception, 18*, 257–264.

O'Regan, K. (in press). Eye movements and reading. In E. Knowles (Ed.), *Eye movements and their role in visual and cognitive processes* (Vol. 4). London: Elsevier.

Ottes, F. P., van Gisbergen, J.A.M., & Eggermont, J. J. (1984). Metrics of saccadic responses to double stimuli: Two different modes. *Vision Research, 24,* 1169–1179.

Plant, G. T., Zimmern, R. L., & Durden, K. (1983). Transient visually evoked potentials to the pattern reversal and onset of sinusoidal gratings. *Electroencephalography and Clinical Neurophysiology, 56,* 147–158.

Sillito, A. M. (1979). Inhibitory mechanisms influencing complex cell orientation selectivity and their modification at high resting discharge levels. *Journal of Physiology (London), 289,* 33–53.

Tinker, M. A. (1963). *Legibility of print.* Ames, IA: Iowa State University Press.

Watt, R. J. (1988). *Visual processing: Computational, psychophysical and cognitive research.* London: Lawrence Erlbaum Associates.

Watt, R. J. (1991). *Understanding vision.* Academic Press: London.

Watt, R. J., Bock, J., Thimbleby, H., & Wilkins, A. J. (1990). Visible aspects of text. British Telecom internal report: *Applying Visual Psychophysics to User Interface Design.* Proceedings of conference at Lavenham. Martlesham: British Telecom.

Wilkins, A. J. (1986). Intermittent illumination from fluorescent lighting and visual display units affects movements of the eyes across text. *Human Factors, 28*(1), 75–81.

Wilkins, A. J., Binnie, C. D., Darby, C. E., & Kasteleijn-Nolst Trenité, D. (1990). Inferences regarding the visual precipitation of seizures, eye-strain and headaches. In M. Avoli, P. Gloor, G. Kostopoulos, & R. Naquet (Ed.), *Generalised epilepsy* (pp. 314–326). Boston: Birkhauser.

Wilkins, A. J., & Clark, C. (1990). Modulation of light from fluorescent lamps. *Lighting Research and Technology, 22*(2), 103–109.

Wilkins, A. J., & Lindsay, J. (1985). Common forms of reflex epilepsy: Physiological mechanisms and techniques for treatment. In T. A. Pedley and B. S. Meldrum (Eds.), *Recent advances in epilepsy* (Vol. 2, pp. 239–271). Edinburgh: Churchill Livingstone.

Wilkins, A. J., & Neary, C. (1991). Some visual optometric and perceptual effects of coloured glasses. *Ophthalmic and Physiological Optics, 11,* 163–171.

Wilkins, A. J., & Nimmo-Smith, I. (1984). On the reduction of eye-strain when reading. *Ophthalmic and Physiological Optics, 4*(1), 53–59.

Wilkins, A. J., & Nimmo-Smith, I. (1987). The clarity and comfort of printed text. *Ergonomics, 30*(12), 1705–1720.

Wilkins, A. J., Nimmo-Smith, I., & Jansons, J. (1992). A colorimeter for the intuitive manipulation of hue and saturation, and its application in the study of perceptual distortion. *Ophthalmic and Physiological Optics.*

Wilkins, A. J., Nimmo-Smith, I., Slater, A. I., & Bedocs, L. (1989). Fluorescent lighting, headaches and eye-strain. *Lighting Research and Technology, 21*(1), 11–18.

Wilkins, A. J., Nimmo-Smith, I., Tait, A., McManus, C., Della Sala, S., Tilley, A., Arnold, K., Barrie, M., & Scott, S. (1984). A neurological basis for visual discomfort. *Brain, 107,* 989–1017.

Wilkins, A. J., & Wilkinson, P. (1991). A tint to reduce eye-strain from fluorescent lighting? Preliminary observations. *Ophthalmic and Physiological Optics, 11,* 172–175.

Willows, D. M. (1974). Reading between the lines: Selective attention in good and poor readers. *Child Development, 45,* 408–415.

21 Processing Text on Monitors

Richard S. Kruk
University of Wollongong

INTRODUCTION

The display of text on computer screens is commonplace for a variety of purposes—electronic journals, library cataloging, computer networks, computer-aided instruction and design, desktop publishing, and electronic-mail are some examples—and the range of day-to-day applications is expanding. As the use of computer monitors for information processing and disseminating activities increases, the importance of maintaining or improving reading performance with text presented on monitors becomes critical. Recent research activity, investigating text displayed on monitors, has focused on questions of legibility and readability. These issues have enjoyed a renewed interest since the introduction of computer monitors to display reading materials; investigators have become aware of the possibility that findings from previous research on printed text may not transfer to computer monitor presentation of text (Daniel & Reinking, 1987). This is evident in data that have shown performance differences between paper and monitor reading. Although the findings are mixed (Reinking & Bridwell-Bowles, 1991), comparison studies of monitor and paper text presentation have shown that reading from a monitor is slower than reading from paper (e.g., Gould & Grischkowsky, 1984; Heppner, Anderson, Farstrup, & Weiderman, 1985; Kruk & Muter, 1984). A number of variables have been proposed to account for the difference, both in terms of the physical characteristics of monitors and in terms of how text is displayed.

Monitor text presentation introduces a number of dimensions not present with paper presentation—not only in the physical aspects of the medium, but also in what can be achieved with software design, including timing, control, flexibility in navigation through text, as well as a wider range of options for information display. This chapter centers on legibility issues and human factors/ergonomics concerns regarding monitor presentation of text, how they might interact with the visual processes of readers, and how these might ultimately affect reading performance.

VISUAL ASPECTS OF MONITORS

The nature of the visual image that appears on a monitor depends a great deal on the technology that makes up the particular system used. As new developments render the quality of the image comparable to paper presentation, the differences currently found between paper and monitor reading will likely be minimized or disappear (Gould, Alfaro, Finn, Haupt, & Minuto, 1987; Jorna & Snyder, 1991). Nevertheless, findings from research examining currently available displays contribute to our understanding the nature of visual factors of text presented on monitors, how they affect reading performance, and what they can tell us about visual processing of text in general.

The most common technology used today is the cathode ray tube (CRT). It involves painting an image electronically onto a phosphor-coated surface repeatedly at a rate of 50 or 60 cycles per second. The monitor is self-luminous, and the text is presented as points of light. Newer technology is moving toward using reflected light to display text; the liquid crystal display (LCD) is one example. Although it is likely that differences exist in how monitors of different types affect visual processing, the discussion here focuses on CRT legibility not only because the bulk of the research activity has focused on CRT screens but also because some general principles may be delineated from that literature.

Monitors present the reader with material that is different in a number of fundamental respects to paper. The typical CRT display of text is a source of light, which is constantly being refreshed. The quality of individual characters currently used with monitors is substantially different from print on paper. Computer-generated characters are made up of discrete picture elements (pixels), which yield lower character resolution compared to print. The CRT presents text in an active manner, and is easily and quickly changed; paper is a passive medium that does not change. This difference, too, might affect reading performance significantly via the visual system (see Kennedy, chap. 10).

How the visual system responds to these differences may to some degree explain the discrepancy among the findings of media comparison studies on a variety of reading-related tasks. Furthermore, the study of reading on monitors can provide useful information in understanding how the visual system responds to degraded visual input.

RESPONSE OF THE VISUAL SYSTEM
TO TEXT PRESENTED ON MONITORS

The manner in which information is taken in by the visual system may be affected by a number of properties of monitors. In order to understand how those properties may affect the visual system, some relevant aspects of the visual system that may be affected are discussed.

The acuity of the visual system increases with luminance, but with increased luminance, flicker sensitivity increases. This may have detrimental effects on reading from CRT monitors, given that screen refresh may be observed as flicker (Thompson, 1984). On many visual dimensions, such as size, shape, color, and movement of stimuli, there are limits to the sensitivity of the visual system. These limits place a constraint on the range of available options for constructing visual displays, while at the same time providing designers with information for the degree to which added visual information becomes redundant and hence can be omitted (Thompson, 1984). Many of these constraints can be traced to psychophysical properties of the visual system, and involve to a large extent spatial and temporal characteristics of the visual image (Harwood & Foley, 1987); Snyder, 1987). Furthermore, the response of the visual system, in terms of two separate but interacting channels that are sensitive to different spatial and temporal frequencies (see Breitmeyer, chap. 5, and Lehmkuhle, chap. 4), may affect how text presented on monitors is processed. As Travis, Bowles, Seton, and Peppe (1990) stated, "interface design can be approached profitably by optimizing visual displays to the visual capacities of users. By understanding the pathways and mechanisms that constitute the human visual system, we are in a relatively strong position to generate general principles for the design of visual interfaces." (p. 147). This point was made by Travis et al. in connection to a study of color displays, but it applies equally well to the study of other factors that may affect visual processes in reading monitor presented text.

However, given the nature of the material displayed and the nature of the reading tasks, other nonvisual processes may in fact compensate for many of the limitations of visual processing and can limit the usefulness of guidelines based on studies of visual processing and human factors (Thompson, 1984). There is, nevertheless, a need for a framework relating visual processes and the quality of input in reading, particularly as it is displayed on monitors (Reinking & Bridwell-Bowles, 1991). Understanding the critical variables that affect visual processing of text displayed on monitors may contribute to the development of a framework.

A number studies have conducted comparisons between hard copy paper and soft copy monitor text presentation, and have yielded conflicting results. A model for monitor legibility would need to account for the discrepancies. This chapter outlines several representative studies looking at a number of aspects of legibility as they relate to monitor reading.

LEGIBILITY AND READING FROM MONITORS

Legibility is a measure of the clarity of textual input and its effects on reading performance. It has been defined as "the ability to detect and discriminate between individual characters" (Cakir, Hart, & Stewart, 1980, p. 97), and is distinguished from readability, which is closely related to the interpretation and understanding of a given piece of text. Legibility provides a measure of how the physical aspects of text, like the size of characters and resolution, affect reading performance and other visual factors, like fatigue (Daniel & Reinking, 1987). A legible text is one that allows for the highest possible reading efficiency. With printed materials, it has generated a great deal of research that spanned several decades from the 1920s to the mid-1960s. The research was conducted primarily by Tinker and his associates, who examined a variety of factors that affect legibility. The bulk of his results are summarized in a book that has become a classic in legibility research (Tinker, 1965). It was concerned more with listing practical guidelines for factors that would ensure best legibility, rather than developing a theoretical account of legibility.

Researchers concerned with delineating guidelines for monitor text presentation, and studying the legibility of monitor text, have found that the same principles outlined by Tinker with hard copy do not always transfer to soft copy CRT reading. In addition, the computer introduces additional degrees of complexity that make the formation of guidelines difficult (Daniel & Reinking, 1987). With regard to reading from monitors, Daniel and Reinking (1987) suggested that characteristics of electronic text be included in the definition of legibility. They proposed a framework that discriminates factors that are related to print legibility, termed "static legibility," factors that are related to the changeability of monitor-presented text, labeled "dynamic legibility," and factors that relate to events that occur in the interface between the reader and the computer, called "interactive legibility." The approach taken in this chapter is slightly different, because the focus is specific to visual processes in reading from monitors, and not with higher level cognitive processes like those involved in comprehension. Factors that affect legibility are divided here into two categories: *hardware-dependent,* which include many static legibility variables, and *software-dependent,* which include many of the factors that Daniel and Reinking classified as dynamic or interactive. However, some additional factors, not considered by Daniel and Reinking, are introduced in both categories.

The following sections present relevant findings and outline hardware-dependent and software-dependent factors that can affect legibility of monitor reading. With the improvement of monitor technology, hardware-dependent factors likely will become less critical in their effects on legibility. Software-dependent factors like pacing, control, and mode of presentation have the potential of improving reading performance.

ASPECTS OF MONITOR PRESENTATION
THAT MAY AFFECT VISUAL PROCESSES
IN READING

Given that research on reading from monitors has indicated that performance in reading speed lags behind reading from paper, what factors mediate reading performance of text presented on computers, and how might possible debilitating factors be addressed? A number of variables can affect the legibility and hence the visual processing of monitor-presented text, and they are listed here under the categories of hardware-dependent and software-dependent.

Hardware-dependent Factors

These factors involve physical aspects of monitors that affect the visibility or resolution of characters presented on the display. The most common form of electronic text presentation currently available is the CRT, which, as discussed earlier, differs in substantial ways from paper text. The effects of these differences on visual processes are important in understanding why reading behavior with text presented on monitors differs from text presented on paper.

The clarity of individual characters on a monitor display can be affected by a large number of variables, including screen resolution, color, brightness contrast, anti-aliasing, flicker, and contrast polarity. These may have both cumulative and interacting effects on image quality (Gould et al., 1987), and ultimately on how the display is perceived by the reader. Although the previous list of display parameters is not exhaustive, it represents those factors that are most relevant to CRTs currently available.

Media comparison studies have yielded mixed results (Reinking & Bridwell-Bowles, 1991). Display characteristics affecting visibility and legibility of text may affect reading performance (as measured by reading speed, comprehension, visual search, or eye movement behavior). A difficulty of conducting media comparison studies centers around the issue of maintaining control over all factors but the one under investigation. In comparisons of CRT and paper displays, it is not always clear that differences that arise, and effects on the visual system, are due to the display characteristics of the monitor (Harwood & Foley, 1987). Nevertheless, some media comparison studies are reviewed, in addition to several that have dealt with the problem by focusing on intra- rather than inter-media comparisons.

One factor that has been investigated extensively in recent years is the resolution of the characters and the effects of character resolution on image quality. Research outlining the effects of the visual quality of individual characters on a variety of tasks including comprehension, proofreading, and visual search performance has shown image clarity to have the greatest potential for accounting for the differences in reading performance between monitor and paper text (Gould, Alfaro, Barnes, et al., 1987; Gould, Alfaro, Finn, et al., 1987; Harpster, Freivalds, Shulman, & Leibowitz, 1989; Jorna & Snyder, 1991). In order to understand the effects of image clarity on visual processes, the question of what variables contribute to image quality on CRTs must be investigated. This has been addressed by a number of researchers who have proposed that the legibility of CRT displays is highly dependent on image quality factors.

Gould, Alfaro, Barnes, et al. (1987) examined a multitude of variables, comparing performance in a proofreading task on CRT and paper, in order to identify factors that contribute to poorer reading performance on CRT. They concluded that the most important factors were those that contributed to the image quality of the characters, font, color, and polarity, but no one factor was found to account for most of the difference. They also suggested that some layout factors may contribute to the differences.

Gould and his associates then turned from a search for explanations of reading speed differences to searching for conditions in which people can read as fast from CRTs as from paper (Gould, Alfaro, Finn, et al., 1987). They looked specifically at areas that affect image clarity, including display polarity, anti-aliasing, display tube characteristics and resolution, CRT fonts, in addition to layout and color of the display. They found comparable performance on a proof-reading task for CRT and paper presentation, and suggested that it was likely that several factors interacted to improve reading performance on CRT. The factors were related directly to the physical attributes of the monitors, namely display polarity, resolution, and anti-aliasing. Each was found to have contributed to the elimination of reading-related differences between paper and CRT.

They studied CRT text that was equivalent to high-quality print on paper, and measured accuracy and speed for proofread text. The CRT had the same character fonts, polarity (dark letters on a white background), size, similar color, and layout as paper. The characters were anti-aliased. Anti-aliasing introduces gray levels to the pixels that make up characters, hence reducing the "jaggedness" of the edges of the characters, and producing the impression of a higher resolution. Furthermore, the monitor that was used had a higher resolution than the monitor used in Gould's earlier study. In a series of six experiments they found that a monitor with higher addressability (higher resolution) eliminated the difference in proofreading rate between paper and CRT. They studied the effects of flicker by comparing 50 Hz with 60 Hz refresh rate monitors, and found no difference in performance. This, though, is a limited range of refresh rates, and they may have found differences if they used a wider range of refresh rates, including a condition that eliminated refresh flicker, or if they used other performance measures (see Kennedy, chap. 10, for a more detailed discussion of flicker on CRTs). They also found that polarity did not affect performance directly, though 12 of the 15 participants were faster with dark characters on a light background. Furthermore, they found that anti-aliasing yielded performance on CRT that was not different from paper, but at the same time it did not differ from aliased CRT presentation. This indicated that anti-aliasing can improve performance, but the evidence was not substantial. Finally, the authors compared proofreading from five different displays—two on paper of different qualities, one anti-aliased high-quality monitor, and two commercially available monitors. Performance with the anti-aliased monitor was as good as with high-quality print, and performance with these two conditions was better than with the commercially available monitors. No explanation for these results based on visual mechanisms was given. However, the authors concluded that the general finding indicated that as image quality on CRTs increases, characters are more easily discriminated.

Hence, ideal conditions were identified for CRT reading under which individuals could read as efficiently from CRT displays as from good quality paper presentation, and variables associated with the image quality of display characters accounted for the reading speed difference found in previous media-comparison studies. Specifically, the variables that contributed to image quality were identified as display resolution, anti-aliasing, and polarity.

In a study of anti-aliasing on recognition performance for objects, Booth, Bryden, Cowan, Morgan, and Plante (1987) found that at higher resolutions anti-aliasing did not improve performance, but at intermediate and low resolutions, anti-aliasing had a facilitating effect. This may explain why anti-aliasing in Gould, Alfaro, Finn, et al. (1987), did not have a clear effect; the monitor resolution may have been too high to have benefited from anti-aliasing to a large extent.

There were several difficulties with the Gould, Alfaro, Finn, et al. (1987) study. First, they did not use an objective measure of image quality. Hence, their findings could have been confounded with unknown variations of image quality. Also, proofreading may not have been an ideal measure of reading performance. These difficulties were addressed by two studies. First, Harpster et al. (1989) carried out a study of the effect of differing screen resolutions on visual accommodation and visual search accuracy for hard copy and monitor-presented letters. They used the resolution/addressability ratio (RAR) as a measure of image quality. This was based on the ratio of width of a pixel profile at half-luminance intensity to peak-to-peak separation between adjacent pixels. Thus, for example, changing the number of pixels across the width of a screen from 320 to 640 doubled RAR. A higher RAR indicated better screen resolution. Accommodation, the change in the curvature of the lens of the eye as it focuses on characters at varying distances, was expected to be degraded as image sharpness, as measured by RAR, decreased. They found similar accommodation with high resolution screens and paper, but low resolution displays yielded poorer accommodation responses. The authors discussed these results in terms of the spatial frequency characteristics of the stimuli, suggesting that low spatial frequency characters provide a less adequate stimulus for accommodation than intermediate and high spatial frequency information that was contained in the high resolution display and on paper. The difference in accommodation was serious enough to impair reading performance, though only correlation evidence was given linking accommodation with task performance. The high resolution screen and paper yielded better visual search speed than the low resolution screen. The results showed that hard copy and CRT displays with different spatial frequency characteristics have different effects on visual processing, and these differences may affect performance on a visual search task. Hence, a clear relationship between legibility of text presented on monitors and the spatial frequency components of the characters displayed was found.

A second study that dealt with the difficulties of Gould's research was carried out by Jorna and Snyder (1991). In a comparison of reading speed and perceived image quality on monitor and hard copy reading, they assessed image quality by measuring the screen's modulation transfer function area (MTFA). This measure of a display's resolution was determined by means of sine-wave test signals of different spatial frequencies. At higher spatial frequencies, the display's ability to resolve the gratings falls, giving a measure of the limit of resolution at different frequencies. The loss of high frequency resolving power in a display manifests itself in blurred-appearing characters. A higher MTFA indicates better image quality. MTFA has been found to have high correlations with task performance and subjective assessments of image quality. The authors controlled for font, visual angle, orientation, polarity, and display luminance in their study. The monitor was high resolution, and filters were used to yield four different MTFA values for monitor and paper presentation. Results showed no difference for display type for reading speed and subjective rating of image quality. Subjects read as fast in the hard copy as in the monitor condition, and had shorter reading times with filter conditions that gave higher MTFA values. Hence, the authors found that reading time did not differ between paper and monitor presentations, and as the quality of the display increased, reading time decreased. They concluded that differences in reading time come about because of image quality and not because of the display technology used.

The aforementioned studies indicate that image quality plays a significant role in accounting for differences in reading performance on monitors. The use of spatial frequency information to measure image quality is consistent with a framework for character legibility put forward by Loomis (1990), who developed a mathematical model for estimating legibility on the basis of spatial frequency components of character sets. A model of this sort may be effective in rating legibility of characters presented on monitors, and it may relate legibility to theories of visual processing that posit two channels that are selective in their sensitivities—one to high and the other to low spatial frequencies in the visual environment. In dealing with monitor reading, adequate stimulation to high spatial frequency channels, which deal with detailed pattern information, may be necessary for good legibility.

Finding equivalence in performance between paper and CRT as image quality increases is not an unexpected result. This research identifies factors that brought about changes in CRT image quality, and these factors do have an effect on the operation of the visual system in reading. Other factors like monitor flicker and color were not directly assessed by these investigators, and they may also have an effect on visual processes. Also, long-term effects of prolonged reading from monitors has not been assessed in relation to the effects of physical factors like screen resolution. Recent research that examined some of these factors is now outlined.

Flicker on CRTs comes about from an interaction between the decay rate of phosphor and the refresh rate of the electron beam that strikes the phosphor. It is not typically perceived by the reader, but may affect visual functioning nevertheless (see Kennedy, chap. 10). Harwood and Foley (1987) studied the effects on the visual system of the temporal characteristics of CRT luminance. They compared CRT displayed text with projections of photographs of the CRT presented material, which were equated for color, contrast, overall luminance, and character size. The work environment and task were the same in both cases. The difference between the two displays had to do specifically with the stability of the image. They measured the temporal resolving efficiency of the visual system by assessing the critical flicker frequency (CFF) of subjects during a 3-hour visual search task for target words. Measurements were taken every hour. Although task performance remained the same for both presentation modes, CFF dropped substantially with the CRT presentation but remained constant with the projection display. This indicated that the temporal characteristics of the CRT display luminance places an added demand on the visual system, and may result in reduced visual functioning.

Harwood and Foley (1987) also found that subjects reported increased task difficulty, problems in maintaining concentration, tired eyes, and an increase in the need to shut eyes with monitor presentation, as opposed to back-projection display. Similar types of reports of subjective difficulty with work on monitors have been reported elsewhere. For example, accommodation and subjective reports of visual fatigue were affected by increases in the intensity of monitor use (Ostberg & Smith, 1987). Cushman (1986) found higher degrees of visual fatigue when dark characters were displayed on a monitor with a light background, in comparison to paper reading. The difference, however, disappeared when light characters on a dark background were used. Gunnarsson and Soderberg (1983) observed evidence of visual fatigue with monitor-based tasks, and Cakir (1980) reported significant correlations between the optical properties of displays and visual strain. However, he also found similar results with paper presentations. Jaschinski-Kruza (1991), in a study of viewing distance, dark convergence, and eye strain, found stronger visual strain when subjects worked at a distance of 50 cm than at 100 cm. He also found that individuals who had more distant dark convergence experienced a greater degree of visual strain at 50 cm. Finally, Matthews, Lovasik, and Mertins (1989) found that subjective reports of visual fatigue were not influenced by the chromatic components of the display. These studies indicate that working with monitors may have effects on the visual system that result in visual fatigue for some individuals. One difficulty in carrying out research of this nature is the absence of an objective measure of the effects of monitor exposure on visual fatigue, which limits the strength of the evidence linking work with monitors and visual fatigue.

A common question regarding CRT text presentation asks which combination of colors yields best legibility. However, chromaticity has been found to have no effect on performance (Matthews et al., 1989; Pastoor, 1990). Studies of this nature, though, often neglect to control all variables associated with color. Travis et al. (1990) attempted to address this issue by looking for general principles of color perception and relating them to reading from monitors, in a well-controlled study. They assessed both chromatic and luminance contrast on detection and discrimination of words and nonwords. The results indicated that any combination of text and background colors is suitable as long as the combination maintains an adequate luminance level, or chromatic contrast level. They determined that a 50% luminance contrast modulation would be adequate for legible reading.

The most important physical aspects of monitor-presented text appear to center about the basic spatial and temporal aspects of the material, which affect the clarity of the image, rather than other less basic issues that involve layout characteristics. Clearly, as the resolution of monitors approaches that of paper, the legibility of both will be similar. Nevertheless, the legibility of monitor and paper displays is also affected by other issues—specifically those concerned with layout and conventional typographic considerations. As mentioned earlier, a great deal of research has been carried out with hard copy presentation, and the findings are summarized in a number of sources. The reader is referred to Tinker (1963, 1965) and Waller (1991) for excellent summaries of the findings of legibility research conducted with hard copy display. In addition to conventional typographic issues, characteristics specific to computers, namely the added dimensions of time, and of interactivity with the reader may affect visual processing in reading. These are discussed together under the rubric of software-dependent factors.

Software-dependent Factors

Much of the early work on reading from monitors focused on layout issues, like letter size, font characteristics, spacing of lines, letters and words, justification, character form, and window size. This work has been summarized in general guidelines for human-computer interface (e.g., Cakir, et al., 1980; Shneiderman, 1987), which include discussions of the effects of layout factors that involve visual processes.

The focus of much of the research looking at typographic issues with monitors was on factors that could explain differences in reading speed between monitor and paper text presentation. The research often found results that did not conform to expectations based on the legibility work with paper presentation. For example, Duchnicky and Kolers (1983) found that very long line lengths were read as efficiently as medium line lengths on monitors, in contrast to recommendations given by Tinker. More typically, though, researchers found that the application of principles of good layout design did improve reading speed for computer-presented text. For example, Kruk and Muter (1984) found improved reading speed with double-spaced text, compared to single spacing; Duin (1988) found that lessons presented in well-laid-out formats were learned more efficiently than lessons laid out in poor format; Trollip and Sales (1986) found that left justification, with a ragged right edge, yielded better reading performance than fully justified text.

Another line of research seeks to examine the unique potential of the computer to accomplish different ways of presenting text that are impossible with paper. Reinking and Bridwell-Bowles (1991) described these as "divergent" studies in reading—studies that seek to find ways to enhance reading performance by emphasizing the differences between paper and computer text presentation. Much of this research is motivated by concerns of cost-effectiveness and efficiency of reading computer-displayed text. Given that improvement in screen technology, involving resolution and other physical factors, may ultimately lead to equalized performance for paper and monitor displays of text, the divergent-type studies of monitor reading have the potential of improving reading performance beyond that which is possible with print.

An important issue that arises when lengthy text is displayed has to do with the means of controlling the flow of text from the display. What distinguishes monitor presentation from paper presentation for these layout issues is the dimension of time. This complicates decisions regarding how text might effectively be presented on monitors, because few guidelines are available to developers for optimum presentation rates (Daniel & Reinking, 1987). Duchnicky and Kolers (1983) studied a variety of layout factors in a scrolling mode of presentation in which readers controlled the pacing of the text. They manipulated line length, character density, and window height (the number of text lines presented), and found equal comprehension for all conditions. Reading speed, however, was 25% faster with medium and long lines, compared to short lines that filled only one-third of the screen. This contradicted findings with paper presentation, in which long lines of text are read slower than medium-length lines (Tinker, 1963). They also found that high-character-density text was read 30% faster than low-character-density text, and that a 4- or 20-line window was read 9% faster than a 1- or 2-line window.

Many studies have examined differences in the manner in which text is presented. One technique, called rapid sequential visual presentation (RSVP), displays text at a quick rate, normally one word at a time, in a fixed location on the screen. The advantage with this form of text presentation is that eye movements are not necessary, and only a small screen area is required. But reader control over the text presentation is usually lost. Muter, Kruk, Buttigieg, and Kang (1988) attempted to increase the degree of reader control by allowing self-pacing of the rate of text presentation, and also permitting regressions. They found that reading speed and comprehension with RSVP and full-screen text presentation did not differ significantly when subjects were able to set their own pace. They found, however, that the use of larger regressions with RSVP resulted in slower reading speed. Furthermore, in an evaluation of long-term reading, lasting for 2 hours, reading speed with RSVP and regressions was about half of that with page presentation. There is clearly a need for additional research to explore other ways of improving reading performance with RSVP, possibly with the use of "intelligent" algorithms that may take into account the nature of the text presented and individual reader characteristics and needs (Just & Carpenter, 1987).

One way in which "intelligent" algorithms may be used involves the segmentation of sentences into units that are most easily comprehended. Pynte and Noizet (1980) found that for sentences made up of short words, fastest reading times were obtained for sentences divided into noun phrase and verb phrase chunks. However, for sentences with long words, the optimum presentation was word-for-word. This type of research provides some guidance for ideal ways of presenting text via alternate display modes, like RSVP.

Another manner of guiding the reader through a page of text that could improve comprehension and reading rate involves the use of typographic cues to direct attention to important parts of text. These factors can be incorporated in monitor text in ways that are impractical on paper. For instance the highlighting of semantic or syntactic word groupings can improve comprehension (L. D. Geoffrion & O. P. Geoffrion, 1983), as can the use of italics, underlining, and color coding (Glynn, 1978). The use of blinking or flashing text is an effective way of drawing attention, as long as the duration of the flashes does not exceed more than one second (Kitakaze & Kasahara, 1987). However, the effectiveness of such devices, in the absence of evidence and theory dealing with differential effects on attention and other visual processing factors as they relate to reading of monitor-presented text, is still largely unknown (Daniel & Reinking, 1987).

TOWARD A THEORY OF LEGIBILITY EFFECTS ON VISUAL PROCESSING OF MONITOR-PRESENTED TEXT

Under some contexts and conditions, text may be presented in different ways on monitors in order to achieve different goals. Examples are library catalogue database lists, and computer-aided learning packages. A question that is raised, in the face of the many uses of monitor text, is what are the ideal visual conditions for text presentation to yield the best legibility for different applications? Answers to questions like this could be guided by models for legibility of monitor-presented text.

Daniel and Reinking (1987) introduced a framework that distinguished three different types of legibility: static, dynamic, and interactive. These types of legibility involved both visual and cognitive processing issues. The factors associated with the legibility of monitor texts, which affect visual processes, were categorized here as either hardware-dependent or software-dependent. These included many of the factors outlined by Daniel and Reinking, but were limited to those specific to visual processes. Hardware-dependent factors were relevant in explaining many of the differences found between monitor and paper reading performance, given the evidence that identified the roles that spatial and temporal frequency characteristics of monitor text played in affecting visual processes in reading. These factors are implicated in theories of visual processing and character legibility that focus on the spatial features of visual input to explain the mechanisms involved. Software-dependent factors are those that do not depend explicitly on the physical nature of the display, and are modifiable by programming. Here, the spatial frequency aspects of how text is laid out on the screen, and issues concerning the rate at which the text is displayed may also be related to more basic theories of visual processing. Theories outlining the basic mechanisms of visual processing may contribute to the development of a model for monitor legibility that could lead to more effective ways of presenting text on monitors, and to a clearer understanding of the factors that affect reading performance with monitor-presented text.

CONCLUSIONS

An important aspect in the study of visual processes for text presented on monitors is legibility. Monitor text is a much more complex area of study than paper text, because reading performance is potentially affected by additional factors that are unique to computers. Two categories of factors that could have had effects on monitor legibility and visual processes in reading were introduced—hardware-dependent and software-dependent. Recent research, examining the effects of monitors that incorporate sophisticated resolution technology, has found that performance differences between paper and monitor text presentation can be eliminated with improved monitor resolution, anti-aliasing, and the use of the same contrast polarity as paper. However, other factors associated with more basic visual functioning, like accommodation, and CCF may be affected by monitor presentation differently than with paper displays, and these may affect reading, as indicated by subjective reports of visual fatigue. Software-dependent factors have the potential to improve reading performance beyond what is possible with paper, and may lead to different ways of presenting text, and to the development of different reading strategies for extracting information. However, clearly delineated theories of monitor legibility are lacking. Frameworks for the mechanisms of basic visual processes may provide some insight into the results obtained, and guide new research initiatives.

REFERENCES

Booth, K. S., Bryden, M. P., Cowan, W. B., Morgan, M. F., & Plante, B. L. (1987). On the parameters of human visual performance: An investigation of the benefits of antialiasing. In J. M. Carrol & P. P. Tanner (Eds.), *Human factors in computing systems* (Vol. 4, pp 13–19). Amsterdam: North Holland.

Cakir, A. E. (1980). Human factors and VDT design. In P. A. Kolers, M. E. Wrolstad, & H. Bouma (Eds.), *Processing of visible language* (Vol. 2, pp. 481–495). New York: Plenum.

Cakir, A., Hart, D. J., & Stewart, T.F.M. (1980). *Visual display terminals.* New York: Wiley.

Cushman, W. H. (1986). Reading from microfiche, a VDT, and the printed page: Subjective fatigue and performance. *Human Factors, 28,* 63–73.

Daniel, D. B., & Reinking, D. (1987). The construct of legibility in electronic reading environments. In D. Reinking (Ed.), *Reading and computers: Issues for theory and practice* (pp. 24–39). New York: Teachers College Press.

Duchnicky, R. L., & Kolers, P. A. (1983). Readability of text scrolled on visual display terminals as a function of window size. *Human Factors, 25,* 683–692.

Duin, A. H. (1988). Computer-assisted instructional displays: Effects on students' computing behaviors, prewriting, and attitudes. *Journal of Computer-Based Instruction, 15,* 48–56.

Geoffrion, L. D., & Geoffrion, O. P. (1983). *Computers and reading instruction.* Reading, MA: Addison-Wesley.

Glynn, S. M. (1978). Capturing readers' attention by means of typographical cuing strategies. *Educational Technology, 18,* 7–12.

Gould, J. D., Alfaro, L., Barnes, V., Finn, R., Grischkowsky, N., & Minuto, A. (1987). Reading is slower from CRT displays than from paper: Attempts to isolate a single-variable explanation. *Human Factors, 29,* 269–299.

Gould, J. D., Alfaro, L., Finn, R., Haupt, B., & Minuto, A. (1987). Reading from CRT displays can be as fast as reading from paper. *Human Factors, 29,* 497–517.

Gould, J. D., & Grischkowsky, N. (1984). Doing the same work with hard copy and with cathode-ray tube (CRT) computer terminals. *Human Factors, 26,* 323–337.

Gunnarsson, E., & Soderberg, I. (1983). Eye strain resulting from VDT work at the Swedish Telecommunications Administration. *Applied Ergonomics, 14,* 61–69.

Harpster, J. L., Freivalds, A., Shulman, G. L., & Leibowitz, H. W. (1989). Visual performance on CRT screens and hard-copy displays. *Human Factors, 31,* 247–257.

Harwood, K., & Foley, P. (1987). Temporal resolution: An insight into the video display terminal (VDT) "problem." *Human Factors, 29,* 447–452.

Heppner, F. H., Anderson, J.G.T., Farstrup, A. E., & Weiderman, N. H. (1985). Reading performance on a standardized test is better from print than from computer display. *Journal of Reading, 28,* 321–325.

Jaschinski-Kruza, W. (1991). Eyestrain in VDU users: Viewing distance and the resting position of ocular muscles. *Human Factors, 33,* 69–83.

Jorna, G. C., & Snyder, H. L. (1991). Image quality determines differences in reading performance and perceived image quality with CRT and hard-copy displays. *Human Factors, 33,* 459–469.

Just, M. A., & Carpenter, P. A. (1987). *The psychology of reading and language comprehension.* Boston: Allyn & Bacon.

Kitakaze, S., & Kasahara, Y. (1987). Designing optimum CRT text blinking for video image presentation. In J. M. Carrol & P. P. Tanner (Eds.), *Human factors in computing systems* (Vol. 4, pp. 1–6). Amsterdam: North Holland.

Kruk, R. S., & Muter, P. (1984). Reading of continuous text on video screens. *Human Factors, 26,* 339–345.

Loomis, J. M. (1990). A model of character recognition and legibility. *Journal of Experimental Psychology: Human Perception and Performance, 16,* 106–120.

Matthews, M. L., Lovasik, J. V., & Mertins, K. (1989). Visual performance and subjective discomfort in prolonged viewing of chromatic displays. *Human Factors, 31,* 259–271.

Muter, P., Kruk, R. S., Buttigieg, M. A., & Kang, T. J. (1988). Reader-controlled computerized presentation of text. *Human Factors, 30,* 473–486.

Ostberg, O., & Smith, M. J. (1987). Effects on visual accommodation and subjective visual discomfort from VDT work intensified through split screen technique. In B. Knave & P. -G. Wideback (Eds.), *Work with display units 86* (pp. 512–521). Amsterdam: North Holland.

Pastoor, S. (1990). Legibility and subjective preference for color combinations in text. *Human Factors, 32,* 157–171.

Pynte, J., & Noizet, G. (1980). Optimal segmentation for sentences displayed on a video screen. In P. A. Kolers, M. E. Wrolstad, & H. Bouma (Eds.), *Processing of visible language* (Vol. 2, pp. 375–385). New York: Plenum.

Reinking, D., & Bridwell-Bowles, L. (1991). Computers in reading and writing. In R. Barr, M. L. Kamil, P. Mosenthal, & P. D. Pearson (Eds.), *Handbook of reading research* (Vol. 2, pp. 310–340). New York: Longman.

Shneiderman, B. (1987). *Designing the user interface: Strategies for effective human-computer interaction.* Reading, MA: Addison-Wesley.

Snyder, H. L. (1987). Counterintuitive criteria for visual displays. In G. Salvendy, S. L. Sauter, & J. J. Hurrell, Jr. (Eds.), *Social, ergonomic and stress aspects of work with computers* (pp. 145–156). Amsterdam: Elsevier Science Publishers.

Thompson, P. (1984). Visual perception: An intelligent system with limited bandwidth. In A. Monk (Ed.), *Fundamentals of human-computer interaction* (pp. 5–33). London: Academic Press.

Tinker, M. A. (1963). *Legibility of print.* Ames, IA: Iowa State University Press.

Tinker, M. A. (1965). *Bases for effective reading.* Minneapolis: University of Minnesota Press.

Travis, D. S., Bowles, S., Seton, J., & Peppe, R. (1990). Reading from color displays: A psychophysical model. *Human Factors, 32,* 147–156.

Trollip, S. R., & Sales, G. (1986). Readability of computer-generated fill-justified text. *Human Factors, 28,* 159–163.

Waller, R. (1991). Typography and discourse. In R. Barr, M. L. Kamil, P. Mosenthal, & P. D. Pearson (Eds.), *Handbook of reading research* (Vol. 2, pp. 341–380). New York: Longman.

VI CONCLUSIONS AND FUTURE DIRECTIONS

22 Visual Processes in Reading: Directions for Research and Theory

Keith Rayner
University of Massachusetts

The chapters in this volume address a number of issues related to visual processes in reading. Whereas some of the chapters deal with neurophysiological, neuropsychological, or psychological aspects of visual processes in normal reading (i.e., Parts II and III), many of the chapters address the role of visual processes in reading disability. There are also chapters that deal primarily with issues such as visual discomfort in reading and ergonomic factors in reading. My task is not to review the book or to discuss in detail any of the chapters. Rather, I was invited to provide some comments on future directions for research and theory in the areas of visual processes in normal and disabled reading.

VISUAL PROCESSING IN SKILLED READING

A number of authors comment that it is obvious that visual processing is important in understanding reading. Information is extracted from the printed page during eye fixations: The neurophysiological mechanisms involved in the initial acquisition of information from the printed page necessarily involve the visual pathways between the retina and the brain. Collectively, the chapters in Parts II and III give a good overview of the kinds of issues that have captured the attention of researchers interested in reading over the past couple of decades.

How much do we really know about the visual processes involved in reading? As someone who recently devoted a fair amount of time to writing a book about the psychology of reading (Rayner & Pollatsek, 1989), my response is that we know quite a bit. But others not so entrenched in the work of cognitive psychologists might not be so optimistic. I feel that we know a lot about eye movements during reading (i.e., such things as what determines where the reader looks next and the factors responsible for how long the reader fixates on different words) and about visual word recognition. Although the puzzle is by no means solved, we have learned some valuable information about the perceptual aspects of skilled reading. The tie between the work done by cognitive psychologists and the underlying neurophysiology is at this point somewhat tenuous, but efforts to forge tighter links are underway (see, e.g., Posner, 1992). I also feel that we know considerably less about how on-line comprehension processes operate; a recent volume that I was associated with attempted to address this issue (see Balota, Flores d'Arcais, & Rayner, 1990).

The chapters that deal with basic visual processes in skilled reading represent a good overview of the work that has been done recently by cognitive psychologists. Future endeavors regarding such topics will primarily serve to further refine the models we already have and fill in gaps in the existing data base so that more complete models can be developed (see Rayner & Pollatsek, 1989). As I argued elsewhere (see Rayner & Pollatsek, 1989), I suspect that a complete understanding of reading will come about by further refinement of the facts that we already know about reading. In other words, I do not think there is going to be a radically new theory or paradigm that changes what we currently believe about the reading process. It will be necessary to put together the information that we know about reading into a coherent model of the process, but such attempts are already underway.

As I already suggested, I think it is highly likely that we will make advances in the next decade of research in terms of understanding the underlying neurophysiological mechanisms related to reading. In the past, attempts to discuss these underlying mechanisms have been highly speculative. With the emergence of the field of *cognitive neuroscience,* people are now actually doing research (see Posner, 1992) to tie together the results of cognitive experiments and neurophysiological studies. Research using Positron Emission Typography (PET), Magnetic Resonance Imaging (MRI), and Event Related Potentials (ERP) techniques, in combination with cognitive paradigms promise to reveal a great deal about the brain mechanisms active during reading. Also, research comparing, for example, eye movement data and ERP data (see Raney & Rayner, 1993) on the same materials promises to reveal interesting relationships about processing during reading.

VISUAL PROCESSING AND DYSLEXIA

In many areas of psychological research, it often seems like there is a pendulum swinging back and forth. For many years, it was assumed that visual and perceptual deficits were a major contributing factor to developmental dyslexia. However, Vellutino (1979) argued rather strongly that the major factor in reading disability was some type of language processing deficit and that visual and perceptual factors were of minor importance. For at least 10 years following the publication of Vellutino's book, the view he espoused was quite dominant among researchers interested in developmental dyslexia. As reflected in some of the chapters in this volume the pendulum has perhaps started swinging back toward some intermediate position between the two extremes.

It is likely that both perceptual and language deficits are contributors to reading disability. I return to this point later. For now, I would like to focus on, as I see it, two major problems with respect to developmental dyslexia research. First, too much of the research is based on the premise that there is an *underlying* cause of dyslexia. Second, and this point is related to the first, an analogy frequently used with dyslexia purports that it is like some specific type of *disease* (and hence we have to find the underlying cause), when it might be more appropriate to use the term *sickness* in the analogy.

An examination of much of the literature on developmental dyslexia reveals that there is a great deal of contradictory evidence (see Rayner & Pollatsek, 1989, for a more complete discussion of the following points). For example, there are studies that demonstrate that dyslexics have a left hemisphere deficit. However, there are other studies showing that dyslexics have a right hemisphere deficit. There are studies that show that there are perceptual deficits, and others that fail to find any such evidence. There are studies purporting to show that erratic eye movements are the major problem of dyslexics, and others that are unable to replicate such results. Most of these studies are based on a *unitary explanation* assumption. There is a problem with the unitary explanation because many researchers have (a) assumed all developmental dyslexics are alike in their symptoms and difficulties; (b) assumed that because developmental dyslexia is a unitary syndrome, it must have a single cause; and (c) developed a theory to explain the one and only cause of dyslexia. The contradictory evidence would seem to me to invalidate such an approach.

There are many reasons why a reader might be dyslexic. Work on acquired dyslexia has demonstrated different types of dyslexics, and some investigators have attempted to make links between developmental and acquired dyslexia (Jorm, 1979; Prior & McCorriston, 1983; Seymour & MacGregor, 1984). Others have argued for the existence of distinct subgroups of developmental dyslexics (see Boder, 1973; Mattis, French, & Rapin, 1975; Mitterer, 1982; Pirozzolo, 1979). This has turned out to be a somewhat controversial topic as some (see Bryant & Impey, 1986) have argued that dyslexia should more appropriately be thought of in terms of a continuum of reading skill, rather than in terms of specific subtypes. Others (see Seymour, 1990) have argued not so much for subtypes as for the idea of heterogeneity in dyslexia. My own experience with some dyslexic readers (see Rayner & Pollatsek, 1989) leads me to believe that there are many types of dyslexia and it is difficult to accurately characterize prototypical dyslexic readers.

This brings me back to my second point. Perhaps it is more appropriate to think of developmental dyslexia as being more analogous to the general term *sickness* than to a *disease*. (Note that I am not equating developmental dyslexia with sickness, but rather forcing a point.) People can be sick for many reasons and they have different symptoms of being ill. There are also many different underlying causes of sickness. Obviously, some sick people are more seriously ill than others. I suspect that similar points can be made about dyslexics. From this perspective then, it would not be surprising to find evidence suggesting that both perceptual and language deficits (as well as attentional and other cognitive deficits) are factors leading to reading problems.

This leads me to one final comment concerning dyslexia. In addition to searching for an underlying cause of dyslexia, many workers interested in reading problems are interested in remediation procedures. In various places (though generally not in the present volume), suggestions have been made for remediation that involve procedures such as (a) having dyslexics read with tinted glasses, (b) varying the contrast between print and background, (c) covering one eye, and so forth. There are some who advocate behaviors such as having dyslexic children walk on balance beams to improve their equilibrium or to have them engage in numerous types of eye exercises. It is assumed that somehow these procedures will make them into better readers. Some of these remediation procedures seem somewhat amusing and far-fetched at times. Yet, in the past few years some respectable scientists have advocated the use of such techniques, largely I assume, because they have seen evidence that such techniques work. The fact that they do work with some people, I believe, is a bit misleading because I am quite certain that none of these remediation techniques will be successful for *all* dyslexic readers. How will wearing tinted glasses help a child whose problem is not at the perceptual level, but at a higher level, read better? Likewise, how will lots of language training (such as teaching children phonemic awareness skills) help a child who has a distinct visual-spatial deficit that is manifest by letter reversals, mirror writing, erratic eye movements, and general visual-spatial disorientation?

Just as physicians would not provide all of their patients with the same drugs or medication irrespective of the nature of their illness, workers interested in the remediation of reading disability need to consider that there are probably many underlying causes of dyslexia. Adopting such a view might make research on dyslexia and its remediation more difficult and challenging, but it would most likely increase the effectiveness of such work.

MODELS OF READING AND DYSLEXIA

We can learn more about dyslexia in two major ways. First, as already argued, researchers need to avoid the unitary explanation in research directed at uncovering the processing difficulties of dyslexics. Second, and more importantly, it is important to develop theories and models of skilled reading and make hypotheses about how various forms of reading disability might result from deficits or problems associated with different aspects of the model.

Although I have not been a big fan of connectionist models to this point, it is possible to explore some interesting hypotheses about acquired dyslexia by lesioning different parts of such models (see Hinton & Shallice, 1991). In principle, it should also be possible to make interesting observations about developmental dyslexia from perturbations of such models (see Seidenberg & McClelland, 1989). In line with my earlier comments about eschewing unitary explanations, once we have good models of the skilled reading process then interesting hypotheses can be suggested (and tested) concerning how deficits in different aspects of the model will lead to poor reading performance.

My point here, of course, is that it may well be the case that the most significant advances in understanding dyslexia will come about once we have a more complete understanding of skilled reading. In other words, once we know how the processing system works during reading, we may be able to better understand how and why it breaks down. This does not mean that research on dyslexia should not be conducted until we have a complete understanding of normal skilled reading. As more data are gathered about developmental dyslexia, we will undoubtedly come to better understand the phenomenon. However, I bet that we will be able to put more of the pieces of the puzzle of dyslexia together if we understand skilled reading than if we do not.

REFERENCES

Balota, D. A., Flores d'Arcais, G. B., & Rayner, K. (1990). *Comprehension processes in reading.* Hillsdale, NJ: Lawrence Erlbaum Associates.

Boder, E. (1973). Developmental dyslexia: A diagnostic based on three atypical reading-spelling patterns. *Developmental Medicine and Child Neurology, 15,* 663–687.

Bryant, P. E., & Impey, L. (1986). The similarities between normal readers and developmental and acquired dyslexics. *Cognition, 24,* 121–137.

Hinton, G. E., & Shallice, T. (1991). Lesioning an attractor network: Investigations of acquired dyslexia. *Psychological Review, 98,* 74–95.

Jorm, A. F. (1979). The cognitive and neurological basis of developmental dyslexia: A theoretical framework and a review. *Cognition, 7,* 19–33.

Mattis, S., French, J. H., & Rapin, I. (1975). Dyslexia in children and young adults: Three independent neuropsychological syndromes. *Developmental Medicine and Child Development, 17,* 150–163.

Mitterer, J. O. (1982). There are at least two kinds of poor readers: Whole-word poor readers and recoding poor readers. *Canadian Journal of Psychology, 36,* 445–461.

Pirozzolo, F. J. (1979). *The neuropsychology of developmental reading disorders.* New York: Praeger.

Posner, M. I. (1992). Attention as a cognitive and neural system. *Current Directions in Psychological Science, 1,* 11–14.

Prior, M., & McCorriston, M. (1983). Acquired and developmental spelling dyslexia. *Brain and Language, 20,* 263–285.

Raney, G. E., & Rayner, K. (1993). Event-related brain potentials, eye movements, and reading. *Psychological Science.*

Rayner, K., & Pollatsek, A. (1989). *The psychology of reading.* Englewood Cliffs, NJ: Prentice-Hall.

Seidenberg, M. S., & McClelland, J. L. (1989). A distributed, developmental model of word recognition and naming. *Psychological Review, 96,* 523–568.

Seymour, P.H.K. (1990). Semantic processing in dyslexia. In D. A. Balota, G. B. Flores d'Arcais, & K. Rayner (Eds.), *Comprehension processes in reading* (pp. 581–602). Hillsdale, NJ: Lawrence Erlbaum Associates.

Seymour, P.H.K., & MacGregor, C. J. (1984). Developmental dyslexia: A cognitive experimental analysis of phonological, morphemic and visual impairments. *Cognitive Neuropsychology, 1,* 43–82.

Vellutino, F. R. (1979). *Dyslexia: Research and theory.* Cambridge, MA: MIT Press.

Author Index

Subject Index

A

abnormal brain development, 66
abnormal eye movements, 382–384, 387–389
abstract letter identities (ALIs), 349, 364
accommodation, 420, 421, 463, 469
achromatic channel, 450
acquired distinctiveness of cues, 53
acquired word blindness, 18, 19
activation models of word recognition, 120, 130
addition errors, 112, 114, 132
addressability, 462
agnosia, 60
ALI coding impairment, 352
alphabet decision study, 245
alphabet modification, 147, 148
alphabetic context, 256
alphabetically based scripts, 61
alphabetically matched/mismatched, 260
alternate display modes, 468
Alzheimer's disease, 89
ambidexterity, 20, 65, 69
ambiguous characters, 242
anagrams, 165, 168, 169, 180, 184
analogy, 166, 170
analytic function
    impairment of, 362, 364
analytic orthographic processing,
    disorder of, 359

anatomical asymmetries, 66
Annett's theory, 68, 69
anti-aliasing, 461–463, 469
array matching, 350, 351
association methodology, 362, 363
asymmetry,
    advantage of, 69
    evolution of, 69
attention,
    orient/maintain, 122, 129
    focused, 129
attentional,
    gradient, 127, 128
    strategy, 320
attentional window account, 127, 128
autoimmune disorders, 67
automated skill, 60
automaticity, 167
aversive pattern, 445, 446

B

b-d confusion, 32, 53
backward masking, 150, 153, 157, 268, 269, 271–273
"balanced polymorphism," 68
between-word saccades, 225
bi-alphabetical, 237
bilateral symmetry, 61, 62

497